Deleuze's Philosophical Lineage

Edited by Graham Jones and Jon Roffe

EDINBURGH UNIVERSITY PRESS

© in this edition Edinburgh University Press, 2009
© in the individual contributions is retained by the authors

Edinburgh University Press Ltd
22 George Square, Edinburgh

Typeset in 11/13pt Adobe Sabon
by Servis Filmsetting Ltd, Stockport, Cheshire, and
printed and bound in Great Britain by
CPI Antony Rowe, Chippenham and Eastbourne

A CIP record for this book is available from the British Library

ISBN 978 0 7486 3299 2 (hardback)
ISBN 978 0 7486 3300 5 (paperback)

The right of the contributors
to be identified as authors of this work
has been asserted in accordance with
the Copyright, Designs and Patents Act 1988.

Contents

Acknowledgements

The preparation of a volume as lengthy as this necessarily incurs substantial debts. We would like to thank Naomi Merritt, for her editorial assistance with the manuscript, and the exceptional cover image. Jack Reynolds, Ashley Woodward and Paul Atkinson have each been particularly supportive and helpful throughout the editorial process. Thanks also to Marg Horwell for her support throughout the assembly of this book.

Many from Edinburgh University Press have also been key parts in the publication of *Deleuze's Philosophical Lineage*. We would like to thank in particular Carol Macdonald, Máiréad McElligott, Tim Clark and James Dale for their assiduity and assistance.

We would also like to thank the Melbourne School of Continental Philosophy, one of the rare contemporary institutions in which a serious reading and teaching of Deleuze can take place.

Finally, we would like to thank the authors who are included in this volume, whose pieces present a very nuanced and attentive version of Deleuze scholarship – the kind of scholarship that this volume aims to promote.

List of Abbreviations

AO	*Anti-Oedipus*
B	*Bergsonism*
D	*Dialogues*
DI	*Desert Islands and Other Texts*
DR	*Difference and Repetition*
ECC	*Essays Critical and Clinical*
EPS	*Expressionism in Philosophy: Spinoza*
ES	*Empiricism and Subjectivity*
F	*Foucault*
FB	*Francis Bacon: The Logic of Sensation*
FLB	*The Fold: Leibniz and the Baroque*
K	*Kafka: Towards a Minor Literature*
LS	*The Logic of Sense*
M	'Masochism'
MI	*Cinema 1: The Movement Image*
N	*Negotiations*
NP	*Nietzsche and Philosophy*
PI	*Pure Immanence: A Life*
PS	*Proust and Signs*
SPP	*Spinoza's Practical Philosophy*
TI	*Cinema 2: The Time Image*
TP	*A Thousand Plateaus*
TRM	*Two Regimes of Madness and Other Texts*
WP	*What is Philosophy?*

Introduction: Into the Labyrinth

Graham Jones and Jon Roffe

Those coming to Deleuze's work for the first time (and even those returning to it anew) find themselves confronted by the dilemma of where to begin, of how to engage with it. Two difficulties present themselves. The first and more immediate one is that, conceptually, Deleuze's work is so richly detailed and complex. Thus on opening one of his books the reader is confronted by a plethora of concepts that already seem to presuppose on the reader's part an intimate familiarity with numerous other related concepts, theories, or thinkers. It is akin, perhaps, to a labyrinth in which one can easily become lost, or frustratingly disheartened at the prospect of navigating such a complex architecture.

This leads into the second, more dangerous, difficulty – the place of commentary in respect to such an encounter. Readers will, not unreasonably, peruse existing interpretations in search of guidance in relation to Deleuze's philosophy. But whatever reassurance they find will often prove misleading, for in the field that can, more or less, be called Anglo-American 'Deleuze Studies', an orthodoxy seems to have installed itself. This orthodoxy or 'Image of [Deleuzian] Thought' has multiple sources, and as a result requires detailed elaboration. In the first instance, it was the case for a long time that few of Deleuze's texts were available in English translation, making it difficult to determine any larger or more accurate 'perspective' on Deleuze's project. Related to this is the fact that the texts were translated in non-chronological order, which made it difficult to assess the development and overall significance of specific concepts and which led in turn to the distortion and sometimes misrepresentation of concepts or terminology (e.g. the 'body without organs') by various critics. Also, and perhaps most significantly, there is the acceptance at face value of Deleuze's own more 'personal' utterances in interviews (the invocation of 'buggery' as his proper method in respect to the history of philosophy, the claim that his philosophical work is to be treated as a toolbox, and so on). This last is a more significant problem than the other two, whose force, in truth, has diminished in recent years, even if their consequences have not – particularly so in respect to the theoretical misconceptions that seem to have permanently lodged themselves under the name of Deleuze within the domain of (so-called) 'cultural applications' of theory. Too often misconceptions are perpetuated by appropriators' reliance on a paraphrasing of Deleuze's ideas drawn from secondary sources and other commentaries (although this is hardly a problem restricted to Deleuze).

In summary, the orthodoxy surrounding Deleuze consists of a hierarchy of at least three concentric rings. The outer and most general ring sees Deleuze's work as advocating an 'anything goes' or 'theory-shopping' approach – an unsystematic, anarchic, 'guerrilla warfare' with concepts.[1] This approach tends to characterise the piecemeal appropriations of Deleuze's concepts within an interdisciplinary field, such as cultural studies, where specific notions can be borrowed with little concern for their original context or their relationship to the writer's *oeuvre* more broadly. In Deleuze's case, this approach is usually mediated via the notions drawn from his later work of the 'rhizome' or the 'nomad'. Indeed, Deleuze's own comments about using theory as a 'toolbox', or of treating it as 'cuts on a record', have unfortunately been interpreted as licence from the 'master' to appropriate, deform, or outrightly abuse his ideas according to personal whim, without any prior understanding of their meaning or context.[2] This explains why at scholarly conferences one often comes across papers employing 'Deleuzian' vocabulary, usually wielded as cudgels or inhaled like hallucinogens, that immediately demonstrate a lack of understanding of the concepts being invoked.[3]

The middle ring or level of this orthodoxy is one which over-estimates the significance of the two volumes of *Capitalism and Schizophrenia*, representing them as the 'essence' or summit of Deleuze's project, the core of the work to which everything else is related as either rehearsal, adjunct or auxiliary. Indeed some critics and commentators go further, often seeing *Anti-Oedipus* itself as but a draft for *A Thousand Plateaus*; the latter achieving a cathartic purging of the vestigial Freudian and Marxist encumbrances of the former – a sort of coital before and after (with a smoking gun replacing the post-coital cigarette). This particular belief, we would suggest, originally stems from, or is compounded by, the order of translation of Deleuze's books overall and, relatively speaking, the long-deferred translation of several of the early works. This resulted in the development during the late 1970s and early 1980s of some very eccentric readings and critical sawhorses that have not been overcome even today. To read such accounts one could easily have believed that *Anti-Oedipus* was an orphan text that had mysteriously appeared from nowhere, and worse, that Deleuze hadn't been writing about philosophy for at least 25 years before its publication. The notion of the 'body without organs' presents the most obvious example of this phenomenon, having largely been interpolated on the basis of crude, almost 'free associative', readings of *Anti-Oedipus*, removed from the historical context and the internal conceptual development and continuity of such earlier works as *Difference and Repetition* and *The Logic of Sense*, or Guattari's pre-'68 essays. Another example concerns the overly literal interpretation and privileging of the concept of machinic desire introduced in *Anti-Oedipus*. Similarly, early responses to *A Thousand Plateaus* were often marked by whimsical or manic interpretations of key concepts and the reification and subsequent valorisation of its terminology.

The central and last ring of this set of orthodoxies is that which prides itself on being the most informed and familiar with the actual body and intricacies of Deleuze's work, and yet which grants an inordinate amount of significance to the influence of Nietzsche and Spinoza in retrospective interpretations of the *oeuvre* as a whole, often to the exclusion of other influences – a view that, to be fair, is in many respects validated by Deleuze himself. Given that neither of these figures have a chapter devoted to them in this volume, it should be clear that in an important respect we do not consider Deleuze necessarily to have been the best judge of his own work's development or significance. Like the second, this last approach often tends to demote or dismiss any notion of genuine development within the *oeuvre*, or to misunderstand the nature of its 'continuity', instead 'flattening' the actual work out into a de-historicised plane, as if the concepts it articulates had always been 'there' as an essence merely awaiting simple realisation or identification.

Contrary to this orthodoxy, and to Deleuze's own intermittent descriptions of his work, we would present the following three characterisations of Deleuze's philosophy, under whose aegis the current volume is presented.

First, Deleuze's thought is one which unfolds internal to an examination of the thought of others. The breadth and depth of the engagements that constitute this method remain an object of serious scholarship, and it is possible that we are just now beginning to come to grips with the strata of Deleuze's own set of investments and interests. In other words, Deleuze's method is primarily a *method of reading*. Although rarely discussed in any direct fashion, his reading practice is clearly one of close, attentive excavation, a careful sieving of the conceptual top-soil in search of latent or even nascent elements beneath. It is a regrettable truth that often too much time is spent by commentators on parroting Deleuze's concepts (and worse still, aping his style) and not enough on grasping their significance, context, lineage, and the manner of their emergence. His reading style is, we believe, as significant for contemporary philosophy and its future as Derrida's better-known approach. However, whereas the latter's is largely etymologically oriented and given to exploiting semantic ambiguities, traces and aporias, Deleuze's strategy is more geared towards conceptual and functional differentiation, exploring the horizons of Ideas (in the Kantian sense) and bringing forth the machinic and operative features of the philosophies with which he engages. Deleuze teases out the text in such a way that the thinkers he engages with express meanings (that is, potential lines of development) which perhaps they never intended, but which striate or traverse their thought, nonetheless, like fissures within glass. It is important, however, to emphasise here that in doing so Deleuze never puts words into the mouths of others – he merely draws forth and synthesises latent strands of implicated meaning, unconscious differences that the thinkers themselves could not or would not discern within their own thought.

One striking piece of evidence in this regard is the extent to which Deleuze will go to extract a structure from the thought of even the most unlikely figures. We need only think of *Nietzsche and Philosophy*, whose systematicity is (in)famous, or his magnificent, and still underrated, reading of Proust. In a quite traditional philosophical fashion, Deleuze's reading of others often unearths an implicit structural level to their work, which is then brought into resonant and dramatic contact with his own (a point that emerges repeatedly throughout the papers in this volume). In this sense there is indeed an implicit or immanent systematicity and structure to Deleuze's approach in general, but there is no system or unity as such. It is neither freewheeling nor fixed, neither homogeneous nor contained. Thus, although the work has an internal consistency and continuity, it is paradoxically also differential in nature.

That is why, despite the fact that Deleuze himself was 'more or less bludgeoned to death with the history of philosophy', (N 5) what we find in his work, given this method of reading, is something very much like the history of philosophy itself – prosecuted, it is true, in a novel and sometimes even perverse fashion, but nonetheless one that does not dispense with the diligent care, attention to detail and contextualising practice that the best examples of works in the history of philosophy demonstrate. In short, we believe that there is no way to grasp the philosophy of Deleuze in itself. It must be approached through the many doorways and intersecting paths provided by the multitude of others with whom Deleuze's work engages.

Second, this volume is concerned to properly locate Deleuze as a philosopher and his work as a genuinely philosophical undertaking. One of the consequences of what we have termed the first level of orthodoxy with respect to Deleuze has been that his thought has much too easily been located outside or beyond philosophy. On the contrary, it is said, to claim that Deleuze is a systematic metaphysician is to risk sounding like the very figure that Deleuze's thought wanted to break away from. Of course, to reject this is not to suggest that Deleuzian thought has not had, or should not have, effects beyond the regime of philosophy. Indeed, Deleuze himself increasingly insisted on the importance of other discourses and practices for philosophy, and of the creative capacity of philosophy to 'interfere' with extra-philosophical points of view.

Finally, rather than moving quickly and unquestioningly towards an applied reading of Deleuze that would betray the very spirit of inquiry that motivates a philosophy of difference – as if all the spade-work was done and our understanding of his work now complete, with little remaining other than some vague obligation to act upon it – this volume is founded on the opposite orientation. There is still so much about Deleuze that remains to be explored, let alone understood. Rather than expanding our vision away from the text itself, we would claim that it is time to turn inwards, and to tread carefully the sometimes obscure pathways that constitute the simultaneous singularity and multiplicity that is Deleuze's philosophical project.

The goal of this book is, then, to place emphasis on these three issues, and to foreground as strongly as possible this approach to reading Deleuze. In what follows, this is undertaken with respect to twenty of Deleuze's key points of reference. Broadly speaking, they fall into two categories. On the one hand, there are those thinkers who are well known on their own terms, but whose role in the Deleuzian text is, or has been, difficult to determine. We might consider Leibniz,

Kant, Marx and Freud to be exemplary in this respect. On the other hand, there are those figures who are not themselves well known in the Anglo-American context, because they are seemingly more historically 'distant' from us, and their work is largely not available in English. As such, Deleuze's use of them presents two levels of difficulty – first in ascertaining the sense of their own thought, and then in regards to examining the way in which Deleuze relates them to his own philosophy. Here, we might note in particular Solomon Maimon, Raymond Ruyer, Gabriel Tarde and Gilbert Simondon. With respect to both groups, and indeed all of the figures who fall between or on either side of them, the approach taken in this volume is the same: to attempt to demonstrate the role and significance they hold for Deleuze's *metaphysics*, and to encourage the reader to explore these connections further.

This volume then is aimed at providing various clear points of entry into the labyrinth of Deleuze's thought, but without sacrificing any of its philosophical complexity or integrity in doing so. Furthermore, it is intended as more than just another addition to the ever-growing flood of introductions that too often serve as a replacement for thinking. As such, this volume of essays is a call to arms on behalf of a philosophy of difference that is only now emerging into the light, and which is too often side-tracked by misguided, utilitarian attempts to appropriate, render and reduce Deleuze's philosophy to a grab-bag of tools, slogans and manifestos for the promotion of this or that cultural agenda. Instead, like 'Ariadne's Thread' (one of the alternative titles for this volume) this collection will ideally provide alternative paths of exploration, all valid yet none of which can be said to be definitive, encompassing, or complete. As a result the reader will encounter in these essays differing, unfamiliar, even controversial versions of Deleuze – an ultra-rationalist Deleuze, a mathematical Deleuze, an esoteric or mystical Deleuze, and so forth: in short, a differential and problematic Deleuze. No longer a 'subject' but a veritable field of endeavour in respect to a philosophy of difference. Not just an ideal Deleuze or a Deleuzian ideal but 'Deleuze' as *Idea*.

Notes

1. This notion appears to have been attached in turn to several different Continental thinkers – Derrida, Agamben, Badiou, etc. – until it is subsequently proven inaccurate by close critical reading, whereupon the characterisation is then attached to some other 'rising star' of theory.

2. Deleuzian studies, as with any field, has attracted its eccentrics (perhaps even a higher proportion than most). Too often, it is true, Deleuze has become the fetish of the 'crank', his philosophy taken up and trumpeted by those who respect and understand it least. The blame for this, however, can hardly be laid at Deleuze's own feet, for his work is never anything other than rigorous in its analysis, development, synthesis and proliferation of concepts. It is, we suspect, merely a phenomenon due, on the one hand, to the nature of public discourse and the demand for 'communication' at any cost and, on the other, to the simple fact that philosophy is too often appropriated, adulterated and *commodified* so as to slake the never-ending thirst of an 'intellectual' market driven by, and pretentiously desperate for, fashionable slogans.

3. This is not to suggest, of course, that there is only one true 'Deleuze' whose real meanings should be preserved and policed at all costs for fear of their prostitution or profanation, but simply an acknowledgment that even a plurality of readings must bear some stronger relation to the original texts than the mere citing of terms and issues. Nor are we suggesting that attempts at 'applying' Deleuze's concepts or terms are necessarily misguided or worthless. Clearly, such undertakings have their place – we are simply advocating that they be pursued with appropriate respect for the original text.

1

Plato

Gregory Flaxman

PART I

The guiding principle behind Gilles Deleuze's commentaries on other philosophers could be summed up with one phrase: 'keep your friends close, but keep your enemies closer'. While Deleuze often treats his philosophical friends in an unexpected and occasionally mischievous manner, as if they were actually strangers ('a *philosophically* clean shaven-Marx . . .'), he treats his enemies with an equally unexpected hospitality, proffering a kind of intimacy, immediacy, and even *immanence* that will make of them familiars and fellow-thinkers (DR xxi). The experience of dipping into Deleuze's commentaries always provokes a moment of astonishment, as if a queer kind of ventrilo-quism had been contrived. How is it possible, we ask ourselves, that this philosopher has been made to speak these words, which are his, but which sound as though he had never uttered them before? How is it possible that an enemy has become an intimate?

Perhaps we feel this sentiment most profoundly in the context of Deleuze's commentaries on Plato, especially given that this particu-lar friendship begins with nothing less than a declaration of war. In *Difference and Repetition* and in the first appendix to *The Logic of Sense*, the very texts where he develops his most extensive analysis of Plato, Deleuze announces that modern philosophy has never had any other task than the overturning (*renversement*) of Platonism.[1] Indeed, Deleuze's own philosophy takes its point of departure as, and its measure from, the repudiation of the enduring Platonic legacy, which he regards as responsible for imposing an overarching image of thought at the cost of real difference, of difference 'in itself'. In effect, Deleuze charges Platonism with having introduced a means of transcendence and a regime of representation into philosophy, and yet this condemnation (no small condemnation!) provides the basis for a reading that seeks to redeem Plato from his worst vices and devices – a reading that will make of Plato an uncanny ally.[2] How can we possibly reconcile the image of this enduring enmity with that of positive friendship?

The logic of our answer, however counterintuitive, or because it is counterintuitive, only begins to emerge when we see Deleuze's relationship to Platonism in light of the legacy of failed critique to which the latter so often gives rise. As Michel Foucault remarks in 'Theatricum Philosophicum', his admiring essay on Deleuze: 'Overturn Platonism: what philosophy has not tried?'[3] No doubt, this question is literally justified inasmuch as the proposal to over-turn Platonism 'seems to mean the abolition of the world of essences and of the world of appearances', for as Deleuze has argued, such a double negation 'dates back to Hegel or, better yet, to Kant' (LS 253). No remark could be more telling, for as long as the overturning of Platonism remains the province of idealism it is destined to fail: this is not an overturning but an attempt to overcome Platonism, and as Deleuze once noted in another context, transcendence is no answer to the transcendent (NP 158). What, then, do we mean by 'overturning'?

Inasmuch as we hope to understand this critical method, the essay to follow is organised around the two basic procedures that distinguish Deleuze's Platonism. In the first place, the return to Plato must bypass all the avatars of representation, especially the spectre of Aristotle's 'corrections', which remain the first and still the most profound attempt to render Platonism a regular and representational framework. In the second place, however, the effort to clear the ground of obstacles and occlusions takes us into the workings of Platonism itself. We can only hope to overturn Platonism *from the inside*, by wheedling ourselves within its logic in order to press its own methods to delirious conclusions. In this sense, as we will see, Deleuze's procedure takes its cue from the sophists who subtly tried to sabotage the Platonic republic: Deleuze slips into Platonism like one of those Greek con artists who make themselves effectively indis-tinguishable from 'proper' philosophers, insinuating themselves into the ranks of its logical, rational and moral machinery. 'The Sophist leads us to the point where we can no longer distinguish him from Socrates himself – the ironist working in private by means of brief arguments' (LS 256).[4] Indeed, the overturning of Platonism consists in the art of producing simulacra, beginning with the simulacrum of Platonism itself; as Deleuze writes, this overturning 'can only occur by virtue of denying the primacy of original over copy, of model over image; glorifying the reign of simulacra and reflections' (DR 66).

In this respect, however, Deleuze's procedures for overturning Platonism derive from a belief that their very conditions of possibility already exist within Platonism itself. The overturning of Platonism 'conserve[s] many Platonic characteristics' (DR 59), and it is this initial paradox with which we must wrestle. On the one hand, Plato assumes the status of an enemy because he founds the philosophical basis for the subordination of difference, namely, the transcendence of the Idea. 'The poisoned gift of Platonism', Deleuze insists, 'is to have introduced transcendence into philosophy, to have given transcendence a plausible philosophical meaning (the triumph of the judgment of God)' (ECC 137). But on the other hand, Plato assumes the status of a worthy enemy, and perhaps even a friend, because he does not develop this subordination *in toto* – or, rather, because he secretly establishes the possibility for the *insubordination of differences*. This is because the Idea, which is capable of reigning over and above the world, is initially 'exercised and situated within the field of immanence', that is to say, within a field of pure or untamed differences liberated from the tyranny of transcendence (ECC 137). Even as Platonism augurs the tradition of philosophy founded upon transcendence, no less the determination of difference as that which is determined by the transcendent, Deleuze insists that its procedures have not yet calcified into the rigid structure (that is, the powers of the One, the Analogous, the Similar and the Negative) that constitutes representation in its mature form. 'The Heraclitan world still growls in Platonism', Deleuze muses. Like 'an animal in the process of being tamed, whose final resistant movements bear witness better than they would in a state of freedom to a nature soon to be lost', Platonism marks a moment of transition, of philosophical mutation, when difference has yet to be domesticated and identities consolidated (DR 59).

At first glance, the suggestion of such a philosophical metamorphosis, as opposed to a metaphysics, seems to echo the critical compromise-formation to which Platonism itself famously lays claim, as if Deleuze had laboured to construct the very agreement that we find, both implicitly and explicitly, in so many of the dialogues. In the *Sophist*, for instance, we are told that between 'the giants and the gods' – that is, between the competing traditions of dynamic materialism and enduring idealism – a kind of 'interminable battle is being fought'. Thus, Platonism appears to negotiate between those philosophers who 'drag everything down to earth out of heaven and the unseen, literally grasping rocks and trees in their hands', and those who are 'very wary in defending their position somewhere in the heights of the unseen, maintaining with all their force that true reality consists in certain intelligible and bodiless forms'.[5] Ostensibly, this epic contest is resolved in the divine myth of the world offered by the *Timaeus*, where Plato acknowledges that 'the father and creator' contrived eternal Ideas *qua* Forms (*eide*) and, from these forms, made copies in the form of 'moving and living' creatures. 'Now the nature of the ideal being was everlasting, but to bestow this attribute in its fullness upon a creature was impossible. Wherefore he resolved to have a moving image of eternity . . .'. By introducing Ideas, then, Plato seems to have struck upon the means to square the chaotic becoming of differences with the certitude of eternal verities, for the empirical vicissitudes of the world henceforth testify to an eternal essence that 'rests in unity'.[6] Or, inversely, we could say that images, which after all compose *this* world, *our* world, are destined to be regarded as little more than empirical afterthoughts, projections cast by the divine *lumen*.

Doubtless, the vast tradition of Platonism unleashes great chains of being, ladders and lineages of remarkable complexity, but at the base of all such gradations we find this caste system, the segregation of the noble Idea from the mongrel differences of the image. As Socrates famously, or infamously, notes in the tenth book of the *Republic*, all imitations refer by virtue of the same name to a single Idea or Form, which we can copy but which belongs to a kind of divine creation. Thus, we can make appearances but not 'the reality and the truth', [7] and this recognition invariably provokes the well-worn Platonic discrimination between good and bad copies. Whereas Socrates traditionally affirms the copy made by a craftsman because it is made with reference to the Idea or Form, he just as surely rejects the copy made by an artist (or sophist) because it is already twice removed from the Idea, a copy of a copy that draws weaker minds increasingly away from the divine. Insofar as it replicates the physical or spatial instantiation of an image that has been fashioned by a craftsman, the work of art potentially exerts the persuasive force of reality when looked upon in a certain way and by certain unwise people. For instance, Socrates admits that 'if he were a good painter, by exhibiting at a distance his picture of a carpenter he would deceive children and foolish men, and make them believe it to be a real carpenter'.[8] In essence, the simulacrum appeals to 'that part of us that is remote from intelligence, and is its companion and friend for no sound purpose'.[9]

This description should already indicate the distance between the predominant tradition of Platonism and 'Deleuze's Platonism', for the former brokers an accord between the Idea and images on the basis of a certitude that Deleuze assuredly recognises and, just as assuredly, seeks to decertify. In 'The Method of Dramatization', which constitutes the text of his dissertation defence, Deleuze evokes the common expectation we bring to the Idea and, thence, to Platonism:

> The Idea, the discovery of the Idea, is inseparable from a certain type of question. The Idea is first and foremost an 'objectality' that corresponds, as such, to a certain way of asking questions. Platonism has determined the Idea's form as *what is X?* This noble question is supposed to concern the essence and is opposed to vulgar questions which point merely to the example of the accident. (DI 95)

If reference to the Idea seems the last word on Platonic difference, however, it is also the first word on Deleuze's procedures for inducing difference and the overturning of Platonism.[10] In effect, what Deleuze will find at the base of Platonism is that the Idea (no less an Idea of the philosopher) effectively participates in differentiation, in *making a difference*. How does this occur? We might say that before the grand question of 'what is . . .?' Platonism displaces all other questions as incidental – as matters of opinion (*doxa*). But in asking this type of question, Platonism often ushers us into logical detours that will draw us further away from anything like the determination of essences and, instead, into all manner of other considerations. Indeed, Deleuze gravitates towards a number of later Platonic dialogues, sometimes called 'aporetic', in which the essential issue, once raised, remains unresolved: in these works, the very question of 'what is . . .?' consists in something closer to a pretence or ruse under which wholly different concerns are smuggled into thought. 'Is it possible that the question of essence is the question of contradiction, that it leads us into inextricable contradictions?' Deleuze asks. 'But when the Platonic dialectic becomes something serious and positive, it takes on other forms: who? in the *Republic*; how much? in *Philebus*; where and when? in the *Sophist*; and in which case? in *Parmenides*' (DI 95).

In these and other dialogues, then, the question of essence gives way to the question of the case, of the circumstance, the accident, and the instance (in the legal terms to which Deleuze occasionally turns, we could say that the Idea becomes less a question of *quid juris?* than of *quid facti?*). By no means mere subsidiaries or derivatives of the essential idea, these new questions – '*who? how? how much? where and when? in which case?*' – constitute the 'sketch for the genuine spatio-temporal coordinates of the Idea' (DI 96). In other words, these questions lead us to the spatio-temporal 'dynamisms' that lie beneath the Idea and constitute the very intensive field of differences from which it emerges. While it will continue to be used to adjudicate between and among particular images, as we will shortly see, the Idea acquires this power by virtue of these dynamisms, such that we must always weigh its ostensible representation against the more profound power to unfold its own 'sub-representative' dramas. Indeed, we must avoid any sense in which the Idea consists in the mere transcendental condition of possibility for experiences and experiments, when in fact the Idea, as we will elaborate it here, finds its conditions in the vertiginous play of spatio-temporal dynamisms, of dramatisations, that it appears to condition. The irony of the Platonic Idea, at least as far as Deleuze is concerned, is that its will to determination should give way at a deeper level to a remarkable *mise-en-scène*.

PART II

This may well constitute the most singularly surprising aspect of Deleuze's Platonism, for he takes Plato's Ideas, which traditionally seem to have cost philosophy its cruelty and ecstasy, and finds in them instead the very spirit of Dionysus. The Idea constitutes 'that zone of obscure distinction which it preserves within itself, that undifferentiation which is no less perfectly determined', Deleuze insists: 'this is its drunkenness' (DI 101). No doubt this is why Deleuze's 'return to Platonism' begins by recovering the latter from Aristotle's subsequent critiques and correctives, which invariably dampen Plato's own flights of intoxication. Our 'mistake lies in trying to understand Platonic division on the basis of Aristotelian requirements', for in so doing we subject the Platonic experiments to Aristotle's sober regime of representation – to epistemological categories and to logical demonstrations (DR 59). In *Difference and Repetition*, Deleuze goes as far as to argue that Aristotle's intervention constitutes a catastrophic turn in the history of philosophy. 'Here we find the principle which lies behind a confusion disastrous for the entire philosophy of difference', Deleuze declares, 'assigning a distinctive concept of difference is confused with the inscription of difference within concepts in general – the determination of the concept of difference is confused with the inscription of difference in the identity of an undetermined concept' (DR 32).

The principle is disastrous because it demands that we submit difference to species and to the method of specification, such that difference will become a mere 'predicate in the comprehension of the concept' (DR 34).[11] Deleuze writes: 'According to Aristotle, it is a question of dividing a genus into opposing species', which demands the reasonable exercise of reason and, thence, the logical intervention of a 'middle term'. But this is precisely what Platonism lacks, operating as it does in the absence of 'mediation – that is, the identity of a concept capable of serving as a middle term'. (DR 59). Platonic division 'not only lacks "reason" by itself, it lacks a reason in terms of which we could decide whether something falls into one species rather than another' (DR 59). And yet Deleuze never ceases to promote this peculiar mode of thinking as the mark (or mask) of a great philosophical innocence. For the absence of the middle term actually constitutes the great ingenuity of Platonism, signalling a kind of fugitive resistance: Plato himself had 'not yet chosen to relate difference to the identity of a concept in general' (DR 59). Instead, what we find in Platonism is that the dialectical method comes to consist in a process of division that never takes its bearing according to the genus, that never makes itself the inverse of generalisation, and that never amounts to the determination of species.[12] As Deleuze remarks, the Aristotelian 'objection clearly fails if Platonic division in no way proposes to determine the species of a genus – or if, rather, it proposes to do so, but superficially and even ironically, the better to hide under this mask its true secret' (DR 59).

Therefore, what Aristotle criticises in the Platonic method, what he takes to be the immaturity according to which it lacks sufficient reason, actually constitutes its subversive 'secret', namely, the very basis of Platonic difference and the last vestige of the Dionysian drive. Precisely because it has yet to assume the overarching sense of 'the concept of an object which submits the world to the requirements of representation', the Platonic Idea constitutes a kind of 'brute presence' that 'has not given up hope of finding a pure concept of difference in itself' (DR 59). Whence Deleuze's remarkable diagnosis of philosophy in the post-Platonic age of the Greeks: 'specific difference refers only to an entirely relative maximum, a point of accommodation for the Greek eye – in particular for the Greek eye which sees the mean, and has lost the sense of Dionysian transports and metamorphoses' (DR 34). In this light, perhaps Deleuze's greatest contribution to the task of overturning Platonism consists in the insight that the Platonic Idea, rather than being simply opposed to the image, actually has as its motive the intoxicating and even vertiginous process of distinguishing between images and selecting from among them. Everywhere in

Platonism the Idea serves as a principle of selection that induces but also intervenes in the dialectical process, cordoning off good images from bad images, genuine images from false ones.

Let us return to the question of 'what is X?' The importance of this question, despite its ostensible promise of demonstration or definition, is that it potentially leads to an entirely different process – what we have heretofore called dramatisation. But what does this mean? 'It is in no way a question of dividing a determinate genus into definite species', Deleuze explains, 'but of dividing a confused species into pure lines of descent, or of selecting a pure line from material which is not' (DR 59–60). In other words, we should understand that Platonic division 'has to do with selecting among the pretenders, distinguishing good and bad copies or, rather, copies (always well-founded) and simulacra (always engulfed in dissimilarity)' (LS 257). Thus, the labour of Platonism places the philosopher in the position of the judge who must decide between litigants: in the *Statesman*, the philosopher's task is to determine the genuine shepherd of men; in the *Phaedrus*, the philosopher's task is to determine the bona fide lover; in the *Sophist*, the philosopher's task is to determine the real sophist. 'The Platonic dialectic is neither a dialectic of contradiction nor of contrariety', explains Deleuze, 'but a dialectic of rivalry (*amphisbetesis*), a dialectic of rivals and suitors.' Platonism is tantamount to a 'philosophical *Odyssey*' (LS 254), since we are forever bound to look out among rivals, among suitors, and ask: which is the real one?

The dialectic of division does not identify, as Aristotle would have us do, but authenticates, and in this regard the operation of division takes on an entirely new significance. Unlike Aristotelian demonstration, where 'representation runs through and covers the entire domain, extending from the highest genera to the smallest species, and the method of division takes on its traditional fascination with specification', Plato's dialectic leads to the production of threads of separation and division that cover the ground of images more like the makeshift filigree of a spider's web than any geometrical architectonic (LS 259). The dialectical method in Plato engenders potentially endless divisions, one delicate strand of thought woven into another, subtending a third, folded back over a fourth, unspooling in ever more idiosyncratic and wandering lines. Precisely because it lacks the overarching rule of reason, the particular pursuit of reason in every dialectical-juridical case elaborates a singularly torturous path. In the *Sophist*, for instance, the discussion eventually lands upon the distinction between the arts of medicine and the labour of the bath-man, for both address the purification of the body, the former inwardly and the latter outwardly. The absurdity of this distinction is by no means inimical to the dialectic, Plato says, because the dialectic does not privilege arts but, instead, 'counts one of them not a whit more ridiculous than another'.[13] This sentiment is echoed in the *Statesmen*, where we reach yet another conclusion 'by our divisions which is not without interest for the comedians'.[14]

In fact, the threat of absurdity or indignity only bears witness to the peculiar procedure of division itself that we are trying to grasp here. Insofar as dialectical division 'is a capricious, incoherent procedure which jumps from one singularity to another', the wonder of this procedure is that it ever lights upon any means of closure at all (DR 59). In other words, these lines of descent would, as Deleuze and Guattari once remarked in a very different context, 'dispatch themselves to the moon' (AO 238) without the imposition of resolution. Thus, the procedures of selection always require some form of *deus ex machina*, and it is in this respect that we must evaluate the status of the Idea once more. For if the Idea conditions the dialectic of division, providing the *mise-en-scène* within which all manner of different (or 'rival') dramatisations will be staged, we must also recognise that in so doing it has also provided the conditions for the judgement of those dramatisations. In other words, *the Idea must be grasped as both the beginning and the end of the dialogue*, for if the Idea carves out the dialogical and dialectical space within which the drama of rival claims will play out, those claims are no less in need of adjudication if the question of 'which one?' is to be resolved. Inasmuch as the Idea initially inspires the dialectical search for the real, then, we are also beginning to come to terms with the fact that the Idea must also intervene in order to delimit this search, to resolve the endless series of divisions. How does this happen?

The practice of authentication drives a labour in which rivals are assembled, divided and finally selected, but as we have seen, Plato's peripatetic lines of descent could conceivably extend into endless exercises, and the selection of the real might never come to fruition were it not for some kind of intervention in the last instance. As Deleuze writes, this explains 'the necessity for Plato to put things in order and to create authorities for judging the validity of these claims: the Ideas of philosophical concepts' (WP 9). In order for this to happen, however, the Idea will have to be imbued with a mythic status in Platonism, effectively providing a story of foundation according to which transcendent criteria are introduced onto the philosophical

plane: in short, myth 'permits the construction of a model according to which the different pretenders can be judged' (LS 255). For
instance, in the *Statesman* the process of authentification takes place
according to the myth of an ancient God who ruled the world, and
likewise in the *Phaedrus* authentification takes place according to
the myth of the circulation of souls who still bear the pale memory
of Ideas. 'When division gets down to the actual task of selection',
Deleuze explains, 'it all happens as though division renounces its task,
letting itself be carried along by a myth' (LS 254). Or, to put it another
way, we could say that in the absence of mediation, Plato resorts to
myth as the ultimate adjudicator to ground the dialectic and thereby
settle the line of inquiry once and for all.

This ground should not be mistaken for a traditional *Grund* or
Abgrund, since the Platonic foundation 'relates difference to the One'
in such a way that we never reach the point of transcendental abstraction or subsumption which this process entails for modern idealisms.
'This role of the ground appears in all clarity in the Platonic conception of participation', Deleuze explains. 'To participate means to have
a part in, to have after, to have in the second place. What possesses
in the first place is the ground itself', or what we have called the Idea,
but the Idea is likewise what provides the ground for testing all other
'claimants', all those who participate to a lesser degree (DR 62).[15]
Given as much, a claimant does not simply lay claim to the ground
like a homesteader or prospector who literally puts down stakes in
order to say, 'This is mine – own it.' The Platonic claim will never
be decided according to who arrived first, to whose claim was filed
first: as we know, the legal process often encourages the worst sorts
of abusers and squatters since the land itself, the ground, provides no
test, affords no means to adjudicate among rivals. The homesteader
and miner test the ground for its value, but what happens when the
ground tests us? When Plato establishes his method of dialectic and
division, the ground must function as both the object of the claim
and the test of the claimant, as if the prospector or homesteader had
put his stakes down only to hear the land itself respond, 'No, you are
not worthy.' Notably, such a rejection, when it does happen, tends to
consist in a regression to some more primitive and ultimately unim-
peachable Law: the land-claim of the family in the film *Poltergeist*
confronts the Law of the Native Tribe, just as the claims of the whites
in *The Last Wave* are met with the claim of the land itself and the abo-
riginal 'people of the land' – that is, the autochthonous. Indeed, these
colonial examples bear witness to a higher or supernatural power of

the ground, which rejects the capitalist claimants *on the very ground* that they are interlopers, pretenders who do not effectively participate in the spirit of the earth . . .

In any event, the surprise of Platonism is that, all reason aside, its method of ranking and differentiation are actually established by recourse to myth. 'It is as though division, once it abandons the mask of determining species and discloses its true goal, nevertheless renounces the realization of this goal and is instead relayed by the simple "play" of myth' (DR 60).[16] The twist here is that the form of this myth is by no means incompatible with or outside of the dialectical process, as if all of a sudden a voice from on high were to announce 'enough of this division – let's get down to the real thing'. Rather, we should understand myth to form the integral element of the dialectic, the element which the dialectic *internally* produces in order to justify the process of selection itself. 'Myth, with its always circular structure, is indeed the story of a foundation', writes Deleuze. 'It permits the construction of a model according to which the different pretenders can be judged' (LS 255).

Part III

Having rehearsed the function of myth in the later Platonic dialogues, we are now in a position to understand why Deleuze's engagement with Platonism culminates with his reading of the *Sophist* as 'the most extraordinary adventure of Platonism' (LS 256). Although it begins in the common spirit of determining the lineage of a particular entity, or because it does so, this dialogue operates in the absence of any grounding myth, as if the promise of any dialectical denouement had been withheld and the philosopher had been brought to a point of incomprehension. 'The reason for this is simple', Deleuze writes. 'In the *Sophist*, the method of division is employed paradoxically, not in order to evaluate the just pretenders, but, on the contrary, in order to define the false pretender as such' (LS 256). As we have already argued of Platonism in general, so in the *Sophist* the philosopher assumes the task of discernment, of 'making a difference', and yet here philosophy finds itself on new ground. In this most uncanny of dialogues, the philosopher's task is no longer to anoint the real pretender, the true lineage, but to seek out the false pretender. The *Sophist* is perverted by virtue of having its task inverted, the selection of the truth having given way to the process of ferreting out the untruth, of hunting down the sophist. Indeed, the peripatetic inclinations that are so evident and available in other Platonic dialogues give way here to a new mission – *search and destroy.*

But wasn't this inevitable, wasn't this tacitly the philosopher's position all along? Without the overarching function of reason to tame difference and subsume it under the Idea, the philosopher is like a bounty-hunter: his authority, derived from the Ideas to which he lays claim, works in the absence of the universal mediator and so always tends towards an independent dialectical logic following its own singular line. In the republic of philosophy, where the Idea must be preserved and its image, its distortion, destroyed, the juridical function of the philosopher reveals itself in the guise of an executioner (at one point in the *Sophist*, the philosopher exhorts, 'Come then, it is now for us to see that we do not again relax the pursuit of our quarry').[17] For this reason, perhaps we ought to admit that Plato's wager here is lost before the game has begun because its motivation ('what is a sophist?' or 'what is an image?') is already a perversion of the traditional Platonic question. On the one hand, as an imitator and maker of images, the sophist cannot possibly be identified with a correlative myth – unless the myth exists to justify the inauthentic itself. On the other hand, without such a myth the pursuit of the sophist cannot possibly succeed, and the sophist will have to be affirmed not simply as a 'bad copy' of the philosopher but as that which places the Idea of philosophy in crisis.

Nevertheless, this very recognition serves to reveal the peculiar path of sophistry that Deleuze will follow in order to befriend Platonism, to become its most intimate friend – its brother (*philia-sophistry?*). Thus, our own 'return to Platonism' via Deleuze would constitute not only an attempt to save Platonism from Aristotle, and from the tradition of external critique, but also, in so doing, an effort to insinuate ourselves into the becomings of the sophist. The diegesis of this task takes shape around an encounter between a Stranger from Elea and Socrates, who lightheartedly solicits the newcomer to expose the Greek 'weakness in philosophical discourse, like a spirit of refutation'.[18] The jest leads to Socrates' admission that one cannot easily discern the figure of the philosopher:

> Such men – the genuine, not the sham philosophers – as they go from city to city surveying from a height the life beneath them, appear, owing to the world's blindness, to wear all sorts of shapes. To some they seem of no account, to others above all worth; now they wear the guise of statesmen, now of Sophists, and sometimes they may give the impression of being simply mad.[19]

Indeed, if a myth does pertain to this dialogue, and to the philosopher in general, it could be said to consist in the belief that the philosopher has been bathed in the *lumen* of the gods. Above all others, Plato so often suggests, the philosopher remains capable of conjuring a prehistoric recollection or *anamnesis*, which thereby qualifies him for the labour of adjudicating over images. Plato lays claim to a 'divine portion' (*theia moira*) that, as Louis Gernet once explained, is at once the consequence and the guarantee of eminent dignity . . .'. It designates a kind of divine election of the philosopher.' As he adds: 'What lasted up to Plato's time, at least on a mythical level, was the ideal of a vision of "another world."'[20] Unlike the sophist, who contrives and dwells in obscuity, the philosopher is endowed with the kind of sight that enables him to see past images to the shining outlines of Ideas.

The confusion into which philosophers fall with respect to sophists can only be addressed by philosophers in general and, as we discover, by the Stranger in particular. Having been schooled by Parmenides, the Stranger is freighted with an expectation that he is uniquely suited to the task at hand, that he (and perhaps he alone) can clarify this nebulous distinction between the philosopher and the sophist according to his teacher's distinction between being and non-being. But this logic soon enough dissipates before the mercurial multiplicity of the sophist. As the Stranger's interlocutor, Theaetetus, admits: 'by this time the Sophist has appeared in so many guises that for my part I am puzzled to see what description one is to maintain as truly expressing his real nature'.[21] How is it possible to capture this slippery creature? Every solution seems to lead to more troublesome questions. 'The pretensions of this art of controversy amount, it seems, to a capacity for disputation on any subject whatever',[22] admits the Stranger, and yet this attribute – 'a capacity for disputation' – also strikes him as the basis for an end-game in which the sophist is sure to be caught. Because he claims to be able to argue any subject whatever, whether on heaven or earth, the sophist's art of disputation (and the fact that he is paid for it) must derive from the belief that he possesses knowledge of all subjects. But if no such overarching knowledge is possible, then 'the Sophist possesses a sort of reputed and apparent knowledge on all subjects, but not the reality'.[23] More to the point, the Stranger adds, this kind of pretension to knowledge is a form of 'imitation' that will allow him to differentiate sophistry from philosophy and to determine the former's identity. In fact, the distinction between the philosopher and the sophist rests upon this very difference between types of imitation, for the difference between good and bad images establishes the task that philosophy undertakes (by divining good images) and sophistry obfuscates (by proliferating bad images).

Indeed, the Stranger offers an essential distinction with respect to imitation, namely, that an image can either be faithful to its model or can only *appear* to be so. The former mode is called a likeness, whereas the latter is called a semblance or, as we will ultimately call it, a simulacrum. Thus, we can now begin to consider what Deleuze takes to be the nature (or, rather, the denaturing, the perversion) of the simulacrum. Whereas the likeness maintains an 'internal' fidelity to the original, the simulacrum maintains an 'external' similarity that only appears to be faithful. As Deleuze writes:

> For if copies or icons are good images and are well-founded, it is because they are endowed with resemblance. But resemblance should not be understood as an external relation. It goes less from one thing to another than from one thing to an Idea, since it is the Idea which comprehends the relations and proportions constitutive of the internal essence. Being both internal and spiritual, resemblance is the measure of any pretension. The copy truly resembles something to the degree that it resembles the Idea of that thing . . . Consider now the other species of images, namely, the simulacra. That to which they pretend (the object, the quality, etc.), they pretend to underhandedly, under cover of an aggression, an insinuation, a subversion, 'against the father', and without passing through the Idea. Theirs is an unfounded pretension, concealing a dissimilarity which is an internal unbalance. (LS 257)

The Stranger initially seemed to suggest that the image-simulacrum is 'bad' because it is a copy of a copy, the beginning of a chain of degradations that will lead us increasingly further away from the Idea. But we would be mistaken to understand this as the threat of the simulacrum. Such degradations *qua* degradations only continue to pay heed to the status of the original, for the differences marked by degradation inevitably sustain the perfection of the model itself. By regarding the simulacrum merely as a copy of a copy, as a copy twice (or however many times) removed from the original, we continue to pay tribute to an original, when in fact the genetic power of the simulacrum to overturn Platonism lies, as the Stranger already intuits, in its capacity to dethrone any such model. The real danger of the simulacrum does not lie in its status as an imitation; rather, the simulacrum emerges out of difference itself – its ostensible likeness is only an outer appearance that, upon closer examination or from a different perspective, bears no resemblance to the original. 'The simu-lacrum seizes upon a constituent disparity in the thing from which it strips the rank of model', explains Deleuze, such that we could define the simulacrum, paradoxically, as a copy without a model, an image without a referent, an image in itself (DR 67).

Needless to say, the simulacrum ranges across different media, but for the sake of clarity we might resort to the well-nigh Platonic suggestion that the threat of the simulacrum is endemic to sculpture, especially to those works of great magnitude. But what is so troubling about the size and proportion of these images? The answer must be sought in the fact that the scope of particularly gargantuan images outstrips the power of perception, potentially leading to a belief in resemblance that may not exist at all. We might consider here the example of Michelangelo's statue of 'David', which is often posed as a paragon of realism and proportion but which, upon closer inspection, demonstrates the basis of Plato's concerns. For as the artist realised, the size of the sculpture was such that, from a distance, the depiction of properly proportioned hands would appear to be almost minis-cule, strangely at odds with the towering body. Hence, the external appearance of resemblance could only be achieved by endowing the statue with abnormally large hands: what appears to be a faithful representation is an image with no likeness, no internal similarity. As Deleuze explains, 'Plato specifies that the simulacrum implies huge dimensions, depths, and distances that the observer cannot master', for such images 'include the differential point of view; and the observer becomes part of the simulacrum itself, which is transformed and deformed by his point of view' (LS 258).

Given all of this, how do we go about deciding which copies are faithful and which are not? How do we know a good copy from a bad one, a likeness from a simulacrum? In returning to Platonism in order to overturn Platonism, Deleuze stresses that making the distinction between these two kinds of images is no easy task. After all, we cannot merely demarcate bad images by virtue of what they lack, by virtue of some identifiable degradation, when their ostensi-ble immorality lies in their capacity to deceive the observer and to *appear* moral. The power of the sophist and the sophistic image, the simulacrum, could thus be said to lie in the power to distort the very basis according to which a traditional distinction could be made and a moral hierarchy established. The sophistic copy, the simulacrum, effectively confutes the criteria of selection, annihilating the basis on which the overarching Idea authenticates. Or, to put it another way:

the simulacrum cannot be hunted down and differentiated in any traditional sense because it is difference itself. Isn't this finally the very definition of Sophistry, namely, the image of Platonism that bears no real resemblance to Platonism, the image that strips Platonism of its rank once and for all? Whence the conclusion to the *Sophist* in which the Stranger is effectively hoist by his own petard, for the pursuit *inevitably* induces the apotheosis of confusion from which Platonism had sought to deliver philosophy. 'Agreed then that we should at once quarter the ground by dividing the art of image-making', the Stranger unwittingly urges, 'and if, as soon as we descend into that enclosure, we meet with the Sophist at bay, we should arrest him on the royal order of reason, report the capture, and hand him over to the sovereign'.[24] But at the very point when the sophist has been chased into his 'lurking place', into the dwelling of imitation, when the division of imitation has been cast, according to good and bad copies, when the quest seems to have been accomplished, the Platonic mission loses its bearings.

Why? As the Stranger explains, if he identifies the sophist with fantastic images, he will have already tacitly granted the being of those images since '[t]he audacity of the statement lies in its implication that "what is not" has being, for in no other way could a falsehood come to have being'.[25] In other words, the Stranger must choose between identifying the sophist with likenesses, which is not the case and which threatens a patent contradiction in the course of the dialectic; or identifying the sophist with resemblances, which he knows will resolve the dialectical contradiction but which, in so doing, will condemn the presentiment of truth itself. Ultimately, the aim of preserving the philosopher's position over and against the sophist leads Platonism to confront its own demise; in Deleuze's words, 'as a consequence of searching in the direction of the simulacrum and of leaning over its abyss, Plato discovers, in the flash of an instant, that the simulacrum is not simply a false copy, but that it places in question the very notations of copy and model' (LS 256). Ultimately, Deleuze returns to Plato not only to recover the originary motive and force of the Idea but to demystify the power of the Idea to adjudicate among rivals, such that the great Platonic dualism of Idea and image, of model and copy, lapses into indiscernibility of depths. Far from seeking a world behind the world, which would simply consist in yet another foundation, we glimpse here the 'unfounding' of foundations whereby the rule of representation would be annihilated by the vertigo of simulacrum: as Nietzsche writes and Deleuze quotes, 'behind each cave another that opens still more deeply, and beyond each surface a subterranean world yet more vast, more strange'.[26]

University of North Carolina, Chapel Hill

Notes

1. See DR 59–64.
2. Indeed, what makes such commentaries so ingenious is that, as Deleuze explains, he never seeks to debate his enemies' basic concepts or refuse the terms their discourses: the task of commentary lies in having learnt to speak a philosopher's idiom, but to speak it in a way that detours its regimented and regular framework into unanticipated eventualities.
3. Michel Foucault, *Aesthetics, Method, and Epistemology 1954–1984, Volume II*, trans. Robert Hurley (New York: New Press, 1999), p. 344. Foucault asks this question at the beginning of 'Theatricum Philosophicum'. Foucault's response to this cynicism, in which he famously anoints Deleuze the philosopher par excellence of the twentieth century, bears witness to the latter's distinct methodology.
4. As Deleuze writes in *Difference and Repetition*, we must submit 'the Same to a conversion which relates it to the different, while at the same time the things and beings which are distinguished in the different suffer a corresponding radical destruction of their identity' (DR 66).
5. Plato, *Sophist*, 246 a-b. Note that while I refer to the standard pagination of Plato's dialogues, all quotations are taken from the *Collected Dialogues of Plato*, edited by Edith Hamilton (Princeton, NJ: Princeton University Press, 1961).
6. Plato, *Timaeus*, 37c–d.
7. Plato, *Republic*, 596e.
8. Plato, *Republic*, 598b–c.
9. Plato, *Republic*, 603b.
10. In order to grasp as much, to evaluate the dramas to which the Idea gives rise, we might begin by recalling the remarkable semantic shift which characterises *eidos* in the centuries prior to its more strictly philosophical deployment. Long before Plato and Aristotle latched onto the term, *eidos* was subjected to transformation that, from our distant perspective, suggests nothing short of an uncanny reversal – a reversal befitting 'the uncanny' (*der Unheimliche*). In the pre-Socratics, *eidos* typically designated the visible shapes and the substance of what we see, and this significance dominates well beyond the precincts of philosophy (in the *Poetics*, Aristotle discusses a passage from Homer describing Dolon, '*hos p e toi eido men heen kakos*', in which '*eido*' refers to the appearance of deformity or ugliness). Later usage progressively linked the term to more general notions of a 'characteristic' or 'type', and this sense still clings to Socrates' occasional invocation of

eidos to distinguish ethical qualities. Hence, even when Plato seems to consummate the transformation of *eidos* from outward manifestation to intelligible place (*topos noetos*), the presence of the former remains, if only mythically, in the soul's dim recollection of its archaic communion with such forms. Above all others, Plato suggests, the philosopher remains capable of conjuring a prehistoric recollection or *anamnesis*, which thereby qualifies him for the labour of adjudicating over images.

11. In this respect, it is worth noting that Aristotle uses the same word to designate 'species' (*eide*) that Plato will use to designate divine Ideas, and this convergence may well provide the basis for surveying the external obstacle that we must bypass if we are ever to contrive an internal relationship to Platonism.

12. Neither abstraction nor synthesis characterise the Idea in Platonism, and while Aristotle saw this as a weakness or immaturity in dire need of correction, Deleuze hails it as the opening for other philosophical possibilities and other philosophical worlds.

13. Plato, *Sophist*, 227c. In short, 'the dialectical art never considers whether the benefit to be derived from the purge is greater or less than that to be derived from the sponge, and has not more interest in the one than the other; her endeavor is to know what is and what is not kindred in all arts, with a view to the acquisition of intelligence; and having this in view, she honors them all alike'.

14. Plato, *Statesman*, 266c.

15. As Deleuze continues: 'The ground is a test which permits claimants to participate to a greater or lesser degree in the object of the claim. In this sense the ground measures and makes the difference' (DR 62).

16. Notably, Deleuze is careful to caution us not to regard the myth as 'an imaginary equivalent of mediation' (DR 61). While myth and dialectic appear distinct, 'this distinction no longer matters once dialectic discovers its true method of division. Division demands such a foundation as the ground capable of making a difference. Conversely, the foundation demands division as the state of difference in that which must be grounded. Division is the true unity of dialectic and mythology, of the myth as foundation and of the logos as *logos tomeus*' (DR 62).

17. Plato, *Sophist*, 235a–b.

18. Plato, *Sophist*, 216b.

19. Plato, *Sophist*, 216b. One might also consider here Deleuze's commentary on the 'acensional psychism' of Plato in *The Logic of Sense*: 'height is the properly Platonic Orient' (LS 127–8).

20. Louis Gernet, *The Anthropology of Ancient Greece* (Baltimore: Johns Hopkins University Press, 1981), p. 358. Anamnesis 'is a "vision" that induces or promotes *enthousiasmos*, and the gift of vision is the characteristic feature of those inspired ancients whose unmistakable heritage

philosophers such as Parmenides were able to preserve and pass on', Gernet writes.

21. Plato, *Sophist*, 231b–c.
22. Plato, *Sophist*, 232e.
23. Plato, *Sophist*, 233c.
24. Plato, *Sophist*, 235b–c.
25. Plato, *Sophist*, 237a.
26. Friedrich Nietzsche, *Beyond Good and Evil*, trans. R.J. Hollindale (London: Penguin Books, 2003), §289. Deleuze quotes this passage in 'Plato and the Simulacrum' to describe the essence of the reversal of Platonism, since 'far from being a universal breakdown', this process 'engulfs all foundations, it assures a universal breakdown (*efondrement*), but as a joyful and positive event, as an unfounding (*enfondement*)'. See LS 263.

2

John Duns Scotus

Nathan Widder

Of all Deleuze's concepts, that of univocity or univocal being remains perhaps the most elusive and liable to confuse contemporary interpreters.[1] Given its literal meaning as a single sense or voice, and despite Deleuze's own formulation of the univocity of being as a univocity of difference, it is easily assumed that the term is meant to suggest an ultimate unity that tempers Deleuze's philosophy of multiplicity. Indeed, this view underpins readings that subsume the univocity of being under a Platonist conception of the One and then accuse Deleuze of closet Platonism.[2] If for no other reason than this, it is crucial to understand the *Aristotelian* origins of the concept of univocity, along with its historical use in medieval thought to resolve lingering problems in Platonist-Augustinian theology. John Duns Scotus, the thirteenth-century Franciscan scholastic known as the 'subtle doctor', is a central figure in this history and, unsurprisingly, the first of the three principal figures Deleuze identifies as forming the philosophical lineage of the concept (DR 39). Deleuze names Spinoza and Nietzsche as the successors to Duns Scotus, although neither thinker uses the term univocity.

Fundamentally, univocity concerns relations established within primary diversity, where differences are related and yet common identity and unity are absent. For Deleuze, such relations constitute a multiplicity or assemblage. Deleuze's most sustained development of univocity, and the place where he engages most extensively with Duns Scotus, is found in the chapter on 'difference in itself' in *Difference and Repetition*. Here Deleuze reproaches metaphysical philosophy for conceiving difference, under the aegis of representation, only in relation to the mediating powers of similarity and identity. Metaphysics discovers 'a merely conceptual difference' (DR 27), rather than a more profound concept of difference in itself:

> As the element of metaphysics, representation subordinates difference to identity, if only in relating it to a third term as the centre of a comparison *between* two supposedly different terms . . . But

metaphysics is unable to think difference in itself, or the importance of that which separates as much as of that which unites. (DR 65)

In contrast, Deleuze argues, we must 'discover in it [difference] a differenciator of difference which would relate, in their respective immediacy, the most universal and the most singular' (DR 32). 'There is a crucial experience of difference' (DR 50), he maintains, where the ascendancy of identity gives way to multiplicity, leaving 'no synthesis, mediation or reconciliation in difference, but rather a stubborn differenciation' (DR 65). This differenciation of difference is what, for Deleuze, speaks univocally across the relations of difference that a multiplicity both brings together and holds apart. Hardly a reduction of difference to unity, Deleuze's univocity expresses an excess of difference that is 'common' to all beings.

This univocal ontology is certainly not Duns Scotus's. Nevertheless, the conception of univocity that Duns Scotus draws from Aristotle and opposes to analogical conceptions of being is what inspires Deleuze's philosophy of univocal difference. Thus, even though Deleuze declares, 'There has only ever been one ontological proposition: Being is univocal' (DR 35), holding that it can be heard throughout the history of philosophy from Parmenides to Heidegger, his elaboration of the concept of difference in itself begins with Aristotle and is followed by Duns Scotus. This chapter will review Deleuze's and Duns Scotus's engagements with the ancient and medieval controversies surrounding the relations possible within primary diversity, demonstrating that even where it is put in the service of Platonist-Christian thought, univocity nevertheless speaks to difference. It will also locate what, from Deleuze's perspective, is the fundamental limitation of the Scotist ontology: its refusal to extend univocity to another concept that Deleuze takes from Duns Scotus – haecceity or individual difference. The removal of this limitation, Deleuze maintains, allows univocal being to express the kind of multiplicity necessary to achieve the inversion of Platonism, a move that Deleuze defines as the task of modern philosophy (DR 59). Despite the brevity of his discussion of Duns Scotus – limited primarily to six pages in *Difference and Repetition* – it is nevertheless central in the development of Deleuze's overall philosophy.

ARISTOTELIAN AND PLATONIST-CHRISTIAN BACKGROUNDS

Rejecting Plato's use of transcendent Forms to secure the identities of individuals, Aristotle seeks to deploy difference in a way that sustains a paradigm of what Deleuze calls 'organic representation'. In Aristotle's schema, difference, in the form of specific difference, delineates identities within larger, indeterminate genera. The specific differentiae 'rational' and 'winged', for example, define the species 'man' and 'bird' within the genus 'animal'. These differentiae literally 'cut up' the genus, 'making the difference' between its various species by constituting their respective essences. As Deleuze says, 'genera are not divided into differences but divided by differences which give rise to corresponding species' (DR 31). Furthermore, differentia are all positive – negative predicates such as 'not-winged' cannot specify, as 'being not-winged' leaves completely open what a thing actually is – and so their relation to one another is a relation of contrariety. These contraries, functioning as specifying differences, demarcate the extreme forms that various species can take while remaining within the common identity of their genus: an animal can be bipedal, quadrupedal, winged, etc.[3] For this reason, Aristotle declares contrariety to be the greatest and most perfect difference (DR 30–2).[4] As Deleuze notes, this is an entirely relative maximum, contrariety being maximal only with respect to the requirements Aristotle sets out for substantial identity (DR 31–2). Strictly speaking, contradiction – the relation between, say, 'existing' and 'not existing', where the second term cannot be given positive formulation and is the absolute negation of the first – is a greater difference than contrariety. But as contradictories cannot both be predicated of species within the same genus, they are imperfect and extraneous to definition and essence (DR 31–2).[5] A certain kind of modern 'orgiastic' or 'infinite representation', exemplified by Hegelian dialectics, goes beyond Aristotle's formulation, holding that contradiction or opposition is compatible with identity and is therefore the greatest difference (DR 44–6, 49–50). For Hegel, a thing's identity is indeed constituted by its negative or contradictory relations to what it is not. Yet because both organic and orgiastic representation analyse difference in terms of its compatibility with identity, Deleuze holds both approaches to stand convicted of never reaching 'difference in itself'.

Setting aside the issue of contradictoriness and what is the 'greatest difference', Aristotle's schema still faces threats of excessive difference coming from two directions. The inadequacy of specific difference as a concept of difference is indicated by the implication that the differences 'above' and 'below' those between species nested within a genus must belong to other orders. Taking the level of the individual first, what ultimately distinguishes two members of a species is a difference signifying each one's ultimate and irreducible 'thisness'. Socrates, for example, is a man who has a variety of particular characteristics, a list of which might indeed be endless; ultimately, however, what must be said of Socrates is that he has these attributes and that *he is this man standing here* or *he is made of this particular matter*. None of these individual differentiations help to specify the essence of an individual: Socrates' essence is his humanity, which is determined at the level of the species and cannot be altered by any further qualifications such as his height, hair and eye colour, nose shape, and so on, let alone by the absolutely final predication that makes him this singular man. Moreover, as this final predicate refers no further than to Socrates himself, it functions as a designation rather than a definitional element.[6] Any definition of Socrates must remain abstract, never quite reaching his concrete individuality, and so, unsurprisingly, Aristotle acknowledges that one can have knowledge of more general categories such as species, but only recognition of individuals as belonging to a species.[7] This means, however, that while two individuals may in one sense belong together in the same species, in another sense, one that speaks truly to their differences, they are irreducibly diverse.

The problematic difference at the other level, and the place where the issue of the univocity or analogy of being is properly located, concerns the relationship among the categories. Above genera such as 'animal' or 'colour' are categories such as substance, quantity, quality, location, time, and so forth. Each is a category of being, but neither 'being' nor any comparable term, such as 'oneness', serves as a common unifying identity; just as modern mathematics discovers that there is no set of all sets, Aristotle demonstrates that there can be no highest genus. His argument, as Deleuze notes, turns on the fact that specific differences *are* (DR 32). A genus is predicated of its species, but not its differentiae: we say 'man is an animal', but not 'winged is an animal'. Being, however, is predicated of all these terms. This is due to the way differentiae both divide a genus into species and belong to their own genera – each is at once a differentia of one genus and a species of another genus. This equivocation, however, extends to being itself: predicated of all beings, being necessarily signifies both identity and difference. And so we do say that 'winged is'. As Aristotle states:

> But it is impossible for either Unity or Being to be one genus of existing things. For there must *be* differentiae of each genus, and each differentia must be *one*; but it is impossible either for the species of a genus to be predicated of the specific differentiae, or for the genus to

be predicated without its species. Hence if Unity or Being is a genus, there will be no differentia of Being or Unity.[8]

Nevertheless, this lack of common identity, which indicates the irreducible diversity of the categories, does not make 'being' a homonymous predicate – that is, one whose various meanings are as disconnected as those of 'dog', which signifies both an animal and a star, or 'bank', which signifies a river's edge and a financial institution. Instead, Aristotle maintains, 'being' still donates, both to its categories and to beings in general, a common sense, which can be glimpsed, for example, in the universality of the law of non-contradiction: whether it is a substance or quality, a category or an individual, no being can both be and not be at the same time and under the same relation. Being therefore still implies a relation or connection across differences, but one that differs from identity. Nevertheless, the form of this connection is left undetermined in Aristotle's texts.

Christian theology introduces a third problem involving the need to bridge heterogeneous differences: that of the relation between an infinite God and His finite creations. The conundrum reflects the Platonist origins of this theology. For Plato, physical beings are ordered in terms of their proximity to the Form they imitate. Knowledge of this Form is the condition for knowingly ranking these particulars: only by knowing the Form of Beauty, for example, is it possible to grade the beauty of different individuals truthfully; otherwise, any judgement is at best mere opinion. The question then becomes how the Forms are grasped, and here Plato famously draws an analogy between knowledge and vision: to know is literally to see clearly. Comprehending the Forms therefore requires something analogous to a source of light and Plato designates this source the Form of the Forms or the Good. It 'illuminates' the soul and allows it to 'see' the Forms, comparable to the way sunlight illuminates physical objects so that they can be discerned by the eye. The Good, however, remains opaque, because it similarly could not be known without being illuminated and the source of that illumination would then require another light to be known, and so on ad infinitum.[9] This failure, however, imperils knowledge at all levels, since, just as the hierarchy of beautiful things requires knowledge of the Form of Beauty, grasping the hierarchy of Form/copy/image that comprises Plato's divided line ought to require knowledge of the Good. This quandary continues in Augustinian theology, where God is the source of illumination, yet He is also mysterious and transcendent. Only through His grace, which enlightens the undeserving soul, is any knowledge possible; but, being infinitely distant from His creation, He remains a matter of mere faith. The only possibility, an absent being able to establish some connection between God and the world that does not reduce Him to finite proportions, is a negative theology in which all that can be said of God is what he is not. Such resignation is unacceptable to Duns Scotus and many other medieval theologians, who instead endeavour to demonstrate that a modicum of rational knowledge of God is naturally possible, even if ultimate knowledge still depends on supernatural grace. This endeavour, in turn, necessitates a way of relating the irreducibly different worldly and divine realms.

THE ANALOGICAL CONCEPTION OF BEING

Univocity and analogy are the two answers to the problem of relating the categories that medieval theology derived from Aristotle's texts after their thirteenth-century reintroduction to the Latin West. The answer given to the problem of the categories governs the answers given for the other forms of primary diversity – between individuals within a species and between finite and infinite being. Regardless, both analogy and univocity remain Christian answers, committed to the transcendence of God even while seeking to secure a degree of human knowledge. They remain thoroughly within the framework of representation, aiming to buttress Aristotelian organic representation rather than moving thought towards a concept of difference in itself.

Aquinas is the figure most closely associated with analogy. Given that being is neither univocal like a genus nor purely equivocal, he holds its various senses to be proportionate to one another. Aquinas follows Aristotle's statement in *Metaphysics* that:

> The term 'being' is used in various senses, but with reference to one central idea and one definite characteristic, and not as merely a common epithet. Thus as the term 'healthy' always relates to health (either as preserving it or as producing it or as indicating it or as receptive of it), . . . so 'being' is used in various senses, but always with reference to one principle.[10]

In the same way, Aquinas maintains, a proportion exists between substance, which is the only category capable of self-subsistence and the one Aristotle holds to define being qua being, and the other categories, which gain their being only by adherence to substances. Even if no identity obtains between the being of substance and that of quality, for example, there remains a relation of derivation and dependence: as Aristotle himself holds, 'it is from the concept of substance that all the other modes of being take their meaning'.[11] Aquinas applies this same reasoning to the relation between God's infinite attributes and His creation's finite attributes, basing this on creatures and their attributes being contingent on God's existence. Concepts such as wisdom are thereby said in a primary way of God and in a subsidiary but related way of His creations, similar to 'the way a word like *healthy* applies to organisms (in a primary sense) and to diets (as causing health) or complexions (as displaying it)'.[12] God's wisdom shares no identity with His creatures' wisdom and the same applies to any other attribute that can have both infinite and finite modes (matter, for example, cannot be predicated of an infinite being and so is excluded from consideration). Nevertheless, the analogical relation of attributes establishes a form of unidirectional resemblance that is comparable to the way 'a portrait can take after a man but a man does not take after his portrait'.[13] Creatures and their attributes, being products of God's power, are marked by this power and so resemble their creator, but God in no way resembles His creatures. Through this resemblance, human reason is able to attain a deficient knowledge of the divine by coming to understand exemplars of perfection in the world, even while the infinite perfection of God remains transcendent. Thus, although God's infinite wisdom eludes human comprehension, the analogical relation of the finite to the infinite makes possible an incomplete knowledge of the divine on earth. Analogy is thereby a middle position between the extremes of univocity and equivocity: 'Words are used analogically of God and creatures, not purely equivocally and not purely univocally.'[14]

However, as Deleuze argues, the analogical solution fails to account for the diversity of individuals within a species, as the individuating differences that establish this diversity cannot be organised in terms of proportion: what makes Socrates this particular man is not somehow analogous to what makes Plato a different particular man, nor does it make him more or less of a man than Plato. As a result, under the analogical conception, the individuality of a being, which constitutes its concrete and unique reality, must be assigned to some inessential or accidental factor – for example, in Aquinas's case, matter:

> It is henceforth inevitable that analogy falls into an unresolvable difficulty: it must essentially relate being to particular existents, but at the same time it cannot say what constitutes their individuality. For

it retains in the particular only that which conforms to the general (matter and form), and seeks the principle of individuation in this or that element of the fully constituted individuals. (DR 38)

In contrast, Duns Scotus both opposes the analogical conception of being and demands a positive principle of individuation. Taken together, these two ideas allow Deleuze to conceive of the univocity among positive individuating differences constituting a nomadic and anarchic multiplicity, such that 'Univocal Being is at one and the same time nomadic distribution and crowned anarchy' (DR 37). Christian considerations of transcendence, however, prevent Duns Scotus from making this Deleuzian move. As will be seen, Duns Scotus keeps his univocity of being and his theory of individuation strictly separate.

DUNS SCOTUS' UNIVOCITY

Analogy pertains to judgement – that is, to the assignment of attributes to a subject through complex propositions such as 'Socrates is white'. Judgement, however, refers back to apprehension – that is, the simple cognition of being – and Duns Scotus maintains that there is no room here for the middle position of analogy: even granting that Socrates is wise analogously to the way God is wise, between the statements 'God is [a being]' and 'Socrates is [a being]', univocity and equivocity are the only possibilities. In the case of equivocity, however, neither natural nor rational knowledge of the divine is possible. With respect to the being of various attributes, analogy may indeed have a role to play. But an analogy, Duns Scotus argues, can only be drawn between beings that are both in some way already known, so that, for the being of the subjects to which attributes are assigned, there must be a relation of univocity.

As with analogy, the univocal conception of being is located at first in the problem of the categories. Since an initial moment of univocity is requisite, analogy is insufficient to account for the various senses of being expressed by the categories. Duns Scotus therefore credits Aristotle with a non-generic univocity, arguing that for Aristotle being is not the highest genus due to any equivocity in its sense but because, by including its differentiae, it is 'larger' than any genus: 'Hence the Philosopher [Aristotle] . . . does not show that being is not a genus because of any equivocation, but because it has a greater commonness and univocation than the commonness of a genus.'[15] Since it is not an identity, this commonness in no way reduces the diversity of the senses of being it covers. On the one hand, being has a quidditative sense, whereby it is predicated *in quid*, signifying the entire essence of a subject. This sense refers specifically to the being of substances, to anything about which it can be asked, 'What is it?', with the answer ultimately being 'It is a being.' On the other hand, being is not predicated *in quid* of specific, individual, or accidental differentiae. The sense of these predicates is rather *in quale*, as they function to modify or qualify essence or otherwise to individuate beings. While no one sense of being is common to all that is intelligible, Duns Scotus holds the quidditative sense to be primary in two respects.[16] First, there is a direct primacy, whereby the quidditative sense applies univocally to all substances that need not share anything in common – hence the statements 'God is' and 'Socrates is' express the same sense of being. Second, there is a virtual primacy, whereby the other senses of being refer to the quidditative sense through the adherence of attributes to substances. The being of these attributes is 'virtually included' under the umbrella of the being of substance, which has the power – the *virtus* – to give them being. The quidditative sense of being thereby traverses all forms of being without eliminating their heterogeneity.

> Hence, all to which 'being' is not univocal *in quid* are included in those to which 'being' is univocal in this way. And so it is clear that 'being' has a primacy of commonness in regard to the primary intelligibles, that is, to the quidditative concepts of the genera, species, individuals, and all their essential parts, and to the Uncreated Being. It has a virtual primacy in regard to the intelligible elements included in the first intelligibles, that is, in regard to the qualifying concepts of the ultimate differences and proper attributes.[17]

Duns Scotus then applies this idea of univocity to the relation between God and the world. It is not through any analogy between the being of divine and worldly attributes, he maintains, but rather due to the common sense of their substantial being that knowledge of things available to the human intellect can enable limited knowledge of the divine:

> In this life already, a man can be certain in his mind that God is a being and still be in doubt whether He is a finite or an infinite being, a created or an uncreated being. Consequently, the concept of 'being' as affirmed of God is different from the other two concepts [infinite and uncreated] but is included in both of them and therefore is univocal.[18]

This univocity of being is transcendental rather than generic. A transcendental is defined by its indifference to the difference between finite and infinite being. It applies to both without invoking a common identity, as opposed to the univocity of a genus in relation to its species, which applies only to the organisation of finite beings. This same reasoning allows the principle of univocity to be extended from being to other predicates that are similarly indifferent to the finite/infinite divide. These predicates need not be said of all things. It is sufficient that they are not subsumed by a genus: 'Not to have any predicate above it except 'being' pertains to the very notion of a transcendental.'[19] Transcendental predicates can be said affirmatively of God or of God and some or all of His creatures without invoking a generic unity and without requiring an analogical relation between the beings so predicated:

> Whatever pertains to 'being', then, in so far as it remains indifferent to finite and infinite, or as proper to the Infinite Being, does not belong to it as determined to a genus, but prior to any such determination, and therefore as transcendental outside any genus. Whatever [predicates] are common to God and creatures are of such kind, pertaining as they do to being in its indifference to what is infinite and finite. For in so far as they pertain to God they are infinite, whereas in so far as they belong to creatures they are finite. They belong to 'being', then, prior to the division into the ten genera. Anything of this kind, consequently, is transcendental.[20]

Goodness, oneness and truth, which, following a Platonist reasoning, are convertible with being, are therefore univocal. So too are disjunctive conceptual pairs such as necessary/contingent and created/uncreated, which together extend across the finite/infinite divide, making them coextensive with being. The statement 'all beings are either necessary or contingent', for example, applies to all finite and infinite beings without establishing a common identity. Finally, there are 'pure perfections' such as wisdom or potency, which cross the finite/infinite divide by virtue of their capacity for modal distinction. In their infinite mode, Duns Scotus holds, these predicates express a formal diversity within the simplicity of the divine essence;[21] in their finite mode, they apply to creatures according to varying degrees of intensity. In their different modes, pure perfections can vary qualitatively and even heterogeneously, but they are nevertheless said univocally of the different beings to which they are attributed. There is thus a common sense between God's wisdom and Socrates' wisdom, but this creates no identity between God and Socrates. Moreover, being itself is said univocally of these perfections, because the finite/

infinite division in no way separates the perfection's modes into different types the way specific differentiae divide a genus. It is therefore the same wisdom, even though God's wisdom infinitely transcends Socrates' and so shares no identity with it. For Deleuze, the extension of univocity to pure perfections means that a common sense exists not only among heterogeneous beings but also individual variations, so that, in a limited way, univocal being is said of difference in itself (see DR 39–40).

UNIVOCITY, INDIVIDUATION AND DIFFERENCE

Duns Scotus addresses the issue of individuation in six questions from his *Ordinatio*.[22] Individuality, he maintains, is an essential quality and essence, that, following Aristotle, must be defined in positive terms. This disqualifies accounts such as the theory of twofold negation, which holds a thing to be individual by virtue of it not being something else and not being divisible into subjective parts,[23] on the grounds that no negation can make a thing formally or essentially incompatible with something else.[24] It further bars accounts that tie individuation to some inessential or accidental factor such as quantity or location, since the individual is a substantial, not an accidental, unity.[25] Matter cannot explain individuality, because as part of the formal composition of an individual's essence, matter is simply another general category, whereas if it is taken as something particular – i.e., Socrates is composed of *this* matter – it begs the question of what individuates this material.[26] Finally, individuality cannot result from an act-of-being or be existentiality added to essence, since 'this man' is singular regardless of any actual existence.[27]

Against these theories, Duns Scotus holds that just as specific difference 'contracts' a genus into a species, the principle of individuation must be a positive difference that further contracts the common nature of a species into a singular individual. This difference or haecceity is neither matter, form, nor a combination of the two and so it cannot be expressed by general predicates such as those that define a species or those that qualify an individual while remaining common to many individuals. It further differs from specific difference in that it does not constitute a whole of which it is a constituent part. In other words, while an indeterminate genus must be contracted into a species to form a unity, making specific difference a necessary and organic aspect of this unity, a species, being an already fully defined whole whose predicates fully exhaust it,[28] is not contracted into an individual *per se* and thus must have something 'added' to it. Consequently, while specific difference constitutes a quiddity, haecceity constitutes a material reality that goes beyond the quidditative. An individual is thus composed of two realities, a quidditative common nature or essence and a non-quidditative singular reality, which are formally distinct.[29] As a formal principle – indeed, it is the principle that constitutes the ultimate actuality of form, without which 'a man' could never become 'this man' – haecceity is intelligible, but in its singularity it transcends the capacities of the finite human intellect, which comprehends reality only at the level of species: 'I grant that the singular is *per se* intelligible as far as it itself goes. But . . . it is not *per se* intelligible to some intellect – say, to ours.'[30]

This haecceity, being an undefinable but fully real and positive excess inhering in individual beings, certainly resonates with Deleuze's concept of difference in itself. However, as with the rest of metaphysical philosophy that Deleuze criticizes, Duns Scotus subordinates individual difference to the common nature that it contracts and to the substance in which it inheres. Common nature is a product of individuals and only the individual exists in the full sense of the term. Nevertheless, Duns Scotus holds common nature, which makes possible the definition of the individual within a higher identity, to be indifferent and therefore prior to the existence of any particular individual: 'Every quidditative entity (whether partial or total) in some genus is of itself indifferent as a quidditative entity to this individual entity and that one, in such a way that as a quidditative entity it is naturally prior to this individual entity insofar as it is "this".'[31] This position is further reinforced by the limitations Duns Scotus places on the univocity of being, whereby it applies only to the quidditative sense of being and to those predicates that, being indifferent to the finite/infinite divide, can be said of God or of God and some or all of His creatures. Since individuating haecceity applies only to finite beings – God's individuality being based on his infinity and simplicity rather than any composition and contraction[32] – it cannot be considered a transcendental. As a non-quidditative reality, haecceity is only virtually included in the quidditative sense of being and does not share this sense. Here Duns Scotus' univocity does no better than its analogical competitors in relating primarily diverse individuals in their diversity. Rather, it simply affirms that fully formed individuals fall within the higher identity of their species, making them apt for representation. Indeed, Duns Scotus acknowledges that individuating differences are primarily diverse, but maintains that the individuals composed by them are not,[33] while promising that haecceity is ultimately intelligible to the divine intellect.

Deleuze holds that by delineating the scope of univocity in terms of indifference, Duns Scotus 'only *thought* univocal being' (DR 39). Furthermore, Deleuze identifies 'the enemy he [Duns Scotus] tried to escape in accordance with the requirements of Christianity: pantheism, into which he would have fallen if the common being were not neutral' (DR 39). Certainly divine transcendence would be impossible if the rule of indifference did not limit univocity to transcendentals; if every predicate were considered univocal, it would be impossible to distinguish those concepts that can be affirmed of God from those that cannot, resulting in either pantheism or a negative theology that Duns Scotus considers incoherent.[34] It is therefore the need to protect divine transcendence, rather than the nature of univocity itself, that prevents the univocity of being from being extended to haecceity. Univocal being, Deleuze insists, must be related directly to individual difference and individual difference, in turn, must be released from the restricted role of serving the requirements of identity by contracting common nature:

> [W]hen we say that univocal being is related immediately and essentially to individuating factors, we certainly do not mean by the latter individuals constituted in experience, but that which acts in them as a transcendental principle: as a plastic, anarchic and nomadic principle, contemporaneous with the process of individuation, no less capable of dissolving and destroying individuals than of constituting them temporarily; intrinsic modalities of being, passing from one 'individual' to another, circulating and communicating underneath matters and forms. The individuating is not the simple individual. In these conditions, it is not enough to say that individuation differs in kind from the determination of species. It is not even enough to say this in the manner of Duns Scotus, who was nevertheless not content to analyse the elements of an individual but went as far as the conception of individuation as the 'ultimate actuality of form'. We must show not only how individuating difference differs in kind from specific difference, but primarily and above all how individuation properly *precedes* matter and form, species and parts, and every other element of the constituted individual. (DR 38)

It is therefore essential to overturn the primacy of substance, of the self-subsistent or the identical, and so too any infinite being that transcends and governs the world of finite beings and becoming. It is necessary to situate a multiplicity from which individual identities emerge and into which they dissolve. With this, individuation (difference) precedes the individual (identity) and an ontology of difference is born. Univocity is no longer limited to fully constituted quiddities that 'share nothing in common', but is said of an immanent difference that escapes representation and that both brings together and holds apart individuals. It is said, in short, of difference in itself.

The path to this univocity of difference continues with Spinoza, whose univocity between substance and modes is expressive, 'an object of pure affirmation', rather than neutral. Nevertheless, Spinoza continues the supremacy of substance, which 'appears independent of the modes, while the modes are dependent on substance, but as though on something other than themselves' (DR 40). This can be overcome

> only at the price of a more general categorical reversal according to which being is said of becoming, identity of that which is different, the one of the multiple, etc. That identity not be first, that it exist as a principle but as a second principle, as a principle *become*; that it revolve around the Different: that would be the nature of a Copernican revolution which opens up the possibility of difference having its own concept. (DR 40–1)

This revolution is carried out by Nietzsche's eternal return, which, Deleuze argues, is not the return of identical events in time but rather the return of difference: 'Returning is thus the only identity, but identity as a secondary power; the identity of difference, the identical which belongs to the different, or turns around the different. Such an identity, produced by difference, is determined as "repetition".' The eternal return is said of a world of the will to power, whose 'pure intensities . . . are like mobile individuating factors unwilling to allow themselves to be contained within the factitious limits of this or that individual, this or that Self'. This world, 'in which all previous identities have been abolished and dissolved', is one of haecceities that are immanent to beings and that compel their self-overcoming (DR 41). It is thus a world of the crowned anarchy of nomadic differences, where the eternal return effects a selection in which only the extreme forms, those forms that overcome themselves, are fit to return:

> In all these respects, eternal return is the univocity of being, the effective realisation of that univocity. In the eternal return, univocal being is not only thought and even affirmed, but effectively realised. Being is said in a single and same sense, but this sense is that of eternal return as the return or repetition of that of which it is said. The wheel

in the eternal return is at once both the production of repetition on the basis of difference and the selection of difference on the basis of repetition. (DR 40–1)

This line of thought that begins with Duns Scotus and culminates with Nietzsche would not have been possible if the concept of univocity in any sense invoked identity. It is because the univocity of being expresses a relationship across irreducible diversity that it links with so many other concepts in Deleuze's philosophy of difference, such as disjunctive synthesis, irrational cut, rhizomatic multiplicity, and differenc/tiation. The obscurity of Duns Scotus as a principal source for Deleuze's thought has often led to interpretations of univocity as a concept that cuts against these other ideas. Ironically, however, univocal being is actually what underpins them and therefore what makes Deleuze a genuine philosopher of difference.

Royal Holloway, University of London

Notes

1. This chapter returns me to issues on the relationship between Duns Scotus and Deleuze that I elaborated earlier in 'The Rights of Simulacra: Deleuze and the Univocity of Being', *Continental Philosophy Review* 34:4 (2001), pp. 437–53; and *Genealogies of Difference* (Urbana and Chicago: University of Illinois Press, 2002), ch. 5.
2. Alain Badiou's *Deleuze: The Clamor of Being*, trans. Louise Burchill (Minneapolis: University of Minnesota Press, 2000) is still the most (in) famous example of this line of criticism.
3. Aristotle, *Metaphysics*, 2 vols, trans. Hugh Tredennick (Cambridge, MA: Loeb Classics, 1933–5), 1018a.
4. Also see Aristotle, *Metaphysics*, 1055a.
5. See Aristotle *Metaphysics*, 1055a-b on the distinction between contrariety and contradiction.
6. With any definition, Aristotle holds that 'the reality of a thing is the last such predication to hold of these atoms', but also that these predicates must belong further than the subject predicated, even though 'all <of them together> will not <belong> further' (Aristotle, *Posterior Analytics*, trans. Jonathan Barnes [Oxford: Clarendon Press, 1975], §II.13).
7. Aristotle, *Metaphysics*, 1035b-1036a.
8. Aristotle, *Metaphysics*, 998b. See also 1059b.
9. Plato, *Republic*, trans. G. M. A. Grube (Indianapolis: Hackett Publishing Company, 1974), 506d-511.
10. Aristotle, *Metaphysics*, 1003a-b.
11. Aristotle, *Metaphysics*, 1045b.

12. Thomas Aquinas, *Summa Theologiae: A Concise Translation*, edited by Timothy McDermot (Westminster, MD: Christian Classics, 1989), p. 32.
13. Aquinas, *Summa Theologiae*, p. 18.
14. Thomas Aquinas, *Selected Philosophical Writings*, trans. Timothy McDermott (Oxford: Oxford University Press, 1993), p. 225.
15. Duns Scotus in R. Prentice, *The Basic Quidditative Metaphysics of Duns Scotus as Seen in His De Primo Principio* (Rome: Antonianum, 1970), p. 54. Returning to the set theory reference made earlier, one could say that in Duns Scotus' reading of Aristotle, being is not a set of all sets but it is rather a proper class – that is, a group of sets that, without being a set, can still be defined by some property that all its members share.
16. John Duns Scotus, *Philosophical Writings*, trans. Allan Wolter (Indianapolis and Cambridge: Hackett Publishing Company, 1987), p. 4.
17. Duns Scotus, *Philosophical Writings*, p. 4.
18. Duns Scotus, *Philosophical Writings*, p. 20. Duns Scotus' particular strategies for establishing this limited human knowledge are not relevant for this chapter. Suffice it to say here that certain strategies available through the naturally hierarchical analogical conception of being are unavailable to him. Rather than suggesting a route to the divine through the proportion between finite and infinite beings and their attributes, Duns Scotus instead relies on the idea of an essentially ordered series of causes, where effects always refer to causes of a higher order and ultimately to a first cause that transcends the entire causal series. For discussion, see Widder, *Genealogies of Difference*, pp. 128–34.
19. Duns Scotus, *Philosophical Writings*, p. 3.
20. Duns Scotus, *Philosophical Writings*, p. 2.
21. In order to strengthen the link between Duns Scotus and Spinoza, Deleuze attempts to characterise Duns Scotus' notion of formal distinction as a precursor to Spinoza's idea of a non-numerical real distinction between attributes (see, in particular, EPS 63–6). To that end, Deleuze holds that formal distinction is a real but not a numerical distinction and that it is a distinction between quiddities: 'Between animal and rational there is not merely a distinction of reason, like that between *homo* and *humanitas*; . . . Formal distinction is definitely a real distinction, expressing as it does the different layers of reality that form or constitute a being. Thus it is called *formalis a parte rei* or *actualis ex natura rei*. But it is a minimally real distinction because the two really distinct quiddities are coordinate, together making a single being. *Real and yet not numerical*, such is the status of formal distinction' (EPS 64; see also DR 39–40). However, this reading is problematic in two respects. First, Duns Scotus famously defines formal distinction as being weaker than the real distinction between real beings but stronger than

the conceptual distinction between beings of reason (see Duns Scotus, cited in Etienne Gilson, *History of Christian Philosophy in the Middle Ages* [London: Sheed and Ward, 1955], p. 765 n. 63). In this sense, formal distinction is neither real nor conceptual – although it might be compared to Deleuze's conception of the virtual difference, which would go some way to supporting Deleuze's interpretation. Second, a quiddiative predicate for Duns Scotus is one that signifies the entirety of the essence of a thing. While the infinite predicates assigned to God may function in this way, this is clearly not the case with the differentiae predicated of finite beings: Duns Scotus would never consider 'rational' to be a quidditative predicate. Indeed, as will be seen, he also holds that there is a formal distinction within the concrete individual between its common nature and its individuating haecceity, but he maintains that haecceity is not quidditative.

22. John Duns Scotus, 'Six Questions on Individuation from His *Ordinatio*, II. d. 3, part 1, qq. 1–6', in V. Spade (ed. and trans.), *Five Texts on the Mediaeval Problem of Universals* (Indianapolis: Hackett Publishers, 1994) The *Ordinatio* is Duns Scotus's major work and is the version of his Oxford lectures on the *Sentences* of Peter Lombard that was revised for publication. It is also known as the *Opus oxioniense*, the title used in Deleuze's references to Duns Scotus's work in both EPS and DR.
23. That is, parts that can be predicated of the whole they divide, as 'Socrates' can be predicated of 'man' and 'man' can be predicated of 'animal'.
24. Duns Scotus, 'Six Questions', §50.
25. Duns Scotus, 'Six Questions', §§66–128.
26. Duns Scotus, 'Six Questions', §§136–41.
27. Duns Scotus, 'Six Questions', §§64–5.
28. In other words, the species, which defines the essence of its individuals, signifies and is signified completely by the combination of its genus and specific differences: a man is a bipedal rational animal and a bipedal rational animal can be nothing other than a man.
29. Duns Scotus, 'Six Questions', §188.
30. Duns Scotus, 'Six Questions', §192.
31. Duns Scotus, 'Six Questions', §187.
32. Duns Scotus, 'Six Questions', §§190–1.
33. Duns Scotus, 'Six Questions', §§185–6.
34. Duns Scotus, *Philosophical Writings*, pp. 15–16.

3

G. W. F. Leibniz

Daniel W. Smith[1]

Gilles Deleuze once characterised himself as a 'classical' philosopher, a statement that was no doubt meant to refer to his indebtedness to (and affinities with) the great philosophers of the classic period, notably Spinoza and Leibniz.[2] Spinoza provided Deleuze with a model for a purely immanent ontology, while Leibniz offered him a way of thinking through the problems of individuation and the theory of Ideas.[3] In both cases, however, Deleuze would take up and modify Spinoza's and Leibniz's thought in his own manner, such that it is impossible to say that Deleuze is a 'Spinozist' or a 'Leibnizian' without carefully delineating the use to which he puts each of these thinkers. Although Deleuze published a book-length study of Leibniz late in his career, entitled *The Fold: Leibniz and the Baroque* (1988), his more profound (and, I believe, more important) engagement with Leibniz had already occurred in *Difference and Repetition* (1968) and *Logic of Sense* (1969).[4] In these earlier works, Deleuze approached Leibniz from a resolutely post-Kantian point of view, returning to Leibniz in his attempt to redefine the nature of the transcendental field. Following Solomon Maimon, Deleuze had argued that, in order for Kant's critical philosophy to achieve its own aims, a viewpoint of *internal genesis* needed to be substituted for Kant's principle of *external conditioning.*[5] 'Doing this means returning to Leibniz', Deleuze would later explain, 'but on bases other than Leibniz's. All the elements to create a genesis such as the post-Kantians demand it, all the elements are virtually in Leibniz' (Seminar of 20 May 1980). One of these other 'bases' was the formulation of a pure principle of *difference*, which alone would be capable of freeing thought from 'representation' (whether finite or infinite), and its concomitant subordination to the principle of identity.[6] In what follows, then, I would like to show how Deleuze uses Leibniz to 'deduce' the necessity of a principle of difference by making his way through the four fundamental principles of Leibniz's philosophy: identity, sufficient reason, indiscernibility and the law of continuity (see Figure 1). What

Principle of Identity

Reason: *ratio essendi* ('reason for being': *Why is there some thing rather than nothing?*)

Popular Formulation: 'A thing is what it is'.

Philosophical Formulation: 'Every analytic proposition is true'.

Principle of Sufficient Reason

Reason: *ratio existendi* ('reason for existing': *Why is there this rather than that?*)

Popular Formulation: 'Everything has a reason'.

Philosophical Formulation: 'Every true proposition is analytic'.

Principle of Indiscernibles

Reason: *ratio cognoscendi* ('reason for knowing')

Popular Formulation: 'No two things are the same'.

Philosophical Formulation: 'For every concept, there is one and only one thing'.

Law of Continuity

Ratio: *ratio fiendi* ('reason for becoming')

Popular Formulation: 'Nature never makes leaps'.

Philosophical Formulation: 'A singularity is extended over a series of ordinary points until it reaches the neighborhood of another singularity, etc'.

Figure 1   *Four Principles in Leibniz*

emerges from Deleuze's reading of Leibniz is, as he himself puts it, 'a Leibnizian transcendental philosophy that bears on the event rather than the phenomenon, and replaces the Kantian conditioning' (FLB 163; PLB 122).[7]

1. *The Principle of Identity*. We begin with the simplest statement of the principle of identity. The classical formula of the identity principle is 'A is A': 'blue is blue', 'a triangle is a triangle', 'God is God'. But such formulae, says Leibniz, 'seem to do nothing but repeat the same

thing without telling us anything'.[8] They are certain but empty: they do not force us to think. A more popular formulation of the principle of identity would be: 'A thing is what it is'. This formula goes further than the formula 'A is A' because it shows us the ontological region governed by the principle of identity: identity consists in manifesting the identity between the thing and what the thing *is*, what classical philosophy termed the 'essence' of a thing. In Leibniz, every principle is a *ratio*, a 'reason', and the principle of identity can be said to be the *ratio* or rule of essences, the *ratio essendi*. It corresponds to the question, 'Why is there something rather than nothing?' If there were no identity (an identity conceived as the identity of the thing and what the thing *is*), then there would be nothing. But Leibniz also provides us with a more technical formulation of the principle of identity, derived from logic: 'every analytic proposition is true'. What is an analytic proposition? It is a proposition in which the subject and the predicate are identical. 'A is A' is an analytical proposition: the predicate A is contained in the subject A, and therefore 'A is A' is true. But to complete the detail of Leibniz's formula, we would have to distinguish between two types of identical propositions: an analytic proposition is true either by reciprocity or by inclusion. An example of a proposition of *reciprocity* is 'a triangle has three angles'. This is an identical proposition because the predicate ('three angles') is the same as the subject ('triangle') and reciprocates with the subject. The second case, a proposition of *inclusion*, is slightly more complex. In the proposition 'a triangle has three sides' there is no identity between the subject and the predicate, yet there is a supposed logical necessity: one cannot conceptualise a single figure having three angles without this figure also having three sides. There is no reciprocity here, but there is a demonstrable inclusion or inherence of the predicate in the subject. One could say that analytic propositions of reciprocity are objects of *intuition*, whereas analytic propositions of inclusion are the objects of a *demonstration*. What Leibniz calls *analysis* is the operation that discovers a predicate in a notion taken as a subject. If I show that a given predicate is contained in a notion, then I have done an analysis. All this is basic logic: up to this point, Leibniz's greatness as a thinker has not yet appeared.

2. *Principle of Sufficient Reason.* Leibniz's originality, Deleuze suggests, first emerges with his second great principle, the principle of sufficient reason, which no longer refers to the domain of essences but to the domain of things that actually exist, the domain of existences.

The corresponding *ratio* is no longer the *ratio essendi* but the *ratio existendi*, the reason for existing. The corresponding question is no longer, 'Why something rather than nothing?' but rather, 'Why this rather than that?' The popular expression of this principle would be: 'everything has a reason'. This is the great cry of rationalism, which Leibniz will attempt to push to its limit. Why does Leibniz need this second principle? Because existing things appear to be completely outside the principle of identity. The principle of identity concerns the identity of the thing and what the thing is, even if the thing itself does not exist: I know that unicorns do not exist, but I can still say what a unicorn is. So Leibniz needs a second principle to make us think existing beings. Yet how can a principle as seemingly vague as 'everything has a reason' make us think existing beings?

Leibniz explains how in his technical formulation of the principle of sufficient reason, which reads: 'all predication has a foundation in the nature of things'. What this means is that everything that is truly predicated of a thing is necessarily included or contained in the concept of the thing. What is said or predicated of a thing? First of all, its essence, and at this level there is no difference between the principle of identity and the principle of sufficient reason, which takes up and presumes everything acquired with the principle of identity. But Leibniz then adds something no philosopher before him had said: what is said or predicated of a thing is not only the essence of the thing, but also the totality of the affections and events that happen to or are related to or belong to the thing. For example: Caesar crossed the Rubicon. Since this is a true proposition, Leibniz will say that the predicate 'crossed the Rubicon' must be contained in the concept of Caesar (not in Caesar himself, but in the concept of Caesar). 'Everything has a reason' means that everything that happens to something – all its 'differences' – must be contained or *included* for all eternity in the individual notion of a thing. 'If we call an "event" what happens to a thing, whether it submits to it or undertakes it, we will say that sufficient reason is what comprehends the event as one of its predicates: the concept of the thing, or its notion. "Predicates or events," says Leibniz' (FLB 41; PLB 55).

How does Leibniz arrive at this remarkable claim? He does so, Deleuze suggests, following Couturat, by reconsidering *reciprocity*. The principle of identity gives us a model of truth that is certain and absolute – an analytical proposition is necessarily a true proposition – but it does not make us *think* anything. So Leibniz reverses the formulation of the principle of identity using the principle of reciprocity:

a true proposition is necessarily an analytic proposition. The principle of sufficient reason is the reciprocal of the principle of identity, and it allows Leibniz to conquer a radically new domain, the domain of existing things.[9] By means of this reversal, the principle of identity forces us to *think* something. The formal formula of the principle of identity ('A is A') is true because the predicate *reciprocates* with the subject, and Leibniz therefore applies this principle of reciprocity to the principle of identity itself. In its first formulation, however, the reciprocal of 'A is A' is simply 'A is A', and in this sense, the *formal* formulation prevents the reversal of the identity principle. The principle of sufficient reason is produced only through a reversal of the *logical* formulation of the principle of identity, but this latter reversal is clearly of a different order: it does not go without saying. Justifying this reversal is the task Leibniz pursues as a philosopher, and it launches him into an infinite and perhaps impossible undertaking. The principle of sufficient reason says not only that the notion of a subject contains everything that happens to the subject – that is, everything that is truly predicated of the subject – but also that we should be able to *demonstrate* that this is the case.

Once Leibniz launches himself into the domain of the concept in this way, however, he cannot stop. At one point in the *Metaphysics*, Aristotle – who exerted a strong influence on Leibniz – proposes an exquisite formula: at a certain point in the analysis of concepts, it is necessary to *stop (anankstenai)*.[10] This is because, for Aristotle, concepts are *general*, not individual. Classical logic distinguishes between the order of the concept, which refers to a generality, and the order of the individual, which refers to a singularity. By nature, a concept was seen to be something that comprehends a *plurality* of individuals; it went without saying that the individual as such was not comprehensible by concepts. Put differently, philosophers have always considered that *proper names* are not concepts. At a certain point, then, the process of conceptual specification must stop: one reaches the final species (*infima species*), which groups together a plurality of individuals. Leibniz, however, does not heed Aristotle's warning: he does not stop. Instead, he attempts to push the concept all the way to the level of the individual itself: in Leibniz, 'Adam' and 'Caesar' are concepts, and not simply proper names. The cry of sufficient reason – 'Everything *must* have a reason' – is the problem that will propel Leibniz into an almost hallucinatory conceptual creation. 'Leibniz pushes the presuppositions of classical philosophy as far as he can, down the paths of genius and delirium' (Seminar of 20 May 1980).

It is not much use to raise objections or to argue against Leibniz, says Deleuze; one first has to let oneself go, and follow Leibniz in his production of concepts. What then is the delirious chasm into which Leibniz plunges?

If everything I attribute with truth to a subject must be contained in the concept of the subject, then I am forced to include in the notion of the subject not only the thing I attribute to it with truth, but also *the totality of the world*. Why is this the case? By virtue of a principle that is very different from the principle of sufficient reason, namely, the principle of *causality*. The principle of sufficient reason ('every-thing has a reason') is not the same thing as the principle of causal-ity ('everything has a cause'). 'Everything has a cause' means that A is caused by B, B is caused by C, and so on – a series of causes and effects that stretches to infinity. 'Everything has a reason', by contrast, means that one has to give a reason for causality itself, namely, that the relation A maintains with B must in some manner be included or comprised in the concept of A.[11] This is how the principle of sufficient reason goes beyond the principle of causality: the principle of causal-ity states the *necessary cause* of a thing but not its *sufficient reason*. Sufficient reason expresses the relation of the thing with its own notion, whereas causality simply expresses the relations of the thing with something else. Sufficient reason can be stated in the following manner: for every thing, there is a concept that gives an account both of the thing and of its relations with other things, including its causes and its effects. Thus, once Leibniz says that the predicate 'crossing the Rubicon' is included in the notion of Caesar, he cannot stop himself: he is forced to include the totality of the world in Caesar's concept. This is because 'crossing the Rubicon' has multiple causes and multiple effects, such as the establishment of the Roman empire and the death of Jesus; it stretches to infinity backward and forward by the double play of causes and effects. We therefore cannot say that 'crossing the Rubicon' is included in the notion of Caesar without saying that the causes and effects of this event are *also* included in the notion of Caesar. This is no longer the concept of inherence or inclu-sion, but the fantastic Leibnizian concept of *expression*: the notion of the subject expresses the totality of the world. Each of us in our concept expresses or contains the entirety of the world. This is the first hallucinatory Leibnizian concept that follows from the principle of sufficient reason.

A second concept follows immediately, since there is a danger lurking here for Leibniz: if each notion of the subject expresses the totality of the world, that could seem to indicate that there is only a single subject, and that individuals are mere appearances of this universal subject (a single substance à la Spinoza, or absolute Spirit à la Hegel). But Leibniz cannot follow such a path without repudiating himself, since his entire philosophy remains fixed on the individual, and the reconciliation of the concept with the individual. To avoid this danger, Leibniz creates another new concept: each individual notion comprehends or includes the totality of the world, he says, but from a certain *point of view*. This marks the beginning of 'perspectivist' philosophy, which would be taken up by later philosophers such as Nietzsche (who nonetheless understood perspectivism in a very different manner than Leibniz). Point of view, however, is such a common notion that one easily risks trivialising Leibniz's conception of perspectivism. Leibniz does *not* say that everything is 'relative' to the viewpoint of the subject: this is what Deleuze calls an 'idiotic' or 'banal' notion of perspectivism. It would imply that the subject is prior to the point of view, whereas in Leibniz it is precisely the opposite: in Leibniz, the point of view is not constituted by the subject, the subject is constituted by the point of view. Points of view, in other words, are the sufficient reason of subjects. The individual notion is the point of view through which the individual expresses the totality of the world.

But here again, Leibniz cannot stop. For what is it then that determines this point of view? Each of us may express the totality of the world, Leibniz tells us, but we express most of the world in an obscure and confused manner, as if it were a mere clamour, a background noise, which we perceive in the form of *infinitely small perceptions*. These minute perceptions are like the 'differentials' of consciousness (Maimon), which are not given as such to conscious perception (apperception). However, there is a small, reduced, finite portion of the world that I express clearly and distinctly, and this is precisely that portion of the world that affects my *body*. Leibniz in this manner provides a deduction of the necessity of the body as that which occupies the point of view. I do not express clearly and distinctly the crossing of the Rubicon, since that concerns Caesar's body; but there are other things that concern my body – a certain relation to this room, this book, this article – which I do express clearly. This is how Leibniz defines a point of view: it is the portion or the region of the world expressed clearly by an individual in relation to the totality of the world, which it expresses obscurely in the form of minute perceptions. No two individual substances occupy the same point of view on the world because none have the same clear or distinct zone of expression on the world.

The problem posed by the principle of sufficient reason thus leads Leibniz to create an entire sequence of concepts: expression, point of view, minute perceptions, and so on. 'In the majority of great philosophers', writes Deleuze, 'the concepts they create are inseparable, and are taken in veritable sequences. And if you don't understand the sequence of which a concept is a part, you cannot understand the concept' (Seminar of 26 November 1980). But the notion of point of view will lead Leibniz into a final set of problems. For the world, Leibniz continues, has no existence outside the points of view that express it. The world is the 'expressed' thing common to all individual substances, but what is expressed (the world) has no existence apart from what expresses it (individuals). In other words, there is no world *in itself*. The difficulty Leibniz faces here is this: each of these individual notions must nonetheless express the *same* world. Why is this a problem? The principle of identity allows us to determine what is contradictory, that is, what is *impossible*. A square circle is a circle that is not a circle; it contravenes the principle of identity. But at the level of sufficient reason, things are more complicated. In themselves, Caesar not crossing the Rubicon and Adam not sinning are neither contradictory nor impossible. Caesar could have not crossed the Rubicon, and Adam could have not sinned, whereas a circle cannot be square. The truths governed by the principle of sufficient reason are thus not of the same type as the truths governed by the principle of identity. But how then can Leibniz at the same time hold that everything Adam did is contained for all time in his individual concept, and that Adam the non-sinner was nonetheless possible? Leibniz's famous response to this problem is this: Adam the non-sinner was possible in itself, but it was *incompossible* with the rest of the actualised world. Leibniz here creates an entirely new logical relation of incompossibility, a concept that is unique to Leibniz's philosophy, and which is irreducible to impossibility or contradiction. At the level of existing things, it is not enough to say that a thing is possible in order to exist; it is also necessary to know with what it is compossible. The conclusion Leibniz draws from this notion is perhaps his most famous doctrine, one which was ridiculed by Voltaire in *Candide* and by the eighteenth century in general: among the infinity of incompossible worlds, God makes a calculation and chooses the 'Best' of all possible worlds to pass into existence, a world governed by a harmony that is 'preestablished' by God. But this rational optimism seems to imply an infinite cruelty, since the best world is not necessarily the world in which suffering is the least.

3. *Principle of Indiscernibles.* This sets us on the path of the third principle, the principle of indiscernibles, which is the reciprocal of the principle of sufficient reason. The principle of sufficient reason says: for every thing, there is a concept that includes everything that will happen to the thing. The principle of indiscernibles says: for every concept, there is one and only one thing. The principle of indiscernibles is thus the reciprocal of the principle of sufficient reason. Unlike Leibniz's first act of reciprocity, this reciprocation is absolutely necessary. (The move from the principle of identity to the principle of sufficient reason, by contrast, was Leibniz's *coup de force* as a philosopher; he could undertake it only because he created the philosophical means to do so.) Banally, this means that there are no two things that are absolutely identical: no two drops of water are identical, no two leaves of a tree are identical, no two people are identical. But more profoundly, it also means – and this is what interests Deleuze – that in the final analysis *every difference is a conceptual difference*. If you have two things, there must be two concepts; if not, there are not two things. In other words, if you assign a difference to two things, there is necessarily a difference in their concepts. The principle of indiscernibles consists in saying that we have *knowledge* only by means of concepts, and this can be said to correspond to a third reason, a third *ratio*: *ratio cognoscendi*, or reason as the reason of knowing.

This principle of indiscernibles has two important consequences for Deleuze. First, as we have seen, Leibniz is the first philosopher to say that concepts are proper names, that is, that concepts are *individual* notions. In classical logic, by contrast, concepts are *generalities* which, by their very nature, cannot comprehend the singularity of the individual. But can we not say that the concept 'human', for instance, is a generality that applies to all individual humans, including both Caesar and Adam? Of course you can say that, Leibniz retorts, but only if you have *blocked* the analysis of the concept at a certain point, at a finite moment. But if you push the analysis, if you push the analysis of the concept to infinity, there will be a point where the concepts of Ceasar and Adam are no longer the same. According to Leibniz, this is why a mother sheep can recognise its little lamb: it knows its concept, which is individual. This is also why Leibniz cannot have recourse to a universal mind: he has to remain fixed on the singularity, on the individual as such. This is Leibniz's great originality, the formula of his perpetual refrain: substance is individual.

Second, in positing the principle of indiscernibles ('every difference is conceptual'), Leibniz is asking us to accept an enormous consequence. For there are other types of difference, apart from conceptual difference, that might allow us to distinguish between individual things. For example, numerical difference: I can fix the concept of water and then distinguish between different drops numerically: one drop, two drops, three drops; I distinguish the drops by number only, disregarding their individuality. A second type of difference: spatio-temporal difference. I have the concept of water, but I can distinguish between different drops by their spatio-temporal location ('not *this* drop, *that* drop over there'). A third type: differences of extension and movement. I can have the concept water and distinguish between drops by their extension and figure (shape and size), or by their movement (fast or slow). These are all non-conceptual differences because they allow us to distinguish between two things that nonetheless have the same concept. Once again, however, Leibniz plunges on; he appears on the scene and calmly tells us, no, these differences are pure appearances, provisional means of expressing a difference of another nature, and this difference is always conceptual. If there are two drops of water, they do not have the same concept. Non-conceptual differences only serve to translate, in an imperfect manner, a deeper difference that is always conceptual.

It is here that we reach the crux of the matter in Deleuze's reading of Leibniz. Although no one went further than Leibniz in the exploration of sufficient reason, Leibniz nonetheless subordinated sufficient reason to the requirements of 'representation': in reducing all differences to conceptual differences, Leibniz defined sufficient reason by the ability of differences to be represented or mediated in a *concept*.

> According to the principle of sufficient reason, there is always one concept per particular thing. According to the reciprocal principle of the identity of indiscernibles, there is one and only one thing per concept. Together, these principles expound a theory of difference as conceptual difference, or develop the account of representation as mediation. (DR 12)[12]

In Aristotle, what 'blocks' the specification of the concept beyond the smallest species is the individual itself: the concept provides us with a *form* for which the individual constitutes the *matter*; in Kant, it will be the forms of space and time that block the concept. Leibniz is able to reconcile the concept and the individual only because he gives the identity of the concept an *infinite* comprehension: every individual substance, or monad, envelops the infinity of predicates that constitutes the state of the world. Where the extension of the concept = 1, the comprehension of the concept = ∞. It is one and the same thing to say that the concept goes to infinity (sufficient reason) and that the concept is individual (indiscernibility). In pushing the concept to the level of the individual, however, Leibniz simply rendered representation (or the concept) infinite, while still maintaining the subordination of difference to the principle of identity in the concept.

For Deleuze, this subordination of difference to identity is illegitimate and ungrounded. We have seen that, in Leibniz, the principle of sufficient reason is the reciprocal of the principle of identity, and that the principle of indiscernibles is in turn the reciprocal of the principle of sufficient reason. But would not the reciprocal of the reciprocal simply lead us back to the identity principle?[13] The fact that it does *not*, even in Leibniz, points to the irreducibility of the principle of difference to the principle of identity. Deleuze's thesis is that, behind or beneath the functioning of the identical concept, there lies the movement of difference and multiplicity within an *Idea*. 'What blocks the concept', writes Deleuze in *Difference and Repetition*, 'is always the excess of the Idea, which constitutes the superior positivity that arrests the concept or overturns the requirements of representation' (DR 289). *Difference and Repetition* in its entirety can be read as a search for the roots of sufficient reason, which is formulated in a theory of non-representational Ideas. But 'the immediate, defined as the "sub-representative," is not attained by multiplying representations and points of view. On the contrary, each composing representation must be distorted, diverted, and torn from its centre' – in order to reveal, not the immediacy of the Given, but rather the differential mechanisms of the Idea that themselves function as the genetic conditions of the given (DR 56).[14] Deleuze understands the term 'Idea' largely in its Kantian sense, except that Kantian Ideas are totalising, unifying and transcendent, whereas Deleuzian Ideas are of necessity differential, genetic and immanent. It on the basis of his post-Kantian return to Leibniz that Deleuze will develop his revised theory of Ideas in *Difference and Repetition*.

4. *The Law of Continuity*. These considerations, finally, bring us to the law of continuity. What is the difference between truths of essence (principle of identity) and truths of existence (principles of sufficient

reason and indiscernibility)? With truths of essence, says Leibniz, the analysis is *finite*, such that inclusion of the predicate in the subject can be demonstrated by a finite series of determinate operations (such that one can say, 'Q.E.D'.).[15] The analysis of truths of existence, by contrast, is necessarily *infinite*: the domain of existences is the domain of *infinite analysis*. Why is this the case? Because if the predicate 'sinner' is contained in the concept of Adam, then if we follow the causes back and track down the effects, the entire world must be contained in the notion of Adam. When I perform the analysis, I pass from Adam the sinner to Eve the temptress, and from Eve the temptress to the evil serpent, and from the evil serpent to the forbidden fruit, and so on. Moving forward, I show that there is a direct connection between Adam's sin and the Incarnation and Redemption by Christ. There are *series* that are going to begin to fit into each other across the differences of time and space. The aim of Leibniz's *Theodicy* was precisely to justify God's choice of *this* world, with all its interlocking series. Such an analysis is *infinite* because it has to pass through the entire series of elements that constitute the world, which is actually infinite; and it is an *analysis* because it demonstrates the inclusion of the predicate 'sinner' in the individual notion 'Adam'. 'In the domain of existences, we cannot stop ourselves, because the series are prolongable and must be prolonged, because the inclusion is not localizable' (FLB 51; PLB 69; translation modified). This is the Leibnizian move that matters to Deleuze: at the level of truths of existence, an infinite analysis that demonstrates the inclusion of the predicate ('sinner') in the subject ('Adam') does *not* proceed by the demonstration of an identity. What matters at the level of truths of existence is not the *identity* of the predicate and the subject, but rather, that one passes from one predicate to another, from the second to a third, from the third to a fourth, and so on. Put succinctly: *if truths of essence are governed by identity, truths of existence, by contrast, are governed by continuity.* What is a world? A world is defined by its continuity. What separates two incompossible worlds? The fact that there is a discontinuity between the two worlds. What defines the best of all possible worlds, the world that God will cause to pass into existence? The fact that it realises *the maximum of continuity for a maximum of difference.*

Now this notion of an *infinite analysis* is absolutely original with Leibniz: he invented it. It seems to go without saying, however, that we, as finite beings, are incapable of undertaking an infinite analysis: in order to situate ourselves in the domain of truths of existence, we have to wait for experience. We know through experience that Caesar crossed the Rubicon or that Adam sinned. Infinite analysis is possible for God, to be sure, whose divine understanding is without limits and infinite. But this is hardly a satisfactory answer. God may indeed be able to undertake an infinite analysis, and we may be happy for God, but then we would ask ourselves why Leibniz went to such trouble to present this whole story about analytical truths and infinite analysis if it were only to say that such an analysis is inaccessible to us as finite beings. And it's here that we begin to approach the originality of Deleuze's interpretation of Leibniz. For Leibniz, says Deleuze, indeed attempted to provide us finite humans with an artifice that is capable of undertaking a well-founded approximation of what happens in God's understanding, and this artifice is precisely the technique of the infinitesimal calculus or differential analysis. We as humans can undertake an infinite analysis thanks to the symbolism of the *differential calculus*. Now the calculus brings us into a complex domain, having to do not only with the relation of Leibniz to Newton, but also with the debates on the mathematical foundations of the calculus, which were not resolved until the development of the limit-concept by Cauchy and Weierstrass in the late nineteenth and early twentieth century.[16] In what follows, I would like to focus on two aspects of Leibniz's work on the metaphysics of the calculus that come to the fore in Deleuze's own reading of Leibniz: the differential relation and the theory of singularities. These are two theories that allow us to think the presence of the infinite within the finite.

5. The Differential Relation. Let us turn first to the differential relation. What is at stake in an infinite analysis is not so much the fact that there is an actually existing set of infinite elements in the world. For if there are two elements – for example, Adam the sinner and Eve the temptress – then there is still a *difference* between these two elements. What then does it mean to say that there is a continuity between the seduction of Eve and Adam's sin (and not simply an identity)? It means that the relation between the two elements is an infinitely small relation, or rather, that *the difference between the two is a difference that tends to disappear*. This is the definition of the continuum: continuity is defined as the act of a difference insofar as the difference tends to disappear. Continuity, in short, is a *disappearing* or *vanishing difference*. Between sinner and Adam I will never be able to demonstrate a logical identity, but I will be able to demonstrate (and here the word demonstration obviously changes meaning) a continuity – that is, one or more vanishing differences.

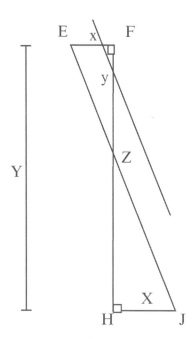

Figure 2

What then is a vanishing difference? In 1701, Leibniz wrote a three-page text entitled 'Justification of the Infinitesimal Calculus by That of Ordinary Algebra', in which he tries to explain that, in a certain manner, the differential calculus was already functioning before it was discovered, even at the level of the most ordinary algebra.[17] Leibniz presents us with a fairly simple geometrical figure (see Figure 2). Two right triangles – ZEF and ZHI – meet at their apex, point Z. Since the two triangles ZEF and ZHI are similar, it follows that the ratio y/x is equal to $(Y - y)/X$. Now if the straight line EI increasingly approaches point F, always preserving the same angle at the variable point Z, the length of the straight lines x and y will obviously diminish steadily, yet the ratio of x to y will remain constant. What happens when the straight line EI passes through F itself? It is obvious that the points Z and E will fall directly on F, and that the straight lines x and y will vanish, they will become equal to zero. And yet, even though x and y are equal to zero, they still maintain an *algebraic* relation to each other, which is expressed in the relation of X to Y. In other words, when the line EI passes through Z, it is not the case that the triangle ZEF has 'disappeared' in the common sense of that word. The triangle ZEF is still 'there', but it is only there 'virtually', since the relation x/y

continues to exist even when the terms have vanished. Rather than saying the triangle ZEF has disappeared, Leibniz says, we should rather say that it has become unassignable even though it is perfectly determined, since in this case although $x = 0$ and $y = 0$, the relation x/y is not equal to zero, since it is a perfectly determinable relation equal to X/Y. *Unassignable, yet perfectly determined* – this is what the term 'vanishing difference' means: it is when the relation continues even when the terms of the relation have disappeared. The relation x/y continues when Z and E have disappeared. This is why the differential relation is such a great mathematical discovery: the miracle is that the differential relation dx/dy is not equal to zero, but rather has a perfectly expressible *finite* quantity, which is the differential derived from the relation of X to Y.

The differential relation is thus not only a relation that is *external* to its terms, but a relation that in a certain sense *constitutes* its terms. It provides Deleuze with a mathematical model for thinking 'difference-in-itself' (the title of the second chapter of *Difference and Repetition*). The differential relation signifies nothing concrete in relation to what it is derived from, that is, in relation to x and y, but it signifies something else concrete, namely a z, which is something *new*, and this is how it assures the passage to limits. Thus, to consider several famous examples, Leibniz can comprehend rest as an infinitely small movement, coincidence as an infinitely small distance, equality as the limit of inequalities, the circle as the limit of a polygon the sides of which increase to infinity. The reason of the law of continuity is thus the *ratio fiendi*, the reason of becoming. Things *become* through continuity: movement becomes rest; the polygon, by multiplying its sides, becomes a circle. This is the source of the popular formulation of the law of continuity in Leibniz: nature never makes leaps (there is no discontinuity in nature). What then is an infinite analysis? An infinite analysis fills the following condition: there is an infinite analysis, and a material for infinite analysis, when I find myself before a domain that is no longer directly ruled by identity, but a domain that is ruled by continuity and vanishing differences.

Now to understand what this theory of the differential relation means in concrete terms, consider the corresponding theory of perception that Leibniz develops in relation to it.[18] Leibniz had observed that we often perceive things of which we are not consciously aware. We recall a familiar scene and become aware of a detail we did not notice at the time; the background noise of a dripping faucet suddenly enters our consciousness at night. Leibniz therefore drew a distinction between conscious perceptions ('apperceptions', or molar perceptions) and unconscious perceptions ('minute' or molecular perceptions), and argued that our conscious perceptions must be related, not simply to recognisable objects in space and time, but rather to the minute and unconscious perceptions of which they are composed. I apprehend the noise of the sea or the murmur of a group of people, for instance, but not the sound of each wave or the voice of each person that compose them. These unconscious minute perceptions are related to conscious 'molar' perceptions, not as parts to a whole, but as what is ordinary to what is noticeable or remarkable: a conscious perception is produced when at least two of these minute and 'virtual' perceptions enter into a *differential relation* that determines a singularity, that is, a conscious perception. Consider the noise of the sea: at least two waves must be minutely perceived as nascent and 'virtual' in order to enter into a differential relation capable of determining a third, which excels over the others and becomes conscious. Or consider the colour green: yellow and blue can be perceived, but if the difference between them vanishes by approaching zero, then they enter into a differential relation (db/dy = G) that determines the colour green; in turn, yellow or blue, each on its own account, may be determined by the differential relation of two colours we cannot detect (dy/dx = Y). The calculus thus functions in Leibniz as the psychic mechanism of perception, a kind of automatism that determines my finite zone of clarity on the world, my point of view. Every conscious perception constitutes a threshold, and the minute or virtual perceptions (infinitely small perceptions) constitute the obscure dust of the world, its background noise. They are not 'parts' of conscious perception, but rather the 'ideal genetic elements' of perception, or what Solomon Maimon called the 'differentials of consciousness'. The virtual multiplicity of genetic elements, and the system of connections or differential relations that are established between them, is what Deleuze terms the 'Idea' of sensibility. It is the differential relations between these infinitely small perceptions that draw them into clarity, that 'actualise' a clear perception (such as green) out of certain obscure, evanescent perceptions (such as yellow and blue). 'The Idea of the world or the Idea of the sea are *systems of differential equations,* of which each monad only actualizes a partial solution'.[19]

In Leibniz, then, the differential calculus refers to a domain that is both mathematical and psychological, a psycho-mathematical domain: there are differentials of consciousness just as there are differentials of a curve. Several important consequences follow. Space and time here cease to be pure *a priori* givens (as in Kant), but are determined *genetically* by the ensemble or nexus of these differential relations in the subject. Similarly, objects themselves cease to be empirical givens and become the product of these relations in conscious perception. Moreover, Descartes' principle of 'clear and distinct' ideas is broken down into two irreducible values, which can never be reunited to constitute a 'natural light': conscious perceptions are necessarily clear but confused (not distinct), while unconscious perceptions (Ideas) are distinct but necessarily obscure (not clear).[20] Indeed, Leibniz can be said to have developed one of the first theories of the unconscious, a theory that is very different from the one developed by Freud. The difference is that Freud conceived of the unconscious in a *conflictual* or *oppositional* relationship to consciousness, and not a *differential* relationship. In this sense, Freud was dependent on Kant, Hegel and their successors, who explicitly oriented the unconscious in the direction of a conflict of will, and no longer a differential of perception. The theory of the unconscious proposed by Deleuze and Guattari in *Anti-Oedipus* concerns a differential and genetic unconscious, and is thus thoroughly inspired by Leibniz.[21]

6. *The Theory of Singularities.* There is a final problem that Deleuze points to in Leibniz's thought. On the surface, there would appear to be a contradiction between the principle of indiscernibles and the law of continuity. On the one hand, the principle of indiscernibles tells us that every difference is conceptual, that no two things have the same concept. To every thing there corresponds a determinate difference, which is not only determinate but assignable in the concept. On the other hand, the principle of continuity tells us that things proceed via vanishing differences, infinitely small differences, that is, unassignable differences. Thus Leibniz seems to be saying, at one and the same time, that every thing proceeds by an unassignable difference, and that every difference is assignable and must be assigned in the concept. So the question is: Is it possible to reconcile the principle of indiscernibles with the law of continuity?

    Deleuze's thesis is that the solution to this problem has to be posed in terms of a theory of *singularities*, which is an extension of the theory of differential equations. In logic, the notion of the 'singular' has long been understood in relation to the 'universal'. In mathematics, however, the singular is related to a very different set of notions: the singular is distinguished from or opposed to the regular: the singular is what escapes the regularity of the rule. More importantly, mathematics distinguishes between points that are singular or remarkable, and those that are ordinary. Geometrical figures, for instance, can be classified by the types of singular points that determine them. A square has four singular points, its four corners, and an infinity of ordinary points that compose each side of the square (the calculus of *extremum*). Simple curves, such as the arc of circle, are determined by a single singularity, which is either a maximum or minimum, or both at once (the calculus of *maxima* and *minima*).[22] The differential calculus deals with the more difficult case of complex curves – the singularities of a complex curve are the points in the neighbourhood of which the differential relation changes sign (focal points, saddle points, knots, etc.): the curve increases, the curve decreases. These points of increase or decrease are the singular points of the curve; the ordinary points are what constitute the series between the two singularities. The theory of singularites provides Deleuze with his final, more technical definition of the law of continuity: the continuum is the prolongation of a singularity over an ordinary series of points until it reaches the neighbourhood of the following singularity, at which point the differential relation changes sign, and either diverges from or converges with the next singularity. The continuum is thus inseparable from a theory or an activity of prolongation: there is a composition of the continuum because the continuum is a product.

In this way, the theory of singularities also provides Deleuze with a model of individuation or determination: one can say of any determination in general (any 'thing') that it is *a combination of the singular and the ordinary*, that is, it is a 'multiplicity' constituted by its singular and ordinary points. Just as mathematical curves are determined by their points of inflection (extrema, minima and maxima, etc.), so physical states of affairs can be said to be determined by singularities that mark a change of phase (boiling points, points of condensation, fusion, coagulation, crystallisation, etc.) and a person's psychology by their 'sensitive' points (points where a person 'breaks down' in anger or tears, states of joy, sickness and health, fatigue and vitality, hope and anxiety, etc.). But such singularites, Deleuze insists, can nonetheless be considered *apart from* their actualisation in a physical state of affairs or a psychological person (see LS 52). Deleuze here reaches a domain that is distinct from, and logically prior to, the three domains that Kant would later denounce as transcendental illusions or Ideas: the Self, the World and God. Each of these Ideas has a determinate place in Leibniz's philosophy: God is the Being who, faced with the infinity of possible worlds, chose to actualise this World, a world that exists only in its individual monads or Selves, which express the world from their own point of view. But what this Leibnizian schema presupposes, Deleuze argues, is the determination of a 'transcendental field' that is prior to God, World and Self, a field populated by singularities that are a-theological, a-cosmic, and pre-individual. It implies a transcendental logic of singularities that is irreducible to the formal logic of predication. Here, for example, are three singularities of the individual 'Adam', expressed in an infinitive form: 'to be the first man', 'to live in a garden of pleasure', 'to have a woman come out of one's rib'. And then a fourth singularity: 'to sin'. We can prolong each of these four singular points over a series of ordinary points such that they all have common values in both directions: a continuity is established between them. But then add a fifth singularity: 'to resist the temptation'. The lines of prolongation between this fifth singularity and the first three are no longer convergent, that is, they do not pass through common values: there is a bifurcation in the series at this singularity, a *discontinuity* is introduced. Adam the non-sinner is thus incompossible with this world, because it implies a singularity that *diverges* with this world.

The theory of singularities thus plays a double role in Deleuze's work on Leibniz. On the one hand, it allows Deleuze to solve the riddle posed by the relation between indiscernibility and continuity within Leibniz's own philosophy. The world 'in itself' is indeed governed by the law of continuity, since continuity is nothing other than the composition of singularities insofar as they are prolonged over the series of ordinaries that depend on them. But the world does not exist 'in itself': it exists only in the individuals that express it. And the real definition of the individual is: *the accumulation or coincidence of a certain number of pre-individual singularities* that are extracted from the curve of the world, each of them being discontinuous and unique, and hence governed by the principle of indiscernibles. Individuation, in other words, 'does not move from a genus to smaller and smaller species, in accordance with a rule of differenciation; it goes from singularity to singularity, in accordance with the rule of convergence or prolongation that links the individual to such and such a world'.[23] On the other hand, Deleuze is not content simply to provide a reading of Leibniz. 'These impersonal and pre-individual nomadic singularities', Deleuze writes, speaking in his own name, 'are what constitute the *real* transcendental field' (LS 109; translation modified). *Difference and Repetition* and *Logic of Sense* are Deleuze's attempt to define the nature of this transcendental field, freed from the limitations of Leibniz's theological presuppositions, and using his own conceptual vocabulary (multiplicity, singularity, virtuality, problematic, event, etc.). In Deleuze, the Ideas of God, World and Self take on completely different demeanours than they do in Leibniz. *God* is no longer a Being who chooses the richest compossible world, but has now become a pure Process that makes *all* virtualities pass into existence, forming an infinite web of divergent and convergent series. The *World* is no longer a continuous curve defined by its preestablished harmony, but has become a chaotic universe in which divergent series trace endlessly bifurcating paths, giving rise to violent discords. And the *Self*, rather than being closed on the compossible world it expresses from within, is now torn open by the divergent series and incompossible ensembles that continually pull it outside itself (the monadic subject, as Deleuze puts it, becomes the nomadic subject).[24]

It is at this point that Deleuze's reading of Leibniz would end, and a reading of Deleuze's own philosophy would have to begin. We have here followed Deleuze's deduction of a principle of difference, within Leibniz's own thought, from the simplest formulation of the principle of identity (A is A). An elaboration of Deleuze's own thought would have to move in the opposite direction, as it were, showing how Deleuze produces his own deduction of concepts starting from the principle of difference: the differential relation and its determinable elements, the resulting singularities that are extended in series (with their connective, convergent and divergent syntheses), which thereby constitute a multiplicity, whose modal status is purely virtual (as opposed to constituting a set of 'possibilities', as in Leibniz), and so on. It would not be an exaggeration to say that almost all of Deleuze's fundamental metaphysical concepts (difference, singularity, multiplicity, virtuality) are derived from this Leibnizian matrix. Classical reason, says Deleuze, collapsed under the blow of divergences, discordances and incompossibilities, and Leibniz's philosophy was one of the last attempts to reconstitute a classical reason. It did so by *multiplying its principles*, relegating divergences to so many possible worlds, making incompossibilities so many frontiers between worlds, and resolving the discords that appear in this world into the melodic lines of the preestablished harmony. But Leibniz's Baroque reconstitution could only be temporary. With the collapse of classical reason, the task of philosophy would be to think without principles, to start *neither* with the identity of God, the Self, or the World, but rather with a transcendental field of differences and singularities that conditions the construction of empirical selves and the actual world. This is the task that Deleuze adopts as his own: 'We seek to determine an impersonal and pre-individual transcendental field that does not resemble the corresponding empirical fields' (LS 102). It is a thoroughly contemporary project, but one that allows Deleuze to reach back into the history of philosophy and make *use* of Leibniz's philosophy and Leibniz's concepts in the pursuit of his own philosophical aims.

Purdue University

Notes

1. An early version of this paper appeared under the title 'Difference, Continuity, and the Calculus', in Stephen Daniel (ed.), *Current Continental Theory and Modern Philosophy* (Evanston, IL: Northwestern University Press, 2005), pp. 127–47.
2. See Deleuze's remark in his *Lettre-préface* to Jean-Clet Martin's *Variations: La Philosophie de Gilles Deleuze* (Paris: Payot & Rivages, 1993): 'I feel that I am a very classical philosopher. I believe in philosophy as a system . . . [But] for me, the system must not only be in perpetual heterogeneity, it must be a *heterogenesis*, something which, it seems to me, has never before been attempted' (p. 7).
3. See EPS 11: 'What I needed was both (1) the expressive character of particular individuals, and (2) an immanence of being. Leibniz, in a way, goes still further than Spinoza on the first point. But on the second, Spinoza stands alone. One finds it only in him. This is why I consider myself a Spinozist, rather than a Leibnizian, although I owe a lot to Leibniz'.
4. Deleuze also devoted two series of sessions of his seminar at the University of Vincennes–St. Denis to Leibniz, first in 1980, and then again in 1987, when he was at work on *The Fold*. My discussion here follows closely the deduction presented in the 1980 seminars.
5. For a discussion of Deleuze's relation to Maimon and the post-Kantian tradition, see Daniel W. Smith, 'Deleuze, Hegel, and the Post-Kantian Tradition', *Philosophy Today*, supplement 44 (2001), pp. 119–31, and Graham Jones, *Difference and Determination: Prolegomena Concerning Deleuze's Early Metaphysic*, unpublished PhD Dissertation, Monash University, 2002.
6. As Maimon had shown, whereas identity is the condition of possibility of thought in general, it is difference that constitutes the genetic condition of *real* thought.
7. References to *The Fold* will be coupled with references to the French original, *Le Pli: Leibniz et le baroque* (PLB)

8. Gottfried Wilhelm Leibniz, *New Essays on Human Understanding*, edited by Jonathan Bennett and Peter Remnant (Cambridge: Cambridge University Press, 1997), p. 361.
9. See Louis Couturat, 'On Leibniz's Metaphysics', in Harry G. Frankfurt (ed.), *Leibniz: A Collection of Critical Essays* (Garden City, NY: Anchor Books, 1972), p. 22: 'The principle of identity states: every identity (analytic) proposition is true. The principle of reason affirms, on the contrary: every true proposition is an identity (analytic)'.
10. See Aristotle, 'Categoriae', in *The Basic Works of Aristotle*, trans. E. M. Edghill, ed. R. McKeon (New York: Random House, 1941), p. 14.
11. See Benson Mates, *The Philosophy of Leibniz: Metaphysics and Language* (Oxford: Oxford University Press, 1986), p. 157: 'To discover the reason for the truth of the essential proposition "A is B" is to analyze the concept A far enough to reveal the concept B as contained in it'. Deleuze, however, would disagree with Mates' statement that Leibniz 'appears to use the terms "reason" and "cause" interchangeably' (p. 158), despite the ambiguities of several Leibnizian texts.
12. On the relation of difference and repetition in the classical theory of the concept, see DR 288: difference is always inscribed within the identity of the concept in general, and repetition is defined as a difference *without* a concept, that is, in terms of the numerically distinct exemplars or individuals that are subsumed under the generality of the concept (x^1, x^2, x^3, ... x^n), and which block further conceptual specification.
13. Seminar of 6 May. http://www.webdeleuze.com/php/texte.php?cle=127 &groupe=Leibniz&langue=1
14. See also DR 222: 'Difference is not diversity. Diversity is given, but difference is that by which the given is given as diverse'.
15. However, Deleuze will argue, against Leibniz himself, that the analysis of essences must itself be infinite, since it is inseparable from the infinity of God. See FLB 42; PLB 56–7.
16. For an analysis of Deleuze's relation to the history of the calculus, see Daniel W. Smith, 'Mathematics and the Theory of Multiplicities: Deleuze and Badiou Revisited', *Southern Journal of Philosophy* 41:3 (2003), pp. 411–49.
17. Gottfried Wilhelm Leibniz, *Philosophical Papers and Letters*, edited by Leroy E. Loemker (Dordrecht, Holland: D. Reidel), pp. 545–6.
18. Deleuze analyses this theory in an important chapter, entitled 'Perception in the Folds', in FLB 85–99; PLB 113–32.
19. See Alberto Gualandi, *Deleuze* (Paris: Les Belles Lettres, 1998), p. 49. Gualandi's book is one of the best short introductions to Deleuze's work, emphasising Deleuze's philosophy of nature.
20. Kant had already objected that Maimon, by returning to Leibniz, thereby reintroduced the duality between a finite understanding (consciousness) and an infinite understanding (the divine), which the entire

Kantian critique had attempted to eliminate. See Immanuel Kant, letter to Marcus Herz, 26 May 1789, in Arnulf Zweig (ed.), *Immanuel Kant: Philosophical Correspondence, 1759–99* (Chicago: University of Chicago Press, 1967), pp. 150–6. Against Kant, however, Deleuze argues that 'the infinite here is only the presence of an *unconscious* in the finite understanding, an unthought in finite thought, a non-self in the finite self (whose presence Kant himself was forced to discover when he hollowed out the difference between a determining ego and a determinable ego). For Maimon as for Leibniz, the reciprocal determination of differentials does not refer to a divine understanding, but to minute perceptions as the representatives of the world in the finite self' (FLB 118–19; PLB 162, translation modified). See also DR 192–3. For an analysis of Deleuze's relation to Maimon, and the manner in which Maimon influences Deleuze's reading of Leibniz, see Graham Jones' magisterial thesis, *Difference and Determination: Prolegomena Concerning Deleuze's Early Metaphysic*. My discussion here owes much to Jones' work.

21. See DR 106–8 (as well as the whole of AO), which contain Deleuze's most explicit advocation of a differential unconscious (Leibniz, Fechner) over a conflictual unconscious (Freud).

22. See Leibniz's analysis of simple curves in '*Tentamen Anagogicum*: An Anagogical Essay in the Investigation of Causes', in Leibniz, *Philosophical Papers*, pp. 477–85.

23. FLB 64; PLB 86; translation modified.

24. See LS 174: 'Instead of a certain number of predicates being excluded by a thing by virtue of the identity of its concept, each "thing" is open to the infinity of predicates through which it passes, and at the same time it loses its centre, that is to say, its identity as a concept and as a self'.

4

David Hume

Jon Roffe

Gilles Deleuze's first book, devoted to David Hume, is often neglected when surveying his work. This is a peculiar state of affairs for any major philosopher, since the early works of important thinkers are frequently rich in meaning in relation to the later *oeuvre*. While none are significant as mitigating factors, there are a number of apparent reasons for the neglect. In the first instance, we cannot help but note the lack of any significant explicit presence of Hume's thought in Deleuze's philosophy. With the exception of a discussion of the Humean account of habit in *Difference and Repetition* (DR 70–4), and a short summary article ('Hume' [1972]),[1] Hume's obvious presence in the Deleuzian corpus is entirely limited to this inaugural volume. It is easy to see his second book, *Nietzsche and Philosophy*, as the true opening moment of Deleuze's mature philosophical endeavour. Not only are the themes broached in the Nietzsche book returned to many times in later works, but Nietzsche himself remains a key point of reference throughout. Correlatively, the philosophical investments that motivate the Nietzsche book are very much closer to the philosophical position which becomes recognisable as Deleuze's own. *Empiricism and Subjectivity* on the other hand, is couched in terms which have no place in the mature Deleuze's work: association, laws of nature, purposiveness, passion and sympathy, all drawn from Hume's philosophy, never feature in any subsequent publication. Nowhere else do we read of the role of God in the organisation of the world of culture, nor the claim that philosophy must renounce its systematic or metaphysical ambitions and become 'the theory of what we are doing, not . . . the theory of what there is' (ES 133).

The aim of what follows is not to dispute any of these points as such. Rather, after presenting the central tenets of *Empiricism and Subjectivity*, I would like to indicate the extent to which this work provides an implicit foundation for what comes after, and in particular the metaphysics of *Difference and Repetition*, with which this inaugural work has, perhaps surprisingly, much in common.

EMPIRICISM AND SUBJECTIVITY

The most general characteristic of Deleuze's reading of Hume is that it completely avoids the epistemological emphasis that has dominated almost the entire history of Hume's reception, beginning with the Kant of the first *Critique* and the *Prolegomena*.[2] For Deleuze, Humean empiricism is *not fundamentally oriented around epistemological questions*. On this matter, Deleuze is extremely direct:

> The classical definition of empiricism proposed by the Kantian tradition is this: empiricism is the theory according to which knowledge not only begins with experience but is derived from it. But why would the empiricist say that? And as the result of which question? This definition, to be sure, has at least the advantage of avoiding a piece of nonsense: were empiricism to be defined simply as a theory according to which knowledge begins only with experience, there would not have been any philosophy or philosophers – Plato and Leibniz included – who would not be empiricists. The fact is, though, that the definition is in no way satisfactory . . . In short, it seems impossible to define empiricism as a theory according to which knowledge derives from experience. (ES 107–8)

In place of this perennial point of interest, Deleuze proposes a fascinating thesis, elaborated on the basis of a thorough reading of, in particular, Hume's key work *A Treatise Of Human Nature* (1739–40).[3] His claim is that the central issue dealt with in Hume's thought is the genesis of subjectivity itself. Deleuze writes that 'the question that will preoccupy Hume is this: *how does the mind become human nature?*' (ES 22). It is only on the basis of this concern that an increasingly ramified series of other issues are addressed, including epistemology, but also the genesis of the entire range of intersubjective states of affairs, including morality, taste, commerce and government, the institution of property and family life.[4] Thus we can already see why, for Deleuze, the central claim of Humean empiricism cannot be reduced to questions of the status and origin of knowledge.[5] This is because these familiar questions – like the nature of our claims about causality,[6] or more generally the problem of induction – already presuppose a distinction between the subject and the object, and it is this that Hume (on Deleuze's account) is principally concerned to give an account of.

Empiricism and Subjectivity turns around this question, returning to it time and time again, reposing it in new ways, representing Hume's answer from new points of views and in increasingly refined ways: 'How does a collection become a system?' (ES 22); 'How does the mind become human nature' (ES 22); 'How does the mind become a subject?' (ES 23); 'How does the imagination become a faculty?' (ES 23); 'How does the imagination become human nature?' (ES 23); 'What factors will transform the mind?' (ES 98); 'When is the subject the product of the principles of human nature?' (ES 109) It is the unity of these questions, and the concepts that they invoke, that give Deleuze's book its coherence.

How does this movement occur in Hume according to Deleuze? Here we arrive at the second key deviation from the traditional reading of Hume, and one that supports the first. The question of induction is presented in the same terms as are used at the opening of both Hume's *Treatise* and the *Enquiry concerning Human Understanding*, namely in terms of the relationship between impressions and ideas. There, Hume presents a familiar account of what is often considered the cornerstone of empiricism: that all 'perceptions' in the mind can be divided into two kinds, distinguishable on the basis of their liveliness or vivacity. On the one hand, impressions are the lively perceptions, which result from sensory experience, or from emotions, and on the other, ideas are 'the faint images of these [impressions] in thinking and reasoning' (T 1; Bk.1 §1). It is this distinction, at least with regards to questions of knowledge and belief, that structures the traditional presentation of Hume.

In place of this emphasis, Deleuze presents what we might call a facultative reading of Hume.[7] Instead of focusing on the impression–idea relationship, Deleuze is interested in the emerging system – the subject itself – which provides the internal rules for the organisation of the chaos which natively exists within the mind. This is why Deleuze does not begin with the impression–idea movement, but with the state of the mind before the elaboration of the subject, which he presents in terms of the faculty of the imagination: 'The depth of the mind is indeed delirium, or – what is the same thing from another point of view – change and indifference. By itself, the imagination is not nature; it is a mere fancy' (ES 23).

This facultative account is effectively split into four moments or aspects of the deployment of the multiple *principles of human nature*. The brief answer to the question 'how is the subject constituted within the given?' is that the principles of human nature give order, regularity and purpose to the chaos of associations, and that through this organisation, the subject emerges as an active part of the organisation itself. Elaborating on Hume's analogy of the mind

as a percussive instrument, Deleuze writes: 'The subject must be compared to the resonance and to the increasingly louder reverberation
of principles within the depths of the mind' (ES 112). At the same
time, this movement is one that involves a transition from passive to
active, or rather the emergence of an active subject under the influence
of the principles: 'the subject is an imprint, or an impression, left by
principles, . . . it progressively turns into a machine capable of using
this impression' (ES 113).

Deleuze compares these principles to Kant's but with a key difference: 'According to Hume, and also Kant, the principles of knowledge
are not derived from experience. But in the case of Hume, nothing is
transcendental, because these principles are simply principles of our
nature' (ES 111–12). The principles of human nature are, in the first
instance, double, constituted on the one hand by the principles of the
passions, but on the other by the famous principles of association:
resemblance, contiguity and cause and effect.

The principles of association are what provide the elementary
structure of the subject by providing constancy to the fleeting and
ungoverned associations in the mind. In particular, the relation of
cause and effect allows us to organise our understanding of the
world around beliefs in permanence, stability and persistence over
time. Through the activity of these principles, 'the mind ceases to
be fancy, is fixed, and becomes human nature' (ES 59). From the
collection of impressions which are associated indifferently and asys-
tematically, the subject begins to emerge as a self-governing system
of tendencies.

The second moment of this account presents an inevitable but del-
eterious consequence of this entirely constructed order in the mind,
an order which relies on no referential content ('things in the world')
for its legitimacy:

> If it is true that the principles of association shape the mind, by impos-
> ing on it a nature that disciplines the delirium or the fictions of the
> imagination, conversely, the imagination uses these same principles
> to make its fictions or its fantasies acceptable and to give them a
> warrant they wouldn't have on their own. In this sense, it belongs to
> fiction to feign these relations, to induce fictive ones, and to make us
> believe in our follies. (PI 41–2)

The (entirely unavoidable) problem here is the following: given that
the consistency and structure of the mind is a fiction, produced not
on the basis of a correspondence with the world but rather according

to the application of principles to the variety of experience, it follows that the consistency and structure thus produced tend towards fictional applications. The 'easy transition' (ES 25) that the principles create from one idea to another is equally in the service of legitimate and illegitimate associations. In other words, the constituted subject is not constituted around a principle of truth, but around a principle of order. And some of the consequences sanctioned by this order are properly speaking products. To put the matter in the Kantian form that Deleuze often uses, the principles of association are *illegitimate and excessive* – they go too far, and sanctify too many things. Perhaps the most famous example, referred to in Hume's own work, is the belief in the reality of cause and effect as a physical law. It is the nature of subjectivity to organise the world on the basis of an association between ideas that assigns one the role of 'cause' and the other its seeming 'effect'. This relationship is legitimately created within the mind in accordance with the principles of association. However, this very legitimacy is then conveyed upon the complex idea of reality as such: the second billiard ball moved because the first one struck it. From the legitimate application of the principles, illegitimate inferences – on the basis of this very application of the principles – are also sanctioned. The same holds for all of the great 'objects' of metaphysical speculation, like space and time (ES 90–2), God (whose status as an object of knowledge and belief is thoroughly examined in Hume's *Dialogues Concerning Natural Religion*) and the world: 'the world . . . is an outright fiction of the imagination' (ES 80). It also holds for the postulation of objects as such, of which Deleuze presents a brief but fascinating structural account (ES 81).

Hume's account, however, does not remain at this initial level. As Deleuze argues, Hume notices that there is a secondary application of the same principles, this time a *corrective* application which reins in this excessive if unavoidable use of association by the subject. This is the role of reason in Hume's philosophy. Reason is the subjective capacity – engendered by the principles themselves – to *reflect on* and *critique* the beliefs that constitute the subject, in accordance with the principles. This is both its proper strength and the source of its ultimate futility. Only reason has the unconcerned and passionless point of view to present such a critique, aligning it with 'a strict calculus of probabilities' (PI 43), a probabilistic analysis of the likelihood of particular fictions in relation to the more general schema of association, and the correction of deviations from this norm. This, however, is all that it can do, having no other strength or mandate. Its capacity 'to reflect on something is exclusively corrective; functioning alone, [it] can do only one thing *ad infinitum* – to correct its corrections' (ES 84).

Furthermore, even given this secondary and corrective activity of the principles of association, Deleuze indicates that we find ourselves in a position whereby the greatest and most widespread illusions are beyond our capacity to correct: 'In a final refinement, or third act, illegitimate beliefs in the Self, the World and God appear as the horizon of all possible beliefs, or as the lowest degree of belief' (PI 44).

> The excessive rules of knowledge openly contradict the principles of association; to correct them amounts to denouncing their fiction. A distinct and continuous world is, from the point of view of the principles, the general residue of this fiction, being situated at a level that makes them impossible to correct. As for the excessive moral rules, they undoubtedly constrain the passions; they also sketch out a wholly fictitious world. (ES 131; translation modified)

So, if reason is the developed capacity to examine and critique the ways in which beliefs relate to our experience of the world, it is developed according to the same processes that present it with problematic instances in need of such critique. For Hume, it is not the sleep of reason which engenders monsters in the mind ('fire dragons, winged horses and monstrous giants' [PI 41]) – these monsters preexist reason, and are given renewed legitimacy by the same principles that lend force to reason itself. This is the first sense in which reason is presented as a weak or auxiliary capacity in Hume's account. The second, as we will now see, concerns the role of the passions in relation to reason.

Now, the principles of association are met, complemented with, supported and exceeded by the principles of the passions.[8] Deleuze strongly emphasises the fact that, for Hume, the passions both give sense to the principles of association and dominate them. Where association constructs relations between ideas, relative causes and effects, what is provided by the passions are the weighting of these relations with respect to *means and ends*. Where the principles of association render the subject consistent, the principles of the passions render it moral. Qualitative distinction is added to quantitative order, providing a capacity for the distinction between causes in terms of a goal. We thus comprehend Hume's famous assertion that reason is the slave of the passions, that 'reason alone can never be a motive to any action of the will' (T 413; Bk.2 §3), and what Deleuze indicates is the single most important sentiment in Hume's philosophy: 'Tis not contrary to reason to prefer the destruction of the whole world to the scratching of my finger' (T 416; Bk.2 §3; cf. ES 33). For the relations of cause and effect that are constituted by the principles of association have no orientation (ES 123), and in themselves suggest no course of action.

More importantly, however, the principles of the passions provide the practical, or, what amounts to the same thing, institutional, solution to the problem of the excessive application of the principles of association. While, as we have seen, the reflexive or corrective use of these principles is of limited capacity, the principles of the passions form the moral and political framework in which the extended use of the associations can be framed, evaluated and judged. This is why Deleuze claims – in a key moment of the text – that 'the problem of the self, insoluble at the level of the understanding, finds, uniquely within culture, a moral and political solution' (ES 64). The principles of the passions thus provide a necessary correlate to the principles of association by orienting them and limiting them according to our social investments, or, as Deleuze has it: 'Association gives the subject a possible structure, but only the passions can give it being and existence. In its relation to the passions, association finds its sense and its destiny' (ES 120). In turn, reason itself, as the corrective moment of the principles of association, finds its ground in the passions. This is why 'reason can always be brought to bear, but it is brought to bear on a pre-existing world and presupposes an antecedent ethics and an order of ends' (ES 33).

Again, however – and this is the fourth moment – the principles of the passions in their primary application are found wanting. This time, instead of extending too far and engaging in illusions, it is a case of them not going far enough. This mechanism is, in the first instance, *sympathy*. It is through my sympathy with others who are like me (here we see one role played by resemblance in Hume's thought) that I can express 'the desire for the pleasure of the Other and . . . an aversion to his or her pain' (ES 37). However, my sympathy for others is naturally limited, since it is partial (ES 38), leaving us with less than the universality implied by the ideas of justice and fairness. This is why Deleuze will claim that 'society is in the beginning a collection of families' (ES 39). Even though '*all the elements of morality (sympathies) are naturally given, . . . they are impotent by themselves to constitute a moral world*' (ES 40).

It is here that one of Hume's greatest strengths lies for Deleuze, for he sees in Hume the elaboration of an account of an entire network of contingent means produced by the inventive movement of the principles of the passions themselves. The whole moral world, or the system of extended means, is literally *created* through the continued activity of the principles. This system is entirely fabricated; it is literally unnatural. The reality of the moral world 'is not natural, it is artificial' (ES 40). This moral world is rich and complex, and Deleuze demonstrates how Hume can present a rich theory of not just politics traditionally understood, but of property, conversation, commerce, taste, taxation, and so forth, all on the basis of the extension of sympathy through the creative movement of the principles of the passions.[9] 'True morality . . . does not involve the change of human nature but the invention of artificial and objective conditions in order for the bad [which is to say, partial, limited] aspects of this nature not to triumph' (ES 50). To make a point that I will return to below, Hume for Deleuze elaborates an entire model of the personal and the social (as two interlinked products of the activity of the principles) in the figure of the *institution*.

> The institution, unlike the law, is not a limitation but rather a model of actions, a veritable enterprise, an invented system of positive means or a positive invention of indirect means. This conception of the institution effectively reverses the problem: outside of the social there lies the negative, lack, or need. The social is profoundly creative, inventive, and positive. (ES 35; translation modified)

Just like the possibility of a rigorous psychology, the possibility of morality, sociology and politics rests on the creative activity of the principles, which themselves work on the delirious maelstrom of the undisciplined imagination. In short, the Hume that emerges in Deleuze's *Empiricism and Subjectivity* presents the entire panoply of intra- and inter-subjective states of affairs as 'veritable production[s]' (ES 48).

HUME'S THOUGHT IN DELEUZE

The next significant direct discussion of Hume in Deleuze's work is found at the beginning of the chapter devoted to repetition in *Difference and Repetition*, discussing habit with respect to the same pair. At issue once more is the constitution of a certain form of subjectivity undergirded by a synthetic moment which is not the act of this subject. However, what is completely absent is any reference to Hume's principles – these will be replaced in the final analysis with

Deleuze's retooled version of the Kantian Idea – and, consequently, the models of the reverberation and complication of the principles in establishing the rich world of the subject and the object will be replaced with the theme of contemplation, and, more profoundly, with the sweeping drama of what Deleuze comes to call *indi-drama-differenc/tiation*. A few years after *Difference and Repetition* Deleuze published his summary article on Hume for a history of philosophy edited by Gilles Châtelet. This piece reprises a number of the main themes of *Empiricism and Subjectivity*, without adding anything distinctive (despite the fact that the piece in question was published in the same year as *Anti-Oedipus*). However, both of these references are relatively insignificant in the general development of Deleuze's thought. It is as though Hume's presence vanishes right after it had first made itself felt in *Empiricism and Subjectivity*.

One might respond that to assume the lack of Hume's significance in Deleuze's thought would mean having to ignore his continual references to and identification with empiricism. But this is not where the real impact of Humean thought on the philosophy of Deleuze is to be felt. As I will argue shortly, Deleuze's project of a properly *transcendental* empiricism is not a descendant of Hume's philosophy in any conventional sense.[10] In fact, we must read *Empiricism and Subjectivity* as the work which sets up a significant number of the issues that Deleuze's mature work is engaged with. Here, I would like to briefly catalogue six of the most important of these, in keeping with the kind of catalogue Deleuze himself proposes with respect to Hume: 'We dream sometimes of a history of philosophy that would list only the new concepts created by a great philosopher – his most essential and creative contribution' (ES ix).

The critique of negativity. A hallmark of Deleuze's thought, particularly in the works of the 1960s and 1970s, is an attempt to revoke – or, to be more precise, properly situate – the power, explanatory or otherwise, of any postulate of negativity. The position elucidated in *Difference and Repetition* is paradigmatic: that the negative is only the ephiphenomenon of actualised difference, an inevitable transcendental illusion; that by taking the negative as fundamental we in fact invert our grasp on the world, animating a shadow play which robs us of the thought of difference. Already in *Empiricism and Subjectivity*, this theme will play a central role. As we have seen, the entire ensemble of institutions – including the subject itself – emerges out of the ramified and reinforced activity of the principles on the given (the indifferent association of the ensemble of ideas in the understanding). From the subject through to the institution and maintenance of private property, then, Hume presents a rigorously positive philosophy. The negative – whether in its Hegelian, Sartrean or psychoanalytic formulations – plays no role in the account of this immense generation of the subject and the intersubjective world.

The figure of the institution. These points about negativity relate to another theme that can be found throughout Deleuze's work, the theme of the institution (*qua* creative construction), often opposed to the idea of instinct (*qua* natural pathway to the satisfaction of drives), where the latter is finally linked, in *Anti-Oedipus*, to negativity once more.[11] As we have seen, for Deleuze the institution names in Hume the inventive aspect of culture as such ('The institution is the figure' [ES 49]): 'The idea that Hume forms of society is very strong . . . the main idea is this: the essence of society is not the law but rather the institution' (ES 45).

The correlate of the rejection of the explanatory power of the negative in Deleuze is the emphasis on the positive construction of reality, whether in relation to the problematic virtual Ideas in *Difference and Repetition*, or the sinuous if repressed movements of the desiring-machines in *Anti-Oedipus*. Indeed, Deleuze's philosophy increasingly emphasises this point, beginning perhaps with *A Thousand Plateaus*, which presents a fully constructivist ontology, and in the course of this presents the infamous question 'How do you make yourself a body without organs?' In the texts that follow, questions of similar timbre occur with increasing frequency: How does Bacon create figures? How can the philosopher creatively respond to cinema? How is a concept, an affect, a conceptual plane of immanence, to be constructed? The least that can be said on this front is that this orientation is first manifest in *Empiricism and Subjectivity*.

'*Relations are external to their terms.*' This claim is championed in each of Deleuze's treatments of Hume. It runs through the whole of *Empiricism and Subjectivity*, and is identified by Deleuze in the Introduction to the English translation as one of Hume's great conceptual inventions (ES x). The strongest and most striking formulation is perhaps the following: 'We will call "non-empiricist" every theory according to which, *in one way or another*, relations are derived from the nature of things' (ES 109). It is particularly striking in comparison with the use to which Deleuze puts this theme later, and particularly in *Difference and Repetition*. For there, this arch-empiricist theme finds its supreme instance in a metaphysical reading of the differential calculus, in which the differential relation dy/dx is maintained as a pure relation even when the respective values are zero.[12] This particular transition indicates the extent to which Deleuze's more general account of empiricism is in keeping with developments within his thought, with no concern for the obvious blocs of opinion which govern the history of philosophy.

The danger for thought within thinking. In *Difference and Repetition*, Deleuze presents a brief history of accounts of error in thinking, beginning with Descartes and Plato. In these figures, external or empirical factors are invoked to explain the possibility that thought might go astray. However, in Kant (but also, in different ways, in Hegel and Schopenhauer [DR 150]), a quite different possibility exists, namely illusion, a threat internal to thinking as such.[13] As Deleuze states in his 'Hume' article, however, 'Kant owes something essential to Hume: we are not threatened by error, rather and much worse, we bathe in delirium' (PI 43). We have seen the important role that this thought plays in Deleuze's reading of Hume in *Empiricism and Subjectivity*: that despite the fourfold activity of the principles of human nature, it is only the plastic and irreducibly contingent socio-political and moral world which holds delirium and madness at bay, since the order which governs the intra- and inter-subjective world is based upon an exercise of these principles which is grounded in the pure indifference of fancy. Thus what Deleuze says of experience in Leibniz might also be said of Hume: that it is 'hallucinatory because [it has] no object', (FLB 93) and is therefore at perpetual risk of being internally undone.

The rules constituted within thought, which govern thought, 'are characterised by the fact that they are extended beyond the circumstances from which they arise. They do not account for the exception, and they misconstrue the accidental, confusing it with the general or the essential' (ES 55). The fact that the social world is integrated into this problematic even suggests that Hume was more advanced than Kant in this respect, for whom reason's internal critique of reason had no fulcrum or basis.[14]

Perhaps the remarkable homology between the ontology of *Anti-Oedipus* ('it should be read as a kind of *Critique of Pure Reason* at the level of the unconscious'[15]) and *Empiricism and Subjectivity* has its key moment in the central and ineliminable role played by unstructured fluidity, the movement which perpetually accompanies all regulation. We can thus perhaps imagine something like a Humean schizoanalysis, which, however limited in scope, would account for the particular habitual and cultural formulations of thinking and 'centers of fixation' (ES 124) in terms of processes which constitute subjects as a part of a fluid milieu, at the heart of which is the threat of the fancy, of delirium and of madness.

The genesis of faculties. Deleuze is perhaps unique among philosophers of the late twentieth century in maintaining an active interest in the theory of faculties, which he considered decisive: 'Despite the fact that it has become discredited today, the doctrine of the faculties is an entirely necessary component of the system of philosophy' (DR 143). Rather than a descriptive interest, Deleuze maintains from his encounter with Hume onwards that faculties themselves do not pre-exist thought, and must, like the subject itself, be formulated within the given. However, if the course of *Empiricism and Subjectivity* follows the unfurling of the faculties of thought on Hume's account, it is in *Difference and Repetition* that this position is presented in its fullest form. Indeed, the centrepiece of 'The Image of Thought', the chapter Deleuze would later speak of as the most significant in that work, is precisely an account of the genesis of faculties or capacities within thinking. If we speak of something like the order of reasons of that account, we begin there with the source point of Hume's own account of thought ('Something in the world forces us to think' [DR 139]). Since, however, Deleuze does not endorse anything like the pre-existence of the principles of nature as static and universal rules to provide the means for the constitution of the active subject, he instead provides an account of how the facultative structures of experience in the Kantian sense (the 'transcendental form of a faculty' [DR 143]) are not native but are generated within thought. This account is pursued with reference to an extremely striking presentation of paradoxical experience, the experience of something which cannot be thought, but which thereby engenders a capacity in thought – assuming it is not, however, excessive to the point of destruction of the thinker.

There remains a final Humean note to this account, however, in the role that Deleuze gives to culture in the formation of faculties in thought. Whereas the postulate of method holds that thinking has a natural course that only needs to be pursued in order to arrive at the truth, Deleuze insists instead on the importance of the each time contingent cultural context, 'an involuntary adventure' (DR 165), in which our capacities to think are embedded. It is the extended network of habituated rules which provides the channels that thought is externally constrained to follow, a violent if nonetheless altogether necessary element in the extension of thinking.

Passive synthesis. This final point is perhaps the most significant of all, returning us as it does to the question of the subject. Indeed, the answer to the various forms of the key question that run through *Empiricism and Subjectivity* concerning the constitution of the self is precisely passive synthesis, the synthesis in the mind of experience which brings about the subject. In his Introduction to that book, Constantin Boundas insists that 'Deleuze will never waver in his conviction that only empiricists have the right access to the problem of subjectivity' (ES 9). In an important sense, this is certainly true, since the three other texts which present formulations of the nature of subjectivity in any detail (*Difference and Repetition*, *Logic of Sense* and *Anti-Oedipus*) all also insist on the *constituted* nature of the subject. What does change is Deleuze's consideration of the key mechanism in this constitution, that of passive synthesis.

Here we find a final theme introduced in Deleuze's reading of Hume that will take on a greater range in subsequent work. In the first place, what shifts is the continuum between passive and active that is attributed to Hume ('the subject is an imprint, or an impression, left by principles, that it progressively turns into a machine capable of using this impression' [ES 113]).[16] Instead, Deleuze's later work emphasises the priority of passivity along with its continued fundamental role. In the chapter *Difference and Repetition* dedicated to repetition itself, for example, in the thorough elaboration of the notion of passive synthesis with respect to the three temporal modalities, the role of active synthesis (which includes the aspects of subjective experience that are involved in Hume's empiricism, including an atomism) has a secondary and subsequently falsifying function.[17] The same point is made in *Anti-Oedipus*, where the passive and unconscious connective and disjunctive syntheses are completed by the passive synthesis of conjunction, and it is on the basis of the latter that 'the subject is produced' (AO 17). Deleuze and Guattari write that

> something on the order of the *subject* can be discerned on the recording surface. It is a strange subject, however, with no fixed identity, wandering about over the body without organs, but always remaining peripheral to the desiring-machines . . . the subject is produced as a mere residuum alongside the desiring-machines.(AO 16; 17)[18]

As is apparent from these references, another key development of the theme of passive synthesis in the works of the 1960s and '70s is the pluralisation of this synthesis. In *Difference and Repetition* and *Anti-Oedipus*, we are presented with three distinct syntheses, and *Logic of Sense* presents a fundamental distinction between static and dynamic geneses which stand prior to any subjectivity, which is produced on the surface produced through these geneses. While in *Empiricism and Subjectivity*, as we have seen, we are presented with two principles (of nature and of the passions), it is their similarity and interplay which is decisive, and the subject is the product of a single complex and ramifying process, a point Deleuze sometimes emphasises by linking the two principles analogically (ES 32; 84; 85; 124).

Furthermore, Deleuze's later accounts of passive synthesis all emphasise a particular mode of this synthesis that is not to be found in *Empiricism and Subjectivity*, namely *disjunctive synthesis*, one of Deleuze's great concepts. Aligned with the eternal return, the body without organs and the virtual, it indicates a synthetic moment in which the differences involved entirely retain their differential status. Arguably, it is one of the keys to understanding Deleuze's philosophy.

Finally, the most important difference: the specific level of the operation of passive synthesis also undergoes an interesting transformation between *Empiricism and Subjectivity* and the texts which close the '60s. In *Empiricism and Subjectivity*, Deleuze is at pains to insist on the particularly *empirical* character of the synthetic activity that constitutes the subject,[19] one which cannot be identified with either a simple psychology (which is itself accounted for on the basis of the empirical constutition of the subject), nor with transcendental philosophy: 'in the case of Hume, nothing is transcendental' (ES 111; see also ES 24: 'nothing is ever transcendental'). As he writes later in the book, 'we defined the empirical problem in opposition to a transcendental deduction and also to a psychological genesis' (ES 119). This claim is reiterated in *Difference and Repetition*, where Deleuze speaks of 'the (empirical) passive synthesis of habit' (DR 81).[20] However, both the general framework of the account of passive synthesis in *Difference and Repetition*, and the syntheses of memory and the eternal return that concern the past and the future, are marked as transcendental in nature. Deleuze will speak, in contrast with the synthesis of habit, of the '(transcendental) passive synthesis which is peculiar to memory itself' (DR 81), and of the eternal return that as 'the third synthesis unites all the dimensions of time . . . and causes them to be played out in the pure form' (DR 115).

These points may even be summarised by saying that the subject, as it appears in Deleuze's mature work, is completely considered as a consequence and not at all as an agent with respect to what provides its support. More than this, though, is the novel and far-reaching elaboration of the absolutely key idea of passive synthesis in Deleuze's mature work.

CONCLUSION: TRANSCENDENTAL EMPIRICISM

If one examines the books published after *Empiricism and Subjectivity*, and after Deleuze's famous hiatus, it is not hard to see both strong departures from and strong criticisms of the Humean picture. The emphasis on philosophy as 'the theory of what we are doing, not . . . the theory of what there is' (ES 133) has given way to an affinity with Bergsonian metaphysics and the beginnings of a philosophy of the virtual, explored both with respect to Bergson himself and to the Nietzschean theme of the will-to-power. We also discover a reading of Proust that aligns itself not just with Bergson but also at points with Jung and Plato, a reading which puts fundamental emphasis on the concept of Essence ('Beyond the sign and the meaning, there is Essence, like the sufficient reason for the other two terms and for their relation' [PS 91]). In *Proust and Signs*, we also see a somewhat ambiguous but nonetheless decisive critique of association (PS 56–8; see also PS 36–7).[21] Deleuze's Nietzsche is not the acute psychologist of the earlier writings, nor really even the far-sighted cultural critic of the middle works – that is, it is hard to think of Nietzsche's 'superior empiricism' (NP 35) on the model of Hume's – but the metaphysically inclined author of *The Will to Power*. The will-to-power as differential kernel of qualities, and above all the eternal return, are the Nietzschean legacy in Deleuze, the two themes in Nietzsche which seem to most radically depart from the constructivist and jurisprudential vision of the world offered in *Empiricism and Subjectivity*. Finally, the works that close the 1960s, and the books with Guattari that follow, stand on the other side of an unbridgeable abyss from Hume's *Treatise*.

In summary, if there is a sense to the term 'empiricism' in the phrase 'transcendental empiricism' with which Deleuze sometimes christens his project, it is not to be drawn from Hume. The great irony of Deleuze's transcendental empiricism is thus that it is derived from Leibniz, Spinoza and Kant – from rationalism and transcendental idealism – much more than from Hume's philosophy itself. Is this then to say that there is here an element of nostalgia in Deleuze, an attempt to express fidelity to a master whose work has long ceased to be relevant?

It is rather the case that Hume's continued influence on Deleuze is irreducible to an homology of doctrine. While the philosophy of association in its Humean form, along with the entire apparatus of rules for the formation and correction of consistency, have no place in Deleuze's transcendental empiricism, his philosophy remains Humean, since the great problems identified there in Deleuze's earliest research continue to inspire and problematise his work throughout. Or, to be more precise, transcendental empiricism is the name given in Deleuze's mature work for the philosophical position which takes up many of the problematics unearthed in his reading of Hume. Transcendental empiricism is not Humean – but it is the supreme consequence of Deleuze's engagement with problems that are marked out in *Empiricism and Subjectivity*. Such is the more fitting cause for claiming the mastery of another philosopher's work in relation to one's own, insofar as the problems, whose genetic status is another of Deleuze's discoveries, that trouble their work find pride of place in what comes afterward.

The Melbourne School of Continental Philosophy

Notes

1. The original French text was published in the volume dedicated to the Enlightenment in Francois Châtelet's *Histoire de la philosophie*; it is also collected in *L'île déserte et autres textes*, edited by David Lapoujade (Paris: Minuit, 2002), pp. 226–37 (DI 162–9). Here, I refer to the translation by Anne Boyman in *Pure Immanence* (PI 35–52).
2. The key passages in Immanuel Kant, *Critique of Pure Reason*, trans. Norman Kemp Smith (London: Macmillan, 1929) are B19–20, A94–5, and A764–9, B792–7. The extent of Kant's familiarity with Hume is still a matter of debate. Certainly, it does not seem that Kant ever read the whole of either the *Treatise* or the *Enquiries*. Having said this, it has been plausibly demonstrated (for example, by Lewis White Beck in 'A Prussian Hume and a Scottish Kant', in *Essays on Kant and Hume* [London: New Haven Press, 1978] that he was introduced to a large number of Hume's ideas via other philosophers, the most likely of which is James Beattie, whose *Essay on the Nature and Immutability of Truth* (which quotes heavily from Hume) was published in German translation in 1772. It is therefore puzzling to observe that Kant remained tied to the very small part of Hume's work which concerns the human knowledge of causation, and he claims in the *Prolegomena* that his reading of Hume 'generalised' this aspect to his own purposes (Immanuel Kant, *Prolegomena to any future metaphysics that will be able to come forward as science*, trans. Gary Hatfield [Cambridge: Cambridge University Press, 1997], p. 29: §5). Later, he states that 'the concept of cause' is '*Hume's* problematic concept (this, his *crux metaphysicorum*)' (p. 65: §29). He even describes the first *Critique* as 'the *elaboration* of the Humean problem in its greatest amplification',

that which is amplified being nothing other than the problem of causation, expanded to the scope of 'the whole of reason' (p. 11: Preface). The *Prolegomena* offers evidence that Kant also knew at least Hume's *Dialogues Concerning Natural Religion* (105: §57; 112: §58), which was published in German translation in 1781. Nonetheless, this only plays a minor role in Kant's discussion here, and beyond it in the *Critique of Practical Reason*. In fact, he demonstrates a clear misunderstanding of Hume's criticisms of deism, which are not aimed to debunk the idea of the deist God as anthropomorphic, but rather to show that God is *necessarily* made in the image of man (see in particular Hume's *Natural History of Religion* [London: Penguin, 1976], p. 9). Deleuze writes: 'Its origin [the origin of religion] is in the events of human life, in the diversity and contradiction we find in it, and in the alternation of happiness and unhappiness, of hopes and fears' (ES 74).

3. David Hume, *A Treatise of Human Nature*, edited by L.A. Selby-Bigge (Oxford: Clarendon Press, 1896 [1739]), cited hereafter as T, followed by page number, then book and section numbers.

4. On this broad set of theoretical consequences which flow from Hume's basic commitments, see also PI 36: 'What is called the theory of association finds its direction and its truth in a casuistry of relations, a practice of law, of politics, of economics, that completely changes the nature of philosophical reflection.'

5. Deleuze in fact addresses the question of knowledge directly, and in a way that is surely more in keeping with Hume's position, by noting the transformation of 'knowing' into 'believing' effected by Hume's thought. Thus – this time in keeping with Deleuze's reading of Hume – the entire issue of knowledge is resituated in terms of the question of belief, its origins and our capacity to guarantee its legitimacy and stability. As he writes in his 'Hume' piece, 'Hume's first displacement is crucial, for it puts belief at the basis and the origin of knowledge' (PI 40).

6. Despite the fact that the standard epistemological account is subordinate to a more thorough reflection on Hume's philosophy, Deleuze will not hesitate to claim that 'Causality enjoys a considerable privilege over other relations' (ES 124).

7. This point among others is argued with particular clarity with respect to the traditional reading of Hume in Robyn Ferrell's 'Rival Reading: Deleuze on Hume', *Australasian Journal of Philosophy* 73:4 (December 1995), pp. 585–93.

8. Deleuze's discussion around the definition of the principles of the passions is to be found at ES 116–19.

9. See the chart at the end of the second chapter of *Empiricism and Subjectivity*, which schematises the initial results of the passions, and their corrected or extended forms (ES 54).

10. Here, I certainly agree with Levi Bryant when, at the opening of his *Difference and Givenness*, he invokes the relative significance of 'Descartes, Leibniz, Kant and Maimon', when compared to that of 'English empiricism' (Bryant, *Difference and Givenness* [Illinois: Northwestern University Press, 2008], p. x). However, aside from the fact that Hume was, of course, Scottish (and that the most well-known of the English empiricists, Locke, is only properly considered an empiricist on the narrow epistemological grounds which don't concern Deleuze), I do not think that Hume need be excluded from this list, once the broader questions of empiricism invoked in *Empiricism and Subjectivity* are taken into account – questions which are *also* what is at issue in Deleuze's reading of Descartes, Leibniz, Kant and Maimon. In short, once again, Deleuze's Hume is not the Hume of the tradition. Likewise, the following claim cannot be maintained in the face of a thorough reading of *Empiricism and Subjectivity*: 'By emphasising Deleuze's debt to empiricism, we risk maintaining the sensible or aesthetic as a passive given for receptivity and thereby miss Deleuze's central point that sensibility is itself the result of productive processes that actually create or produce the qualities of sensibility' (Bryant, *Difference and Givenness*, p. 9). After all, Deleuze's key concern in his Hume book is precisely to account for this genesis itself, if in terms that deviate from his mature thought (if anything, this remark is *too* Kantian).

11. Also key here is Deleuze's Introduction to his edited collection of texts, *Instincts et Institutions* (Paris: Hachette, 1955); this text is included in Deleuze, *L'île Déserte*, pp. 24-7 (DI 19–21). We read there: 'If it is true that tendency is satisfied within the institution, the institution is not explained by tendency. The same sexual needs will never explain the multiple possible forms of marriage. Niether will the negative explain the positive, nor the general the particular' (p. 25). On this occasion, Deleuze links the opposition in question to debates in biology and ethology. This aspect is very presciently discussed in Christian Kerslake, 'Insects and Incest: From Bergson and Jung to Deleuze', *Multitudes* 25 (Summer 2006), available online at http://multitudes.samizdat.net/Insects-and-Incest-From-Bergson.html?var_recherche=deleuze(accessed 16/5/2008).

12. On this point, see Daniel W. Smith in this volume; Gilles Deleuze, Lecture Sur Spinoza, 17 February 1981, available online at www.webdeleuze.com (accessed 6/5/2008); Simon Duffy, 'Schizo-Math', *Angelaki* 9:3 (2004), pp. 199–215, especially pp. 207–8.

13. Deleuze makes this point about Kant on a number of occasions, but none as memorable as 'On four poetic formulas that might summarise the Kantian philosophy', reproduced in both *Essays Critical and Clinical* and the English version of *Kant's Critical Philosophy*.

14. On the question of the ends of reason and critique in Kant and Deleuze, see Christian Kerslake, 'Deleuze, Kant, and the Question of Metacritique', *The Southern Journal of Philosophy* 42 (2004), pp. 481–508.
15. Gilles Deleuze, *Deux régimes de fou et autres texts*, edited by David Lapoujade (Paris: Minuit, 2004), p. 289.
16. Interestingly, this passage in fact begins: 'To speak like Bergson . . .' (ES 113).
17. Let me note that *Empiricism and Subjectivity* also deals with the question of synthesis with respect to time: 'Habit is the constitutive root of the subject, and the subject, at root, is the synthesis of time – the synthesis of the present and the past in light of the future' (ES 92–3). Likewise we find a double account of the present that is also exhibited in *Bergsonism* and *Difference and Repetition*: 'Recollection is the old present, not the past. We should call "past" not only that which has been, but also that which determines, acts, prompts, and carries a certain weight' (ES 95). Certainly Hume, like Locke and Berkeley before him, was interested in the phenomena of memory in the light of his more general account of the subject, but we must certainly express at least surprise when we read the following in Deleuze's account:

> Anticipation is habit, and habit anticipation: these two determinations – the thrust of the past and the élan toward the future – are, at the center of Hume's philosophy, the two aspects of the same fundamental dynamism. It is not necessary to force the texts in order to find in habit-anticipation most of the characteristics of Bergsonian *durée* or memory. (ES 72; translation modified)

18. It is interesting to note the role of the subject in *Anti-Oedipus* – as a rootless consequence which later, thanks to the illegitimate use of the synthesis becomes the centre of the organisation of desire – in relation to the manner in which the subject in *Difference and Repetition* goes from a contemplative compound riven by time to dominant fixture. What is also striking is the inclusion in both books of a claim about the fact of consciousness: 'Every spatio-temporal dynamism is accompanied by the emerge of an elementary consciousness which itself traces direction, doubles movements and migrations, and is born on the threshold of the condensed singularities of the body or object whose consciousness it is' (DR 220). This sentiment is very close to the self-consciousness produced by the conjunctive synthesis as it is outlined in *Anti-Oedipus*.
19. Deleuze's reading of Hume is often remarked on as being explicitly or even excessively Kantian in nature. Certainly, much evidence can be found in *Empiricism and Subjectivity* to support such a view: an emphasis on the productive nature of the imagination, the internal nature of the threat to thinking posed by illusion (as I have already noted above),

the emphasis on the great tropes of God and the World as regulative idealities rather than objects of experience ('The idea of God, as originary agreement, is the thought of something in general' [ES 77]; 'The World is an Idea' [ES 80]), the very idea of thought's self-regulation, and the phenomenal character of time and space ('Space and time are in the mind' [ES 91]), not to mention the fundamental role of synthesis itself. However, the empirical character of the syntheses in the Hume book already provide an indication of how Deleuze plans to deviate from Kant's transcendental idealism in his later work.

20. We should be careful here not to confuse Deleuze's (admittedly somewhat difficult to understand) association of the first passive synthesis of time (*habitus*) with the empirical, on the one hand, with the *active* synthesis of the present that is based upon it, which Deleuze sometimes designates as having an 'empirical character' (e.g. DR 83), on the other. Nor, it might be added, should we confuse it with the 'empirical content' of time which the third passive synthesis evicts (DR 89).

21. We do indeed find claims cautioning a simple rejection of association ('Associationism is less outmoded than the critique of associationism' [PS 56]), which duplicate similar remarks in both *Empiricism and Subjectivity* (ES 105–8) and *Difference and Repetition* ('Associationism possesses an irreplaceable subtlety' [DR 71]). Nonetheless, there is still a sharply critical attitude evident in *Proust and Signs* towards the philosophy of association.

5

Immanuel Kant

Melissa McMahon

In his popular work, *Modern French Philosophy*, Vincent Descombes opens the section on Gilles Deleuze with the statement: 'Gilles Deleuze is above all a post-Kantian.'[1] In justifying this claim he identifies three main areas of contention shared between Deleuze and 'the great Chinaman of Königsberg',[2] which will also form the main threads of the examination of the relationship presented here. The first is their rejection of the idea that thought requires a transcendent entity (the soul, the world, God) to serve as its foundation: 'No experience can justify us in affirming a single substantial self, a totality of things and a first cause of this totality.'[3] The second is their emphasis on the active and autonomous nature of thought, substituting a practical ideal of thought as a form of *determination* for a speculative one based on *representation*: '*Liberation of the will* is the significance of the critical idea . . . Deleuze gives the name "philosophy of being" to the old, pre-Kantian metaphysics, and "philosophy of will" to the metaphysics born of the accomplished critique.'[4] Third, they identify the true problem of 'difference' as the difference between a conceptual order and a non-conceptual one rather than the difference between two concepts or identities: the one which obliges thought to introduce difference into its identities, particularity into its general representations, and precision into its concepts. The real difference is that which exists between concept and intuition, between the intelligible and the sensible, between the logical and the aesthetic.[5]

A commitment to philosophy as a form of *critique*, in the specific sense Kant gave this term, is a recurring motif in Deleuze's work, from his earliest monograph on Hume in 1953 to his late collection of essays entitled *Critique et clinique*. Deleuze's last published piece, 'Immanence: A Life', opens with a characterisation of the 'transcendental field', another distinctively Kantian concept which recurs throughout his work.

In many places Deleuze's 'Kantianism' is 'felt' rather than stated: suggested by a turn of phrase or piece of terminology rather than an explicit reference, as is often the case with Deleuze's influences. Elsewhere it is an explicit topic, as for example in his work on Hume, *Empiricism and Subjectivity*, *Nietzsche and Philosophy* (1962) and *Difference and Repetition* (1969), aside of course from his 1963 work dedicated to Kant, *Kant's Critical Philosophy*. The account of the relationship presented here will mostly draw on these resources, but will aim to present the key concepts and problems that animate Deleuze's relationship with Kant in such a way that their broader impact on Deleuze's philosophy is made visible and, where practical, explicitly indicated.

Kant is undoubtedly the most canonical of the philosophers to whom Deleuze devotes a book, and his relationship to Kant is strongly marked with ambivalence. Deleuze described *Kant's Critical Philosophy* as a book on an enemy, and many of his references to Kant's insights carry the qualification that these are either misconceived at the outset or inadequately developed. Deleuze casts Hume, Nietzsche and finally himself in the role of a rival to Kant for the successful realisation of the critical project. The tension between a 'true' and 'false' critique however is also one that is identified by Deleuze as internal to Kant's own *oeuvre*. Kant's philosophy, from any perspective, is nothing if not plural, with its three separate critiques, each with their striking divisions, subdivisions and revisions; and indeed it is characterised by a pluralism on other levels (the different interests of reason, the different faculties) that will become a significant for Deleuze. There is also the fact that Kant's critique was written as a philosophical 'call to arms' that by its nature implies a destiny beyond the work of a single thinker. As the symbol of a 'revolution' for modern philosophy, Kant's philosophy is both an event that marks a definite rupture between a 'before' and an 'after', and one whose precise nature, meaning and moment remain a source of continuing dispute. Deleuze's relationship with Kant is in this sense compatible with a whole tradition of 'Kantianisms' that maintain a selective relationship with the historical figure and letter of Kant in order to better bring into focus what they understand as the spirit of critique.

IMMANUEL KANT (1724–1804)

The first radical gesture that inaugurates Kant's rupture with a classical metaphysics is, as indicated above, his rejection of the idea that the validity of thought derives from its being 'anchored' or grounded in a transcendent identity: that the truth of thought depends on its approximation of the nature of things 'in themselves' or as they appear to a divine understanding. What exists or is given to thought, 'by right', on such a classical model, is this determined nature or understanding, and the task of thought is to reflect or re-present this implicit state of affairs in an explicit form. Kant reverses this model: the status of the nature of things or the divine is entirely dependent on their ability to be determined by our reason, and the task of philosophy is to identify the necessary and universal terms and conditions according to which reason is able to determine its objects. These are not the conditions of thought as they exist 'in fact', as part of our 'human' condition relative to the divine, or as examined from a psychological or scientific perspective, for example, but as dictated 'by right' relative to the immanent demands and interests of reason. The most obvious analogy is perhaps with the way logic or mathematics present internal conditions of validity that exist 'by right' independently of empirical variables. The 'plane of right' that belongs to reason, however, is not limited to the abstract domains of logic and mathematics but more especially concerns the principles by which the material of actual experience is 'synthesised' to form the objects of a true science and a true morality. Kant uses the term 'transcendental' to designate this plane occupied by the immanent principles of reason in their application to experience, and 'critique' is the operation by which the transcendental status and scope of reason's principles are established for a given area.

Kant's first major work, the *Critique of Pure Reason* (first edition 1781, second edition 1787), seeks to identify the universal and *a priori* conditions under which reason constitutes the domain of Nature, the field of the theoretical exercise of reason. These firstly consist in the pure concepts of the understanding, or the 'categories', grouped under four headings: Quantity (unity, plurality, totality), Quality (reality, negation, limitation), Relation (substance/accident, cause/effect and community) and Modality (possibility/impossibility, existence/non-existence, necessity/contingency). In the second place, they consist in the pure forms of sensibility, or space and time. The irreducible duality for Kant of concepts on the one hand and existence in space and time on the other, and the requirement that these must however be synthesised in a necessary way, represents Kant's other major departure from previous traditions. For Kant, concepts and existence in space and time are irreducible to one another: one cannot, following the rationalist tradition, arrive at any truths about sensible experience or what actually exists by analysing concepts,

nor can one, following the empiricist tradition, 'derive' any necessary truths from experience. Both traditions indeed tend to rely on
an enveloping concept or entity such as God or Nature in which the
unity of concepts and spatio-temporal existence could be grounded.
Having rejected this solution on principle, however, Kant faces the
problem of showing how a coherent and necessary relationship can
hold between orders that differ in nature – how a truth can be both
a priori and *synthetic*.

Two main approaches to this problem can be drawn from Kant's
first critique, whose terms will be taken up by Deleuze. On the one
hand, Kant addresses the problem of grounding the coherence of
concepts and spatio-temporal forms by drawing inspiration from
mathematics and geometry. In another radical hypothesis that will be
discussed further below, Kant claims that geometrical and mathematical concepts are pure constructions of space and time, without there
being any separation of the conceptual and spatio-temporal element,
and he extends this model to philosophical concepts by means of
the notion of the 'schematism', which 'translates' pure concepts into
spatio-temporal forms. In the Transcendental Doctrine of Judgement,
Kant shows how the categories can be schematised as pure determinations of time – time being the ultimate form for all intuitions, inner
and outer – in order to be applied to experience. On the other hand,
in the Transcendental Deduction, Kant attempts to ground the objective necessity of the relationship between concepts and intuitions in
the unification of the sensible manifold under the general form of an
object, and the unification of experience in a transcendental subject.
Here again, Kant outlines a series of syntheses that unify the field of
experience in time: the *synthesis of apprehension in intuition*, the
synthesis of reproduction in imagination, and finally the *synthesis of
recognition in a concept*. This last synthesis allows us to consider a
series of representations as the manifestations of a single object – the
object or concept = x – and this is the objective correlate of my ability
to consider all representations as belonging to a single transcendental
subject, what Kant calls the 'transcendental unity of apperception'.
For Kant, the schematisation of the categories outlined in the Doctrine
of Judgement is ultimately dependent on the unification of experience
as outlined in the Deduction.

The domain of 'possible experience' formed at this intersection of
the universal concepts of the understanding and the universal forms
of space and time is a narrow one: it is not a question of seeking the
conditions of 'experience' in the psychological sense of the conditions

of 'perception', but the grounding of an objective Nature such as would be the domain of exercise of the physical and mathematical sciences. There are obvious limits on what can be determined *a priori* – that is, in advance – about experience: all Kant can say of any *possible* experience is that it will necessarily be in space and time, show unity, causality, and so on. What falls outside this domain are, in one direction, the pure Ideas of reason, because of their *unconditional* nature, and, in the other direction, the specificity and singularity of *actual* experience. These areas will also be important for Deleuze's revision of the critical apparatus.

In the first case, the Ideas are concepts that in virtue of their unconditional nature can't be an object of experience and which thus remain 'indeterminate' from a theoretical perspective. These include the 'total' concepts mentioned above, namely God, the soul and the whole of nature, but also the 'thing-in-itself', freedom, and in general any concept that represents an unconditioned limit or totality of a series of conditions. Experience is by its nature partial, limited and conditioned, and such concepts are therefore by definition excluded as objects of possible experience. Ideas are not simply fancies of the imagination for Kant, but are necessary and involuntary representations of reason, which always seeks to establish the unconditioned principle for any partial series presented to it – hence the tendency of reason to fall prey to the 'transcendental illusion' that such Ideas represent a form of knowledge, that is, a representation of an existing thing. While Ideas are necessarily indeterminate from a theoretical perspective (they can and must be *thought*, but not *known*), they serve certain *practical* functions, and both determine and are determined by our actions in certain ways. In the context of the first critique, the Idea of the totality of nature, for example, serves what Kant calls a *regulative* purpose for organising our theoretical endeavours, providing principles of unity, diversity and community as guidelines for organising our empirical concepts of nature, and he speaks in this context of an 'indirect' and 'reciprocal' determination of the Ideas in relation to the activities of our understanding. In Kant's second critique, the *Critique of Practical Reason* (1788), the Ideas of God and the soul also have a regulative role in relation to our moral endeavours, and the Idea of our freedom is fully determined from a practical perspective, the conditions of its lawful exercise constituting an autonomous domain.

In the second case, there are all the elements of *actual* experience that remain undetermined from the perspective of the *a priori* conditions of *possible* experience. The 'nature' of possible experience is of a very 'generic' or general kind – a Newtonian universe of physical bodies bound by the laws of causality. What remains undetermined in this model is, in the first place, nature in its *specificity* or diversity: while physics deals with the laws of matter en masse, we also encounter *organised* matter, living bodies whose nature and relations can't be adequately understood on a purely causal model, nor can they be determined in advance. Kant may be able to say, in other words, that experience will necessarily be causal, but not that it necessarily includes elephants, nor will Newtonian-style laws be much help for understanding elephants specifically, even though they are subject to these laws. In the second place, there is nature in its *singularity*: not just elephants, but *this* elephant, taken in its singular *quiddity* apart from its being a member of a species. Deleuze sometimes says that he is interested in the conditions of *actual* experience rather than *possible* experience, and he means it in this sense of conditions that are no 'larger' than what they condition, principles that especially address and respond to this singular level of experience rather than remaining at a level of generality.

These levels of experience are addressed in Kant's last major critical work, the *Critique of Judgement* (1790), which assigns *a priori* principles for *reflection* on actual experience in its specificity and singularity. The *Critique of Judgement* has its title because 'judgement', in the non-legislative sense of the 'art of judgement', is for Kant the ability to adapt or invent principles in response to actual experience. The second part of the work, the Critique of Teleological Judgement, assigns the principle of nature as a 'system of purposes' for reflecting on specific or organic natural forms. The first part of the work, the Critique of Aesthetic Judgement, presents the principles for reflecting on what is singular in experience, for judgements of the beautiful and the sublime. Only aesthetic judgements express the principle of judgement in its purity – its higher, transcendental form – as they refer to no determinate concept, idea or purpose, and are in this sense 'disinterested' – they are not grounded by any intellectual or moral concept. In aesthetic experience we don't so much 'make' a judgement as a judgement 'happens' to us: we experience a necessary agreement or accord between our powers of thought and a singular object without this being 'constrained' by any determinate rule or concept. It is this *event* rather than the object that is properly described as beautiful or sublime, and it is its involuntary character that leads us to 'feel' (as opposed to demonstrate) that aesthetic judgements are universal as well as singular in nature.

The 'discovery' of the realm of the transcendental by Kant is compared by Deleuze in *Difference and Repetition* to the act of a great explorer, a discoverer 'not of another world, but a mountain or underground of this one'.[6] The notion of an autonomous plane that provides an area of thought with an immanent consistency and virtual field of deployment, by demarcating what belongs to it 'by right', is one of the defining features of a discipline as presented in Deleuze and Guattari's *What is Philosophy?*, alongside its constructions (concepts, percepts . . .) and personae. There, as in Kant, it is a matter of assigning a foundation to thought that is independent of the field of 'fact', whether empirical givens or 'established values': 'The image of thought implies a strict division between fact and *right*: what pertains to thought as such must be separated from contingent features of the brain or historical opinions . . . The image of thought retains only what thought can claim by right' (WP 40/37). There are two 'sides', however, as Deleuze and Guattari present it, to philosophy's repudiation of this world of 'fact' in favour of a plane of right, according to whether this is simply the traditional rejection of the variabilities of 'this world' in favour of a transcendent realm of essential being 'behind' it, or a genuinely critical impulse that institutes a plane on which new values and forms are truly engendered.

In Kant, this is the problem of the 'transcendental illusion' of reason, which is constantly tempted to ascribe its tendency to go beyond experience to a transcendent source instead of seeing this same tendency as a positive expression of its own power. One of the important functions of critique is to diagnose and restrict this illegitimate or transcendent 'use' of reason, and the idea of this internal 'duplicity' of thought, with a productive side that tends towards the production of difference and an 'entropic' side that makes difference a function of a pre-existing identity, is a persistent one in Deleuze. It appears in his reading of critique – in the works on Nietzsche and Kant in particular – as the key question of whether a given thought expresses a 'high' (transcendental, superior, active) or 'low' (empirical, inferior, reactive) form of the will, according to whether it affirms and determines itself or is determined by an external object or end. When the will is considered to be dependent on an external representation that would be its object, our conception of the will, and of thought, is degraded as it represents only a struggle for power or recognition in the arena of established values. Deleuze uses this critical notion of the will as an end in itself to mark the difference between Nietzsche's 'will-to-power' and a *desire for* power, and it is also a key to Deleuze and Guattari's rejection of the notion that a philosophy of desire must be a philosophy of *lack*, as this depends on desire being understood as a dependence on a transcendent object.

Deleuze's early writings on critique focus on this notion that thought occupies an autonomous plane that is the site of an active transformation of 'givens'. In *Empiricism and Subjectivity*, both 'transcendental' (Kantian) and 'empirical' (Humean) critique are united in their repudiation of 'a philosophy of Nature' (ES 94/88), which is to say speculation as to the 'real' nature of things as they exist in themselves, in order to concentrate rather on the principles by which thought transforms what is given to it. After discussing Hume's notion of the 'intentional finality of nature' as a potential ground underlying the 'accord' between our ideas, Deleuze tranquilly dismisses the idea in recognisably critical terms:

> This accord can only be thought; and no doubt it is the most empty and impoverished thought. Philosophy must constitute itself as the theory of what we do, not as the theory of what is. What we do has its principles, and Being can never be grasped except as the object of a synthetic relation with the very principles of what we do. (ES 152/133, translation modified)

A critical philosophy for Deleuze is above all one where the 'nature of things' is what is constituted through the action of thought and thus results *from* it, rather than *preceding* it in any determinate sense. Where Hume is more radical than Kant in this respect is that his empiricism is understood as an account of the constitution of *human* nature as much as any objective domain, and thus does not presuppose even the subject as condition of thought. While 'transcendental' critique starts from the perspective of an already constituted subject and asks under what conditions the *object* is constituted from the given, Hume's 'empirical critique' starts from the immanent field of passions and impressions and asks how a *subject* capable of knowledge and morality is constituted (ES 91–2/86, translation modified).

The transformative notion of critique is pursued in *Nietzsche and Philosophy*, where critique is identified with a pluralist philosophy of *value*: Nietzsche's 'genealogical' critique expresses an 'active science' that approaches phenomena from the perspective of the actor who bestows their value and sense. The thinker as 'actor' is understood in a dramatic as much as a practical sense: Deleuze introduces here his notion of the 'dramatic' method in philosophy, which displaces the question of essence – *what is x?* – with the more primary question *who?*, as the mark of a centre of evaluation which gives sense or value to a thing. The shift from the question of essence to that of sense is identified by Deleuze in his seminars on Kant as one of the key innovations of the critical method.[7] The Kantian notion of the 'phenomenon' is not an 'appearance', which would imply that it concealed an essence, but is rather 'what appears in so far as it appears', or an 'apparition', which does not refer to an essence but rather to its conditions or sense: 'something appears, tell me what is its sense or – and this amounts to the same thing – tell me what is its condition?'[8] These conditions refer not only to the identifiable principles of reason within a given point of view, but also to the variety of possible arrangements of the subjective and objective 'roles' according to whether it is a matter of the intellectual, practical or aesthetic interest of reason.

Kant fails as a critical philosopher, on Deleuze's account, when he seems to reintroduce on a transcendental level the categories, relations and values whose transcendent status he has rejected: the categories of subject and object, the relations between the faculties, the values of truth and morality, are treated as 'givens' rather than being truly engendered. Deleuze broadens the scope of the 'transcendental illusion' to include the concept of identity per se as a ground of thought, whether this is identity in the form of a metaphysical and transcendent entity (God, world, soul), or the formal transcendental identities of subject and object as ground of the relation of thought. In his last work on 'Immanence . . .', what distinguishes the transcendental field from the field of experience is that 'it does not refer to an object nor belong to a subject (empirical representation)', and his 'transcendental empiricism' is defined in 'opposition to everything that constitutes the world of subject and object'.[9] The categories of subject and object are in one sense *too* empirical: they belong to an already constituted world of experience whose constitution is supposed to be accounted for on the transcendental level rather than simply reproduced on this level as already given. On the other hand they are not empirical enough, as they tether experience to the habitual forms and concepts under which it is *recognised*, rather than those under which it is *encountered* – the 'unconscious' of experience lies as much in its 'immediate givens' as in anything 'beyond experience' in the ordinary sense.

These two problems combine so that what is required are the conditions of a true *genesis* of thought in confrontation with those elements within experience that are not determinable or 'identifiable' from a categorical perspective: something that impels the necessity of thought, the synthesis of its internal and external elements, without this necessity taking the form of some underlying identity that determines the path of thought in advance, whether this identity be that of the subject, the object or a Being that underlies their relationship. Deleuze's approach to this problem consists to a great extent in developing parts of Kant's philosophy that give substance to the notion of a 'problem' as such, as a positive and generative instance at the core of thought rather than a relative stage that is overcome in its development. It is a classical critical move to address the validity of a theory by addressing the validity of the problem or question it implies. Deleuze takes this tenet literally, challenging the primacy of Kant's theoretical synthesis by unearthing the 'problematic' dimensions within Kant's own thought that lie beneath and beyond the concept of identity – the schema, the Idea and the framework of aesthetic experience. The 'problematic' has a special sense for Deleuze, but even in its everyday sense we can anticipate how it will help Deleuze reorient Kant's transcendental critique in a more 'empirical' direction, while retaining its essential autonomy. Problems confront thought from outside, beyond the habitual categories of thought, and yet address thought intimately as its special task or quest. They impose their own necessity and awaken the internal necessity of thought, while remaining allied to what is most contingent and singular in experience. And they confront and compel thought in virtue of their positive *in*determinacy, an indeterminacy that nevertheless provokes thought to its highest powers of determination.

REWRITING CRITIQUE: THE PROBLEMATIC

The original sense of a 'problem' in geometry is most simply rendered by the Concise Oxford definition: 'a proposition in which something has to be done'. The problem is opposed in geometry to the *theorem*, which is 'a proposition to be proved by a chain of reasoning'. The difference between a theorem and a problem is that while the first involves a deductive process deriving some essential properties of a figure from its definition, a problem requires a material process of construction or transformation, in the course of which properties of a figure come to light which cannot be deduced from its concept. The existence of problems was cause for a certain amount of scandal in discussions of geometry,[10] as mathematics and geometry had long presented an ideal of a purely analytic knowledge, deducible from first principles and offering necessary and universal truths independent of the material world of becoming in space and time. Kant reprised this scandal when he argued in the *Critique of Pure Reason* that mathematical and geometrical concepts owe their necessity and universality to the fact that they are entirely *synthetic*, pure constructions of space and time with no separation between the conceptual and intuitive elements. Whereas an ordinary empirical or philosophical concept (e.g. 'dog') can be broken down into a general conceptual definition on the one hand and particular existing examples on the other, for Kant there is no meaningful 'definition' or concept of a triangle, for example, apart from its actual *construction* in space (even if only in the imagination), and, conversely, any given triangle yields immediate, necessary and universal truths concerning its properties: concept is immediately intuition and vice versa. The relationship of concept to intuition in geometrical knowledge is not an *external* one between a general concept and a particular instance but an *internal* relationship where a single instance embraces the universal scope of the concept.[11]

The pure *a priori* plane of space and time that is home to the geometrical and mathematical concept is, however, independent from the material plane of actual existences. Kant broke with the opposition that placed the intelligible and eternal realm on the one side, and the material world with space and time on the other, by positing this independent realm of pure space and time that is both irreducible to traditional concepts and independent of material content, whose reality is demonstrated by the internal 'diagrammatic' unity of the intelligible and the spatio-temporal in the geometrico-mathematical concept. This immediate unity cannot however be shared by philosophical concepts like 'dog' or 'causality', which must be connected to an external, material element to have any meaning. Here the pure form of space and time has a paradoxical status as both what separates the concept from material existence and the only form under which concepts can be determined at all in relation to experience. Kant distinguishes between the geometrical or mathematical knowledge that proceeds via the 'construction' of concepts, under a 'mathematical synthesis' of pure space and time, and knowledge 'from concepts' or 'according to concepts', where the concept has to be synthesised with the material content of intuition in a 'dynamical synthesis'. Kant, however, attempts to extend the logic of geometrical concepts to philosophical ones by positing the notion of the 'schema' as a 'rule of construction' for all concepts in space and time, whether mathematical or not. He elaborates how the various categories may be 'schematised' in temporal terms – causality is schematised as 'time-order', for example – but leaves the details of how more empirical concepts – like 'dog' – are schematised in spatio-temporal terms rather vague. As mentioned above, he ultimately falls back on the unifying force of the subject and object = x as the necessary ground for unifying concepts and intuitions.

In his lectures on Kant in the 1970s, Deleuze defines the schema as following a 'rule of production', demarcating an autonomous 'bloc' of space-time (what he calls in *Difference and Repetition* an 'erewhon' [DR 3/xx–xxi]), as opposed to the 'rule of recognition' that governs the synthesis.[12] Deleuze is clearly inspired by the geo-metrical or 'schematic' understanding of a concept as *a diagrammatic mode of occupying space and time*: the idea that a thing's concept or essence is a set of distinctive points or movements that mark out a territory, instead of being a purely intelligible identity. In his 'Method of Dramatisation', for example, Deleuze contends that the distinguishing character of a thing lies not in its conceptual definition, but in its 'remarkable points and regions', the way it 'determines and differenciates a whole exterior space, as in the hunting ground of an animal' (DI 92). He also, however, respects and indeed highlights the way that philosophical concepts involve a material and contingent element coming from 'outside', which cannot be determined *a priori*, and which must contend with the 'pure and empty form of time' as an essential condition of their determination.

The 'umbrella' that gives the elements of this synthesis its ultimate coherence for Deleuze is not the form of identity in the transcen-dental subject and object, but rather the enveloping horizon of the problem-Idea. The condition of Deleuze's rethinking of the schematic construction of the concept is that it be considered a *dramatisation* of an Idea-problem rather than a *schematisation* of a concept, as he signals in *Difference and Repetition*: 'The Kantian schema would take flight, and overcome itself towards a conception of the differen-tial Idea, if it were not unduly subordinated to the categories which reduce it to a state of simple mediation in the world of representa-tion' (DR 365/285, translation modified). The 'dramatisation' of the Idea consists in staking out coordinates at the intersection of the ideal relationships of the problem and the field of its resolution. The relationship between the problem-Idea and its solution is described by Deleuze in the same terms as that attributed to the geometrical concept: an internal relation between a singular instance with universal scope:

> the problem or the Idea is a concrete singularity no less than a true universal. Corresponding to the relations which constitute the universality of the problem is the distribution of remarkable and singular points which constitute the determination of the conditions of the problem. (DR 211/163, translation modified)[13]

This model, however, requires a certain reconfiguration of the Kantian notion of the Idea as well as the image of thought in a direction other than that provided by Kant in the first critique.

The Kantian Idea does not look at first glance to be a very promising candidate for inclusion in Deleuze's revised transcendental apparatus. As outlined above, an Idea for Kant is a pure representation of reason that by its nature goes beyond experience because it is a representation of the ultimate condition of all experience, the most well-known examples being those of the Soul, God and the totality of the Universe. Kant calls such Ideas of reason 'problematic', because their status as existing things can be neither affirmed nor denied from the perspective of the understanding. These Ideas, of course, are precisely the kind of centering, holistic ideals that are no longer real 'problems' for Deleuze in a critical philosophy, even if taken in an 'immanent' sense. But what if, in aspiring to reach the limits of experience, reason is not presented with an enlarged identity such as a supreme being or soul, but the framework of a problem or the unconditional impact of an event? What if the indeterminacy of the Idea, and its activating and compelling characteristics, derived not from the fact that it is a pure concept for which there is no intuition, but from *a pure intuition for which there is no concept*? The Idea would then be something that could – and must – be actually encountered, while remaining 'outside' experience in the sense of not being part of the world of well-constituted objects and subjects.

This understanding of the Idea does in fact exist in Kant: it appears in the *Critique of Judgement* as the 'aesthetic idea', a presentation that is 'unexpoundable' by concepts, inverting the structure of rational ideas, which are concepts that are 'indemonstrable' in intuition.[14] Aesthetic judgements express the transcendental principles of *pleasure and pain*, which are vital principles for Kant: they consist in the enhancement or inhibition of our 'feeling of life'. Aesthetic experience and judgements take place on this level of the stimulation of forces: while all of our faculties are engaged in aesthetic judgements – reason, understanding, imagination, sensibility – they are engaged only as pure powers or tendencies since they don't determine, and aren't determined by, any particular concept. The 'dynamic' of the aesthetic is that we are confronted by something that both stimulates our powers of thought but can't be resolved in any definitive way by these same powers – a formula that could equally be reversed, i.e. we are confronted by something that can't be resolved by our ordinary powers of thought and which thus stimulates these same powers. It is not simply a case of being stupefied in aesthetic experience: on the contrary, we are provoked and compelled to exercise our powers of thought, but our attempts to resolve or determine the presentation do not exhaust its suggestive powers. There is a necessarily temporal dimension to aesthetic experience, as the faculties persevere in this dialectic between attempted determinations and objective indeterminacy.

The aesthetic experience is as much sustained by a certain *discord* between our powers of thought and a given presentation as a feeling of *accord*, and Kant writes elsewhere that any enduring pleasure in fact consists in a perpetual oscillation between pleasure and pain. This oscillation is particularly evident in the Kantian sublime, where the imagination is commanded by reason to comprehend something that exceeds its powers of presentation. In the sublime, according to Deleuze, Kant comes close to a 'dialectical conception of the faculties',[15] where the faculties are genuinely awakened and enter into a relationship that is not based on the representation of an identity:

> [The sublime] brings the various faculties into play in such a manner that they struggle against each other like wrestlers, with one faculty pushing another to its maximum or limit, to which the second faculty reacts by pushing the first toward an inspiration it would not have had on its own. One faculty pushes another to a limit, but they each make the one go beyond the limits of the other. The faculties enter into relationship at their deepest level, where they are most foreign to each other. They embrace each other from their greatest point of distance. (ECC 48–9/34, translation modified)

This interpretation of the sublime forms the background to Deleuze's account of the *event* of thought, which combines the notion of undergoing a violence and at the same time realising a higher freedom: we are faced with a presentation that is 'too big for me', and our faculties are expanded in response.

In *Difference and Repetition*, Deleuze brings these elements of the problem together in his model of the determination of the Idea-problem as the new transcendental synthesis of thought. This determination has a three-part structure comprising, first, the encounter with the Idea as an 'objective indeterminacy', a problematic 'instance' or sign that is both unthinkable and compelling to thought; second, the search for the conditions of resolvability or determinability of the problem engaging the pure forms of space and time – 'the adjunctions which complete the initial body of the problem, as such, whether varieties of multiplicity in all dimensions, fragments of an ideal future or past event which renders the problem solvable' (DR 246/190, translation modified); and finally the determination of a case of resolution of the problem, 'fusing' or 'condensing' the two parts or 'sides' of the problem (its initial instance and the conditions of its resolvability) into a new entity or 'body' that constitutes a response to the problem but does not efface its essential indeterminacy. Deleuze interprets these moments of the Idea as constituting the process of *learning*, which he opposes to *knowledge* as the goal of thought.

As an account of the relationship between the faculties, the three parts of the determination of the problem-Idea have a particular connection for Deleuze with sensibility, memory/imagination, and thought or reason, respectively. The encounter with a problematic instance is first experienced on the level of intuition and its force is transmitted to the other faculties in turn (memory, reason), in a transmission or 'relay' which proceeds via the differentiation of the faculties rather than via a form of identity that mediates the relationship of the faculties to each other and to their object. But each of these faculties themselves have to be engendered in response to a problem, and Deleuze outlines a synthesis for each showing its own internal problematic structure, mode of learning and 'schema' of space and time: sensibility constituted in a 'living present' of duration from the contraction and retention of impressions; memory and imagination constituted in a 'pure past' that envelops the contractions of the present and establishes resonances between them; and thought that confronts the pure event as force of the future, which 'expels' the substance of all prior conditions and retains of their effects only what contributes to an aesthetic coherence like that of the work of art (DR 125/94).

THE NEW SYNTHESIS: A LIFE ON THE PLANE

Deleuze sometimes suggests that his revision of Kant is the attempt to combine the two senses of the 'aesthetic' in Kant: the aesthetic of the first critique which outlines the pure forms of space and time as conditions of sensibility, and the aesthetic of the third critique that attempts to formulate principles for thinking vital singularities that defy categorisation. In his writings on Kant, Deleuze identifies the aesthetic apparatus of the third critique as the site of the true 'deduction' of the relationship between the faculties, between the inside and outside of thought. In many ways Deleuze's revision of critique can be seen as a logical extension of Kant's own major critical premises. When Kant declares that no transcendent identity can be evoked to ground the validity of thought as a matter of principle, and not just as a confession of inability, thought is necessarily reconfigured as a confrontation with pure indeterminacy – the 'chaosmos' described in Deleuze and Guattari's last work together. And how can the result of such a confrontation not be both violent and creative, since no path is determined for it in advance?

Deleuze affirms this absence of identity as the presence of a difference – Kant's 'discovery' of a concept of difference 'no longer as empirical difference between two determinations, but transcendental Difference between the Determination as such [*LA détermination*] and what it determines' (DR 116/86, translation modified). This 'difference' is not simply a 'gap' but the place of pure space and time as the forms under which any object is determinable in thought – Kant's other major contention. Space and time are not indifferent milieus 'in which' thought takes place, but the essential dimensions 'with which' thought constructs its objects; but neither is their role as 'means' of construction just a mediating one: they form an autonomous plane which can only be inhabited as a set of singularities, a collection of movements, rhythms, postures and passages. This is the terrain that Deleuze returns to in his last piece on 'Immanence: A Life': the state of pure immanence characterised by what is essentially 'in between', the 'passage' from one moment to another, the hovering between life and death, a transcendental 'determinability' where 'the life of the individual has given way to an impersonal life, and yet singular, which extracts a pure event liberated from the accidents of internal and external life'.[16] The indefinite article, 'a', in 'a life', is the 'index' of the transcendental: what is not, or not yet, attributed to or actualised in the transcendent figures of subject or object, Being or Act. A proper name is also for Deleuze a singularity, and with Kant, as for all the other names in history that form Deleuze's solitary crowd, Deleuze has sought out those elements that give contingency its necessary weight, and necessity its contingent life.

Notes

1. Vincent Descombes, *Modern French Philosophy*, trans. J. Harding and L. Scott-Fox (Cambridge: Cambridge University Press, 1980), p. 152.
2. As Hugh Tomlinson and Barbara Habberjam describe Kant in their translators' preface to Deleuze's *Kant's Critical Philosophy* (London: Athlone Press, 1983), p. xv.
3. Descombes, *Modern French Philosophy*, p. 152.
4. Descombes, *Modern French Philosophy*, p. 156.
5. Descombes, *Modern French Philosophy*, p. 153.
6. DR French 176/English 135; hereafter citations of Deleuze's texts will give the French pagination first followed by the page number of the English edition.
7. Gilles Deleuze, First Lesson on Kant, 14 March 1978, available online at http://www.webdeleuze.com/php/texte.php?cle=58&groupe=Kant& langue=1
8. Deleuze, First Lesson on Kant, para. 18.
9. Gilles Deleuze, 'L'immanence: une vie . . .', *Philosophie* 47 (1995), p. 3.
10. For example, in the neo-Platonic philosopher Proclus' commentary on Euclid's *Elements*, which Deleuze often refers to.
11. 'The [intuition] must . . . be a *single* object, and yet none the less, as the construction of a concept (a universal representation), it must in its representation express universal validity for all possible intuitions which fall under the same concept.' Immanuel Kant, *Critique of Pure Reason*, trans. Norman Kemp Smith (London: Macmillan, 1990), A713/B741.
12. Gilles Deleuze, Fourth Lesson on Kant, http://www.webdeleuze.com/ php/texte.php?cle=57&groupe=Kant&langue=1, para. 5.
13. See also WP 27/22, in which Deleuze and Guattari develop their theory of the creation – the construction – of concepts: 'Constructivism unites the relative and the absolute.'
14. Immanuel Kant, *Critique of Judgement*, trans. Werner S. Pluhar (Indianapolis: Hackett Publishing Company, 1987 [1790]), pp. 342–4.
15. Gilles Deleuze, 'The Idea of Genesis in Kant's Aesthetics', trans. Daniel W. Smith, in *Angelaki: Journal of the Theoretical Humanities*, 5:3 (2000), p. 63.
16. Deleuze, 'L'immanence: une vie . . .', p. 5.

6

Solomon Maimon

Graham Jones

Who was Maimon?[1]

Shlomo ben joshua (1753–1800) was a Polish-Russian rabbi from a humble, poverty-stricken background. Never having been to university he learnt philosophy through the Talmudic tradition and his own eclectic reading, and took the name Maimon in homage to the Spanish, Jewish philosopher Moses Maimonides whom he greatly admired. Exiled from his Polish community because of his heretical views, Maimon travelled throughout Europe before finally settling in Germany where, socially inept, uncouth and evil-tempered, it is said he would recount, in the taverns where he wrote most of his works, his disgrace for the price of a drink. There, filled with ambition, he immersed himself in various intellectual debates whilst working his way through the history of philosophy. After reading Kant, who claimed to have resolved the dispute between rationalism and empiricism, Maimon set out to write a commentary on Kant's *Critique of Pure Reason*, which would also outline the general principles of his own philosophy (which he referred to as a 'Koalition-system'), an ingenious attempt at synthesising and reconciling the differing and seemingly incompatible positions of Leibniz, Hume and Kant. This document, called the 'Essay on Transcendental Philosophy',[2] both mammoth in size and written in idiosyncratic German, was eventually passed on to the ageing Kant who grudgingly acknowledged 'that none of my opponents had understood me so well, but that very few could claim so much penetration and subtlety of mind in profound inquiries of this sort'.[3]

The Kantian Context

Kant's 'Copernican revolution' in his *Critique of Pure Reason* was to claim that the 'world' conforms to our thoughts rather than the reverse. For something (an object) to be determined it must be 'thought', as it is cognition which provides object-ivity and thus produces objects.

In elaborating his account of such determination Kant introduced several key innovations. First, he placed synthesis at the centre of his account, inasmuch as for something to be an 'object' it must be the result or product of a synthesis of some kind (of a 'joining' or 'uniting' of elements). The notion of synthesis was not unique to Kant's philosophy however. Indeed it was commonplace within empiricism. Kant's innovation was to place synthesis at a transcendental level, as *a priori* – as independent of experience and as the condition of the possibility of experience in general.

Kant's second innovation was to claim that a thought without a corresponding sensible component (to which it is linked through the intermediary of the Imagination), is merely empty and formal – for only sensation denotes something as 'actual', making of such a synthesis a real occurrence or event in respect to the object's 'appearing'. Thus although determining an object means that we must 'think' it, we can only 'know' it on the condition that it is a possible object of experience (i.e., there must first be a received intuition or sensible contribution, linked to the forms of time and space, that is then subsumed under a set of *a priori* rules provided by the faculty of understanding). Without the contribution of sensibility an object of thought is but a metaphysical speculation, a potentially misleading fiction.

This suggests Kant's third innovation: the distinction he draws between phenomena (objects of experience) and things in themselves. The latter are the independent entities that provoke or stimulate our senses (those mysterious things which 'affect' us). We have no direct or unmediated grasp of these entities, nor can we have such a grasp – that is, we cannot know them as they truly are in themselves, only in respect to how our cognitive apparatus makes its own sense of them, according to its own form and nature.

The fourth innovation was to claim that the efforts of the faculties of sensibility, imagination and understanding converge 'upon' the empirical object of cognition such that collectively they identify the object in an act of recognition (it is the same chair before me that I see, remember, understand, etc.), and correspondingly that their efforts converge in the opposite direction on a centre or locus that co-ordinates and unifies their efforts – the transcendental unity of apperception or transcendental subject.

The fifth innovation was to split thought in two – dividing its powers (and concepts) between two faculties, understanding and reason. The former can produce possible objects of experience. But the latter, reason, is the faculty of pure thought as such and has no direct relationship with sensibility. Its own concepts, the Ideas, pose problems in their most general form. These Ideas have no empirical equivalent (no corresponding element in experience): instead the Ideas concern the problematic or perplexing aspects of experience – from whence does experience ultimately arise? from what it is ultimately made? what is its true nature? why does it exist at all? why does it take the form that it does? and so on. In short, Ideas concern the problem of the underlying conditions that provide or support the unity, consistency, conformity and necessity of nature in general. Such Ideas include the Soul, God, the totality of the cosmos, things in themselves, freedom and so forth – they are the 'unconditioned conditions' (i.e., causes that are themselves seemingly uncaused or self-causing) that we fall back on in order to explain the ultimate nature of things. According to Kant, such Ideas are ideals or themes: hypothetical or speculatively inferential concepts that empirically we can neither prove nor disprove, yet which function as helpful foci in respect to organising and systematising the various, disparate pieces of knowledge that objective experience provides. They are, then, necessary means of making sense of, or providing a broader unity and arrangement to, the 'world'. However, in this sense, they are not constitutive things or real causes, merely regulative guidelines for further research.

Maimon will critique and revise each of these inter-related notions (as, in turn, will Deleuze). However, what is remarkable about Maimon's account, as will become evident, is that he overcomes the deficiencies of Kant's account through a *return* to the rationalist legacy of Leibniz and Spinoza, reintroducing several of the same (or modified) metaphysical features that Kant had been so careful to expunge from his own work.

MAIMON'S CRITIQUE

Maimon directs his initial attentions towards the inadequacies of Kant's 'Transcendental Deduction' in the *Critique of Pure Reason*, wherein Kant argued that transcendental, *a priori* concepts called 'categories', provided by the faculty of understanding (and acting in accordance with transcendental principles), extrinsically condition or subsume sensory impressions provided by the faculty of sensibility. In doing so the categories determine or provide the continuity, objectivity and order of such impressions.

Against this Maimon argues that there is no convincing evidence that the synthetic *a priori* principles or concepts proposed by Kant necessarily apply to *a posteriori* sense intuitions – necessity and universality being the two preconditions that Kant insists ground the objectivity of experience and derive from thought.[4] He insists that Kant is unable to find a justifiable criterion with which to determine when synthetic *a priori* concepts apply, for he has no way of distinguishing those cases in which these concepts do apply in experience from those in which they do not, and as such all 'the evidence of our senses, as Hume argued, shows us only a constant conjunction between distinct events but never any universal and necessary connections'.[5]

From these sceptical beginnings Maimon extends his critique of Kant's philosophy, focusing on the insufficiency of Kant's dualism. He questions how the two fundamentally distinct, heterogeneous faculties of sensibility and understanding – one passive and receptive and the other active and spontaneous – can genuinely interact.

Maimon's solution is to reject the dualism of the Transcendental Deduction. He observes that none of these difficulties concerning the application of *a priori* concepts to sensible intuitions would exist if both were merely different yet related aspects of the same thing, arising from a common source or constituting a continuum in which they represent opposing tendencies – that is, if either the understanding created intuitions as well as concepts according to its own laws or, alternatively, sensibility also created concepts as well as intuitions. In short, either 'sensualised' concepts or 'intellectualised' intuitions.[6] But rather than a sensualised intellect as the empiricists proposed (for Maimon asks, how can something intelligible be made from the unintelligible?), he instead embraces the more satisfactory Leibnizian alternative of intellectualising the senses – that is, by assuming that the understanding is the source of *both* the form and the content of experience, and that sensibility is not itself a separate source of knowledge but rather a *confused form of thought*.[7] In this fashion, Maimon turns the qualitative difference between sensibility and understanding into a quantitative one such that they differ only in degree, where a decrease in the former can be said to reflect a proportional increase in the latter.[8] Thus, the indistinctness, confusion and obscurity that characterises the intuition gives way to the clarity and distinctness of the concept – for the more we truly know 'the less we are affected'.[9]

Maimon's solution to Kant's dilemma, however, raises potential difficulties of its own concerning the nature of our perceptions and how we experience them. We would be justified in asking how then

are we to adequately explain the given-ness, irreducibility and independence of – that is, the lack of conscious choice that we have in
respect to — our perceptions, and the fact that 'sensations' seem to
be perceivable *only* by the senses and not directly or solely by the
understanding? Maimon overcomes this difficulty with his ingenious
theory of 'differentials'.

INFINITESIMALS AND DIFFERENTIALS

Kant in the *Critique of Pure Reason* describes the raw matter of sensation in terms of an intensive magnitude denoting the degree to which
the passive sensory apparatus is affected. This intensive magnitude is
without extension, consisting merely of degrees or gradations of intensity existing potentially in a continuum between infinity and zero, and
undergoing changes of augmentation and diminution (although intensive magnitude is never *actually* experienced as reducible to zero).

Maimon similarly regards the matter of sensation (the manifold
content of a perception) as consisting of such extension-less degrees,
of gradations or constitutive *differential* elements. Moreover, he
argues that these lie below the threshold of conscious recognition:
they are unconscious elements, imperceptible in themselves. As
Frederick Beiser notes of Maimon's account:

> [These units] consist in the lowest possible degree of intensity of a
> sensation, which is the basic element of all consciousness. The addi-
> tion of these units increases the degree of consciousness, and their
> subtraction decreases it. We approach such units . . . by continually
> diminishing the degree of consciousness of sensation. Since these
> units are infinitely small, however, the analysis of sensation only
> approaches but never reaches them.[10]

Maimon relates these imperceptible elements to Leibniz's differential
and integral calculus. In his development of the calculus Leibniz theo-
rised that differences (signified by the symbol dx), or points which
he called 'infinitesimals', could be infinitely sub-divided into smaller
units whereupon they seemed to vanish (i.e., become indiscernible)
without ever reaching zero – such as in the asymptotic relation of
a line tangent to a curve. More significantly, however, Leibniz also
found that even when the values denoting rates of change of the differential dx in respect of x and of dy in respect of y (i.e., dx/dy) were
reduced towards zero ($0/0$) the *differential relation* dx/dy would itself
never equal zero.[11]

Maimon takes up Leibniz's terminology, referring to the divisible, dimensionless elements of intensive magnitude as infinitesimals. More importantly though, he views their inter-relations in terms of a differential (relation) in which, although no longer perceivable by the senses they are still determinable by the Understanding (even if beneath the threshold of consciousness), in a manner akin to the way that the differential equation defines the properties of a curve through its analysis in terms of an infinite division of points. In such a manner Maimon extends Leibniz's mathematical account into a direct metaphysical claim concerning the nature of infinitesimals and differentials (thus arguably making explicit what was perhaps already implicit in Leibniz's thinking).[12]

In respect to the unconscious and imperceptible nature of these differential elements Maimon also links them to Leibniz's theory of 'petit perceptions'. Leibniz had argued that mental activity was a continuous activity, much of which went on below the threshold of consciousness (i.e., he suggested that in some sense we are still thinking when quiescent, asleep, or even comatose), and in line with his belief that sensory perceptions were in fact confused or unclear forms of mental activity on the part of monads he subsequently suggested that our conscious perceptions, although seemingly homogeneous, were, in fact, built up from numerous 'little impressions' or micro-perceptions of which we were not 'conscious'.[13] Whilst at some level we still remain aware of, or sense, all of these separate micro-perceptions (no matter their number), their singularity or the distinctness of their respective individual contributions lies beneath the threshold of conscious recognition, making 'imperceptibles' of them at least at the global or molar level. In this respect, for Maimon, sensations as intensive magnitudes similarly consist of infinitesimal degrees of subliminal mental activity – they are merely the products of the *subconscious* workings and laws of the understanding (sensations 'appearing' given and contingent, and as 'confused' representations, only because their actual production lies beneath or beyond the threshold of individual consciousness).

Because they are 'productive' in their relations Maimon claims that infinitesimals or differentials are *a priori* elements of intuition and thus the 'necessary condition of the unity of the manifold that makes up conscious perception',[14] in contrast to the 'given' of experience which is the product of their synthesis. Indeed, it is the combination of the reciprocal or determinate relations of these infinitesimal points, or rather the *integration* of their differences or 'differentials', which results in a particular finite perception, thus granting it extension as well as a degree of quality:

> What distinguishes one sense quality from another . . . is the rule for its production or genesis, the rule for the combination or aggregation of its basic units. All the differences between the various sense properties will then be determinable from the differences between their rules of production; and, furthermore, all the relations between sense properties will be determinable from the relations between the rules of production.[15]

Moreover, it is these differentials and the differences between them, their aggregates or *syntheses*, which account for the diversity of phenomenal objects, such that 'in the difference of the infinitesimals lies the foundation of the variety of perceptions'.[16] For the relations between objects reflect the relation of these various immanent rules of generation, of their qualitative differentials, at a broader level of integration, inasmuch as the relations between *a priori* differentials constitute the seeming relations between the objects that differentials produce, for they are, strictly speaking, 'not parts of objects but the *ultimate lawful relations of objects*'.[17]

Ultimately, such synthesis takes place not in relation to a simple homogeneous substrate, but to an immanent differentiating medium in which the *differential* between such infinitesimals provides both the *smallest unit with which to analyse sensations*, as well as the *rule of their combination*.[18]

In this regard, the 'given' is merely a mark of the limitation of our faculty of thought (something not yet thought through or overcome within thought itself), whereas, in contrast, the infinitesimals and differentials are the building-blocks and chain-like laws of thought itself that we must discover (i.e., think) by way of understanding. As such, empirical objects are thought by way of *a priori* rules or laws that govern the creation of those same objects and the 'essence of thought thus consists in thinking of an object, not as already existing, but as resulting from a process of creation' or genesis – that is, as becoming.[19] In such a fashion then, Maimon is able to solve Kant's difficulty in respect of determining the necessary applicability of the categories to intuitions: by claiming that their relations are *internal* to thought itself and that the sensory aspect of intuition merely involves those elements of thought not yet sufficiently cognised, not yet dissolved in to the pure thought that is the concept (as lawfulness).

In addressing the inadequacies of extrinsic conditioning through this alternative account of 'intrinsic' conditioning, or more accurately, immanent genesis, Maimon is also obliged to either modify or reject other crucial aspects of Kant's account: namely, things in themselves, and his account of time and space. In respect to the first, Maimon develops Kant's (often inconsistent) terminological distinction between a 'thing-in-itself' and a noumenon. The former denotes those independent yet mysterious entities that 'affect' our senses – mysterious because we can know nothing of their true nature, and can have no unmediated apprehension of them as they are in themselves. The latter, noumena, denote pure objects of thought – such as the Ideas of reason (God or the Soul) that act as hypothetical yet useful representations for making general sense of experience – that have no equivalent in empirical experience. There is a potential overlap between the two concepts, however, inasmuch as the notion of a thing-in-itself can function noumenally – we can 'think' it (i.e., mentally represent it as an Idea) without empirically 'knowing' it – and it is this overlap that Maimon exploits.

He argues that such noumena are synonymous with the differentials of thought (although they are, in fact, Ideas of understanding rather than of reason),[20] and objects are their corresponding products or phenomena.[21] Indeed, differentials are noumenal inasmuch as they constitute determinate relations imperceptible in direct experience, and present 'principles for the explanation of the genesis of objects . . . [which] act according to the rules of the understanding'.[22] They are the *a priori* genetic conditions of such experience – that which gives or produces the given (the content and form of intuitions) – whilst being *immanent* to cognition (i.e., we are not conscious of them, only of their integrals). However, Maimon claims that such differentials can also function as things in themselves, but on the proviso that we no longer mistake being affected by or conscious of 'something' as meaning that we are conscious of something *existing by itself outside of, or independently of*, consciousness. Maimon's account of immanent genesis allows him to totally discard the notion of 'independence' in respect to things in themselves – it is unnecessary because both intuitions and concepts arise from within thought – there is no 'external', independent stimulus as such. Understanding ultimately provides all the forms and content of experience and cognition. Thus, on the one hand, the differential as noumenon refers to something emergent or created within the field of consciousness, a process whereby a multiplicity of elements is stitched together or synthesised as an intuitive representation within imagination whilst, on the other, as a thing-in-itself it can still denote that unclear element or 'X' in experience that we do not yet fully understand. In the latter sense the thing-in-itself functions as a useful ideal or 'limiting concept' akin to a Kantian Idea, for it merely marks the potential perfection, completeness and clarity of understanding – of grasping all the underlying rules for the production of experience – for which we must continually (and never-endingly) strive, and in the absence of which we feel only perplexity.[23]

Turning now to space and time, we see, given that Maimon agrees that intensive magnitude concerns only the matter of intuition, that he must supplement his theory of differentials as noumena with a corresponding account of the *a priori* forms of space and time in respect of his revised account of the workings of the understanding. His account seeks a middle ground between Kant and Leibniz. He agrees with Kant that time and space are *a priori* forms of consciousness but not that they are *a priori* forms of intuition. They are merely forms of the understanding represented in a confused manner: that is to say, space and time are (as Leibniz argued originally) solely conceptual in nature in the way that we represent them to ourselves, and 'they are necessary conditions not of *sensation* but of the objectivity [and objectality] of experience. . .'.[24] They are differential concepts that are the minimal conceptual conditions for the thinking of diverse objects.[25] Indeed, the concept in which space is grounded is the very notion of *difference*, for when

> we perceive two bodies in space by means of our senses, we picture the fact of their being conceptually different from each other. The conceptual difference underlying the given objects is pictured, or generally perceived by our senses, as an occurrence at different points in space and time.[26]

An intuition thus 'represents' or illustrates (i.e., expresses) a concept – and in doing so it makes of space a picture of difference, but one that differs from difference in itself. Space and time then, for Maimon, are neither simply independent forms nor ideal fictions: they are conceptual properties expressed or represented as objects, their relations and production, rather than pre-existing fields into which objects are then inserted.[27]

IMMANENCE

So far I have examined the confused nature of sensibility and its relation to differentials in respect to intrinsic conditioning or genesis, but Maimon sought to ground these in a monistic notion of immanence and it is to this that we now turn. Maimon offered two different (yet compatible) accounts here – one transcendental and the other ontological. Even though the former was a later addition I will deal with it first so that its relation to the second makes more sense.

Maimon claims that the systematic unity of reason and knowledge must be grounded in a manner that can account for things as they are (their real conditions), rather than in their mere possibility (as Kant sought to do). He argues that a critical philosophy that seeks such a transcendental ground will require a new logic; one that reflects its own concerns and which is derived from a *single* principle. For although the differentials in the form of the Ideas of understanding are the rules for the production of objects, they need, nonetheless, to be unified within an *a priori* 'principle of determinability'.[28]

Maimon argues that formal logic with its categorical reliance on the Aristotelian 'principle of (non)-contradiction' does not have anything of value to say about the application of judgements in a real, material world (referring only to that which is formally true of all possible worlds). The role of this principle is then, according to Maimon, to deduce the real categories and to assess the validity of synthetic *a priori* claims to knowledge in respect of the world as it exists – to provide the criterion by which we can, on the one hand, ascertain objective knowledge of reality as distinct from merely subjective or habitual perceptions, and on the other, distinguish 'real thought or necessary connection' as distinct from 'formal or arbitrary thought'.[29]

More significantly, Maimon's principle of determinability provides some insight into the way he believes judgements (conscious representations) concerning *objects are determined*. The principle demands that the terms of a proposition concerning some thing or state of affairs must, somewhat akin to Leibniz's account of 'conceptual containment' or 'inesse principle', exist in an asymmetrical or non-reciprocal relation of dependence (unlike the reciprocal relations of the differentials themselves). That is, in respect of two terms or elements, one must be sufficiently independent of the other such that it is conceivable without it. For example, in the proposition 'X is Y', X must be independent of Y and therefore conceivable without Y, whereas Y must be within or entail X in such a way that it is inconceivable without it.[30]

In essence the principle of determinability is Maimon's attempt to deduce the transcendental, categorical 'necessity' that he argued Kant was unable to provide in his own account. It is the principle that underlies intrinsic conditioning, and which explains how all the elements of experience (and knowledge) can derive from an internal, transcendental logic or foundation.

The second and more significant notion of immanence that Maimon introduces, and which traverses all his work, embraces a modified version of Leibniz's notion of a God who is able to perceive and apperceive the universe in its totality, wedded to a Spinozan monistic notion of a God indistinguishable from nature (i.e, as the entirety of nature and as a single, self-causing substance). This infinite mind or 'infinite understanding' as Maimon usually refers to it, serves to ground the relation of intuitions and concepts, of noumena and phenomena, in an ontological notion of the infinite. It replaces Leibniz's account of an infinite number of irreducible monads with an infinite continuum of which we are all but 'parts' – partitions or sections. As such the notion of infinite mind is a totality both immanent to (as subconscious cause) and (imperceptibly) transcendent of finite understanding – it is the 'unconditioned condition' of the world of experience and thus a Kantian Idea which spurs us on towards greater understanding but which by its very nature remains forever beyond our reach.

In contrast, what defines finite understanding is its incomplete 'conscious' knowledge, that is, experience. The faculty of sensibility, now linked by degrees to the faculty of understanding, merely characterises the perplexed, confused and limited knowledge of a finite understanding that embraces and yet also presupposes the un-experienceable totality of infinite understanding as the source of all its representations. That is to say, from our own limited perspective we are unable for the most part to comprehend how our intuitions stem from this same partiality of our understanding (and its finite partitioning within infinite mind). We intuit objects whilst striving to understand their underlying or immanent laws of production. But infinite understanding has no need of intuitions (objects) at all. It grasps reality directly – not by apprehending the totality of given objects as such but rather through apprehending the totality of the relations prevailing among their differentials. Implicitly it knows, so to speak, the determinate laws or intrinsic formulae that constitute all such objects. In fact, it *contains* all the complete rules (concepts) for generating such necessary objects because it is ultimately their totality.

Deleuze

Turning now to the relevance of Maimon's work for Deleuze's 'philosophy of difference', we will find that the latter adopts, and reconfigures where necessary, a number of Maimon's own revisions of the Kantian transcendental framework – namely, the common origin of concepts and intuitions; the clear/confused distinction in respect to sensibility; Ideas as differentials; the principle of determinability; and infinite understanding. I will restrict my discussion here to Chapter 4 of Deleuze's *Difference and Repetition*, where the significance of these five concepts is especially foregrounded.[31]

In this chapter, titled 'Ideas and the Synthesis of Difference', Deleuze agrees with Maimon that Kant's failure stems from his reliance on the fundamental division between intuition and concept:

> Such a duality refers us back to the extrinsic criterion of constructability . . . and the renunciation of any genetic requirement . . . [for] difference remains external and as such empirical and impure, suspended outside the construction 'between' the determinable intuition and the determinant concept. Maimon's genius lies in showing how inadequate the point of view of conditioning is for a transcendental philosophy: both terms of the difference must equally be thought – in other words, determinability must itself be conceived as pointing towards a reciprocal determination. (DR 173)

The key phrase here is that 'both terms of the difference must be thought'. As we saw earlier, Maimon's solution was to intellectualise the sensuous: to claim that concepts and intuitions only differ in degree and that the latter are but a confused version of the former, derived from differentials in a process of intrinsic conditioning or immanent genesis. Deleuze similarly embraces the notion of the differential, but with certain modifications concerning its nature and function, that will enable him to argue that it 'overcomes concept and intuition by interiorising both' as a determination within a differential unconscious (DR 174).

The Idea

Deleuze begins by expanding the association that Maimon introduced between the differential and the Kantian Idea. For Kant the Ideas of the faculty of reason had three key characteristics: their speculative and problematic nature, their concern with pure thought and 'unconditioned conditions', and their synthesising function. It is these very same aspects of the Idea that Deleuze takes up, drawing out their implications and transforming them in the process.

First, Deleuze claims that although Ideas concern problems – perplexing underlying conditions – this does not suggest a lack, insufficiency or absolute indeterminacy on their part. That they are not determinable in experience does not mean they are not determinable as such. Indeed to say that the problem (as ideal) is a no-thing is far from saying that it is simply 'nothing'. Thus the problematic – as something 'unknown' (or unavailable in experience) – does not denote an absence or negativity, but rather marks an 'X' that is not part of or yet integrated into experience as a representation. This, however, makes it no less real or replete than any actual 'given' object of perception. Indeed, the problem-(matic) has a positive and fecund or overflowing nature that Deleuze describes in terms of a ?-being or [non]-being, so as to distinguish it from the traditional notion of non-being as limitation (and of difference reduced to lack).

Secondly, Deleuze points out that if 'thought', by way of the understanding, produces objects then so too must reason, as the faculty of pure thought: that is, the Idea must also have an object of some sort.[32] Indeed, we must not confuse saying that the Idea (as problem) has no *corresponding empirical object* with claiming that it therefore has no object at all, for the problem (as unconditioned condition) *is* the object of the Idea. It does have a corresponding object of sorts: not one given in experience, yet, nonetheless, an object somehow representable or determinable within thought (objects always being, for Kant, the result of syntheses) (DR 169).

Of what does this problematic object consist? What is its nature? Here Deleuze links the Idea to Bergson's notion of a qualitative, non-numerical, *virtual* multiplicity consisting only of pure co-existing and interpenetrating differences or vibrations – differences in kind – that transform in nature (become 'other') once measured or actualised.[33] Such a multiplicity does not have an identity of its own (that is, although we can speak of it in terms of a continuity involving interpenetration of its 'parts', we cannot yet speak of its elements as constituting a unity or of any of its elements as having identities in themselves). It is more thematic than defining, for the Idea as 'Multiplicity tolerates no dependence on the identical in the subject or in the object . . . [nor does it] *allow any positing of an essence as "what the thing is"'* (DR 191, emphasis added).

It is the differential – that is, non-identical – elements of this immanent, virtual domain that the Idea synthesises, that make of the Idea a multiplicity itself, consisting of differential elements, differential relations between those elements, and the various singularities corresponding to those relations. The Idea contracts elements of the multiplicity, or more accurately perhaps, it relates or places in resonance such differences (or differentials), linking them to one another without imposing any unity, identity or meaning upon them, either collectively or individually. In this sense, the Idea as a positive, synthesising multiplicity functions as a structure or complex theme.[34] But what is this structure in respect to the Idea as problem? It is a differential structure of determinability, one that characterises pure thought in respect of the real conditions of experience, and 'has the differential relation as its object' (DR 173). The Idea as such is an ideal and genetic structure – real and yet non-empirical – that constitutes a 'system of multiple, non-localisable connections between differential elements which is incarnated in real relations and actual terms' (DR 183). It provides the ensemble of conditions that determine experience, and thus the potential production of and interrelation of all empirical objects. Unlike its Kantian precursor then, the Idea as virtual multiplicity is fully constitutive, ontological and immanent.

DETERMINABILITY

It is here in his account of determination that Deleuze finally links the Maimonian differential to his revised account of the Kantian Idea.[35] The Idea as differential (or determinate) encompasses, or synthesises, all of the elements so far discussed – the Idea as problem, virtual multiplicity and ideal structure – thus clarifying their inter-relations. This differential Idea consists of three key moments:

1) Determinability (in respect to the undetermined).
2) Reciprocal determination (in respect to the determinable).
3) Complete determination (in respect to the determined).

Collectively these moments constitute a process of 'progressive determination' or 'differentiation' that, Deleuze claims, will provide the immanent and genetic conditions that determine the production of actual or empirical objects.[36]

As noted earlier, Maimon sought a 'principle of determinability' for a transcendental philosophy, a single immanent principle or law for the production – by way of differentials – of real experience as distinct from possible experience. The first of these moments, concerning the 'undetermined', is Deleuze's radical reworking of this notion.

Drawing upon Bergson, he claims that this immanent 'principle of determinability' is the *virtual* and concerns virtual elements – i.e., the reservoir or ensemble of pure differences contained in the virtual that are subsequently synthesised or connected in Ideas as determinate differentials. However, no longer envisaged in terms of infinitely divisible 'points' (i.e., Maimon's infinitesimals), these pure differences which have 'neither sensible form nor conceptual signification' are 'ideal elements – in other words, elements without figure or function, but reciprocally determined within a network of differential relations (ideal non-localisable connections)' (DR 278).

These differences, subsisting and interpenetrating within the virtual multiplicity, have no identity as such – they constitute but a single, intensive continuum of heterogeneous elements, prior to all quality and quantity, space or extension. As they are without identities these differential elements cannot be said to be 'essences': they are inessential (DR 187). This is why Deleuze insists that the development of the Idea is built up from the inessential (and the determinable from the undetermined), providing an answer of sorts to Maimon's question: 'how can the intelligible be made from the unintelligible?'

This first moment, determinability, implies yet another in turn, a further moment that also has its roots in Maimon's account. Here an ensemble or assemblage of such pure, inessential differences reciprocally constitutes a differential relation that determines or produces a corresponding value. These inessential elements then provide the raw material for syntheses, which although undetermined in themselves are, nonetheless, infinitely *determinable* in respect of one another.

Deleuze, like Maimon before him, draws inspiration here from the differential relation of Leibniz's calculus, wherein the relation dy/dx remains viable or determinative even when the respective values of dx and dy are indiscernible (i.e., $0/0$), for in 'relation to x, dx is completely undetermined, as dy is to y, but they are perfectly determinable in relation to one another' (DR 172). Deleuze adopts $0/0$ as the symbol of the differential as reciprocal determination and dx as the symbol of immanent, virtual difference in itself (of ?-being, or to make a pun, the '(non)-things in themselves'), undetermined and yet capable of determination.

It is important to grasp here that although the *reciprocal* determinations of the 'differential' *determine particular values*, the contributing elements do not in themselves constitute values for they are inessential and without identity (hence the symbol $0/0$). In short, the resulting values derive from the relation itself and not directly from the elements of the relation – it is simply the very difference(s) between the latter that contribute to modulating the overall relation. In this regard, however, the elements of the differential relation are neither deficient or negative (in any Hegelian sense), merely *contrastive*. Indeed, Deleuze is adamant that we must substitute everywhere the notion of *differential relation* for one of 'distinctive opposition' or contradiction if we are to enable determination to relinquish or escape any negative conception, for each 'term exists absolutely only in its relation to the other: it is no longer necessary, or even possible, to indicate an independent variable' (DR 172).

These differentials *between* virtual or 'inessential' elements constitute the variables that designate or assign corresponding values, reciprocal relations and distributions of those values and relations, and which demarcate a transcendental 'topological' field from which physical or material relations are subsequently derived, in the form of qualities, extension, species and parts.[37] But it is their reciprocal relations that provide the determinate 'laws' for the development of such differentials of thought, as the source of *both* intuitions and concepts. It is here that Maimon's ambition of overcoming the insufficiency of extrinsic conditioning is perhaps finally fulfilled: that we must determine both intuition and concept together in a relation internal to 'thought' and that this be achieved through reciprocal determination *within* the non-empirical synthesis of the virtual, differential Idea.

This second moment of reciprocal determination, however, also implicates a third, complete determination – a notion that Deleuze derives from Kant, who in turn borrowed it from Christian Wolff. In the *Critique of Pure Reason* Kant radically revises Wolff's claim that existence is the final predicate that perfects an object (i.e., for it to be actual it must be determined in all its 'parts'). He links this principle of completion back to the regulative faculty of reason as a means of providing completion in the form of the Idea of 'totality' or a systematic unity in respect of not just individual objects but of all objects of possible experience. In this sense, different objects are likened to and related to one another through a determinate and reciprocal process of analogy (A is to B as B is to C), such that all phenomenal objects in experience can be said, in respect of the encompassing web of their causal relations, to thus imply an objective unity, although as a totality it is not experienceable.[38]

For Deleuze, these two respective notions of the expression of the object in its entirety and of an implied totality in respect to all phenomena are bridged via the virtual multiplicity and the corresponding distribution of values which will form (to use Leibnizian-Maimonian terminology) a complete 'law of the series' able to both individuate objects and produce an enfolding or complementary field of perceptual phenomena. Deleuze agrees with Kant that this 'totality' of relations is not accessible in the actual phenomena (even in the form of intuitions), but rather presupposed transcendentally (DR 175). But nonetheless, Deleuze insists that the Idea as differential, in consisting of all its inessential elements and their differential relations, is complete and thus must be distinguished from the actual object produced from that structure. The problematic object as an ideal, virtual structure is already complete, fully determinate and real – but this is not the same as saying that it 'exists', that it is actual or empirical.

Deleuze's key insight is that the virtual is fully determinate; however, the 'object' is not whole or entire if by this we mean that it has 'existence' – it is not explicated; it is without extensity or quality. Thus Deleuze insists that such a virtual synthesis can be completely determined (in structural terms) 'without, for all that, possessing the integrity [integration] which alone constitutes its actual existence' (DR 46–7). That the structure virtually subsists rather than exists marks no deficiency or imperfection in the Idea itself. In effect, the differential synthesis of the Idea as structure generates a corresponding integration which then forms the empirical object, but the virtual structure itself bears no resemblance to what it produces. The Idea is not a 'possible' identity simply awaiting realisation (like a Platonic Form), but a principle of transformation.

In drawing this distinction Deleuze is referring to two quite different processes in respect of the production of the object, one purely on the side of the virtual and structural determination (which he calls differentia*t*ion), and the other characterised by actualisation itself (which he calls differen*c*iation):

> [Where] differentiation determines the virtual content of the Idea as problem, differenciation expresses the actualisation of this virtual and the constitution of solutions (by local integrations). Differenciation is like the second part of difference . . . [thus] in order to designate the integrity or the integrality of the object we require the complex notion of different/ciation. (DR 209)

In this regard every 'whole' or existing object consists of two complementary yet unequal, non-resembling components[39] – one imperceptibly virtual, problematic and ideal (its *noumenal* structure), and the other actual and empirical (its *phenomenal* expression) (DR 210).

This reflects the fact that for Deleuze 'reality' consists of two different and asymmetrical yet related sides or *halves* (rather than two different worlds as Plato proposed).[40] Together these two halves make up an object of experience in its entirety but only one half, the virtual, and its corresponding transcendental field provides its *sufficient reason*, its internal difference or differential. [41]

This distinction also enables Deleuze to finally address the issue of clarity and confusion raised by Maimon in his characterisation of concept and intuition. Deleuze's account is far more nuanced and faithful to the notion of difference in this regard, as the relation is no longer one between intuition and concept, but between the virtual Idea in respect of its complete determination and the actualised object as a whole empirically individuated entity – that is, the distinction between differentiation and differenciation.

Deleuze notes that Descartes believed that only those perceptions which we perceive *clearly* and *distinctly* are valid – clear inasmuch as a perception is present and accessible to the attentive mind and distinct when it can be easily differentiated from other perceptions (i.e., it is more distinct the 'clearer' it is). For Leibniz, in contrast, the 'senses' merely perceive in a confused manner the metaphysical and intellectual reality that the mind apprehends more clearly, and are subject to the obscurity of 'unconscious' petit perceptions (as increments which once sufficiently synthesised or integrated cross a threshold and emerge within consciousness as an integrated or blended phenomenon).

Deleuze refashions Leibniz's account of 'petit perceptions' such that we need no longer speak of monads and their perceptions, but only of differentials and the subjects they generate (nomads). He argues that the clear is not related to the distinct but to the confused, and conversely that the distinct is related to the obscure.[42] Integrating this distinction into his account, Deleuze claims that the *fully determinate* nature of the noumenal, virtual Idea (its reciprocal and complete synthesis) is what we should call 'distinct', but because it is not yet 'actual' it is also therefore what we might call 'obscure'. The 'distinct-obscure' thus describes the differentiated inasmuch as pure differences are distinct from one another, *real and determinate in their relations within the Idea* whilst still being indiscernible and immaterial from the point of view of the actual where they have no identity, location, or discretion – for there is no 'confusion within the Idea, . . . [merely the] internal problematic objective unity of the undetermined, the determinable and determination' (DR 170). The 'clear-confused', in contrast, describes the nature of differenciated phenomena which are 'clear' inasmuch as they are actual and perceivable entities (distinguishable and representable with the aid of concepts) but whose relations to the underlying or implicit continuity of the virtual Idea are 'confused' (i.e., cannot be empirically grasped or represented in themselves). In short, phenomena are clear-confused in form and nature but the distinct-obscure Idea is 'precisely *real without being actual, differentiated without being differenciated, and complete without being entire*' (DR 214).

DIFFERENCE AND THE DIFFERENTIAL UNCONSCIOUS

This leads us finally to Deleuze's reworking of Maimon's notion of an infinite understanding and its partitioning as finite consciousness. For Maimon the relationship between these two aspects (of totality and section) is reflected in the relationship between the two faculties of sensibility and understanding. The latter relation was one of continuity in which an increase in the clarity of understanding led to a proportional decrease in the confusion of sensibility (and vice versa), and where the clarity of finite understanding finds its completion in infinite understanding (inasmuch as to know – to understand clearly – is to accurately grasp reality).

Obviously, in the face of the above revisions concerning Ideas, differentials, and determinability, Maimon's original claims that sensibility is but confused understanding, and that intuitions are derivatives of concepts, is unsustainable. Throughout *Difference and Repetition* Deleuze's constant refrain is that a philosophy of difference must be faithful to difference, must be founded in the primacy of difference, that such a foundation ('a groundless ground') must be transcendental and ontological, genetic and immanent – but most significantly, that it must always precede identity (see DR 40–1). Although Maimon's philosophy pushes in this direction – indeed, goes further than most – nonetheless, it is still tainted with residues of the most conservative aspects of Leibniz's and Kant's respective philosophies that must be purged.

Given Deleuze's claim that the fundamental elements of a philosophy of difference cannot be grounded in any form of identity, Maimon's reliance on concepts obviously then presents difficulties. Non-empirical concepts are rules for the construction of representations (for Kant they make intuitions conform to universal forms). They ultimately impose identities on the products of Maimonian differentials, inasmuch as the sensible sacrifices its singularity to the purity, clarity and dominion that is the underlying concept. It is impossible then to see how concepts could provide a genuinely convincing foundation for difference. Instead Deleuze seeks a difference – a positive, genetic, immanent difference – that engenders, inhabits and motivates the concept in general without being reducible to it. Maimon is thus right to see concepts and intuitions as meeting in a common source but incorrect in assuming that one (or for that matter, the other) can be the source itself. To make the concept potentially capable of encompassing everything in the manner of Leibniz (or even in the fashion of Hegel) only betrays what is at stake – for they are both but aspects, or expressions, of something more fundamental, something immanent. Intrinsic conditioning cannot overcome extrinsic conditioning if it is still grounded in the concept itself. It is only the pre-conceptual, sub-representative Ideas of pure thought that can provide such a foundation, that can give the 'given' in all its diversity. Thus Deleuze acknowledges that concepts and intuitions have a common origin but not one in which intuitions are revealed to be confused concepts – for both elements originate from the side of the virtual, from within Ideas (as the rules of their production), with issues of obscurity and distinctness, confusion and clarity now marking the relation between virtual and actual, differen*tia*tion and differen*cia*tion, and not the relationship of intuition and concept, or sensibility and understanding.[43]

These issues also stem from another difficulty that has its origins in Kant's original conception of synthesis. True, Kant's genius was to see that synthesis is primarily transcendental and *a priori*, however, he betrayed this insight by assuming that only syntheses that occur in respect to mental cognition and its production of representations – grounded in the conditioning power of the understanding and the unity of the transcendental unity of apperception – are valid (and concern the real). Deleuze rejects this assumption as unfounded. He distinguishes between the active syntheses of a self-reflexive consciousness (the cogito that affirms itself as self-identical: *I* think, *I* feel, *I* remember, *I* decide, etc.), whose stock in trade is intuitions cut to the generic cloth of representational concepts, and the 'passive' yet constitutive *a priori* syntheses upon which such active syntheses are founded. These syntheses are passive because they take place within the mind but are not undertaken or initiated by it – in fact the mind (consciousness and agency) is a by-product of such contractile processes (DR 70–4). In place of Kant's assumption that syntheses ultimately presuppose or stem from a subject, Deleuze claims that we find that the reverse is the case.[44] In order to remain faithful to a philosophy of difference, what precedes consciousness (or the cogito) must be viewed as arising from a synthesis that has neither the unity nor the identity of a subject – for only a passive synthesis or set of syntheses is able to produce such a unity. These passive syntheses are the condition of subjectivity without themselves being subjective – instead they characterise an immanent, non-spatial, problematically objective and trans-subjective field that constitutes and traverses all subjects. Fundamentally, the province of such 'unconscious' passive syntheses is the domain of the Idea, of virtual multiplicity, and of determination.

Returning to Maimon we see that Deleuze is prepared to accept a distinction between finite consciousness and something *a priori* and transcendental but on the proviso that we do not conceive of the latter in terms of unity, or understanding, or a cogito. Despite his own prioritising of synthesis and the unconscious differential relation, Maimon's ontological account of infinite understanding teeters uncertainly on the edge of a model of identity. Yes, it describes differentials and synthesising ideas, and yes, the infinite understanding is subconscious, immanent and genetic, but ultimately it still privileges elements – concepts and understanding – that potentially threaten the integrity of the entire philosophical edifice. Moreover, it remains inconsistent and unclear concerning to what degree infinite understanding is self-reflexive, to what degree it is an 'I' analogous to consciousness, and merely universalised in its scope. This ambiguity marks the two different paths that follow from it. One path was taken by the German idealists Fichte, Schelling and Hegel, who saw in the notion of infinite understanding the possibility of the transcendental subject or cogito simply writ-large (thus replacing the plurality of such subjects with a single all-encompassing 'I' in which everything was ultimately or potentially united), whilst the other path, different and less travelled, was taken by Deleuze. In this latter odyssey – implicit throughout *Difference and Repetition*, and virtually threaded throughout its every word and concept – infinite thought remains unconscious in its most important sense: not as a universal mind, but a purely differential, structural unconscious of Ideas, devoid of the self-reflexive unity ascribed to it by Kant, no longer characterised by the purified, complete understanding of Maimon, and divorced from the substantive, repressed alter-ego reified by Freud in his worst moments. Instead, just an immanent virtual multiplicity, both ideal and real, differentiated and differentiating, that structures and systematises all of these elements without constituting a centre – a pure genetic thought of the undetermined, the determinable, and the determined. The Idea of Ideas.

It is this Idea of a differential unconscious as the source of our Ideas, I believe, that overcomes and supplants Kant's 'Copernican revolution' with another yet more profound, more far-reaching and more 'untimely'. And perhaps of all Deleuze's myriad and enduring contributions this, ultimately, is his allusive and elusive legacy to philosophy.

Notes

1. There are variant spellings of both his first and last name (for example, Salomon Maïmon). Here I have simply used one of the most common spellings.
2. *Versuch über die Transcendental-philosophie, mit einem Anhang über die symbolische Erkenntniß und Anmerkungen*, dating from 1790.
3. Cited in Frederick Beiser, *The Fate of Reason: German Philosophy from Kant to Fichte* (Cambridge, MA: Harvard University Press, 1987), p. 285. Today Maimon is a largely forgotten figure, infrequently discussed and often overlooked (with but a few notable exceptions). None of his major philosophical works are available in English and he is rarely mentioned in philosophical dictionaries or histories of philosophy, and yet, ironically, his work has exerted a truly profound, if little acknowledged, influence on the development and future direction, not just of post-Kantian thought, but of continental philosophy in general. It is no exaggeration to say that the works of Fichte, Schelling and Hegel could not have existed in the forms that we know them today without Maimon's contribution. Indeed, Fichte said of him: 'My respect for Maimon's talents knows no bounds. I firmly believe that he has completely overturned the entire Kantian philosophy as it has been understood by everyone until now . . . No one noticed what he had done: they had looked down on him from their heights' (cited in Frederick Beiser, 'Maimon and Fichte', in *Salomon Maimon: Rational Dogmatist, Empirical Skeptic – Critical Assessments*, edited by Gideon Freudenthal, Dordrecht: Kluwer Academic Publishers, 2003 p. 232).
4. 'In his definition of the concept of *a priori* Maimon differs from Kant. Whereas for the latter, a concept that is logically prior to and independent of sensation and perception belongs to the *a priori* mode of cognition, for Maimon *a priori* is only that mode of cognition which precedes cognition of the object itself . . . [and] when the cognition of objects

must precede cognition of their relations to one another, it is *a posteriori* (Samuel Atlas, *From Critical to Speculative Idealism: The Philosophy of Solomon Maimon* [The Hague, Nijhoff, 1964], pp. 133–4).

5. See Beiser, *The Fate of Reason*, pp. 288–90, for an excellent summary and discussion pertaining to these issues.
6. Beiser, *The Fate of Reason*, p. 291.
7. Beiser, *The Fate of Reason*, p. 293.
8. Beiser, *The Fate of Reason*, p. 305.
9. Mier Buzaglo, *Solomon Maimon: Monism, Skepticism, and Mathematics* (Pittsburgh: University of Pittsburgh Press, 2002), p. 107.
10. Beiser, *The Fate of Reason*, p. 296.
11. See Daniel W. Smith's chapter on 'Leibniz', in this volume, for a discussion of this matter.
12. Atlas, *From Critical to Speculative Idealism*, p. 110.
13. For instance, the famous example which Leibniz employs in his 'Preface to the New Essays' describes how when we hear the ocean we only *consciously* perceive a monolithic crescendo of sound, where all the different, individual sounds arising from the movement of the surf merge into a single indistinct susurration within our perception (Gottfried Wilhelm Leibniz, *New Essays on Human Understanding*, edited by Jonathan Bennett and Peter Remnant [Cambridge: Cambridge University Press, 1997], p. 295).
14. See Atlas, *From Critical to Speculative Idealism*, pp. 109, 124, 129. Of necessity a given intuition arises gradually over time but the rule by which its manifold is *united, ordered and determined arises instantaneously* – that is to say, outside of empirical time in a kind of transcendental 'ideal' time. See also Samuel Bergman, *The Philosophy of Solomon Maimon*, trans. Noah J. Jacobs (Jerusalem: Magnes Press, 1967), pp. 63–4.
15. Beiser, *The Fate of Reason*, p. 297. See also Bergman, *The Philosophy of Solomon Maimon* for a discussion of this.
16. Atlas, *From Critical to Speculative Reason*, p. 109.
17. Bergman, *The Philosophy of Solomon Maimon*, p. 62 (emphasis added).
18. See Beiser, *The Fate of Reason*, p. 297. It is worth noting, however, that in his later work Maimon seems to waver on the issue of whether infinitesimals are merely a useful and creative hypothesis (which he calls a 'fiction'), or a genuine metaphysical reality.
19. 'Actually, however, the process of imagination is not a representation (*Vorstellung*) of something existing outside the mind, but rather the presentation (*Darstellung*) of something as existing, which in fact did not exist before' (Atlas, *From Critical to Speculative Reason*, p. 111).
20. See Beiser, *The Fate of Reason*, p. 309.
21. Atlas, *From Critical to Speculative Reason*, p. 110.

22. Beiser, *The Fate of Reason*, p. 298.
23. As Atlas says: 'The infinitesimals constitute the basic elements of our conscious perception of an object. They . . . are a determining factor and an integral part of our perception. The thing-in-itself, on the other hand, is a problem, an X, or an idea, that is, the ideal of the final and complete solution of all problems relating to an object' (*From Critical to Speculative Reason*, p. 115).
24. Beiser, *The Fate of Reason*, p. 301.
25. Maimon succinctly sums up his own differences from Kant: '[I]n Kant's opinion, space is merely a form of intuition, whereas in my opinion space, as a concept, is the form of all objects in general and, as an intuition, it is the picture of this form' (cited in Buzaglo, *Salomon Maimon*, p. 89). For discussion of Maimon's view of time and space also see Peter Thelke's 'Intutition and Diversity: Kant and Maimon on Space and Time', in Freudenthal (ed.), *Salomon Maimon: Rational Dogmatist, Empirical Skeptic*.
26. Buzaglo, *Salomon Maimon*, p. 90.
27. See Beiser, *The Fate of Reason*, p. 303; Buzaglo, *Salomon Maimon*, p. 92; and also Jan Bransen, *The Antinomy of Thought: Maimonian Scepticism and the Relation between Thoughts and Objects* (Dordrecht et al: Kluwer Academic Publishers, 1991), pp. 65–80. The upshot of Maimon's argument is that the subject–object dualism can no longer be said to exist between two different kinds of entity. The distinction now provides a contrast between two different kinds of thought (i.e., objects *and* their rules of production), or two different mental states (representations *and* presentations, respectively) (Beiser, *The Fate of Reason*, p. 308). In this regard, a presentation is something fully or completely cognised or determined by the mind (in respect of its relations and lawfulness), whereas a representation is something incompletely or only partially cognised. For infinite mind full cognisance would thus mean simply 'knowing' the rule(s) of production of an object – i.e., its differential or presentation – whereas, in contrast, the 'object', matter, time and space, are all characteristics of finite consciousness and its dependence on representations, that denote its incomplete understanding.
28. Kant also speaks of a 'principle of determinability', which he derives from the work of Leibniz's follower, Christian Wolff. Little more than a version of the traditional Aristotelian 'principle of contradiction', it demands that in determining a possible object and thus applying a category to it that the presence or absence of a specific predicate should logically exclude its opposite (and every predicate or thing subsequently dependent on either the former predicate's presence or absence); see Etienne Gilson's *Being and Some Philosophers* (Toronto: Pontifical Institute of Medieval Studies, 1952), pp. 114–15, 117.

29. As Beiser notes: 'So what the principle of (non)contradiction is to the form of a judgement, the principle of determinability is to its content' (*The Fate of Reason*, p. 313).
30. See Beiser, *The Fate of Reason*, pp. 314, 316.
31. However, if evidence were required of a broader Maimonian influence on Deleuze's philosophy, one need merely mention the following three aspects of Maimon's thought that Deleuze reiterates (surprisingly without acknowledgement): first, that Maimon describes his aim as going beyond the possible conditions of experience in general in search of the 'conditions of real experience' (a claim that Deleuze himself repeats almost word for word on several occasions); second, that Maimon privileges difference over opposition and claims that the latter derives from the former and not the other way around – another claim that Deleuze subscribes to; and finally, that Deleuze describes his own work as a philosophy of the 'middle' (or the 'between') – essentially the same characterisation that Maimon presents of his own work.
32. Deleuze claims that problems as 'Ideas are both immanent and transcendent' (DR 169) – 'transcendent' in respect to representation or conceptual knowledge, and 'immanent' in respect to thinking as an unconscious movement of (passive) synthesis. He also draws an analogy between problematic Ideas and the way mathematical problems function in respect to the production of solutions (DR 163–4) – see Simon Duffy's chapter later in this volume for discussion of this matter.
33. Bergson characterises this multiplicity in terms of an ontological past – see Deleuze's *Bergsonism* for his elaboration of this concept.
34. For an insight into Deleuze's thoughts about structure see his paper 'How do we recognize structuralism?', trans. Melissa McMahon and Charles Stivale, in *The Two-Fold Thought of Deleuze and Guattari: Intersections and Animations* (New York and London: Guilford Press, 1998)
35. In fact, I would go so far as to claim that each and every one of Deleuze's works concerns this issue of determinability in respect to a different domain: of determining the conditions of social formations, of desire, of painting, of cinema, of signs, etc.
36. They are called moments because they occur, or constitute a series, within an enfolded or *ideal temporality* (i.e., the virtual as coexistence) as distinct from the unfolding time of actualisation (i.e., empirical or experiential succession). See DR 210–11.
37. In a sense, the world of experience is the result of the expression of such transcendental co-ordinates, of an ontological combinatory or calculus that is expressed in different physical and symbolic domains (and modified accordingly). The value of the mathematical calculus is that it foregrounds this differential relation which Deleuze sees as intrinsic to Ideas. However, we should carefully note that in making this claim

Deleuze does not directly conflate mathematics with ontology (DR 179), as do certain other philosophers.

38. Immanuel Kant, *Critique of Pure Reason*, trans. Norman Kemp Smith (London: Macmillan, 1990), A572–4/B600–2; A581–2/B609–10.

39. Unfortunately, I do not have space here to examine the particular processes outlined in Chapter 5 of *Difference and Repetition* that Deleuze claims characterise differenciation – namely, *individuation* and *dramatisation* – processes that engender the process of actualisation from the transcendental field thus allowing the virtually determined to actualise itself in qualities and extensities, and species and parts. Suffice to say that they involve the production of an accompanying or corresponding empirical space and time (and proto-consciousness) in respect to the engendered object; see DR 206–7.

40. Here Deleuze returns to a notion first introduced in his earlier study of Proust (PS 26). This also in turn evokes Deleuze's discussion of the two asymmetrical tendencies in his paper 'Bergson's Concept of Difference' (DI 32–51) and in the later *Bergsonism*.

41. As such the virtual is a diffuse field of interpenetrating, overlapping and fluidly shifting multiplicities which create and *inter-relate* diverse, individuated phenomena. Thus, Deleuze suggests, the relation of one empirical object to another – say, one billiard ball striking another – is not simply due to a physically causal or mechanical relation existing between them but is a relation internal to the virtual itself. Or as Maimon might have said, it is the relation of the differential of one intuition to the differential of another. In this sense, causality is but the shadow of real immanent relations.

42. Here Deleuze is drawing upon distinctions established in Leibniz's 'Meditations on Knowledge, Truth and Ideas'; see Leibniz, *New Essays on Human Understanding*, pp. 219–20.

43. This explains why Deleuze argues that Ideas do not originate within the faculty of understanding (as Maimon claimed) or within Reason (as Kant originally proposed) but emerge through all the faculties – as each cognitive faculty expresses in its own fashion aspects of the immanent Idea (DR 192).

44. Such passive syntheses relate to the three moments of determinability, i.e., the three moments of progressive determination directly correspond to the three passive syntheses of time (and to the three, less frequently discussed, syntheses of space).

7

G. W. F. Hegel

Bruce Baugh

In a perceptive review of Gilles Deleuze's influential *Nietzsche and Philosophy* (1983), Jean Wahl remarks that Deleuze's resentment[1] and "ill feeling" (*mauvaise humeur*) towards Hegel[2] sometimes impair Deleuze's otherwise brilliant critique of Hegel. Of all the major philosophers discussed by Deleuze (including Plato, Lucretius, Leibniz, Spinoza, Kant, Nietzsche and Bergson), Hegel receives by far the least sympathetic treatment; whereas in all the other cases, Deleuze is able to retrieve something useful for his own philosophy, his critique of Hegel is almost unrelentingly negative. In a philosophy that celebrates the affirmation of difference, such negativity may come as a surprise, and even seem ironic.

Yet Deleuze's rejection of Hegel, from start to finish, rests on the firm conviction that Hegel's philosophy has betrayed difference by making difference into something negative (negation, opposition, contradiction), and it is against this Hegelian negativity that Deleuze so tirelessly inveighs. Deleuze's Nietzschean critique of Hegel is well known: the negative conception of difference is the expression of the *ressentiment* of those who suffer because they turn their own forces against themselves and make 'reaction' their 'creative act'.[3] 'For the affirmation of difference, [Hegel's dialectic] substitutes the negation of that which differs; for the affirmation of self, it substitutes the negation of the other; and for the affirmation of affirmation, it substitutes the famous negation of the negation' (NP 96). But his critique of Hegel neither begins nor ends here. From the beginning, Deleuze sought to construct an ontology and a logic of affirmative difference that would resist the famous Hegelian 'identity of identity and difference' which makes 'difference' into a passing 'moment' of Being 'contradicting itself' via its multiple determinations in the 'Absolute Idea'.[4]

DIFFERENCE AND CONTRADICTION

Deleuze's objections to Hegel emerge as early as his 1954 review of his teacher Jean Hyppolite's book, *Logic and Existence*. Deleuze agrees with Hyppolite that 'Being is difference', but disagrees with Hyppolite's 'completely Hegelian' thesis that difference cannot remain at Otherness or pure Difference, but must be carried up to the absolute, that is, to contradiction. Deleuze counters: 'Could one not construct an ontology of difference which would not go all the way to contradiction because contradiction would be less than difference and not more? Is not contradiction the phenomenal and anthropological aspect of difference?'[5]

In his *Science of Logic*, Hegel continually finds negations underlying difference, and his dialectic consists in making negations more and more internal. Thus, to begin with, a being is something determinate only to the extent that it differs from or is not another thing, and not-being an other is thus a constitutive 'moment' of its own identity as 'the negation of the negation'.[6] But just as for the first thing (A), the second (B) is the other, so the first (A) is the other of the second (B), and each thing is then both itself and an other,[7] and in that respect, they are indistinguishable and each passes into its other, such that each takes its otherness into itself and becomes other-than-self. If the other is then conceived apart from its relation to a determinate something, and becomes 'the other as such' (*to heteron*), it becomes pure externality, the external relations which obtain in being which is external to itself: nature as space, time and matter, which is always altering (becoming) and yet remains the same as itself.[8]

This 'natural' progression is taken up at a higher level in the form of principles of thought or logic. The law of identity (A = A) can also be expressed negatively (A *is not equal to* not-A), so that A affirms itself by distinguishing itself from not-A, or by negating its negation; but in negating its negation (not-A), it has nothing from which to distinguish itself, and so becomes self-related negativity, that is, no longer difference from another, but absolute difference.[9] Absolute difference is 'difference identical with itself' or *self*-related difference, and thus contains both difference and identity in its relation to itself,[10] but as difference and identity negate each other, absolute difference 'falls apart' into diversity, in which two terms are identical to themselves but different from each other; this difference is then external to the two terms, and the two terms are indifferent to one another.[11] But in external difference, the difference vanishes inasmuch as each term, being equally like itself, is the same as the other, and cannot affirm its difference; rather, external difference relies on a comparison made by a third party which assesses the similarity or dissimilarity of the two terms with respect to a common element that connects them as being 'more or less' similar or dissimilar to each other. It is only when this common 'mediating' element is internalised that difference becomes opposition between 'two sides' opposed to each other (as positive and negative) without reference to a third term. In opposition, the different is not confronted by *any* Other but by *its* Other.[12] Opposed to its contrary, each opposite 'has within itself its relation to its other moment; it is thus the whole, self-contained opposition', each contrary both containing but also excluding its opposite in affirming itself: 'It is thus contradiction.'[13] In positing itself by negating the opposite through which it defines itself, it makes its being depend on the opposite it negates, and implicitly takes that opposition into itself, becoming 'the negation not of another but of itself'.[14] Or, as Hegel puts it in the *Phenomenology of Spirit*, 'the object is *in one and the same respect the opposite of itself*; and *it is for another, so far as it is for itself*'.[15] Contradiction is thus difference internalised, 'essential difference' which, as self-relating, is also self-identical, that is, identity, the opposite of difference;[16] when this contradiction is posited and becomes explicit or 'for-itself', the inherently self-contradictory becomes 'the contradiction resolved',[17] difference returning into itself from otherness, a unity of contradictory moments sustained by the infinite movement of negation underlying all finite determinations.[18]

It is easy to see the basis for Deleuze's criticism that Hegel's account of difference subordinates difference not just to negation, but to the 'identity of identity and difference': reduced to the negative, 'difference is already placed on a path . . . laid out by identity' (DR 44–50), already destined to the development of opposition into contradiction and the resolution of contradiction (NP 157). In two 1956 articles,[19] Deleuze's first counter-move to Hegel relies on Bergson's 'duration' as an 'internal difference' which 'does not go, and does not have to go, as far as contradiction, alterity and negativity' (DI 39). Difference is neither the purely external difference of one thing from another (diversity), nor the difference of a thing from everything it is not (DI 25, 42), nor the differences of species sharing a common element (DI 30–4). Rather, being is difference as duration, 'heterogeneity, what differs from itself' and in itself (DI 26–7). Time is neither an undifferentiated whole nor a series of moments external to each other but a single self-differentiating process, 'an internal succession that is both heterogeneous and continuous' (B 37): not abstract otherness (difference outside itself) but differential relations in duration or virtuality (DI 27) and alteration as a process (25) of differentiation through developmental tendencies that differ in nature (26, 34), resulting in real differences in actual things (28). In virtue of its duration and the tendencies it incarnates, then, 'the thing differs from itself *first, immediately*', and not, as in Hegel, 'the thing differs from itself because it first differs from everything it is not' (42).

'Contradiction' and 'opposition' are illusions based on a comparison of two actualised, completed things that result from the differential actualisation of the virtual in divergent tendencies (DI 42). 'We will see in one the negative of the other' (B 101) because difference has been replaced by a sterile opposition between the completed results considered without respect to the processes that generated them (DI 42; NP 157). 'The negation of one real term by another is only the positive actualization of a virtuality that contains both terms at once . . . It is our ignorance of the virtual that makes us believe in contradiction and negation' (DI 42–3). Difference is taken to be negative only insofar as it involves the diversity of actual things, the products of difference, rather than difference itself understood as duration, differentiation into tendencies, and the actualisation of those tendencies.

We find the same theses in *Difference and Repetition*: 'Difference is not diversity. Diversity is given, but difference is that by which the given is given . . . as diverse', that is, as the actual products of differential processes which precede all constituted differences (DR 222, 38). 'Limitation' and 'opposition' arise only within what has been actualised as effects separated from 'the principle and real movement of their production' (DR 207) in 'the extended' (*l'étendue*) insofar as the increase in one extension necessitates a decrease in another, and in qualities insofar as the contrariety of qualities (hot and cold, light and dark, etc.) arises only with respect to already constituted qualities; both extension and qualities mask and cancel out the differential processes that gave rise to them so as to present negative relations of opposition (DR 235–6). 'Contradiction' is the difference between two completed actualities which can oppose each other only through a generic common ground (extension, quality, etc.) that relates them to each other and through which each contrary 'internalises' its opposite: difference as a function of 'the identity of contraries' which necessarily leads contradiction back to identity (DR 263). This is equivalent to setting one point of view or opinion against another, without regard to the 'problem' for which the opinions are proposed as answers. When it sees a 'confrontation between opposing, contrary or contradictory propositions', the dialectic forgets the genesis of divergent tendencies from ontological difference (DR 164, 202–3) and confuses philosophical knowledge with the interplay of rival opinions (WP 80). 'Opposition' and 'negation' are then only illusory epiphenomena of difference (DR 52, 117).

Deleuze finds the same confusions in Hegel's famous dialectic of 'being' and 'nothingness', according to which pure and simple 'being' is being without any determinations or differentiation, or being in an unqualified sense, which is, with respect to its absence of determinations and qualities, the same as nothingness, such that being and nothingness pass over into one another and develop into 'becoming'.[20] Following Bergson, Deleuze considers the 'dialectic of being and nothingness' to be a 'false movement' among ill-defined terms. Indeterminate and general 'being' is a generality opposed to nothingness (DI 24), which is itself a mere pseudo-idea (35), and both are solutions to the false problem of 'why is there something rather than nothing?', rather than the genuine problem of 'why this rather than something else? . . . Why this tension of duration? Why this speed rather than another?' (24). 'The idea of non-being appears when, instead of grasping different realities which are indefinitely substituted for one another, we muddle them together in the homogeneity of a Being in general, which can then only be opposed to nothingness' (B 20; see 46–7). The dialectic is thus a 'false movement' of abstract and unreal contraries which pass back and forth through imprecision (B 44; DR 182; WP 7; D viii), establishing fictitious oppositions in order to resolve them in an entirely fictitious manner (NP 158, 15).

THE CRITIQUE OF NEGATION

We have seen how contradiction is the merely *phenomenal* aspect of difference; it remains to be seen how this phenomenon is grounded in anthropology.[21] 'Negation is not added to what it negates, but only points to a weakness in who it is that negates' (B 19). The question is then: *who* negates, or for whom is negation primary?

It is only from the point of view of 'reactive forces' and *ressentiment* that differential and genealogical forces become opposition, negation and contradiction (NP 56). For the slave – the person of *ressentiment* in whom reactions dominate actions – begins with the negative, needs 'to conceive a non-Ego, then to oppose himself to this non-Ego, in order to finally posit himself as self'; this is pseudo-affirmation through 'the negation of the negation' rather than the genuine affirmation of difference (NP 121; DR 268). Rather than being logical operations, 'affirmation' and 'negation' are first 'qualities of becoming', 'becoming active' (affirmation) or 'becoming reactive' (negation), expressed in affirmative or negative evaluations of life (NP 54), and the slave or reactive person is one who experiences the suffering of life as 'negative' and in need of redemption because he is unable to make use of that suffering and affirm it, and so instead condemns and accuses life in the name of so-called 'higher values', values transcendent to life (NP 14–15, 17, 34, 121–2). 'Such a force negates all that it is not and makes this negation its own essence and the principle of its existence' (NP 9). By contrast, the affirmative will, that of the master type, begins with a feeling of its own strength or power, affirms its existence, and draws a supplementary feeling of pleasure in contemplating its 'good fortune' or superiority over the weak or reactive; 'negation' is here an afterthought, the consequence of an 'affirmation of affirmation', the enjoyment of difference and superiority, the affirmation of distance and of what it distances (NP 8–9, 121; LS 172–3; DR 54). Hegel's dialectic distorts negation and affirmation by making them into symmetrical logical operations; 'Negation is *opposed* to affirmation, but affirmation *differs* from negation', as the affirmative will (the master) does not negate the slave but affirms and enjoys his difference from the slave in affirming himself (NP 68, 188–9), whereas the slave must negate the master to achieve the pseudo-affirmation of the negation of the negation (DR 52).

MASTER–SLAVE DIALECTIC

Because master and slave differ in nature (as active and reactive), the Hegelian dialectic of master and slave, in which slave and master emerge from a 'struggle for recognition', establishes a false parity between the two and results in a false resolution.

For Hegel, the nature of human desire is that it desires to enjoy its own independent consciousness or subjectivity, but since consciousness is an entirely fluid process of negating its object, it cannot find any stability in itself or objectify itself on its own.[22] Consequently, consciousness seeks itself in the form of another consciousness, and desires the other consciousness as subjectivity, that is, as desire; what consciousness desires is the desire of the Other, through which the Other *recognises* it as consciousness. Since it wants to enjoy or possess itself, consciousness seeks to compel the Other to recognise it; the Other, which wants the same thing, engages in the same movement, and there ensues a 'struggle for recognition'.

The victor of this struggle is the master, who is prepared to sacrifice his life in order to gain recognition of his freedom; the loser is the slave, who is more attached to life than to freedom. However, in the long run, it is the slave who triumphs through work: by transforming nature, the slave elevates himself above nature and life, and creates culture. Only when both Self and Other have risen above natural needs can there be a 'mutual recognition' of two subjectivities who freely recognise each other rather than being compelled to do so by attachment to life and the fear of death. Through the free mutual recognition mediated through human cultural institutions (morality, law, custom), each is for itself what it is for the Other, and each thus returns into itself from out of the Other and realises the truth implicit in the Self–Other relationship, Spirit, '"I" that is "We" and "We" that is "I".'[23]

Deleuze regards this whole dialectic as involving only slaves: 'Beneath the Hegelian image of the master, the slave always peeks out' (NP 10), for the Hegelian master's desire for recognition makes him a slave from the outset. Only a slave regards power as something one is granted or recognised in accordance with established values, rather than an affirmative capability which creates new values (NP 81; DR 136); from the standpoint of a genuine master, power as creative will has no need of being recognised in order to have value (NP 11). The Hegelian 'master' who receives recognition is nothing but a slave who has 'made it' according to established values (NP 11, 80–2), that is, a conformist. The recognised 'I' is only the Everyone of 'everyone knows' or 'everyone recognises', that is, the person who conforms to the status quo, and the 'We' is only the social consensus surrounding current values: this identity of the conformist with the social consensus is the outcome of the struggle for recognition.

The conservative and reactionary reconciliation of the 'I' and the 'We' receives its political-moral expression in the Kantian-Hegelian doctrine of rational autonomy, according to which 'obedience to a law one gives oneself is perfect freedom'. When the slave frees himself from nature through labour, he does so by placing reason over instinct and natural inclination; and in obeying the moral law arising from reason, the subject likewise subordinates instinct and inclination, and is truly self-governing or autonomous, and thus free. Hegel's essential addition to Kant's theory of moral autonomy is to ground the universal in concrete historical circumstances so that it becomes 'the concrete universal': universality with a particular, historically determined content, customary ethics or mores (*Sittlichkeit*). This reaches its highest rational expression in the form of the State, which constitutes the self-consciousness of individuals in their universal and rational aspect. Whereas in Kant the highest ethical duty was to will one's duty simply because reason demands this, in Hegel, the highest duties of individuals is to participate in the State's rational self-governance as citizen-subjects with both duties and legal rights recognised by the State.[24]

Deleuze sees 'rational autonomy' as the establishment of a new servitude, servitude to reason itself, the subjection of 'the living being' to 'the rational being'. 'Understanding and reason have a long history; they are the authorities (*instances*) which still make us obey when we no longer want to obey anyone. When we stop obeying God, the State and our parents, reason shows up and persuades us: you are the one giving the orders' (NP 92). Reason persuades us that in submitting to reason, we move from being merely natural beings of instinct and inclination to reasonable beings, but this is the subjection of life and the living being to values and laws beyond life which negate and devalue life (NP 92). We are still subjugated, then; we are still asked to obey, 'to submit, to take on burdens, to recognize only reactive forms of life and accusatory forms of thought',[25] to internalise the laws and established values which command us (NP 93). The 'autonomy of the subject' merely internalises the laws and rational organisation of the modern state (NP 93) and makes *obedience* the value *par excellence*: 'In so-called modern philosophy, in the so-called modern or rational State, everything revolves around the legislator and the subject . . . Always obey. The more you obey, the more you will be master, for you will only be obeying pure reason, in other words, yourself' (TP 376). In fact, this is '*nothing but bearing, assuming,* acquiescing to the real as it is' (NP 181), the false 'affirmation' of life-negating reactive forces (NP 178–82; DR 120–1). 'Rational autonomy' is not then, as Kant and Hegel claim, the development of freedom, culminating in the rational State, but 'preserving, organizing and propagating reactive life' (NP 139).

Only a genuinely affirmative will can create, and creation requires a critique of current values and the destruction of reactive forces both within and outside oneself (NP 55, 107, 174–7). Revolution is 'the social power of difference' that creates new social forms and values (DR 208), whereas contradiction, far from being the weapon of the proletariat, is the bourgeoisie's means of safeguarding its right to determine what has importance or value by letting the struggle be merely a struggle for a share of established values (DR 268), the struggle against 'alienation' (NP 59). The difference between conservative values and creative difference is not between old and new but between order and creative disorder, between the 'average' and the 'exceptional' (DR 54), between consensus (I = We) and the dissenting 'private thinker' (DR 52, 258–61; TP 351–6, 376–7). It is not the dialectical labour of the negative which is creative, but the playful affirmation of difference; not the assumption of 'recognised' duties and rights, but the invention of new problems; not the reconciliation of opposites, but the differentiation of difference (NP 9, 16–19, 157–8, 190; DR 43, 236).

SUFFERING, NEGATIVITY AND THE UNHAPPY CONSCIOUSNESS

'The discovery dear to the dialectic is the unhappy consciousness, the deepening of the unhappy consciousness, the resolution of the unhappy consciousness, the glorification of the unhappy consciousness and its resources'; 'the unhappy consciousness is the subject of the whole dialectic' (NP 159, 196). Following Jean Wahl,[26] Deleuze takes the Hegelian figure of the 'unhappy consciousness' to be the protagonist of the entire Hegelian dialectic of negation and the negation of the negation, but he denounces the unhappy consciousness (*conscience malheureuse*) and its sufferings as merely the 'bad conscience' (*mauvaise conscience*) of the guilty and resentful person.

In the *Phenomenology of Spirit*, the 'unhappy consciousness' follows the master–slave dialectic, in which the slave discovers his power of transforming and negating nature within and outside himself. This power of negation is deepened in consciousness' discovery of itself as 'absolutely dialectical unrest', the power of negating itself and all its determinations:[27] absolute negativity aware of itself as nothingness and as a mere vanishing particular. Over against this vanishing particularity is the universality of what immutably and eternally endures: God, the formless and wholly Other, infinite Being as an infinite beyond and the object of an infinite yearning.[28] In truth, says Hegel, this is a conflict within the self of two aspects of the self which have become separated and opposed: the self's changeable, perishable and individual aspects (finitude) over against its universal and eternal aspects (infinite thought). The unhappy consciousness thus reveals the essence of Absolute spirit, which transcends and negates itself, or 'suffers violence at its own hand',[29] in order to return to itself in an 'absolute knowing' which redeems every opposition and division – and the suffering that results from them – by showing them to be necessary to a realisation of a self that surmounts and encompasses them as 'moments' of its own development. It is the sufferings of the self which motivate the self to reconcile itself with itself,[30] and for that reason, suffering is the driving force behind every dialectical progression, and the 'unhappy consciousness' is the protagonist of the entire *Phenomenology*.[31]

From Deleuze's standpoint, this shows that the dialectic is simply 'the natural ideology of *ressentiment*' (NP 159). If difference is suffering and hence evil (*le mal*), then one can affirm only by expiating through further suffering, whether that suffering be Man's or God's; affirmation can be attained only through the long detours of all the unhappiness of division and dismemberment (DR 53). But Deleuze opposes 'the idea of a value of suffering and sadness . . . manifested in division (*scission*) and dismemberment (*déchirement*)' (NP 195) along with the presupposition that suffering is evil or in 'contradiction' to life (NP 11–16). Suffering is 'evil' only for a reactive being who is unable to make pain a stimulus to action, and so instead internalises it as remembered pain, as *ressentiment*, which is then directed towards another as the impulse to revenge, and when it finds no satisfaction or outlet in that fashion (because of the inability to act), is introjected as 'guilt', or vengeance against oneself for one's own sufferings, here interpreted as wrong-doings or evil (NP 128–32). This complex of suffering, and suffering to expiate suffering (guilt), is what Nietzsche calls 'bad conscience', the source of all antinomies (NP 87–8) and the truth of Hegel's 'unhappy consciousness' (NP 18–19, 157–8). 'Bad conscience' is the real 'motor of history' in its Christian-Hegelian form, that is, the history of the triumph of reactive and nihilistic forces, the depreciation of 'life' by a 'beyond', by nothingness (NP 34, 152, 161).

SENSE-CERTAINTY

'Hegel wanted to ridicule pluralism, identifying it with a naïve consciousness which would be content with saying "this, that, here, now" . . . In the pluralist idea that a thing has many senses, that there are many things and "this and then that" goes for a single thing, we see philosophy's highest conquest, the conquest of the true concept' (NP 4). As Deleuze specifies, 'pluralism' is identical with 'empiricism', and 'empiricism' is concerned with 'the concrete richness of the sensible' (D vii, 54; DR 284–5; ES 99). Hegel's critique of pluralism is thus a critique of knowledge as this is obtained through the sensory apprehension of an empirical given in the 'here and now'.

In the 'sense-certainty' chapter of the *Phenomenology*,[32] Hegel says that sensory experience wants to grasp the actuality of the object through pure receptivity to an empirical object independently of any contribution from the subject, such as the categories of the understanding; it wants to grasp the object in its immediacy, as pure being, without any determinations or predicates. But in doing so, consciousness can only point to its object: this, here, now. However, every 'this' is as much a 'this' as any other, and yet each this is also not other 'thises' in the same way that the other thises are neither it nor any other this: with respect to its utter indeterminacy and lack of content, pure being, as grasped through pure sensory receptivity, is equivalent to nothing, just as in the *Science of Logic*, pure being passes over into nothingness.[33] When consciousness tries to grasp hold of the truth of what it apprehends through sensation by expressing it in language, it undergoes the same dialectical reversal: the words 'now', 'here', 'this' do not designate any particular 'now', 'here' or 'this', but any 'now', 'here' or 'this' in general; that is, they designate the universal rather than the particular that was meant: 'it is just not possible for us to express in words a sensuous being that we *mean*'.[34] The truth of 'sense certainty' is perception, which grasps the sensuous being through the mediation of universals: time and space as the forms of intuition, the categories of the understanding, and the unity of the 'I' as a synthesis of faculties and a synthesis over time.

Deleuze objects that in this movement, the singular here-now-this is indeed not captured in the abstract universals of the dialectic, but is stripped of all its concrete richness and determinations (DR 51–2). The sensible is rather 'the stubbornness of the existent in intuition which resists every specification of the concept' (DR 13–14). There is, says Deleuze, a 'being of the sensible' which is not a particular sensible being, and is not 'the given' (a sensible particular) but 'that by which the given is given' (DR 139–40), something that can only be sensed as what forces sensation (DR 144–5).

'What is a sensation? It is the operation of contracting trillions of vibrations onto a receptive surface' and is manifested in consciousness as the sensing of a quality in a spatially located and spatially extended object (B 74). Sensation is a product of forces acting 'from without' on the sensibility of the subject, or on a capacity to be affected that is itself a degree of power (NP 62; EPS 93–4, 217–21, 231, 245–6, 253, 261, 306–7; F 49–51). These interacting forces are the sufficient reason for what is sensed: both for *that* it is sensed and *how* it is sensed (B 28–9). It is these forces which give each sensation and each sensible thing a singularity which escapes the concept: 'difference, difference of potential, difference of intensity as the reason for qualitative diversity' form the objects of investigation for a 'superior empiricism', a 'transcendental empiricism' (DR 56–7).

Intensities exist as singular points in a system of differential relations (DR 209), or virtual systems, a 'system of liaisons or differential relations among particles and of singularities corresponding to the degrees of variation of these relations' (DR 165). An intensity is an element whose 'value' is a function of both the difference within the ordinal series to which it belongs and of the difference of one series from another (DR 117); each intensity, as it were, passes through all the others at each moment (DR 57; NP 6–7), constituting an intensive field, 'differences of intensity distributed at different depths', a material system (DR 96–8). However, each intensity is also internally differentiated in the form of a differential series of variable ratios; every intensity is by nature unequal to itself or heterogeneous in itself (DI 97; DR 235) in the manner of Bergson's duration (DR 239). In that way, 'since intensity is already difference, it refers to a series of other differences which it affirms by affirming itself' (DR 234), and 'returns to itself' not as an 'I' recognised by another, but as a differentiated difference within a field of differences (DR 241), as difference with self prior to the difference between one and the other (NP 188). Sensible qualitative differences are merely the effect on the consciousness, the distorting surface reflection of these subterranean differences (DR 236–9; DI 97); 'intensity is never given in a pure experience' but 'it gives all the qualities with which we make experience' (B 92; see DR 238). Conscious awareness of qualitative difference is, however, a second-order effect; the sensibility of the subject is itself constituted by a transcendental and unconscious field of intensity, a capacity to be affected or pure receptivity that is itself a material system, and which registers the effects of external intensities acting upon it at an unconscious level (DR 58, 151). Intensity is something imperceptible (*insensible*), which can only be sensed inasmuch as it 'awakens' or 'arouses' the unconscious sensibility (DR 152, 230, 236).

As well as grounding qualitative sensible difference, intensity functions as an individuating factor in both subject and object. The individuation characteristic of things is an intrinsic determination, an intensive quantity or difference of intensity (EPS 196–7; DR 39), but this individuation takes place within fields of intensive forces (DR 151) as the actualisation of the distribution of potentials within that field: 'Individuation is the act by which intensity determines differential relations to become actualised' (DR 246). The result is not an empty 'this' or 'I' which would be a repeatable particular instance of a general category, but bears the determinateness of the forces or intensities which determine it. Individuation is the product of divergent processes of actualisation or differentiation of a multiplicity or manifold of intensities, multiplicity being 'an organisation pertaining to the many (*le multiple*) as such', in which elements are 'other without being several' inasmuch as their being is determined only through their relation to each other (DR 182; B 42–3, 95). A multiplicity is not actual, but is a fully real system of differential elements and relations, a structure (linguistic, genetic, physical, etc.) that is completely determined prior to the actualisation that expresses it (DR 209–15). Even similarities among actualities must be accounted for through different and divergent lines of development, much as the eye and analogous organs in invertebrates can be accounted for as divergent 'solutions' to the organic 'problem' of how to respond to light, in which the solutions do not negate either each other or the problem that gives rise to them (DR 117, 212; B 97, 106). Actualisation is not the specification of a generality – which would be a negative determination (B 46–47) – but individuation through the differential development of a determinate virtual field of intensities, the positive differentiation of difference (DR 214–15).

'The conditions of real experience' are 'indistinguishable from intensity as such' (DR 232), and 'transcendental' or 'superior' empiricism is precisely the search for conditions of real experience that are no broader or more general than the conditioned (DR 285; B 23–30; NP 50): not the empty universals of '"now" "here" "this"' which Hegel ridiculed, but now-here complexes of space-time generated by the dynamic interplay of intensities, and which can only be sensed and encountered rather than known or recognised (DR 285).

Anti-Hegel?

Is Deleuze an anti-Hegelian? His *oeuvre* does include some appreciative remarks on Hegel's philosophy. Hegel showed that 'variability in the function' requires not just a change in values or undetermined values ($a = 2b$), but that one variable be a higher power ($y2/x = P$), which makes the relation a differential one in which each variable is a function of the other (dx/dy),[35] although elsewhere Deleuze criticises Hegel for regarding the mathematical series of differential calculus as being merely a 'bad' or 'spurious' infinity, merely an indefinite continuation *ad infinitum* lacking the genuine determinacy of the concept (DR 43);[36] Hegel criticises dogmatic thought, which asks questions for which the answer is a simple proposition, confusing thought with opinion and truth with correct opinion or orthodoxy (DR 150),[37] although Hegel is guilty of this very dogmatism insofar as he makes the differences between opposing opinions or points of view 'moments' of the concept (WP 80); Hegel's *Phenomenology* depicts an extraordinary apprenticeship or self-development through the positing and solving of problems, but this 'remains subordinated . . . to the ideal of knowledge in the form of absolute knowledge', a final end that is given in advance (DR 166); Hegel and Schelling rightly focus on the philosophical concept as a self-positing Figure with constitutive Moments, the Figures being the phenomenological historical appearances of the concept (*Phenomenology of Spirit*), the Moments being the concept's absolute self-movement (*Science of Logic*), but Hegel over-extends philosophy by including the arts and sciences within the philosophical concept (WP 11–12). Anything Deleuze gives Hegel with the one hand he seems to take back with the other.

Yet the question of Deleuze's relation to Hegel cannot be solved simply by collecting citations and toting up the balance of positive and negative remarks. For all his criticisms of Hegel, there remains an element in Deleuze that is profoundly Hegelian: a notion of 'alienation' that stems from Deleuze's 'vitalism'. Thus we read that 'every solution' in the form of an organ 'is a relative success in relation to the conditions of the problem or the environment' but is nevertheless 'a relative failure (*échec*) in relation to the movement which invents it'; 'Life as *movement* alienates itself in the material *form* that it creates; by actualising itself, by differentiating itself, it loses "contact with the rest of itself"' (B 104). Similarly, insensible intensities are 'always covered by a quality which alienates or contradicts' them by levelling out and homogenising their constitutive differences (DR 236, 241); consciously recollected memories are 'images' extracted from an ontological and unconscious past which cannot be represented (B 71); there is a single, vital time of the virtual prior to its differentiation into differing fluxes of duration, a single virtual multiplicity underlying the plurality of lived durations (B 81–3). Deleuze seems to hold that the actual can only betray the virtual it actualises by constituting the extensive and qualitative elements which are subject to negation through limitation and the dialectic of contraries (see DR 188). The virtual 'knows nothing of negation' (DR 202–3, 207); these arise only at the level of the actual. Hence the privilege of the 'fractured I' of schizophrenia – which opens Being directly onto difference without the mediation of concepts – over the identity of the 'I' of the 'I think' (DR 58); hence the valorisation of Dionysian dismemberment in the eternal return, in which 'the thing is reduced to the difference which fragments it and to all the differences implicated in it and through which it passes' (DR 67); hence the privileging of the 'body without organs' over the body differentiated into organs and functions which limit and alienate the intensive vital 'flows'. It is as if actual life were a degradation of virtual life; as if virtual life were a value higher than actual life and through which actual life is denounced.

There is a Hegelian type of circularity involved here as well. Larval, embryonic life, the body without organs: all represent a primary origin, a difference prior to identity. The making of the body without organs, or the search for the virtual point prior to which duration differentiates itself into diverging tendencies, seems to amount to a search for lost and alienated life, for Paradise Lost. In making a primal origin into a goal, Deleuze seems to enact the 'circular' movement of return that he denounces in Hegel, for whom Spirit rejoins itself after going through all the separations from itself necessary to its full development. While it sometimes appears that Hegel begins with the simple or the One, whereas Deleuze begins with difference and multiplicity, Hegel's Absolute, which is there from the beginning,[38] is disparate from the beginning,[39] and without this difference-from-self, the Absolute would be inert and homogeneous substance, rather than a Subject which differentiates itself and then takes these differences back into itself: the Absolute is neither one nor many, but in fact a multiplicity, a 'one' that is said 'of' the many, as Deleuze says. It remains the case that Hegel seeks unity, the 'identity of identity and difference', whereas Deleuze seeks the differentiation of difference, fragmentation rather than unity, the dissolution of identity through difference returning to itself. However, that makes Deleuze's circle a different circle from Hegel's 'monocentric' one (LS 260); it has a different teleology, a different finality; but it is no less circular and teleological for all that. To that extent, it represents the persistence of Hegel in this most anti-Hegelian philosopher.

Thompson Rivers University

Notes

1. Jean Wahl, 'Review of *Nietzsche et la philosophie* by Gilles Deleuze,' *Revue de métaphysique et de morale* 68 (1963), p. 353.
2. Wahl, 'Review of *Nietzsche et la philosophie*', p. 370.
3. Friedrich Nietzsche, *Untimely Meditations*, trans. R. J. Hollingdale (Cambridge: Cambridge University Press, 1997), p. 22.
4. Jean Hyppolite, *Logic and Existence*, trans. Leonard Lawlor and Amit Sen (Albany: State University of New York Press, 1997), pp. 186–7.
5. Gilles Deleuze, 'Review of *Logique et existence* by Jean Hyppolite', in *Revue philosophique de la France et de l'étranger* 94 (1954), p. 460.
6. G. W. F. Hegel, *Hegel's Science of Logic*, trans. A. V. Miller (Atlantic Highlands, NJ: Humanities Press, 1989), p. 115.
7. Hegel, *Science of Logic*, p. 117.
8. Hegel, *Science of Logic*, p. 118.
9. Hegel, *Science of Logic*, p. 413.
10. Hegel, *Science of Logic*, p. 417.
11. Hegel, *Science of Logic*, pp. 418–20.
12. G. W. F. Hegel, *Hegel's Logic. Being Part One of the Encyclopedia of the Philosophical Sciences*, trans. William Wallace (Oxford: Oxford University Press, 1975), p. 172.
13. Hegel, *Science of Logic*, p. 431; see Hegel, *Hegel's Logic*, p. 173.
14. Hegel, *Science of Logic*, pp. 432–4.
15. G. W. F. Hegel, *The Phenomenology of Spirit*, trans. A. V. Miller (Oxford: Oxford University Press, 1977), p. 76.
16. Hegel, *Hegel's Logic*, p. 173.
17. Hegel, *Science of Logic*, p. 442.
18. Hegel, *Science of Logic*, pp. 442–3.
19. 'Bergson, 1859–1941' and 'Bergson's Conception of Difference' – both to be found in *Desert Islands and Other Texts*.
20. Hegel, *The Science of Logic*, pp. 82–105.
21. Deleuze, 'Review of *Logique et existence*', p. 460.
22. Hegel, *Phenomenology*, pp. 109–10.
23. Hegel, *Phenomenology*, pp. 104–19.
24. G. W. F. Hegel, *Elements of the Philosophy of Right*, edited by Allen W. Wood, trans. H. B. Nisbet (Cambridge: Cambridge University Press, 1991), pp. 191–7, 275–81.
25. Gilles Deleuze, *Nietzsche* (Paris: PUF, 1965), pp. 21–2.
26. Jean Wahl, *Le Malheur de la conscience dans la philosophie de Hegel* (Paris: Rieder, 1929).
27. Hegel, *Phenomenology*, p. 124.
28. Hegel, *Phenomenology*, pp. 126–38.
29. Hegel, *Phenomenology*, pp. 51–2.
30. Wahl, *Le Malheur de la conscience*, pp. 7, 82f, 107f.

31. Wahl, *Le Malheur de la conscience*, pp. 187f.
32. Hegel, *Phenomenology*, pp. 58–66.
33. Hegel, *Phenomenology*, pp. 81–4.
34. Hegel, *Phenomenology*, p. 60.
35. See Hegel, *Science of Logic*, pp. 251–3.
36. See Hegel, *Science of Logic*, pp. 246–9.
37. See Hegel, *Science of Logic*, p. 23.
38. Hegel, *Science of Logic*, p. 47.
39. Hegel, *Science of Logic*, p. 21.

8

Karl Marx

Eugene Holland

The first page of Deleuze's most important philosophical work, *Difference and Repetition*, lays the groundwork for his analysis of capitalism. There are, he insists, two enemies of the difference he champions. They are representation and exchange, 'the qualitative order of resemblances and the quantitative order of equivalences' (DR 1). Capitalism plays one against the other: the cash nexus of the market decodes representation and thence frees desire from its repression by codes; 'all that is solid melts into air', as Marx put it.[1] But capital also recaptures desire and subjects it to the demands of private accumulation through commodity production and exchange. Marx's analyses of capital were thus crucial for Deleuze throughout his career. Indeed, Deleuze not only insisted that he and Guattari remained Marxists (N 171), he also planned to devote what would have been his last book to 'the greatness of Marx' – although he was not able to write it due to health problems.[2] From the first pages of *Difference and Repetition*, then, it is clear that Deleuze shared with Marx what Marxists would call a 'dialectical' evaluation of capitalism, one that assesses both its benefits to humankind and its liabilities. But already, a crucial difference emerges. What Marx admired most about capitalism was its socialisation of production relations and the attendant development of human productive forces, which offered humankind the historical prospect of overcoming necessity and realising freedom. What Deleuze admires most about capitalism is the ways in which the socialisation of production, the development of productive forces, and the spread of the market actively promote difference. By constantly decoding representation and continually expanding the division of labour, capital constitutes an immensely powerful difference-engine. In relation to two of the other difference-engines constituting human being – the evolution of biological life and the expression of linguistic sense – the capitalist difference-engine is important for Deleuze because it accelerates processes of differentiation already active in the living body and in expressive language, by, respectively, grafting labour diversification and specialisation onto humans' already extremely adaptable biological makeup, and by subjecting any and all linguistic and cultural representations to market decoding.

Yet this overall agreement about the importance of analysing capitalism risks obscuring a more profound affinity between Deleuze and Marx, which involves the centrality both assign to economics, or more specifically to what Deleuze, following the French Marxist philosopher Louis Althusser, calls the 'economic instance' (DR 186).[3] Although Deleuze agrees with Marx and Althusser that economics must be considered the ultimately determining instance, his formulation of the problem differs significantly from theirs, given his own distinctive understanding of the practice of philosophy. In a nutshell, the function of political philosophy is to create new concepts in response to ever-changing situations. Concept-creation involves, for one thing, selectively borrowing concepts or elements of concepts from previous philosophies while rejecting other concepts or elements – as Deleuze does with respect to Marxism. But more important, concept-creation involves responding to problems arising outside philosophy, by adapting selected concepts and elements to new situations. Existence poses problems, and the task of political philosophy is to formulate such problems as productively as possible in concepts, so as to improve our capacity to address them in the actual world. Now social problems are by no means the only problems humans face, but the problems that are social, Deleuze insists, are always economic:

> In all rigour, there are only economic social problems, even though the solutions may be juridical, political or ideological, and the problems may be expressed in those fields of resolvability. . . . In short, the economic is . . . the totality of the problems posed to a given society . . . (DR 186)

Althusser had already suggested that the economic instance structurally determines which other instance is dominant in a given social formation, and is therefore never fully present in its own right: 'the lonely hour of the last instance never comes'.[4] Deleuze agrees:

> Althusser and his collaborators are, therefore, profoundly correct in showing the presence of a genuine structure in *Capital*. . . . That is why 'the economic' is never given properly speaking, but rather designates a differential virtuality to be interpreted, always covered over by its forms of actualisation; a theme or 'problematic' always covered over by its cases of solution. (DR 186)

In terms very different from the base–superstructure model familiar from orthodox Marxism,[5] Deleuze poses the relation of the economic instance to social reality in terms of virtual problems and actual solutions: 'The problems of a society, as they are determined in the infrastructure in the form of so-called "abstract" labour, receive their solution from the process of actualisation or differenciation (the concrete division of labour)' (DR 207). The economic is the problematic virtual structure to which various societies (or a given society at various times) propose differing actual solutions (in much the same way that bird wings, fish fins, mammalian legs provide differing actual solutions to the biological problem of locomotion (see DR 211)).

At the most abstract level, and given a multitude of differences as a starting point (differences of gender, age, ability, skill, etc.), the fundamental social problem is how to organise social relations so as to maximise the positive potential of the social multiplicity thereby created. In more recognisably Marxist terms, the basic social problem is how to organise social relations so as to maximise the enhancement of production and consumption arising from the *technical* and *social* division of labour, while minimising the risks arising from a *political* division of labour conducive to gross inequalities of wealth and power, and to exploitation, oppression and repression.[6]

There are two further points of fundamental agreement between Deleuze and Althusserian Marxism, both deriving from the preference for Spinoza over Hegel that they shared. For alongside Toni Negri and Althusser and his collaborators (especially Pierre Macherey),[7] Deleuze represents one important version of an anti-Hegelian, Spinozian Marxism.[8] This means that, for one thing, Deleuze's Marxism will be as staunchly anti-historicist as Althusser's, although as we shall see, Deleuze's mode of anti-historicism is far more complex than Althusser's structuralist mode. Nonetheless, Deleuze insists that 'Althusser and his collaborators are . . . profoundly correct . . . in rejecting historicist interpretations of Marxism' inasmuch as the virtual structure of a society 'never acts transitively, following the order of succession in time [but] rather . . . acts by incarnating its varieties in diverse societies' (DR 186), varieties which, as we have seen, represent so many actual solutions to the virtual problem posed by that society. Furthermore, 'this structure [also] acts . . . by accounting for the simultaneity of all the relations and terms which . . . constitute the present' of a social totality. This means, for another thing, that Deleuze's anti-Hegelian Marxism will eschew 'dialectical' versions of totality based on negation and contradiction. 'Those commentators on Marx who insist on the fundamental difference between Marx and Hegel', Deleuze maintains, citing precisely Althusser et al's *Reading Capital*, 'rightly point out that in *Capital* the category of differenciation (the differenciation at the heart of a social multiplicity: the division of labour) is substituted for the Hegelian concepts of opposition, contradiction and alienation' (DR 207). Indeed, Deleuze goes further in this respect than Althusser, who still retained the category of contradiction in his concept of an over-determined, structural totality. Deleuze is categorical: 'the negative is always derivative and represented, never original or present: the process of difference and of differenciation is primary in relation to that of the negative and opposition' (DR 207). These two points of agreement with Althusser regarding history and totality bring us to two Marxian categories where Deleuze's engagement with Marx is sustained and deep: the mode of production and universal history.

It is not difficult to see, given his commitment to the notion of the economic instance as a virtual structure determining the actual organisation of social relations, why Deleuze would adopt and adapt Marx's notion of the mode of production. It is one of the cornerstones of Deleuze's first collaborations with Guattari, *Anti-Oedipus*, which is arguably the most completely Marxist work in Deleuze's entire *oeuvre*. It is also the work in which the notion of universal history figures most centrally. By the time Deleuze and Guattari write the sequel to *Anti-Oedipus*, in their two-volume *Capitalism and Schizophrenia*, however, the category of the mode of production has been superseded (though not eliminated): 'We define social formations by *machinic processes* and not by modes of production (these on the contrary depend on the processes)' (TP 435). Also in *A Thousand Plateaus*, Deleuze's anti-historicism comes to the fore (although here too, as in their last collaboration, *What is Philosophy?*, the notion of universal history by no means disappears). The transformations wrought by Deleuze and Guattari on Marx's concept of the mode of production in their first collaboration are so extensive that we must start there, before going on to see what happens to the concept in the second volume of *Capitalism and Schizophrenia*.

Given that the mode of production in general is now defined as a virtual structure posing fundamentally economic problems, Deleuze and Guattari delineate three historical solutions to these problems, which they call 'coding', in the savage mode of production; 'overcoding', in the barbarian mode of production; and 'axiomatization', in the civilised or capitalist mode of production. Significantly, these solutions involve ways of managing debt, for whereas Marx considers production to be primary, Deleuze and Guattari (drawing here more on Nietzsche than Marx) instead consider debt to be the primary element in any actual social formation. (Against the grain of Marx's dialectical derivation of surplus from production and of finance capital from industrial capital, their view gives finance capital priority over industrial capital.) How does society manage the problems of economics? By organising a system of debt relations driving production and exchange: a patchwork of finite and temporary debts in the case of savagery; an infinite debt owed to the despot, head priest or king in barbarism; an equally infinite debt owed to capital in capitalism. These solutions may be false (illusory, 'ideological'), but they are nonetheless effective in organising production and exchange relations.

Perhaps an even more important transformation of the concept of mode of production than the position assigned to debt in relation to production is the redefinition of production itself proposed by Deleuze and Guattari. For production in general now includes libido as well as labour-power: what they call 'production' is the investment of human energy in any and all activity, whether psychical or physical or both. And it is distinctive of capitalism to have separated the two components of production ('psychological' and 'economic') from one another, with the emergence of economics as an actual social field in its own right, attendant on the emergence and dominance of abstract labour in the capitalist mode of production, and with the segregation of reproduction in the nuclear family.

Where the conceptualisation of the two other modes of production derived from Nietzsche, Engels and Lewis Morgan, Deleuze and Guattari draw heavily on both Marx and Freud (by way of Lacan) for their analysis of the capitalist or 'civilised' mode of production. But it is Marx who predominates. This is principally because in privatising productive property, capitalism separates human reproduction from production, and segregates reproduction in the nuclear family. At the same time that abstract labour predominates in the field of privatised production, abstract libido prevails in the privatised field of reproduction: the nuclear family and its Oedipus complex are therefore, according to Deleuze and Guattari, strictly capitalist institutions. As theorist of abstract libido, 'Freud is the . . . Adam Smith of psychiatry' (AO 271), and just as Marx brought Smith and bourgeois political economy to the point of revolutionary auto-critique, Deleuze and Guattari bring Freud and bourgeois psychiatry to the point of revolutionary auto-critique in what they will call *schizoanalysis*.

Much the same can be said of Lacan. Lacan described the process whereby parental care-giving gives particular zones of the infant body erotic value in terms of 'territorialisation'. But the plasticity of the human organism is such that any given territorialisation of the body, any specific system of erogenous zones, can be deterritorialised and psychic energy re-invested or reterritorialised in a new system of organisation. Drawing on this view (but importing a term from French playwright Antonin Artaud), Deleuze and Guattari call the locus and limit of psycho-somatic deterritorialisation the 'body without organs': it designates the moment when psychic energy is detached from fixed connection to any specific organ, sign, image or object, and becomes free to invest other objects indiscriminately. But crucially for Deleuze and Guattari, such psycho-somatic deterritorialisation is in fact a secondary effect of socio-economic deterritorialisation, which they insist is primary. Just as libidinal energy can be detached ('de-cathected') from one object and focused on another, so too can labour-power be detached from one object (fields and command land, in the classic case of the Enclosure Acts cited by Marx)[9] and re-focused on another (mechanical looms of the nascent textile industry). Indeed, capitalism becomes famous for 'constantly revolutionising the means of production' as Marx says[10] – famous, that is, for constantly deterritorialising labour-power and reterritorialising it on ever-newer means of production and consumption as capitalism expands and intensifies in response to the falling rate of profit. Because abstract labour has become the very basis of capitalist social organisation, 'the quantitative order of equivalences' prevails over 'the qualitative order of resemblances', freeing desire from capture and repression by the social codes of what Lacan calls the Symbolic Order. So it is the revolutionising, deterritorialising tendency of capital that empties the Symbolic Order of its erstwhile centre (the '*sujet-supposé-savoir*' or possessor of the phallus, in Lacan's terminology) and makes the body without organs as the index of psycho-somatic deterritorialisation increasingly evident and available throughout capitalist society.

In *Anti-Oedipus*, deterritorialisation and reterritorialisation designate the two moments of the specifically capitalist debt-management process Deleuze and Guattari call 'axiomatisation', whereby flows of abstract (or 'liquid') wealth (in money form) and abstract labour (labour-capacity in commodity form) are brought together and endowed *ex post facto* with concrete content in order to produce a surplus to pay the infinite debt. And although in their subsequent collaborations the concepts of deterritorialisation and reterritorialisation will take on a far broader range of meanings, in *Anti-Oedipus* they derive directly from Marx's analysis in the third volume of *Capital* of the rhythms of capitalist development.[11] In a first moment, according to Marx, a wave of new, more productive capital-stock transforms the pre-existing apparatuses of production and consumption: capital's 'continual revolution of the means of production' deterritorialises pre-existing labour and capital in order to devote them to new forms of production and consumption, and in the process spawns de-coding throughout society. But in a second moment, this progressive movement is abruptly stopped, and everything is reterritorialised: the evolving apparatuses of production and consumption alike are tied down to what is now obsolete capital-stock, solely in order to valorise it and realise profit on previous private investment. A wave of deterritorialisation liberates all kinds of creative energies (in consumption as well as in production) at the same time that it revolutionises and socialises productive forces; but then reterritorialisation supervenes, yoking the relations of production and consumption to the dead weight of private surplus-appropriation.[12] As Marx puts it: 'Capitalist production seeks continually to overcome these immanent barriers, but overcomes them only by means which again place these barriers in its way and on a more formidable scale. The *real barrier* of capitalist production is *capital itself*.'[13] For Deleuze and Guattari, this tension between increasingly socialised production and private appropriation is key, more or less completely superseding other dynamics analysed by Marx (such as the struggle between classes or the tension between forces and relations of production). Just five years before his death, Deleuze recalls the centrality of this analysis for himself and Guattari:

> Félix . . . and I have remained Marxists, in our two different ways, perhaps, but both of us. You see, we think any political philosophy must turn on the analysis of capitalism and the ways it has developed. What we find most interesting in Marx is his analysis of capitalism as an immanent system that's constantly overcoming its own limits, and then coming up against them once more on an expanded scale, because its fundamental limit is Capital itself. (N 171, translation modified)

In line with this dynamic, capitalism is described as the mode of production that constantly defers its own crisis: older capital becomes relatively less productive and the rate of profit approaches zero; but then newer, more productive capital intervenes to restore (for a time) the rate of profit, thereby displacing the limit. On this view, there is no solace to be found in history – via the immiseration of the proletariat, for example, or the exhaustion of natural resources – for 'all [capitalism ever] confronts are its own limits (the periodic depreciation of existing capital); all it repels or displaces are its own limits (the formation of new capital, in new industries with a high profit rate)' (TP 463). And all the while, capitalist deterritorialisation implacably 'strips of its halo' all pre-existing coded meaning, fostering the kind of free-form investment of desire based on difference rather than identity that Deleuze and Guattari call schizophrenic in *Anti-Oedipus*, and nomadic in *A Thousand Plateaus*.

By fostering difference in this way, capitalism frees labour and libido from illusory objective determinations and thereby inaugurates the *possibility* of universal history. But at the same time, capitalism prevents and defers the *realisation* of universal history by re-subjecting free productive energy to the alienations of private property and the privatised family, to capital and the Oedipus.[14] Deleuze and Guattari's notion of universal history is quite specific, based not on the familiar Hegelian philosophy of history, but on a set of comments Marx makes in the *Grundrisse*. 'Universal history is nothing more than theology', Deleuze and Guattari insist, 'if it does not seize hold of the conditions of its contingent, singular existence, its irony, and its own critique' (AO 271). Marx refers first of all to the 'legitimation of chance' in historical understanding: even if world history 'appears as necessary development', in fact 'world history has not always existed; history as world history [is] a result'.[15] Universal history is therefore a history of contingency. Indeed, following Fernand Braudel among others, Deleuze and Guattari insist that the emergence of capitalism in early modern Europe was an historical accident, which could have happened elsewhere, or nowhere at all. The emergence of capitalism appears on this view as a contingent bifurcation-point: capitalism in fact emerged from the conjunction of 'free' labour and liquid wealth, and this fact changes everything. But it could equally well not have happened, or happened otherwise. Once it does occur, however, history becomes universal, and the dynamic of capital accumulation endows it with a certain linearity. The irony of schizoanalytic universal history, meanwhile, derives from the 'essential difference' between capitalism and previous modes of production. 'Bourgeois economics supplies the key to the ancient', Marx claims in a famous passage, in much the same way that 'human anatomy contains a key to the anatomy of the ape':

> But not at all in the manner of those economists who smudge over *all* historical differences and see bourgeois relations in all forms of society. . . . Although it is true . . . that the categories of bourgeois economics possess a truth for all other forms of society, this is to be taken only with a grain of salt. They can contain them [relations from earlier social forms] in a developed, or stunted, or caricatured form etc., but always with an essential difference. . .[16]

This retrospective and ironic relation to the past, finally, is only possible, Marx insists, once a certain degree of self-criticism is at work in capitalist society – in this case, only when bourgeois political economy has reached a point of self-criticism regarding abstract labour as the subjective essence of wealth. Like universal history for Marx, schizophrenia and the body without organs for Deleuze and Guattari arise only at the end of history – as capitalism reveals the common essence of desire and labour, and then becomes capable of self-criticism regarding the ways it nevertheless continues to re-alienate that essence, through capital and Oedipus. Yet that common essence is itself not fixed or determinate: production freed from alienating forms of external determination (viz. increasingly developed division and composition of labour freed from oppressive capitalist command; increasingly decoded desire freed from repressive Oedipal representation) is the motor of permanent revolution, a movement of perpetual transformation and differentiation: post-capitalist economics as difference-engine.

From the retrospective of *A Thousand Plateaus*, the view of history presented in *Anti-Oedipus* seems far too linear – despite Deleuze and Guattari's insistence that the source of that linearity, the capitalist mode of production,[17] arose by chance, and that the universal history revealed by capitalism appears only as a result, and still requires critique and revolutionary transformation to be realised. So the second volume of *Capitalism and Schizophrenia* is organised in an explicitly anti-linear manner, with dated plateaus appearing in no discernable (and certainly not chronological) order, and indeed belonging to very different time-scales. And in *A Thousand Plateaus*, the critique of linear Marxist historicism or 'historical materialism' is far more explicit: 'Economic evolutionism is an impossibility' (TP 430). Invoking models of non-linear development from the hard sciences, Deleuze and Guattari criticise older models of history which continue

to inform much Marxist thought: rather than a continuous development of productive forces punctuated by revolutions ushering in new
modes of production, Deleuze and Guattari conceive of history in
terms of reverse causalities, bifurcation-points and thresholds.

They reject not only linear historical materialism, but orthodox
Marxist dialectical materialism as well. Nowhere is this clearer than
in the case of money. Marx's presentation of the relations among
exchange, money and capital can give rise (and has given rise) to the
impression that money exchange evolved from barter and then into
capital proper. The historical record, Deleuze and Guattari insist,
shows otherwise: money first arose as a vehicle for imposing and
collecting the infinite debt, in connection with imperial tribute and
taxation (TP 427–8, 443 *passim*), and only much later became a
medium of commodity exchange and then wage payments. It is therefore 'not the State that presupposes a mode of production', Deleuze
and Guattari affirm against the grain of a certain Marxism, but
'quite the opposite, it is the State that makes production a "mode"'
(TP 429). This might seem to evacuate the primacy of the economic
that Deleuze and Guattari share with Marx, but not if we follow
Althusser's lead (as Deleuze and Guattari do) so that the economic
instance can determine politics (the state) to be dominant. All social
problems are economic in essence, but they are given different cases of
solution by different social formations or modes of production. The
main irreducible break for Deleuze and Guattari is between primitive
communism (called savagery in *Anti-Oedipus*) and what Marx called
the Asiatic mode of production (which Deleuze and Guattari call des-
potism in *Anti-Oedipus* and the imperial state form in *A Thousand
Plateaus*) (427). The imperial state form entails two apparatuses of
capture – tribute or taxation and ground rent – to which capitalism
adds a third apparatus: capital (TP 437–48). Capture is the machinic
process whereby a direct comparison (of land, labour, or goods)
enables a monopolistic appropriation (of rent, profit, or tribute), the
first moment presupposing an established stock constituted by the
second moment. So instead of surplus arising from production, as in
conventional Marxist accounts, production according to Deleuze and
Guattari arises from surplus:

> [I]t is by virtue of the stock that activities of the 'free action' type
> come to be compared, linked, and subordinated to a common and
> homogeneous quantity called [abstract] labour. . . . [T]here is no so-
> called necessary labour, and beyond that surplus labour. Labour and
> surplus labour are strictly the same thing; the first term is applied to

the quantitative comparison of activities, the second to the monopolistic appropriation of labour by the entrepreneur. Surplus labour is not that which exceeds labour; on the contrary, labour is that which is subtracted from surplus labour and presupposes it. (TP 442)

This is why Deleuze and Guattari consider debt to be more important for the organisation of social relations than production, and why they prefer to 'define social formations by *machinic processes*' rather than by the modes of production that depend on them (TP 435): modes of production are defined by a combination and hierarchy of apparatuses of capture. And, in explicit agreement with Marx (TP 447) the stock involved in the comparison of labour activity and the appropriation of profit – capital – must initially originate in another apparatus of capture, through the process of so-called 'primitive accumulation'.[18]

Deleuze and Guattari also agree that, once capitalism constitutes itself 'in a single stroke' (TP 453) through the conjugation of labour and capital, everything changes. The state henceforth becomes subordinate to capital as the dominant apparatus of capture; the transcendent, imperial state transforms into modern or 'civilised' states which now serve as so many different 'models of realisation' for worldwide capitalist axiomatisation – the socialist model, the liberal model, the dictatorial model, and so on. The economic (as social problem) is, as always, determinant, but it now determines the capitalist economy itself and the capture of surplus value to be dominant, rather than the state.[19] The imperial state had furnished the original 'primitive accumulation' of stock that eventually became capital; now capitalist axiomatisation furnishes the worldwide market, to which modern states must all relate as models of realisation. Axiomatisation fosters deterritorialisation, but also imposes reterritorialisation in the service of private accumulation, according to the rhythm outlined by Marx in *Capital* (Volume 3), as we have seen. And whereas the focus in *Anti-Oedipus* was on family reterritorialisation which produced Oedipal subjects for capital, in *A Thousand Plateaus* it is the state apparatus that serves as the main apparatus of reterritorialisation and subjectification: 'It is . . . proper to State deterritorialization to moderate the superior deterritorialization of capital and to provide the latter with compensatory reterritorializations' (TP 455). In the terms of *Anti-Oedipus*, capital has replaced the body of the state despot as socius (with the figure of the despot migrating into the nuclear family to become the Name of the Father); in the terms of *A Thousand Plateaus*, capitalist profit has superseded ground rent and despotic tribute as the dominant apparatus of capture, with the state serving as point of subjectification and compensatory reterritorialisation for the superior deterritorialising power of capitalist axiomatisation.

In *A Thousand Plateaus*, Deleuze and Guattari outline two processes of subject-formation correlated with the deterritorialising force of the worldwide capitalist market and the reterritorialising tendency of state models of realisation. State reterritorialisation produces citizen-subjects through the process of social subjection; axiomatisation manages flows through a process called machinic enslavement. Consider for example commercial or political marketing campaigns. Social subjection is measured by opinion polls, where voters or consumers are asked their opinions about products or candidates. Here, a certain degree of consciousness mediates the circulation of information from subject to pollster. Machinic enslavement is revealed in tests of galvanic skin response or pupil dilation in response to candidates or products: here, the desired information flows directly from the body to the pollster, without the mediation of consciousness or subjectivity. Despite the apparent difference in scale (worldwide vs. state boundaries) and the difference in technologies (machinic enslavement involving cybernetics), 'we have the privilege of undergoing the two operations simultaneously. . . . Rather than stages, subjection and enslavement constitute two coexistent poles . . . two simultaneous parts that constantly reinforce and nourish each other' (TP 459, 458). This important contribution to the Marxist analysis of contemporary society, first adumbrated in *A Thousand Plateaus*, is further developed in Deleuze's essay on 'control societies'.[20]

There, building on Foucault's analysis (in *Discipline and Punish*), Deleuze distinguishes three forms of power: sovereign, disciplinary and control. Sovereign power corresponds to the despotic or imperial state, and involves the right to tax and to take life. Disciplinary power, as Foucault himself also acknowledged, corresponds to an early form of capitalism, and involves the right to profit and the disciplining of life to maximise its productivity and reproductivity. It operated, as Foucault showed, by disciplining subjects in specific, relatively discrete institutions whose function was to reproduce certain models of behaviour: the model worker, husband, student, and so on. Profit was captured at the factory, with other institutions playing merely supporting roles in preparing workers and consumers for their respective positions in the economic system. Control corresponds to the contemporary form of capitalism, characterised by the complete subsumption of society by capital, and by its increasingly high speeds of de- and re-territorialisation. Capital has by now completely saturated social life; as Deleuze and Guattari explain in *A Thousand Plateaus*:

> In the organic composition of capital, variable capital defines a regime of subjectification of the worker (human surplus value), the principal framework of which is the business or factory. But with automation comes a progressive increase in the proportion of constant capital; we then see a new kind of enslavement [control]; at the same time the work regime changes, surplus value becomes machinic, and the framework expands to all of society. (TP 458)

All activity is now merely a moment in the circulation of capital; profit can be captured anywhere and everywhere, not just at the factory. Furthermore, the turnover rate of capital (in its increasingly frenetic drive to forestall the falling rate of profit) increases dramatically, becoming so rapid that disciplinary institutions cannot possibly keep pace. Control power operates not by means of the relatively fixed models of discipline, but via continual modulation. The values of currencies, labour-power, fashion styles, brands, musical trends, and so on are allowed to float, because the computer-powered cybernetic apparatus of capture is fast enough to appropriate surplus value without fixed values. Indeed, the constant pressure of de- and re-territorialisation in fact requires the constant churning of standards of value to ward off overproduction and profit-rate stagnation.

It is important to be clear here about what Deleuze and Guattari do and do not mean by 'machinic surplus value' in the control regime of advanced, high-speed capitalism. They do mention that each of the forms of power outlined in the 'control societies' essay has a corresponding form of machine – simple machines for sovereign power, mechanical machines for disciplinary power, and computers for control power (TP 457–58). But they insist that it is never these technical machines that are determinant, but rather the social machines or assemblages of which they are a part that really differentiate among the social formations and their corresponding forms of power. Following Lewis Mumford, they have (consistently, since *Anti-Oedipus*) considered society itself to be a kind of machine (or 'megamachine', in Mumford's terminology) – so the reference to machinic surplus value characteristic of control capitalism in contrast to the human surplus value of classical or disciplinary capitalism must not be misunderstood as attributing value-creation to machines themselves – that is, to technical machines. Machinic surplus value prevails, as the quotation above suggests, when the proportion of constant to variable capital reaches a critical threshold. Marx had discussed this in connection with what he called the real (rather than merely formal) subsumption of work by capital – that is, the transformation of the work process itself through the introduction of machinery. Instead of doing all the work themselves, workers in the regime of relative surplus value operate or oversee increasingly complex machines which 'do' the work for them. Marx was primarily concerned with the implications of this tendency for the production of surplus value and the rate of profit. But in a passage from the *Grundrisse* known as 'the Fragment on Machines'[21] which became very important to Deleuze and Guattari, Marx also discusses machines and production technology in terms of the 'general intellect': constant capital embodies not just economic value, but also the collective intelligence of the species. Machinic surplus value in Deleuze and Guattari must therefore not be understood as value produced solely by machines, but value produced by an assemblage that includes the contributions of generations of knowledge-workers embedded in machines, as well as the contributions of present-day workers. This is one reason why Deleuze and Guattari attach such great importance to the continued expansion of the international division of labour (and why they consider the differenciation of labour, as we saw above, to be more important than contradiction in the definition of the capitalist mode of production): it represents the continuing enhancement of productive forces stemming from the development and operationalisation of the general intellect. Social co-operation is no longer only imposed from above on the shop floor by managers, but is embedded in the production technology itself. So in the control regime of advanced capitalism, computer technologies not only enable the high-speed capture of continual modulation, but also and conversely embody social co-operation – a machinic form of co-operation that no longer depends entirely on the subjective consciousness of workers, since much of it is embedded in technical machines. This is another important sense in which advanced capitalism adds an element of machinic enslavement to social subjectifcation – inasmuch as capital has saturated the entire social field and the line between human and machine has become blurred, with both serving capital in the production and private appropriation of surplus value:

> [i]n the capitalist regime, surplus labour becomes less and less distinguishable from labour 'strictly speaking,' and totally impregnates it. . . . How could one possibly distinguish the time necessary for

reproduction and 'extorted' time, when they are no longer separable in time? This remark certainly does not contradict the Marxist theory of surplus value, for Marx shows precisely that surplus value *ceases to be localizable* in the capitalist regime. That is even his fundamental contribution. It gave him a sense that . . . the circulation of capital would challenge the distinction between variable and constant capital . . . It is as though human alienation through surplus labour were replaced by a generalized 'machinic enslavement,' such that one may furnish surplus-value without doing any work (children, the retired, the unemployed, television viewers, etc.). (TP 491)

Deleuze's analysis of the control regime of contemporary capitalism thus remains consistent with, and is indeed based on, Marx's analysis of the regime of relative surplus value and the real subsumption of all of society by the circulation of capital.

Yet this analysis of contemporary capitalism has important implications for the vision of politics that emerges from the political philosophy of Deleuze and Guattari. And along with their rejection of ideology, nothing seems further from conventional notions of Marxist politics than Deleuze and Guattari's devaluation of class struggle. In their view, class struggle is not in itself revolutionary because there is actually only one class: the class of all those constituted by their – admittedly very different, even opposed – relations to capital and its axioms, whether as worker, manager, technician, owner, or whatever. The regime of real subsumption means that any activity of any person is susceptible to axiomatisation, to the extent that it can be formalised or quantified. This includes factory workers, who as producers and consumers are merely incarnations of capital as it circulates in various forms throughout control society. Deleuze and Guattari conceive of 'Fordism', for example, as a set of worker axioms – including axioms of consumption: the single-family house, the power boat in the driveway, as well as axioms of production: the technology of the assembly-line – that effectively incorporate workers into and subordinate them to capital. 'Keynesian economics and the New Deal were axiom laboratories . . . [as was] the Marshall Plan' (TP 462). But it equally includes, say, hip-hop music, which gets captured and becomes a fashion standard of consumption and a source of surplus value, more or less completely voiding its apparent outlaw or contestatory stance. The same is true of the legal system, inasmuch as it treats or constructs subjects as formally equally citizens before the law – as for example when a viable protest movement degenerates into a demand that the state itself add axioms to grant and enforce the 'rights' of movement members to be treated as full-fledged citizens. Axiomatisation is the way capitalist enterprise and the 'civilised' state manage subjectification and enslavement to capture surplus value throughout control society.

Hence the imperative to create *minor* lines of flight: to avoid capture. Deleuze and Guattari's concept of the minor must be understood in relation to the norms or standards managed by axiomatisation, as that which differs from and escapes the norm, not in a statistically defined opposition of minority to majority. As they never tire of pointing out, the standard (for example, white male European) can be and indeed often is a statistical minority, and yet still represents the norm. Conversely, a statistical minority can be standardised, as for example when ethnic groups seek recognition and civil rights from the state in the form of 'identity politics', or unionised workers seek state recognition and bargaining rights vis-à-vis capital in the form of 'class struggle'. The minor, by contrast, is defined as a non-denumerable set, an *ad hoc* group or movement whose cohesion defies formalisation and quantification:

> What characterizes the nondenumerable is neither the set nor its elements; rather it is the *connection*, the 'and' produced between elements, between sets, and which belongs to neither, which eludes them and constitutes a line of flight. The axiomatic manipulates only denumerable sets . . . whereas the minorities constitute 'fuzzy,' nondenumerable, nonaxiomatizable sets, in short, 'masses,' multiplicities of escape and flux. (TP 470)

The capture function of the advanced capitalist control regime has become so rapid, supple and all-encompassing that escaping axiomatisation has become the top priority for Deleuze and Guattari. Only denumerable sets are manageable by axioms, which operate by homogenising elements and programming relations from the outside, in conjunction with some other denumerable set(s). Minor, non-denumerable sets, by contrast, group heterogeneous elements together via *ad hoc* connections (this *and* that *and* the other *and*. . .) that cannot be formalised, and that therefore escape capture precisely insofar and for as long as they remain unformalised and hence nonaxiomatisable.[22] And the point of becoming-minor is to 'promote compositions [of social relations] that do not pass by way of the capitalist economy any more than they do the State-form' (TP 470). This may seem quite distant from a Marxian politics premised on the organisation of industrial workers at the 'point of production', but in fact the complete saturation of control society by high-speed capital means, as we have seen, that surplus value is produced throughout society, so that resisting axiomatisation becomes a political priority for everyone: 'Minority as a universal figure, or becoming-everybody/everything (*devenir tout le monde*)' (TP 470). Deleuze and Guattari remain Marxist in this sense, too, however – that the principal struggle is always the struggle against capitalism. If minorities are revolutionary, they insist,

> it is because they carry with them a deeper movement that challenges the worldwide axiomatic. The power of minority . . . finds its figure or universal consciousness in the proletariat. . . . [A]s long as the working class defines itself by an acquired status [e.g. unionized workers], or even by a theoretically conquered State, it appears only as 'capital,' a part of capital (variable capital) and does not leave the *plan(e) of capital*. . . . It is by leaving the plan(e) of capital, and never ceasing to leave it, that a mass becomes increasingly revolutionary and destroys the equilibrium of the denumerable sets. (TP 472)

This is not to say that struggle over axioms themselves is unimportant, for Deleuze and Guattari insist on the contrary that it is very important, even 'determinant' (TP 471, translation modified). Despite the extraordinary 'recuperative' power of the control regime, they stress that 'the constant adjustments of the capitalist axiomatic . . . are the object of [legitimate] struggles' (TP 463) – and they offer a wide-ranging list of examples: 'women's struggle for the vote, for abortion, for jobs; the struggle of the regions for autonomy; the struggle of the Third World; the struggle of the oppressed minorities in the East or West. . .' (TP 471). In the same vein, they stress the 'fundamental difference between living flows and the axioms that subordinate them to centers of control and decision making', and maintain that 'the pressure of the living flows, and of the problems they pose and impose, must be exerted inside the axiomatic' (TP 464). Nevertheless, the best chances for resisting axiomatisation and creating viable lines of flight from the plane of capital lie with the becoming-minor of nondenumerable sets or multiplicities. This is because of what Deleuze and Guattari call 'the deepest law of capitalism', which is, as we have seen all along, that 'it continually sets and then repels its own limits, but in doing so gives rise to numerous flows in all directions that escape its axiomatic' (TP 472). At their best, struggles against capitalist control are bi-valent (or what Deleuze and Guattari call 'undecidable' (TP 471–3): 'the struggle around axioms is most important when it manifests itself opens, the gap between two types of propositions, propositions of flow and propositions of axioms' (TP 471). These two types of propositions, too, stem from the fundamental law or paradox of capitalism:

> *At the same time that capitalism is effectuated in the denumerable sets serving as its models [of realisation], it necessarily constitutes nondenumerable sets that cut across and disrupt these models.* It does not effect the 'conjugation' of the deterritorialized and decoded flows without these flows going farther ahead; without their escaping both the axiomatic that conjugates them and the models that reterritorialize them; without their tending to enter into connections . . . [and to] construct *revolutionary connections* in opposition to the *conjugations of the axiomatic.* (TP 472–3)

From Marx's analysis of the paradoxical dynamic of capitalist development, Deleuze and Guattari derive a political imperative to bring the pressure of nondenumerable minorities to bear on the struggle over axioms, to the point of escaping from capitalist axiomatisation altogether, and ultimately altering the global balance of power between connections and conjugations in favour of the former.

Ohio State University

Notes

1. Karl Marx and Friedrich Engels, *The Communist Manifesto*, in *Marx/Engels Collected Works*, Vol. 6 (London: International Publishers, 1976), p. 12.
2. Gilles Deleuze, 'Le "Je me souviens" de Gilles Deleuze', *Le Nouvel Observateur* 1619 (1995), pp. 50–1.
3. Althusser produced a sophisticated version of Marxism compatible with French structuralism and poststructuralism, partly by rejecting Hegel's philosophical influence on Marx in favour of views adapted from the early-modern philosopher, Baruch de Spinoza. Deleuze and Althusser cited one another in their respective philosophical works.
4. Louis Althusser, *For Marx*, trans. Ben Brewster (London: New Left Books, 1969), p. 113.
5. In some versions of Marxist materialism, the economic base was understood to determine unilaterally the superstructure, which was comprised of laws, political institutions, culture, etc.
6. I use 'technical' to refer to the specialisation and distribution of tasks within an enterprise, 'social' to refer to the specialisation and distribution of tasks throughout society, and 'political' to refer to class or power divisions in society.

7. See Pierre Macherey, *Hegel ou Spinoza* (Paris: Maspero, 1979)
8. On the impact of Spinoza on Deleuze's Marxism, see Eugene W. Holland, 'Spinoza and Marx', *Cultural Logic* 2:1 (1998), http://clogic. eserver.org/2-1/holland.html, and my *Deleuze and Guattari's Anti-Oedipus: An Introduction to Schizoanalysis* (New York: Routledge, 1999), Chapter 4.
9. See Karl Marx, *Capital*, in *Marx/Engels Collected Works*, Vol. 1 (London: International Publishers, 1976), Chapter 27, 'Expropriation of the Agricultural Population from the Land'.
10. See Marx and Engels, *The Communist Manifesto*, p. 13.
11. See Marx, *Capital*, Vol. 3, in *Marx/Engels Collected Works*, Vol. 1, (London: International Publishers, 1976), pp. 249–50; see also Karl Marx, *Grundrisse: Introduction to the Critique of Political Economy*, trans. M. Nicolaus (New York: Vintage, 1973 [1939]), pp. 618–23, especially the following: 'In one period the process appears as altogether fluid – the period of the maximum realization of capital; in another, a reaction to the first, the other moment asserts itself all the more forcibly – the period of the maximum devaluation of capital and congestion of the production process' (p. 623).
12. See Holland, *Introduction to Schizoanalysis*, especially Chapter 3.
13. See Marx, *Capital*, vol. 3, p. 50.
14. On the splitting of the subjective essence of human life into abstract labour and abstract desire under capitalism, see AO 337.
15. Karl Marx, *Grundrisse*, p. 109; for an exposition of Deleuze and Guattari's view of universal history, see Jason Read, 'Universal History of Contingency: Deleuze and Guattari on the History of Capitalism', in *Borderlands E-journal* 2:3 (2003), online at http://www.borderlandse-journal.adelaide.edu.au/vol2no3_2003/read_contingency.htm
16. Karl Marx, *Grundrisse*, p. 106
17. For a similar view of linear history as a product of capitalism, see Michel Foucault, *The Order of Things* (New York: Vintage, 1994), p. 255.
18. On the compatibility of Marx's account of 'primitive accumulation' with Deleuze and Guattari's views on non-linear history, see Eugene W. Holland, 'Nonlinear Historical Materialism and Postmodern Marxism', *Culture, Theory, Critique* 47:2 (2006), pp. 181–96; see also Jason Read, 'Primitive Accumulation' in *Rethinking Marxism* 14:2 (2000), pp. 24–49, and *The Micro-Politics of Capital: Marx and the Prehistory of the Present* (Albany: State University of New York Press, 2003).
19. On Deleuze and Guattari's agreement with Althusser on the relations of determination and dominance within a social formation, see AO 247–8.
20. See Gilles Deleuze, 'Postscript on Control Societies' (N 177–82).
21. Karl Marx, *Grundrisse*, pp. 690–712. For an informative discussion of this passage from Marx, and of the relations between Deleuze and Marx

in general, see the excellent work by Nicholas Thoburn, *Deleuze, Marx and Politics* (New York: Routledge, 2003).

22. Throughout *A Thousand Plateaus*, set theory replaces what in *Anti-Oedipus* was couched in terms of 'groups-in-fusion' opposed to serialised groups – an opposition borrowed directly from Jean-Paul Sartre (AO 256–7).

9

Hoëne Wronski and Francis Warrain

Christian Kerslake

At least up until the publication of *Difference and Repetition* in 1968, Deleuze could with accuracy be described as a proponent of 'the philosophy of difference'. In the notoriously dense fourth chapter of *Difference and Repetition*, 'The Ideal Synthesis of Difference', Deleuze develops at length the thought that differential calculus can serve as the universal formal instrument for the theory and practice of 'differentiation'. Deleuze argues that differential calculus offers a formal clue to a possible 'dialectic of problems' which can replace the Hegelian dialectic of the Concept. 'Just as we oppose difference in itself to negativity, so we oppose dx to not-A, the symbol of differ- ence (*Differenzphilosophie*) to that of contradiction' (DR 170). Since Deleuze's philosophy of difference rests in part on his development of models from differential calculus, the question of the precise meaning and use he ascribes to the calculus is an important one. 'A great deal of heart and a great deal of truly philosophical naivety is needed in order to take the symbol dx seriously', says Deleuze, looking us in the eye, at the outset of his discussion of the calculus in *Difference and Repetition*. 'For their part, Kant and even Leibniz renounced the idea' (DR 170). But why exactly must a philosopher be naive to take the differential calculus seriously as an instrument of the philosophy of difference?

In the introduction to the discussion of the calculus in *Difference and Repetition*, Deleuze announces that he specifically wishes to focus on an 'esoteric history of differential philosophy', in which 'three names shine forth like bright stars . . . Salomon Maïmon, Hoëne Wronski and Jean Bordas-Desmoulin'. Maimon (1753–1800) and Wronski (1776–1853) were the two main protagonists in the imme- diate context of post-Kantian philosophy to argue for the centrality of differential calculus as an instrument of determination. Maimon, says Deleuze, 'paradoxically sought to ground post-Kantianism upon a Leibnizian reinterpretation of the calculus', while Wronski, he says, was a 'profound mathematician who developed a positivist, messianic and mystical system which implied a Kantian interpretation of the calculus' (DR 170).[1] Deleuze expresses a preference for Wronski's properly Kantian approach to the calculus, over Maimon's approach, which he acknowledges falls back into pre-critical metaphysics. It has been assumed that by 'esoteric' Deleuze simply means 'obscure'; and it is true that the figures of Solomon Maimon, Hoëne Wronski and Jean Bordas-Desmoulin are rarely referred to in standard histories of the mathematical calculus. Wronski is also rarely referred to in standard histories of post-Kantian philosophy, which only adds to the mystery of how Deleuze ended up appealing to his ideas to ground his philosophy of differentiation. It is certainly true that Wronski is an obscure figure in this sense. But it is also possible that when Deleuze refers to 'the esoteric history of differential philosophy', he means something more specific.

Wronski's peculiar synthesis of mathematics and philosophy is acknowledged by a number of sources to have played an important role in the constitution of the modern Western revival of interest in 'esotericism' in its more specific sense. Although the question of Wronski's 'esotericism' was contested by his followers after his death,[2] the role his ideas played in the revival of a self-identified 'occultist' esotericism in mid-late nineteenth century France is well documented. Alphonse-Louis Constant (the self-styled 'Eliphas Lévi') is often held to have inaugurated the modern revival of 'occultism' in the 1850s with his *Doctrine and Ritual of High Magic* (translated into English as *Transcendental Magic*), but numerous sources (including Lévi himself) attest that Lévi was himself first 'initiated' into 'occultism' by Wronski, and that prior to the year he spent with Wronski, he had been a utopian socialist.[3] Moreover, one of the leaders of the esoteric movement of Martinism, Gérard Encausse (aka 'Papus'), also regularly appealed to Wronski in his theoretical works. Given the young Deleuze's own early work on Johann Malfatti de Montereggio's *Mathesis*, another fundamental work in the history of nineteenth-century esotericism, also mined by the Martinists,[4] it is at least possible that the 'esoteric' use of the calculus to which Deleuze refers really *is* esoteric, as in 'esotericist', as in 'occultist', a term that is perhaps preferable in these circumstances, since it gets rid of the ambiguity of the term 'esoteric'. In his *History of Occult Philosophy*, Sarane Alexandrian connects both Malfatti's account of 'mathesis' and the philosophy of Wronski with an older occult tradition of 'arithmosophy'.[5] Pythagoreans, cabbalists, Indian occultists and Renaissance thinkers such as Ramon Lull and Giordano Bruno all developed the use of combinatorial techniques involving metaphysical elements (often in the form of divine attributes or names). It was this same 'science of numbers', claims Alexandrian, which 'was completely renovated in the 19th century by Hoëne Wronski, mathematician, inventor and philosopher . . . , whose remarkable work rests entirely on practical reason and on the most rigorous scientific methods'.[6] He goes on to claim that 'Wronski holds in occult philosophy the place of Kant in classical philosophy'.[7] Although some mathematicians and historians have contended that Wronski's central idea, the 'Law of Creation' [*Loi de création*], is no more than an abstruse formulation of a properly mathematical idea about infinity, or, more precisely, a formulation of a particular kind of series expansion – the Polish mathematician Stefan Banach, for instance, claims that Wronski's so-called Law of Creation ended up finding its proper application in topology, in the theory of *orthogonal polynomials*[8] – the esotericist interpreters of Wronski claim that the meaning of the Law of Creation was never explicitly spelled out in his mathematical works. So when we see Deleuze returning to the notion of mathesis in *Difference and Repetition*, explicitly appealing to ideas from Wronski, and making a clear statement that he is concerned with an 'esoteric' use of the calculus, we need to take a step back and ask whether we have at our immediate disposal all the necessary means to understand what is going in Deleuze's philosophy of difference.

As well as the references to esoteric and 'gnoseological' (DR 170) uses of the calculus, there are other passages in *Difference and Repetition* which also directly appeal to esoteric theories of space, time and number. Take for instance the dense paragraph (DR 20–1) which summarises the theses of Matila Ghyka's *The Golden Number: Pythagorean Rites and Rhythms in the Development of Western Civilization* (*Le nombre d'or: rites et rhythmes pythagoriciens dans le développement de la civilisation occidentale* [1931]). There Deleuze can be found murmuring about the rhythmic properties of pentagrams as an example of a 'pure dynamism which creates a corresponding space' to Ideas. In *Le nombre d'or*, as well as in *Etudes sur le rhythme* (1938), and the 1946 English language selection from these volumes, *The Geometry of Art and Life*, Ghyka had explored the difference between the hexagonal forms of inorganic nature and the pentagonal morphology of organic forms. In his passage on Ghyka, Deleuze takes this same 'dynamic symmetry which is pentagonal and appears in a spiral line or in a geometrically progressing pulsation – in short, in a living and mortal "evolution"' as a clue to the formation of the 'evolutionary cycles or spirals' found in nature, in which 'creatures weave their repetition and receive at the same time the gift of living and dying' (DR 21). In the language of contemporary philosophy, what type of *claim* is being made in passages such as this? Are they merely poetic, or are they up to something philosophically? Or – and this is obviously the darker thought – are they the lineaments of some clandestine occult scheme underpinning the ideas of that famously obscure book bearing the somewhat blank and neutral title of *Difference and Repetition*. . .? *Le nombre d'or* is after all itself full of explicit detail in its last chapters about esoteric and occult ideas of number and form, and their development in ritual practices.[9] Could some of Deleuze's ideas have been a little more *specific* than we might have expected for someone engaged in the practice we know, or at least we think we know, as 'philosophy'?

A crucial piece in this puzzle is the work of Francis Warrain (1867–1940), a contemporary of Bergson, who published several major studies of Wronski, as well as editing the collection of papers by Wronski to which Deleuze refers in *Difference and Repetition*.[10] Deleuze was aware of Warrain's own philosophical work; in a footnote to his discussion of Wronski, he refers the reader in search of an account of Wronski's philosophy to Warrain's edition of Wronski, stating that 'Warrain undertakes the necessary comparisons with the philosophy of Schelling' (DR 324). Warrain does indeed draw out the comparisons between Wronski and Schelling in his 1933 edition of Wronski, but in what follows I will suggest that it is Warrain's earlier works, published in the first decade of the twentieth century, that may turn out to be more significant for understanding Deleuze's avowedly 'esoteric' interpretation of the differential calculus. In 1906, Warrain published *Concrete Synthesis: A Study of the Metaphysics of Life* [*La synthèse concrète: Étude métaphysique de la Vie*], in which he claimed that Wronski's philosophy should be understood in a precise sense as a 'mathematics of life'.[11] A year before Bergson published his own major 'vitalist' work, *Creative Evolution*, Warrain had developed in this neglected work a powerful version of metaphysical vitalism that focused on the idea of a 'non-organic life'. Warrain takes up Bergson's proposal, first sketched out in his 1903 essay on 'Life and Consciousness', that his own durational philosophy of time could combine with contemporary energetics and biology to generate a new form of 'vitalism', according to which it would be legitimate to posit an immaterial 'life in general',[12] manifesting itself through waves of evolutionary differentiation. Warrain claimed that Bergson had misunderstood the nature of vitalism, and had mistakenly modelled his metaphysical notion of 'Life' on the *organism*, when this latter should be seen as the mere shell, even an obstacle, to the ultimately *non-organic* pulse of differentiation. 'What characterises life', he says, 'is rather that it represents an absolutely concrete synthesis. This is pure life, absolute and ideal. *No organism can realise it completely.*'[13] He specifies that 'with M. Bergson, we consider the body as being the work of the soul, its exterior manifestation, its objectivation';[14] but there is a contradiction in Bergson's conception of vitalism, insofar as he claims on the one hand that the organic body is merely the *means* utilised by some sort of 'life in general', while 'still also conceiving it as engendered by an organism'.[15] It is only if we look *beyond* the form of the organism, argues Warrain, that we become able to perceive the real polarisations, rhythms and vibrations that carry the ongoing evolution of 'life'. And for this, we need Wronski's 'mathematics of life'. Armed with this highly specific 'mathematics', we can arrive at an authentic, detailed, metaphysical vitalism, where 'vibration is the physical expression of Life',[16] and through which we can discover the true patterns of the 'Vibration-Thought' that is activated by embodied rational beings.

Warrain's metaphysics of vibration and rhythm appears to be *both* immanently philosophical *and* esoteric, and suggests a way in which the potential clash of principles between philosophy and the 'esoteric' might be resolved. Warrain illustrated his chapter on Wronski's Law of Creation in *Concrete Synthesis* with a diagram which correlates the elements of Wronski's system one-by-one with the cabbalistic sephiroth of Jewish mysticism.[17] In one of the most far-seeing passages of his 1907 treatise on *Space* (subtitled *The Universal Modalities of Quantity*), he claims that under certain conditions it is possible to apprehend a 'superior spatial order' akin to the models of Riemann and Lobachevsky, in which 'the phases of existence on diverse planes' unfold, and which allows one 'to account for the thesis of the esotericists, and of mystical visions telling of joys, paradisiacal gardens, celestial animals, and anthropomorphic divinities'.[18] Warrain's later works, including his magnum opus on Wronski, *The Metaphysical Armature of Hoëne Wronski* (*L'Armature métaphysique de Hoëne Wronski* [1925]), also continue to stress the esoteric significance of Wronski's philosophy, contending that the 'irradiation' of Wronski's 'Law of Creation' recalls cabbalistic notions of immanence.[19] Despite all this, Warrain's work suggests how Wronski's own brand of mathematicised philosophy should ultimately be understood as neither completely exoterically mathematical, nor completely 'esoteric'. His claim is that 'the schema of reality established by Wronski is nothing else than the determination of Life in its most general conception; it is the formula of concrete synthesis'.[20] For Warrain, Wronskian metaphysics is an instrument for assessing currents of vitality, for gauging creative power against the forces of preservation and conservatism, and for generating new 'non-organic' forms of life, such as music, poetry and machines, all of which are able to sustain complex 'rhythms' and 'vibrations' that human organisms can only participate in for limited durations.

> Machines and works of art are the tangible proof of the objective reality of syntheses; for the machine realises in matter the act emanating from an idea-force, and the work of art disengages, from the virtualities of matter, the expression of the idea. And this double involutive and evolutive current is what we approach in the concrete character of vital synthesis.[21]

Wronski himself contended that he was sketching out the tenets of a future 'sehelian' religion (*sehel* is 'reason' in Hebrew), which would no longer be a revealed religion, but a *proven* religion: the religion of the Absolute.[22] Indeed, it seems to have been this feature of Wronski's philosophy that attracted Eliphas Lévi, and prompted him to construct a revived occultism, based, so he said, on Wronskian principles. In his obituary for Wronski, Lévi wrote that Wronski had 'placed, in this century of universal and absolute doubt, the hitherto unshakeable basis of a science at once human and divine. First and foremost, he had dared to define the essence of God and to find, in this definition itself, the law of absolute movement and of universal creation.'[23] This appears to be an odd thing for an avowed 'occultist' to say. The notions of the 'esoteric' or 'occult', in the popular mind at least, are usually related to belief in spiritual and demonic beings. But Lévi is saying here that Wronski's contribution to 'science' is 'to dare to define the essence of God', and then from that definition to generate the 'law of universal creation'. This appears to be a very *rationalist* project. Defining the essence of God and seeing what follows from it was the hubristic enterprise of Spinoza's and Leibniz's rationalism. In fact, rather than attempting to 'unveil' the esoteric truth of Wronski's philosophy, it may in fact be more revealing to go the other way, and to show that what we call modern 'esotericism' and 'occultism' has its intellectual roots in the reaction to Kantian philosophy. In the first half of the nineteenth century, as a result of the influence of Kant, philosophy underwent some extraordinary metamorphoses, and figures like Wronski and Malfatti believed they were legitimately extending post-Kantian philosophy in its systematic form with their researches into *mathesis universalis* and esotericism. Perhaps Deleuze's work is, in part, a continuation of this relatively unknown, 'bastard' line in German idealism. The rest of this essay is devoted to reconstructing Wronski's and Warrain's ideas about the 'true matter' of the calculus, which we shall see involves a 'transcendental' conception of 'life' in its twin aspects of 'spontaneity' and 'passivity', 'creation' and 'preservation', 'knowledge' [*Savoir*] and 'being' [*Être*] – Wronski and Warrain's Kantian prototype of Bergson's basic polarity between 'duration' and 'matter'.

JÓZEF-MARIA HOËNE WRONSKI AND MESSIANISM

Wronski was born in 1776 in Wolsztyn in Poland and lived in Marseilles and then Paris from 1800 until his death in 1853. After beginning his adult life with a series of military escapades in the aid of Polish independence, in 1797 Wronski inherited a large sum of money and set out on a voyage to Königsberg, to study philosophy with the great Kant, but since Kant was no longer teaching at that time, Wronski ended up studying at Halle and Göttingen. However, the philosophical revolution that was taking place in Jena during the years Wronski spent in Germany (1797–1800) did not pass him by, and, in parallel with Fichte, Schelling and Hegel (but apparently unbeknownst to them), Wronski soon found himself embarked upon his own search for a new, post-Kantian philosophical Absolute. In 1800, he enrolled at the Polish Legion in Marseilles, studying with the astronomer Jerôme Lalande, resulting in his first scientific publication, *Memoirs on the Aberration of the Mobile Stars and on the Inequality in the Appearance of their Movement* (*Mémoires sur l'aberration des astres mobiles et sur l'inégalité dans l'apparence de leur mouvement* [1801]). One of the central applications of the differential calculus at the time was in celestial mechanics, and it provided Wronski with the instrument for his account of the real and apparent movement of the 'mobile stars' (the sun, moon and the planets). Already in this early work, Wronski was preoccupied with the formation of celestial objects, and ultimately with the problems of the origin of the solar system, of the universe, and of the metaphysical relation of energy and matter.

On the 15 August 1803, while he was attending a ball in Marseilles to celebrate Napoleon's birthday,[24] Wronski had an intense vision of the nature of the Absolute. As Piotr Pragacz puts it in a recent biographical article: 'As he described it, he had a feeling of anxiety and certainty, that he would discover the "essence of the Absolute". Later, he held that he had understood the mystery of the beginning of the universe and the laws which govern it. From that time on he decided to reform human thought and create a universal philosophical system.'[25] Wronski was to become convinced that this 'intuition' was fully in conformity with the results of the Kantian philosophy in which he had immersed himself.[26] Alexandrian suggests that the intuition specifically arose from the idea that 'the absolute, as condition of the relative, is a postulate of reason'.[27]

In the same year as his vision, Wronski published his first book of philosophy, entitled *The Critical Philosophy Discovered by Kant, Grounded on the Ultimate Principle of Human Knowledge* (*Philosophie critique découverte par Kant, fondée sur le dernier principe du savoir humain*); this was the first detailed presentation of Kant's critical philosophy in French at the time.[28] Like Schelling and Hegel, Wronski now believed he had spotted a doorway in Kant's system that led to a new kind of 'absolute', speculative theory and practice of Reason.

Kant's Copernican turn had inverted traditional expectations that knowledge was supposed to correspond with an external object. The real problem, according to Kant, was to get to the bottom of how we *justify* our knowledge claims; that is, what are the *criteria* (both intellectual and sensible) by which we judge an event to be 'objective'? When we ask ourselves how we know something, we must have a set of implicit criteria to which we make appeal. Kant had shown that knowledge was governed by a specific set of rules, such as the 'category' of causality. Given that we have no direct intellectual intuition which gives us access to the noumenal truth, and given that sensible representations do not unify themselves, it must be such rules of the intellect that are the conditions for the possibility of knowledge, and experience in general insofar as it is ordered and coherent. What was needed now, claimed Wronski, following Fichte, Schelling and Hegel, was access to the *unconditioned* principle that lay at the basis of knowledge and cognition in general. Wronski's distinctive approach was to bring about an identification of Kant's theory of Reason with an algorithmic form of mathematics, in such a way that the spontaneity that Kant held to be at the basis of the subjective conditions of cognition could be liberated and redirected into an algorithmic theory and technique of reason. 'The spontaneous character' of reason, Wronski stated, 'is hyperlogism, in other words, the independence of every prior condition'.[29] Wronski maintained that by appealing to the methods of the differential calculus, with its possibility for complete 'horizontal' determination (the reciprocal determination of dx/dy), alongside its capacity for 'vertical' differentiation through the generation of power series, it was at last possible for Reason to assume its proper form: that of a concrete mathematics. Wronski thought that the construction of Taylor series (power series) allowed for an *a priori* 'generation of knowledge about quantity'. His first published presentation of his mathematical theory, his 1811 *Introduction to the Philosophy of Mathematics and the Technique of Algorithms* (*Introduction à la philosophie des mathématiques et technie d'algorithmie*), was an attempt to generate and develop the basic propositions of mathematics out of a theory and practice of algorithms. Exponential and logarithmic series in geometry, mathematics and the differential calculus provided Wronski with examples of an internal, self-generated ideal order that, he claimed, could be elaborated across the entire horizon of human knowledge.

Wronski argued that Kant had not drawn the full consequences of his own theory of reason. Kant's theory of 'regulative ideas gives us, beyond all expectation so to speak, the rules for generating knowledge itself about quantity; which incontestably is the most sublime use of our faculties of knowledge'.[30] The Kantian *horizon* of the Ideal, once penetrated by mathematics, opens up the space in principle for a final reconciliation of reason and energy. As Warrain puts it, in Wronski's system, 'energy and Reason are the two faces of the active principle: the power of Energy shows itself in the development [*devenir*] of the act; the power of Reason in the immutability of principle'.[31]

Kant's problem was that he had allowed the power of Reason to become obscured by procedures more appropriate to the Understanding. But if there is a rational *mundus intelligibilis*, argued Wronski, it must be adequately conceived:

> No mortal before Kant had approached so close to the true object of philosophy. But unfortunately, it was still only a hypothesis: Kant's error is the same as that of his predecessors, he still takes knowledge *on the model of being* [*il considère toujours le savoir* à l'instar de l'être], in ascribing it conditions or forms which make us misrecognise its sublime character of *spontaneity* or *unconditionality*. Despite Kant's erroneous hypothesis, the results of his philosophy, guaranteed by the character of *necessity*, are true, for the most part at least, in the inferior region of the universe, that is, in the realm of things, where this character of necessity is applicable.[32]

It was by giving primacy to the role of practical reason in the realisation of the rational capabilities of finite beings that Kant had completed the Copernican revolution in philosophy and truly turned the world inside out. What has *unconditioned* reality in the Kantian system is ultimately the act of self-determining reason, not the conditioned matter of appearances. With the unconditional act of self-legislating autonomy at the heart of Kant's system, the realm of appearances inevitably begins to lose some of its dignity, and only stands to have it restored by becoming the space for moral action. As Deleuze shows in *Kant's Critical Philosophy*, Kantian reason already has its own, intrinsic set of ends. At the summit of Kant's system, there is an 'absolute unity of *practical finality* and *unconditioned legislation*'. The 'supreme end' of reason 'is the organization of rational beings under the moral law, or freedom as reason for existence contained in itself in the rational being'.[33] Wronski's contribution was to develop Kant's claim that reason only had unconditional validity in practical action (and not in knowledge claims, where the understanding had to rule), by inferring that practical reason, taken in its status as *unconditioned*, is not just creative because it is synthetic, but rather that the *spontaneity* Kant ascribes to it renders it *ontologically creative*. It is on this Kantian basis that Wronski lays claim – in the words of Philippe d'Arcy, author of the last philosophical book to be written on Wronski – to 'a philosophy of creation'.[34] Insofar as it is a free act, to realise a rational idea in a practical action is to make a genuine difference to the world as it is given, to modify it and determine it by reference to an ideal. It is therefore only properly in the act of creation, Wronski reasoned, that thought properly assumes unconditioned status. It is only when reason licenses itself to reconstruct material reality in the light of ideas and 'virtualities' that it takes on the consequences of its proper 'achrematic' status (*chrema* is Greek for 'thing').[35]

Wronski's project becomes to convert Kantianism into what he calls a 'messianism' of Absolute Reason. As D'Arcy puts it, Wronski claims that 'creation is for each being a law, or a duty [*devoir*], . . . each being must create, . . . the only real *beings* are those which can create, engender effects, consequences, and, in the case of man, the acts through which he accomplishes and engenders himself (autogenesis)'.[36] There is only one *de jure* destination for finite rational beings: towards the assimilation of the 'creative virtuality' of reason, and its deployment in the service of absolute creation. The ultimate destination of Wronski's messianism is a kingdom of rational beings, whose capability for taking themselves and each other as ends-in-themselves rests on their dual capacity to regressively recapitulate their individual formation, and to progressively determine the incarnation of the Good and True, with the practical goal of bringing about a kingdom of ends on the Earth.

It is this *autogenic* power of reason, Wronski claims, that allows us to rediscover the *laws* proper to creativity itself, and to locate the true 'indifference-point' (to use Schelling's terms) of thought and being. Deleuze directs those who are interested in Wronski's philosophy to the collection of papers edited by Warrain in 1933 entitled *The Philosophical Work of Hoëne Wronski (L'Oeuvre philosophique de Hoëne Wronski)*. These three hefty volumes are mostly filled with curious tables, all based on the same 'schema'. In its most general form, Wronski terms this schema 'The Table of the Law of Creation of All Systems of Reality'.[37] He always presents his 'Law of Creation' in a double form, on the one side under the heading of 'Theory' or 'Autothesis', and on the other side, under the heading of 'Technics' [*Technie*] or 'Autogeny'. He gives Kant's distinction between theoretical and practical reason a new formulation: there is a 'theoretical constitution' and a 'technical constitution' of reality. Theory concerns *that which is given* in the existence of a reality'; it concerns the *individual content* of a being, and articulates an 'individual generation (in mathematics, taken in its transcendental sense [in which] the essence of the content is part of absolute reality, which receives a being for the establishment of this individuality'.[38] The practical or 'technical' constitution of reality, on the other hand, involves *'that which must be done* for the accomplishment of a reality'.[39] It is in the properly autogenic determinations of finite rational beings that one finds the most developed and self-differentiated acts of creation, their ideal movement liberated from the inertia of the relatively 'inferior order' of constituted phenomenal nature.

Wronski contends that Kant's opposition between Reason and Understanding should really be mapped onto a more primordial opposition between the 'Element of Knowledge' (*Élément Savoir*), and the 'Element of Being' (*Élément Être*). In 'The Table of the Law of Creation of All Systems of Reality', these two elements of Knowledge and Being are the poles that generate the initially triadic relationship that Wronski puts forwards as his basic transcendental matrix. The third element is what Wronski calls the 'Neuter' (*Élément neuter*), in that it 'neutralises' the opposition or polarity between Knowledge and Being. For Wronski, the basic opposition between *Élément Savoir* and *Élément Être* has a specific dynamism of its own. The Element of Knowledge is characterised by its 'spontaneity' or 'autogenic determination', while the Element of Being implies 'inertia' or 'autothetic determination'. Knowledge and Being are opposed as creation to inertia, as spontaneous calculation versus preservation and petrifaction. Given this context, we can imagine the creative principle and the preservative principle combining in a principle of transformation. In a text collected in the posthumous *Apodictic of Messianism*, Wronski describes the ensuing double polarisation as follows:

> The influence of Being within Knowledge introduces a sort of inertia into the spontaneity of Knowledge and gives to Knowledge the fixity of Being. Knowledge finds itself as conditioned as Being, and is submitted to fixed and determinate laws. [Conversely] the influence of Knowledge in Being introduces spontaneity into the inertia of Being and grants to Being the variability that belongs to Knowledge. Being now finds itself susceptible to modifications and determinations.[40]

There is no space here to account for how Wronski develops his four final components of his septenary: Universal Being (UE), Universal Knowledge (US), Transitive Being (TE) and Transitive Knowledge (TS). Suffice only to say that Wronski takes the doubling of Being in Knowledge and of Knowledge in Being to give him access to two inversely doubled series composed of properly 'intensive' relations. Warrain goes on to develop Wronski's theory of intensity at length throughout his work: 'intensity', he claims, must be grasped as 'the primordial state of quantity by virtue of which matter penetrates into the intelligible'.[41] The 'Law of Creation' is intended to express a dialectic that is inherent to 'spontaneous generation'.[42] It expresses the form of an ontological convulsion: each creative advance falls back into petrification or inertia, becoming its own opposite. But in turn, being is internally modified by spontaneity, tending to become *its* own opposite. Every act of creation is constrained by this fundamental dialectic. As living beings, Wronski and Warrain claim, we are caught in a gigantic, implicate order of determinations, our existence composed of multiple planes, physical, organic, psychic, each containing further, concentrated septenaries. Alexandrian says that Wronski 'deduced one hundred and eighty systems of reality interlinked by prolongation and ramification'[43] from his 'Law of Creation'. As *rational* living beings, we are able to penetrate the 'virtuality' of the real and elicit its lines of differentiation. In his 'messianic' meditations, Wronski imagines the daily lives of future rational beings as being governed by a weird kind of vitalist calculus, in which the petrification of knowledge itself (of Knowledge in Being and Being in Knowledge) can be countered by generating creative possibilities through algorithmic thought.

Why was Wronski so entranced by the philosophical potential of serial, exponential mathematical forms (expansionary and geometrical series, etc.)?[44] In 1810, he had presented his *The Supreme Law of Mathematics* [*La loi suprême des mathématiques*] to the Parisian Académie des Sciences. This work presented Wronski's claim to have discovered a supreme algorithm of mathematics, which he expressed thus:

$$Fx = A_0\Omega_0 + A_1\Omega_1 + A_2\Omega_2 + A_3\Omega_3 + \ldots$$

Wronski's later works contain fabulous engravings of radiating suns inscribed with this formula; in one the formula is inscribed on the plinth of the Sphinx. The Academy apparently made an acknowledgement that Wronski's formula encompassed all series expansions known until that time, including Taylor's theorem, but refused to grant the universality of Wronski's claim. Between 1810 and 1820, Wronski entered into a strange debate with some of the leading contemporary theorists of the calculus, such as Joseph-Louis Lagrange, who had just published his major work on the calculus, the *Theory of Analytic Functions* (1797). As Boyer puts it, Wronski 'protested with some asperity against the ban on the infinite in analysis which Lagrange had wished to impose. He criticised Lagrange not so much for the absence of logical rigour in his free manipulation of infinite series . . . as for his lack of a sufficiently broad view'.[45] Clearly, the possibility of mathematically expanding functions of one variable into a series excited something profound in Wronski, but he was not successful in communicating it to Lagrange and the Academy of Sciences. His insistence that his 'supreme algorithmic law' was 'not mathematically derived, but given by transcendental philosophy'[46] was probably the source of most of the confusion felt by Lagrange and Laplace when confronted with his tracts. Not being versed in recent developments in Kantian philosophical idealism, they could not see why calculus had this profound, awe-inspiring metaphysical significance for Wronski.

The one point Deleuze explicitly develops from Wronski in *Difference and Repetition* is this insistence on a 'Kantian interpretation of the calculus'. According to this interpretation, the differentials must be the objects of reason, not of the understanding. 'Finite quantities bear upon the objects of our knowledge, and infinitesimal quantities on the very generation of this knowledge; such that each of these two classes of knowledge must have laws proper [to them], and it is in the distinction between these laws that the major thesis of the metaphysics of infinitesimal calculus is to be found.'[47] It is only when calculus is taken as rigorously ideal in the Kantian sense that its relations with infinity and its ontological significance become apparent. Differentials have ontological value for Wronski precisely because they are *not* taken as empirically real, but are rather taken as absolutely *ideal*, as virtual curves composed of singularities.

In his *History of the Calculus*, Carl Boyer notes that Wronski was convinced this fundamental algorithm could *generate* pure quantities, prior to the positing of any empirical quantities:

> Wronski asserted that the differential calculus constituted a *primitive algorithm* governing the *generation* of quantities, rather than the laws of quantities *already formed*. Its propositions he held to be expressions of an absolute truth, and the deduction of its principles he consequently regarded as beyond the sphere of mathematics. The explication of the calculus by the methods of limits, of ultimate ratios, of vanishing quantities, of the theory of functions, he felt constituted but an indirect approach which proceeded from a false view of the new analysis.[48]

Deleuze's comments on Wronski take up these remarks by Boyer: 'if it is true that the understanding provides a "discontinuous summation", this is only the matter for the generation of quantities: it is only "graduation" or continuity that constitutes their form, which belongs to Ideas of reason'. And this, he goes on to say, is 'why differentials certainly do not correspond to any engendered quantity, but rather constitute an unconditioned rule for the production of knowledge of quantity, and for the construction of series or the generation of discontinuities which constitute its material' (DR 175).

Boyer goes on to remark on the fact that Wronski's implied 'direct approach' to the generation of quantities was through the elaboration of the concept of *intensive magnitudes*. He says that 'followers of this school of thought' (although he does not say who these followers were) 'were to attempt to retain the concept of the infinitely small, not as an extensive quantity but as an intensive magnitude'.[49] The Wronskians accepted that 'mathematics has excluded the fixed infinitely small because it has failed to establish the notion logically', but they drew attention to the fact that 'transcendental philosophy has sought to preserve primitive intuition in this respect by interpreting it as having an *a priori* metaphysical reality associated with the generation of magnitude'.[50] The Wronskians claim that the 'primitive intuition' of the 'fixed infinitely small' has a special *'a priori* metaphysical reality', one that, if elaborated in its full complexity, allows the transcendental philosopher to legitimately restore continuity to our discontinuous experience of things.

Deleuze's project in *Difference and Repetition* to produce a new synthetic *a priori* account of the relationship between Ideas and intensive difference appears to be in full conformity with this Wronskian trajectory. In his remark on Warrain in *Difference and Repetition* ('Warrain undertakes the necessary comparisons with the philosophy of Schelling'; DR 324), Deleuze indicates however that he considers an understanding of Schelling's account of the relationship between metaphysical and mathematical powers to be necessary in order to fully grasp what Wronski is doing in his synthesis of the ideal and the intensive. Deleuze's main references to Schelling are to the 1810 *Stuttgart Lectures* and to the drafts of the *Ages of the World*. In these lectures, Schelling had outlined the shift he envisaged from a dialectic of contradiction to a dialectic of powers. He stated that the 'transition from identity to difference has often been understood as a *cancellation of identity*; yet that is not at all the case . . . Much rather it is a doubling of the essence, and thus an intensification of the unity [*Steigerung der Einheit*].'[51] For Schelling, the notion of powers can help formulate how unity can be maintained throughout differentiation without being lost. Unity can be 'intensified'; 'power' is the key to the *Steigerung der Einheit*. The merely negative relations of the concept will now be undergirded by metaphysical use of the mathematics of power. Using the notion of power, differentiation no longer implies a cancellation of identity, but a doubling, an intensification, formally expressed through the mathematical notion of power. Here Schelling too is taking up Boehme's idea that the cosmos is to be understood as an *involution*[52] of ideality into matter, followed by progressive *evolution* back upward to ideality. This movement of intensive doubling through power appears to provide a new model of dialectical transformation, capable of incorporating Hegelian *Aufhebung* within a vertical, progressive hierarchy. The preservation of a vertical (and 'virtual') hierarchy of 'powers' allows for a greater, more living Absolute than the Hegelian model, which has no effective virtuality.

The importance of Wronski's philosophy hinges on his elaboration of a dimension of 'creative virtuality' [*virtualité créatrice*] proper to the Absolute.[53] And whereas Schelling increasingly came to focus on the mythological origins of human thought, Wronski instead trained his vision on the possibilities for future existence opened up by the discovery of achrematic thought.

Wronski's major tome, *Messianism*, published in 1831 (subtitled *The Final Union of Philosophy and Religion, Constituting the Absolute Philosophy* [*Messianisme: Union finale de la philosophie et de la religion, constituent la philosophie absolute*]),[54] proposed that human evolution should be divided into a series of epochs, in which human beings become progressively conscious of their powers of reason. Wronski believed he was writing in the thick of a 'critical' and transitional epoch, in which human beings start to come to consciousness of the role of the mind in shaping their experience of nature. The critical epoch was making possible a new kind of 'comprehensive consciousness', with a special 'transcendental' dimension, in which awareness of the rules of thought themselves can be generated. Wronski was convinced that it was possible to deduce from this a future, higher destination of consciousness. In the epoch of the Absolute (the sixth and seventh periods of human historical development), 'human reason will exercise the full plenitude of its creativity, will recognise in its reason the virtuality of creation, and will obtain within itself the clear and immanent consciousness of the Word';[55] the seventh stage will herald the 'reproduction of the accomplishment of the creation of the universe'.[56] In this final stage, there will be absolute consciousness or consciousness through creativity itself.

Taking up the perspective of a realised Kantianism, Wronskian Messianism resonated with the call that we bring about an epochal shift in relation to traditional meanings of what constitutes 'reality'. As D'Arcy puts it, 'Wronski sensed that an epoch in which one defines reality by inertia is an epoch which has fundamentally chosen, in the domain of thought, stupidity and death.'[57] Wronski believed that he had glimpsed the possibility of a future transformation of critical consciousness, in which we will come to grasp our given, *discontinuous* experiences as fragments of a greater, continuous self-differentiation of creative becoming, and embark on the process of situating ourselves in relation to its curve, isolating its levels or planes, its bifurcations and ramifications, its rotatory spirals. In order to clarify further the true, 'ideal' *matter* of this peculiar 'calculus', we turn finally to Warrain's explicitly vitalistic version of Wronskianism.

FRANCIS WARRAIN ON DIFFERENCE AND REPETITION IN WRONSKI'S LAW
OF CREATION

Wronski's idea of a post-Kantian 'philosophy of creation' was not without its internal problems. In the recently unearthed lecture series *What is Grounding?*, Deleuze himself notes emphatically that post-Kantianism replaces all rationalist and theological versions of 'the idea of creation' with new concepts modelled around the demands of 'constitutive finitude'.[58] Wronski's philosophy only manages to save the notion of 'creation' for post-Kantianism by grounding it in the productivity of practical reason (and despite what he says in *What is Grounding?* Deleuze too will go on to make qualified use of the notion of creation in his discussions of artistic and philosophical activity). Nevertheless, Wronski suggests throughout his numerous tables of the 'Law of Creation' that this 'Law' can be multiplied and diversified through a series of implicate orders, that one can ascribe an identical 'spontaneity' and 'creativity' to reality itself insofar as it is engaged in a process of quantifiable becoming or development, and that along with processes such as cultural formation (*Bildung*), physical 'vital' processes, including sexual reproduction, are instances of this identical 'creativity' in nature itself. But how is this to be understood? How is the 'creativity' of sexual reproduction analogous to the 'creativity' of practical reason? Can an ideal creative virtuality be ascribed to organic processes *per se*, or is the meaning of such an ascription dependent on the status of such processes as material fore-shadowings of the achrematic essence of the law of creation, which, as Wronski indicates in his 'messianic' theory, only emerges *de facto* in human history?

In his 1906 work *Concrete Synthesis*, Warrain elaborates Wronski's 'philosophy of creation' as a metaphysical theory of 'evolution' and 'life' (the subtitle of the book is *A Study in the Metaphysics of Life*).[59] As we recalled at the outset, in his own vitalist works (contemporary with Warrain's), Bergson defends the idea that the term 'life' can be applied to non-biological phenomena insofar as they are 'creative' (as, for instance, in the intensive states of energy in the inflationary period of the formation of the universe). Explicitly *contra* Bergson, Warrain takes up the project of producing a Wronskian vitalism of *non-organic life*. What Wronski's philosophy shows us, he claims, is that the life of 'organisms' is really the *vessel* for a true, metaphysi-cal, non-organic 'life' that can be ascribed rather to *vibration* and *rhythm*. This non-organic life is eminently mathematicisable, since it is fundamentally composed of vibratory movements which can be expressed in mathematical terms. If the world is mathematicisable, Warrain argues, that is because it vibrates. 'Movement is the mathematical expression of Life; it is the synthesis of algorithm and geometry. Vibration is the physical expression of Life; it is the synthesis of action and resistance.'[60] In his 1907 *Space*, Warrain goes on to develop an elaborate non-Euclidean theory of space and of the evolution of the universe (more than twenty years before Einstein combined Riemannian geometry with relativity physics to produce the general theory of relativity). In one of the first chapters, entitled 'Characteristics of Non-Euclidean Spaces', Warrain outlines the nature of 'The Curve in Non-Euclidean Spaces':

> One could say that the two spaces of Riemann and Lobatschewsky are the characteristics of *the curve as such*, taken in its first principle. The curve is that which corresponds to the presence of an extrinsic influence on an object which is developing in extension. Whether one considers a psychic perception or a mechanical realisation, there is only a curve where a determining condition of the line is not constantly in the same relation with this line. Differential calculus answers to this notion through the correspondence which it establishes necessarily between the curve and the functions of derived variables.[61]

For Warrain, Wronski is the discoverer of a 'mathematics of life', the object of which is not the organism as such, but movement itself, considered in its complex and implicate structure of vibration and rhythm.

Warrain's account in *Concrete Synthesis* of the nature of Wronski's central algorithm is especially intriguing for our purposes, due to the key role it gives to the concepts of 'difference' and 'repetition'. He argues that it is 'the combination of Repetition and Differentiation [*différenciation*]' that 'leads to Organization, which is the means by which the being gets the power to persist and progress across Time and Space'.[62] He goes on to elaborate constructions of geometrical and mathematical forms, of elementary 'rhythms' that govern the development and periodic convulsions of living organisms, and of the complex 'vibrations' that compose thought itself,[63] culminating in the products of thought, machines and works of art. Wronski's supreme 'Law of Creation' provides the basic schema, he says, for this combinatory process of repetition and differentiation: '*Every Repetition presents itself originarily in the form of the mixed algorithm of reproduction*', states Warrain, explaining that in his 'mathematics of life', 'Wronski traces every algorithm back to the three fundamental algorithms,

that is, to the opposition between Summation (discontinuous generation) and Gradation (continuous generation), reconnected through a
neutralising algorithm, Reproduction'.[64] With these three algorithms
for summation, gradation and reproduction, one can then generate
an entire system of algorithms, taking the fullest advantage of the
connections made possible by the vertical power series generated
for each function. Warrain's elucidation of this 'algorithm' is worth
citing in full:

> Every repetition presents itself originarily under the form of this
> mixed algorithm of reproduction. In appearance, it is an increasing
> juxtaposition of similar elements; in reality, it operates through the
> continuous growth of a single element which pluralises its type; in its
> act it is a veritable graduation. And, if the reunion of these similar
> unities furnishes a sum, the multiplicity of this same type expresses
> the power [*puissance*] of this type. But, from the fact that this power
> is manifested explicitly, no longer in intensive unities, but in an
> elementary plurality – division follows; here we find simple genera-
> tion through cellular reproduction. 'Repetition therefore expresses
> the transposition of the continuous energy that characterises immate-
> rial force in the discontinuity of the resistances which define matter.
> And the exponent or logarithm marks the degree of continuity, the
> measure in which matter has enfolded itself [*la mesure dans laquelle
> la matière a pu s'y plier*], the degree of penetration of life in matter,
> its hierarchical level [*son rang hiérarchique*] . . . And the more
> complex the organism becomes, the more Repetition is replaced by
> Differentiation, proliferation by structure, assimilation by functions
> of relation.[65]

For Warrain, a vitalistic theory of 'evolution' must reconstruct the
algorithmic patterns of repetition or 'reproduction' which bring about
ever more complex resolutions of the fundamental, 'mathematical'
polarisation between ideal continuity and discontinuous summation.
At the limit, 'life in its perfect form consists in the absolute continuity
of these degrees and in the infinity of orders of synthetic relations'.[66]
On Warrain's Wronskian architectonic, life is composed of a series of
levels of reality, each a rhythmical and dynamic compromise between
continuity and discontinuity, each with its own 'universal problem'
[*problème universel*] (how to find a dynamic equilibrium for opposing
forces), each with its own secret harmonies. For Warrain, this 'life'
is the true matter of the transcendental calculus. In order to find out
whether this is also true of Deleuze's own 'gnoseological' and 'esoteric' theory of calculus, and to assess whether it succeeds in escaping the potential ambiguities of Wronski's own theory of creation,

a renewed reading of Chapter 4 of *Difference and Repetition* in the light of further research into the ideas of Wronski and Warrain, in all their peculiarity and 'untimeliness', is required.

Middlesex University

Notes

1. The third 'star' in the esoteric history of the calculus, Bordas-Desmoulin, seems to have a less important role than Maimon and Wronski. See Simon Duffy, 'Schizo-Math: The logic of different/ciation and the philosophy of difference', *Angelaki: Journal of the Theoretical Humanities* 9:3 (2004), pp. 199–215 for a brief account of his contribution.

2. The main proponents in this dispute appear to be Nicholas Landur and Lazare Augé, who wrote tracts on Wronski's philosophy in the period following his death.

3. Paul Chacornac, *Eliphas Lévi: Rénovateur de l'occultisme en France* (Paris: Chacornac, 1926), pp. 131–9; Christopher McIntosh, *Eliphas Lévi and the French Occult Revival* (London: Rider, 1972), pp. 96–100; Thomas A. Williams, *Eliphas Lévi: Master of Occultism* (Alabama: University of Alabama, 1975), pp. 66–70. Lévi's references to Wronski are scant and ambiguous, however, apart from one passage in *Doctrine and Ritual of High Magic*, where he indicates his debt to Wronski. Cf. Eliphas Lévi, *Transcendental Magic* (London: Rider, 1896 [1855]), pp. 52, 30–5. Lévi is more critical of Wronski in his 1860 *History of Magic* (Eliphas Lévi, *History of Magic*, trans. A.E. Waite (London: Rider, 1913 [1860]), pp. 330–2), but his criticism focuses on Wronski's paranoiac behaviour.

4. See Christian Kerslake, 'The Somnambulist and the Hermaphrodite: Deleuze, Johann Malfatti de Montereggio and Occultism', *Culture Machine*, 'Interzone' section (2007).

5. Sarane Alexandrian, *Histoire de la philosophie occulte* (Paris: Seghers, 1983), pp. 109–39.

6. Alexandrian, *Histoire de la philosophie*, p. 133.

7. Alexandrian, *Histoire de la philosophie*, p. 133.

8. Piotr Pragacz, 'Notes on the Life and Work of Józef Maria Hoene-Wronski,' Institute of Mathematics of the Polish Academy of Sciences, available online: www.impan.gov.pl/-pragacz/download, p. 14.

9. Matila Ghyka, *Le nombre d'or: rites et rhythmes pythagoriciens dans le développement de la civilisation occidentale*, Tome 1: Les rythmes; Tome 2: Les rites (Paris: Gallimard, 2000 [1959]). See, in particular, Tome 2, pp. 151–86.

10. Francis Warrain (ed.) *L'oeuvre philosophique de Hoëne Wronski*, three volumes (Paris: Vega, 1933).

11. Francis Warrain, *La synthèse concrète* (Paris: Chacornac, 1910 [1906]), p. 33.
12. Henri Bergson, *L'évolution créatrice* (Paris: Felix Alcan, 1910), p. 26.
13. Warrain, *La synthèse concrète*, p. 131; emphasis added.
14. Warrain, *La synthèse concrète*, p. 156.
15. Warrain, *La synthèse concrète*, p. 157.
16. Warrain, *La synthèse concrète*, p. 126.
17. For a reproduction of the diagram, and a more detailed account of Wronski and Warrain, see Christian Kerslake, *Deleuze and the Problem of Immanence: Kant, Post-Kantianism and the Philosophy of Difference* (Edinburgh: Edinburgh University Press, 2008).
18. Francis Warrain, *L'Espace* (Paris: Fischbacher, 1907), p. 123.
19. Francis Warrain, *L'Armature métaphysique de Hoëne Wronski* (Paris: Alcan, 1925), pp. 186–7, 194; cf. Warrain, *La synthèse concrète*, pp. 182–5.
20. Warrain, *L'Espace*, p. 5.
21. Warrain, *La synthèse concrète*, p. 130.
22. Józef-Maria Hoëne Wronski, *Messianisme: Union finale de la philosophie et de la religion, constituent la philosophie absolue* (Paris: Depot des ouvrages de l'auteur, 1831), p. 71.
23. Cited in McIntosh, *Eliphas Lévi*, pp. 97–8.
24. Pragacz, 'Notes . . .', p. 3.
25. Pragacz, 'Notes . . .', p. 3.
26. Z. Zalewski, 'Introduction', in Warrain (ed.) *L'oeuvre philosophique de Hoëne Wronski*, p. iv; cf. Alexandrian, *Histoire de la philosophie*, p. 134.
27. Alexandrian, *Histoire de la philosophie*, p. 134.
28. He was preceded by Charles Villers' *Philosophie de Kant* (1801). Wronski's work gets a nominal mention in J.E. Erdmann's classic idealist history of philosophy, *A History of Philosophy*, 3 volumes, trans. W.S. Hough (London: George Allen & Unwin, 1890), Vol. II, p. 435.
29. Cited in Alexandrian, *Histoire de la philosophie*, p. 135.
30. Józef-Maria Hoëne Wronski, *Philosophie de l'infini: contenant des contre-refléxions sur la métaphysique du calcul infinitésimal* (Paris: Depot des ouvrages de l'auteur, 1814), p. 35; cited in Michael Blay, *Reasoning with the Infinite: From the Closed World to the Mathematical Universe* (Chicago: University of Chicago, 1998), p. 158.
31. Warrain, *La synthèse concrète*, p. 143.
32. In Warrain (ed.), *L'oeuvre philosophique*, vol. 1, p. 60.
33. Gilles Deleuze, *La philosophie critique de Kant* (Paris: PUF, 1963), p. 72.
34. Phillipe D'Arcy, *Wronski: Philosophie de la creation. Présentation, choix de textes* (Paris: Seghers, 1970).

35. Cf. Józef-Maria Hoëne Wronski, *Apodictique Messianique* (Paris: Depot des ouvrages de l'auteur, 1876), p. 4.
36. D'Arcy, *Wronski*, p. 5.
37. Warrain, *La synthèse concrète*, p. 186.
38. Cf. Warrain, *La synthèse concrète*, p. 186.
39. Warrain, *La synthèse concrète*, p. 186.
40. Wronski, *Apodictique Messianique*, p. 9; cited in Warrain, *La synthèse concrète*, p. 174.
41. Warrain, *L'Armature métaphysique*, p. 279; cf. 'The comparison of that which is qualified with that which remains unqualified consists in establishing the relative predominance of Quality or Quantity, of activity or of resistance, and, in its first indistinct and primitive result, is what constitutes Intensity. Intensity, magnitude and number are the three modes of Quantity. And we see that Quantity results from the first contact of spiritual activity with material passivity, and that it rests on the divisional multiplication of the One-All' (Warrain, *L'Espace*, p. 6).
42. Wronski, *Apodictique Messianique*, p. 1.
43. Alexandrian, *Histoire de la philosophie*, pp. 134–5.
44. Deleuze remarks that power series are essential to the calculus. 'Power is the form of reciprocal determination according to which variable magnitudes are taken to be functions of one another. In consequence, calculus considers only those magnitudes where at least one is of a power superior to another' (DR 174).
45. Carl Boyer, *The History of the Calculus and its Conceptual Development* (New York: Dover, 1949), p. 261.
46. Boyer, *History of the Calculus*, p. 261.
47. Wronski, *Philosophie de l'infini*, p. 35, cited in Blay, *Reasoning with the Infinite*, p. 158.
48. Boyer, *History of the Calculus*, p. 262.
49. Boyer, *History of the Calculus*, p. 263.
50. Boyer, *History of the Calculus*, p. 263.
51. F. W. J. Schelling, 'Stuttgart Lectures', trans. T. Pfau, in Schelling, *Idealism and the Endgame of Theory* (Albany: SUNY, 1994 [1810]), p. 425.
52. Schelling, 'Stuttgart Lectures', pp. 440–1.
53. Deleuze alludes to Schelling's theory of powers in a fascinating passage of *Difference and Repetition* (DR 191).
54. It was divided into a *Prodrome to Messianism* (Vol. 1) and a *Messianic Metapolitics* (*Métapolitique messianique*) (Vol. 2, published in 1839).
55. Józef-Maria Hoëne Wronski, *Messianisme, ou Réforme absolue du savoir humain* (Paris: Depot des ouvrages de l'auteur, 1847), Vol. I, p. 56; cited in Auguste Viatte, *Les sources occultes du Romantisme*, two volumes (Paris: Honoré Champion, 1928), Vol. II, p. 254.

56. Józef-Maria Hoëne Wronski, *Prospectus de la philosophie absolue et son développement* (Paris: Depot des ouvrages de l'auteur, 1878), p. 73.

57. D'Arcy, *Wronski*, p. 5.

58. Post-Kantian systematic philosophy 'does not claim to occupy the place of God . . . When Hegel talks of an absolute knowledge he says to us that "this reveals to us no other world than our own". Absolute knowledge is knowledge of this world here. What is involved here is the substitution of the transcendental imagination for the infinite intellect. The systematic point of view replaces the concept of the infinite intellect with the transcendental imagination that belongs to constitutive finitude. So many notions can no longer be conserved. For instance, the notion of creation, which is a theological idea which can only be understood starting from the postulation of an infinite intellect and will. If the latter falls, then the concept of creation cannot be maintained. It is absurd for an atheist to conserve the idea of creation because he cannot avail himself any longer of concepts that are inseparable from the idea of God. From that moment on, philosophy, in its difference from theology, and *as* philosophy, cannot recover the idea of creation. Gilles Deleuze, 'What is Grounding?', available online http://www.webdeleuze.com/php/texte.p hp?cle=218&groupe=Conf%E9rences&langue=1, p. 40.

59. In his 'Exposition of Wronski's System of Reality', an appendix to *Concrete Synthesis*, Warrain remarks that 'the transitive elements are of the highest importance from our point of view in this study'; that is, in the study of what he calls 'life'. In Transitive Being (TE), Being 'makes a function of Knowledge'; while in Transitive Knowledge (TS), 'Knowledge manifests itself as Being' (Warrain, *La synthèse concrète*, p. 182). Warrain states that these two transitive elements 'correspond to that which constitutes life in matter. We find in them the point of transformation of the universal into the individual, of alterity into ipseity, the transformation of spiritual energies into material forms and movements, and finally the passage from quantity to quality' (Warrain, *La synthèse concrète*, p. 173).

60. Warrain, *La synthèse concrète*, p. 126.

61. Warrain, *L'Espace*, pp. 37–8.

62. Warrain, *La synthèse concrète*, p. 32.

63. Warrain, *La synthèse concrète*, pp. 127, 153.

64. Warrain, *La synthèse concrète*, p. 33.

65. Warrain, *L'Espace*, pp. 34–5.

66. Warrain, *L'Espace*, p. 131.

10

Bernhard Riemann

Arkady Plotnitsky

Mathematics played a major role in Gilles Deleuze's thought, beginning with his engagement with calculus and Gottfried Leibniz, who was also a major *philosophical* influence on Deleuze. Bernhard Riemann may, however, be the most significant *mathematical* influence on Deleuze, especially in his later works, such as the *Cinema* books, and in his collaborations with Félix Guattari. The conjunction of Riemann's mathematics and Deleuze's philosophy is a remarkable event in the history of twentieth-century philosophy, and it has major implications for our understanding of the relationships between mathematics and Deleuze's thought, and between mathematics and philosophy in general. Riemann's thought, however, is also part of the *philosophical*, and not simply *mathematical*, lineage of Deleuze's thought. Born from philosophy with the pre-Socratics, mathematics has a great philosophical potential, even though this potential is not always utilised in the disciplinary practice of mathematics. Riemann's work represents one of the greatest cases of exploring this potential and creating it, to begin with, in part by fusing philosophical ideas, such as those extending from post-Kantian philosophy, with his mathematical thinking. Deleuze, I would argue, takes advantage of both Riemann's mathematical and philosophical concepts in building his own philosophical concepts. Thus, the relationship between Riemann and Deleuze not only represents a remarkable conjunction of mathematics and philosophy but also establishes a philosophical friendship, as Deleuze and Guattari see it in *What is Philosophy?* (WP 4–5, 9–10).

MATHEMATICS AND PHILOSOPHY IN RIEMANN

Bernhard Riemann (1826–66) was one of the greatest mathematicians of the nineteenth century and one of the greatest mathematicians who ever lived. His work rivals and sometimes outshines even that of such legendary figures as Sir Isaac Newton, Karl Friedrich Gauss (Riemann's teacher) and Evariste Galois, before him, and

Henri Poincaré and David Hilbert after him (often listed, along with Riemann, as the greatest mathematicians of the modern era). Riemann's ideas, moreover, had arguably the greatest impact (even compared to those of Poincaré and Hilbert, his main competitors in this respect) on mathematics in the twentieth and twenty-first centuries. Riemann also made a significant philosophical contribution, perhaps comparable to that of other mathematicians such as Pythagoras and Euclid, whose ideas have had, and continue to exert, a powerful philosophical impact. In particular, we can see the import of Riemann's non-Euclideanism on Deleuze. This claim concerning Riemann's philosophical contribution is somewhat unorthodox and requires qualification.

Although his extraordinary mathematical capabilities became apparent early on, Riemann, who was born to a Lutheran pastor's family, was initially trained in philology and theology. Later in his life he became well versed in post-Kantian German philosophy. These theological and philosophical (and earlier philological) interests had their impact on his mathematical ideas. Riemann, however, was not a philosopher, unlike, say, Descartes and Leibniz who, by and large, practised philosophy and mathematics as separate fields of inquiry, although their thought was shaped by a complex traffic between both fields. Riemann's philosophical concepts were developed primarily through his mathematical concepts. This may of course also be said of Descartes' and Leibniz's mathematical concepts, or of those of other mathematicians such as those listed above. But Riemann's capacity for developing and utilising this philosophical potential of mathematics is especially remarkable and his significance for Deleuze in this respect is unmatched – although Leibniz, Galois, Niels Henrik Abel, and Karl Weierstrass make similar contributions to Deleuze's work.

In his short mathematical career (he died of tuberculosis at the age of forty), Riemann made fundamental contributions to most areas of modern mathematics – algebra, analysis, geometry, topology and number theory. It would be impossible to do justice to these contributions even from the more limited philosophical perspective of this essay. One might argue, however, that from this perspective and as concerns his significance for Deleuze's philosophy Riemann's greatest contributions are, first, his concept of spatiality, and, secondly, his capacity of combining different fields in approaching problems apparently belonging to a single field. What I call non-Euclideanism, mathematical or philosophical, is conceived on the model of Riemann's thought and practice, as defined by these two phenomena.

Riemann's concept of spatiality as manifoldness allows one to define certain spaces as patchwork-like assemblages of local spaces, without, in general, the overall space possessing the same type of structure as these local subspaces do, while the latter may differ from each other as well. These qualities give a Riemannian space heterogeneity, which is, however, interconnected by virtue of the overlapping between local spaces. In particular, these local spaces can be considered as infinitesimally Euclidean, while the overall space is, in general, not a Euclidean space. The overall space may be given a global determination. In particular, it may be given an overall metrical structure, determined by the formula for measuring the distance between points that varies locally and that, infinitesimally (that is, when the two points in question are close to each other), converts itself into the formula for measuring distances in the Euclidean space. Such a space may have a constant curvature, as for example in the case of a two-dimensional sphere, which is a Riemannian manifold, or it can be a space as variable curvature, similar to a rolling-hill landscape. The Euclidean space of a given dimension, such as the two-dimensional plane or three-dimensional space as we ordinarily perceive them, would be trivial cases of manifoldness in which both the local spaces involved and the overall spaces are Euclidean. Modern mathematics considers spaces, whether Euclidean or Riemannian, of any number of dimensions, including the infinite-dimensional spaces, and Riemann considered such spaces as well.

The second main component of non-Euclideanism is defined by the theoretical practice – mathematical or philosophical – of combining different fields in approaching objects defined or problems formulated within, and apparently belonging to, a single field. Riemann's concept of a manifold was developed by bringing together algebra, analysis and geometry, and thus by means of a multiple or *manifold* – heterogeneous yet interactive – theoretical practice that he deployed and expanded throughout his work. Riemann's multi-field approach to mathematical problems exemplifies the rise of a new type of mathematical practice, defined by the multiply interactive and yet heterogeneous workings of different mathematical fields – geometry, topology, algebra, analysis, and so forth – in dealing with a single concept or problem, without there necessarily being a wholeness or oneness governing this multiplicity. One can thus easily perceive shared features in the 'space' of practice and in Riemann's concept of spatiality as manifoldness, and certain aspects of Riemann's thinking are manifest in both. While it would be difficult to simply map

Riemann's concept of spatiality onto his practice, this type of spatial thinking and this type of practice often go hand in hand and variously overlap, and hence can partially map each other, in non-Euclidean thinking, whether mathematical, such as that of Riemann, or philosophical, such as that of Deleuze.

Thus understood, mathematical non-Euclideanism extends far beyond the ideas that led to the alternative geometries with which the term 'non-Euclidean' originated, important as their discovery in early 1800s was in this context. Riemann discovered one type of such geometries – those of positive curvature. There are also those of negative curvature, and Euclidean geometry itself has zero curvature, that is, is flat. Riemann's concept of the manifold allowed him to encompass both Euclidean and non-Euclidean geometry within a single more general concept, which also enabled it to serve as the mathematical basis for Einstein's non-Newtonian theory of gravity, known as general relativity. One finds certain ingredients of non-Euclideanian plural practice in ancient Greek mathematics, specifically in the relationships between arithmetic and geometry. Indeed, the unresolved complexity of these relationships has continued to haunt mathematics ever since, with algebra having eventually supplanted arithmetic, and Riemann's thought and his concept of manifolds reflect this complexity. Nevertheless, the eruptive emergence of plural mathematics on a large scale in the early 1800s, roughly at the time of Gauss (Riemann's teacher and precursor in this respect as well), was one of the most significant developments in the history of mathematics. One finds this mathematics at work throughout the nineteenth century and then, with ever increasing effectiveness, in the twentieth and twenty-first centuries.[1]

Riemann's thought is among the greatest early manifestations of non-Euclideanism not only in mathematics but also in philosophy, using the term philosophy in Deleuze and Guattari's sense of the invention of new concepts, or even concepts 'that are always new' (WP 5). This sense is also defined by a different *concept* of the philosophical concept itself. A philosophical concept is not an entity established by a generalisation from particulars or 'any general or abstract idea' (WP 11–12, 24) but a multi-layered conglomerate entity: 'there are no simple concepts. Every concept has components and is defined by them. It therefore has a combination [*chiffre*]. It is a multiplicity [manifold(ness)?] . . . There is no concept with only one component' (WP 16). Each concept is a multi-component conglomeration of concepts (in their conventional senses), figures, metaphors, and so forth,

which form a unity or have, as Deleuze's own concepts often do, a
more heterogeneous, if interactive, architecture that is not unifiable.
The architecture of Deleuze and Guattari's concept of the concept
is itself defined in part by Riemannian spatiality as manifoldness by
linking the very invention of philosophical concepts to a spatial and,
in part, Riemannian concept – the plane of immanence – thus making
the space of functioning of a given concept a Riemannian space. This
concept of a concept is traceable to Deleuze's earlier texts, and the
activity of creating concepts may be seen as defining Deleuze's work.
Equally significantly, each concept is also seen as a problem, another
hallmark of Deleuze's philosophy. From *Difference and Repetition*
to *What is Philosophy?*, philosophical thinking is seen, on a mathematical model, as *problematic* (thinking defined by posing problems)
rather than *theorematic* (thinking proceeding by deriving propositions from axioms according to proscribed rules, in the manner of
Euclid's *Elements*, rather than by posing problems). *Difference and
Repetition* appeals to Abel's and Galois' mathematical or, again,
mathematical-philosophical practice as paradigmatic examples, and
states that 'Ideas are essentially "problematic"', while 'conversely,
problems are ideas' (DR 168).

   Certain forms of mathematical thought, such as that of Riemann,
may be seen in Deleuze and Guattari's philosophical terms. That is,
one can extend to mathematical thinking, as Deleuze and Guattari in
effect do, their definition of philosophical thinking and of philosophical concepts themselves, even though, as I shall discuss presently, they
are also right to stress the disciplinary difference between mathematics and philosophy (WP 117–18). According to Deleuze:

> There are two sorts of scientific concepts. Even though they get mixed
> up in particular cases. There are concepts that are exact in nature,
> quantitative, defined by equations, and whose very meaning lies in
> their exactness: a philosopher or writer can use these only metaphori-
> cally, and that's quite wrong, because they belong to exact science.
> But there are also essentially inexact yet completely rigorous concepts
> that scientists can't do without, which belong equally to scientists,
> philosophers, and artists. They have to be made rigorous in a way
> that's not directly scientific, so that when a scientist manages to do
> this he becomes a philosopher, an artist, too. This sort of concept's
> not unspecific because something's missing but because of its nature
> and content. (N 29, translation modified)

Thus, a *philosophical* concept corresponding to a mathematical or
scientific object could also be discovered by mathematics and science,

now working as philosophy on Deleuze and Guattari's definition. Thus, as they contend, 'when an object – a geometrical space, for example – is scientifically constructed by functions, its philosophical concept, which is by no means given in the function, must still be discovered' (WP 117). On the other hand, it is a complex question where and how, and in what order of invention, among mathematics, physics and philosophy, a given philosophical concept of space, say, Euclidean or Riemannian, has emerged. In particular, Riemann may be seen as primarily responsible not only for many key mathematical (geometrical and topological) features of his concept of space as manifold but also for many of its key philosophical aspects, even though both Leibniz before him and Einstein after him contributed significantly on both scores. Deleuze's appeal to the numerical or quantitative nature of scientific concepts may have been made with the question of mathematical versus philosophical spatiality, and Riemann as well as Bergson, in mind. Deleuze and Guattari juxtapose the (qualitative) concept of distance and the (quantitative) concept of magnitude, related to the juxtaposition (due to Pierre Boulez) of the smooth and the striated spaces in *A Thousand Plateaus* (TP 483–4). Similarly to Deleuze and Guattari's use of Riemann's concept of manifoldness, Bergson's duration may be seen as, in part, a distillation of an inexact, qualitative concept from Riemann's 'metric manifoldness or the manifoldness of magnitude' (TP 483; translation modified).[2]

Hence, Deleuze is both cautious concerning the use of mathematics and science in philosophy, and yet also defends its use. As he says in *Cinema 2* – which, like *Cinema 1* (guided by Bergson's philosophy), uses the idea of Riemannian spaces, to which this statement also refers:

> We realize the danger of citing scientific propositions outside their own sphere. It is the danger of arbitrary metaphor or of forced application. But perhaps these dangers are averted if we restrict ourselves to taking from scientific operators a particular conceptualizable character which itself refers to non-scientific areas, and converge with science without applying it or making it [simply] a metaphor. (TI 129)

PHILOSOPHY AND MATHEMATICS IN DELEUZE AND GUATTARI

In *What is Philosophy?* Deleuze and Guattari define thought in terms of its confrontation with chaos, a great enemy and a great friend of thought and its indispensable ally in its yet greater struggle against opinion, *doxa* (WP 201–2). Mathematics or science, philosophy and art, are particular forms of thought in this confrontation (WP 118, 201–18). Chaos itself is given a particular concept as well:

> Chaos is defined not so much by its disorder as by the infinite speed with which every form taking shape in it vanishes. It is a void that is not a nothingness but a *virtual*, containing all possible *particles* and drawing out all possible forms, which spring up only to disappear immediately, without consistency or reference, without consequence. (WP 118)

The difference between philosophical and scientific, including mathematical, thinking, as confrontation with chaos, is defined by their determination in terms of, respectively, concepts and functions. (Mathematically, functions rigorously relate numbers or other entities to each other according to specified rules.) According to Deleuze and Guattari:

> The object of science is not concepts but rather functions that are presented as propositions in discursive systems. The elements of functions are called *functives*. A scientific notion is defined not by concepts but by functions or propositions. This is a very complex idea with many aspects, as can be seen already from the use to which it is put by mathematics and biology respectively. Nevertheless, it is this idea of the function that enables the sciences to reflect and communicate. Science does not need philosophy for these tasks. On the other hand, when an object – a geometrical space, for example – is scientifically constructed by functions, its philosophical concept, which is by no means given in the function, must still be discovered. Furthermore, a concept may take as its components the functives of any possible function without thereby having the least scientific value, but with the aim marking the differences in kind between concepts and functions. . . . Philosophy wants to know how to retain the infinite speed while gaining consistency, by *giving the virtual a consistency specific to it*. The philosophical sieve, as a plane of immanence that cuts though chaos, selects infinite movements of thought and is filled with concepts formed like consistent *particles* going as fast as thought. Science approaches chaos in a completely different, almost opposite way: it relinquishes the infinite, infinite speed, in order to gain *a reference able to actualize the virtual*. By retaining the infinite, philosophy gives consistency to the virtual through *concepts*; by relinquishing the infinite, science gives a reference to the virtual, which actualizes it through *functions*. Philosophy proceeds with a plane of immanence and consistency; science with a plane of reference. In the case of science it is like a freeze-frame. It is a fantastic *slowing down*. (WP 117–18; translation slightly modified)

Philosophy's thought, thus, tries to hold to a concept that traverses a plane of immanence with the infinite speed of thought and to give this plane consistency. The plane of immanence is itself a complex multi-component philosophical concept (WP 35–61). The main point here is that, in contrast to philosophy, science 'freezes' chaos in slow motion or freeze-frames – sometimes, especially in physics, literally photographs the physical processes considered. By so doing science creates a plane of reference or co-ordination that it requires as science.

While, however, the differences between philosophy and science, or between either and art, appear to be irreducible, the interaction between them appears to be unavoidable as well. Thus, philosophy's thought may sometimes *hold* to a virtual concept by slowing-down or freeze-framing it. Conversely, science sometimes proceeds with the philosophical infinite speed on (and by creating) the plane of immanence, in order to create a *philosophical* concept corresponding to a mathematical or scientific object or in order to create this object. Philosophy and science appear to need each other, as Deleuze and Guattari say in closing their discussion of the difference between philosophy and science in *What is Philosophy?* According to them:

> If philosophy has a fundamental need for the science that is contemporary with it, this is because science constantly intersects with the possibility of concepts and because concepts necessarily involve allusions to science that are neither examples nor applications, nor even reflections. Conversely, are there functions – properly scientific functions – of concepts? This amounts to asking whether science is, as we believe, equally and intensely in need of philosophy. But only scientists can answer that question. (WP 162)

The answer, I would argue, would be positive, at least if one asks good scientists. Deleuze and Guattari suggest as much in closing their book, by noting that science at least 'tries' to create 'functions of concepts, as Lautman demonstrates for mathematics insofar as the latter actualizes virtual concepts' (WP 217).

MANIFOLDS IN RIEMANN AND DELEUZE AND GUATTARI

According to Riemann, in his habilitation lecture 'On the Hypotheses which Lie at the Bases of Geometry', which introduced the ideas of manifold and Riemannian geometry:

The concepts of magnitude are only possible where there is an antecedent general concept which admits of different specializations. According as there exists among these specializations a continuous path from one to another or not, they form a *continuous* or *discrete* manifoldness [*Mannigfaltigkeit*]; the individual specializations are called in the first case points, in the second case elements, of the manifoldness. Concepts whose specializations form a *discrete* manifoldness are so common that at least in the cultivated languages any things being given it is always possible to find a concept in which they are included. . . . On the other hand, so few and far between are the occasions for forming concepts whose specializations make up a *continuous* manifoldness, that the only simple concepts whose specializations form a multiply extended manifoldness are the positions of perceived objects and colours. More frequent occasions for the creation and development of these concepts occur first in the higher mathematics.[3]

Riemann thus defines manifolds not in terms of ontologically pre-given assemblies, 'sets', of points and relations between them, but in terms of concepts. Each concept has a particular mode of determination, such as a discrete versus a continuous manifold, whose elements, such as points, are related through this determination. Thus, beyond giving an essential priority to thinking and specifically to thinking in concepts over calculational or algorithmic approaches – to the point of, in this case, containing only one (!) formula in the whole lecture – Riemann's mathematical thinking is *structurally* conceptual, which brings it close to philosophical thinking in Deleuze and Guattari's sense. It is based on specifically determined concepts, as against the set-theoretical mathematics that followed him or the mathematics of formulas that preceded him.[4] Continuous and discrete manifolds are given different conceptual determinations, and thus become, in effect, *different* concepts, the point noted by Deleuze and Guattari (TP 32). It is significant, and adds to the conceptual difference between two types of manifoldness, that Riemann speaks of 'points' only in the case of continuous manifolds, and in the case of discrete manifolds uses the term 'elements', for the simplest constitutive entities comprising manifolds. This is astute, since, phenomenally, points *qua* points only appear as such in relation to some continuous space, ambient or background, present or implied, such as a line or a plane. Riemann primarily pursues the conception of space as a continuous manifold, for which the modern mathematical usage of the term is primarily reserved as well.[5] A manifold is, as I said, defined as a conglomerate of local spaces, which can be infinitesimally mapped by a (flat) Euclidean or Cartesian map without allowing for a global Euclidean map or a single co-ordinate system for the whole, except in the case of the Euclidean space itself. In other words, every point has a small neighbourhood that can be treated as Euclidean, while the manifold as a whole in general cannot.

As noted above, one of the starting points of Riemann's reflection on space was the possibility of non-Euclidean geometry, which also led him to a particular new type of non-Euclidean geometry, that of positive curvature. This also means that there are no parallel shortest or, as they are called, geodesic lines crossing any point external to a given geodesic. In Euclidean geometry, where geodesics are straight lines, there is only one such parallel line, but in non-Euclidean geometry of negative curvature or the hyperbolic geometry of Gauss, Johann Bolyai and Nikolai I. Lobachevsky – the first non-Euclidean geometry discovered – there are infinitely many such lines. Riemannian geometry encompasses all of these as special cases. Significant as the discovery of non-Euclidean geometry was for the history of mathematics and intellectual history, it was also in retrospect, as Hermann Weyl argued, 'a somewhat accidental point of departure' for Riemann's radical rethinking of the nature of spatiality.[6] Riemannian geometry is that of (continuous) manifoldness, an approach that makes both Euclidean and non-Euclidean spaces only particular cases of this more general understanding of space. Weyl speaks of Riemannian geometry as 'a true *geometry*': 'This theory . . . is a true *geometry*, a doctrine of *space itself* and not merely like Euclid, and almost everything else that has been done under the name of geometry, a doctrine of the configurations that are possible in space.'[7] Deleuze and Guattari agree and take the point further by also crediting Riemann with the creation of a new philosophical conceptuality: 'It was a decisive event when the mathematician Riemann uprooted the multiple [manifold] from its predicate state and made in to a noun, 'manifold' [*multiplic- ité*]' (TP 482–3; translation modified). They also acknowledge the role of discrete manifolds in Riemann, and the significance of still other spaces, such as porous spaces, in mathematics and elsewhere. Citing Lautman, they describe, Riemannian or Riemann spaces as (continuous) manifolds as follows:

> 'Riemann spaces are devoid of any kind of homogeneity. Each is characterized by the form of the expression that defines the square of the distance between two infinitely proximate points. . . . It follows that two neighboring observers in a Riemann space can locate the points

in their immediate neighborhood but cannot locate their spaces in relation to each other without a new convention. Each vicinity is therefore like a shred of Euclidean space, *but the linkage between one vicinity and the next is not defined and can be effected in an infinite number of ways. Riemann space at its most general thus presents itself as an amorphous collection of pieces that are juxtaposed but not attached to each other.*' It is possible to define this multiplicity without any reference to a metrical system, in terms of the conditions of frequency, or rather *accumulation*, of a set of neighborhoods; these conditions are entirely different from those determining metric spaces and their breaks (even though a relation between the two kinds of space necessarily results). In short, if we follow Lautman's fine description, Riemannian space is pure patchwork. It has connections, or tactile relations. It has rhythmic values not found elsewhere, even though they can be translated into a metric space. Heterogeneous, in continuous variation, it is a smooth space, insofar as smooth space is amorphous and not homogeneous. We can thus define two positive characteristics of smooth space in general: when there are determinations that are part of one another and pertain to enveloped distances or ordered differences, independent of magnitude; when, independent of metrics, determinations arise that cannot be part of one another but are connected by processes of frequency or accumulation. These are the two aspects of the *nomos* of smooth space. (TP 485; translation modified)

The cartographical terminology and conceptuality, crucial to Deleuze (and Foucault, whom Deleuze discusses from this perspective in *Foucault*), are not accidental and have their own history. Gauss arrived at his ideas, extended by Riemann, through his work in land surveying. The spatial architecture here outlined can be generalised to spaces that are not manifolds, that is, to spaces that are defined as patchworks of local spaces that are not infinitesimally Euclidean. These local spaces could be, in the language of *Cinema 1*, 'any spaces whatever'. This architecture is, however, inherent in Riemannian manifolds, from which it was in part developed historically, since manifolds are in the first place topological (non-metrical), rather than only geometrical (metrical) spaces. The function of Riemannian spaces as *smooth* spaces (in Deleuze and Guattari's sense) is defined by their topology, by their (in Boulez's and Deleuze and Guattari's language) 'rhythmic' properties, rather than by their geometry or their 'metric' (this language is also mathematical) properties (TP 485). In contrast to geometry (geo-*metry*), which has to do with measurement, topology disregards measurement and scale, and deals only with the structure of space *qua* space and with the essential shapes of figures. Insofar as one deforms a given figure continuously (that is, insofar as one does not separate points previously connected and, conversely, does not connect points previously separated) the resulting figure is considered the same. Thus, all spheres, of whatever size and however deformed (say, into pear-like shapes), are topologically equivalent. They are, however, topologically distinct from tori. Spheres and tori cannot be converted into each other without disjoining their connected points or joining the disconnected ones. The holes in tori make this impossible. Such qualitative topological properties can be related to certain algebraic and numerical properties associated with these spaces, which topology indeed must do as a mathematical discipline, unlike philosophy, where this is not necessary, as Bergson's or Deleuze's qualitative use of Riemann's ideas shows. Anticipated by Leibniz, these ideas were gradually developed in the nineteenth century by – in addition to Riemann – Gauss, Poincaré and others, establishing topology as a mathematical discipline by the twentieth century.

Topological spaces need not have any metric structure or striation, either global or local. Global Euclidean/Cartesian striations are not found in Riemannian spaces (apart, again, from special cases, such as those of Euclidean spaces), while local ones are allowed but not required. This is why Deleuze and Guattari say above that Riemannian space 'has rhythmic values not found elsewhere, even though they can be translated into a metric space' and hence that 'a relation between the two kinds of space necessarily results' in Riemannian space (TP 485). When we consider the discussion of space in *A Thousand Plateaus*, we can see that, smooth (nomadic) spaces almost inevitably give rise to local striations (reterritorialisation), even as they simultaneously arise from them (deterritorialisation) – in other words, they again lead to Riemannian spaces as both smooth and (locally) striated. The nomos of the smooth space (as against the logos of the striated space) is defined by the rhythmic interplay of connectivities between neighbourhoods, which defines topological spaces in general rather than Riemannian spaces, defined by local Euclidean striations. Accordingly, it appears that the underlying mathematical model of 'Riemann space *at its most general*' and, by extension, of smooth space in Deleuze and Guattari, is a general topological space, which, however, underlies any Riemannian space.

Deleuze takes advantage of these ideas throughout his work. The Cinema books are built in part upon Riemannian spatiality, via

Bergson, whose ideas were indebted to Riemann. *Cinema 2* offers spectacular examples of this 'Riemannianism' as against Euclideanism: 'Riemannian spaces in Bresson, . . . topological spaces of Resnais' (TI 129). It also explores the far-reaching implications – aesthetic, philosophical and cultural, including political – of Riemannianism.

MANIFOLDNESS AND MATERIALISM IN RIEMANN AND IN DELEUZE AND GUATTARI

Riemann's radical rethinking of spatiality offers an extension of Gauss's ideas concerning the *internal* geometry of curved surfaces, that is, a geometry independent of the ambient (three-dimensional) Euclidean space where such curved spaces could be placed. This view of space also allows one to extend Leibniz's ideas concerning the relational nature of all spatiality. The actual space is now no longer seen as a given, ambient (flat) Euclidean space or, in Weyl's words, a 'residential flat' (flat is a fitting pun here), where, phenomenally, geometrical figures or, physically, material things are placed.[8] Instead it emerges as a (continuous) manifold, whose structure, such as curvature, would be determined *internally*, mathematically or materially (for example, by gravity, as in Einstein's general relativity theory, based on Riemannian mathematics), rather than in relation to an ambient space, Euclidean or not. From this point of view, the concept of empty space might be entertained mathematically or phenomenally, but, as Leibniz grasped, it is difficult to apply this concept to the physical world. According to Leibniz, space cannot be seen as a primordial ambient given, as a container of material bodies and the background arena of physical processes, along the lines of Newton's concept of absolute space in his *Principia* – the most influential and, in many respects, defining form of Euclideanism in all of modernity. Einstein gave a rigorous physical meaning to these ideas and extended them by arguing that space, or time, are not given but arise, are the effects of our instruments, such as rods and clocks, and, one might add, of our perceptual and conceptual interactions with those instruments. Space is thus possible as a phenomenon (or a concept) by virtue of two factors. The first is the presence of matter and technology, such as rods and clocks (or natural objects that function in this role). The second is the role of our perceptual phenomenal machinery, a role that one might argue to be the primary condition of the possibility of space, along with time, which machinery is still due to the materiality of our bodies.

Riemann offers extraordinary intimations of Einstein's theory, based on his ideas discussed here. According to Weyl:

> Riemann rejects the opinion that has prevailed up to his own time, namely, than the metrical structure of space is fixed and [is] inherently independent of the physical phenomena for which it serves as a background, and that the real content takes possession of it as of residential flats. *He asserts, on the contrary, that space in itself is nothing more than a three-dimensional manifold devoid of any form; it acquires a definite form only through the advent of the material content filling it and determining its metric relations.*[9]

It would be more accurate (and closer to Riemann) to say that space may be given phenomenally at most as a three-dimensional manifold, as a kind of free smooth space with possible striations. Physically, it may be and, in Riemann's and Einstein's or Leibniz's view, could only be, co-extensive with matter. Weyl adds: 'Looking back from the stage to which Einstein brought us, we now recognize that these ideas can give rise to a valid [physical] theory only after *time* has been added as a fourth dimension to the three-space dimensions.'[10] The gravitational field determines the manifold in question and its in general variable curvature. The reverse fact, that the gravitational field shapes space and shapes it as a Riemannian manifold, remains crucial, however. Different spaces become subject to investigation in their own terms, on equal footing, rather than in relation to an ambient or otherwise uniquely primary space. This view radically transforms our philosophy of space and matter, and of their relationships, by leading to a horizontal rather than vertical (hierarchical) science of space as 'a typology and topology of manifolds', which Deleuze and Guattari associate with the end of dialectic and extend to spaces that are philosophical, aesthetic, cultural, or political (TP 483; translation modified).

Deleuze and Guattari's 'physical model' of the smooth and the striated converts this transformation into a grand conceptual and historical conjunction of physics and political economy, and of both with geometry (TP 490). The technological model – specifically that of textile technology, a 'weaving' model (from Plato on) – is seen in these terms as well, in part given that the origins of the capitalist economy and labour can be especially traced to textile manufacturing in Florence, to the 'space', smooth and striated, of the Renaissance. The Renaissance (if one can still speak of one) was also a Renaissance of geometry in mathematics, science, philosophy and art; and 'perspective', a great Renaissance striation, is only one of its aspects. The overall situation can be traced back to Galileo or to the ancient Greek mathematicians, specifically Archimedes, and to the role of geometry and physics as state, major sciences of (and in) striated spaces and as nomad, minor sciences of (and in) smooth spaces, and their interactions (TP 362). Both Galileo and Archimedes were military engineers (as was Leonardo), and Newton became a powerful state figure, the president of the Mint, thus moving from mathematics to money. From ancient Greece onwards, 'Geometry lies at the crossroads of a physics problem and an affair of the State' (TP 489). The terms of this sentence are transposable: 'Physics lies at the crossroads of a geometry problem and an affair of the State.'

Gaspar Monge, a key representative of state mathematics in *A Thousand Plateaus*, was instrumental in setting up, in the late eighteenth century, the famous École Politechnique as a state Institution (in either sense), where the most rigorous training in pure mathematics was combined with equally rigorous training in applied sciences and engineering. A major role in this programme was given to the new discipline of differential geometry, which combined geometry and calculus. Calculus, especially in the work of Newton and Leibniz, can, as both a major and a minor science, be considered from this perspective. Differential geometry, however, became a minor science in Gauss's work, eventually leading to Riemann's geometry and then to Einstein's physics. The nineteenth century brought physics and geometry into a new conjunction, under equally revolutionary developments of both the politico-economic history of capitalism and of the social and economic sciences, from Adam Smith onward.

The same type of matrix, interactively Riemannian and materialist, defines a vertiginous landscape, from brain to politics, that emerges in *Cinema 2* and towards the end of *What is Philosophy?* The Riemannianism of *What is Philosophy?* is more implicit, and yet equally powerful. The philosophised concept of Riemannian spaces appears by name at a crucial juncture, that of the interference of mathematics and philosophy (WP 217). The space of such interference is defined by and manifest in the ultimate dynamics of thought as a confrontation with chaos and, through that confrontation, 'extracted from chaos', the shadow of a political world yet to come, in which even philosophy, art and science may dissolve, while still leaving space for thought itself as a confrontation with chaos (WP

216–18). 'In this submersion [of brain into chaos] it seems that there is extracted from chaos the shadow of the "people to come" in the form that art, but also philosophy and science, summon forth: mass-people, world-people, brain-people, chaos-people' (WP 218). The same type of intersection of the brain, thought, chaos and a 'people to come' defines the closing chapters of *Cinema 2*, especially Chapter 8, 'Cinema, Body and Brain, Thought' (TI 189–224).

I can only briefly sketch here the Riemannian dimensions of these extraordinary pages of both books. Roughly, at stake here are the complex – heterogeneously interactive and interactively heterogeneous – relationships not only between neighbourhoods in a Riemannian space, but also between such spaces themselves. Our mathematics and physics on the one hand, and our neuroscience on the other, tell us that, to the degree that the processes that define nature and life, and our brains (neural networks), can be mapped, they are likely to be mapped in terms of Riemannian spaces, and of the interplay of the smooth and the striated within them. The same mapping needs to be deployed when we approach our politics and culture. It is not only a matter of mirroring such Riemannian manifoldness from inanimate nature to life to bodies to brains to thought to culture to politics, but also and primarily that of contiguous relations that manifoldly connect these manifolds. This is a new kind of 'landscape architecture', the architecture of many landscapes, in which these spaces co-exist and horizontally interact, without necessarily mirroring each other.

Leibniz's monadology could be viewed from this perspective as well, and Deleuze and Guattari juxtapose 'monads' to 'the unitary Subject of Euclidean space' (TP 574, n. 27). This monadology must, however, become nomadology in the new, post-Riemannian Baroque, as against the old, Leibnizian Baroque. Leibniz's monads ultimately interact with each other only through their interaction with the world, whose overall interactive architecture is, in the Leibnizian Baroque, containable in and converging upon a harmony, fully available to, or calculable by, only God (see FLB 26). The divergent harmonies of the new Baroque retain the fold, made mani*fold*, but convert monadology into nomadology, which contains but is not reducible to monadology (FLB 137). The chapter in *A Thousand Plateaus*, 'The Smooth and the Striated', may also be read in terms of this link between 'Riemannology' and nomadology in various models of the smooth and the striated – especially dramatically in the musical and the aesthetic models. The first is exemplified by the work of Boulez, who introduced the language of 'the smooth and the striated' and who is also a key figure of the new Baroque in *The Fold*; the second by the work of Cézanne and the painters who came after him (TP 477–8, 493–4). This conversion of Leibniz's monadology into Riemann's nomadology is expressly linked to Riemannian space, against Euclidean space:

> All of these points already relate to Riemannian space, with its essential relation to 'monads' (as opposed to the unitary Subject of Euclidean space). . . . Although the 'monads' are no longer thought to be closed upon themselves, and are postulated to entertain direct step-by-step local [Riemannian] relations, the purely monadological point of view proves inadequate and should be superseded by a 'nomadology' (the identity of striated spaces versus the realism of smooth space). (TP 573–4)

We can now readily perceive why Deleuze and Guattari see Riemann's mathematics of manifolds as implying a kind of horizontal rather than vertical, hierarchical science of space as 'a [nondialectical] typology and topology of manifolds' (TP 483; translation modified). This view suggests a new – horizontal – space of science itself, or a new space of thought and different ways to think, either within a given discipline, such as mathematics or philosophy, or (but this is now the same) between and among disciplines. We can think of spaces or landscapes of thought and culture in an interactively heterogeneous way – in terms of distinct and varied but actually and potentially interactive maps, arranged and related horizontally rather than vertically or hierarchically. Anticipated by Riemann's practice of mathematics through the interactions of different fields – topology, geometry, algebra, analysis, and so forth – this practise defines non-Euclideanism, mathematical and philosophical, such as that of Deleuze.

It is difficult to avoid the conclusion that the passage on Riemannian space cited above also describes the chapter 'The Smooth and the Striated', with its different but, again, interactive models – the technological, the musical, the maritime, the mathematical, the physical, the aesthetic (nomad-art), etc. – and *A Thousand Plateaus* as a whole. I list only those expressly named by Deleuze and Guattari, whose analysis implies many other possible models, a thousand models. In part these different models are necessary to establish certain general or shared aspects of (more) abstract concepts of the smooth and the striated (TP 475). Most crucial, however, is that these models enable an exploration of various aspects of each type of space and of the relationships between them, and of spaces, heterogeneously interactive assemblages, of such spaces, *manifolds of manifolds* (TP 475). Remarkably, this type of concept was introduced by Riemann in considering the families of the so-called Riemannian surfaces (such as tori). This type of object, known as 'moduli spaces', is one of the most extraordinary conceptions in modern mathematics; it was, for example, instrumental in proving Fermat's last theorem, by Andrew Wiles, one of the greatest achievements of contemporary mathematics. This concept, however, cannot be only mathematical, or only mathematical and philosophical. It is something more than either or both. Mathematics proves itself to be more like thought and life (which is more complex than thought) than thought and life prove to be like mathematics – that is, mathematics understood, as it has been all to often, as an abstraction from the richness, the manifoldness, of life. The idea of a manifold of manifolds is a product of thought as a confrontation with chaos and part of a shadow of the future – of things, thoughts, and the people to come.

Purdue University

Notes

1. I have considered the subject in more detail in *The Knowable and the Unknowable: Modern Science, Nonclassical Thought, and the 'Two Cultures'* (Ann Arbor: University of Michigan Press, 2002), pp. 126–36, 266–8, and nn. 24–6).
2. The English translation by Brian Massumi uses 'multiplicity' to render the French '*multiciplité*'. The English mathematical term is manifold, which also preserves the 'fold' of Riemann's *Mannigfaltigkeit*.
3. Bernhardt Riemann, 'On the Hypotheses which lie at the Bases of Geometry', trans. W. K. Clifford, *Nature* 8 (1873), section #1; translation modified. The lecture, given in 1854, was published posthumously in 1868. The English translation I cite is available at http://www.maths.tcd.ie/pub/HistMath/People/Riemann/Geom/WKCGeom.html.
4. Cf. D. Laugwitz, *Bernhard Riemann: Turning Points in the Conception of Mathematics*, trans. A. Shenitzer (Boston: Birkhäuser, 1999), pp. 303–7, which, however, takes a more conventional view of Riemann's conceptual mathematics.
5. Technically, Riemann considered the so-called differential manifolds, meaning that one can define differential calculus on them.
6. H. Weyl, *Space Time Matter*, trans. Henry L. Brose (New York: Dover, 1952 [1918]), p. 92.
7. Weyl, *Space Time Matter*, p. 102.
8. Weyl, *Space Time Matter*, p. 98.

9. Weyl, *Space Time Matter*, p. 98.
10. Weyl, *Space Time Matter*, p. 101. The resulting spaces are significant in the context of the question of temporality in Bergson and in Deleuze, especially in *The Logic of Sense*.

11

Gabriel Tarde

Éric Alliez

In a coincidence too happy to be properly counted as one, Gabriel Tarde has been republished in recent years under the imprint *Empêcheurs de penser en rond*[1] – which is, let's admit, an easier thing to say than to *be*. In effect, the *empêcheurs* will be sufficiently eccentric with respect to their time, improper for them from the point of view of History (they will found no 'school'), in order to become actively untimely in our own ... It is, then as now, an affair of *tendencies* and *relations*. Let's pose a general rule, whereby it is necessary to end badly (historically speaking) in order to *return* – in order to *properly become*.

Thus, in the sociological field, it is supposedly known that Tarde was the unfortunate adversary of Durkheim in his role as heir to an 'individualistic' and 'psychologistic' tradition that was incompatible with the methodological requisites of the new science or with the vision of founding a 'scientific morality'. To object – as the accused Tarde himself did, continually – that this was decidedly not the case since, on the contrary, it was a question of an 'interpsychology' and of an 'inter-mental' (or 'inter-cerebral') psychology investing the Social, the *logic of the social*, on the basis of trans-individual Relations, so that the latter might better endow the former with a power of invention that exceeds the Individual on all sides and that projects society to the rank of a *collective brain*, to object that the "desire of association" is composed in an immanent fasion . . . all of this would be pointless (Tarde himself never ceased to define every individual subject as the always provisory integration of an innumerable number of differentials, or 'individual variations').[2] Precisely because of the crushing domination of the analysis of systems of social representation, as the reality independent of individuals (hence Durkheim's *motto* concerning the founding transcendence of the social), the rare French defenders of Tardian sociology almost always present themselves as advocates of a 'methodological individualism' – or else rapidly fall back into the traditional terms of sociological interactionism . . . So that it would have to await Bruno Latour's recent *acting out*, which raised Tarde to the rank of a *forefather* of Actor Network Theory (ANT), for the scene to change, at least on the margins of the discipline, in any significant fashion.[3]

Braving the Durkheimian interdiction of any 'metaphysical' interference in the field of sociology (of sociology *'tout court'*), on a philosophical plane – more favourable in principle given that Tarde is widely recognised as the most 'metaphysical' of sociologists,[4] elected in 1900 to the Chair of Modern Philosophy at the Collège de France – Tarde's *neo-monadology* clearly played an absolutely determining role. With and *beyond* Leibniz:[5] if the whole of Tarde's demonstration – which takes as its point of departure the affirmation of difference as 'the substantial aspect of things' and the motor of an absolutely universal activity – is grounded on the Leibnizian principle of the metaphysical immanence of *substance-force* (all substance, insofar as it is living, is force *in itself*), with its spontaneity providing each body with its internal principle of action (in the sense of an *internal power of expansion*, synonymous with an original *activity*) and its irreducible *intensive* properties, it is in order to better radicalise monadology in its principle of *productive activity* by liberating it from that preestablished harmony which would forbid all real action, any mutual physical influence between beings, and *collective constutituion* as such – all in order to reserve for the God of the Theodicy the full and radical compossibility of things.

With and *beyond* Maine de Biran:[6] if we are obliged to remark that Tarde encountered, in Maine de Biran, his first 'master' – in particular in *The Exposition of the Philosophical Doctrine of Leibniz* (1819) – and the idea of this rewriting of Leibnizianism, it is essential to underline the difference between their two points of view. While Maine de Biran is concerned with 'the *truth* of consciousness' and the expressions of the *self* as causal origin of all force in order to make the soul the vector of a pure psychology, Tarde will to the contrary seize on Leibniz's elementary animism, identifying in the relational activity of monads *the metaphysical institution of the social* under the primitive form of 'molecular cohesions or affinities' which express *'the tendency of monads to assemble'* . . .

With and *beyond* Nietzsche: Tarde will translate the 'philosophy of values' into a *sociology of values* by the definition of social quantities founded on the powers of desire and belief – *belief-force* and *desire-force, belief* as *static force* and *desire* as *dynamic force* . . .

With and *beyond* Bergson, finally, since Tardean neo-monadology

is based on Bergson's conception of a *creative energy* – 'always double
. . . at each superposed stage of universal life' – according to 'that
great distinction between the static and the dynamic, which also contains the distinction between Space and Time, [such that it] divides
the entire universe into two'.[7] This basis is affirmed, however, in order
that the question of the production of the new finds in the *virtual relations* between affective forces, in which the infinitesimal dynamic of
social invention is generated, its condition of collective reality. Upon
Tarde's death in 1904, Bergson would pay a glowing tribute to the
thinker 'who opened so many horizons to us'. . .

But what, unsympathetic minds will ask, is the connection between
the man who is presented as a strangely 'missing' link in late nineteenth-century metaphysics and today's philosophical scene, (still
largely) dominated by a moral and political thought of a 'Germano-
Anglo-Saxon' persuasion, piloted by the presiding figures of Rawls
and Habermas? To assert here for example (as a philosopher addressing his colleagues) that Tarde could be this Third Man who would
enable us – on the plane of the history of philosophy! – to take a fresh
look at the question of the *sense* of the 'relations' between Nietzsche
and Bergson and beyond is of little use. To add that the splendour
of their 'wedding' announced the philosophical (and even aesthetic)[8]
contemporaneity of a vitalist constructivism, in which Tarde identified the constituent power of the social defined afresh once again . . .
this can only damage one's standing in the eyes of the Academy.

And as is also the case, the 'cultural' debate is periodically dominated – and today in France, at least, Sarkozy obliges, more than
ever! – by the persistent question of la *Pensée 68* and of the *cattivi
maestri* whose symbolic execution seems decidedly interminable . . .
Amongst them, a philosopher named Gilles Deleuze, to whom the
most significant rediscovery and rehabilitation of Tarde's *oeuvre* is
entirely due. We are in 1968, the book is called *Différence et répétition*, and must be conceived as the taproot of Deleuzian philosophy.
It is here that Deleuze confers the greatest importance upon the
'philosophy of Gabriel Tarde'. To the point of attributing *de facto* to
Tarde the formula enveloped in the title: *repetition as the differenciator of difference*, implying Tarde's double construction: 'repetition
is therefore the process by which difference . . . "goes on differing"
and "is its own goal"'.[9] And Deleuze emphasises, in the final pages of
his Introduction, that 'Tarde proposes to substitute this differential
and differenciating repetition for opposition in every domain' (DR
39 n.1/307–8 n.15). Because more fundamental than the polemic

against Durkheim's sociology is the critique of Hegel's philosophy, in particular in *L'Opposition universelle*,[10] where Tarde makes the continued constitution of the social depend upon the 'Imitation' (that is, Repetition) of the differential relation between affective forces (a difference Tarde calls 'Invention' so as to posit, reciprocally, that 'invention means imitated invention') . . . It is as if it were *only as a Tardean* that Deleuze could have, and had to, set forth the renewed conditions for a *philosophy of difference* in a denunciation of the dialectic which presents a travesty of difference mediated by representation.

Conditions that he would explore, along with Félix Guattari, through a politics of desire, in the guise of a *biopolitics of multiplicities and of becoming*, in *Anti-Oedipus* and *A Thousand Plateaus*. Now, if Tarde is nominally absent from *Anti-Oedipus* (but, in truth, virtually present throughout on account of the overarching thesis of the coextension of the social field and desire), *A Thousand Plateaus* not only contains an 'Homage to Gabriel Tarde' (TP 267/218–19) in which the sociologist of *Les lois de l'imitation* is associated with the molecular domain of flows (as opposed to the molar domain of representations to which Durkheim limits himself, who thereby 'presuppos[es] exactly what needs explaining') and celebrated as the inventor of a 'micro-sociology' attentive to the active forces of desire and of beliefs[11] (*imitation is the propagation of a flow, invention is the connection of imitative flows*). Its title is also absolutely Tardean in that the term 'plateau', referred back to its use in Bateson ('a continuous plateau of intensity'), depends in fact upon Tarde's denunciation of its 'triumph' in the field of statistics in which it translates – as a term *traced* from 'uniform reproduction of the same numbers' signifying 'equilibrium', 'mutual arrest of concurrent forces' – the *inverse image* of the dynamic multiplicities that the process of counting cannot but disregard. (In fact, as Tarde explains, '*plateaus* are always unstable equilibria'[12].) Beyond Bergson, the consequence can be read in Deleuze and Guattari: 'number systems attached to some particular dimension of multiplicities' (TP 32–3/22)[13] – which are always 'social quantities' (in Tarde's words) turning the desire that works through them into an assemblage (and here one will not be able to avoid thinking of the differend between Deleuze and Badiou with respect to this question of multiplicities, thought respectively from the 'diagrammatic' and 'axiomatic' point of view). All this, finally, as though the critique of structuralism, and its surpassing by an affective ontology of multiplicities bearing upon 'an entire realm of subrepresentative matter' (TP 267/219) depended secretly on the *reactualisation* of this

Tardean thinking, bringing together a 'universal sociology' and an 'infinitesimal philosophy of nature' in the form of a *universal bio-politics*. A thinking that we will only be able lightheartedly to hazard calling – with René Schérer – 'Deleuzian *avant la lettre*',[14] when we have assessed its *constitutive*ly inspirational status for Deleuze himself – something that deserves all the more attention given that Deleuze himself was the first to recognise in Tarde that type of 'precursor' whose most untimely topicality he knew how to explore.

That topicality, in the form of a new *zeitgeist* in those areas of the social sciences more attentive to 'small' complex relations than to 'grand' dialectical structures, more open to plastic differences than to substantial identities,[15] is certainly not unconnected to the fact that the edition of *Oeuvres de Gabriel Tarde* that I have the privilege of directing in the series of the *Empêcheurs de penser en rond* has encountered a considerable response. So much so that one could hear tell – not without some exaggeration, bitterness and regret – of the *Tardomania* of the year 1999 which saw the publication of the first four volumes; a year also dubbed 'Tarde's year' in the issue of the *Revue d'Histoire des Sciences Humaines* (2000/3) devoted to him. The contrast could not be more striking with the opening lines of Jean Milet's doctoral thesis, published in 1970, *Gabriel Tarde et la philosophie de l'Histoire*, which even today remains the only work to present (despite its title) the entire development of Tardean thought, right from that Dissertation of sorts entitled 'La Différence universelle' published in 1870 by the young magistrate of Sarlat. I quote Milet's first paragraph in full:

> History commits strange injustices. It has been particularly hard on Gabriel Tarde. This man was hailed by his contemporaries as one of the greatest thinkers of his time. He was awarded the most coveted honours: he was professor at the Collège de France with Henri Bergson; he was a member of the *Institut*; he was President of the International Societies of Sociology and of Law. His *oeuvre* totals more than fifteen volumes, which thanks to numerous editions and translations extend his renown as far as Russia and America. At his death, he was compared to Auguste Comte, to Taine, to Renan, even to Darwin and Spencer; and Bergson, although somewhat sober in his tribute, held him as an eminent master. And yet, the same man, a few years after his death, was inexplicably forgotten. A heavy silence settled upon his *oeuvre*. Over the last fifty years, only a very few studies and articles (and these often of foreign origin) even recall the existence of this great sociologist and philosopher.[16]

But can such oblivion – I will not say unexplained but *inexplicable* – be comprehended? Is it not what our author himself did that is inexplicable, his inexplicable omission of Durkheim's name in these introductory lines to Tarde's intellectual biography? This is certainly not the case for Laurent Mucchielli in his vigorous attack upon the contemporary figures of 'Tardean hagiography' and its 'presentist transgressions'. We read:

> Durkheim succeeded in incarnating a certain form of rationality – *scientific rationality* – that consists of methods, of examples, of the logic of reasoning, of standardised procedures for validation and argumentation, all things that are not to be found in Tarde, whose thinking belongs more to traditional philosophy, even sometimes to a form of writing and argument that is closer to journalism. For, in the expression 'social science', there is the word 'science'.[17]

In all the anti-philosophical brutality of its expression, this selected passage is remarkable because it explains Tarde's 'oblivion' – and the repression of the resounding *Hypotheses fingo* put in place by the sociologist-metaphysician at the outset of *Monadologie et Sociologie* – reciting the reasons for it on the basis of a positivist ideology of science and society that was foundational for the birth of sociology outlined by Durkheim (in *Les règles de la méthode sociologique*, published in 1895) and his school (grouped together around the review *Année sociologique*, launched in 1896–7). Now, we know that the 'functionalism' of Durkheimean sociology served to reinforce all the social and human sciences in their struggle against 'psychologism' and 'anthropologism' – right up to structuralism and the 'epistemological revolution' that celebrated in Durkheim the *Galileo of the social sciences* (Bourdieu[18]): according to the wishes of the author of *Les règles de la méthode sociologique*, it is a question of 'extending scientific rationalism to human conduct'. And, finally, it may explain the following: the rediscovery of Tardean intuitions is contemporary with the critique of structuralism voiced on the one side by Foucault, and on the other by Deleuze/Guattari: the former leading it towards a *microphysics of power* (which Deleuze will explicitly associate with Tarde's micro-sociology [F81 n.6/142]), the latter two making their own the project of a *molecular revolution in thought* 'where the distinction between the social and the individual loses all meaning' because all things are continually constituted from relations of forces, because each force is itself a relation between differential elements, and because the very concept of force is derived from desire. Or, again to use the words of Tarde, whose profound Nietzscheanism avoids in advance the psychologist-individualist confinement to which Durkheim sought to consign him: '[e]very thing is a society, every phenomenon is a social fact' – 'up to and including the infinitesimal that becomes the key to the entire universe' with the Socius as a paradigm of Life, 'source of this stream of varieties that dazzles us'. This having been asserted, then on the level of sociology, 'it is social changes that must be caught as they happen and examined in great detail in order to understand social states, not the other way around'. [19] For the historical process only engages the molar domain of representations and of collective signifiers (as Durkheim objected to Tarde) [20] in a derivative manner: first of all it is played out at the infinitesimal level of beliefs and of desires, of the power of affection of these associative, attractive, collectively inventive forces that *do not subjugate individuals without subjectivising them*, without forming the possibility of new assemblages, without reopening totally new processes of individuation. Thus 'micro-sociology' is not merely an area of social science, a sort of discipline dubbed (somewhat provocatively) 'interpsychology' – rather it defines the field of action of a *social thought* that is truly, otherwise, materialistic. Either a *sociology of events in process*[21] according to which 'a social field is always animated by all kinds of movements of decoding and deterritorialisation affecting "masses"' and which 'take flight' (or not) from their reterritorialisation as 'classes', with their binary organisation, their molar resonance, and so on, making *flows* fall back into *segments* (TP 268–70/220–1). Whence the properly constitutive distinction between the molecular aspect and the molar aspect, which takes up the political difference of a macro-history and a micro-history of the present. Here, it must be emphasised, Tarde has more of an immediate affinity with the Chicago School (hence Tarde's influential career in America,[22] even whilst he was entirely absent from the European scene), or even to William Burroughs' *Electronic revolution* (was Tarde not the first thinker of the 'viral' power of the media, which he compared to an 'intercerebral' form of 'magnetism'?), than with Regis Debray's 'Mediology' with its (deterministic) allure as the 'chronicle of an [*automatic*] cataclysm'.

A materialism that is vitalist through and through, advocating the transversal-machinic principles of a political ontology of difference opposed equally 'to the automation of capitalist axioms and to bureacratic programming' (TP 590/472): this is the lesson, indissociably *expressionist* (the vital expression of forces) and *constructivist* (the machinic connection of fluxes), of Gabriel Tarde. A lesson entirely in tune with the open process of a Socius which, as we are beginning to understand, is entirely *biopolitical* as a constituent cooperative power.[23] And in which '[e]very struggle . . . constructs *revolutionary connections* in opposition *the conjugations of the axiomatic*' (TP 591/473).

Middlesex University

Notes

1. *Empêcheur de penser en rond*: i.e., a spoilsport and nuisance to established thought.
2. Read, with the inevitable effect of hindsight, Tarde's extremely optimistic declaration in *Les lois sociales*: 'As for other objections that have been made to me, as they all stem from a most incomplete understanding of my ideas, I shall not dwell upon them. They will disappear of their own accord, in the eyes of whomsoever adopts my point of view. I therefore refer you back to my works.' *Les lois sociales* (Paris: Les Empêcheurs de penser en rond/Institut Synthélabo, 1999 [1898]), p. 61.
3. Bruno Latour, 'Gabriel Tarde and the End of the Social', in P. Joyce (ed.), *The Social in Question: New Bearings in History and the Social Sciences* (London: Routledge, 2002), pp. 117–32. This article appeared previously in French and in German translation in 2001.
4. See especially Tarde's article 'Monadologie et sociologie' (*Monadologie et sociologie*, with a preface by Éric Alliez and a postface by Maurizio Lazzarato [Paris: Les Empêcheurs de penser en rond/Institut Synthélabo, 1999]). In his 'Discours sur Gabriel Tarde' (12 September 1909), Bergson says that 'Tarde derived [his grand sociological ideas] from certain profound metaphysical views on the nature of the universe, of the elements that compose it and of the actions that these elements exert on one another.' It should be pointed out here that, in his study on *La théorie bergsonienne de la religion* Swedish theologian Hjalmar Sunden noted the importance of Tarde in the development of Bergson's thought: see Hjalmar Sunden, *La théorie bergsonienne de la religion* (Uppsala: Almqvist & Wiksell, 1940).
5. See my preface to *Monadologie et sociologie*: 'Tarde et le problème de la constitution'.
6. On Maine de Biran, cf. Gabriel Tarde, *Maine de Biran et l'évolutionnisme en psychologie*, with a preface by Anne Devarieux (Paris: Les Empêcheurs de penser en rond/Institut d'édition Sanofi-Synthélabo, 2000).
7. Gabriel Tarde, *les lois de l'imitation*, with a preface by Jean-Philippe Antoine (Paris: Les Empêcheurs de penser en rond/Le Seuil, 2001), pp. 205–6. Tarde had previously referred in a note to the *Essai sur les*

données immédiates de la conscience published by Bergson in 1889, an essay 'so in touch . . . with our manner of thinking'.

8. See Éric Alliez and Jean-Claude Bonne, *La Pensée-Matisse. Portrait de l'artiste en hyperfauve* (Paris: Le Passage, 2005).

9. Gilles Deleuze, *Différence et Répétition* (Paris: PUF, 1968), pp. 104–5 n.1, p. 313 n.3 in English translation. References to both the original text and its translation will be cited hearafter, with the French pagination given first.

10. See Gabriel Tarde, *L'Opposition universelle. Essai d'une théorie des contraires* (1897), republished as Volume III of the *Oeuvres* (Paris: Les Empêcheurs de penser en rond/Le Seuil, 2001).

11. Cf. Gabriel Tarde, 'La croyance et le désir', *Revue philosophique* 10 (1880), pp. 150–80; 264–83, to appear in *Oeuvres de Gabriel Tarde*. This was, as Tarde himself said, his 'first philosophical publication'.

12. Tarde, *Les lois de l'imitation*, p. 175.

13. Cf. Tarde, *Les lois de l'imitation*, pp. 173–91; Jean-Philippe Antoine, 'Statistique et métaphore. Note sur la méthode sociologique de Tarde', in Tarde, *Les lois de l'imitation*, pp. 20–5.

14. 'Tarde, a Deleuzian before Deleuze', writes Schérer in his preface to the republication of Gabriel Tarde, *Fragment d'histoire future* (Paris: Séguier, 1998), p. 24.

15. See Bruno Latour, *Reassembling the Social: an Introduction to Actor-Network-Theory* (Oxford: Oxford University Press, 2005); Christian Borch, 'Urban Imitations: Tarde's Sociology Revisited', *Theory, Culture & Society* 22:3 (2005), pp. 81–100; not forgetting the older article by F. Balke, 'Eine frühe Soziologie der Differenz: Gabriel Tarde,' in P. Zimmermann and N. Binczek (eds), *Eigentlich könnte alles auch anders sein* (Cologne: Walther König, 1998).

16. Jean Milet, *Gabriel Tarde et la philosophie de l'Histoire* (Paris: Vrin, 1970), p. 9 (emphasis mine). In 1973, Milet, together with A.-M. Rocheblave-Spenlé, published an initial collection of texts by Tarde entitled *Ecrits de psychologie sociale*. Preceded by *La Philosophie pénale* (in 1972), a number of republications were to follow in random order (*Les lois de l'imitation, L'Opinion et la foule, Fragment d'histoire future*, etc.) but without ever making any appreciable impact. It is true that Tarde's rehabilitation essentially depended upon the 'methodological individualism' championed by Raymond Boudon.

17. Laurent Mucchielli, 'Tardomania? Réflexions sur les usages contemporains de Tarde', *Revue d'Histoire des Sciences Humaines* 3 (2000), p. 181.

18. On Bourdieu's 'Durkheimeanism', see Loïc Wacquant, 'Durkheim et Bourdieu: le socle commun et ses fissures', *Critique* 579/580 (August–September 1995), pp. 646–60.

19. Tarde, *Monadologie et sociologie*, p. 58.

20. See the lengthy note on 'l'ingénieux système de M. Tarde', in Chapter 1 of *Règles de la méthode sociologique* (Paris: PUF, 1973 [1895]), p. 12 n.1.

21. Cf. A. Barry, 'Events That Matter', Paper for the workshop on Gabriel Tarde, University of London, 1 December 2005.

22. In his preface to *Les lois sociales*, Isaac Joseph points out that 'Tarde, along with Simmel and Durkheim, is one of the key reference authors in Robert Park and Ernest Burgess' famous sociology manual, *Introduction to the Science of Sociology* (Chicago University Press, 1921), which was to be the sociological bible for two generations of American students from the 20s to the 40s' ('Gabriel Tarde: Le monde comme féerie', in Trade, *Les lois sociales*, p. 12 n.2). Cf. Isaac Joseph, 'Tarde avec Park. A quoi servent les foules?', *Multitudes* 7 (December 2001), pp. 212–20.

23. Cf. Maurizio Lazzarato, *Puissances de l'invention. La psychologie économique de Gabriel Tarde contre l'economie politique* (Paris: Les Empêcheurs de penser en rond/Le Seuil, 2001), particularly Chapter 8 ('La politique de la multiplicité').

12

Sigmund Freud

Ronald Bogue

In the 1960s, French interest in Freud increased dramatically, in large part due to the teachings of Jacques Lacan, whose seminars on Freud and psychoanalysis had been drawing a growing body of adherents since their inception in 1953. With the publication of Lacan's *Ecrits* in 1966 that interest redoubled, and by the end of the decade a veritable 'psychoanalytic culture' had begun to take shape in France.[1] Like many of his contemporaries, Deleuze was intrigued with the possibilities offered by Freud for the creative reconfiguration of philosophical issues, and in *Masochism: Coldness and Cruelty* (1967), *Difference and Repetition* (1968), and *The Logic of Sense* (1968) Deleuze took up several Freudian concepts and gave them a prominent position in his thought. After May '68, however, Deleuze began a collaboration with Félix Guattari, a Lacanian psychoanalyst and activist in the anti-psychiatry movement, and in 1972 the two of them produced *Anti-Oedipus: Capitalism and Schizophrenia*, a thoroughgoing critique of Freud and the Freudian tradition of psychoanalysis. Save for a chapter of *Kafka: Toward a Minor Literature* (1975), a short section of *A Thousand Plateaus* (1980), and a few brief papers in *Essays Critical and Clinical* (1993), Deleuze made little mention of Freud in his subsequent writings. Despite this silence, however, the influence of Freud remained in his work, for whatever the shortcomings Deleuze saw in Freud and the Freudian psychoanalytic movement, they provided him with the key insight that desire and the unconscious are fundamental constituents of thought.

Deleuze's first major venture into psychoanalytic commentary is his *Masochism: Coldness and Cruelty*, a lengthy introduction to a French translation of *Venus in Furs* (1870), a novel by Leopold Ritter von Sacher-Masoch, whose name was used by Kraft-Ebbing in 1886 to designate the perversion of masochism. In medicine Deleuze sees a distinction between symptomatology and aetiology, arguing that symptomatology belongs 'as much to art as to medicine', and that 'the writer or artist can be a great symptomatologist, just like the best doctor' (DI 132). Symptomatology is an art of reading signs, and among the great symptomatologists Deleuze ranks Sade and Masoch. Unlike Sade, however, Masoch has not been given his due, says Deleuze, primarily because he and his works have been assimilated within a false clinical category – a syndrome, or collection of signs, called sadomasochism – the end result being that Masoch is treated as a mere adjunct to Sade. Deleuze's basic claim is that sadism and masochism are separate phenomena, and in *Masochism* he sets out to differentiate sadism from masochism and to demonstrate the formal coherence of these two distinct domains.

Sade's world is that of the cruel father at war with the mother and all procreative processes. He seeks a nature of pure negation that obliterates the impure nature of constant creation and destruction, birth and death. Such a pure nature is a delusional Idea, 'but it is a delusion of reason itself' (M 27). With cold apathy, the Sadean torturer pursues this delusional Idea, inflicting suffering as if he were demonstrating a mathematical truth. If he occasionally allows himself to be tortured, it is not to extract a masochistic pleasure, but to surrender all personal desires and submit himself to the impersonal principle of pure negativity. Masoch's world, by contrast, is that of the son in league with the severe mother in a war against natural sensuality. Deleuze distinguishes three female figures in Masoch: a procreative, uterine mother who spreads confusion and disorder through promiscuous sexuality; a sadistic, Oedipal mother who inflicts pain; and an oral mother, at once 'cold-maternal-severe, icy-sentimental-cruel' (M 51).[2] The first two belong to a nature of violent struggle between men and women, but the oral mother represents another nature, a supersensual domain of rigorous, frigid order. Like Sade's nature of pure negativity, Masoch's supersensual nature is a delusional Idea, but a delusion of the imagination rather than reason. Its mode of application is that of dialectic persuasion rather than analytic demonstration. The male victim instructs the dominatrix, forms a contract with her, and through this alliance transcends sensuality to reach a supersensual dimension. In the masochistic torture scene, the oral mother humiliates the father in the person of the son-victim, annihilates the son's sensual desires, and makes possible the parthenogenetic rebirth of the son as a new man, beyond sensuality, at one with the oral mother in a pure nature, 'icy-sentimental-cruel'.

Deleuze sees disavowal, suspension, waiting and phantasy as the dominant elements in masochism.[3] Deleuze concurs with Freud in his analysis of the fetish, so important in masochism, as a symbol of the maternal phallus. Through the fetish, the masochist is able simultaneously to deny and to admit that the mother is castrated; this strategy for maintaining such contradictory beliefs Freud labels 'disavowal' (*Verleugnung*).[4] For Deleuze, disavowal informs the entirety of masochism, not simply the fetish, for through disavowal, the masochist at once contests 'the validity of that which is', provides a 'defensive neutralization' of a reality that threatens the masochistic phantasy, and gives a 'protective and idealizing' quality to that phantasy (M 31–2). This suspension of disbelief is echoed by literal suspensions within the masochistic phantasy – bodies tied up, hung, crucified – and by a suspended time of frozen scenes and perpetual delay. Masochistic time is one of 'waiting in its pure form' (M 71), a dual time of awaiting a pleasure that is always deferred while expectantly awaiting the pain that will hasten that pleasure. 'The anxiety of the masochist divides therefore into an indefinite awaiting of pleasure and an intense expectation of pain' (M 71). And it is in the phantasy that disavowal, suspension and waiting find their proper element, for disavowal 'transposes [the real] into phantasy', suspension 'performs the same function in relation to the ideal', and waiting 'represents the unity of the ideal and the real, the form or the temporality of the phantasy' (M 72). In its Freudian conception, the phantasy is an imaginary scene expressing a desire,[5] and in Masoch those scenes resemble *tableaux vivants*, frozen images of an aestheticised and idealised 'supersensuality'. Hence, masochism may be said to be 'the art of the phantasy' (M 66), an aesthetic product of the imagination that stages desire in a temporally suspended milieu, in which the ideal is protected and imbued with a hallucinatory reality.

Masochism is commonly thought to be the product of a hypercritical, punishing superego, but Deleuze argues that masochism belongs to the realm of the ego, whereas sadism is the domain proper to the superego. Freud assumes that sadism and masochism are transformations of one another, masochism being an externally directed sadism that has been transformed into self-directed violence, or sadism being a primary masochism that has been transformed into an outer-directed violence, and behind that assumption is the belief that the ego and superego are intertwined in sadomasochism, merely changing their positions within various transformations.[6] Deleuze proposes instead that perversion, unlike neurosis or spiritual sublimation, is 'related not to the functional interdependence of the ego and the superego, but to the structural split between them' (M 117). In *The Ego and the Id* (1923), Freud speaks of the 'desexualisation' of libido in the formation of the ego and the superego, a process whereby libido is detached from an overtly sexual object (desexualised) and directed to another object. Deleuze assigns a different function to this process in the perversions of sadism and masochism than in neuroses and sublimation, and he posits as well a complementary 'resexualisation' of libido as a constituent of those perversions.[7] In sadism, the superego reigns supreme. The superego arises through an identification with the father, whereby an internal 'ego-ideal' (*idéal du moi*), or authority figure, takes shape, and in sadism, 'the sadist's superego is so strong that he has become identified with it; he is his own superego and can only find an ego in the external world' (M 124). The sadist's primary victims are the mother and the external-ised ego. For the sadist, all libido has been detached from specifically erotic objects – hence Sadean apathy – and put at the service of a neutral energy of negation, but it has also been reattached to (and hence resexualised in) the Idea of negation. At the heart of sadism, then, 'is the sexualization of thought and of the speculative process as such, insofar as these are the product of the superego' (M 127). In masochism, by contrast, the ego prevails, and the superego's seeming dominance is only a ruse. The ego arises, not through identification with the father, but through 'a mythical operation of idealization, in which the mother-image serves as a mirror to reflect and even produce the "ideal ego"' (M 129). That 'ideal ego' (*moi idéal*), in contrast to the 'ego-ideal', is an all-powerful, narcissistic self.[8] In the masochistic phantasy, the female dominatrix is a manifestation of the ideal ego, a narcissistic, grandiose mother-self in collusion with the son, who stages the humorous mockery and humiliation of the superego-father through the son's own punishment. For the masochist, as for the sadist, libido has been desexualised, detached from specific erotic objects, but it is disavowal, not negation, that is 'the form of desexual-isation particular to masochism' (M 128). Disavowal is 'nothing less than the foundation of [the] imagination, which suspends reality and establishes the ideal in the suspended world' (M 128). The coldness of masochism is evidence of this desexualisation, but in the phantasy there is a simultaneous resexualisation 'in the narcissistic ego, which contemplates its image in the ideal ego through the agency of the oral mother' (M 128). One may say, then, that sadism eroticises reason as the paradigmatic superego function, whereas masochism eroticises the imagination, as the faculty proper to the ego.

In some ways, Deleuze's *Masochism* may be seen as an interven-tion within Freudian psychoanalytic discourse. Deleuze clarifies the role the artist should assume in psychoanalytic research, arguing that writers like Sade and Masoch are not simply bearers of symptoms but themselves symptomatologists. He offers detailed analyses of Freud's statements about sadomasochism, pointing out their limitations and inconsistencies (see especially M 103–10). He borrows concepts from Freudian analysts who have proposed modifications in Freud's theory of masochism, notably Theodor Reik and Edmund Bergler. And he offers his own account of sadism and masochism, couched in the psychoanalytic terminology of ego, superego, desexualisation, orality, Oedipal mother, and so on. Yet in at least one regard Deleuze's approach to masochism runs counter to the psychoanalytic enterprise, and that is in the valorisation of perversion. For Deleuze, perversion is something to be explored rather than cured. As Deleuze makes clear in *The Logic of Sense*, he sees perversion as one means of 'thinking otherwise', of going beyond orthodox thought and inventing new possibilities for life.[9]

Such a valorisation of perversion is finally part of Deleuze's larger aim, which is to use psychoanalytic discourse as a component of his fundamental philosophical project. This is especially apparent in his interpretation of Freud's concept of the death instinct, which Deleuze sketches in *Masochism* and develops further in *Difference and Repetition*. Freud's primary text on the death instinct, *Beyond the Pleasure Principle*, is a 'masterpiece', says Deleuze, in which Freud 'engaged most directly – and how penetratingly – in specifically philosophical reflection' (M 111). In Deleuze's reading, Freud's quest beyond the pleasure principle is not to find exceptions to the principle, but to determine the condition under which pleasure becomes a principle, that is, to identify the transcendental condition of possibility of the principle. The death instinct is such a condition, and Deleuze sees it finally as an essentially temporal condition, one that Freud only partially and inadequately articulates and that Deleuze seeks to develop more fully within a general theory of time.

In *Difference and Repetition* Deleuze identifies three transcendental conditions that underlie our commonsense experience of time, which he labels 'passive syntheses' of time. The first passive synthesis belongs to the present; it is a synthesis linking discrete moments (a, b, c, . . .) such that the present (b) is at once a retention of a previous moment (a) and a projection towards a future moment (c). This synthesis is a necessary condition of the present as a temporal category, since without it each moment would have no relation to any other (and what meaning does the present have outside its relation to past and future?) and the present would never pass or be succeeded by a new present. Yet '*there must be another time in which the first synthesis of time can occur*', claims Deleuze, and this time 'refers us to the second synthesis' (DR 79), the synthesis of the virtual past. Following Bergson, Deleuze argues that the past of memory is qualitatively different from the present. The past exists as a single co-existing domain that stretches back indefinitely and extends forward into the present. It is real, but it is not actual, as is the present. Rather, it is virtual, a domain with its own mode of existence. Since it is qualitatively different from the present, it is not made up of previously present moments. It is a past that has never been present. And yet it is a past that is constantly being constituted as something that includes within it the moments that are passing in the flow of time. Hence, for every present moment there must exist a virtual double, a 'present of the past'. In a sense, time splits in the present moment, an actual present thrusting towards the future, a virtual double of that moment simultaneously emerging and forming part of the vast expanse of the virtual past. Beyond this second synthesis, however, Deleuze sees the need of a third synthesis, one that he identifies as 'the empty form of time' (DR 88), a mysterious groundless ground of time, a chaotic 'time out of joint' (DR 88), which is the time of an open future. This is the time of the death instinct.

In Deleuze's analysis, biopsychical life 'implies a field of individuation in which differences in intensity are distributed here and there in the form of excitations', and what Freud calls the Id is 'a mobile distribution of differences and local resolutions within an intensive field' (DR 96). Pleasure is a process whereby tensions are reduced, but the question is, how does a haphazard, locally manifested process become a principle, a regular rule or practice? What makes such a principle possible is the linking of moments in a set sequence, and that linking presumes the first passive synthesis of time. The first synthesis is that whereby habits are contracted, and through the formation of habits 'we pass from a state of scattered resolution to a state of integration, which constitutes the second layer of the Id and the beginnings of organization' (DR 96). Thus, 'habit, in the form of a passive binding synthesis, precedes the pleasure principle and renders it possible' (DR 97).

In the contraction of these habits, the infant focuses its desires on various objects, but Deleuze argues that its desires engage both actual objects and virtual objects. These virtual objects are related to what Melanie Klein calls 'partial objects' (and Lacan calls '*objets petit a*').

Klein's partial objects are such things as 'the good breast', 'the bad breast', 'the good penis', or 'the bad penis' – symbolic body parts that the infant takes in and expels in a confused, phantasmal fashion in the first four months of life. Deleuze sees such objects as virtual objects that are 'shreds of [the] pure past' (DR 101). They are simulacra, what Plato calls *phantasma*, entities that are neither models (Ideas) nor copies, but troubling, furtive appearances that resist any fixed identity and seem to differ from themselves, forever engaged in a process of becoming-other. The virtual object is elusive, always existing where we do not seek it, 'essentially displaced in relation to itself, being found only as lost' (DR 103). It is also essentially different from itself, the good breast, for example, being always simultaneously the bad breast. The virtual object never exists in the actual present, for it '*is always a "was"*' (DR 102), a fragment of the pure past. And it is Eros that 'tears virtual objects out of the pure past and gives them to us in order that they may be lived' (DR 103). It is the virtual nature of such objects that explains the effects of infantile desires in the adult psyche. In dreams, phantasies, symptoms, and so on, an infantile experience and an adult experience are brought together, but not as an original experience repeated in the present. Rather, the virtual object, as part of the pure past, co-exists with the infant and the adult in a single realm, bringing together the actual infant that formerly existed and the actual adult that now exists. In this realm, there is no genuine beginning, no point of origin. It is the realm of *phantasma*, of simulacral fragments of the pure past, a domain that emerges through the second passive synthesis of time.

If the first passive synthesis of habit ensures 'the foundation of the pleasure principle', the second synthesis of Eros 'functions as the ground [*fondement*] of the pleasure principle' (DR 108). Through its engagement of virtual objects, the infant brings together the various satisfactions regulated by the first synthesis, the totality of co-existing virtual objects coalescing with the desiring self to form a narcissistic ego, a fusional self that is at once desirer and desired, ego and virtual objects. As the narcissistic ego forms, however, that ego also necessarily becomes the object of thought, and the only means of thinking the self is as an 'other'. At this point, there is an essential split in the 'I', the I as subject, and the I as object. According to Kant's interpretation of the Cartesian formula *cogito ergo sum*, the form under which the cogito (the thinking subject) takes itself as an object of thought (*ego sum*) is that of time, and in Deleuze's reading of Kant, the time of the 'split I', the self as cogito and ego, is that of the empty form of

time. This empty form of time is the undifferentiated and unorgan-
ised dimension of the temporal per se, within which specific kinds of
time may emerge – those being the time of the passing present (first
synthesis) and the virtual past (second synthesis). The blank form of
time is the 'groundless' dimension that brings forth the ground of time
(second synthesis) and the foundation of time (first synthesis). When
the narcissistic ego that emerges through the second synthesis takes
itself as an object of thought, it becomes 'the phenomenon which
corresponds to the empty form of time' (DR 110). Libido invested in
various partial objects is abstracted from them and fixed on the narcissistic ego itself. In this process, libido is desexualised and rendered
a neutral, displaceable energy. That neutral energy is subsequently at
the service of the death instinct, which, argues Deleuze, is precisely
'time empty and out of joint' (DR 111).

     In Deleuze's ontology, the Many does not issue from the One. There
is no originary unity from which the multiple entities of the world
derive. Primary instead are multiplicities of difference, self-differing
differences that generate further differences through a process of
self-differentiation. Unities are secondary effects produced by self-
differentiating differences. The time of the third synthesis is that of
such self-differentiating differences, a time that Deleuze identifies
with Nietzsche's eternal return. The eternal return, Deleuze argues,
is not a return of the same, but a return of difference. Deleuze calls
this return 'repetition', but it is perhaps more easily conceived of as
'reiteration', each moment being a reiteration of the generative force
of self-differentiating differences. Each iteration of difference is without commonsense temporal co-ordinates or stable identities, itself
a groundless medium producing other kinds of time within which
diverse entities take shape. In its generative, creative capacity, this
groundless medium is the time of the new, and hence the time of the
future. In Freud's association of the death instinct with the repetition
compulsion Deleuze finds evidence that Freud is nearing a conception
of the time of the third passive synthesis. Deleuze agrees with Freud
that the death instinct is unconscious and that it only manifests itself
directly in conjunction with Eros, always in elusive disguise. But he
does not concur that the death instinct is an impulse of organic matter
to return to a previous inorganic state, for the death instinct 'is not a
material state' but instead 'corresponds to a pure form – the empty
form of time' (DR 112). The unconscious knows no death (as Freud
himself says), at least in the material sense of the word. Rather, the
'death' proper to the unconscious 'refers to the state of free differences

when they are no longer subject to the form imposed upon them by an I or an ego, when they assume a shape which excludes *my* own coherence no less than that of any identity whatsoever' (DR 113). If there is a subject in the third synthesis, it is an anonymous 'narcissistic ego without memory, a great amnesiac' (DR 111), through which passes an energy no longer bound up with Eros, and hence one that is desexualised and neutral.

Clearly, in his reading of the Freudian death instinct in *Difference and Repetition* Deleuze ventures well beyond the customary purviews of psychoanalysis, and in *The Logic of Sense*, one finds a similar extension of Freudian concepts into a broader philosophical domain. *The Logic of Sense* is an exploration of the relationship between sense and nonsense in the constitution of language. Deleuze's point of departure is the Stoic distinction between bodies and 'incorporeals', one such incorporeal being the *lekton*, sometimes translated as the 'expressible'. For the Stoics, bodies alone have real existence, whereas incorporeals have merely a quasi-existence, a 'subsistence' or 'insistence'. In the Stoic analysis of language, sound bodies issue from a speaker's mouth and strike a listener's ears, but what makes the sound bodies more than incoherent noises (as when we listen to an unintelligible language) is the *lekton*, an incorporeal 'sense' or 'meaning', which subsists or insists like a surface emanation of the sonic bodies. From this Stoic distinction Deleuze develops the concept of 'sense' as a surface effect between bodies and words, sense being both an emanation of words that cannot be subsumed within standard linguistic or logical categories, and an emanation of bodies in the form of the 'event', an impersonal, temporally undifferentiated becoming, a pure infinitive ('to battle' as surface effect hovering over the various bodies interacting on the battlefield). Deleuze argues that sense is a transcendental field, or metaphysical surface, that serves as an incorporeal membrane interrelating words and things, and much of his analysis is focused on the way nonsense, as a self-differentiating difference, generates this metaphysical surface through a 'static genesis' within thought. Late in the book, however, Deleuze turns to the 'dynamic genesis' of sense, or the developmental process whereby the infant comes to distinguish sound-bodies from words, and it is here that he formulates a psychoanalytic theory of the relationship of language to desire.

Deleuze distinguishes three phases in the infant's psychic development, which he associates topologically with depths, heights and surface. Adopting an essentially Kleinian framework, Deleuze sees the infant's earliest psychic world as a tumultuous, chaotic domain in which 'orality, mouth, and breast are initially bottomless depths' (LS 187).[10] In these depths of digestion and excretion, partial objects (good-breast, bad-breast, and so on) are ingested and expelled, the whole constituting a mother-infant fusional 'system of mouth-anus', in which 'bodies burst and cause other bodies to burst *in* a universal cesspool' (LS 187). Deleuze argues, however, that in addition to these violent, persecutory objects, there exists within the depths 'an organism without parts, a body without organs, with neither mouth nor anus' (LS 188). Two depths, then, must be distinguished: a hollow depth of partial objects, and a full depth of the body without organs, the two in a tension that foreshadows the conflict between id and ego. Words in this primal world are experienced as bodies, either as partial objects, 'word-passions, splintered excremental bits', or as sonic bodies without organs, 'word-actions, blocks fused together' (LS 189).

In the second phase of the infant's development, a new object emerges, 'a good object which holds itself aloft' (LS 189), one that is qualitatively distinct from the partial objects of the depths in that it is a complete object. From this complete object of the heights arises the superego, the ideal with which the infant ego identifies, yet which the ego also experiences as persecutory, since the ego retains a degree of its connection with the primal depths upon which the aerial superego looks with hatred. In this second phase, language attains a new dimension, that of the Voice, not yet a vehicle of articulated meaning, but simply the Voice of authority, imbued with emotion (the voice that soothes, scolds, praises, condemns). At this point, sound 'is no longer a noise, but is not yet language' (LS 194).

The third phase is that of the surface. As the infant derives various satisfactions, erogenous zones emerge, local surfaces of pleasure that take on a coherence that differentiates them from the depths. Each zone is 'inseparable from a partial object "projected" onto the territory' (LS 197), the infant's erogenous body surface resembling a 'Harlequin's cloak' (LS 197) of heterogeneous sites of excitation. That patchwork of zones becomes organised and unified through the infant's identification with the phallus, the ideal, complete object of the heights, which is projected onto the erogenous surface. The infant's initial intention is to unify its fragmented body (and thereby heal the wounded maternal body of the depths which is projected from below onto the surface) and reconcile itself with the superego by giving presence to the authority that always threatens to withdraw itself. Such good intentions are subsequently punished, however, for the third phase of the surface is the Oedipal phase, when sexual differences are established. The penis as disconnected partial object of the depths, and the penis as simple symbol of parental authority (male or female), becomes the phallus possessed by the father and missing in the mother. Once this sexual division takes place, the line traced by the phallus across the erogenous body surface no longer heals but instead draws the castrating line of a narcissistic wound. Nevertheless, a 'polymorphously perverse' surface remains, and as the infant begins to acquire language, that erogenous surface is doubled by a metaphysical surface, that of sense. First, the infant differentiates phonemes from the continuous flow of the voice, still without attributing any meaning to the sounds. Then it forms various proto-words with proto-meanings, those proto-words functioning as do the nonsense words of Lewis Carroll: esoteric words, which 'integrate phonemes into a conjunctive synthesis of heterogeneous, convergent, and continuous series' ('y'reince', a contraction of 'Your royal highness'); and portmanteau words, which 'enact a disjunctive synthesis' (LS 231) – 'snark' as 'shark + snake'. The infant thus proceeds 'from the phonemic letter [the unit extracted from the flow of the voice] to the esoteric word as morpheme, and then from this to the portmanteau word as semanteme' (LS 232). From this libidinally invested surface of proto-sense the linguistic surface of fully articulated sense eventually emerges.

Deleuze argues that if in Kleinian terms the first phase of the depths is 'paranoid-schizoid' and the second of the heights is 'depressive' (LS 187), the third phase of the surface is 'sexual-perverse' (LS 197), in that it is the phase of sexual differentiation and polymorphous perversity. The erotic surface is the site of perversion and phantasy, and it is on this surface that the worlds disclosed by Sade and Masoch unfold. It is also the domain in which the death instinct and the third passive synthesis of time become manifest, as libido is desexualised and fixed on the narcissistic ego of the surface (LS 208). In *Masochism* Deleuze says that the perversions of sadism and masochism serve to resexualise desexualised libido, and in the instantaneous leap from desexualisation to resexualisation, within phantasy scenes of incessant repetition, the mute and invisible death instinct, in its ceaseless reiteration of self-differentiating difference, comes close to a direct appearance (M 115–20). In *The Logic of Sense* Deleuze states that there is a perilous relationship 'between the two extremes of the original depth and the metaphysical surface, the destructive cannibalistic drives of depth and the speculative death instinct' (LS 239). The greatest danger is that the surface will merge with the depths and be consumed in a schizophrenic chaos. The greatest promise of this relationship, however, 'lies in the constitution, beyond the physical surface, of a metaphysical surface of great range, on which even the devouring-devoured objects of the depths are projected' (LS 240). Deleuze's conclusion in *The Logic of Sense*, then, is that only on the surface of perversion and phantasy, which is the dual surface of an erogenous body and the incorporeal emanation of linguistic sense, can the chaotic forces of the world be captured and made effective components of thought.

In *Anti-Oedipus*, Deleuze and Guattari's first collaboratively written book, however, Deleuze abandons the surface to plunge into the depths, and by way of that plunge, the entire Freudian apparatus comes under attack. Deleuze's guide to the psyche is no longer perversion but psychosis, the psychological state that Freud judged inaccessible to psychoanalytic treatment. Deleuze and Guattari replace Freud's id–ego–superego with a psychotic triad of desiring machines, body without organs and nomadic subject. Desiring machines are like the partial objects of the Kleinian depths, but now modelled after hallucinatory experiences of the body in disintegration, of persecutory organs, of strange connections between the inner and outer world (controlling radio waves, voices from dogs). Desiring machines are heterogeneous elements – psychic, somatic, material, natural, industrial, and so on – assembled in a connective synthesis through which pass flows of various sorts. The body without organs is like the catatonic body of the schizophrenic, a static, viscous, egg-like body, miraculously self-sufficient, upon which desiring machines trace their course and enter into disjunctive syntheses that paradoxically interrelate flows while simultaneously differentiating them. And the nomadic subject is like the self of a perpetually shifting multiple personality disorder, a roving site of ecstatic intensity traversing the circuits of desiring machines that cover the body without organs, each intensity being the locus of a conjunctive synthesis that creates an ephemeral self.

Deleuze and Guattari's object is not to romanticise psychosis – Guattari's extensive experience in psychiatric institutions made him acutely aware of the grim realities of mental illness – but to extract from the reports of psychotics the principles that govern the workings of the unconscious. For Deleuze and Guattari the unconscious is not so much non-conscious as it is non-rational, and here they depart significantly from Freud. The Freudian unconscious is ultimately inaccessible save through its representatives, whether they be dream images, symptoms, parapraxes, sublimated ideas, and so on. Deleuze and Guattari's unconscious, by contrast, is directly accessible, for it does not represent but instead functions. Desiring machines, bodies without organs and nomadic subjects synthesise diverse flows in a perpetual process of 'desiring-production'. The functioning of the unconscious is this process of desiring-production, and it is immanent within the real. 'For the unconscious itself is no more structural than personal, it does not symbolize any more than it imagines or represents; it engineers, it is machinic. Neither imaginary nor symbolic, it is the Real in itself' (AO 53). The unconscious is the agency of desire, but not an agency seeking to fill a lack. Rather, unconscious desire is positive libido or sexual energy that permeates inner experience as well as the processes of interaction among individuals and their surroundings. 'Desire is the set of *passive syntheses* [performed by desiring-machines, the body without organs and the nomadic subject] that engineer partial objects, flows, and bodies, and that function as units of production' (AO 26). The 'great discovery of psychoanalysis', according to Deleuze and Guattari, 'was that of the production of desire, of the productions of the unconscious' (AO 24). Unfortunately, psychoanalysis also betrayed that discovery, replacing the model of the 'unconscious as a factory' by an unconscious 'that was capable of nothing but expressing itself – in myth, tragedy, dreams' (AO 24).

For Freud, unconscious desires are organised by the Oedipus complex, and this universal pattern of psychic development involving father, mother and individual subject is the key to all human relations. Deleuze and Guattari counter that the Oedipus complex is not universal but instead a product of modern capitalist societies, and that this complex is the principal means whereby such societies discipline, restrict and regulate desire. Desire is immediately social for Deleuze and Guattari, not familial. The family, far from being a closed unit that structures external social relations, is 'eccentric, decentered', itself permeated by extended circuits of interaction.

> The father, the mother, and the self are at grips with, and directly coupled to, the elements of the political and historical situation – the soldier, the cop, the occupier, the collaborator, the radical, the resister, the boss, the boss's wife – who constantly break all triangulations, and who prevent the entire situation from falling back on the familial complex and becoming internalized in it. (AO 97)

The function of the Oedipus complex is to reduce social desire to familial desire and to instil guilt and lack in desiring subjects through the castration complex. Psychoanalysis does not invent the Oedipus complex, for 'the subjects of psychoanalysis arrive already oedipalized, they demand it, they want more' (AO 121). Rather, it merely reinforces existing tendencies, adding 'a last burst of energy to the displacement of the entire unconscious' (AO 121).

Early in their critique of psychoanalysis, Deleuze and Guattari offer a reading of three texts by Freud, which they see as symptomatic of the shortcomings of the entire enterprise. The first is Freud's 1911 'Psychoanalytic Notes on an Autobiographical Account of a Case of Paranoia (Dementia Paranoides)', Freud's reading of Daniel Paul Schreber's *Memoirs of My Nervous Illness* (1903). In this textual analysis (Freud never met Schreber), Freud offers his only extended commentary on a case of psychosis. Though he finds few references to Schreber's father in the text, Freud concludes that the key to Schreber's disorder is his anxiety over homoerotic feelings towards his father. Freud also dismisses Schreber's lengthy remarks on his secret connections to various peoples, races and historical personages. For Freud, such material is merely the residue of mythic and religious narratives, and as much symptomatic of the Oedipus complex as Schreber's personal narrative. For Deleuze and Guattari, by contrast, Schreber's cultural and historical delirium is evidence of the immediately social nature of desire, just as Schreber's delusions (such as those of miraculating rays of the Sun and talking birds) testify not to homoerotic feelings towards the father but to the direct connection of the unconscious with the natural world.

Exhibit number two is Freud's 1919 paper '"A Child Is Being Beaten": A Contribution to the Study of the Origin of Sexual Perversions'. Here Freud uncovers three stages in the generation of a common sadomasochistic phantasy, the most important of which stages is never reported by Freud's patients, but only revealed through analysis: 'My father is beating me.' As Deleuze and Guattari observe, 'never was the paternal theme less visible, and yet never was it affirmed with as much passion and resolution. The imperialism of Oedipus is founded here on an absence' (AO 58). The phantasy as initially reported to Freud is generally that 'some boys are beaten by someone – the teacher, for example – in the presence of the little girls' (AO 59). Yet Freud ignores the group nature of the phantasy, as well as its institutional dimension. For Freud, then, the phantasy is individual and focused on the Oedipalising father. Deleuze and

Guattari, however, insist that the phantasy is irreducibly collective, embedded in a social setting (school, teacher, discipline, authority), and libidinally invested in both boys and girls (evidence not simply of the unconscious' bisexuality, but of its polysexuality, its investment in people, things, images, ideas, and so on).

The third text Deleuze and Guattari examine is 'Analysis Terminable and Interminable', Freud's 1937 reflection on the disquieting realisation that psychoanalytic treatment seems never to result in a final cure, and hence to come to an end. The obstacle to a completed analysis, Freud eventually concludes, is that certain subjects 'have such a *viscous* libido, or on the contrary such a *liquid* one, that nothing succeeds in "taking hold"' (AO 65). Here Deleuze and Guattari find Freud imperfectly glimpsing the oppressive, disciplinary function of psychoanalysis. Viscous libidos are those that resist Oedipalisation, refusing to answer 'Papa-Mama-Me' whenever summoned, whereas liquid libidos gladly acquiesce to any Oedipal interpretation, subverting the analytic process by agreeing to all interpretations and settling on none. What Freud cannot see, then, is that the Oedipus complex is produced, not discovered, and that the resistance to Oedipalisation manifest in viscous and liquid libidos is not an obstruction to treatment but the sign of a potential opening of the subject towards genuine desiring-production.

After *Anti-Oedipus*, Deleuze's comments on Freud diminish significantly. Deleuze and Guattari devote one chapter of *Kafka* (1975) to a refutation of psychoanalytic readings of Kafka, arguing that Kafka's quintessentially Oedipal 'Letter to the Father' is actually a parody of the complex that humorously destroys it through exaggeration, but the rest of the book addresses other matters. Although *A Thousand Plateaus* (1980) purports to be a sequel to *Anti-Oedipus*, with its subtitle *Capitalism and Schizophrenia II*, only the short plateau 'One or Several Wolves?' – a critique of Freud's reading of the Wolfman case – focuses directly on psychoanalytic questions. And *Essays Critical and Clinical* (1993), despite the title's reference to the project Deleuze first proposed in *Masochism* – that of studying writers as great psychological symptomatologists – contains only a few essays of psychoanalytic import, chief of them being 'What Children Say', a counter-reading of Freud's case of Little Hans in terms of a social rather than a familial mapping of desire.

Clearly, *Anti-Oedipus* marks a watershed in Deleuze's approach to Freud. In *Masochism, Difference and Repetition* and *The Logic of Sense* Deleuze uses Freudian materials to build a relatively consistent psychological model, making certain minor modifications in the structure as he proceeds. The domains of the id, superego and ego are those of the depths, heights and surface. A Kleinian framework informs the developmental movement from the chaotic depths of partial objects and the body without organs, to the heights of the complete object and the ego-ideal, to the surface of erogenous zones and the ideal ego. The infant's acquisition of language follows this developmental course. The three syntheses of time provide linkages among psychic processes, the first turning pleasure into a principle, the second grounding the pleasure principle in Eros, the third supplying the 'groundless ground' of the death instinct. The surface is the realm of phantasy and perversion.[11] In sadism the superego is dominant, in masochism the narcissistic ego, and in both a resexualisation of desexualised libido brings the death instinct near the surface. With *Anti-Oedipus*, this Freudian edifice collapses. Little remains save the depths of partial objects and the body without organs. Freud and psychoanalysis are shown to be enemies of desire, whose social function is to discipline subjects by Oedipalising them within the familial confines of castration, guilt and lack.

After mounting this thorough critique of Freud and psychoanalysis, Deleuze has no need of continuing the critique and no interest in making further use of Freudian terminology in his thought. It would be a mistake, however, to stress too heavily the break of *Anti-Oedipus*. At no point is Deleuze an orthodox Freudian. If Freud's primary focus is neurosis and its cure, Deleuze's is first perversion in *Masochism*, *Difference and Repetition*, and *The Logic of Sense*, and then psychosis in *Anti-Oedipus*, and in neither case does he worry about cures. From the beginning, Deleuze's purposes run counter to the therapeutic ends of psychoanalysis, for he sees perversion and psychosis not as disorders to be normalised, but as positive means of inventing new modes of thought.

Yet if Deleuze is never truly Freudian in the proper sense of the term, in a broad sense he may be deemed Freudian to the end. Freud's greatness, say Deleuze and Guattari, 'lies in having determined the essence or nature of desire' (AO 270), and though Freud was also 'the Luther and the Adam Smith of psychiatry', mobilising 'all the resources of myth, of tragedy, of dreams, in order to re-enslave desire' (AO 270–1), his discovery of desire and the unconscious opened the way to Deleuze's conception of affect and the non-rational as central constituents of being and thought. Throughout his work, Deleuze stresses the involuntary nature of genuine thought. To think differently

– and for Deleuze this is philosophy's proper task – requires a violence to thought, a disorienting, unsettling shock to common sense and orthodoxy. New thought is necessarily 'para-doxical', beyond *doxa*, and hence beyond commonsense rationality. And if genuine thought as process is paradoxical, so too are the objects of that thought. The shock of thought is always a paradox that impinges on ordinary consciousness from the outside. The instigation of thought is never consciously chosen, and that which impinges on thought is never part of the field of ordinary consciousness. In both its process and its objects, then, genuine thought is unconscious. And yet this unconscious disruption is experienced directly, always as an intensity, a sensual alteration in affectivity. The domain of intensities is one of desiring-production, in which the body's powers of affecting and being affected are directly experienced, tested, and perhaps extended through a process of experimentation initiated by genuine thought. It is this enduring conception of the unconscious and desire as primary elements of genuine thought that allows us to characterise Deleuze, if only in this one regard, as a Freudian philosopher.

University of Georgia

Notes

1. I take the phrase 'psychoanalytic culture' from Sherry Turkle, who provides a useful history of the French reception of Freud in her *Psychoanalytic Politics: Jacques Lacan and Freud's French Revolution*, 2nd edition (New York: Guilford, 1992). For a more detailed and less sociological treatment of the subject, see Elisabeth Roudinesco, *Jacques Lacan & Company: A History of Psychoanalysis in France, 1925–1985*, trans. Jeffrey Mehlman (Chicago: University of Chicago Press, 1990).
2. Deleuze derives the concept of the oral mother from elements of Edmund Bergler's theory of orality and masochism, as outlined in his *The Basic Neurosis: Oral Regression and Psychic Masochism* (New York: Grune and Stratton, 1949). Deleuze also makes frequent use of Theodor Reik's analysis of masochism in *Masochism in Modern Man*, trans. Margaret H. Beigel and Gertrud M. Kurth (New York: Grove Press, 1941).
3. In keeping with the practice of some psychoanalytic writers, I have chosen to adopt the spelling 'phantasy' rather than 'fantasy' to render Freud's concept of *Phantasie*. Deleuze himself uses the term 'phantasme' rather than 'fantasme' throughout *Masochism*. I have silently emended the translation of *Masochism* throughout to conform to this spelling. On the problems of translating Freud's *Phantasie*, see Jean Laplanche and Jean-Baptiste Pontalis, *The Language of Psycho-Analysis*, trans. Donald Nicholson-Smith (New York: Norton, 1973), pp. 314–15.

4. See Laplanche and Pontalis, *The Language of Psycho-Analysis*, pp. 118–21, for a summary of Freud's views on disavowal.
5. For a concise exposition of Freud's understanding of phantasy, see Laplanche and Pontalis, *The Language of Psychoanalysis*, pp. 314–19.
6. For a lucid summary of Freud's complicated and sometimes contradictory speculations about sadomasochism, see Laplanche and Pontalis, *The Language of Psychoanalysis*, pp. 401–4.
7. 'The transformation of object-libido into narcissistic libido which thus takes place obviously implies an abandonment of sexual aims, a desexualization – a kind of sublimation, therefore.' Freud, *The Ego and the Id*, in *The Standard Edition of the Complete Psychological Works of Sigmund Freud*, edited by James Strachey (London: Hogarth, 1961), Vol. 19, p. 30. The concept of desexualisation does not seem to be one that Freud developed at any length, and I have not found it in any dictionaries of psychoanalytic terminology.
8. The terms 'ego-ideal' and 'ideal ego' come from Freud, but it is Daniel Lagache who has proposed a systematic alignment of the ego ideal with the superego and the ideal ego with the ego. See Laplanche and Pontalis, *The Language of Psychoanalysis*, pp. 144–5, 201–2.
9. See especially LS 304, 320–1.
10. Melanie Klein identifies two stages in the infant's development, a 'paranoid-schizoid position', from birth to four months, and a 'depressive position', from four months to one year. Deleuze's proposal of a third 'sexual-perverse' phase is his own invention. For a succinct account of Klein's two positions, see Laplanche and Pontalis, *The Language of Psychoanalysis*, pp. 114–16 and 298–9.
11. In *The Logic of Sense* Deleuze situates both sadism and masochism within the surface of perversion, which he also characterises as the domain of phantasy and the narcissistic ego. In *Masochism* Deleuze identifies masochism with the narcissistic ego and phantasy, opposing it to sadism and its identification with the superego. The placement of sadism and masochism within a single surface of perversion would seem to represent an alteration in his conception of the two perversions, but nowhere does he provide clear indications of how his earlier account might be modified to conform to this new topography of depths, heights and surface.

13

Henri Bergson

Paul Atkinson

Henri Bergson (1859–1941) was perhaps the most popular Western philosopher in the first decade of the twentieth century, with his works being translated shortly after the appearance of the French editions and his lecture tours extending as far as the United States.[1] The esteem in which his work was held could be attributed to both the artfulness of his prose – he won the Nobel Prize for literature in 1927 – and the timeliness of his ideas. His most celebrated argument that time must endure was a response to the evolutionary theories of Herbert Spencer but, more importantly, presented an alternative to the widespread influence of mechanism in the natural sciences. His theory of memory, which accepted that there is always a retention of the past in the present, led to his radical reworking of the mind–body dualism and, by a circuitous route, to the belief that evolution is driven by a creative impulse (*élan vital*).

Gilles Deleuze is largely responsible for the renewed interest in the philosophy of Bergson, which was laid to rest in many circles as far back as 1962, only fifty years after the height of its popularity.[2] In the early part of the twentieth century Bergsonism had influenced a range of fields including the phenomenological tradition,[3] artistic practice[4] and even social policy.[5] The waning of interest in Bergson's work was not a gradual process, where each of his arguments was tested in a philosophical context; rather, there was a sudden and vehement rejection of the philosophy as a whole, so great that Western philosophy in the period following the Second World War has been characterised by some thinkers as anti-Bergsonian.[6] There are a number of reasons for this sudden change in favour, many of which can be attributed to a change in mood following the two World Wars, a period in which Bergson's processual optimism seemed out of place, but also to a misreading of his philosophy as both vague and primitive. Maurice Merleau-Ponty argued that in France many groups from all areas of academic life tried to compartmentalise Bergson's thought and effectively reduce it to a collection of incoherent and incompatible ideas.[7]

The element in his work most often misunderstood was 'intuition', because it is irreducible to either language or the dialectical method: 'Identified with the vague course of spiritualism, or of some other entity, the bergsonian intuitions lose their bite; they are generalized, minimized.'[8] The critique followed a similar path in the English-speaking world, with detractors such as Georges Santayana arguing that in Bergsonism there is an epistemological regression in the confla-tion of intuition, intellect and instinct and that because it recoils from any attempt to establish universal laws, it can only succeed in describ-ing the natural world through vague, mystical conceptions such as the *élan vital*.[9] In contrast, Deleuze commends Bergson for his unwilling-ness to posit universal laws and carefully dissociates Bergson's phi-losophy from the charge of vague 'spiritualism' through a thorough repositioning of his theory of intuition. Deleuze's two articles on Bergsonism – 'La Conception de la différence chez Bergson' in *Les Études Bergsoniennes*, and 'Bergson 1859–1941' in Merleau-Ponty's edited collection on key philosophers, *Les philosophes célèbres*, written in the same year (1956) – and the monograph *Bergsonisme* ten years later, all refute the claim that Bergsonism lacks a coherent methodology. These three texts form the core of Deleuze's work on Bergsonism but the *fin-de-siècle*'s philosopher's ideas are refracted throughout Deleuze's *oeuvre*, most notably in the two *Cinema* books and *Difference and Repetition*. This refraction takes a number of forms: implicit reference in the examination of other philosophies as in Nietzsche's and Heraclitus' 'affirmation of multiplicity' (NP 24); the development of new concepts such as perplication (DR 187); or more directly the use of Bergsonian examples including the imma-nence of colour in white light (DR 207) and time as a simultaneity of flows (MI 20). Bergson's philosophy resonates throughout Deleuze's *oeuvre*, but it is the propaedeutic created in the early writings, with its integration of Bergson's diverse range of metaphors, methods and lines of thought, that serves as the ground for this resonance.

Deleuze's attraction to Bergson's work relates to the latter's mar-ginal place within the history of philosophy and to Deleuze's preference for those writers 'who escaped from it in one respect, or altogether: Lucretius, Spinoza, Hume Nietzsche, Bergson' (N 6). Deleuze redraws and extends those features of Bergsonism that remain unassimilable within traditional philosophical dualisms, including his qualitative account of becoming and the theory of 'coexistent multiplicities' (D 14–15). In an often quoted passage from 'I Have Nothing to Admit', Deleuze mischievously claims that in *Bergsonism* he has taken Bergson from behind and produced a monstrous child that mimes Bergson's words but in a way that is contrived by the puppet master Deleuze (N 6). For those familiar with Bergson's writings, reading Deleuze's analyses of his work is disconcerting because all the theoretical elements are there, including many of the examples, but there is a change in emphasis with incidental metaphors often raised to the status of concepts. Terms such as 'nuance', 'virtual', 'actual', and 'possible' are certainly used by Bergson but they are not consistently grouped in the form of a recognisable methodology because they remain attached to specific examples or arguments. Bergson is rarely intent on producing stand-alone philosophical concepts; some are consistently applied and regularly used as part of his critique, for example the 'possible', while others change with context, including the much celebrated 'virtual' which has been used to describe both potentiality and possibility.[10] Furthermore, Bergson's work is decontextualised in that Deleuze only briefly acknowledges the bio-historical shifts in his work, usually in the form of a broad synthesis, and rarely makes reference to Bergson's interlocutors and the theoretical fields that served as springboards for his philosophical investigations, although he does introduce peripheral figures such as Riemann (B 39–40). There is little discussion of the importance of Bergson's writings on aphasia, the Special Theory of Relativity, or natural selection, as Deleuze directs his attention inward to the methodological and ontological lines that can be drawn through Bergson's work and which can be said to constitute the articulations of their monstrous child.[11]

Deleuze is not faithful to the Bergsonian *oeuvre*, if what is meant by this is a closed set of writings comprising essays, books, letters and lectures, but in another sense he is faithful to the open and emergent features of Bergson's philosophy and their capacity to unravel in unforeseen ways. To write about Bergson, if one is also to accept his method, is akin to the act of remembering, where the past is altered as it is brought into the service of a continually changing present. George Mourélos, with reference to Bergson, states that a philosopher's work has a 'double character of being at once a bygone and outdated past and a ceaselessly renewed present' which in a reappraisal involves a continuous process of reorientation.[12] For Deleuze, this reorientation entails the integration of Bergson's ideas via the intuitive method that leads eventually to a reformulation of his ontology. Intuition is a series of procedures each of which is integrated in the articulation of differences in kind, which in their turn become species of a vital movement of differentiation. This process mirrors Bergson's contention that his philosophy should form the basis for an integration of the sciences in which physics and chemistry are realigned with the vital movement of biology.[13] Philosophy must take the next step of integration because it is only the intuitive method which can attend to the changing form of the thing in itself.[14]

In the two summaries of Bergson's philosophy, 'Bergson 1859–1941' and *Bergsonism*,[15] Deleuze begins with an examination of Bergson's method of intuition and its role in the adjudication of false problems in philosophy. The article on the concept of difference follows a similar structure, and uses many of the same examples, except that intuition is framed by a theory of difference. This contrasts with the format of most summaries of the philosopher's work[16] that begin with Bergson's critique of the spatialisation of time in science and philosophy and how this leads to his alternative theory of time as duration (*durée*).[17] In taking intuition as his starting point, Deleuze avoids the overemphasised dualism between duration and space but also one of the key problems faced by Bergson: the difficulty in describing the positive features of duration without reference to consciousness or to the negative aspects of spatialised time. Despite its pivotal role in his philosophy, there are very few direct discussions of duration in Bergson's work because its processual movement resists description in natural and philosophical languages, where the emphasis is on the substantive. Most of the positive discussions of duration have a psychological bearing and this is most explicit in the published thesis, *Essai sur les données immédiates de la conscience* (translated into English as *Time and Free Will*):

> Pure duration is the form which the succession of our conscious states assumes when our ego lets itself *live*, when it refrains from separating its present state from its former states. For this purpose it need not be entirely absorbed in the passing sensation or idea; for then, on the contrary it would no longer *endure*. Nor need it forget its former states: it is enough that, in recalling these states, it does not set them alongside its actual state as one point alongside another, but forms both the past and the present states into an organic whole, as happens when we recall the notes of a tune, melting, so to speak, into one another.[18]

Duration is here aligned with a notion of consciousness unhinged from any form of external determination and comparable to the immanent plenitude of a phrase of music that is unbounded by formal notation and exists only in time. To 'let itself live', the ego must not linger on a single perception, idea or object but instead attend to the flow of the whole defined only by a seamless integrity: 'succession without distinction, . . . a mutual penetration, an interconnection and organisation of elements, each one of which represents the whole, and cannot be distinguished or isolated from it except by abstract thought'.[19] Although *Time and Free Will* is an early work, the image of consciousness as an interpenetration of psychic states remains the source of most positive descriptions of duration, even in the late, controversial[20] book on Einstein's Special Theory of Relativity, *Duration and Simultaneity*, where Bergson argues that time is 'at first identical with the continuity of our inner life'.[21] This is not to say that Bergson assumes a coincidence between consciousness and duration in all his works, as ontology outruns psychology in his two introductions to *Creative Mind*, *Creative Evolution* and the latter half of *Matter and Memory*, but it must not be forgotten that Bergson arrives at duration through imagining time in consciousness and it is only in his pursuit of synthetic lines of thought that this connection is diminished.

This positive image of duration as a given in consciousness, however, can only function as a *telos* because Bergson acknowledges that duration is mediated by our conception of time outside of consciousness – it is a composite form, an 'admixture of extensity'.[22] In most of Bergson's accounts of duration, there is the spectre of 'space' as an impurity that must be removed through a process of division, that is, duration can only be apprehended through stripping away, methodologically and phenomenologically, the architecture of space. The role of philosophy is to co-ordinate the effort by which we expel from our mind of all those features that link it to the spatial field of perception. In *Duration and Simultaneity*, the sensual world must be foreclosed in an act of sensual reduction:

> A melody to which we listen with our eyes closed, heeding it alone, comes close to coinciding with this time which is the very fluidity of our inner life; but it still has too many qualities, too much definition, and we must first efface the difference among the sounds, then do away with the distinctive features of sound itself, retaining of it only the continuation of what precedes into what follows and the uninterrupted transition, multiplicity without divisibility and succession without separation, in order finally to rediscover basic time [*le temps fondamental*].[23]

In this example, Bergson again uses the metaphor of the melody because it describes a movement whereby the sounds yield their discreteness to the whole but in this case duration is 'rediscovered' rather than given. Its rediscovery is only possible through the application of a method where external difference accedes to an internal difference of a qualitative multiplicity. Depending on the example used, duration is either the source of Bergson's method, the given into which all phenomena are integrated, or what remains after the impurity (extensity) has been removed through a retroactive process of division. It is the second of these two approaches that Deleuze adopts, but always with the expectation that the division itself will lead eventually to a comprehensive integration; though unlike Bergson he does so without recourse to psychological or phenomenological argument.

In *Bergsonism*, Deleuze states that there are three 'major stages of Bergson's philosophy' 'Duration, Memory, *Élan Vital*' (B 13), but rather than examining how each stage is presented as part of Bergson's ontology, he argues instead that intuition should form the basis of their integration. So unlike Bergson, who wavers between the methodological and phenomenological, Deleuze states clearly that intuition as a method is primary because 'it is likely to inform us as to the nature of bergsonian problems'.[24] Ontologically Deleuze recognises that 'intuition . . . is second in relation to duration or to memory' but that its primacy is essential if there is to be methodological 'precision' (B 13). Methodology precedes ontology in order to disengage Bergson's philosophy from the problems inherent in psychologism or any other method based on givenness either in consciousness or perception.[25] This precision is necessary because Bergson's reduction does not provide a sufficient ground for knowledge, since in duration there are no lines of differentiation or integration, and as such 'it would remain purely intuitive, in the ordinary sense of the word' (MI 14). In highlighting the methodological precision of Bergson's theory of intuition and in contrasting it with 'feeling', 'disorderly sympathy' and 'inspiration' (MI 14), Deleuze is responding to the increasing neglect of Bergson's work, discussed above, as both vague and mystical. Deleuze's task, however, is made all the more difficult by Bergson's persistent claim that intuition is the 'direct vision of the mind by the mind',[26] a claim that is regularly made in opposition to the role of the intellect with its utilisation of 'ready-made' [*déjà faites*] concepts that are applied in any circumstances irrespective of the object.[27] In this opposition, Bergson responds to the push by both science, in the form of Laplacean physics, and philosophy, via concepts such as 'Substance, Ego, Idea, Will', to articulate a coherent unity into which any new fact can be readily placed.[28] Despite stating that intuition is a 'method',[29] Bergson is reluctant to set out the principles of intuition because in such a context it could be misconstrued as a collection of 'ready-made' concepts.

For Bergson, intuition does not utilise ready-made concepts because it attends to the object in its specificity, giving each an 'explanation which would fit it exactly, and it alone'.[30] In its 'fit', the object cannot be separated from the 'precise' concept, or rather the percept that is coincident with the object over time. Consequently, intuition 'signifies first of all consciousness, but immediate consciousness, a vision which is scarcely distinguishable from the object seen, a knowledge which is contact and even coincidence'.[31] It is the unmediated apprehension of the object that proceeds from 'contact' with its surface to 'coincidence' with its internal movement and, in doing so, reaches across the boundaries between bodies to a state of spiritual connection:

> Between our consciousness and other consciousnesses the separation is less clear-cut than between our body and other bodies, for it is space which makes these divisions sharp. Unreflecting sympathy and antipathy, which so often have that power of divination, give evidence of a possible interpenetration of human consciousnesses. It would appear then that phenomena of psychological endosmosis exist.[32]

Lawlor argues that for Bergson, sympathy is only 'self-sympathy', where an understanding of the self in duration leads to sympathy with all things in the form of an expansion of consciousness.[33] In this argument, the movement of intuition is vertical in that it proceeds from the self outwards, eventually reaching a point where it is one with the whole and intuition dissolves in the firstness of duration. It is this all-encompassing notion of interpenetration and sympathy that Merleau-Ponty critiques in the *Phenomenology of Perception* where he argues that in 'discovering an "inner" layer of experience', the actual experience of multiplicity is 'really abolished'. The distinction between the parts of a movement, spatial regions and even the qualitative difference between the past, present and future are effectively erased because when 'the phases of movement gradually merge into one another, nothing is anywhere in motion'.[34] Merleau-Ponty argues that there is a loss of actual difference because duration is not grounded in the phenomenal body, and, despite failing to provide a detailed study of Bergson's conception of difference, makes it clear that this vertical passage of intuition into duration undermines Bergson's philosophical method.

Deleuze does not dismiss Bergson's suggestion that consciousness is expanded via intuition into a processual whole but returns the consciousness, duration and the immediate to their proper place in a series of intuitive procedures. In this respect, intuition is pragmatic in that it cleaves or articulates lines of difference rather than apprehends duration. This horizontal aspect of intuition is discussed by Bergson when he states that intuition does not require ready-made concepts but rather '"mobile concepts" destined to guide other men through th[e] same intuition or put them on the path',[35] and as such its role is indexical rather than referential. When grounded in a series of methodological 'acts', intuition, and by extension philosophy, will rival science because it 'will demand a new effort for each new problem'.[36] It is not a matter of effortless immediacy since intuition must exert itself against two main sources of resistance, the overwhelming weight of philosophical and scientific history and our perceptual and intellectual habits. Deleuze sets out three main 'acts' of intuition: 'the first concerns the stating and creating of problems; the second, the discovery of genuine differences in kind; the third, the apprehension of real time' (B 13). In contrast to the vertical path of intuition, Deleuze places the 'apprehension of real time' third in the list after the reconfiguration of philosophical problems and the cleaving of matter according to differences in kind, even though duration underpins the articulation of problems in a Bergsonian metaphysic. The direct apprehension cannot come first because an explanation is required as to how we have lost the immediate connection to things in themselves and this 'second characteristic of intuition' is a return or restoration of the thing where philosophy 'regains rather than invents'.[37] There is a process of forgetting incorporated in every act because the totality of memory cannot be sustained in consciousness – an argument similar in many respects to Nietzsche's vis-à-vis historical man who is paralysed by the 'insomnia' of reflection.[38] This loss is not simply an intellectual or psychological illusion but an ontological movement whereby the apprehension of time as duration is lost in language, intellectual acts, perceptual orientation, causality and even in the fragmentation of matter into solid bodies; for Deleuze 'things begin by losing themselves in order that we finish by losing them, it must be that forgetting is found in being'.[39] Intuition must push against this tide of forgetting, be a remembering of the present, if duration is to become anything more than a conception.

This act of remembering involves a speculative process of concept creation which circumvents the philosophical tradition of problem solving, passed down through the teaching of philosophy. Solving existing problems often occludes the fact that the problem was badly phrased in the first place, in which case, a solution is only possible by re-examining the structure of a problem or rephrasing a question (B 15). In an extension of Bergson's argument, Deleuze and Guattari argue that philosophy is the 'discipline that involves *creating* concepts' which is a continual and immanent process cultivated in the time of the philosopher (WP 5, 11). As a movement, creating concepts can be compared to the *élan vital* (vital impetus, vital spirit) that compels an organism forward only for it to be constantly confronted by 'obstacles' in the material world that it must overcome or solve in order to continue its movement.[40] The act of rephrasing 'false problems' is central to intuition and these problems can be divided into two types: 'nonexistent problems' (Deleuze refers to the problems that Bergson isolates, such as the relationship between order and disorder), and 'badly stated problems' that 'arbitrarily group things that *differ in kind*' (such as the conflation of sensation and intensity) (B 18–19). One of the most interesting features of Bergson's work is the way he approaches problems – rather than addressing the problems on their own ground he rephrases them with respect to duration. Aporias that have plagued philosophy for centuries often lose their status as questions, including the famous paradoxes of Zeno which Bergson believes involve a 'badly stated problem' because they confuse time and space in the imaginary form of the instant. The instant is a timeless abstraction derived from the line that subtends movement that bears no resemblance to the concrete movement of the arrow or the indivisible steps of Achilles.[41] The 'arbitrary' grouping of 'badly stated problems' is also central to Bergson's critique of psychophysics, a discipline that confuses the psychological state with a change in the value of an external cause. Psychophysics extracts a measurable quantity from a sensible quality, or psychic state, and wrongly argues that qualitative change is effectively determined by quantitative difference. But all this tells us is that the subject experienced a change, which we choose to call a change in intensity and that by convention it is matched by a change in an extensive magnitude.[42] In his critique, Bergson argues that changes in intensity are actually qualitative changes and uses the example of muscular effort, which is not simply an increase in force but a change in the state of the body such that a greater number of muscles are implicated in an action. [43] This kinaesthetic change cannot be described in terms of more or less but rather as a qualitative change in the overall musculature.

Bergson also analyses the metaphysical suppositions of a number of 'nonexistent problems' that have had a decisive impact on philosophical and scientific thought, of which the most famous are the analyses of order/disorder and being/nothingness in *Creative Evolution*. Bergson argues that these oppositions are 'theoretical illusions' that involve a false movement from 'absence to presence'.[44] The opposition of being and nothingness is often phrased as a problem: 'why does this principle exist rather than nothing', with many derivatives including such questions as 'why is there something rather than nothing?' Nothingness is either the origin of being in *ex nihilo* arguments, or the 'eternal' ground of existence, but in either case, being is that which fills the void and the void the eternal receptacle of being.[45] The effect of this way of stating the problem is that metaphysics seeks an explanation of being that will raise it to the status of the eternal, comparable to the eternity of nothingness, and in doing so overcome the idea of nothingness.[46] Rather than directly refute the concept of nothingness, Bergson plots how the concept could have emerged, that is he imagines it within the positivity of becoming in the form of a genetic argument. The problem is first addressed through the body and consciousness, a feature of many of Bergson's critiques, where he asks how one can imagine nothingness and proposes that one can either extinguish the 'external perception' of things or the 'internal perception' of consciousness. In both cases, there is a residual state of consciousness such that it is impossible to posit both at the same time and the only way to imagine nothingness as a generalised state is through the alternation of attention from one invocation of nothingness, 'partial nought' (*néant partiel*), to another.[47] This is a typical Bergsonian turn, where nothingness is conceived in terms of time, in the alternating form of the subject's attention, rather than space with its absolute separation of presence and absence, being and non-being. [48] Nothingness is a figure of expectation and regret, for expecting one object in the place of another turns the attention from the present object to the absent one and thus transforms the former into a 'virtual absence':[49] 'The conception of the void . . . is only a comparison between what is and what could or ought to be, between the full and the full.'[50] Nothingness might serve as the condition for imagining the eternal in philosophy but for Bergson it is actually produced from within the plenitude of perception and memory, as the 'virtual absence' is carved out of the perceptual continuity of 'radical becoming' by a recollection projected onto the present. This is expressed in the form of the question, 'why is this object here rather than the other recollected object?', and underlying this question is an imagined substitution where the absent object takes its place. If an object can be substituted it can also be excluded, that is, imagined as absent from the plenitude and this becomes the foundation for a general concept of nothingness as the extrapolation of this possible exclusion to all things.[51] In this critique, contrary to most metaphysical accounts, Bergson argues that there is actually more in the concept of nothingness than in being because it combines recollection and perception. This is also true of negation which is comprised of an affirmation of being, in the form of an existential statement, to which is added the judgement that it does not exist.[52] However, the negation is qualitatively different to the affirmation because it is not an existential statement about a particular object, or a particular moment in becoming, but a judgement of a judgement.[53] This asymmetry serves as the ground for Bergson's distinction between the actual and the possible where the actual is what passes and is affirmed – noted or noticed (*noter*)[54] in experience rather than conceptualised – whereas the possible is always a secondary judgement on objects that have already been abstracted.

Bergson's examination of nothingness is underpinned by the 'second characteristic of intuition' in that it describes a return to the actual via a critique of the possible but it also reveals how the two types of 'false problems' are connected. The 'theoretical illusion' of nothingness serves as the basis for the amalgamation of differences in kind inasmuch as nothingness is the ground for both space and time in notions of eternity and of course in Newton's conception of absolute space and time. However, only space is derived from the extrapolation of the 'partial noughts' because it serves as the background to the substitution or exclusion of objects.[55] It is the unalterable ground of possibility, the general container of being, and the blank field that joins together discrete objects in a quantitative multiplicity. This conception of space is so stripped of any connection to the actual movement of becoming that displacement and change can be understood solely as differences in degree – what is more or less can be plotted against a line, plane or volume. It is to this conflation of the two problems that Deleuze alludes when he states that 'conceiving everything in terms of more and less, seeing nothing but differences in degree or differences in intensity where, more profoundly, there are differences in kind is perhaps the most general error of thought, the error common to science and metaphysics' (B 20). Throughout Deleuze's work, he has exposed this error and sought to re-imagine philosophy from the perspective of difference or actual differences in kind and stresses the importance in his own method of examining difference without recourse to opposition. However, philosophy is not restricted to the critique of 'false problems' and any method requires a second act of intuition, the 'discovery of genuine differences in kind', which provides a means of specifying as well as arbitrating between 'genuine differences'. Without this second act, philosophy would be no more than a discipline that lists or 'notes' an infinite procession of actual differences.

The recovery of 'genuine differences in kind' involves a reorientation of philosophy from difference as 'altérité', usually in the form of contradiction and opposition, to difference as 'altération'[56] – that which both differs from itself and differs in kind.[57] Difference as 'altération' does not adhere to the external surface of things, which yields an infinite number of points of view, but instead expresses an *'internal difference'*[58] where difference is stabilised in the unity of a process, such as the integration of memory with the present. The difficulty for philosophy is how to enact a shift from the external and endlessly juxtaposed differences to genuine differences, without positing an unreachable thing in itself. For Deleuze, and to a lesser degree Bergson, this requires a methodological procedure, and consequently Deleuze interpolates into the act of discovering 'genuine differences' two characteristics of intuition that are intermittently employed by Bergson, 'articulations of the real' and 'lines of facts'[59]

> The articulations of the real distribute things according to their differences of nature, they constitute a differentiation. The lines of facts are directions, each of which are followed to the end, directions which converge on one and the same thing; they define an integration, each one constitutes a line of probability.[60]

The 'articulations of the real' are differences that relate to the natural function and development of an object and are most easily understood in the example of living bodies which have developed their form according to an internal movement or a broader evolutionary movement. In *The Two Sources of Morality and Religion* Bergson argues that science should be judged by the 'way it first dissects its object' – good science will find the 'natural joints' and not depend on broad, ill-fitting categories.[61] It is always an act of differentiation, where intuition functions like a scalpel cleaving an object into parts that already have a natural division. The accurate dissection does not, in itself, provide an understanding of 'internal difference' but an object's natural articulations are central to understanding its movement and direction. Drawing on a Bergsonian example, Deleuze calls this process of articulation *'decoupage'* (carving up or cutting out), and argues that it forms only the beginning of a more extensive process of *'recoupage'* (recutting or matching up)[62] where differences in kind are extended as 'lines of fact'.[63]

The 'lines of fact' form the basis of Bergson's empiricism and describe the 'gradual ascent' from the articulations of the object to states of higher probability.[64] Experience is the starting point for the 'lines of fact' but the intellect expands the experience along a line of probability well beyond the immediately given.[65] The clearest example of this process is in Bergson's essay 'Life and Consciousness', which begins with a brief account of consciousness as a given; however, unlike in the above examples, there is no vertical expansion of consciousness into a durational whole but rather the intuition of a number of key features or 'articulations'. Consciousness can never be defined in an instant – there are no snapshots or cross sections of consciousness – and has a definite duration in which there is both the retention of the past and the preparation for the future held together in the continuity of memory.[66] Bergson then follows this line of facts outside the body arguing that non-human species have consciousness of some form because their actions resemble our own, 'from that external resemblance you conclude by analogy there is an internal likeness'.[67] There is high probability that they are conscious in that there is a degree of anticipation in all organisms and, consequently, the presence of some form of memory. The resemblance is further supported by the fact that all species are part of the continuum of evolution. In the expansion beyond experience, Bergson has removed from consciousness the condition of self-awareness and it is little more than a mnemonic bridge, a 'hyphen' between the past and present,[68] but a line of facts is not sufficient in itself to understand an object as it must converge with other lines.[69] He begins by rejecting the commonly accepted idea that the brain houses consciousness – an argument derived from the relationship between brain death and a loss of consciousness – and argues instead that we should look to its proper function as an articulation in the long evolution of the nervous system. In this context the brain's role is to induct sensations, the movements of matter, and transfer this movement to the body, that is, to conduct the stimulus to a particular response.[70] The brain is an 'organ of choice' because there is the capacity to redirect movement down a variety of channels.[71] In the simplest unicellular organism there is a degree or 'zone of indetermination' which expands in the more complex organisms where there is a greater range of possible actions. In this there is a convergence of two lines of facts because consciousness is 'co-extensive' with choice and voluntary movement insofar as both involve an anticipation of the future.[72] Bergson adds a third lines of facts arguing that material difference is contracted according to utility – the perceptual field and the array of difference is reduced through action – and this is linked to the other lines of facts because contraction depends on the mnemonic range of the subject.[73] The greater the scope and number of material events that are held together in the present consciousness moment, the tension of memory, the greater the control the subject has over its perceptual environment.[74] In the final analysis, the three lines of facts are integrated into the general evolutionary movement of 'consciousness flowing against matter' with increasing force as the mnemonic range of each species develops.[75] This evolutionary argument is in turn integrated in a higher level of movement where the tendency of life pushes against the inelasticity of matter.

Deleuze highlights this argument because it decentres Bergson's ontology despite the fact that it begins with consciousness. Intuition isolates the 'lines of facts' which are like mathematical differentials, lines of movement tangential to consciousness, that must be integrated or resolved in a new conception of consciousness as part of a broader tendency. For Deleuze, integration is one reason why Bergson maintains an interest in the infinitesimal calculus despite his critique of the spatialising language of mathematics.[76] Integration takes a portion of a line describing motion and extends this to envisage the whole line, in the same way that philosophy should take a portion of experience and 'broaden' it. In following the 'lines of facts' along the curve of experience, there is both an attention to the presentness of experience and a movement towards what Deleuze states are the 'conditions of experience', the true object of philosophy (B 27–8). The brain is not an object that can be analysed in itself – a container for consciousness or an object that is revealed by morphology alone – but the meeting point of two tendencies, the space opened up in matter by the movement of life. The explanation, however, is not located in the present but in an indefinite future, 'a virtual point' where the 'lines of facts' conjoin to serve as the 'sufficient reason of the thing'.[77] The 'lines of facts' and the tendencies they reveal are not restricted to any one field but cross and intersect in the general movement of life and it is for this reason that Bergson can employ arguments on the nature of instinct and the vital impetus to explain the mystical tradition in religion.[78]

In isolating the movement of experience, Bergson is not describing a clear, abstract or smooth concept as suggested by the image of mathematical integration, rather it is, as Deleuze reiterates, the movement of a 'percept' (B 28). The simplicity of the tendency does not inhere in the clear form of the curve of experience but in its explanatory power to correlate and integrate the widest range of differences in kind.[79] Bergson uses the example of an artillery shell which is shot into the air and bursts into fragments, each of which continues to divide until it hits the ground. The shape and path of the fragments is a product of the interaction of the 'explosive force of the powder' with the resistance of the metallic shell casing. The aim is to understand the movement of the trajectory rather than simply plot the individual objects. By analogy evolutionary theory must recognise that the tendency of life is manifest as a force which proceeds through the division of matter. The difficulty lies in the fact that '[w]e perceive only what is nearest to us, namely, the scattered movements of the pulverised explosions. From them we have to go back, stage by stage, to the original movement.'[80] The movement of the trajectory is something that is readily understandable as a continuity of change but this process of alteration is not readily yielded in the examination of the individual parts. Raymond Ruyer discusses a related problem in biology where the detailed examination of morphology, and its mechanical explanation of bodily function, can actually lead to difficulties in understanding the development of organisms, where there is a difference in kind between the movement of morphogenesis and the detailed examination of structure in relation to function.[81] Likewise for Bergson, the movement of the tendency cannot be understood through the analysis of a cross-section. The tendency resists any analytical decomposition due to its simplicity, which derives from the concrete interpenetration of unity and multiplicity in the interiority of an act.[82] In this unity of integration, the interpenetration of one moment with the next ensures the continuity of the line. In short, intuiting the line beyond experience involves the vertical integration of its movement, the path of the curve, and a horizontal integration of matter itself in the form of the percept.

Tendencies are concrete movements in the world and in their broadest expression describe the movement of matter and the movement of life otherwise conceived with reference to the second law of thermodynamics as, respectively, the act of '*unmaking itself*' (material dissolution) and '*making itself*' (creation).[83] This seems far removed from the action of intuition posited at the beginning of this chapter as an awareness of duration in the immediately given, but Bergson stresses that intuition is a dynamic principle that must 'coincide with the act of generating reality'.[84] Deleuze foregrounds these methodological acts because it is only through the recognition of differences in kind – differences that extend beyond the psychological – that we can arrive at duration as the 'apprehension of real time'. This requires a final act of intuitive integration and Deleuze argues that one tendency can serve as the basis for the integration of the other, that is, there must be a dominant tendency in all mixtures and the question is how to choose the 'right one'.[85] In the two tendencies discussed above, there is on the one hand the movement of matter as the expenditure of energy – as a 'descent' in which all future states can be intellectually apprehended in the present because there is only a quantitative change in the distribution of energy – and on the other hand the movement of life as an 'ascent' or process of emergence, differentiation and complexification whose future states are unforeseeable.[86] The difference between the two tendencies is insurmountable if we presuppose that the differences in kind are somehow located *between* the two tendencies, where the quantitative dispersal of space is juxtaposed with the qualitative complexification of time. Deleuze reconciles the two tendencies, not by invoking the concrete features of duration as Bergson so often does, but by taking difference itself as the principle. In this regard there is clearly a dominant tendency insofar as the 'ascent', the movement of the *élan vital*, describes difference in its simplest (most highly integrated) form as differentiation or the movement that 'differs from itself'.[87] This incorporates all the other forms of movement and change in Bergson's work including the accumulation of the past, the movement of life, and so on, because it unifies duration as both an account of time *and* substance: 'Duration, tendency is the difference of self from self; and what differs from itself is *immediately* the unity of substance and subject.'[88] For Deleuze this ceaseless and immanent differentiation underpinning all other actual, real or possible differences is the virtual.[89] The simplicity of the virtual is that it provides a necessary and sufficient explanation of substance as the generation of differences in kind without recourse to external explanations such as first or final causes.[90] In the virtual, there is a singular and immediate movement of actualisation – unlike the immediacy of the whole which lacks lines of actualisation – in the creative act of differentiation where the present does not resemble the past (DI 101).

The 'apprehension of real time' that follows is the third act of an intuitive method because it integrates the other acts and prevents any dissolution of intuition into a vague monism – the methodology acts as a temporal scaffold of genuine differences in kind. Furthermore, it is only by means of the intuitive method that an appropriately post-psychological understanding of duration can be reached, for Bergson's philosophy is 'not psychological in itself', insofar as psychological apprehension is only one manifestation of a process of differentiation.[91] One must follow the lines of facts beyond experience to understand that the self-conscious intuition of duration is actually the product of the differentiation of the virtual, describing that point where life reflects on itself.[92] Deleuze states that Bergson's thought evolved such that 'Duration seemed to him to be less and less reducible to a psychological experience and became instead the variable essence of things, providing the theme of a complex ontology' (B 34–5). The method of intuition redraws the lines of Bergson's work such that the 'complex ontology' underpins the 'apprehension of real time' as a series of ideas integrated, or folded, into the whole.[93] It is only in recognising the openness of the whole, found here in the virtual, that the radical nature of duration can be fully realised.

Bergson also performs a similar integration, although without an explicit methodology, when he argues that the simple movement of life and duration incorporates the infinite complexity of the real because into it 'everything will be restored, and into movement everything will be resolved'.[94] But unlike Deleuze he does not posit a single genetic principle, such as the virtual, because he remains tied to the qualitative features of duration and the metaphors he has used to develop his philosophy of time. Bergson argues that the 'ascending movement' of life '*endures* essentially, and imposes its rhythm' on the descending movement of matter,[95] with the emphasis on the integrated temporal whole of rhythm rather than the iterative process of differentiation. The metaphorical basis of so much of Bergson's work contrasts markedly with Deleuze's integration of Bergsonian ideas in the methodology of intuition because Deleuze looks to distil concepts from Bergson's heuristic examples, for example, in the elevation of '*nuance*' as the sufficient explanation of the 'essence' of the thing.[96] In contrast to its invocation in the encyclopaedia entry,[97] there is an examination in the 'Difference' essay of the other meaning of the term '*nuance*' to refer to a shade or colour and how the shade should be placed within a broader spectrum of white light.[98] There is a distinct difference in the way Bergson and Deleuze treat the same examples. Bergson's metaphors do not readily yield concepts or lines of integration and many of his arguments are actually formed in the space between metaphors. Indeed, Bertrand Russell criticised Bergson for his use of 'similes' and 'analogies' and remarked that an argument using such techniques cannot be refuted any more than a work by Shakespeare can be considered incorrect.[99] In the 'Introduction to Metaphysics' Bergson expands upon a series of metaphors to describe duration, including: the movement towards death in the 'unrolling of a spool'; the accumulation of memory in the winding of a ball of string; the proliferation of differences in kind in the metaphor of the spectrum and its shades; and the tension of memory as the contraction into an 'infinitely small piece of elastic'.[100] Bergson acknowledges the insufficiency of each metaphor, stating that duration 'cannot be represented by images', and argues instead that duration should be imagined as an amalgamation of all these metaphors.[101] While acknowledging the insufficiency of metaphor, Bergson proscribes the use of concepts because the abstraction will actually obstruct the cultivation of an intuitive disposition that can successively resist the 'utilitarian habits of mind'.[102] This capacity to integrate metaphors and percepts into a non-contradictory intuitive act is pivotal to Bergson's method, and in one of his speculative passages in *Creative Evolution* he imagines that a prolonged intuition 'would not only make the philosopher agree with his own thought, but also all philosophers with each other'.[103] This expansion of intuition beyond the turn of experience is the aim of Bergsonism and it is Deleuze who gives it the precision of a methodology through the integration of the intuitive acts.

The integration of Bergson's theory of intuition into the genetic movement of the virtual leaves open the question as to the form that future Bergson scholarship might take. It is noteworthy that Bergson himself does not perform a similar reappraisal of his own method, although there are many beginnings, including the two introductions to *Creative Mind* and the articles on 'The Perception of Change', 'The Possible and the Real' and the 'Introduction to Metaphysics', but for the most part his approach is heuristic and synthetic. Bergson constantly wandered into new fields of enquiry using intuitive acts of the kind later outlined by Deleuze. Bergson's resistance to a Deleuzian-style methodological integration probably issues from his suspicion of ready-made concepts which have the capacity to alienate an idea from its empirical context. It is noteworthy that Bergson wrote only one book addressing the work of a single philosopher, his Latin doctoral thesis on Aristotle, preferring to develop new concepts rather than provide detailed critiques of existing methods.[104] Like Deleuze, Bergson maintained his interest in scientific change, and most of his works begin with a discipline-specific scientific problem – psychology in both *Time and Free Will* and *Matter and Memory*, biology in *Creative Evolution*, and physics in *Duration and Simultaneity*. This describes a possible path for the continuation of Bergson's philosophy, as the recent changes in the fields of physics and biology provide fertile ground for the investigation of the fine-grain of the virtual – the 'larval subjects' and infra-empirical intensive concepts that had yet to emerge in Bergson's biologism (DI 96). Another path would be to return to Bergson's philosophy and find further differences in kind, as Deleuze does in the *Cinema* books with his differentiation of the theses on movement before their inevitable integration in a cinematic ontology. In this differentiation, it is not so much a question of remaining faithful to the philosopher, to what was said, but of discussing what might have been had he followed the same lines in his own work.[105] Bergson's heritage, like his philosophy, is dynamic, and to return to the past should always result in the extension of new lines of differentiation beyond the turn of experience.

Monash University

Notes

1. Mark Antliff, *Inventing Bergson* (Princeton, NJ: Princeton University Press, 1992), pp. 3–4.
2. Edouard Morot-Sir, 'What Bergson Means to us Today', in T. Hanna (ed.), *The Bergsonian Heritage* (New York: Columbia University Press, 1962), pp. 35–8.
3. Morot-Sir, 'What Bergson Means', pp. 40–1.
4. See A. E. Pilkington, *Bergson and His Influence: a Reassessment*, (Cambridge: Cambridge University Press, 1976).
5. During the First World War, Bergson was sent as an ambassador to the United States and may have played some part in its decision to enter the war. See R. C. Grogin, *The Bergsonian Controversy in France, 1900–1914* (Calgary: Calgary University Press, 1988), pp. 200–2.
6. Morot-Sir, 'What Bergson Means', pp. 40–1.
7. Maurice Merleau-Ponty, 'At the Sorbonne', in T. Hanna (ed.), *The Bergsonian Heritage*, pp. 133–5.
8. Merleau-Ponty, 'At the Sorbonne', p. 134.
9. George Santayana, *Winds of Doctrine and Platonism and the Spiritual Life* (Gloucester: Peter Smith, 1971), pp. 66–8.
10. Bergson argues that in terms of traditional logic, the colours red and yellow always existed potentially (*virtuellement*) in the colour orange.

See *Oeuvres*, edited by André Robinet (Paris: Presses Universitaires de France, 1959), p. 1267.

11. A similar approach can be traced in the *Cinema* books, where Deleuze draws the ontological limits of the cinema using Bergson's philosophy and in doing so minimises the importance of both industrial factors and the role of the audience in the development of film form.

12. My translation of 'double caractère: d'être à la fois un passé révolu et périmé et un présent qui se renouvelle sans cesse', in G. Mourélos, *Bergson et les niveaux de réalité* (Paris: Presses Universitaires de France, 1964), p. 15.

13. He also states that this metaphysical goal is not 'realisable' because the vital movement is still marked by an indeterminacy not found in its derivatives. See Bergson, *Creative Evolution*, trans. Arthur Mitchell (New York: Random House, 1944 [1907]), p. 38.

14. Moore states that Bergson's criticism of philosophy's endeavour to unify the sciences in his essay 'Philosophical Intuition' could be levelled at his own *Creative Evolution*. See F. C. T. Moore, *Bergson: Thinking Backwards* (Cambridge: Cambridge University Press, 1996), p. 10.

15. This was written as an undergraduate text alongside the books on Hume and Nietzsche, and as such the main impetus was exegesis. See P. Perry, 'Deleuze's Nietzsche', *boundary 2*, 20:1 (1993), p. 176.

16. This is true of most of the early summaries of his work but also those published post-Deleuze, including John Mullarkey, *Bergson and Philosophy* (Edinburgh: Edinburgh University Press, 1999) and A. R. Lacey, *Bergson* (London: Routledge, 1989).

17. I will use the English translation 'duration' hereafter but it is worth noting that it is usually used to indicate a measurable period of time not the concrete movement of time as envisaged by Bergson. Moore argues that 'duration' omits a fundamental sense in the French of '*the fact or property of going through time*', its continuance, and has chosen instead the archaic English expression 'durance', Moore, *Bergson*, pp. 58–9.

18. Bergson, *Times and Free Will: An Essay on the Immediate Data of Consciousness*, trans. F. L. Pogson (London: George Allen and Unwin, 1910 [1889]), p. 100.

19. Bergson, *Times and Free Will*, p. 101.

20. Bergson 'did not wish any further editions to be published in the thirties, since he felt that he could not defend adequately the technical and mathematical parts of his argument', Moore, *Bergson*, p. 11.

21. Bergson, *Time and Free Will*, p. 44.

22. Bergson, *Times and Free Will*, p. 102.

23. Bergson, *Duration and Simultaneity: With Reference to Einstein's Theory*, trans. Leon Jacobson (Indianapolis: Bobbs-Merrill, 1965 [1922]), p. 44.

24. My translation of 'elle est susceptible de nous renseigner sur la nature des problèmes bergsoniens', Deleuze, 'Bergson 1859–1941', in *Les philosophes célèbres*, edited by Maurice Merleau-Ponty (Paris: Editions d'Art Lucien Mazenod, 1956), p. 292.
25. In *Cinema 1*, film serves as a model for decentering consciousness and perception, see MI 57.
26. Bergson, *The Creative Mind*, trans. M. L. Añdison (New York: Philosophical Library, 1946), p. 35.
27. Bergson, *Creative Mind*, pp. 40–1.
28. Bergson, *Creative Mind*, pp. 34–5.
29. Bergson, *Creative Mind*, p. 33.
30. Bergson, *Creative Mind*, p. 35.
31. Bergson, *Creative Mind*, p. 36.
32. Bergson, *Creative Mind*, p. 36.
33. Leonard Lawlor, *The Challenge of Bergsonism* (London: Continuum, 2003), p. 66.
34. Maurice Merleau-Ponty, *Phenomenology of Perception*, trans. Colin Smith (London: Routledge & Kegan Paul, 1962), p. 276 n.1.
35. My translation of '"concepts mobiles" destinés à guider les autres hommes à travers cette même intuition ou à les mettre sur la voie'; letter to W. R. Boyce Gibson, 9 February 1911: Gibson Papers, University of Melbourne Archives, Melbourne.
36. Bergson, *Creative Mind*, p. 35.
37. My translation of 'retrouvée plutôt qu'inventée', Deleuze, 'Bergson 1859–1941', p. 293.
38. Friedrich Nietzsche, *Untimely Meditations*, trans. R. J. Hollingdale (Cambridge: Cambridge University Press, 1997), p. 74.
39. My translation of 'choses commencent par se perdre pour que nous finissions par les perdre, il faut qu'un oubli soit fondé dans l'être', Deleuze, 'Bergson 1859–1941', p. 293.
40. Bergson, *Creative Evolution*, p. 16.
41. Henri Bergson, *Matter and Memory*, trans. W. S. Palmer and N. M. Paul (New York: Zone Books, 1991), p. 191.
42. Bergson, *Time and Free Will*, pp. 63–4.
43. Bergson, *Time and Free Will*, pp. 22–4.
44. Bergson, *Creative Evolution*, p. 296.
45. Bergson, *Creative Evolution*, p. 300.
46. Bergson, *Creative Evolution*, pp. 300–1.
47. Bergson, *Creative Evolution*, p. 303.
48. Bergson, *Creative Evolution*, pp. 297–8.
49. Bergson, *Creative Evolution*, p. 299.
50. Bergson, *Creative Evolution*, p. 307.
51. Bergson, *Creative Evolution*, p. 310.
52. Bergson, *Creative Evolution*, p. 311.

53. Bergson, *Creative Evolution*, p. 316.
54. In an earlier passage Bergson uses the adjective 'constatée' to describe the actual and this is contrasted with the possible, where existence is only ever thought. See *Oeuvres*, p. 740.
55. It is noteworthy that Bergson wrote his first thesis on Aristotle's conception of place and in this text discussed the division between a notion of place in which form and matter are intimately entwined and one with 'la forme libre et indépendante'. See Bergson, *Mélanges*, edited by A. Robinet (Paris: Presses Universitaires de France, 1972), p. 51.
56. In Aristotle's categories, alteration is distinguished as the only form of motion that does not have a natural contrary unless one states that the contrary is to 'rest in its quality' or to find in the quality its contrary (black vs. white, for example). See Aristotle, 'Categoriae', *Organon*, trans. E. M. Edghill, in *The Basic Works of Aristotle*, edited by R. McKeon (New York: Random House, 1941), pp. 36–7. For Bergson there is no state of rest, only states of relative stability, and qualities are never truly contrary, that is, there is no absolute black only states of becoming black and becoming non-black.
57. Deleuze, '1859–1941', p. 295.
58. Deleuze, 'Bergson's Conception of Difference', trans. Melissa McMahon, in J. Mullarkey (ed.), *The New Bergson* (Manchester: Manchester University Press, 1999), p. 43.
59. Deleuze, 'Bergson's Conception of Difference', p. 43.
60. Deleuze, 'Bergson's Conception of Difference', pp. 43–4.
61. Henri Bergson, *The Two Sources of Morality and Religion*, trans. R. Ashley Andra and Clondesley Brereton (Westport: Greenwood Press, 1963), pp. 105–6.
62. The word has a similar duality to the English word 'cleave', which means both to separate and to cling or adhere to. Moreover, Deleuze is interested in the relationship between division and the whole in his other works, including *Cinema 1*, where he argues that the frame unifies in the act of dividing (the 'dividual') by joining the image to other frames (MI 14).
63. Deleuze, 'Bergson's Conception of Difference', p. 44.
64. Henri Bergson, *Mind-Energy Lectures and Essays*, trans. H. Wildon Carr (London: Macmillan, 1920), pp. 3–4.
65. Bergson, *Two Sources*, p. 248.
66. Bergson, *Mind-Energy*, p. 5.
67. Bergson, *Mind-Energy*, pp. 6–7.
68. Bergson, *Mind-Energy*, p. 6.
69. Bergson, *Two Sources*, p. 248.
70. Bergson, *Mind-Energy*, pp. 8–9.
71. Bergson, *Mind-Energy*, p. 9.

72. Bergson, *Mind-Energy*, p. 13.
73. Bergson, *Mind-Energy*, pp. 16–17.
74. Bergson, *Mind-Energy*, pp. 15–16.
75. Bergson, *Mind-Energy*, p. 21.
76. In the second introduction to *Creative Mind*, Bergson openly praises Newton's theory of fluxions (the differential) as a true intuition in that it reunites the immobility of matter with real change (p. 37).
77. Bergson, *Creative Mind*, pp. 28–9.
78. Bergson argues that there is a common movement between instinct and intuition which has been maintained in the mystical tradition despite its suppression by the intellectual structures of organised religion. See *Two Sources*, pp. 249–50.
79. Deleuze, 'Bergson's Conception of Difference', p. 44.
80. Bergson, *Creative Evolution*, p. 109.
81. Raymond Ruyer, *La genèse des formes vivantes* (Paris: Flammarion, 1958), pp. 8–9. Ruyer argues that: '*Il ne peut y avoir isomorphisme entre une forme et une formation, mais seulement entre forme et forme, ou entre formation et formation.*' In morphogenesis, the difficulty lies in explaining how one type of structure becomes another – how the nervous system develops from an egg that does not resemble a nervous system.
82. Mourélos, *Bergson et les niveaux*, p. 70.
83. Bergson, *Creative Evolution*, p. 267. In *Creative Evolution*, Bergson accepts the general principle of entropy but rather than accepting it as a purely energetic principle, premised on the dissipation of heat, he regards it is a tendency that works inversely against creation, that is, works against qualitative change and evolutionary complexification (pp. 267–8).
84. My translation of 'coïncide avec l'acte générateur de la réalité'; Bergson, *Mélanges*, p. 773.
85. Deleuze, 'Bergson's Conception of Difference', p. 47.
86. Bergson, *Creative Evolution*, p. 14.
87. Deleuze, 'Bergson's Conception of Difference', p. 48.
88. Deleuze, 'Bergson's Conception of Difference', 48.
89. Deleuze, 'Bergson's Conception of Difference', 51.
90. Deleuze, 'Bergson's Conception of Difference', 53.
91. Deleuze, 'Bergson's Conception of Difference', 55.
92. Deleuze, 'Bergson's Conception of Difference', 51.
93. An allied argument is proffered in *Cinema 1*, where the single cinematic frame invokes duration as a whole in proportion to its separation from the spatial infinity of actualised frames (see MI 18).
94. Bergson, *Creative Evolution*, p. 273.
95. Bergson, *Creative Evolution*, p. 14.
96. Deleuze, 'Bergson's Conception of Difference', 46.

97. Here he makes reference to the spectral context discussed in Bergson's article on Ravaisson. See Deleuze, '1859–1941', p. 294.
98. This excision of this other sense is maintained in the translation where the term 'nuance' is translated directly as 'nuance' rather than 'shade'; Deleuze, 'Bergson's Conception of Difference', p. 46. Bergson acknowledged in a letter to his Polish translator that recreating the 'images' central to his work is a difficult task. See Bergson, *Mélanges*, p. 960.
99. Bertrand Russell, *A History of Western Philosophy*, 2nd edn (London: Counterpoint), pp. 761–4.
100. Bergson, *Creative Mind*, pp. 192–93.
101. Bergson, *Creative Mind*, p. 194.
102. Bergson, *Creative Mind*, p. 195.
103. Bergson, *Creative Evolution*, pp. 260–1.
104. In one of his first published speeches Bergson criticised those thinkers who only attend to a very limited area of expertise rather than opening their gaze to broader areas of knowledge. See Bergson, 'La Spécialité', in *Mélanges*, pp. 257–64.
105. Based upon his arguments concerning the image as movement in *Matter and Memory*, Bergson could have developed an ontology that fully decentres the subject if he was not tied to the critique of cinematic perception (see Deleuze, MI 57–8).

14

Edmund Husserl

Alain Beaulieu

DELEUZIAN DRAMATURGY

Deleuze attributes three very distinct functions to the various philosophers he quotes, studies and uses. First and foremost, there are
the subjects of his monographs which, with the exception of Kant, he
transforms into true and untimely heroes of thought (Hume, Spinoza,
Leibniz, Nietzsche, Bergson, Foucault). Then come the genuine enemies
against whom he fights philosophical battles (Hegel, Freud starting in
the 1970s, Kant to some extent, and more implicitly Wittgenstein).
Phenomenologists (namely, Husserl, Heidegger and Merleau-Ponty)
hold a place of honour in Deleuzian dramaturgy. They fulfil a third
function that is neither heroic nor strictly antagonistic. Deleuze
does not fight *against* phenomenology, rather he struggles *with* it.
Defying phenomenology does not imply turning towards other veins
of thought. On the contrary, he must struggle with phenomenology,
on its own ground. Deleuze has broken away from Hegelian idealism
and psychoanalysis, but despite a certain interpretative belief, he does
not place his thought 'above' phenomenology. The status he reserves
for phenomenology is complex and unique in the Deleuzian corpus
since the 'science' that stems from Husserl's works is not made the
subject of a specific study, though phenomenological themes remain
omnipresent in Deleuze's development.[1]

For Deleuze, phenomenology is neither a trusted friend nor a hated
enemy. But strangely, it corresponds to the kind of 'well-loved enemy'
that Deleuze also needs. Phenomenology is an enemy, because it
presents an intelligibility of meaning that lends a sort of religious coherence to an ideal world of meaning and signification. With Guattari,
Deleuze considers this an insidious infiltration of the transcendent
within immanence (WP 46). But phenomenology is also beloved by
Deleuze in that it delimits the area in which Deleuze's philosophical
fights take place. An enemy, because it establishes a 'royal science';

beloved, because it provides the grounds for defining the most important moments in Deleuzian thought. To the question 'Why was Deleuze
interested in Husserl and in phenomenology?', we would respond that
it was essential for Deleuze to maintain a detached relationship with
a friend/enemy capable of keeping him in suspense up to the end. The
function he gives to phenomenology arises from a Nietzschean tem-
perament that suggests the adoption of an admiring attitude towards
a genuine opponent.[2] It is indeed Nietzschean, but it is also Sadean.
For something resembling a sadistic pleasure can be seen in this love/
hate relationship. Deleuze subjects phenomenology to Chinese water
torture, thereby leaving it to suffer indefinitely while he incessantly
accuses it of all sorts of crimes of which it considers itself innocent.
The sentence Deleuze imposes ultimately resembles an unlimited
postponement. He condemns phenomenology while taking a sinister
pleasure in deffering the exposition of his ultimate and biggest accusa-
tion. Even the late-coming argument about the 'transcendent within
immanence' does not seem definitive. Deleuze indefinitely puts off his
last assault because, ultimately, he needs a phenomenological land-
mark to orient his thought, to give his work an expressive power and to
measure the value of his concepts. In sum, the three functions Deleuze
assigns to philosophers are the following: heroism (declared love),
antagonism (sworn enemies), and sadism (game partners/opponents).
Phenomenology is connected with the third of these functions.

From the 1960s onwards, Deleuze does not think twice about com-
paring phenomenology with a 'modern scholasticism' (NP 195; see
also F 113), thus stepping out of several decades of howling debates
on phenomenology's theological turn. Here again several parallels
with Nietzsche are most interesting. Deleuze sees phenomenology
in a manner similar to the way in which Nietzsche sees Christianity.
Phenomenology for Deleuze and Christianity for Nietzsche hold a sick
fascination throughout each thinker's works. The two philosophers
never really dispensed with their eternal adversary. Deleuze's battles
with phenomenology find no ultimate outcome and would have
been perpetuated in all the books he never wrote. Deleuze respected
and admired his heroes, he denigrated his true enemies, but he saw
phenomenology through the eye of an obsessive player. Of course,
Deleuze upheld to the very end the objective of victory. The battle with
phenomenology – one of the most respected philosophical currents of
its time – afforded Deleuze the opportunity to constitute his untimeliness. This ongoing task of combating the dominant thought was, for
Deleuze, the surest means of building his strength. A battle between

David and Goliath that one would imagine lost from the start, but also the kind of confrontation that is most likely to generate power (*puissance*). Phenomenology is the essential rival to Deleuzian philosophy, which needs majority criteria to bring about a series of minority and revolutionary developments. Thus it constitutes a central element in the formation of Deleuzian thought. Without joining forces with it, Deleuze nonetheless played with phenomenology. To become untimely, it is necessary to win. But the intensity of the game must hold strong. We must acknowledge that this playful view of a battle tending towards victory without ever quite reaching it remains inoperative in the monographs dedicated to the victorious community of thinker-heroes. Yet it is also absent from relationships with his true enemies, with whom he had practically finished from the start.

The most sceptical will say that the phenomenologists condition nothing in Deleuzian thought. The most seriously formulated objection in this respect is to say that, in philosophy in the twentieth century, it is Bergson, and not phenomenology, that is in fact the true catalyst of Deleuzian thought. These critiques reconnect with the legendary opposition between Husserl and Bergson, who benefited from being contemporaries. In choosing the Bergsonian method, Deleuze would have lost interest in the phenomenological access in the goal of affirming 'the thing itself'. But the hypothesis of this anti-Husserlian and truly Bergsonian Deleuze is only partly true. As is the case with other philosophers to whom he dedicated monographs, there is a Deleuzian conspiracy about Bergson that takes this latter along a path different from that of his original intention; in other words, towards the *raison d'être* of things in the process of happening. Deleuze subverts Bergson's spiritualist evolutionism by presenting a new rationalist principle. Furthermore, Deleuzism reached a climax in its experimentation with non-progressive changes peppered with disjunct singularities (Baconian figures, *faux-raccords* in cinema, stammering in language, etc.) that surprisingly do not suffer from any lack of rational explanation.

The many references to phenomenological themes that riddle the Deleuzian corpus bring us not to consider Deleuze as a disciple of the Husserlian school but to analyse the particular status of phenomenology in the development of Deleuzian thought. Supporting the idea that phenomenology plays no positive function on the Deleuzian agenda means considering Husserlian science and Deleuzian thought as independent from one another; considering that there is an appropriate balance among the statuses that Deleuze attributes to Husserl, Freud and Hegel; and considering that there would have been Deleuze with or without the phenomenological breakthrough. We believe, on the contrary, that the 'phenomenological function' made the most important Deleuzian innovations possible. Not only did Deleuze almost invariably take care to situate his philosophical inventions in relationship to phenomenological thoughts, but the constancy of his struggle with phenomenology also serves to give Deleuzian thought its unity. The paradoxical nature of this connection can be seen as follows: on the one hand, for Deleuze, phenomenology is a treasure chest of shiny ideas to overthrow; on the other hand, the turbulence he inflicts on these phenomenological ideas is the primary consolidating force and revolutionary character of his philosophy. Even more so, we believe that Deleuze's most important conceptual innovations are new answers to the issues phenomenologists raise – new answers that undermine, to a great extent, the very basis of the phenomenological movement but that would never have come about without it. The question, 'Is Deleuze a phenomenologist?', must be replaced by: 'In what way does Deleuze need phenomenology?' The answer: the most decisive proposals of Deleuze's thought, from its conceptual creations to its most particular relationship with the history of philosophy, were decided in an energetic, virulent and drawn-out struggle with phenomenological propositions. In addition, by placing Deleuzian philosophy, as one does frequently, in relation to a particular category (immanence, ontology, the virtual, the event, vitalism, etc.) one is limiting a more general pattern connected to the incessant battle Deleuze leads with phenomenology. A combat that is not just one struggle among many, given that all the other Deleuzian struggles are subordinate to the conflictual relationship he maintains, with a kind of sadistic joy, with his phenomenological rival.

In what follows, we will present a few of the most decisive lines of the contact in the one-on-one struggle between Deleuze and Husserl. Deleuze read Husserl, and he quoted and commented on many of Husserl's works.[3] However, it is *Cartesian Meditations* that seems to play the most influential role in Deleuzian dramaturgy. Husserl's *Cartesian Meditations* will therefore serve us as a guide. We shall draw from each of the five meditations an essential notion dreamed up by Deleuze.

FIRST MEDITATION: ANEXACT SCIENCE

The definition of science is the first meditation's central issue. Husserl deplores the lack of unity in scientific research and would like to bring to research efforts a common beginning point. Following a now well-known process, Husserl makes transcendental reduction the first step towards this absolute basis. The *épochè*, or bracketing, of the natural attitude gives rise to a pure consciousness distinct from the Cartesian *cogito* in that the evidence does not address the outside world, but rather the content of consciousness. The first meditation presents intentional objects as 'unreal'; in other words, neither exact nor inexact, simultaneously constitutive and relative to the pure consciousness to which they appear. Elsewhere Husserl states that '*the phenomena of transcendental phenomenology will be characterized as non-real (irreal)* . . . The *element* which *makes up the life of phenomenology as of all eidetical science is "fiction"* . . . Concepts are *essentially and not accidentally inexact*.'[4] This leads us to suppose, according to the Principle of all principles,[5] that an imaginary entity, such as a chimera or a unicorn, can be 'a source of authority for knowledge' as long as it 'presents itself in "intuition" in primordial form'. For example, a unicorn can appear 'in-person' in the living present of children's intentional consciousness and become the 'object' of phenomenological knowledge, while being deprived of reality outside consciousness. These considerations lead back to the distinction Husserl established between *real* (mundane reality of what exists according to the natural thing's way of being) and *reell* or *wirklich* (characterising the components of lived experiences in opposition to the reality of the natural thing because of their 'fictional' aspect).

Deleuze (with Guattari) is fascinated by the Husserlian invention of an 'anexact' or 'vagabond' science: 'It [vagabond science] is neither inexact like sensible things nor exact like ideal essences, but *anexact yet rigorous*' (TP 367). The German term '*inexakt*' that Husserl used and that translators render literally by 'inexact', became for Deleuze 'anexact' (TP 555 n. 32). In this way, Deleuze points out that we place ourselves above and beyond true and false, a bit like the way we talk of 'amorality' to designate what is neither moral nor immoral. Husserl and Deleuze's philosophical undertakings meet in the practice of an anexact science that does not probe objective *real*-ity. This redefinition of science is at the centre of the phenomenological revolution, and Deleuze learned from it. It is in a similar register of fiction and unreality that Deleuze situates his vagabond science. Does this mean that there is only one anexact science that can be either Husserlian or Deleuzian? Not exactly. Deleuze (with Guattari) salutes Husserl's discovery of vague essences: 'Husserl brought thought a decisive step forwards when he discovered a region of *vague and material* essences (in other words, essences that are vagabond, anexact and yet rigorous), distinguishing them from fixed, metric and formal essences' (TP 407). But he also deplores within Husserl's thought a desire for the hegemony of anexact science over thought and other sciences. In the development of a Deleuzian anexact science, the autonomy of other sciences is preserved. Deleuzian anexactitude is not rigorous in the sense that it is at the core of all other sciences. For Deleuze, it is not a question of opening up the field of anexactitude to make it a common denominator for all exactitudes. Therefore, Deleuze maintains that there is a difference in nature between the exact sciences and the anexact science where Husserl wishes to make uniform all sciences on the side of a triumphant non-exactitude. This Deleuzian science, which authorises a passage between exactitude and anexactitude without granting any privilege to one or the other or setting one above the other, is named 'nomad science'. This is because it grants bestows such an absolute primacy to the non-exact over the exact that Deleuze might have labelled Husserlian science despotic. In contrast to Husserl's royal science, Deleuze's nomad science is not constrictive or repressive of so-called exact science, for each science (exact and anexact) can lay out (*tracer*) its own plane.

Nomad science is confronted with change by following the 'connections between singularities', and the vague essences that it comes across 'are nothing other than haecceities' (TP 369); in other words, non-personal singularities (an hour of the day, a sky blue, a refrain or *ritournelle*, etc.). It does not seek any generality of the type 'individual essence' or 'universal singularity' (these are the pride of phenomenological science). Rather, it lets itself be carried by the intense currents of individuation in which the nomad experimenter can measure the degree of intensity at any point in the current. The more variations there are, the more nomad science is in its element. These variations are not 'eidetic variations' but rather the 'intensive variations' free of any finality (particularly constitutive finally). Nomad science shows a particular interest in the abrupt passages and transitions between states of being that provoke unforeseen meetings between singularities: '*There are itinerant, ambulant sciences that consist in following a flow in a vectorial field across which singularities are scattered like so many "accidents"*' (TP 372).

The exact sciences study the natural world, while Husserl's anexact science studies the phenomenal unrealities at the foundation of reality, and Deleuze's nomad science wanders in a chaosmic Nature experimenting with the degrees of intensity at various points along the way. Moreover, Deleuze transposes the Husserlian theme of the non-exact onto linguistics: 'in order to designate something exactly, anexact expressions are utterly unavoidable' (TP 20).

Husserl's scientific mind contrasts with Heidegger's position for which science, in its natural and Husserlian forms, remains caught in the ontical world: it does not think. Deleuze defines a nomad science while adopting Heidegger's assertion that 'we are not yet thinking' (NP 108 and elsewhere). For Deleuze, transcendencies are dangerous illusions that keep one from thinking about and experimenting with immanence by imposing themselves as abstract figures. Deleuze makes a strange synthesis between Husserl and Heidegger that opens up the possibility of a nomadic *and* thinking science.

SECOND MEDITATION: TRANSCENDENTAL EMPIRICISM

The second meditation is devoted to the transcendental experience where the pure ego becomes the object of its own experience. The phenomenological reflection probes the current of multiple *cogitationes* (imaginations, memories, empathy, and eventually kinesthesis, etc.) that can be found within a 'stream of experience'. Transcendental phenomenology thus experiments with unrealities to create a 'pure description'. The phenomenological experience where the ego becomes a 'non-participant onlooker at himself'[6] corresponds with a transcendental self-experience, among other things, in the sense that 'it uncovers the self through which and for which there is a *history* of experience'.[7]

In Deleuze's thinking, everything begins with the experience of the chaosmos made by a 'fractured I' (*je fêlé*). As in Husserl's thinking, Deleuzian empiricism has a transcendental status. The expression 'transcendental empiricism' (DR 56, 143; TRM 384–90), which Deleuze sometimes associated with a 'superior empiricism' (NP 50; B 30) or a 'radical empiricism' stemming from William James's pragmatism,[8] remains paradoxical to Hume and Kant's points of view: Humean empiricism has no transcendental elements insofar as it has no theoretical basis that explains the necessity of a cause/effect union; Kantian transcendentalism is not empirical either in that it is less focused on experience than on the theoretical conditions of the possibility of experience. For Husserl and Deleuze, the conditions of the possibilities of experience are created by the very becoming of experimentation. What, in the *The Origin of Geometry*, Husserl designates as the 'historical *a priori*' makes possible a science of that which is a continual state of variation, at the cost, of course, of becoming anexact – in other words, breaking with the objectivity of evidence.

For Husserl as for Deleuze, there is no independent truth (non-intentional, Husserl would say; transcendent, Deleuze would say) and the 'truth' becomes relative to the arbitrariness of experience. Of course, a fundamental difference remains: For Husserl, it is the transcendental 'I' immersed in the life-world that is his experience, while for Deleuze it is the impersonal forces that become the objects and conditions of experience.

Concrete and immaterial forces intervene repeatedly within Deleuze's demonstrations by simultaneously playing the double role of explicative causes and experienced effects. Critical philosophy, Deleuze tells us, remains always in possible and general conditions of experience without ever accessing concrete experience (NP 91; B 23). Deleuze wants to go beyond the conditions of experience that were only possible and move in the direction of concrete conditions in the goal of accessing the experience of intensifying forces that condition and that are expressed by singularities, thus allowing non-sensible forces to become sensible on their own. Husserlian phenomenology manages to shake up Kantian critical philosophy's presuppositions, thus destroying the reference to the ahistoric *a priori* in favour of a new transcendental field of experience that is subject to its own historicity. But this also reactivates the quest for generalities by seeking to determine the universal conditions of knowledge. The transcendental ego becomes the centre of the primordial individuation that is at the very basis of the conditions of possible experience. In a phenomenological scheme, the transcendental field always makes possible a foreseeable experience (constitution of an object, bodily perception, etc.), whereas the Deleuzian transcendental field – which is always populated with forces with effects of singular and unforeseeable intensities – conditions the unexpected meetings that remain invariably exterior to the nomadic haecceities that they assemble. 'Only when the world, teeming with anonymous and nomadic, impersonal and pre-individual singularities, opens up', says Deleuze, 'do we tread at last on the field of the transcendental' (LS 103). Such anonymous singularities are never made possible by determined generalities (e.g., the transcendental ego) but rather by the concrete forces that condition attainment by giving rise to meetings that exceed all prior general determination.

Deleuze recovers a conception of transcendental philosophy from Husserl that is not opposed to empiricism; the difference that separates the meaning they intend to give experience can also be seen.

Phenomenological experience remains internal and ante-predicative; it is integrated into a stream independently of its degree of 'veracity' or 'falsity'. Deleuze's empiricism could also be perceived as ante-predicative. However, it is never the sovereign consciousness that experiments with variations, but rather the 'fractured I', the 'dissolved self' or the 'larval subject' (or any other haecceities making up the Deleuzian Nature) that experiments with impersonal forces. It is, in fact, the exact meaning Deleuze gives the term 'transcendental field', thought of in terms of streams of consciousness that are 'a-subjective', 'pre-reflective' and 'impersonal' where experiences become independent of the classic relationship between subject and object.

We see that there remains a certain degree of consciousness in Deleuzian empiricism (TRM 384–90), and the Husserlian 'stream of experience' is indeed characterised by the 'anonymous'.[9] This minimal Deleuzian consciousness (to bring us closer to James' term *stream of consciousness* and Whitehead's *superject*) is mobilised by a continual movement at a variable speed that neutralises any attempt at intentional immobility, which by default interrupts experimentation. Husserlian lived experiences flow well through a partly extra-subjective stream, but pure consciousness intentionally attaches an element of the stream of experience to temporarily block the flow and participate in the undertaking of constitution. Husserlian experimentation remains too basic from a Deleuzian point of view, while intentional relationships are always too connected with a vision of almighty consciousness.

One way of drawing the dividing line might be to distinguish Deleuze's anti-humanist transcendental empiricism with *minimal consciousness*, on the one hand, and Husserl's transcendental empiricism with *maximal consciousness*, on the other. A few examples punctuate the anti-humanism of the Deleuzian method: the contemplation of plants, the Earth, rocks and rats, the deterritorialisation of lobsters, the world of the tick, bird-artists, etc. (WP 184, 212–13). In a sense, minimal consciousness is no less present in plant, animal and mineral kingdoms than it is in the human one. And it is this minimal consciousness that allows singularities to experience the transcendental. Minimal human consciousness is just a particular modality of Deleuze's transcendental empiricism, the thought of which, for political reasons Husserl and his direct successors do not grasp, tends towards a degree of ego-culture equivalent to zero.

Resorting to empiricism gave rise to a confrontation with Husserl, who was the first to try to destroy the opposition between empiricity and transcendentality without seeking his salvation in absolute idealism. Deleuze took on as his own the Husserlian idea of an empirical-transcendental co-generativity. But this revival is only partial, since the structure of experience does not have an intentional model for Deleuze. A good part of *The Logic of Sense* is dedicated to explaining the insufficiency of the noetic–noematic correlation in *Ideen I*. If noesis tends to be only partly determinant for Deleuzian empiricism, is it possible to maintain the autonomy of a noematic project when the noetic is removed? This question gives rise to one of the most vigorous struggles between Deleuze and Husserl, with Deleuze going so far as to ask himself whether phenomenology was not, in fact, the rigorous science of surface effects that he was seeking. But, in the end, Deleuze turned to the Stoics to think through that which can be experienced and the conditions under which it appears. Over Husserl's 'meaningful' noeme he preferred the paradoxical event, freely inspired by the Stoics.[10]

THIRD MEDITATION: IMMANENCE

Despite its brevity, the third meditation proves to be crucial to all of the analyses. Evidence is presented as the possibility of appearing from a 'state of affair'. It is not a necessary case, but rather just a possible or accidental case of the life of consciousness that Husserl distinguishes from simple subjective abstraction (personal conviction, opinion, etc.). Evidence is therefore not a possibility among others, but rather a fundamental possibility. Intentional objects can seem fictional from the viewpoint of natural attitude, but from the phenomenological angle the fundamental possibility of evidence constitutes the phenomenological reality that Husserl compares to 'an *ideal immanence*, which refers us to further complexes of possible syntheses'.[11]

The conceptuality of the third meditation is largely debated within Deleuzian thought: immanence, abstraction, ideality, state of affair, etc. Deleuze's revival of the conceptual frame of the third meditation is, of course, neither exhaustive nor dogmatic. Notably, it proves to be critical vis-à-vis the notions of 'truth' and 'possibility'. Husserl finds 'truth' in an ante-predicative sense while Deleuze only acknowledges as ante-predicative the experience that can and must be exempt from judgement. For Deleuze, the modern conception of truth emanates from a predicative judgement; he discards this notion of truth from his system and seeks to resituate it in the context of problems (which can be true or false). And, in terms of possibility, Husserl distinguishes that which is not fundamental (personal conviction) from that which is fundamental (evidence), while Deleuze can only admit the necessary action of forces that precisely force the differentiation process to arise. This is what brings Deleuze to oppose the possible (such as the determination of a form of identity) with the virtual (DR 211–12).

Deleuze's notion of the virtual – 'real without being actual, ideal without being abstract' (B 96; DR 208; WP 156) – could almost agree with the Husserlian 'fundamental possibility' that remains just as 'real without being actual' while being 'ideal without being abstract'. However, Husserlian possibility and the Deleuzian virtual cannot be entirely superimposed, since they are each committed in different ways to the conquest of immanence.

Distinguishing, as Husserl does, the fundamental possibilities from the non-fundamental ones comes to mean accrediting the millennia-old doctrine of judgement that Deleuze had hoped to be done with. If Husserl's pure consciousness is able to judge reality, it is because it is endowed with a transcendental value. This is what Husserl asserts when he compares the transcendental Ego to 'a *quite peculiar* transcendence', and to '*a transcendence in immanence*'.[12] Even under the imperative of reduction, Husserl needs this 'unsuspendable' transcendence to make his phenomenology work. Deleuze (with Guattari) does not go beyond what Husserl advances by renouncing the injection of the transcendent in Husserlian theories: 'Immanence becomes immanent "to" a transcendental subjectivity . . . This is what happens in Husserl and many of his successors who discover in the Other or in the Flesh, the mole of the transcendent within immanence itself' (WP 46).

Rudolf Boehm distinguishes three types of immanence in Husserl's work – pure, intentional and real (*reelle*) – as well as two types of transcendence – pure and real (*reelle*).[13] The ambiguous uses of the concepts of immanence and transcendence comes from the fact that Husserl uses them first in their traditional meaning and then later in a new meaning. The complexity (and even the confusion and equivocation) of the overlapping of the various types of immanence and transcendence in Husserl's work did not hold any interest for Deleuze, who seemed unaware of the new meaning Husserl accorded to immanence, being instead content with critiquing all of the traditional uses. The new function Husserl assigns to immanence consists of thinking the immanence in correlation with transcendence; in other

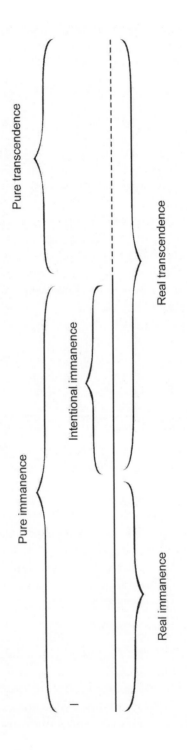

Figure 1   Immanence and Transcendence in Husserl

words, the intersection between pure immanence (contents immanent to pure consciousness) and real transcendence (that of intentional objects). Boehm designates this intermediary sphere as 'intentional immanence'.

Deleuze had reasons to affirm that phenomenology compromises itself with transcendence; but it is a relative compromise, since phenomenology only makes pacts with real transcendence, thus stepping around the essentialism of traditional metaphysics (an enemy common to Husserl and Deleuze) that naively takes on the task of thinking absolute, eternal and universal truths.

Husserl's 'plane of immanence' overlaps with transcendence, insofar as it is a real, relative and intentional transcendence. The Husserlian challenge is not to avoid (as Deleuze does) all compromise with transcendence, but rather to remove the strict opposition between immanence and transcendence in order to create an intermediary zone that they share at least partly. This contrasts with Deleuze's position, which maintains the traditional dualism between immanence and transcendence. He lays out a plane to glorify the first, looking to exclude the second more radically than phenomenology does. In Husserlian terms, the Deleuzian plane would correspond with a doxical *'reale Immanenz'*, since it is constructed without respect for pure consciousness, reduction and intentionality. This reading assimilates Deleuze's philosophy into a manifestation of the natural attitude. But, really, all philosophers are led to this natural attitude, according to Husserl, who himself struggles to destroy it within his corpus, which develops like a series of introductions to phenomenology. The Husserlian type of interpretation of Deleuzian immanence does not consider the minimal value that Deleuze (for whom personal convictions did not play any determinant role) attributed to consciousness. Deleuze invites us to another logic of immanence that at least has the merit of proposing an effective community model, and not one that is abstract, absent or yet to come.

The ambivalence Deleuze demonstrates towards phenomenology, and which brings him to ask 'Could phenomenology be this rigorous science of surface effects?' (LS 21), comes in part from recognising a tension with the immanence inherent in the phenomenological discourse. Phenomenology tends towards immanence without ever attaining it since it remains attached to the sphere of real transcendence. Deleuze can not be fully seduced by phenomenology because it perspicaciously maintains a connection with a form of transcendence.

Deleuze's rapport with immanence is not just tendential or relative; rather, it is the whole field of experience that is absorbed by immanence. In Deleuze's plane of immanence, the distinction between fundamental and non-fundamental possibilities no longer holds. In fact, there is nothing fundamental, foundational or founding in the actions and effects of the forces. As its name would indicate, the plane is a surface with neither height nor depth, lacking vertical hierarchy which infinitely stretches out horizontally. Foundationalism leaves room for constructivism.

Deleuze liked to draw, as his sketches in his books on Leibniz and Foucault illustrate, as well as those in *Qu'est-ce que la philosophie?* where we can see his typical pencil drawings. It is surprising, then, that he did not try to give a graphic image to his thoughts on immanence. This is all the more surprising given that his descriptions would lend themselves well to this kind of illustration. In *Qu'est-ce que la philosophie?*, Deleuze and Guattari distinguish the planes of philosophy (plane of consistency), science (plane of reference) and art (plane of composition) that each hold their own specificity while nonetheless building a similar constructivist logic. The conceptual plane or the immanent plane of philosophical consistency is said to be 'holed' (*troué*) in that it risks being pierced through by the somewhat proliferating illusions that are transcendence, universals, the eternal and the discursive. The purest plane is that which is the least holed. The more holes, the more it decomposes, blurred and chipped away by illusions that, eventually, completely destroy it, thus causing a purely transcendental order to appear.

With Husserl, Deleuze remains the greatest thinker on the distinction and the rapport between immanence and transcendence. It is surely audacious to bring the Deleuzian determination of the immanence plane to Husserlian reduction,[14] but it is true nonetheless that Husserl opens the way for thought on radical immanence. Though Spinoza (along with other Deleuzian heroes) can be called one of the greatest experimenters of immanence, Husserl remains the only precursor in the conceptual exploration of immanence.

FOURTH MEDITATION: PASSIVE SYNTHESIS

In the fourth meditation, Husserlian reflections on passivity develop around the notion of the quest for the origins of constitution. Originally, constitution is shared between the voluntarist and 'judging' actions of the transcendental ego (the active side of genesis)

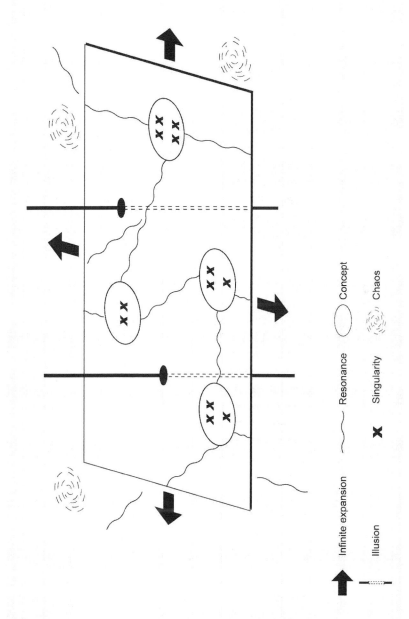

Figure 2 *Conceptual and Immanent Plane of Philosophical consistency*

Infinite expansion

Illusion

Resonance

Singularity

Concept

Chaos

and the simple reception of the 'ready-made'[15] found object (the passive side of genesis). Husserl brings back to himself the paradox of the constitution of 'ready-made objects', the appearance of which chronologically precedes the active intervention of the subject, according a constitutive value to the passivity of syntheses. This is not the first contortion of language Husserl invites us into. A true king of the oxymoron, he has made us accustomed to expressions as apparently contradictory as 'anexact science', 'phenomenal unreality' or 'transcendental empiricism'. The notion of 'passive synthesis' is not a simple linguistic provocation. Of course, it contradicts the Kantian theory according to which synthesis is an *act* of the imagination bringing representations together, but passive synthesis has the advantage of lending the ante-predicative sphere a consistency highlighting the existence of a passively 'pre-given' life that 'activity necessarily presupposes'.[16]

Deleuze integrates passivity into his system but, for him, it is neither the activity's mere precondition (the past for Husserl) nor the condition of an ideal state yet to come (the future for Heidegger). In Deleuze's work, passivity finds its temporal space, on the one hand, in the 'living present' (DR 71) through the involuntary and the machination of desire (AO 26, 324–6), and on the other, in the experience of contemplating the world, from which arise the 'passively synthesized contractions of habits' (DR 70 ff., 98 ff.).

Deleuzian passive synthesis, operating in contemplation, is not exclusive to humankind. The third of the *Enneads* by Plotinus, which Deleuze admired greatly, already took contemplation out of the strictly human frame. 'All things are striving after Contemplation, says Plotinus, looking to Vision as their one end – and this, not merely beings endowed with reason but even the unreasoning animals, the Principle that rules in growing things, and the Earth that produces these.'[17] Plant, mineral, animal: all contemplate and contract as they exist. 'All is contemplation!' (DR 75), Deleuze exclaimed. And even in his last texts, Deleuze wrote in tribute to Plotinus that 'even when one is a rat, it is through contemplation that one "contracts" a habit' (WP 213).

The Deleuzian system integrates the Husserlian notion of passive synthesis and goes so far as to beatify it (DR 74). But, towards phenomenology, Deleuze admits a contracting passivity in the present moment of contemplation and does not develop a hierarchic theory of passivity and activity by according each with its own importance.

FIFTH MEDITATION: THE OTHER

The fifth meditation introduces the theme of the Other within contemporary thought. Husserl conceives that inside the '*community of monads*, which . . . constitutes *the one identical world*',[18] there could be different perspectives among the constituent monads. These different perspectives ideally communicate: 'The Other as phenomenologically a "modification" of myself.'[19] *Ego* and *alter ego* enter into an analogical rapport that allows them to bring about an '*original "pairing"*'[20] represented by a spatial movement following which the ego is at liberty to transpose itself ideally to a space occupied by otherness, and to 'convert any There into a Here'.[21] Husserlian intersubjectivity eliminates any possibility of an incompatibility between monadic perspectives. It rejects the presence of a singular and irreducible view of the world. The analogical rapport between the ego and the Other becomes the weapon of a battle against solipsism and the philosophy of world-views.

Deleuze did not assume the role of defender of a pure perspectivism, nor did he argue for the incoherence of a radical whole. He left room for differences between points of view without, however, breaking into a Dionysian celebration of chaos or encouraging a festival of interpretations. The Deleuzian theory of otherness is not entirely phenomenology's heir, certainly no more than it is Nietzschean. Rather, Deleuze elaborated a redefinition of the relationship between the concept of the world and the plurality of individual universes within it.

What is the Other for Deleuze? 'The Other is neither an object in the field of my perception nor a subject who perceives me: the Other is initially a structure of the perceptual field' (LS 307). Deleuze did not aim to stitch together points of view within a common world. For him, the Other is neither subject nor object, but rather a structure among others that each time expresses a possible world: 'The Other, as structure, is *the expression of a possible world*' (LS 308; see also DR 260–1, 281). The Deleuzian structure of the Other is not relative to humankind. Deleuze distinguished the *a priori* Other (*Autrui a priori*), who is always impersonal or non-human (object, animal, plant, etc.), from the 'concrete Other' (*cet autrui-ci, cet autrui-là*), who always has a personal character. We must therefore see here an implicit questioning of phenomenology for which the Other is never more than a 'human spirit' (eventually divine) endowed with intelligence. For Deleuze, the Other had an independent existence vis-à-vis personal experience, and it creates possibilities. What does it make possible? 'The Other . . . does not restore transcendence to another self', but 'it is the condition for our passing from one world to another' (WP 48; see also WP 18). The phenomenological world has no homologue and it is always unique. It is a world without other possible worlds that eliminates the *a priori* Other.

For Husserl, there is only *one* world that can be seen from several angles. The example that he presents – that the six faces of a die truly exist even though we can never see more than a few at a time[22] – resembles the Leibnizean convergence of viewpoints on the same city.[23] Husserl's cube and Leibniz's city symbolise the unique character of the only possible world created; in other words, this is a solitary and absolute coherence towards which all faces turn. In Deleuze's work, there is not an infinite number of perceptive fields with the same structure, but there is an infinite number of structures each with a perceptive field. All possible worlds are real: 'Each point of view must itself be the object, or the object must belong to the point of view' (DR 56). Therefore, for Deleuze, there are *some* cubes and *some* cities: 'Another town corresponds to each point of view, each point of view is another town, the towns are linked only by their distance and resonate only through the divergence of their series, their houses and their streets. There is always another town within the town' (LS 174).

Deleuze plays Nietzschean perspectivism against the doctrines (Leibnizian, phenomenological, etc.) of unified points of view. He thinks a form of perspectivism against phenomenology. Nietzsche admits an infinity of interpretations, none of which can claim to have more value than the others. Therefore, there is no longer a supreme and unifying truth unifying all the points of view on the world. Nietzsche thus considered the crumbling of the world and its loss without thinking of the hypothesis of a real infinity of worlds. However, Deleuze makes Nietzsche into the thinker of divergence, disjunction and the multiplicity of worlds created. 'Nietzsche's perspective – his perspectivism – ', Deleuze writes, 'is a much more profound art than Leibniz's point of view; for divergence is no longer a principle of exclusion, and disjunction no longer a means of separation. Incompossibility is now a means of communication' (LS 174).

In Nietzsche's eyes, there is always *just one* world. The difference between the Nietzschean world and the world of Leibniz or the phenomenologists is that a unique world for Nietzsche lost its coherence: '*Chaos sive natura*'.[24] Nietzsche's new world remains One by taking on an incoherent character and by becoming an interpretative fable. Thus, it is already the result of Deleuze's interpretation of the Nietzschean perspective to see at work in his philosophy a number 'n' of coherent wholes replacing the lost unique world. In reality, for Nietzsche, the lost 'coherent one' is replaced by an 'incoherent one'. There is an infinite number of interpretations for Nietzsche, but these interpretations take place within the same chaotic unity. Therefore, Deleuze innovated in regards to Nietzsche by thinking a multiplicity of worlds that can be incoherent amongst themselves; in other words, that possess incompatible laws without being deprived of their own logic. This thesis of the multiplicity of worlds is a perspectivism, but a modified perspectivism. Unlike Nietzsche, the Deleuzian world is not considered a sum of interpretations. It is rather each of these interpretations that each time reveals the existence of a possible world. For Deleuze, it is not a question of deploring the relativity of realness, but rather of joyously affirming the truth of the relativity of worlds, the inter-incoherence of which in no way limits the coherence of each: 'Perspectivism as a truth of relativity (and not a relativity of what is true)' (FLB 21).

Deleuze gave an affirmative meaning to the notion of the world by relating it to the concept of the Other, who is never considered analogue to oneself. Rather, the Other refers to a not necessarily human entity expressing a possible world, the laws of which can be applicable only to him without making his existence illegitimate in consequence.

CONCLUSION

Deleuze is not a simple follower of Husserl, but he takes from Husserl a certain orientation of thought that gives a new twist to the major themes of *Cartesian Meditations*. Husserl's universal science is founded on a cogito-judge to whom passively given information appears, the most original of which can ideally be shared with the *alter egos*. Deleuze's nomad science experiments with the intensity of haecceities activated by the desubjectivating forces of virtual chaos. Deleuze was not orthodox when it came to phenomenology, but he showed a certain debt towards Husserl, who discovered vague essences, opened the way to transcendental empiricism, initiated the theoretical exploration of immanence, pushed back the boundaries of the opposition between activity and passivity, and began a new series of investigations into the relationships between monads. Deleuze's debt to Husserl is characteristic of the rather particular relationship Deleuze maintains with the history of ideas. We might say that the general movement of machination carried out by Deleuze brings him closer now to the de-anthromorphisation of Husserlian phenomenology by introducing a Nietzschean notion of force that is absent from phenomenological reflections.

Deleuze's silence on many central themes in Husserlian phenomenology, such as reduction, constitution and the atmosphere of crisis, illustrates the distance between the two thinkers. At other times, attacks are explicit and virulent, as was the case for intentionality, *Urdoxa* or the *Leib*. As for other elements in Husserl's doctrine, Deleuze was more nuanced and led one to believe that Husserl was on the right track but without being able to bring about the right results. Notably, this shows the attraction Deleuze felt to the Husserlian theories of the noeme (LS series 3, 14) and multiplicity (B 122 n. 4; DR 182; F 13; TP 483–4). On these last points, Deleuze ended by giving his respectful assent to the Stoics and to Bergson. Finally, Deleuze did not directly address other points of interest he shares with Husserl. Here, we are thinking of the great Deleuzian theme of 'disjunctive syntheses' that Husserl anticipated in his analyses of the *disjungierende Synthesen* as an elementary form of logical connection,[25] or of their common metaphysical quest[26] that remains a rarity in a panorama of contemporary thought dominated by a desire to reverse, destroy, go beyond or deconstruct Western metaphysics.[27]

Laurentian University

Notes

1. Alain Beaulieu, *Gilles Deleuze et la phénoménologie* (Mons/Paris: Sils Maria/Vrin, 2004).
2. Friedrich Nietzsche, *Thus Spoke Zarathustra*, Part I, 'War and Warriors', trans. R.J. Hollingdale (Cambridge: Cambridge University Press, 1961).
3. Namely, *The Philosophy of Arithmetic, Logical Investigations, The Phenomenology of Internal Time-Consciousness, Ideen I, Cartesian Meditations, Krisis, Experience and Judgment, Formal Logic and Transcendental Logic*, and *The Origin of Geometry* (B 122 n. 4; DR 66, 182; LS 20–2, 96–9, 101, 113–17, 122, 212, 298, 308, 341 n. 2, 344 n. 6; F 13, 151 n. 49–50; FLB 107–9; TRM 349–51, 384–90; TP 192, 367, 407–10, 483–4, 545 n. 85, 555 n. 32; WP 46, 85, 97–8, 142, 226–7 n. 9, 228 n. 6).
4. Edmund Husserl, *Ideas: General Introduction to Pure Phenomenology* (London/New York: George Allen/Macmillan, 1958), p. 44, 201 and 208. *Husserliana. Gesammelte Werke*, dir. S. Ijsseling, The Haag, Martinus Nijhoff Verlag, 1950. Further references to volumes of

the *Gesammelte Werke* will be abbreviations of the form: *Hua*, III, p. 6.

5. *Hua*, III, §24.

6. Edmund Husserl, *Cartesian Meditations* (The Hague: Martinus Nijhoff, 1960), p. 37 (*Hua*, I, p. 75).

7. Ludwig Landgrebe, 'The Phenomenological Concept of Experience', *Philosophy and Phenomenological Research*, 34:1 (1973), p. 13.

8. David Lapoujade, 'From Transcendental Empiricism to Worker Nomadism: William James', *Pli*, 9 (2000), 190–9. Salomon Maimon could be considered as another reference for Deleuze's transcendental empiricism. See Daniel W. Smith, 'Deleuze, Hegel, and the Post-Kantian Tradition', *Philosophy Today*, vol. 44 (2000) (suppl.), pp. 119–31.

9. Husserl, *Cartesian Meditations*, p. 47–8 (*Hua*, I, pp. 84–5).

10. Alain Beaulieu, 'Gilles Deleuze et les Stoïciens', in A. Beaulieu (ed.), *Gilles Deleuze. Héritage philosophique* (Paris: PUF, 2005), p. 45–72.

11. Husserl, *Cartesian Meditations*, p. 60 (*Hua*, I, p. 95).

12. Husserl, *Ideas*, pp. 173, 178 (*Hua*, III, pp. 138, 143).

13. Rudolf Boehm, 'Les ambiguïtés du concept husserlien d'"immanence" et de "transcendance"', *Revue philosophique de la France et de l'étranger* 84 (1959), pp. 481–526.

14. René Schérer, 'L'impersonnel', in É. Alliez et al., *Gilles Deleuze. Immanence et vie* (Paris: PUF, 1998), p. 70.

15. Husserl, *Cartesian Meditations*, p. 78 (*Hua*, I, p. 66).

16. Husserl, *Cartesian Meditations*, p. 78 (*Hua*, I, p. 66).

17. Plotinus, *The Enneads* (London/New York: Penguin Books, 1991), p. 233.

18. Husserl, *Cartesian Meditations*, p. 107 (*Hua*, I, p. 90).

19. Husserl, *Cartesian Meditations*, p. 115 (*Hua*, I, p. 97).

20. Husserl, *Cartesian Meditations*, p. 112 (*Hua*, I, p. 94).

21. Husserl, *Cartesian Meditations*, p. 116 (*Hua*, I, p. 99).

22. Husserl, *Cartesian Meditations*, §17–19 (*Hua*, I, §17–19).

23. Gottfried W. Leibniz, *New Essays on Human Understanding*, edited by Jonathan Bennett and Peter Remnant (Cambridge: Cambridge University Press, 1996), III, 3, §15.

24. Friedrich Nietzsche, *Sämtliche Werke. Kritische Studienausgabe*, Hrsg. G. Colli und M. Montinari (München: Deutscher Taschenbuch Verlag, 1967ff), §11[197] from 1881.

25. Husserl, *Ideas*, §118 (*Hua*, III, §118). See also Husserl *Logical Investigations*, §67 (*Hua*, XVIII, §67).

26. Husserl, *Cartesian Meditations*, p. 156 (*Hua*, I, p. 182). See also (*Hua*, VII, p. 188, note); Deleuze's answers in Arnaud Villani, *La guêpe et l'orchidée* (Paris: Belin, 1999), p. 130.

27. This article was supported by a grant from Laurentian University Research Funds (LURF).

15

A. N. Whitehead

James Williams

There is no 'Deleuze's Whitehead' in the same way as there is 'Deleuze's Hume' or 'Deleuze's Nietzsche'. He neither wrote a major book on Whitehead, as he did for Spinoza or for Leibniz, nor did he refer to Whitehead regularly to allow a critical or sympathetic position to emerge. This does not mean there is no value or basis in reflecting on the Deleuze and Whitehead connection. On the contrary, I will give four reasons for returning to this link in terms of Deleuze's and Whitehead's philosophies and in terms of wider philosophical problems. The first reason is biographical and historical. Deleuze has roots in an early French reader of Whitehead through the work of his teacher and colleague Jean Wahl.[1] These roots then extend through Deleuze's teaching to thinkers who worked alongside him or closely on his philosophy and now trace a novel Deleuzian lineage. I want to comment in detail on one of these philosophers, Isabelle Stengers, but I will also refer readers to others, such as Éric Alliez, Steven Shaviro and Jean-Claude Dumoncel. All have written at length on Deleuze and on Whitehead and have investigated rewarding overlaps and tensions. Their texts provide a rich and varied philosophical timeline running through Deleuze's study of Whitehead.

Second, Whitehead turns up infrequently and marginally in Deleuze's early and middle period work (roughly up to 1969 with the publication of *Difference and Repetition* and *The Logic of Sense*, then from 1969 to 1979 with the capitalism and schizophrenia works with Félix Guattari). However, in the lectures preparing for and then in the full text of his Leibniz book *The Fold: Leibniz and the Baroque*, Whitehead takes on a full and important role. This occurrence is interesting because it illuminates the concept of the event, a longstanding feature of Deleuze's work, dating back to *The Logic of Sense* for its earliest extended treatment. Chapter 6 of *The Fold* is a development of a lecture given on 10 March 1987 at the University of Paris VIII Vincennes–St Denis.[2] Subsequent lectures on 17 March, 4 April, 19 May and 20 May extend and complicate this first lecture.

Isabelle Stengers was one of those present at the lectures and she entered into debate with Deleuze during them. Wahl and Dumoncel's works are cited in the Whitehead chapter of *The Fold*. There is much more material in the lectures than in the Leibniz book. They were among Deleuze's last, a point he makes very movingly during them, contributing to the appealing thought that close work on Whitehead was perhaps still in his plans.

Third, during the investigation of the event in the Leibniz lectures, Whitehead is the catalyst for a rare moment of bile in Deleuze's lectures and writing, where he accuses a group of thinkers of having 'assassinated' another philosopher. I shall not yet say who the perpetrators were, but the victim was Whitehead. According to Deleuze, his philosophical legacy was silenced for a period of over fifty years. This foray into academic politics fits Deleuze's understanding of the political machinations, baseness and stupidity running parallel to a dominant doxa, seeking support from it and propping it up in return. The remarks are significant in understanding certain silences in Deleuze's own work and in situating his thought with respect to other dominant strands of twentieth-century thought. They also help us to complete the puzzles of the strikingly low profile of Whitehead over a long period since the early reception of his best-selling and influential work. This trend is now reversing and part of this reversal stems from work done by thinkers formed by Deleuze.

Finally, there is the much broader and less text-based question of whether it is possible to consider Deleuze and Whitehead as belonging to the same school or to similar movements. The first stab at an answer could consider sets such as 'process philosophers', 'superior empiricists', 'post-Hegelian speculative metaphysicians' and 'transcendental metaphysicians'. This kind of nominalism might have a useful educational or wider explanatory role to play, but it is so far removed from Deleuze's and Whitehead's approaches to education and to explanation that it would be unseemly to take this approach. They are both deeply critical of an idea of explanation as the correct ascription to sets, for this is a blunt instrument destructive of the things it assigns and falsely supportive of the illusory sets it assigns to. Explanation is about connection and not boxes. Learning is about tracing new links and transformations, rather than confirming stultifying grids. So I will look at whether the Deleuze and Whitehead connection allows us to trace lines and concepts which evolve out of their works, thereby offering novel critical and creative ways of thinking about process, about immanence and about forms of real reciprocal conditions connecting ideas and actual things.

The chapter 'What is an Event?' in *The Fold* is an extremely dense moment in an already highly complex book. Deleuze is working fast on material he is very familiar with, much of which dates back to his late-sixties masterworks *Difference and Repetition* and *The Logic of Sense*. The content can be seen on a simple level as unfinished business. It is an answer to the question 'What is your full relation to Leibniz, given your many references to him and his closeness to your concepts and metaphysical structures?'[3] However, this route into the book is unsatisfactory for an interaction with the Whitehead material, since the published matter for the Whitehead and Leibniz connection is even thinner than the Whitehead and Deleuze one. This is not to say that there is no interest in drawing the links, but rather that this is not the most revealing entrance to Deleuze's chapter. It makes some comparisons between Whitehead and Leibniz and closes on a very important contrast between the direct contact of metaphysical components in Whitehead and their isolation in individual incompossible worlds in Leibniz.[4] The comparison is not, though, a reflection on their relation, but rather a juxtaposition around a wider problem.

This extended problem is somewhat hidden in the title to the chapter. At first glance, the chapter could simply be an exposition of the meaning of the concept of 'event' in Whitehead and in Leibniz. Were this the case, the answer would be an abject failure at simple definition: overwrought, unclear, gnomic and incomplete. But Deleuze is responding to a quite different question, or rather to a problem as detailed in his novel definition of the term.[5] A problem is a complicated series of relations between questions crossing over with one another yet resisting organisation into rank or order of importance. The questions included in such problems are twofold expressions of affect, or bodily and emotional transformation, and intellect, or consistency-seeking yet also creative thought. This dual aspect means that a problem is determined not only by its questions but also by underlying tensions between ideas, affects and desires, and their expression in actual states, both historical and contemporary. The title of the chapter is therefore more like the expression of a pressing series of puzzles and tensions, of the kind we sometimes encounter after a long but inconclusive quizzing. The problem is the coming together of the following questions:

1. If events occur in infinitely connected series, which themselves subdivide infinitely, does this not commit you to a grounding chaos resisting all sense and order?
2. If there are manifold events, how do these relate to one another without allowing us to break them into final components, and thereby contradicting their infinite divisibility and interconnections?
3. How are different series of events distinguished from one another, if there is not a single chain of events?
4. If there are novel events, or if there is novelty in each event, under what conditions can this take place and what is this novelty like?
5. How can we distinguish between positive or good events and negative and evil ones, if all series of events are connected and if there is no external measure to judge them by?
6. Does this philosophy of events commit you to becoming without being, or to process without permanence? If it does not, where is the permanence in your structures?
7. If there are different series of events, are these related or are they radically different? If they are related, why can't they be reduced to one series? If they are not related, can they ever be said to be in touch in any way or to belong to the same universe?

For example, while pulling a rusty nail out of the ground, you cut yourself, contracting tetanus. You die. Where are we to situate the event? Do we include your earlier refusal of an immunisation booster injection? Or when an even earlier injection was botched and gave you a deep fear of needles? Do we put it at the cut itself, or at the death? Or perhaps it should be at the diagnosis that death has become inevitable, or in the successful propagation of bacteria in manure? *Maybe life should now be written from the point of view of bacteria?* Does the event now include this writing about it and medical textbooks and discoveries? Should we also include events now cut off by the death: events that may have happened, but now cannot? Or those now opened up by it? Or is there one event which makes up the whole of existence? If so how do we make sense of this event? Or is it closed to us? Was the cut a truly new event, or is the continuity of disease, inoculation and later similar events a sign of similarity and like-for-like repetition between cuts and infections? Is there a proper scale for events? Do they happen to things that aren't themselves simply events? Or if there are no such permanent things, how can we speak of events at all, since they are but change?

The first answer Deleuze derives from Whitehead is that events do not emerge from a pure chaos, even if we assume that all is event, and even if we assume that divisibility and divergence are inherent properties of events. This is because the idea of a pure chaos is a false abstraction from a necessary condition whereby chaos only appears when accompanied by a sieve introducing differential properties.[6] These properties allow for a positive definition of chaos, not then as a mystical limit, but rather as the reverse of the condition: differential processes appear against the background of a chaos constituted of all the other potential conditions, but the chaos only appears when taken with given differential processes.[7] It is as if we had a wall of palimpsests where the oldest were so faded and intermingled as to be illegible, but where we could begin to trace back through them thanks to later and more clear engravings. The clarity comes through and must be read with the obscure background, the obscure background only makes sense as a palimpsest thanks to the most readable top layers.

The critique of abstraction[8] and the way the background is carried by any emerging difference are important because they also allow for an answer to the second problematic question. The components of Whitehead's, Leibniz's and Deleuze's metaphysics are not discrete elements. We cannot say that there is a self-sufficient entity without depending upon a false abstraction of the kind made when positing a pure chaos. Yet the resulting interdependence is not indeterminate, in the sense where we would have to say that everything is connected in an indecipherable manner because any determinate connection would also be an abstraction. On the contrary, how components belong to others is carefully charted by Whitehead and by Leibniz. Connections take the form of vibrations or patterns extending along series, and these patterns have intrinsic properties that allow them to be distinguished from one another. So, though we have no legitimate independent elements, we have legitimate differences between the patterns. These are the conditions for any subsequent abstraction into elements; they are also the way to unpick and criticise this abstraction.[9] For example, though each statement in a palimpsest would be an abstraction from those around it, this does not mean that we have to work with all of them at the same time and therefore tackle an indistinct mass of statements. On the contrary, we can trace patterns through the statements, for example, regarding the counting of time or the waning of hope on a prison wall. Hope in one statement is a falsifying abstraction, but the variation of intensities of hope through series of statements allows us to begin to determine the palimpsest.

This in turn allows us to make selections within series of events according to the intrinsic properties of the patterns running through them. For example, though it is contingent and abstract to focus on an element of the chain in the event of the contraction of tetanus, the variation in intensity running through the chain as a whole – an increase or a decrease in a value – allows for distinctions to be drawn between different paths (the different effects of survival or death along the series, for instance). This is not yet the full basis for making selections. All we have at this stage is a well-founded difference (something is occurring along the chain, rather than at a point), and not a principle for moving one way or another (towards the bacteria or towards the human, say). This principle appears with the concept of the individual which combines the extension of the event as pattern with a special form of abstraction expressed in Whitehead's concepts of concrescence, prehension and nexus. An individual is a concrescence of prehensions, that is, a coming together of ways a thing includes another thing in a novel process (in the way the bacteria take hold of the human body, or the way a doctor takes hold of the molecular structure of the bacteria). On the one hand the event is extended without limit, but on the other it is made actual and determinate according to the ways things prehend one another. This prehension is itself dual because the prehension is public, since it is available to be taken as that prehension in many other prehensions (in the way bacteria might thrive on the original one, or in the way a branch of medicine might develop around a particular discovery). But it is also private in the way the prehending thing feels it to be novel (*my* struggle with infection). Events are therefore extended patterns and sets of individual concrescences (nexès) which themselves have public and private sides. There is the way an event is new for an individual and therefore private. There is the way the event can be taken as given and as public and therefore as available to be taken in a different novel manner. There are also the extended reverberations beyond both of these limited takes through the series of all events.

Novelty therefore becomes the principle determining individuals: there is an individual where there is a new take on given prehensions. Novelty is also the explanation for changes in patterns running through events; they change because individuals emerge when things are taken differently. Finally, novelty becomes the principle determining better or worse selections. It is better to increase the potential for novelty than to decrease it, because it is the source of greater enjoyment and lesser evil in the relations of individuals in societies. Deleuze then goes on to discuss the problem of permanence through the role played by 'eternal objects' in Whitehead's philosophy. A parallel is drawn between these objects and their potential to be taken up in novel actual occurrences (similar to the way we recombine words in novel ideas or poems, say). The object has no existence independent of these actual occurrences or – to use Deleuzian terms – independent of actual expressions of virtual potentials. The reverse is also true: the actual occurrence is partial unless it is viewed with the eternal objects it brings into play anew. The discussion of eternal objects is perhaps the place where there the gap between Whitehead and Deleuze is at its widest, since according to Whitehead an eternal object can 'cease to be incarnated'. This would imply a discontinuity at the level of this potential reserve contradicting Deleuze's account of the variegated continuity of virtual ideas and intensities.[10] He does not pursue this critical difference except in drawing the distinction between Leibniz and Whitehead in answering the final question on the connection of individuals through events where he contrasts a dappled world of bifurcations and disaccord (Whitehead) with a universe of incompossible worlds out of touch with one another except through God (Leibniz).[11] This leads to the distinction drawn between an immanent God as process and a transcendent one as selector of the best of all possible worlds.

THE LEIBNIZ–WHITEHEAD LECTURES

Are Deleuze's lectures on Whitehead and Leibniz worth consulting given that we have the *The Fold: Leibniz and the Baroque* where the oral presentations are set down in careful and definitive form? The answer is 'Yes' for the following reasons:

1. The lectures show the development of Deleuze's thought and therefore contain more material and different material than the later book.[12]
2. Deleuze's lectures were not monologues pronounced ex-cathedra, but communal efforts to work round texts and questions. His Whitehead lectures include debates with other readers of Whitehead and other thinkers, notably Stengers.
3. The recordings of Deleuze's lectures show him as a teacher, taking chances in explaining and conveying his ideas in ways he could not risk in finished texts (perhaps for fear of the kind of

misinterpretation where a simplified idea or example, or tentative thesis, is taken as the last word).

4. The lectures take more time on examples that only appear fleetingly in the book.

5. In his teaching, due to the need to recapitulate and keep projecting forward and back within lectures and across lectures, but also due to an effort to give close but different openings on to difficult ideas, Deleuze gives many similar but not reducible variations on ideas. These extend his reading considerably beyond *The Fold*.

6. The Leibniz book quotes Whitehead very little and gives very few references. It could be concluded that Deleuze did little research on Whitehead. Such a conclusion is directly contradicted in the lectures where Deleuze takes his audience through Whitehead's texts – whilst admitting to difficulties in English (humorously, in his pronunciation of *many*, a word he clearly loves but cannot pronounce).

For example, in the lectures Deleuze draws out a difficult problem that he does not make explicit in the book; it explains why he focuses his enquiry into events on the vocabulary of prehensions, nexus, concrescence and eternal objects. How do we explain the genesis of actual occasions, not only in terms of their conditions, or what must obtain for there to be actual things, but more directly in terms of which principles allow us to trace the genesis of this or that individual?[13] It is important not to confuse the object of this question with the genetic fallacy of providing a philosophical account of the relations of cause and effect that give rise to a given individual. Deleuze is concerned with a possible gap in Whitehead's metaphysics which would admit to series of events and to series of eternal objects, but could not explain how these give rise to different significant actual occasions and to different significant individuals. So the lectures add to the background of the account found in *The Fold* by making a sub-problem of the claim that all is event explicit and by showing the many facets of this problem:

> First problem: we began with conjunctions, that is, with actual occasions, we gave ourselves events and a world of events. Can we trace the genesis of the event? How do we come to conjunctions? Are they given just like that? It is not straightforward that there are conjunctions in this world. What is going to explain that there are?[14]

Answers to this problem are constructed around novelty: the new in an event makes it distinguishable from others and significant. This distinction requires the genesis of individuals as sites for that novelty. An event is something new for an individual.

The lectures are particularly rewarding for the examples they provide for events and for novelty. These appear in the book, for instance in the proposition 'There is a concert tonight', but Deleuze makes them more lively in his oral presentations. He dramatises the statement with the additional twist of characterisation: 'You know this person is giving a concert tonight.'[15] We then sense the novelty that drives the desire to see the concert and the excitement at getting tickets. It will be a one-off and we'll have missed it forever if we don't go. So though it combines eternal objects – sounds, ideas, notations – it brings them into a unique conjunction that vibrates through series of prehensions: the musician on the instrument, the instrument on the surrounding atmosphere, the audience on the carried vibrations, their take on the emotions of those around them, and so on without limit. The concert is unique but reverberates through the whole world, sometimes in tune with other events and sometimes in disharmony, thereby leading to the dappled universe Deleuze draws from Whitehead:

> The event is the actual occasion. Once more: there is a concert tonight. The first problem for Whitehead was: What are the conditions for the emergence of events? You sense that it is a very particular world; it is a particularly new world. Events never stop rising up; and they are always new events. The problem of philosophy will become the forming of novelty. This is very important. There are so many philosophies that have presented themselves as philosophies of the determination of eternity.[16]

> In this process the creativity, universal throughout actuality, is characterised by the datum from the past; and it meets this dead datum – universalised into a character of creativity – by the vivifying novelty of subjective form selected from the multiplicity of pure potentiality.[17]

The first passage is by Deleuze; the second by Whitehead. They meet around the problem of how the eternal and the actual are necessarily combined in the new and are necessary for the new (the past is carried by eternal objects for Whitehead). The opposition drawn between the task of determining what is eternal (Platonic forms, for example) and forming the new (the creation of philosophical concepts as described in Deleuze and Guattari's *What is Philosophy?* for instance) leads to a further important contrast between the Leibniz book and the lectures. In the latter, Deleuze reflects on how Whitehead's metaphysical novelty maps on to scientific accounts of reality. This is a very important topic, because it adds to the complicated and many-sided discussion of the exact relation of Deleuze's philosophy to science. This is in turn supported by the relation of Whitehead's philosophy to physics and to mathematics. There is still much work to be done on these questions, but there is no doubt that the Whitehead and Leibniz lectures provide important material for them.

STENGERS ON WHITEHEAD AND DELEUZE

Deleuze's work on Whitehead and Leibniz is carried through to Isabelle Stengers' original and comprehensive recent work on Whitehead, *Penser avec Whitehead: une libre et sauvage création de concepts*.[18] The book opens with an exergue from Deleuze and Guattari's *What is Philosophy?* where the idea of the free and savage creation of concepts in English philosophy is first coined; it is the central idea of Stengers' book not only in terms of the interpretation of Whitehead's works, but also in terms of its own writing style and aims.[19] The book creates with Whitehead's concepts and, to a lesser extent, in dialogue with Deleuze – a discussion already present in his Whitehead lectures. Unfortunately, the record of Stengers's interventions at those lectures has been lost, since the microphone, turned towards Deleuze, failed to pick up her words. We are therefore left only with his summaries of her remarks and it is thanks to these that I will select a passage from *Penser avec Whitehead* representative of the distinctions to be drawn between the three thinkers around the concept of God and its role in Whitehead's *Process and Reality*.

Here is Deleuze's gloss on what is a stake in their interpretations, or more precisely, between the problems that interest them and the concepts and processes they select to develop them:

> . . . I think that the genesis of conjunctions, or the genesis of actual occasions, a physical-mathematical genesis, is something that Whitehead does not give up on, so long as that genesis fully respects the demand that Isabelle reminds us of, that is, that it must not be a genesis such that the actual occasion derives, or follows, or results from its genetic components. It must be a genesis that takes account of this: that the only law of the actual occasion is to always be a novelty in relation to its own components.[20]

In short, the actual occasion is always a novelty beyond its conditions, to the point where these cannot be traced within it as that which it derives from. A novel creation brings such a degree of novelty to the processes it flows from that their relations are changed to the point where it does not make sense to say that the initial relations are components of the latter novelty.[21] Though a series of ideas and past actual occasions leads into a new one, and can be described as such, the novelty can never be accounted for in terms of its sources. Thus, if we take the example of historical events, a change in history cannot be explained fully in terms of its causes, or in terms of the conditions that gave rise to it, but instead, we also have to find the novelty that goes beyond causes and conditions and changes them retrospectively.

Deleuze and Stengers respond to this problem in different ways, and on a close reading of *Penser avec Whitehead* it becomes clear that their difference is not strictly on the role of physical-mathematical genesis, but rather on diverse versions of that genesis in relation to the concept of God. This distinction is prefigured in Deleuze's lectures: 'Isabelle thinks that [Whitehead] had renounced or became less interested in genesis and instead took to the problem from the level of a finality and from a very particular conception of God which, finally, operates on the level of actual occasions.'[22] Of course, Deleuze did not have the benefit of reading Stengers' book, but this should not take away from another sign of the interest in the Deleuze and Whitehead connection: the effort to think God differently after Whitehead and in relation to mathematical functions is taken to a deeply original and fruitful level first by Deleuze and then much further by Stengers. Her chapter 'God and the World' in *Penser avec Whitehead* refers to Deleuze's work, to *The Fold*[23] and to *Difference and Repetition*,[24] in order to explain a double function of God (much closer to Deleuze's overall approach than his remarks would let us conclude) itself explained not so much through mathematical genesis as such, but rather by adopting mathematical methods for philosophical interpretation and concept construction. Whitehead's God becomes a mathematical operator deployed in two different ways in order to draw a productive and irreducible two-way connection between eternal ideas and actual occasions.[25]

Stengers makes use of a shift from the concept of derivation to the concept of induction, and their different roles in the resolution of problematic functions in mathematical creativity, in order to show exactly how Deleuze's original intuition regarding the lack of result from condition to occasion can be brought into the concept of God. A condition can induce a further state, but is not its necessary and sufficient condition (Stengers uses the example of induction through hypnosis to support her study).[26] So while a change in relation of eternal objects can be said to induce actual occasions, the latter does not supervene on the former and we cannot trace back from one to the other. This then allows her to strip this concept of all theistic and theological aspects, whilst maintaining it as a necessary condition for creative (and beneficial) novelty. God becomes process without human projections, without divine providence and judgement, and without mystical or interpretable parallels between originator and creation. This effort of 'secularisation', as she calls it, draws the last chapter of *Process and Reality* back into Whitehead's work as whole and opens new avenues for his philosophy. Were we then to object that this merely goes to show that the concept of God is redundant, the answer would come back that the concept of God is necessary to connect novelty in any actual occasion to the eternal objects it springs forth with, without reducing one to the other, yet giving well-determined principles for explaining their reciprocal relations:

> The ways of God are not impenetrable because the hybrid physical feeling is not the enigmatic sign of a 'way'. It is not a matter of 'track marks', of indications offered by God to the world in the hope that it will take the path that he himself envisages as the best. Divine induction has no other reach than the rising up of the answerer that he thirsts for, of the occasion that, in one way or another, will confer its effective signification upon what is 'proposed' as eventually pertinent.[27]

The concept of God explains why there is novelty and why it is valuable, because it is the goal of the reciprocal relations of eternal objects and perishing actual occasions. Thereby, Stengers connects to Whitehead's discussion of Good and Evil in *Process and Reality*, but on her reading novelty and the Good are not beholden to God in any religious sense. This then allows her to make the, at first sight, very surprising step of relating Whitehead on God and on evil to Deleuze's work on the event in *The Logic of Sense* and to his important concept of counter-actualisation. Deleuze and Whitehead rely on a difference drawn between the *numerical* distinction of events, which allows for probabilistic calculation relating them, and their *formal* distinction, which by separating radically in terms of calculation makes each one the affirmation of the whole of chance or, in Deleuze's terms, one Event expressed by all events. It is because an event is incomparable that it affirms that special form of chance in every event.[28]

FOR A TIME TO COME

Deleuze said he would have liked the voice recorders to have been turned off when he made his severe remarks about Whitehead having been assassinated by English analytic philosophy.[29] They weren't, so a record exists in his 10 March 1987 lecture as stored at webdeleuze.com. However, since we have his wish, it would be inaccurate to take his spoken words as having the same status as the Leibniz book. At the very least, we would need to develop a theory as to why he wished to keep those words off the record. Any such conjecture would likely be airy and without secure basis. It is very hard to know whether he was being provocative, or tactfully avoiding direct criticism of colleagues in print, or letting off steam, or working towards some rhetorical aim such as drawing attention to a problem at the beginning of a lecture. Even if we had a stable view of his intentions, this would itself be highly dubious when viewed against Deleuze's writing methods and ideas on the process of writing: '. . .since each one of us was many. . .'.[30] Instead, I shall work back from the book to the lectures tracing two strands of questions within the wider topic of the Deleuze and Whitehead connection. First, what can we learn from Deleuze's remarks on the political and philosophical conflicts which lead to periods of relative hegemony for one philosophical movement and a consequent overlooking of others? Second, which areas of common interest provide us with a strong potential for the development of novel philosophical concepts and approaches?

The first question should make us feel uncomfortable given Deleuze's work on the event and on time. This is because his thought is not consistent with arguments that make judgements on the value and effects of actual occurrences based on their prominence at a given time. Any such judgement would be, at best, a minor part of a much more important response to events through their combination in new creations. At worst, it would illegitimately hinder the adoption of past events in new ones through the straightjacket imposed by value-judgements – irrespective of whether these are positive or negative. This point came out strongly in my discussion of Deleuze on Whitehead's concept of the event in relation to eternal objects. Changes in the relations between eternal objects in new creations would be inhibited by judgements that fixed these relations on the basis of a past association with actual occurrences. Furthermore, proximity in time and space is not a condition for creations that carry and reveal the potential of earlier events. On the contrary, Deleuze often insists on the imperceptible and distant work of events.[31] It would therefore be a profound mistake to draw a negative conclusion on a philosophy for its lack of effects in its time. No event occurs in that kind of time to the exclusion of any other. Instead, according to Deleuze's philosophy of time, every event takes place in a paradox-driven dialectics between an eternal time in touch with the past and the future, and an actual one. Such a dialectics will not have a preset logic allowing for predictions or inferences, hence its dependence on paradoxes generating attempts at resolutions, but also undoing any such attempts – thereby calling for a continual renewal of our thinking about the relation between two forms of time.[32]

There is therefore a view on the relation between philosophies and their historical epochs in Deleuze's work, but it is much closer to Nietzsche's concept of the untimely[33] than to any sense of a philosophy as dependent on its historical epoch. By setting itself at odds with its time, a philosophy grows against it and seeks to change it, for 'a time to come'. The key to the untimely lies in the open nature of the expression 'a time to come', which neither allows for a firm logic for determining when that time will be, nor a well-determined representation for what that time will be like. For Deleuze and Guattari, philosophies draw up their own 'planes of immanence' and 'conceptual personae', and these are neither wedded to the times and places where they are formed, nor dependent on a close response from those times.[34] Ideas, intensities and singular turning points can remain latent for long periods of actual time, but this in no way implies a lack of potential, or interest, or novelty. This means that Deleuze's concern with the deliberate ignoring of Whitehead's work is not primarily about its snuffing out, since, according to his philosophy, even a tepid dish served too late has a side in eternity and an ideal potential to be drawn out anew. Instead, rather than with the actual published works, the worry lies with the possible later effects that could have taken place but did not due to a form of academic repression. Deleuze's anger is caused by what a time lost because it was not allowed to create with Whitehead, rather than how long it took for a later epoch to find Whitehead again.

In *The Fold*, when Deleuze laments the 'mists, sufficiency and terror'[35] spread by the disciples of Wittgenstein he is not worried about the assassination of Whitehead, neither is he attacking Wittgenstein. The intemperate remarks in the lecture give way to a different worry about the imposition of hegemonic views and methods within universities and societies. There should be no such hegemonies because they necessarily reduce the opportunities for different creative expressions. There never really was a Wittgensteinian hegemony anyway and analytic philosophy maintains great differences within it.[36] Deleuze is worried about the more general elimination of speculative metaphysics and its power to create new concepts, methods and fields. Not in order to then impose a final one and to freeze all future creativity, or to dominate an actual field, but rather in order to affirm a multiplicity of creative responses to events and ways of following on from them. This pluralism of novelty and metaphysical invention invites two classic critical responses. Are there not truths and methods for discovering truths which stand above others and which reveal them to be lesser and thereby destructive and worthy of destruction? Is it not a waste of resources to affirm multiple creations, when we have the right one?

If we are to counter the claim that Deleuze and Whitehead's metaphysical creativity turns away from more grounded and commonsensical truths – and their capacity to align with demystification – then general claims about process philosophy, or superior empiricism, or transcendental metaphysics will do little to advance a case for the defence. In many eyes it will merely bring down a negative judgement all the quicker. However, if we use the vast resource of concepts, arguments, examples and studies they both provide – and if we use these rigorously and with precision to show contrasting yet related lines of argument and emerging useful and interesting ideas, none of which contribute to mystification, but on the contrary serve multiple critical arguments – then the Deleuze and Whitehead connection will have worked on their own terms, not in the establishment of a school, but rather in prompting critical evaluations of what we take to be common sense, or ostensible matters of fact, or common ideas. Thereby, the metaphysical presuppositions behind such claims and the different takes on reality lying in wait in different models and concepts will also be shown at work. In turn, this will demonstrate the value of philosophical creativity as the careful construction of metaphysical systems in relation to culture, to contemporary lives, to history and to the sciences – to the exclusion of none of them. Deleuze drew one of these connections in renewing our reflection on the concept of event. Stengers draws another through the idea of a secularisation of God. Many others remain to be drawn out and to do this will be a better way of bringing the two philosophers together. For Deleuze's anger at Whitehead's 'assassination' was in the name of a radical pluralism in thought and, therefore perhaps, in universities: 'Progress is founded upon the experience of discordant feelings. The social value of liberty lies in its production of discords.'[37]

University of Dundee

Notes

1. Jean Wahl's *Vers le concret: étude d'histoire de la philosophie contemporaine, William James, Whitehead, Gabriel Marcel* (Paris: Vrin, 2004 [1932]) first introduces Whitehead into France in 1932. Wahl taught and was a colleague of Deleuze's at the Sorbonne.
2. http://www.webdeleuze.com/php/texte.php?cle=140&groupe=Leibniz &langue=1 (Accessed 27 August 2007).
3. Daniel Smith has argued for this deep relation between Leibniz and Deleuze in his 'The Conditions of the New', *Deleuze Studies*, 1:1 (2007), pp. 1–21, esp. pp. 8–14.
4. Deleuze, *Le pli: Leibniz et le baroque* (Paris: Minuit, 1988), pp. 110–11.
5. See LS 54.
6. This discussion of chaos and the chaosmos can be traced back to *Différence et répétition* (DR 161), where the literary references are shared with *The Fold* (Borges and Gombrowicz), and to Deleuze and Guattari's *What is Philosophy?* where the concepts of chaosmos and chaos are discussed in depth, drawing a direct connection to Deleuze's discussion of the necessity of a sieve between chaos and actual occasions in Whitehead.
7. Deleuze, *Le pli*, p. 104.
8. See A.N. Whitehead, *Science and the Modern World* (Cambridge: Cambridge University Press, 1927), Chapter X, for a much more complex account of abstraction as both necessary and a source of falsely incomplete representations of reality: 'Eternal objects are thus, in their nature, abstract . . . To be abstract is to transcend particular concrete occasions of actual happening. But to transcend an actual occasion does not mean being disconnected from it' (p. 197).
9. Deleuze, *Le pli*, p. 105.
10. Deleuze, *Le pli*, pp. 108–9.
11. Deleuze, *Le pli*, pp. 110–11.
12. This free resource is due to Richard Pinhas and others, and to the generous permissions given by the Deleuze family. Their self-less work reflects the same values in Deleuze's philosophy.
13. See similar work on genesis and the same problem in the much earlier *The Logic of Sense* (LS 118–27, 186–90).
14. http://www.webdeleuze.com/php/texte.php?cle=140&groupe=Leibniz &langue=1 (Accessed 29 August 2007, my translation).

15. http://www.webdeleuze.com/php/texte.php?cle=140&groupe=Leibniz&langue=1

16. http://www.webdeleuze.com/php/texte.php?cle=142&groupe=Leibniz&langue=1

17. A.N. Whitehead, *Process and Reality* (New York: The Free Press, 1978), p. 164.

18. Isabelle Stengers, *Penser avec Whitehead: une libre et sauvage création de concepts* (Paris: Seuil, 2002)

19. There is a broader discussion of Deleuze and Guattari's work in relation to novelty and speculative metaphysics in Éric Alliez's *The Signature of the World: What is Deleuze and Guattari's Philosophy?* (London: Continuum, 2004), pp. 53–9. Alliez is particularly good at drawing out the connections between Deleuze and Whitehead on questions around the organism and philosophies of life and of biology

20. http://www.webdeleuze.com/php/texte.php?cle=140&groupe=Leibniz&langue=1 (Accessed 31 August 2007).

21. Steven Shaviro gives an extended treatment of novelty in terms of Whitehead and Deleuze in his essay 'Deleuze's Encounter with Whitehead'   http://www.shaviro.com/Othertexts/DeleuzeWhitehead. pdf (accessed 3 September 2007) which will be part of a new book on Whitehead. The great strength of Shaviro's work lies in the connection drawn to other thinkers and their influences on Deleuze and Whitehead, most notably, Bergson, Kant and James. See also the 2005 conference 'Deleuze, Whitehead and the Transformation of Metaphysics', Cloots and Robinson (eds) (Brussels: Koninklijke Vlaamse Academie van Belgie voor Wetenschappen en Kunsten, 2005) with papers by Stengers, Debaise, Cloots, Halewood, Goffey, De Bolle, Wambacq, Palin, Williams, Sha Xin Wei, Faber, Robinson, Meyer and Dumoncel. Shaviro rightly makes strong use of Keith Robinson's work. See also my *The Transversal Thought of Gilles Deleuze: Encounters and Influences* (Manchester: Clinamen, 2005), Chapter 5, 'Deleuze and Whitehead'.

22. http://www.webdeleuze.com/php/texte.php?cle=140&groupe=Leibniz&langue=1 (Accessed 31 August 2007).

23. Stengers, *Penser avec Whitehead*, p. 516.

24. Stengers, *Penser avec Whitehead*, p. 511.

25. Jean-Claude Dumoncel's work provides a contrast to readings that focus on mathematics; see, for example, his remarks on nature and machines as a connection between Deleuze and Whitehead in *La pendule du docteur Deleuze: une Introduction à l'anti-oedipe* (Paris: Cahiers de l'Unebévue, 1999), p. 20. See also Dumoncel, *Les septs mots de Whitehead, ou l'aventure de l'être: créativité, processus, événement, object, organisme, enjoyment, aventure: une explication de processus et réalité* (Paris: Cahiers de l'Unebévue, 1998).

26. Stengers, *Penser avec Whitehead*, p. 510.

27. Stengers, *Penser avec Whitehead*, p. 527.

28. Stengers, *Penser avec Whitehead*, pp. 542–5.

29. http://www.webdeleuze.com/php/texte.php?cle=140&groupe=Leibniz &langue=1

30. Gilles Deleuze and Félix Guattari, *Mille plateaux* (Paris: Minuit, 1980), p. 8.

31. See Deleuze and Guattari's discussion of haecceities and becoming imperceptible in *Mille plateaux*, pp. 318–42.

32. For an account of such forms of time as 'Aion' and 'Chronos' related through series of paradoxes, see LS 162–7. See also My *Gilles Deleuze's Logic of Sense: a Critical Introduction and Guide* (Edinburgh University Press, 2008), Chapters 2 and 3.

33. 'That much, however, I must concede to myself on account of my profession as a classicist: for I do not know what meaning classical studies could have for our time if they were not untimely – that is to say, acting counter to our time and thereby acting on our time and, let us hope, for the benefit of a time to come.' Friedrich Nietzsche, *Untimely Meditations* (Cambridge: Cambridge University Press, 1983), p. 60.

34. See Gilles Deleuze and Félix Guattari, *Qu'est ce que la philosophie?* (Paris: Minuit, 1991), pp. 38–81, esp. p 58.

35. Deleuze, *Le Pli*, p. 76.

36. For good discussions of these historical and philosophical schools and oppositions see Simon Glendinning's *The Idea of Continental Philosophy* (Edinburgh: Edinburgh University Press, 2006) and Simon Critchley *Continental Philosophy: a Very Short Introduction* (Oxford: Oxford University Press, 2001).

37. A.N. Whitehead, *Adventures of Ideas* (Harmondsworth: Penguin, 1948), p. 296.

16

Raymond Ruyer

Ronald Bogue

To the casual observer Raymond Ruyer might seem a minor contributor to Deleuze's enterprise. Deleuze first mentions Ruyer in *Difference and Repetition* (1969), quoting him briefly and listing him in the annotated bibliography as a source for information about 'biological differenciation' (DR 342). Deleuze and Guattari make reference to Ruyer in *Anti-Oedipus* (1972), *A Thousand Plateaus* (1980) and *What Is Philosophy?* (1991), but without discussing his thought in any detail. Deleuze's most extended treatment of Ruyer appears in *The Fold* (1981), and though remarkably dense and concise, it nevertheless occupies only two or three pages of the book. Yet, despite such evidence, one might well claim Ruyer as one of the most important influences on Deleuze's philosophy of biology, and a significant force in the development of Deleuze's ontology as a whole. If 'the world is an egg', as Deleuze asserts in *Difference and Repetition* (DR 251), it is through an examination of the thought of Ruyer and its appropriation by Deleuze that one may most easily grasp the full implications of this assertion.

Born in 1902, Raymond Ruyer began his studies at the Ecole normale superieure in 1921, completing his *docteur ès lettres* in 1930. For most of his career, he taught at the Université de Nancy. Ruyer's doctoral thesis appeared in two volumes in 1930, *L'humanité de l'avenir d'après Cournot*, a study of the philosophy of Antoine-Augustin Cournot (1801–87), and *Esquisse d'une philosophie de la structure*, in which Ruyer developed Cournot's insight into the centrality of structure as the guiding light in all objective cognitive investigation. In the course of pursuing this line of thought, however, Ruyer came to recognise the need for distinguishing 'structure', or the disposition and operation of already functioning components, from 'form', or the self-generating and self-sustaining relation among elements such as one encounters in biological entities. The rest of Ruyer's career may be seen as a continuing meditation on that distinction and its implications in the domains of epistemology, ontology, axiology and theology. In 1937, Ruyer turned to the venerable mind-body problem in his *La conscience et le corps*, here articulating for the first time his key notion of consciousness as a self-forming form in 'overflight' (*survol*) across an 'absolute surface' or 'absolute domain'. From 1940 to 1945, Ruyer was interned at Oflag (*Offizierslager*) XVII-A, a German Army prisoner-of-war camp for officers. In this remarkable prison camp, the inmates, many of them distinguished scholars, established their own university, and besides teaching his own courses, Ruyer advanced his studies in biology with the eminent scientists Alexis Moyse and M. Etienne Wolff, among others. During his internment Ruyer drafted the text of a systematic exposition of his philosophy of biology, which was published in 1946 as *Eléments de psycho-biologie*. Further elaborations of this philosophy appeared in *Néo-finalisme* (1952) and *La genèse des formes vivantes* (1958). His consideration of living entities as goal-directed agents led him to develop a general theory of values, which he articulated in *Le monde des valeurs* (1948) and *Philosophie de la valeur* (1952), and his reflection on the differences between organisms and machines inspired both *La cybernétique et l'origine de l'information* (1954) and *Paradoxes de la conscience et limites de l'automatisme* (1960). In his later work, Ruyer turned to the examination of social and political issues, first situating human culture within the biological world in *L'animal, l'homme, la function symbolique* (1964), and then considering the consequences of that position in four subsequent volumes from 1969 to 1979. Perhaps Ruyer's moment of greatest public attention came in 1974, with the publication of his *La Gnose de Princeton: des savants à la recherché d'une religion*, in which he playfully reported his transactions with a purported organisation of American scientists intent on formulating a new religion compatible with contemporary science. On his death in 1987 he was at work on a manuscript titled *L'Embryogénèse du Monde*, which has yet to appear in print.[1]

One might loosely describe Ruyer's philosophy of biology as a Leibniz-inspired 'panpsychism', though Ruyer preferred the terms 'psycho-biology' and 'neo-finalism' to characterise his position, since 'panpsychism' carries with it romantic mystical connotations he sought to avoid. The basic elements of his psycho-biology are laid out in the four books upon which Deleuze concentrates his attention: *La conscience et le corps* (1937), *Eléments de psycho-biologie* (1946), *Néo-finalisme* (1952), and *La genèse des formes vivants* (1958).

In *La conscience et le corps* Ruyer reviews various formulations of the relation between mind and body, describing his own position as 'the inverse of epiphenomenalism',[2] an approach he sees as first suggested by Leibniz and roughly in accord with the views expressed by Russell in *The Analysis of Matter* (1927) and *An Outline of Philosophy* (1927). In *Néo-finalisme* Ruyer recapitulates the arguments of *La conscience et le corps*, there offering the clearest exposition of his approach to the problem.[3] The hidden – and mistaken – assumption in most analyses of consciousness is that consciousness must be observed as an object in order to be understood. E. A. Abbott, in his popular and widely discussed *Flatland* (1884), imagines what the world would be like for creatures who inhabit a two-dimensional space, such as the surface of a piece of paper. If they encountered a circle inscribed on the surface, they would experience it as an impenetrable wall, and they would be unable to comprehend it as a circle (at least as we understand circles). If, however, an inhabitant of Flatland were able to rise above the surface into a third dimension, that individual would have no difficulty surmounting the supposed wall of the circle and would gain a full understanding of Flatland's geometrical characteristics. Abbott's purpose is to propose that a fourth-dimension would provide the same transformed perspective for those of us who inhabit a three-dimensional world, but Ruyer's use of this parable is to suggest that analyses of consciousness typically assume the necessity of something like a fourth-dimensional observer to understand consciousness. As an example, Ruyer imagines an adult (himself), seated at checkerboard-patterned table, looking at the table surface. The standard assumption is that an observer, a disembodied 'eye' of some sort, whether just behind the adult's head or inside his head, must be invoked in order to describe consciousness. Of course, such reasoning leads to an infinite regress, since the additional 'eye' must itself be observed by yet another 'eye', ad infinitum. Ruyer insists, however, that consciousness does not operate this way. The seated adult is in immediate possession of the table surface of its perception – indeed, there is no difference between perceiving subject and perceived object, between having the perception and being the perception. Contrary to Husserlian phenomenological analyses, consciousness is not consciousness *of* something. Consciousness *is* something.

The seated adult's consciousness is in 'self-enjoyment' of the table surface, present at every point of the table as if in a ubiquitous 'overflight' (*survol*) across the surface.[4] If the table were to be photographed, a camera would have to be situated at a sufficient distance from the table, and if the camera were moved closer or further, or from side to side, the surface would appear larger or smaller, or its sides altered to form a trapezoid. The seated adult's optical apparatus likewise requires that a certain distance be maintained if he is to see the table as a whole, but his conscious 'self-enjoyment' of the surface entails no supplementary third-dimension, and the surface shape does not change as consciousness 'flies over' the surface. Nor does consciousness relate the details of the surface to one another by simple contiguity. Each square of the table's checkerboard is separate from the others, and connected to the others only along the edges of the immediately surrounding squares. For consciousness, however, all the squares are grasped at once as a single thing, yet without their multiplicity being reduced to an undifferentiated unity. 'It is a surface seized in all its details, without third dimension. It is an "absolute surface", which is relative to no point of view exterior to itself, which knows itself [*se connaît elle-même*] without observing itself'.[5]

The table's checkerboard squares, when considered from the vantage of a single square, are interrelated by mere contiguity, or in Ruyer's favourite phrases, *partes extra partes* (Latin 'parts outside parts'), '*de proche en proche*' (literally, 'from close to close', perhaps idiomatically approximated as 'by degrees', 'closer and closer', 'little by little', or 'piece by piece'). And even when considered '*de proche en proche*', contiguous squares are not genuinely connected to one another. If a given square were to be connected to an adjoining square, rather than simply juxtaposed against an opposing surface, some sort of glue would need to hold them together. But this glue, when considered as discrete molecules *partes extra partes*, would itself require a glue of some kind to connect its components. What this ultimately suggests to Ruyer is that 'connections [*liaisons*] are always inferred, never observed'.[6] The difference between a 'structure' and a 'form' is that a structure may be observed, but only as a collection of entities *partes extra partes*, whereas a form is a set of interconnected elements whose *liaisons* cannot be observed. Most scientific analyses of phenomena, focused as they are on observation, deal with structures and ignore forms, and implicit in such analyses is an essentially mechanistic understanding of the world as a collection of entities interacting *de proche en proche*.

Yet connections genuinely exist, and though they cannot be observed, they can be known, directly through our experience of consciousness, and indirectly through our recognition of consciousness as the fundamental '*force de liaison*' throughout the physical world.[7] Ruyer finds support for this view in the discoveries of quantum physics, according to which atomic particles are less things than activities, zones of forces sustaining a given form. An atom is 'not a structure' but 'a *structuring activity*', and when atoms combine to form a molecule, 'the connecting and interacting electrons are not localisable'.[8] Modern chemists speak of molecular bonds in terms of 'maps of electronic density', and according to this model, in a given molecule, 'two regions, neighboring in the map of electronic density, conjointly "structure one another" ["*se structurent*"] according to their energy of interaction and resonance'. Thus, the molecule 'is a domain where energies interchange [*s'échangent*], where energy structures itself, where a structural state "chooses itself", among an essential multiplicity of possible states'.[9]

Atoms, in short, are genuine *forms*, self-sustaining activities in which there is no distinction between shape and force, between what it is and what it does. Molecules have a structure, since their components may be observed, but they too are forms, in that they are self-sustaining activities whose interconnecting *liaisons* are unobservable. Every form, from atoms to molecules, viruses, bacteria and more complex organisms, is a self-sustaining configuration of forces of connection. Each of these forms, according to Ruyer, is a consciousness. Identifying form with consciousness must at first seem far-fetched, but Ruyer's point is not that all the attributes of human consciousness are present in atoms. Rather, he argues that human consciousness is merely a complex, highly developed, self-aware version of the primary self-forming activity that manifests itself in varying degrees of complexity throughout the physical world. The amoeba, for example, is a self-sustaining form that exhibits the properties of a basic subjectivity. 'It is capable of auto-conduction, of conditioned reflexes, of habits, of "learning", of adaptation, of instinctive actions appropriate to circumstances',[10] and though it lacks the many specialised body components of a human being, including a central nervous system, its actions exhibit the primary characteristics of consciousness – perception, self-generated and goal-directed action, memory, learning, adaptation and invention. What human consciousness makes accessible to us, and hence knowable (if not observable as an external object), is the fundamental nature of form as a self-enjoying 'absolute surface' in 'auto-overflight', whose elements are connected through ongoing activity. It is this, our immediate experience of consciousness, that allows us to understand the amoeba, not as a mechanism, but as a living form.

Forms, then, extend from atoms to molecules to all the diverse types of organisms on our planet. All are living, and all are manifestations

of 'consciousness-force'.[11] They are to be contrasted with 'aggregates', collections of disconnected forms, such collections not imbued
with a single consciousness in overflight that would give them their
own form. A bucket of sand is an aggregate; a cloud is an aggregate,
as is a set of billiard balls on a pool table. Geological formations in
general are aggregates, in that mountains, mesas, even planets, are
mere accretions of atoms and molecules that take on various shapes
according to mechanical laws of adhesion, erosion, and so on. Many
of the phenomena in our world involve the interaction of separate
bodies as components of aggregates. Aggregates are structures rather
than genuine forms, and hence they are observable; their elements,
relative positions to one another, and functions may be described;
and the future states of their functioning may be predicted. Most
of the advances of modern science have come through the study of
aggregates, and they have given us invaluable knowledge about the
world, but they have also encouraged a mechanistic view of reality
as nothing but a collection of discrete objects interacting according
to the laws of classical physics, which are laws governing aggregates.
Ruyer recognises the importance of the scientific study of aggregates,
but argues that sciences based on such study are secondary sciences,
whereas those that study forms are primary sciences.

Classical mechanistic science, the science of aggregates, treats
the structure and function of entities in terms of *partes extra partes*,
interacting by contiguity, *de proche en proche*, the overall shape and
regular operation of any entity (say, a dog) emerging simply via the
deterministic and theoretically predictable assemblage of machine-like
constituents (atoms and molecules) interconnected solely via contact
with their immediately surrounding co-constituents. Obviously,
according to such a model the whole is merely the sum of its parts.
Advocates of Gestalt theory, which was especially popular in the
1940s and 1950s when Ruyer was articulating his psycho-biology,
are among those who recognise the difficulties of this extreme position. They assert that the whole is greater than the parts, and that
the whole, or *Gestalt* (German 'form'), may be explained in terms
of the dynamic interaction of its parts and the *Gestalt*'s 'equilibrated
totality of forces'.[12] Gestaltists sometimes propose the soap bubble
as a simple model of a form as 'equilibrated totality of forces', but
Ruyer points out that such an entity is not a genuine form. Despite
talk of 'dynamism' and 'equilibration of forces', the structure of the
soap bubble is that of an aggregate, a collection of parts related to
contiguous parts *de proche en proche*. What Gestalt theory does is to

recognise the problem of the existence of genuine forms but obfuscate the inadequacies of mechanistic explanation through imprecise and ambiguous terminology that masks the movement from pseudo-forms (aggregates) to true forms.

For Ruyer, the difficulty faced by Gestaltists is that of deriving a living, self-sustaining form from the interaction of particles of brute matter according to the laws of a mechanistic physics. He sees theories of 'emergence' in general as further vain efforts to explain how lifeless, billiard-ball like atoms can somehow give rise to living organisms or sentient beings endowed with self-consciousness, as if in some way at various stages of organisation certain 'wholes' suddenly take on properties that are qualitatively different from the functioning of the separate parts. Ruyer sees no mystery in the development of life from inorganic matter or in the emergence of consciousness, since for him all genuine beings are alive and conscious, in the sense that atoms, molecules and organisms are all self-sustaining forms. He does, however, see a mystery in the origin of self-replicating forms, and especially those that undergo morphogenesis – forms that are born, grow, reproduce and die. He makes no claim to having solved the mystery of how such forms came into being, but he does propose ways of understanding morphogenesis that expand our comprehension of consciousness and its relationship to biology.

To understand morphogenesis, we must add to Ruyer's concepts of 'overflight' and 'absolute surface' that of 'verticalism'. It is relatively simple to grasp an organism's morphology, that is, the structure and functioning of its diverse components, but its morphogenesis is much more difficult to fathom. A morphological analysis may treat the organism as a complex machine, with already-formed parts operating in regular circuits of interaction. An organism, however, is a machine that builds itself, and during its self-construction it manages to function even at stages when it lacks the parts essential to the functioning of the completed machine (such as the human embryo, which manages to survive while 'building' the brain, heart and lungs without which it cannot live once it is born). We may observe the various stages of morphogenesis, perhaps photographing a limb at representative moments as a hand gradually emerges and takes on its fully developed shape, and we may then sequentially arrange those photographs along a horizontal time line. But we will thoroughly misconstrue the growth process if we do not add what Ruyer calls a 'vertical' dimension to our analysis, one that recognises the continuous, goal-directed activity that co-ordinates the multiple processes of morphogenesis in the unified task of shaping a hand. The hand is not formed simply like our snapshots on the time line, point by point, *de proche en proche*, by an accretion of contiguities. Rather, the incipient hand and the completed hand are starting point and end point of a continuous line of development, that line best thought of as something like a musical melody. A melody unfolds in time, moment by moment, but the listener only knows it fully when it is completed, and only recognises it as a genuine melody (as opposed to a random sequence of notes) when its overall design is grasped, that design or shape being immanent within the melody from beginning to end. In a sense, the melody as shape exists outside chronometric time, as an idea that manifests itself moment by moment in performance. Rather than represent the melody as a horizontal sequence of notes on a score, one might represent it vertically, first note to last, one on top of the over, all present at the starting point of a given time line of performance, and all of them continuing to be present at each consecutive point on the horizontal performance time line. The actual performed melody, then, would be a temporal unfolding of an atemporal melody-idea. In like fashion, according to Ruyer, a vertical, atemporal developmental melody-idea directs the morphogenesis of every self-replicating organism. Hence, if a genuine form is a self-sustaining activity, an organism is a self-sustaining and self-shaping activity. And if a form is an absolute surface in auto-overflight, a self-forming form that 'builds' itself is an atemporal absolute surface in auto-overflight unfolding chronologically as a developmental melody.

Ruyer is not advocating a conventional idealism, we must note, for a developmental melody is not an idea residing in some ethereal great beyond. Rather, it 'never loses contact with the spatio-temporal plane', even though it 'is not constrained to actualise in space, at every moment, the totality of the structure which it is capable of constructing'.[13] At an embryo's conception, for example, its developmental melody exists largely as a potential form only minimally actualised, but as the organism grows, the developmental melody becomes increasingly 'embodied' in the spatio-temporal world. If the organism dies without reproducing, the developmental melody-idea dies also. If the organism reproduces, however, the developmental melody continues, the self-forming formative activity enacting a succeeding organism's morphogenesis. Yet at no point is the idea-form detached from the spatio-temporal physical world. Though actualised only by degrees during an organism's morphogenesis, the organism's idea-form is immanent within the organism throughout its diverse

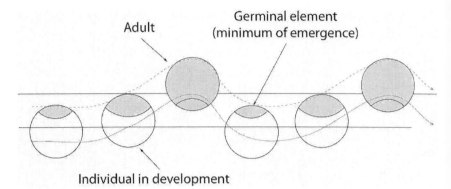

Figure 1   *The Morphogenesis of Two Generations of an Organism*

actualisations, and never totally separated from the actual organism. To illustrate this point, Ruyer offers a diagram (see Figure 1) of two successive generations of an organism.

The first three spheres represent one organism, the last three a succeeding organism. The shaded areas of each circle represent the portion of the completed organism that has been actualised. The dotted line traces the sequence of structures functioning in space-time (the object of mechanistic science's observation), whereas the continuous line maps the developmental melody of the form-idea.

We should also avoid seeing in Ruyer's developmental melody a version of preformationism. The developmental melody is not like the perforated paper roll of a player piano that mechanically generates the piano's performance of the actual organism. Rather, the developmental melody is best thought of as a musical theme in the process of forming itself as a variation of that theme.[14] Each organism that undergoes morphogenesis, each self-forming form, exhibits memory and invention in its development.[15] A cat embryo possesses the memory of its 'catness' and how to make itself into a cat, but its self-development is an action, a task, and a genuine process of invention, not fully predictable, open to disturbances, adjustments and improvisation, the eventual mature cat being a novel variation of the 'catness' immanent within its developmental melody. 'The organism forms itself with risks and perils; it is not formed. . . . The living being forms itself directly according to the theme, without the theme having first to become idea-image and represented model.[16] And a complex organism – such as a cat – is itself a hierarchy of self-sustaining and self-forming forms. Each of its organs, for example, is a self-forming form, which is under the dominance of the 'cat form'. The cat is, as it were, a co-ordinated group project involving a hierarchy of agents. The line between 'organ' and 'individual' is not always easily drawn, and in fact 'the hesitation between "being an individual" and "being the organ of an individual" is found throughout the organic domain'.[17] If, as Ruyer claims, every self-forming form is a subject, an 'I', then we may say of every human being, as of every complex living organism, '"I" am made of all the other I's that I have already produced as if through a sort of cellular division of internal and dominated reproduction. I am a colony, both psychological and biological.'[18] Given the 'colonial' nature of hierarchically organised, complex self-forming forms, it is no wonder that morphogenesis entails risks, perils, improvisations and invention.

Ruyer finds evidence against preformationism and in favour of morphogenetic invention and improvisation in the phenomenon of 'equipotentiality'. Early in embryological studies, researchers found that grafting cells from one sector of an embryo into another (or from other embryos, even in some cases from embryos of different, though closely related, species) did not necessarily disrupt normal morphogenesis. If the graft was made early in development, the cell often simply assumed the function appropriate to its new location in the embryo. If, however, the graft was made later in development, the grafted cell developed as if it were in its old position. This suggested that initially embryonic cells are 'equipotential', capable of developing in a number of ways – to become a lung, a foot, or an eye – and that as development proceeds, cells become more specific in their function, such that at a certain point a given cell might be capable of forming only a limb, or even later, of forming only a right thumb. Ruyer sees in 'equipotentiality' simply another name for consciousness, or a self-forming form in auto-overflight of an absolute surface, and he regards morphogenesis as an incremental specification of areas of restricted potentiality as the organism takes shape. 'Primitive embryonic equipotentiality thus disappears progressively; it distributes itself into increasingly restrained areas; the theme of organs, in becoming more precise, ceases to be a theme in order to become a structure.'[19] Something of the embryo's equipotentiality continues to exist in the diverse components of an organism, in that development never ceases while the organism lives, even if that development is in a steady-state of maintenance, repair and regular cell replacement, or in a state of decline as death approaches. Given that equipotentiality is but another name for consciousness, Ruyer can say of the various components of an organism: 'Each area is equipotential in itself, and to each equipotentiality corresponds a precise consciousness.'[20] But Ruyer argues as well that in humans, at least, a good deal of equipotentiality continues to exist in the brain throughout an individual's life. Citing numerous studies supporting the view of brain functions as distributed across intricate, modifiable and not strictly localisable networks, and noting the remarkable plasticity of the brain in remembering, learning, reasoning, inventing, and so on, Ruyer concludes that 'the brain, in the adult organism, is an area that has remained embryonic'. Hence, 'the brain is an embryo that has not completed its growth. The embryo is a brain, which begins to organise itself before organising the external world.'[21]

These are but the rudiments of Ruyer's philosophy of biology, incomplete, admittedly, but perhaps sufficient to suggest the richness of his thought. At this point, then, though the effort will be equally rudimentary, a brief critical review of Deleuze's citations of Ruyer will have to suffice to indicate some of the complexities of the Ruyer–Deleuze connection.

In the paragraph of *Difference and Repetition* that opens, 'The entire world is an egg' (DR 216), Deleuze makes use of Ruyer's analyses of embryological equipotentiality in remarking that 'when a cellular migration takes place, as Raymond Ruyer shows, it is the requirements of a "role" in so far as this follows from a structural "theme" to be actualized which determines the situation, not the other way round' (DR 216). Deleuze adds a footnote to this sentence, observing that 'Ruyer, no less than Bergson, profoundly analysed the notions of the virtual and actualization. His entire biological philosophy rests upon them along with the idea of the "thematic"' (DR 328). This is indeed a fair appraisal of Ruyer's biological philosophy, though Ruyer speaks most often of the actualisation of 'potential' rather than 'virtual' forms. But whether termed 'potential' or 'virtual', what is crucial is that Ruyer distinguishes between the vertical domain of self-forming forms and the horizontal domain in which they are actualised. Just as Deleuze maintains that the virtual and the actual are both real, and that the virtual is immanent within the actual, so Ruyer insists that self-forming forms are real and immanent within their actualisations. At times in *Difference and Repetition* Deleuze speaks of the virtual in terms of Ideas as problems, and Ruyer likewise refers to self-forming forms as 'ideas', stressing that such ideas are not static Platonic forms but thematic activities, goal-directed projects that constantly require improvised solutions to unanticipated problems. Deleuze does not refer to the virtual as consciousness, though one cannot avoid hearing an echo of Ruyer's 'I am a colony' in Deleuze's references to 'larval subjects' (DR 78) or to 'souls' that contract habits, such that 'a soul must be attributed to the heart, to the muscles, nerves and cells' (DR 74). Obviously, Deleuze is not simply repeating Ruyer – Ruyer never engages the issues of difference, repetition, multiplicities, and so on, which are fundamental to Deleuze's conception of biological processes – yet if treated with caution, Ruyer's biological studies may be read as an extended demonstration in the domain of biology that indeed 'the entire world is an egg', one in which virtual self-forming forms are everywhere actualising themselves.[22]

Deleuze and Guattari cite Ruyer in *Anti-Oedipus* in the course of reiterating the differences between the molar and the molecular. Their formulation of the opposition adheres closely to Ruyer's distinction between molar aggregates/structures and genuine forms, the latter being manifest at the molecular level and maintained in every self-forming form, whatever its size or complexity. Deleuze and Guattari correctly note that 'these themes are developed at length by Ruyer in *Néo-finalisme*' (AO 286). Ruyer states there, for example, that 'a field of consciousness, or of subjectivity, is a domain of *liaisons*, according to which model we must conceive the domains of microscopic *liaisons* that assure the coherence of physical individualities'. Since all organisms are made up of atoms and molecules, we may say that 'the elephant is, if you will, a macro-microscopic being'.[23] Whatever the actual scale of the entities under consideration, there is a qualitative difference between forms and aggregates, the one manifest even in an individual atom, the other evident only in assemblages of forms, such assemblages at any given scale always being 'macroscopic' in relation to the 'microscopic' forms that constitute the given aggregate. Hence, Ruyer can quip, 'the elephant is, despite all appearances, more "microscopic" than a soap bubble'.[24] This judgement accords well with Deleuze and Guattari's repeated insistence throughout *Anti-Oedipus* that their fundamental distinction between the molar and the molecular is qualitative rather than quantitative, having nothing to do with size.[25]

In *A Thousand Plateaus* Deleuze and Guattari again cite Ruyer's opposition of molar aggregates and molecular forms (TP 42, 334–5), but they also refer to Ruyer's discussions of an organism's inner 'developmental themes' and the developmental role played by the organism's behavior in its external environment: 'Raymond Ruyer has demonstrated that the animal is instead prey to "musical rhythms" and "melodic and rhythmic themes" explainable neither as the encoding of a recorded phonograph disk nor by the movements of performance that effectuate them and adapt them to the circumstances' (TP 332). Deleuze and Guattari cite Ruyer here merely to buttress a subsidiary point in their argument, but if one consults Ruyer's *La genèse des formes vivantes*, one finds many parallels between his and Deleuze and Guattari's exploitation of musical metaphors to discuss biological systems. In the penultimate chapter of *La genèse*, Ruyer differentiates three kinds of forms: the primary forms of atoms, molecules and simple organisms (Form I); the forms of organisms endowed with representational consciousness, specialised perceptual organs and motor schematisation (Form II); and the forms possessed of self-consciousness, that is, humans (Form III). Every form is a Form I; every Form II is both a Form I and a Form II; and every human is at once a Form I, Form II and Form III. Ruyer sees every form as an activity aimed at mastering space and time. The simpler the form, the smaller its domain of space-time control. The movement from Form I to Form III is one of increasing mastery of space-time, increasing flexibility and increasing autonomy. Using von Uexküll's analyses of environmental patterns as contrapuntal melodies in a grand symphony (analyses that Deleuze and Guattari also exploit in the Refrain plateau), Ruyer reviews the incremental changes evident in Forms I, II and III in terms of various organisms' inner developmental melodies and their external contrapuntal relations. He describes the amoeba's restricted domain of control, the broader domains of the spider, the mole, birds and various territorial animals, and the extensive domain of humans, noting that the expansion of space-time control brings with it increased specialisation of functions and increased freedom of activity. And throughout this discussion Ruyer maintains the musical metaphors of themes, melodies and counterpoint to frame his analysis. If one were to substitute 'refrains' for Ruyer's 'themes' and 'melodies', and speak of varying degrees of space-time mastery and autonomy in terms of relative degrees of deterritorialisation, it would not be hard to see Ruyer's discourse on Forms I, II and III as a precursor of Deleuze and Guattari's entire treatment of refrains in the natural world.[26]

In *The Fold*, Deleuze offers a brilliant synopsis of Ruyer's philosophy (FLB 102–4) – judicious, incisive and, I would venture to guess, virtually impenetrable to the majority of readers unfamiliar with Ruyer. (One of the primary goals of this essay, in fact, has been to render Deleuze's difficult few pages relatively comprehensible.)

Deleuze claims Ruyer as 'the latest of Leibniz's great disciples' (FLB 102), and though Ruyer frequently expresses his differences with Leibniz, he would no doubt have welcomed the accolade, especially since Deleuze's reading of Leibniz's thought makes evident its similarities with Ruyer's own.[27] There is no need to rehearse Deleuze's summary of Ruyer, but it is worth noting the mutual illumination of Leibniz and Ruyer that Deleuze provides in this conjunction of the two. Deleuze cites Ruyer in a chapter devoted to the relationship between monads and bodies, and Ruyer's primary function in the chapter is to demonstrate the viability of a monadological approach to contemporary biology. But Leibniz helps enrich our understanding of Ruyer as well. One of the problems Leibniz addresses is the relationships among hierarchically organised monads, specifically those among dominating and dominated monads (such as the various monads of a human body's organs that are dominated by the monad of the body as a whole). Deleuze pursues this question at length, as well as the related issue of how, why and in what way monads 'have' bodies, offering an ingenious reading of Leibniz that provides significant tools for approaching the thorny issue of what constitutes a biological 'individual'. Deleuze's analysis of this dimension of Leibniz's thought could well guide one in extending Ruyer's theory of forms into this largely unexamined region of his thought.

Intimations of Ruyer appear early in *What Is Philosophy?* when Deleuze and Guattari state that 'the concept is in a state of *survey* [*survol*] in relation to its components' (WP 20), but it is only in the book's concluding chapter that they explicitly refer to Ruyer. There they characterise the brain as '*the junction* – not the unity – *of the three planes*' (WP 208) of philosophy, the arts and the sciences, and they argue that the brain is a Ruyerian form. Scientific descriptions of the brain typically follow two models, conceiving of neural connections either as 'pre-established' or as 'produced and broken up in fields of forces', and treating processes of integration as either 'localized hierarchical centers' or as 'forms (*Gestalten*)' (WP 208). Yet 'both schemas presuppose a "plane", not an end or a program, but a *survey* [*survol*] *of the entire field*. This is what Gestalt theory does not explain, any more than mechanism explains preassembly [*prémontage*]' (WP 209). The brain

> is a primary, "true form" as Ruyer defined it: neither a Gestalt nor a perceived form but a *form in itself* that does not refer to any external point of view . . . it is an absolute consistent form that surveys *itself* independently of any supplementary dimensions, . . . which remains

> copresent to all its determinations without proximity or distance, . . .
> and which makes of them so many inseparable variations on which it
> confers an equipotentiality without confusion. (WP 210)

The brain, in its guise as 'absolute form, appears as the faculty of
concepts' (WP 211) proper to philosophy. In this role, 'the brain is the
mind [esprit] itself', a 'subject – or rather "superject", as Whitehead
puts it' (WP 211). The brain of the arts involves a process of contraction that is 'the correlate of the survey *[survol]*', this brain-subject
being 'called *soul [âme]* or *force*', not a 'superject' but 'an *inject*'
(WP 212). The brain of the arts is one that contracts sensations, and
that contraction of sensations takes place not only in humans but
throughout the physical world. 'Not every organism has a brain, and
not all life is organic, but everywhere there are forces that constitute
microbrains, or an inorganic life of things' (WP 213). And the brain
of the sciences 'is neither a form nor a force but a *function*', and in
this capacity 'the subject now appears as an "eject"' (WP 215).

Ruyer characterises the human brain as a self-forming form in
absolute overflight that has maintained its equipotentiality. As such,
it is but one manifestation of the process of self-formation that
pervades the physical world. Deleuze and Guattari's notion of the
tripartite brain of philosophy, the arts and the sciences may seem to
relate solely to the domain of human cognition, but there are signs
that their concept of the brain, like Ruyer's concept of self-forming
form, extends into the world at large. Deleuze and Guattari express
qualified approval of phenomenology's movement 'beyond the
brain toward a Being in the world' (WP 210), though they see the
phenomenological account of the interfolding of man and world as
anthropocentric. Rather than asserting that 'Man thinks, not the
brain', Deleuze and Guattari declare, 'It is the brain that thinks and
not man – the latter being only a cerebral crystallization' (WP 210).
Philosophy, the arts and the sciences 'are not the mental objects of an
objectified brain but the three aspects under which the brain becomes
subject, Thought-brain' (WP 210). The Thought-brain of philosophy
bears on the virtual domain of events, which Deleuze and Guattari
describe as 'forms of a thought-Nature that surveys *[survolent]* every
possible universe' (WP 177–8). What the phrase 'thought-Nature'
suggests, I believe, is that Deleuze and Guattari share Ruyer's view
that human cognition, and specifically the practice of philosophy,
is a highly specialised manifestation of the phenomenon of auto-
overflight of an absolute surface that is everywhere present in the

world. I find support for this conjecture in Deleuze and Guattari's reference to ubiquitous 'microbrains' (WP 213) that exist wherever sensations are contracted, and in their characterisation of each microbrain as a 'a *soul* or *force*' (WP 211) – an attribution that cannot help but recall Deleuze's remark in *Difference and Repetition* that for every contraction of a habit there is a 'soul', such that 'a soul must be attributed to the heart, to the muscles, nerves and cells' (DR 74).[28] Final confirmation of this hypothesis I discern in the comment that 'not all life is organic' (WP 213), an apparently paradoxical statement that makes perfect sense from a Ruyerian perspective, in that for him all atoms are living, acting, self-sustaining forms, and hence all molecules, whether organic or inorganic, as self-sustaining forms, are likewise forms of life.

In a 1988 interview, Deleuze said, 'I want to write a book on "What Is Philosophy?"', and then added, 'Also, Guattari and I want to get back to our joint work and produce a sort of philosophy of Nature' (N 155). The project of a 'philosophy of Nature' never came to fruition, and in the absence of such a study it is difficult to establish with certainty the contours of the Ruyer–Deleuze connection. Significant conceptual and terminological differences separate the two, but in their pursuit of a philosophy of biology that avoids mechanism and vitalism, they are united. Ruyer rejects vitalism by making living force, 'consciousness-force', a constituent of matter, rather than some mysterious 'life force' added to inert matter. But for him, the primary enemy is mechanism, and hence he wages a relentless battle against the notion of the organism as a machine. Deleuze, by contrast, embraces the machine model, though he does frequently caution that the 'machinic' is not 'mechanistic', and that what we usually call machines are mere 'technological machines', a subset of the general category. When he and Guattari first introduce the machine model in *Anti-Oedipus*, their primary goal is to counter psychoanalysis' humanism and its obsession with signifiers and interpretation. But the machine model also undermines distinctions between psyche and body, and between body and world. 'There is no such thing as either man or nature', Deleuze and Guattari claim, 'only a process that produces the one within the other and couples the machines together. Producing-machines, desiring-machines everywhere, schizophrenic machines, all of species life' (AO 2). This view of nature as a multiplicity of machines invites a conception of all life forms as part of a continuum of activity, a conception Deleuze and Guattari develop in *A Thousand Plateaus*. The machine model is not entirely abandoned in that book, but talk of 'desiring machines' tends to give way to discussion of such things as 'assemblages' and 'refrains'. In *A Thousand Plateaus* they avoid the terms 'subject', 'mind', and 'consciousness' when characterising nature, and in *What Is Philosophy?* also those terms are largely absent. It is significant, however, that the brain is said to operate, if not as a 'subject' (a concept replete with undesirable philosophical associations), then as a 'superject', 'inject', or 'eject', and that each such agent is, respectively, an *esprit* (which may be translated either as 'mind' or as 'spirit'), an *âme* (soul), or a function. This description of what one would assume to be the physical brain in terms of such seemingly mental agencies as superjects, injects and ejects, and such supernatural entities as spirits and souls, is finally just one more effort to escape mechanism and dualism, in this instance, by thwarting mechanism's tendency to see all physical entities, including the brain, as nothing but assemblages of deterministic physico-chemical processes. Ultimately, what Deleuze and Guattari and Ruyer are trying to do is to develop new concepts of matter and life. For Ruyer, every entity that has genuine being is at once matter and mind, form and force, a consciousness-force-matter-form actively sustaining and forming itself. For Deleuze, the world is an egg, but it is also a machine, as well as a brain that operates as a spirit/superject, soul/inject or function/eject. For Ruyer, as for Deleuze and Guattari, matter is always formed by forces of *liaisons* in auto-overflight, and life is, in Deleuze and Guattari's terminology, 'anorganic' (TP 503), in that it is present in organic and inorganic molecules alike. Thus I would conclude that though Deleuze is no mere disciple of Ruyer, his fundamental views of nature and those of Ruyer are broadly consonant with one another. And though Deleuze's explicit references to Ruyer are few, it is safe to say that Ruyer's philosophy of biology was an essential and far-reaching stimulus in the development of Deleuze's conception of nature, and perhaps in the formation of his ontology as a whole.

University of Georgia

Notes

1. Ruyer was a prolific writer, authoring twenty-two books and over one hundred articles. His publications appeared in distinguished venues, and his work was highly regarded by a small but distinguished group of scholars. Nonetheless, he never received the acclaim of many of his contemporaries in philosophy, perhaps in part because of his peripheral position at Nancy. (On more than one occasion, he was reported to have graciously declined offers to join the faculty of the Sorbonne, preferring

instead the quiet life outside Paris.) As a result, his thought is not well known today, even in France. A few of his books have been translated into other languages – Spanish, German, Portuguese, Czech, Arabic – but none has appeared in English translation. An invaluable guide to his work is a description of his philosophy that he himself prepared for radio broadcast and subsequently published in *Les philosophes français d'aujourd'hui par eux-mêmes*, edited by. Gérard Deledalle and Denis Huisman (Paris: CDU, 1959), pp. 262–76. Other than a brief article by Maurice Gex in 1959, 'La psycho-biologie de Raymond Ruyer', *L'age nouveau* 105, pp. 102–9, a modest sketch of his thought in André Vergez and Denis Huisman's *Histoire des philosophes illustrée par les textes* (Paris: Fernand Nathan, 1966), pp. 423–6, a short essay by Alain de Benoist in *Vu de droite: anthologie critique des idées contemporaines* (Paris: Copernic, 1977), pp. 443–6, and a commentary by Max Morand on the physics of Ruyer's *La Gnose de Princeton*, 'Reflexions d'un physicien sur la Gnose de Princeton', *Cahiers Laïques* 174 (1980), pp. 123–43, Ruyer's work received little critical commentary until the publication of a collection of essays titled *Raymond Ruyer, de la science á la théologie*, edited by. Louis Vax and Jean-Jacques Wunenburger (Paris: Kimé, 1995). The first monograph devoted to Ruyer, Laurent Meslet's *Le psychisme et la vie. La philosophie de la nature de Raymond Ruyer* (Paris: L'Harmattan), appeared in 2005. With the exception of Paul Bains's excellent essay on Ruyer and Deleuze and Guattari, 'Subjectless Subjectivities', in *A Shock to Thought: Expression after Deleuze and Guattari*, edited by Brian Massumi (London and New York: Routledge, 2002), pp. 101–16, very little has been written about Ruyer in English.

2. *La conscience et le corps* (Paris: Alcan, 1937), p. 2. All translations of Ruyer are my own.

3. *Néo-finalisme* (Paris: PUF, 1952). See especially, pp. 80–117.

4. Ruyer says that he borrows the term 'self-enjoyment' (which he never translates into French) from Samuel Alexander's 1920 tome *Space, Time and Deity* (*Néo-finalisme*, p. 81), but his use of the term primarily signals his sympathetic appreciation of Whitehead, who himself appropriated the term from Alexander. As the translators of Deleuze and Guattari's *What Is Philosophy?* note, the word *survol* poses special problems for the English translator. The verb *survoler* means literally 'to fly over', and a *survol* is a 'flight over' something. Deleuze's translators quite reasonably opt for 'survey' as its English equivalent, but I have chosen to render it as 'overflight' in order to retain something of the literal sense of the French term, with apologies to those who might find the neologism barbaric.

5. Ruyer, *Néo-finalisme*, p. 98.

6. Ruyer, *Néo-finalisme*, p. 87. In *Néo-finalisme*, Ruyer remarks that 'the notion of *liaison* has been greatly neglected' (p. 110). Bernard

Ruyer, Raymond's son and himself a philosopher, observes in his essay 'La notion de liaison dans la philosophie de Ruyer', (in Vax and Wunenberger's *Raymond Ruyer, de la science á la théologie*, pp. 45–54), that 'the notion of *liaison* is present throughout the Ruyerian *oeuvre*' (p. 45), and he suggests that Ruyer's philosophy may be seen as one extended exploration of the implications of that notion. The word *liaison* is a common enough term, translated often as 'connection', 'joining', or 'binding'. To stress the concept and its special significance in Ruyer's thought, I have chosen to leave the word untranslated often (though not always). The centrality of the notion of *liaison* is in some ways parallel to the crucial role played by the concept of *relation* in Deleuze, though obviously, *liaison* is a subset of *relation*. See Paul Bains's *The Primacy of Semiosis: An Ontology of Relations* (Toronto: University of Toronto Press, 2006) for a brilliant discussion of the role of relations in Deleuze's philosophy.

7. Ruyer, *Néo-finalisme*, p. 113.
8. Ruyer, *La genèse des formes vivantes* (Paris: Flammarion, 1958), p. 58.
9. Ruyer, *La genèse*, p. 59.
10. *Eléments de psycho-biologie* (Paris: PUF, 1946), p. 22.
11. Ruyer, *Eléments*, p. 293.
12. Ruyer, *Eléments*, p. 9.
13. Ruyer, *Eléments*, p. 13.
14. Ruyer wrote before a number of the remarkable recent advances in genetic research had occurred, and many might regard his analyses of self-forming forms as hopelessly out of date. He objected to the notion of a genetic 'code' and to the belief that our understanding of DNA fully explains morphogenesis. He recognised DNA as an important component of morphogenesis, but its role he saw as that of a signal rather than a cause. The theory of a genetic code or program he viewed as a disguised version of preformationism, and the typical explanations of the operation of DNA he regarded as informed by the mechanistic logic of development *de proche en proche*. Lest one think that Ruyer's speculations are as outmoded as treatises on phlogiston, one should consult such recent works as Susan Oyama's *The Ontogeny of Information*, 2nd edition. (Durham: Duke University Press, 2000), Evelyn Fox Keller's *The Century of the Gene* (Cambridge: Harvard University Press, 2000), Lenny Moss's *What Genes Can't Do* (Cambridge: MIT Press, 2003) and Jason Scott Robert's *Embryology, Epigenesis and Evolution: Taking Development Seriously* (Cambridge: Cambridge University Press, 2004), which voice criticisms of the deterministic model of DNA and the 'genetic code' that are remarkably reminiscent of Ruyer's earlier objections (which are not cited by any of these authors).
15. Ruyer, *La genèse,* p. 46.

16. Ruyer, *La genèse*, p. 261–2.
17. Ruyer, *La genèse*, p. 95. This problematic relationship between organs and bodies, especially in species that form colonies that function as 'supraindividuals', leads Ruyer to posit that human groups, too, may function as supraindividuals, or self-forming forms, for which reason he classifies Sociology as a Primary Science, as opposed to classical political science and economics, which study the interactions of aggregates.
18. Ruyer, *La genèse*, p. 97.
19. Ruyer, *Néo-finalisme*, p. 44.
20. Ruyer, *Néo-finalisme*, p. 77.
21. Ruyer, *La genèse*, p. 73.
22. Deleuze also cites an essay of Ruyer's during a discussion of the concept of depth (DR 236). While perhaps interesting in itself, the passage in my judgement does not touch on issues that are central to either philosopher's thought.
23. Ruyer, *Néo-finalisme*, p. 112.
24. Ruyer, *Néo-finalisme*, p. 227.
25. Deleuze and Guattari also cite Ruyer's chapter on Markov chains in *La genèse des formes vivantes* (pp. 170–89) as a useful exposition of the concept of 'aleatory phenomena that are partially dependent' (AO 289). Deleuze later makes use of the concept of the Markov chain in F 86 and 117.
26. For a more extended discussion of the similarities between Ruyer's exposition of Forms I, II, and III and Deleuze and Guattari's treatment of the refrain, see my *Deleuze on Music, Painting, and the Arts* (New York: Routledge, 2003), pp. 62–6.
27. Ruyer regularly acknowledges that his philosophy of biology is inspired by Leibniz. Bernard Ruyer, in 'La notion de liaison dans la philosophie de Ruyer', concurs in this judgement of his father's work, though he qualifies that judgement by commenting, in implicit allusion to Leibniz's dictum that monads have neither doors nor windows, that 'the Ruyerian metaphysics is in many regards a monadology, in which the monads are nothing but doors and windows' (p. 48).
28. In presenting the notion of microbrains, Deleuze and Guattari say that 'Vitalism has always had two possible interpretations: that of an Idea that acts, but is not – that acts therefore only from the point of view of an external cerebral knowledge (from Kant to Claude Bernard); or that of a force that is but does not act – that is therefore a pure internal Awareness (from Leibniz to Ruyer)' (WP 213). This statement seems to draw on Chapter 18 of *Néo-finalisme* (205–27), in which Ruyer critiques Kant, Claude Bernard and other 'organicists' for separating a directing 'idea' from physical force. Whether in fact Ruyer advocates a 'force that is but does not act' is a difficult question, dependent on what one means by 'act'. My suspicion is that Ruyer would not have

been happy with the formulation, since he always stresses the concept of consciousness-force as activity. Deleuze describes the Leibnizian 'force that is but does not act' in Chapter 8 of *The Fold*, concluding that 'the soul is the principle of life through its presence and not through its action. *Force is presence and not action*' (FLB 119).

17

Martin Heidegger

Constantin V. Boundas

In Deleuze's writings one finds frequent acknowledgements of the importance of Heidegger's rejection of the old image of thought and the significance of his new beginning. 'The Heidegger question', he wrote, 'did not seem to me to be "Is he a bit of a Nazi?" (obviously, obviously) but "What was his role in this new injection of history of philosophy?"' (D 12). Although there is more wholehearted acknowledgement in his early works and more nuances and qualifications later on, their generosity cannot be disputed. Deleuze's references to Heidegger reveal interesting points of proximity but also significant lines of divergence between the two philosophers. They praise Heidegger for his role in the transformation of the old image of thought (DR xvi–xvii); for the priority he assigns to questions and problems over answers and solutions (DR 200–1); for his refusal to follow the old philosophical line that considers thinking a natural endowment of human beings (DR 144, 275; F 116); for standing up with Duns Scotus for the univocity of Being (DR 35); for having contrasted memory with the forgetting of forgetting that makes of forgetting the impossibility to return and discovers in memory the necessity of renewal (F 107–8); for having displaced intentionality through the fold (F 111–13; N 112); for causing language to stutter in an etymological procedure that borders on madness (N 107); and for having assigned to difference the prominent philosophical role that distinguishes it from the negative, the identical and the equal, unhinges it from the modalities of representation and lets it be thought in association with the question and the fold (DR 64–5).

On the other hand, the lines of divergence between the two thinkers have ultimately the upper hand. Deleuze criticises Heidegger for having rendered philosophy indistinguishable from its own history, planting it in the land of the Greeks – the *autochthon* of Being's territory (DR 94–5); for having thought that the form of the Same suffices in the fight against identity and equivalence, and that *philia* rather than shock and paradox should govern the process of repetition

(DR 66, 321 n. 11); for having allowed shades of representation to weaken the univocity of Being that he himself had championed (DR 66); for limiting the force of his fold by never really freeing it from the embrace of intentionality, and by appointing it to the origin of the visible and the utterable, at one and the same time (F 59, 110–13, 119; N 107, 112); for having chosen the world over the planetary, the 'rational' over strategy, and being and truth over errancy (DI 161); and finally, in his politics, for getting hold, through his 'abject reterritorialisation', of 'the wrong people, earth, and blood' (WP 108–9).

Now, gathering references may be helpful in compiling concordances but it cannot be a substitute for seriously confronting the 'battle of the giants over difference' (*gigantomachia peri t s diaforas*). In order to remedy this deficiency I want first to focus on those issues in Deleuze's and Heidegger's writings where similarities in thematic choice are likely both to mask and to reveal important differences in their thinking: finitude/infinity, temporality/*Chronos–Aion*, eternal recurrence of the Same/eternal return of difference, *Ereignis*/event, death/*metamorphosis*, and ethics of wanting to have a conscience/ethics of becoming worthy of the event – these are the issues that I have in mind. Only later will I venture to put Deleuze's 'yes' and 'no' up against Heidegger in the context of a more general characterisation of their differential ontologies.

DEATH AND FINITUDE

In Heidegger's *Being and Time* (Division Two), death appears initially as a response to the quest for a standpoint that would permit the circumscription of Dasein *as a whole*. Dasein's existential analytic, undertaken for the sake of discovering the Being of that being for which Being is a question, is destined for a major embarrassment in front of the essential incompleteness of Dasein: As long as Dasein is, death is not yet and this 'not yet' is constitutive of Dasein and, as such, ineliminable. The project therefore of a fundamental ontology, which depends on the tabulation of all the possibilities of Dasein, cannot be signed and delivered. But, at the same time, Dasein's finitude is also Dasein's essential possibility. Heidegger's solution to the riddle posited by Dasein's incompleteness is a distinction between, on the one hand, the *event of death* that replaces the 'not-yet' with the 'no-more' and, on the other, the *possibility of death* – Dasein's foremost possibility – that Dasein can either flee from, in distraction and inauthenticity, or learn to anticipate resolutely by wanting to be guilty and, as a result, by emerging authentically as a Self. In the running ahead of itself towards the possibility that Dasein already is – a situation that he characterises as *'having been presently future'* – Heidegger discovers the structure of temporality.[1]

As soon as we turn to Deleuze, we are struck by his refusal to accept death as an end in light of which the meaning of present experience is determined.[2] With him, death – the end of personal life – is not man's essential possibility; it is always an accident, something extrinsic, due to the dissolution of the structure of a mode's extensive parts, the outcome always of 'bad encounters' – that is, the outcome of bodies encountering other bodies with which they are not compatible. 'It is a disgrace', he writes, 'to seek the internal essence of man in his bad extrinsic encounters' (SPP 72). With respect to personal death or to the annihilation of the organism, the Stoics had it right. As long as I am alive, death has not yet come; when death comes, I am no longer there. Personal death always approaches from the outside and there is no reason whatsoever to fabricate on its account the notorious drive. But there is another death, the importance of which Deleuze is ready to acknowledge: the death of the 'I' and of the organic – the death that releases the impersonal, the inorganic and the molecular.[3] From its vantage point, one never ceases to die, one is already always dying. One may think that Deleuze's view on death repeats Heidegger's gesture: death is always double; but, in Deleuze, its duplicity acquires a non-Heideggerian sense and function. Death is the moment 'when I disappear outside myself' and also the moment 'when death loses itself in itself' because a singular life is substituted for mine.[4] Neither one of the Deleuzian senses of death (the accidental and the becoming-imperceptible) justifies Heidegger's dictum that death is 'always mine'.

Heidegger's concept of death finds no place in Deleuze's theory of time either. Life – and we must remember that life, for Deleuze, is lived according to the quantity and the quality of interacting forces – is eternal, if lived with the maximum of intensity in the moment. Eternity does not outlast or come after death. It is contemporaneous with life and 'can be the object of direct experience' (EPS 314). Bruce Baugh, therefore, is correct when he writes that 'duration necessarily involves a beginning but not an end, making birth and death asymmetrical . . . Death is not the horizon of time.'[5] And also: 'The future', for Deleuze, 'is not a possibility that folds back on the present, but something virtual that coexists with the present: in fact, the future is eternity itself . . . the repetition of difference.'[6] Given this attitude with respect to death and life, Deleuze, unlike Heidegger, is not concerned with human finitude and with its relation to Being. Speaking in his Appendix to the book on Foucault of the reassemblage of forces that could precipitate the 'post-historical' and the 'post-human', Deleuze leaves his readers with this question:

> What would be the forces in play, with which the forces within man would then enter into a relation? It would no longer involve a raising to infinity or finitude but an *unlimited finity*, thereby evoking every situation of force in which a finite number of components yields a practically unlimited diversity of combinations. (F 131)

This '*unlimited finity*' is the productive and creative work of the virtual as it differentiates itself inside the actual – the triumph of an inorganic life situated worlds apart from the sombre brooding of Heidegger's Dasein.

On the other hand, death, as Heidegger understands it, finds no place in Deleuze's ethics either, where wanting to assume one's onto-logical guilt has been replaced by the invitation to become worthy of the event. This does not mean, however, that death, in Deleuze's sense of metamorphosis and becoming-imperceptible, has no place in his ethics. In his 1967 essay, 'A Theory of the Other', which was reproduced as an appendix to his *The Logic of Sense*, Deleuze argued that the structure-other and the structure-self mutually imply each other. And that, consequently, for the first time the bracketing of 'the other' of the phenomenologist permits the bracketing also of the Self. The *altruicide* of the thinker of radical difference precipitates a form of *suicide* and ushers in the elemental and the *autrement qu'autre*.[7] Then and only then the elemental and the 'otherwise other' become constitutive of the becoming-imperceptible – the kind of becoming that crowns all other becomings in an ethology of the impersonal, the pre-personal and the larval selves.

TEMPORALITY

The importance that Heidegger assigns to time does not come from the fact that we live in it or that it is an *a priori* form of all our intui-tions; it comes from the fact that time is constitutive of our being. With the locution 'in time' being consigned to the 'vulgar' notion of time, which is derivative and secondary, primordial or ontological time is best understood in terms of the existential analytic of Dasein and in terms of Dasein's *ecstasies*: the *having-been* (past), the *to-come* (future) and the *making-present* (present).[8] These are not to be confused with the now, the now that is no longer and the now that is not yet of the derivative notion. It is in the second division of *Being and Time* (BT IV, 68) that Heidegger attempts to elucidate these points. He begins by making a distinction between the time of the existential analytic and the derivative notion of time by calling the former 'temporality'. He then goes on to argue that temporality is not an entity and to underline this point with the expression '*temporality temporalizes*'. Earlier sections have already shown that Dasein discloses its structure in understanding, in mood (attunement), in falling prey (becoming entangled) and in discourse. If Heidegger could now show that these modes of disclosing and being disclosed are constituted through temporality, he could establish that temporality is a condition for Dasein's being. And this, in fact, is what he does. The entire structure of Dasein is constituted by temporality. Moreover, through Dasein's temporalisation, a World emerges in temporality. Without the temporalising and temporalised Dasein, there can be no temporal World.

To the extent that understanding is the being-projected towards a potentiality-of-being for the sake of which Dasein exists, the *being-projected* would make no sense without the future (the *to-come*). The meaning of 'temporality temporalises' hinges on the fact that each one of the three temporal ecstasies involves the other two (the whole of temporality); temporality, unlike time, is not characterised by succession, but by the co-existence of all these modalities of temporalisation. For example, to the extent that the future is essential for the understanding of the '*to be*,' the '*having-been (past)*' and the '*making-present (present)*' are co-implicated in the following way: understanding projects me towards a potentiality-of-being. In the project (expectation or anticipation) the idea of futurity is indispensable. But also in the potentiality of being (my own finitude, lived authentically or inauthentically) the idea of this potentiality, being always already mine, is indispensable. The project brings me back to the one that I have been all along. The project and the Dasein that does the projecting are 'futurist recollections'. The fact that I will be as I have been shows the past in its co-ordination with the future. As for the 'having-been', it can be lived authentically, in anticipation, in the mode of retrieval; or it can be lived inauthentically, in expectation, in the mode of forgetting, being understood not as the obliteration of memory but rather as a backing off. Finally, in the temporality of understanding, the present is not without its own weight. Dasein, in being futurist recollection, is not merely dreaming to become the entity that it is; rather, Dasein wants to bring together the project and the potentiality to the present. And, once again, this may happen in two ways: through the mere 'making-present' of the idle or frantic 'everyday busi-ness' (inauthenticity) or through being one's own potentiality-of-being (instead of having it) in the context of authenticity. It is the latter choice that Heidegger calls 'the Moment'. What is essential in all this is that the understanding temporalises from the vantage point of the future.

A similar existential analytic scrutiny of attunement (mood) will help unpack the sense and the direction of the temporalisation that it renders possible (BT 312–17). Using fear, angst and hope as examples, Heidegger will conclude that moods, which, as he argued in earlier chapters, bring Dasein before the *That* of its thrownness, temporalise from the vantage point of the *having-been always already* (thrown). But, although in this temporalisation primacy is given to the past, mood temporalises, that is, co-ordinates, in its own modality or style, all three *ecstasies*. For example, angst, in turning away from the uncanniness and homelessness of being thrown, also discloses thrownness as something to be possibly retrieved (in the context of a to-come). And, at the same time, the present of angst holds the Moment in readiness.

We find the same co-imbrication of all three ecstasies in Heidegger's discussion of the temporality of falling prey and becoming entangled in the everydayness and inauthenticity of the 'they-self' (BT 317–20). With curiosity as his example, he attempts to illustrate that falling prey keeps close to what is nearest or strives to make present what is nearest. The modality of this temporalisation is the present, which orchestrates in an inauthentic way all three *ecstasies*, as a continuous succession of present, past and future 'nows'. Forgetting is the inauthentic possibility of this temporalisation, but to the extent that 'forgetting' is not a simple case of amnesia but rather a kind of backing off, it is the Moment that 'falling prey' and 'becoming entangled' function both as covering up and as disclosing.

As for Deleuze's views on time, they are given in his Bergson-inspired paradoxes of time, in his theory of repetition (whether naked or disguised) and in his ingenious adaptation of Nietzsche's riddle of the eternal return to his own purposes. I have always maintained that Deleuze's choice of the title 'Difference and Repetition' for his most important philosophical text was meant as a response to Heidegger's 'Being and Time'. 'Difference' is asked to eliminate the last vestiges of identity in 'Being' and Time turns into the Repetition of the *eventum tantum* in the eternal return of infinite different/ciation. Becoming, in defence of which Deleuze's entire work is mobilised, cannot be constituted through a concatenation of 'immobile cuts'. Such a concatenation has always been responsible for the hieratic and static world of Being. Rather, forces seized *in actu* are better candidates for a diagrammatic mapping out of becoming; but for this mapping to be successful we need a plausible theory of time and space – one that will be capable of doing so without subjects steering the process of becoming (or being steered by it), without substantive names designating 'blocks' in motion, and without points of origin or destination marking the allowed trajectory. No adequate theory of transformation and change can be contemplated as long as it is predicated on a process conceived as a mere sequence of multiple states of affairs. Deleuze's claim that transformation goes from (actual) states of affairs to (virtual) tendencies and back to (actual) states of affairs prevents the time of transformation from collapsing into discrete temporal blocks and from destroying the kind of continuity and mutual imbrication necessary for an adequate characterisation of the duration of processes.

It seems to me that Deleuze has all the necessary blocks for the right theory of time – a theory which, through an ingenious rereading of Bergson's *durée*, will articulate the structure of time in accordance with the requirements of his ontology of processes and will permit Deleuze to advance the following claims: actual presents are constituted simultaneously as both present and past; in every present, the entire past is conserved in itself; and there is a past that has never been present, as well as a future that will never be present (DR 70–128). If the idea of the constitution of each present as simultaneously present and past is reminiscent of the phenomenological inclusion of retention in every present-lived moment, the conservation of the entire past within each present signals the rejection of the *sine qua non* of phenomenology – 'the lived' and consciousness – and the decision to speak of time without the qualifications of the 'subjective' or the 'objective'. As for the ideas of a past that has never been present (the immemorial past), as well as of a future that would never turn into a present, the reason for their postulation is this: any philosophy that puts a premium on the de-actualisation of the present, in order to tap the resources of the past or the future, risks reifying the past (as in Plato's recollection) and also the future (as in the case of apocalyptic eschatologies). To prevent this reification from taking place in a way that will contradict the very idea of radical becoming, the notions of 'immemorial past' and 'messianic future' – Deleuze prefers to talk of the pure past and of the eternal repetition of the different – are brought to safeguard the idea of a process that can be conceived without the dead-weight of tendencies determining it *a tergo* or *ab ende*.

EVENT

My reading of Heidegger leaves me with two possible interpretations of his *Ereignis*. Either '*Ereignis*' designates the emergence of a new world, a new epochal disclosure of Being,[9] as well as the being 'enowned' or appropriated by this disclosure; or *Ereignis* is the *a priori* event of the opening up of the open. Speaking of this *a priori* event, Thomas Sheehan has this to say: It is 'neither "Big Being" nor "Léthé", operating from some "beyond" and heteronomously appropriating us into a place other than ourselves. Rather, our finitude is the absence that opens the open.'[10] The first interpretation of the event carries with it the advantage of displacing the last vestiges of anthropologism present in Heidegger's early work in favour of 'something' that draws Dasein into the open as it always already withdraws. The trouble with this interpretation is that it prepares and legitimises the recent turn in French phenomenology, where the search for the conditions of phenomenality lead to a hybrid discourse of givenness and grace, to renewed speculations on God beyond God, messianicity without Messiahs and to a further entrenchment of equivocity and transcendence.[11] From a Deleuzian point of view, such a price for this interpretation is too costly, given the weight of hermeneutic piety that ushers in. The second interpretation – Sheehan's – has the advantage of demystifying Heidegger's discourse on Being, of carefully following the complex etymology of *Ereignis* that Heidegger himself offers in his *Contributions to Philosophy (From Enowning)*, and in persuasively linking finitude as the *a priori* event of our openness to the open with Heidegger's assignation of fundamental guilt to Dasein, and with his ethical imperative that one must want to be guilty. As Steven Watson, in anticipating Sheehan's interpretation, aptly put it.

> No longer would it be possible . . . simply to think "appropriation" (*Ereignis*) as a species of Being . . . Instead, in default of a guarantee which might maintain representation intact, a "transformed interpretation" resulted, one by which the hermeneutic in question, the "sending and extending" which "hermeneutic" appropriation "explicates," involves equally a "self-withholding" and "expropriation" (*Enteignis*).[12]

I am doubtful that this expropriation would suffice to deconstruct the anthropological foundations of Heideggerianism.

When we turn our attention to Deleuze's theory of the event the landscape changes diametrically. The event is now a sense-event that arises from a particular state of affairs in the world. Being between words and things (subjects and objects), the event insists in a time that is never present (always past and always just to come). 'It neither shifts, transforms, mutates over time nor is it a static structure that remains the same across time. It is that which repeats but repeats differentially.'[13] The event, being virtual, actualises itself in different states of affairs as it differenciates itself.

Given this notion of the event, Deleuze cannot accept Sheehan's interpretation of Heidegger's *Ereignis* as one that advances the cause of difference: it would rather lock the event within the problematics of Dasein than liberate it from an older anthropomorphic conception, and would make it depend on the negativity of a finitude that falls short with respect to Being. There is no space, in Deleuze's ontology, for the withdrawal that Sheehan's reading requires. Rather, the entire past co-exists with the present – and, as I am going to show below, Deleuze's ritornello is not advocating Heidegger's 'futurist recollection', but rather the 'remembering to forget'. After all, we do not repeat because we forget; we forget because we repeat. We often falsely claim that unless we remember the past we are destined to repeat it. But it is not the remembrance of time past that will affect the future; it is the creation of the new that will prevent the sterile repetition of the Same. We must indeed heed Deleuze's advice and strive to create a memory of the future, but between his advice and Heidegger's 'futurist recollection' there is only a verbal similarity.

On the other hand, presented with the dominant interpretation of *Ereignis* as the horizon of the epochal disclosure of Being, Deleuze has no choice but to repeat what he said on the notion of light, present in both Heidegger's and Foucault's writings: 'Foucault's light-being', he wrote, 'is inseparable from a particular mode, and while being *a priori* is none the less historical and epistemological rather than phenomenological' (F 59). This phrase, adapted to the issue of understanding the event, would read as follows: Unlike Heidegger's *Ereignis*, the event, as Deleuze intends it, while being *a priori*, belongs nonetheless to becoming and to joyful wisdom, rather than to a thinly disguised phenomenology looming behind fundamental ontology. When all is said and done, as I will argue later on, it is their radically different assessments of Nietzsche's vision of the eternal return that motivate the disagreement of the two ontologists over *Ereignis* and event.

Suppose now, for the sake of moving the discussion ahead, that there is a third alternative, apart from the dominant interpretation of *Ereignis* and apart from Sheehan's own: an alternative that eliminates 'big Being' but also and at the same time the captivity of *Ereignis* to Dasein's incompleteness and to the 'to and fro' of *aletheia*. Let's suppose that *Ereignis* is difference and different/ciation and that Heidegger's *Ereignis* and Deleuze's different/ciation of the *eventum tantum* address one and the same thing. For the sake of our argument, let us even suppose that the late Heidegger succeeded in eliminating the foundationalist presupposition of an anthropomorphised Dasein (Deleuze, let me make it clear for the record, is not prepared to make this concession). Even after all these concessions are made, the differences between Heidegger and Deleuze will not go away. Even if Dasein were to be displaced, a behind the scenes operating intentionality will entrench the kind of *sensus communis* which, by presupposing an agreement – *philia* – between thinking and Being, perpetuates a fraudulent conception of the transcendental, conceived and articulated according to the image and the resemblance of the empirical.[14]

ETERNAL RETURN

The distance between Deleuze and Heidegger is best appreciated in the context of a discussion of the radically different postures the two philosophers strike in their discussion of Nietzsche.[15] In Heidegger's eyes, Nietzsche, given the key concepts of his philosophy, such as the will to power, nihilism, the eternal recurrence of the same, the overman, justice and so on, is a metaphysician – actually, the last metaphysician. And this judgement applies, with particular force, to his notion of the eternal return: 'The eternal recurrence of the same', which constitutes 'the concealed essence of Time', is 'the last metaphysical name of Being', writes Heidegger in *What is Metaphysics?*. Nietzsche remains mired in the metaphysical tradition, attempting with his teaching of eternal recurrence to 'eternalize the moment' within a single, heroic act of the will.

On the other hand, nothing could be more foreign to Deleuze's homage to Nietzsche than Heidegger's transcription of Nietzsche's will to power as the will to will, and the ensuing conscription of the bard of Zarathustra to the cause of the Western nihilist metaphysics.

To Heidegger's Nietzsche, as the last metaphysician, Deleuze coun-
terposes Nietzsche as the creator of a 'new image of thought', or even
better as the creator of a thought without an image. I have no space
here to document this chasm that separates the two thinkers in all
its amplitude. It has been done already by François Laruelle in his
Nietzsche contre Heidegger,[16] and the interested reader can consult
this text profitably. Here, I will focus my attention on Heidegger's and
Deleuze's sharply diverging readings of Nietzsche's eternal return and
on the impact this divergence has on their thoughts on difference.

Neither Heidegger nor Deleuze mean by 'return' or 'repetition' a
recurrence of the factually historical, a reenactment of incidents in
the life of an individual or a society. Speaking of Heidegger, Calvin
Schrag expresses this point with these words: 'repetition is a matter
of *reclamation* rather than recurrence, and what is reclaimed are
possibilities rather than factual historical incidents. Repetition is the
handing-over and *appropriation (berlieferung)* – that is to say, a
going back to the possibilities of the Dasein that has been there.'[17] It
implies a counter-claim (*Wiederruf*). There is a superficial similarity
between this reclamation and Deleuze's reading of repetition – but
we should not be misled. If repetition, in Deleuze's text, governs
counter-actualisation, which is a central element of his philosophy, it
is not for the sake of reclaiming possibilities. It is rather for the sake
of releasing the virtual. Arguably, the pivotal point of the difference
between Heidegger and Deleuze lies precisely at their assessment of
the ontological status of the eternal return, especially of its ethical
and selective function. Heidegger never allowed the eternal return to
be the thought of Being. In his writings, the experience of the eternal
return does not threaten the world. He no sooner turns his attention
to the eternal return than he introduces a consciousness that can
think it, having failed to call into question consciousness itself. In
fact, Heidegger links the eternal return with the moment of decision
(with the affirmation of it or the failure to heed it). But then this
affirmation alters only the phenomenological experience of Dasein –
the relation of Dasein to its possibilities – not its reality, let alone the
ontological determination of the being of Dasein.[18] The fact that he
entrusts the doctrine of the eternal return to the saga of consciousness
explains Heidegger's anxiety over the inevitable (for him) return of
the 'little men': after all, the little men are not devoid of consciousness; they too are able to affirm their own return. Arguably, it is the
anxiety stemming from linking eternal return with consciousness that
prevents Heidegger from ever appreciating the power of the eternal

return to guarantee the return of difference only, and to function as the selective principle that weeds out reactive forces.

As far as Deleuze is concerned, the eternal return is to the philosophy of difference what recollection is to the philosophy of identity. It is the pivotal point of Nietzsche's ontology, a veritable memory of the future provided that – and Deleuze always insisted on this point – it is not taken in the sense of the eternal return of the same, but rather in the sense of the eternal repetition of difference. A repetition of origins seals the ontology of Being while epistemologically and ethically separating and selecting the original from the copy. A repetition of the future seals the ontology of Becoming and performs the epistemological and ethical selection of the simulacra that have freed themselves from the dialectic of models and copies (DR 297–301). Deleuze is, from the very beginning, clear over the fact that Nietzsche's eternal return is not about the world of things and subjects – not about extended magnitudes and the law of nature that describes their relationship. The eternal return is, in a first approximation, about forces and force-fields that do not 'world' worlds in the way of Heidegger, but rather steer the errancy of a chaos-cosmos – *chaosmos*. The eternal return, as Daniel Conway says, is the marriage of chance and necessity, which does not turn these two into one more binary opposition.[19] Being always plural, dominating and dominated, active and reactive, forces, for Deleuze, for whom consciousness is an 'opaque blade in the heart of Being', are essentially unconscious. To use the more technical ontological vocabulary of Deleuze, the eternal return is not about the actual states of affairs, bodies and their mixtures, but rather about the intensities and the virtual events that insist in the actual and constitute the necessary condition for it to be what it is. If repetition has to do with memory, memory must be memory of the future – the sort of memory that must be created in the purifying fires of the eternal return. Deleuze was aware of the temptation to turn *mnemosyne* into Plato's *anamnesis* (DR 109–10) – in fact, he thought that it is hard to escape this temptation as long as the conservation of the entire past is not yet qualified with the help of the ungrounding (*effondement*) that only the thought of the eternal return can precipitate (DR 297).

Now, Deleuze claims that the eternal return is 'the principle of selection [that] is neither yours nor mine'; that selection belongs to the eternal return itself: 'The eternal return is the principle of selection, which screens the identical and allows the differentiated manifold to return. But this principle of selection is not mine or yours – the eternal

return itself selects' (NP 68–71). Reactive forces operate at the level of
the law of nature, creating average forms and generalisations of the
diversity of force (in accordance with) local or specific assemblages
of force.[20] It is the nature of reactive forces to select themselves out;
as long as they fashion themselves as Being they do not return.[21] It is
therefore clear that, in the case of Deleuze, the eternal return has a real
effect on being – an effect that does not require the intentionality of
consciousness. The negative and reactive assimilation of difference is
not repeated, only the affirmative release of difference repeats itself.

I foresee an objection being raised at this point. If the criticism of
Heidegger is based on his preventing the doctrine of the eternal return
from going as far as it can and on not realising that the eternal return
is itself responsible for the dispersion of Dasein and its replacement by
a multitude of intensive pre-personal and pre-individual forces, a *tu
quoque* type of argument may still be leveled against Deleuze. When
he writes that 'Being is the affirmation as the object of an affirmation
[; that] as first affirmation, it is becoming, but as an object of a second
affirmation it is Being [; and that] Becoming is raised to the power of
Being' (NP 186–9), it is legitimate to ask: What does it mean to make
the eternal return the object of a double affirmation? Can there be
affirmation without someone doing the affirming?

I believe that the answer to this question demands a correct understanding of Deleuze's position on counter-actualisation.[22] Becoming
worthy of the event – Deleuze's ethical imperative – was never meant
to be a call for our acquiescence to whatever state of affairs chance
brings our way. Counter-actualisation was meant to be the process
by means of which the virtual tendencies insisting in the actual state
of affairs were grasped for the sake of a new creation. One page from
Deleuze and Guattari's '*Mai '68 n'a pas eu lieu*' suffices to set the
record of counter-actualisation straight. Here it is:

> In historical phenomena such as the revolution of 1789, the Commune,
> the revolution of 1917, there is always one part of the event that is
> irreducible to any social determinism, or to causal chains. Historians
> are not very fond of this aspect: they restore causality after the fact. Yet
> the event is itself a splitting off from, or a breaking with causality; it is
> a bifurcation, a deviation with respect to laws, an unstable condition
> which opens up a new field of the possible. . . . In this sense, an event
> can be turned around, repressed, co-opted, betrayed; but there still is
> something there that cannot be outdated. . . . May '68 is more of the
> order of a pure event, free from all normal or normative causality. . . .
> There were a lot of agitations, gesticulations, slogans, idiocies, illusions

in '68, but this is not what counts. What counts is what amounted to a visionary phenomenon, as if a society suddenly saw what was intolerable in it and also saw the possibility for something else. . . . The possible does not pre-exist, it is created by the event . . . The event creates a new existence, it produces a new subjectivity (new relations with the body, with time, sexuality, the immediate surroundings, with culture, work . . .) When a social mutation appears, it is not enough to draw the consequences or effects, according to lines of economic or political causality. Society must be capable of forming collective agencies of enunciation that match the new subjectivity, in such a way that shows that it desires the mutation. That's what it is, a veritable redeployment.[23]

This page, representative as it is of Deleuze's formal distinction between history and becoming, clearly envisages counter-actualisation as a line of deterritorialisation that must be constructed for the sake of repeating the virtual and 'repotentialising' it for the sake of the discovery of new weapons, new insights and the incentive for renewed efforts. Vicediction, rather than prediction, is still capable of grounding a new *phronesis* and of guiding the process of our becoming worthy of the event. Vicediction/counter-actualisation is capable of having the ethical and political implications that Deleuze has reserved for it only if it involves a double affirmation: we begin by affirming (rather than fleeing) 'the destiny' of the causally constituted series of the actual states of affairs confronting us; and then, in a process of de-stratification of the actual, we seize, that is, we welcome and affirm, the virtual tendencies in the actual – we affirm the chance in the virtual – we learn to coincide with it, becoming thereby its co-genitors in the production of the new. To Heidegger's intuition that Being cannot be without Dasein nor Dasein without Being, Deleuze juxtaposes his own: Radical difference can certainly do without Dasein (in a sense, one wishes that it can be so), but Dasein with its organism and organisation is certainly capable of blunting the forces of creation, of precipitating lines of flight, deterritorialisation and transformation down black holes, and of multiplying disjunctions of the exclusive type. To counter-actualise is to overcome the human only because becoming is 'anti-memory' and 'insistence' of the virtual, rather than *Zukunftiges Erinnerung* and historical anamnesis.[24]

ETHICS

I want to conclude these diagnostic soundings of the relationship between Heidegger and Deleuze with a couple of points about the ethical projects that seem to emerge from their texts. Commenting on Heidegger's ethical project, Miguel de Beistegui writes:

> In a sense, as Heidegger once suggested, ethics can only mean this attempt to return man to his "proper dignity" ... What is great in and about the human is that it is made to enter into a relation with that which is greater than it, which it can neither generate nor circumvent, neither appropriate nor contain, yet which is the very condition of its own freedom and power.[25]

Once again, there is an initial similarity between this talk about something that the human can neither generate nor appropriate and Deleuze's suggestion that ethics transform itself to a pedagogy that shows us how to become worthy of the event and how to find the dignity of being human in this pedagogy. But the similarity does not go any further. In Heidegger's case, the ethics of dignity is tied to resoluteness and wanting to have a conscience. Heidegger and Deleuze confront us with two different decisions. In the case of Deleuze, the imperative that one become worthy of the event has been prepared by, and embedded in, a demystificatory naturalism and an ethic of joyful affects – both of which lead back to Spinoza (SPP 25–9). Heidegger's invitation to the dignity of the human in the new beginning, on the other hand, incorporates (and attempts to overcome) something very old and nasty – the moment of radical evil grounded in the rage of Dasein's inability to be its own foundation (BT 258–66). It seems to me then that any claim to proximity between Heidegger and Deleuze in the name of human dignity risks dooming the Deleuzian flight, which is meant to be a flight away from the judgement of God, and bringing about a violent reterritorialisation upon the striated space occupied by the Heideggerian God that 'may still be'.[26]

And since we are on the topic of ethics, which can only be for both Heidegger and Deleuze an ethology, one final point about the modality of the givenness of the Ereignis/event. I suggest that each time we are inclined to locate the trace of both Heidegger and Deleuze in the beautiful expressions, 'es gibt Sein' and the donation of Being, we pause to think for a while longer. It seems to me that the piety of the Heideggerian 'es gibt' should not be allowed to obscure the paganism that marks the Deleuzian gift and theft.[27] The Heideggerian Being under erasure is not the Deleuzian Being-question mark (Being?). The Heideggerian donation is still too Kierkegaardian for Deleuze's taste – it has not yet learnt the steps of Nietzsche's dance. To the Christian theological question of the status and the authority of the Word of

God/call of Being (is it human words about God that we are being given
or is it rather the Verbum Dei?), Karl Barth[28] and Martin Heidegger,
albeit through different pathways, give the same answer: Most definitely it is the Word emitted by God/Being and transmitted by man! As
for Deleuze's infrequent use of the 'es gibt Sein', it signals that emission
and transmission coincide in the multiplicity of multiplicities that is
none other than Spinoza's substance in the act of expressing itself in its
attributes and in its modes. A quotation from de Beistegui's book sums
up the distance between Heidegger and Deleuze admirably: 'This . . .
is where Heidegger's most problematic assumption lies: in having ultimately "attuned" being to the human, in having interpreted the event
of being in terms of a gift, when it is more akin to a shock.'[29] This is why
Heidegger's fundamental ontology can accommodate difference, but
not radical difference.[30] As an ontologist of radical difference Deleuze
has no rivals. He never wavers in his conviction that thought and the
real are indeed born of a certain violence. But this violence is not a
mere propaedeutic to the advent of philia. The resonance that makes
possible the deterritorialisations and reterritorialisations of becoming
is different from the accommodating (recognitive and representation-
loving) philia of the old image of thought – to which, I maintain,
Heidegger's philosophy succumbs in the end.

CONCLUSION

Heidegger's ontology is sometimes credited with the discovery of a
robust differential ontology. I have summarised Deleuze's reasons
for remaining sceptical with respect to giving Heidegger such credit
and strove to explain my own reasons for finding this scepticism
compelling. It cannot be denied that Heidegger's letting Being be in
its verbal mode shifted our attention away from things (designated
by substantive nouns) and replaced essences with 'essencing' and with
informative answers to the question 'how?' Heidegger allowed us to
move away from the flower towards flowering; away from the green
tree towards the greening of the tree, from world to 'worlding' and
from truth to 'truthing' in the palinodic movement of concealing and
revealing. Such a preference for an ontology written with the help of
infinitives is also to be found in the work of Deleuze. But Heidegger
no sooner made this move than he ruined the chances that infinitives offer to a process philosophy that wants to be the vehicle of the
thought of difference: He ruined these chances because he planted
Dasein in the centre of his meditations. But then the existence of a

privileged moment or site – in Heidegger's case, the human site by another name – in a differential ontology, which cannot, by definition, tolerate privileged moments and first principles, leads to the conclusion that Heidegger's famed forestry paths are doomed to repeat the palinodic movement of revealing (the Same) and concealing (the Same) and to reactively prevent lines of deterritorialising and creative flight from carrying on the de-sedimentation of our *doxic* strata as far as their intensity would permit.

Trent University

Notes

1. Bruce Baugh, 'Death and Temporality in Deleuze and Derrida', *Angelaki* 5:2 (August 2000), p. 75.
2. For Deleuze's views on death, see LS 145, 152, 153, 222; see also AO 330–1; and DR 111–15.
3. Deleuze's views on death have been influenced by Xavier Bichat and Maurice Blanchot. See, on these influences, Leonard Lawlor's 'Life: An Essay on the Overcoming of Metaphysics', http://www.pucp.edu.pe/eventos/congresos/filosofia/programa_general/viernes/plenariamatutina/LawlorLeonard.pdf (accessed 1 July 2008)
4. Baugh, 'Death and Temporality', p. 79.
5. Baugh, 'Death and Temporality', p. 79.
6. Baugh, 'Death and Temporality', p. 81.
7. Constantin V. Boundas, 'Foreclosure of the Other: From Sartre to Deleuze', *The Journal of the British Society for Phenomenology* 24:1 (1993), pp. 32–43.
8. Martin Heidegger, *Being and Time*, trans. Joan Stambaugh (New York: State University of New York Press, 1996), pp. 308–21. Cited hereafter in the text as BT.
9. As Slavoj Žižek puts it in 'Notes on a Debate "From Within the People"', *Criticism* 46:4 (Fall 2004), p. 665.
10. Thomas Sheehan, 'A Paradigm Shift in Heidegger Research', *Continental Philosophy Review* 34 (2001), pp. 198, 199.
11. I have argued elsewhere that caution must be taken against the syncretist tendencies that tend to identify the structures of the Deleuzian and the Derridean temporality; see Constantin V. Boundas, 'Between Deleuze and Derrida: A Critical Notice', *Symposium* (Spring 2005). A useful meditation on (Pauline) temporality that I found very helpful in my reading of Deleuze is Giorgio Agamben's 'The Time that is Left', *Epoché* 7:1 (Fall 2002), pp. 1–14.
12. Stephen H. Watson, 'Heidegger: The Hermeneutics of suspicion and the Dispersion of Dasein', unpublished manuscript, p. 43.

13. C. Colwell, 'Deleuze and Foucault: Series, Event, Genealogy', *Theory and Event* 1:2 (1997), p. 3.

14. Deleuze has often denounced the postulation of a transcendental ground, which, on close inspection, looks like an unnecessary duplication of the empirical realm. For him, the transcendental should never be the ghostly reflection of the empirical that it is supposed to account for. See, for example LS 105, 123; DR 143.

15. For Heidegger's reflections on Nietzsche, see his *Nietzsche* (four volumes), trans. David Farrell Krell (San Francisco: Harper Collins, 1991). For Deleuze's encounter with Nietzsche, see his *Nietzsche and Philosophy*.

16. François Laruelle, *Nietzsche contre Heidegger* (Paris: Payot, 1977).

17. Calvin Schrag, 'Heidegger on Repetition and Historical Understanding', *Philosophy East and West* 20:3 (July 1970), p. 289.

18. Alexander Cooke, 'Eternal Return and the Problem of the Constitution of Identity', *Journal of Nietzsche Studies* (June 2005), p. 23.

19. Daniel Conway, 'Tumbling Dice: Gilles Deleuze and the Economy of *Répétition*', *Symploke* 6:1 (1998), p. 9.

20. Conway, 'Tumbling Dice', pp. 28–9.

21. Conway, 'Tumbling Dice', p. 28.

22. See my 'The Ethics of Counteractualisation', *Concepts*, hors série 2 (2003), 170–99.

23. Gilles Deleuze and Félix Guattari, 'Mai '68 n'a pas eu lieu', *Les nouvelles*, 9 May 1984, pp. 233–4.

24. Véronique Bergen, *L' Ontologie de Gilles Deleuze* (Paris: L'Harmattan, 2001), p. 411.

25. Miguel de Beistegui, *Truth and Genesis: Philosophy as Differential Ontology* (Bloomington: Indiana University Press, 2004), pp. 339–40.

26. I am aware, of course, that Heidegger, unlike those who speak today about the 'return of the religious', meant to maintain a distinction between fundamental ontology and theology. (See his 'Phenomenology and Theology' in *Pathmarks*, edited and translated by W. A. McNeill [Cambridge: Cambridge University Press, 1998] pp. 39–62.) But in his fundamental ontology I cannot help but see the imposing shadow of a 'demythologised theology'.

27. On gift and theft being discussed as the unthought of the economy of exchange, see Deleuze and Guattari's AO 185–7.

28. The resonance between Heidegger's attempt to free the language of Being from its humanistic shackles and Karl Barth's efforts to cut the Word of God loose from its anthropomorphic moorings strikes me as uncanny.

29. De Beistegui, *Truth and Genesis*, p. 282.

30. Laruelle, *Nietzsche contre Heidegger*, p. 161.

18

Pierre Klossowski

Ian James

> Repetition as a conduct and as a point of view concerns non-exchangeable and non-substitutable singularities. Reflections, echoes, doubles and souls do not belong to the domain of resemblance or equivalence.
>
> Gilles Deleuze, *Difference and Repetition*

DELEUZE'S BIBLIOGRAPHY

At the end of original French edition of *Difference and Repetition* Deleuze's bibliography divides itself into three columns indicating the name of the author, the work cited and, in the final column, 'the sense in which the work is cited' (DR 334). Of the hundred and twenty-three authors listed, thirty-five are cited explicitly in relation to the motif of repetition. These include major thinkers for whom repetition plays a key role in their philosophy, for example Bergson, Derrida, Foucault, Freud, Kierkegaard, Lacan, Marx and Nietzsche. Three well-known names are cited, along with a number of other figures, as thinkers of repetition in the unconscious. They are: Derrida, Freud, and Lacan, and are accompanied by names such as Ferdinand Alquié, Sandor Ferenczi, Serge Leclaire and Jacques-Alain Miller. Marx is cited along with writers such as Pierre-Simon Ballanche, Joachim de Flore, Harold Rosenberg and Giovanni-Battista Vico as thinkers of repetition in history. A number of literary writers and essayists are also cited in relation to repetition (including, amongst others, Butor, Joyce, Klossowski, Péguy and Proust).[1] Along with these proper names a diverse range of concepts are associated with repetition throughout this bibliographical list, most obviously those already mentioned – difference, the unconscious and history – but also memory, habit, freedom, chaos, phantasm and equality.

From this array of philosophical, psychoanalytic and literary references one specific constellation of terms stands out has having a particular importance for Deleuze's thinking of difference and repetition in the late 1960s. Under the entries for Nietzsche, Klossowski and Foucault repetition is associated with the following: eternal return, simulacrum and 'loss of identity'.[2] Of these three proper names Klossowski will undoubtedly appear to be the least well known. Yet he is a recurring point of reference for Deleuze who, from 1966 onwards, repeatedly cites Klossowski as a key figure in the contemporary French reception of Nietzschean philosophy, and, in particular, as a key interpreter of the doctrine of eternal return.[3] Interestingly, of the three pieces authored by Foucault listed in Deleuze's bibliography, one, 'La Prose d'Actéon', is itself an essay entirely devoted to a critical-philosophical reading of Klossowski's work.[4] The name of Klossowski, undoubtedly less well known than that of Foucault, nevertheless has a silent presence in the more famous philosopher's bibliographical entry. Under Klossowski's own entry the motifs of repetition, simulacrum, eternal return and loss of identity are given together in a way they are not for either Nietzsche, Foucault or any other entry on Deleuze's list of references.

Klossowski, then, has in interesting double presence, one explicit and one more veiled, in the bibliography of *Difference and Repetition*. He also, as will become clear, has a marginal, yet arguably very important presence in key sections of the text itself. Deleuze himself devotes a full-length essay to Klossowski in the appendix to *The Logic of Sense* (1969), and it is here that clues can be found as to his importance in relation to Deleuze's thinking of simulacrum, eternal return and loss of identity, and, in turn, to his thinking of difference and repetition.[5] If Deleuze inherits from Klossowski he does so by way of repeating a thought of repetition which Klossowski himself repeats in his readings of Nietzschean eternal return.

'KLOSSOWSKI OR BODIES-LANGUAGE'

The opening of 'Klossowski or Bodies-Language' immediately affirms, as its title might suggest, that an 'astonishing parallelism between body and language' (LS 280) lies at the centre of Klossowski's work. In this writing, Deleuze asserts, reason is an operation of language, and is conceived in its essence to be theological. As a theological operation of language, reason, for Klossowski, takes as its primary form the disjunctive syllogism. Pantomime on the other hand is the operation of the body. This reflection of language in the body and the body in language goes on to form the focus of Deleuze's subsequent discussion in which he touches on nearly all aspects of Klossowski's

theoretical and fictional writing.[6] From the outset Deleuze's emphasis is on the gesture of mimicry or of simulation which pantomime
in Klossowski affirms. As language is reflected in the body and the
body in language, he argues, the discrete operations of both become
blurred: 'The most abstract argumentation is mimicry, but the body's
pantomime is a sequence of syllogisms. One no longer knows whether
it is the pantomime which reasons, or reasoning which mimics' (LS
280).

Pantomime and the associated motifs of mimicry and simulation
appear, initially at least, to offer the guiding threads for Deleuze's
reading of Klossowski in *The Logic of Sense*. If there is a gesture of
pantomime and mimicry articulated in the body-language or language-
body of Klossowski's writing, such a gesture does not simply give
this writing a comic or burlesque character. Rather the pantomimic
force of simulation in Klossowski has a rather heavy philosophical
outcome: 'Klossowski's entire work moves towards a single goal: to
assure the loss of personal identity and to dissolve the self. This is the
shining trophy that Klossowski's characters bring back from a voyage
to the edge of madness' (LS 283). The reference to madness here might
suggest that the loss of personal identity and dissolution of self attributed to Klossowski occurs by way of an ecstatic self-dispossession
such as it is thought, for example, by Bataille in relation to 'inner
experience', that is, as 'laughter, vertigo, nausea', and 'loss of self to
the point of death'.[7] Yet the emphasis Deleuze places on mimicry and
simulation in his reading of Klossowski suggests otherwise. After this
strong affirmation of dissolution of the self Deleuze adds: 'The self
is subject to dissolution only because, in the first instance, it is dissolved' (LS 283; translation modified). The self or personal identity
is lost, this suggests, not so much in a rending of Dionysian ecstatic-
self-dispossession, but rather in the manner in which the principle of
identity is dissolved across a series of pantomimic gestures or masks
that are staged in Klossowski's writing.

According to Deleuze's reading, then, loss of personal identity
in Klossowski is inseparable from a logic of repetition. That which
is repeated – i.e. 'doubles, simulacra, or reflections' (LS 284) – is
repeated, not according to a logic of sameness, but rather to one of
difference:

> In short, the double, the reflection, or the simulacrum opens up at last
> to surrender its secret: repetition does not presuppose the Same or the
> Similar – these are not its prerequisites. It is repetition, on the con-
> trary, which produces the only 'same' of that which differs. (LS 289)

This reading of repetition in Klossowski is clearly itself a repetition of the logic of difference and repetition elaborated in the earlier work by Deleuze which bears that name. Repetition is always a repetition of difference and the simulacrum is not a poor imitation of an original identity, rather it internalises and repeats a difference in itself. Deleuze, of course, makes this point many times throughout the text of *Difference and Repetition*.[8] In light of this it would appear that Deleuze is reading Klossowski very much through the lens of his own philosophical concepts and is interpreting the Klossowskian corpus (or 'bodies-language') as paradigmatic, or exemplary, of those concepts.

Yet what might at first appear to be an eminently Deleuzian reading of loss of identity, repetition and simulacrum, in Klossowski emerges as a perhaps more complex engagement when the Nietzschean doctrine of eternal return is discussed in the final pages of Deleuze's essay. Here Deleuze refers to Klossowski's essay 'Forgetting and Anamnesis in the Lived Experience of the Eternal Return of the Same', a paper which was first given at the Royaumont conference on Nietzsche in 1966. Describing Klossowski's essay as a 'fine analysis' of Nietzsche, Deleuze indicates that what is at stake in the Klossowskian reading of eternal return is a relation of signification, or of the linguistic sign, to the fluctuation and intensities of libidinal drives. Here the sign is not, as Saussure would have it, a differential element in a structure which exists without positive terms.[9] Rather it exists as a relation to, or function of, the repetition of bodily intensity or libidinal drive. Klossowski, Deleuze remarks, interprets the sign: 'as the trace of a fluctuation, of an intensity, and "sense" as the movement by which intensity aims at itself in aiming at the other, modifies itself in modifying the other, and returns finally onto its own trace' (LS 298). Deleuze sees in Klossowski's reading of eternal return a description of the way in which, prior to linguistic signification or any relation between signifier and signified, sense emerges as a repetition of a singular bodily intensity. As a repetition of singular intensity, sense emerges here only in difference, since repetition occurs in the movement whereby a singular intensity, in making sense of itself, only ever results in the production of another different singular intensity which is repeated as a differential trace of that which has been repeated. At one further remove from intensity the linguistic sign exists as a differential trace or repetition of 'sense'.

According to this reading the linguistic sign emerges from bodily intensities or libidinal drives as a double movement of repetition in difference. Sense exists as a trace, repetition in difference, or simulation of intensity. The linguistic sign exists as a trace, repetition in difference, or simulation of sense. This movement of repetition in Klossowski's reading of eternal return, Deleuze suggests, offers: 'an entire "phenomenology"', one which diverges from that of Husserl and which describes a 'passage from intensity to intentionality' as well as a passage 'from sign to sense' (LS 298). What this initial presentation of Klossowski's reading of eternal return suggests is that Klossowski interprets Nietzsche's doctrine as a thinking in which sense and signification emerge as a function of repetition in difference. Deleuze's discussion of pantomime, simulacrum and loss of identity in 'Klossowski or Bodies-Language' might at first appear to be a reading of Klossowski entirely through the lens of those concepts developed in *Difference and Repetition*. Yet the account he gives of Klossowski's 1966 essay on eternal return suggests that Klossowski himself is deeply engaged in a thinking of difference and repetition. Repetition in difference, then, is not simply a Deleuzian conceptual framework which is brought to bear on Klossowski's writing; it is a framework developed quite explicitly in that writing. In this context the possibility arises that Deleuze is not repeating the logic of *Difference and Repetition* in order to read Klossowski in his appendix to *The Logic of Sense*. Rather it may be that the logic of *Difference and Repetition* is itself a repetition of Klossowski's reading of eternal return.

'FORGETTING AND ANAMNESIS IN THE LIVED EXPERIENCE OF THE ETERNAL RETURN OF THE SAME'

In 'Forgetting and Anamnesis in the Lived Experience of the Eternal Return of the Same' Klossowski reads Nietzsche's doctrine, as Deleuze later suggests, as a description of the relation between intensive bodily drives (the term used in French is 'impulsions' which translates the German 'Triebe'), sense, and linguistic signs. He does so, however, by arguing that the doctrine of return itself is a sign which exists as a trace of a lived experience of the 'highest intensity'. In this essay Klossowski formulates eternal return on two levels; firstly as a direct experience or a revelation that Nietzsche underwent at Sils-Maria and secondly as the presentation of the doctrine or 'sign' of the 'Vicious Circle'.

It is in relation to the first level of revelation that Klossowski speaks of an experience of the 'highest intensity'. Here the revelation of eternal return is lived as an affirmation of the imperative that Zarathustra formulates in 'On Redemption' and 'Of Old and New Law-Tables' in *Thus Spoke Zarathustra*.[10] In these chapters Zarathustra brings together the possibility of 'will' and of 'necessity', 'necessity' referring here to the irreversibility of past moments of life (and therefore by implication the necessity of all present and future moments). Zarathustra speaks of the affirmation of a lived life which would repeat itself eternally as an imperative: 'To redeem the past and to transform every "it was" into an "I wanted it thus!"'.[11] Importantly though, if the past is irretrievable, then to will it as it was is paradoxically to will necessity – to will that which is beyond will. This means that in the moment of revelation the conscious individual apprehends itself as being a 'fortuitous case', that is, a singular instance, in excess of any possibility of autonomous self-determination or fixed personal identity. In the revelation of return the self undergoes a process of passing through previous instances of self each affirmed as fortuitous and arbitrary until the self for whom the thought of return is revealed is also affirmed as fortuitous. Here a paradox constitutive of the doctrine of eternal return is encountered, for how can conscious thought become conscious of its own fortuity when the fact of that fortuity itself undermines the integrity of conscious thought?

On the second level, Klossowski speaks of eternal return as a sign or a doctrine to which the conscious self adheres. If the revelation of return voids thought of its content (by affirming its fortuity) then it is an experience which is radically incommunicable. Since, for Klossowski, the illusion of a stable consciousness exists only within language, to destroy the one is equally to abolish the other. The sign of the Vicious Circle is also an instance of irreducible paradox since it is a sign which in some way voids itself of its own content as a sign.

In order to think this paradoxical status of both the lived experience and the doctrine or sign of eternal return Klossowski suggests that what happens in the moment of revelation, when necessity is willed and every 'It was' becomes an 'I willed it thus and thus would I will it', is that the present conscious self is rendered inactive and the whole preceding series of selves (singular fortuitous instances) is passed through (each a single 'It was'). This whole process is possible because of forgetting and remembering which are essential to the way Klossowski constructs eternal return in this later essay. Forgetting, he argues, is crucial to the possibility of a coherent self being able to establish itself through the fixity of what he calls the 'code of everyday signs', that is of everyday language and representational categories. Because, according to Klossowski's interpretation of Nietzsche, the self is nothing other than a discontinuous series of non-identical and fortuitous instances, any one instance can only establish itself as a coherent consciousness in the forgetting of all the other moments in the series, or, as Klossowski puts it, 'my present consciousness will be established only in the forgetting of my other possible identities' (VC 58). The lived experience of eternal return is therefore a forgetting (disactualisation) of the current self, and a remembering of the others each in turn until one returns to the self which first underwent the revelation of return. Klossowski articulates this moment as follows:

> Eternal Return is a necessity that must be willed: only he who I am now can will the necessity of my return and all the events that have led to what I am – insofar as the will here presupposes a subject. Now this subject is no longer able to will itself as it has been up to now, but wills *all* prior possibilities; for by embracing in a single glance the necessity of Return as a universal law, I deactualize my present self in order to will myself in *all the other selves whose entire series must be passed through* so that, in accordance with the circular movement, I once again become *what I am in the moment I discover* the law Eternal Return. (VC 57–8)

As each past moment is passed through, each past self is rewilled, but rewilled as a necessary instance, as an instance which was not produced itself by a moment of conscious will but as a fortuitous instance, as a singular 'fortuitous case'. This means that when the circle is closed and the revelation returns to the point in the series when the revelation itself occurred something radical happens:

> All that remains, then, is for me to re-will myself, no longer as the outcome of these prior possibilities, no longer as one realisation among thousands, but as a fortuitous moment whose very fortuity implies the necessity of the integral return of the whole series.
> But to re-will oneself as a fortuitous moment is to renounce being *oneself once and for all*; since it is not once and for all that I had renounced being myself and I had to will this renunciation; and I am not even this fortuitous moment *once and for all* as long as I have to re-will this moment . . . *one more time!* (VC 58)

What eternal return as a lived revelation represents is an apprehension of the self in all its separate moments as a series of 'fortuitous cases'. It is the revelation of the non-identity of identity and difference but here it is also a revelation of existence as repetition, a motif which is recurrent in Klossowski's thinking from the 1930s onwards. The vision of return reveals the span of a human life to be nothing other than a repeating series of random dice throws prior to all will and conscious intentionality. The self apprehends its own dissolution as a conscious and fixed self. Again one can see the way in which this is an irreducibly paradoxical moment in that consciousness is consciously apprehending the dissolution of its own consciousness. More seriously it thereby renders the status of the revelation as an experience itself paradoxical if not impossible. Indeed how can the experience of return be an experience at all if, by definition, it lies outside the realm of experience (i.e. that of a thinking self-aware subject)? The title of the essay 'Forgetting and Anamnesis in the Lived Experience of the Eternal Return of the Same' therefore carries with it a certain irony, firstly because 'eternal return' as an experience is always an impossible experience and secondly because it overturns 'the same' and places experience under the sign of repetition and difference.

It is here that the importance of the construction of eternal return as a sign, that of the Vicious Circle, becomes apparent. If eternal return lies outside the possibility of language and experience then in fact the process just outlined, which Klossowski described as the 'revelation' of return, is always already a formulation of the doctrine (since it is being described in language). The parodic or simulacral aspect of the doctrine of return now fully asserts itself. It is parodic because it is always describing something which escapes that description. As that which reveals the non-identity of experience it can never be coincident with anything at all, not even its own revelation. Yet this paradoxical moment still subsists when Klossowski speaks of the Vicious Circle as the sign of eternal return. The Vicious Circle is a sign which voids the identity of whoever speaks it. 'I' (as a coherent self-same identity) am nothing in this sign which overturns all identities. Despite this, what is essential about the sign of the Vicious Circle is that it places the entirety of individual experience, of meaning and language, under the law of repetition, non-identity and discontinuity. By existing under the parodic sign of the 'Vicious Circle' our apprehension of existence changes and the nature of one's positioning as regards that illusory unity of self is radically altered. Irrespective of one's conscious intentionality existence under the sign of return changes the very substance of experience. It also, crucially, changes the nature of thought and writing, because again even though one writes from within the perspective of meaning and identity, writing, under the sign of the Vicious Circle, is deployed in such a way as to affirm its own lack of foundation, its absence of self-identity, its status as parody.

Eternal return emerges, then, as a doctrine or a sign which is affirmed by the conscious subject. As a lived experience, though, it is, paradoxically, in excess of, or without, a conscious subject. It exists as an experience in excess of experience. As Deleuze puts it in his essay on Klossowski in the appendix to *The Logic of Sense*: 'The true subject of eternal return is intensity and singularity' (LS 300; translation modified).[12] It is only insofar as the doctrine of return voids both subject and sign of their content that it grounds existence in the groundless and fortuitous flux of intensities and makes any instance of self, meaning, or signification a simulacral repetition or differential trace of flux or intensity.

DIFFERENCE AND REPETITION

The Nietzschean doctrine of eternal return is central to Deleuze's thinking in both the 1962 work *Nietzsche and Philosophy* and in *Difference and Repetition* in 1968. Yet the manner in which he thinks this doctrine changes in the interval that separates these two works.[13] In the earlier work the key emphasis is on eternal return as a selective doctrine which affirms that only that which is different or new will return and therefore affirms also the becoming of active over that of reactive forces. The thinking of return in *Difference and Repetition* is developed in terms which repeat and modify those of Klossowski's 'Forgetting and Anamnesis' essay of 1966. Deleuze makes a number of explicit references to Klossowski's reading of Nietzsche in *Difference and Repetition*. In a note on page 312 he refers to 'two articles which renew the interpretation of Nietzsche' (DR 312 n. 19), these being the 'Forgetting and Anamnesis' essay and Klossowski's 1957 essay 'Nietzsche, Polytheism and Parody'.[14] Later Deleuze specifically cites Klossowski's interpretation in the following terms: 'Pierre Klossowski has clearly noted this point . . .: taken in its strict sense, eternal return means that each thing exists only in returning, copy of an infinity of copies which allows neither original nor origin to subsist' (DR 66–7). Later still he also once again explicitly cites Klossowski's interpretation of eternal return as a simulacrum of a doctrine (DR 95).[15] In the text of *Difference and Repetition*, then, Deleuze very clearly acknowledges and affirms the importance of Klossowski's renewal of the French interpretation of Nietzsche in the 1960s.

    Yet, although Deleuze's explicit references to Klossowski in *Difference and Repetition* are relatively few, the traces of the

Klossowskian 'renewal' of Nietzsche are far more pervasive through-out certain sections of the text. This can be seen, for instance, in the various terms that are associated with repetition and eternal return, for example the mask, the circle and the simulacrum. Each of these terms has a key place in Deleuze's thinking of difference and repetition in the work which bears that name.

Mask

This discussion began by citing as an epigraph Deleuze's affirmation at the very beginning of *Difference and Repetition* that 'Repetition as a conduct and as a point of view concerns non-exchangeable and non-substitutable singularities. Reflections, echoes, doubles and souls do not belong to the domain of resemblance or equivalence' (DR 1). References to reflections, doubles and souls can be found throughout Klossowski's published work from the late 1930s onwards.[16] In each case these references articulate a thinking of the self which, reflected, doubled and repeated in a series of images, is affirmed as a mask or as a role which is fortuitously received and thus exists in excess of any principle of identity. This is not, therefore, a mask which conceals any true or authentic self, but rather one which is only ever repeated as a series of masks in which all possibility of an originary self or identity is overturned. This thinking is most explicitly articulated by Klossowski in his 1957 essay on eternal return entitled 'Nietzsche, Polytheism and Parody'. As in the later essay on forgetting and anam-nesis Klossowski interprets the Nietzschean doctrine of return as an apprehension of the self as a fortuitous instance. Rather than using the language of the 'fortuitous case' as he does in *Nietzsche and the Vicious Circle*, in 1957 Klossowski implicitly invokes the language of the mask. The doctrine of return he affirms 'immediately concerns Nietzsche's own identity in so far as it is considered to be fortuitously received and thus assumed as a role that can be assumed – as one role, which, chosen over others, could also be rejected as a mask in favour of another taken from among the thousand masks of history' (SFD 218). As has been indicated, this reading of Nietzsche repeats in the mode of quasi-theoretical exposition key aspects of Klossowski's nov-elistic writing in which identity is staged as role play, or as a theatrical multiplication of fantastical figures or masks.

In the introduction to *Difference and Repetition* Deleuze invokes the figure of the mask in relation to Freud when the question of the relation of repetition to the death instinct is posed. The death instinct in Freud, Deleuze points out, is discovered directly in relation to phenomena of repetition. In this context Deleuze highlights the theatrical character of unconscious fantasy in Freud, the way in which the subjects of the case studies find the role they play in their unconscious fantasies distributed across a series of roles. In this context: 'The disguises and the variations, the masks or costumes, do not come "over and above": they are, on the contrary, the internal genetic elements of repetition itself, its integral and constituent parts' (DR 16–17). The dissolution of identity in a series of images conceived as roles, variants, or doubles appears to be what allows Deleuze to affirm that 'the death instinct may be understood in its relation to masks and costumes' (DR 17). This thus allows him to relate the death instinct to an originary affirmative repetition of difference. Here Deleuze draws some wider conclusions which relate to 'the essence of repetition' (DR 19), namely:

> Repetition is truly that which disguises itself in constituting itself, that which constitutes itself only by disguising itself. It is not underneath the masks, but it is formed from one mask to another, from one privileged instant to another, with and within the variations. The masks do not hide anything except other masks. (DR 17)

This formulation recalls, or rather in a certain way repeats, both Klossowski's quasi-theoretical exposition of the self as mask in his 1957 essay on Nietzsche and his *mise-en-scène* of self-identity as mask or role play in his novels: 'The mask is the true subject of repetition' (DR 18). Yet if the mask is the subject of repetition it is a subject without origin or identity since, as mask, it can only ever be 'signified, masked by what signifies it, itself masking what it signifies' (DR 18).

This repetition of the figure of the mask which persistently recurs in Klossowski's fictional and theoretical writing is itself, of course, a repetition of a figure of repetition, or more precisely, of repetition as always the repetition of difference. Yet in repeating Klossowskian figures of repetition Deleuze also diverges somewhat from Klossowski. The 1957 essay on Nietzsche and parody does not, for instance, engage with Freud or with the concept of the death drive. Klossowski links the figure of the mask to the doctrine of eternal return in his philosophical essay on Nietzsche and to the staging of fantasy in his fiction, but in many ways sidelines or disengages with psychoanalytic discourse.[17] In this context, then, Deleuze repeats a key Klossowskian figure of repetition, but does so in a divergence from Klossowski and therefore repeats him also in a mode of difference. This logic of repetition in divergence can also be seen to inform Deleuze's thinking of eternal return as a circle in *Difference and Repetition*.

Circle

In *Nietzsche and Philosophy* Deleuze draws on Nietzschean imagery such as the labyrinth or the wedding ring to describe the movement of eternal return.[18] The image of circular movement is used in relation to Heraclitus (NP 33), but Deleuze insists, of course, that Nietzsche was always critical of the notion of eternal return as a cyclical time in which the same events would repeat themselves eternally (that is, return as the repetition of the same and the becoming of reactive forces) (NP 55). When seen as an ethical selective doctrine which affirms the becoming active of forces *as Being* (as selective ontology) (NP 81), the doctrine of eternal return is not associated with the figure of the circle in *Nietzsche and Philosophy* in any sustained way (perhaps because of its association with the notion of a circular movement thought in terms of a cycle of the same).

However, Deleuze persistently uses the figure of the circle in relation to the doctrine of eternal return in *Difference and Repetition*. If he does so though, he takes pains to differentiate the circularity of return from any circular or cyclical movement which would imply the repetition of the same: 'For if eternal return is a circle, then Difference is at the centre and the Same is only on the periphery' (DR 55). The image of the circle here is, as it is in Klossowski's essay on 'Forgetting and Anamnesis', used to figure a cycle or circular movement of repetition. Yet in this movement the notion of an origin or anchored centre point which would give the circular series a fixed identity is overturned. For Klossowski this overturning of origin or centre is affirmed in the paradoxical viciousness of a circle which excludes the subject in the very moment that the subject comes to think the circle itself (thought as a cycle of selves remembered as a series of fortuitous instances which culminates with the self who remembers). Deleuze explicitly cites this aspect of Klossowski's thinking of the Vicious Circle in relation to eternal return: 'As Klossowski says, it is the secret coherence which establishes itself only by excluding my own coherence, my own identity, the identity of the self' (DR 91). In this context he once again repeats the figure of the circle in relation to eternal return and once again explicitly differentiates it from the circularity of a cycle of sameness. He does this, however, in slightly different terms than does Klossowski. In contrast to a circle in which the same repeats itself, the circle of return is 'a less simple and much more secret, much more tortuous, more nebulous circle, an eternally excentric circle, the decentred circle of difference' (DR 91). Throughout *Difference and Repetition* Deleuze's circle of return is not vicious, rather it is tortuous. It is a 'constantly decentred, continually tortuous circle which revolves only around the unequal' (DR 55), or as Deleuze also puts it: 'the circle of eternal return, that of difference and repetition . . ., is a tortuous circle in which sameness is said only of that which differs' (DR 57).

In the wake of Klossowski's interpretation of Nietzschean return under the sign of the Vicious Circle, the circle becomes a principle figure in the Deleuzian thinking of difference and repetition in the late 1960s. In both *Difference and Repetition* itself and in *The Logic of Sense* Deleuze repeatedly invokes the figure of the circle to describe the temporality of return, and with that the becoming of sense, the repetition in difference of elements in a series and the non-identity of thought and being. All these elements come together in his commentary on Klossowski in the appendix of *The Logic of Sense* when he affirms that:

> The phantasm of Being (eternal return) brings about the return only of simulacra (will to power as simulation). Being a coherence which does not allow mine to subsist, eternal return is the non-sense which distributes sense into divergent series over the entire circumference of the decentered circle. (LS 301)

Yet, as with Deleuze's repetition of the Klossowskian language of the mask, of role play and theatricality, this repetition of the language of the circle is once again repeated, not in the exact terms used by Klossowski, but in a way which diverges from Klossowski in the very moment of repetition. Klossowski's vicious circle is repeated as Deleuze's tortuous circle. It is as if Deleuze has doubled the figure of the circle in Klossowski with the image of the labyrinth which he draws from Nietzsche in the earlier *Nietzsche and Philosophy*. Once again, it seems, Deleuze repeats Klossowski's figures of repetition, but does so only in a marking or affirmation of difference.

Simulacrum

In the light of this it might be tempting to read Deleuze's repetition of Klossowski as itself a simulacrum, that is a repetition that internalises a difference, a reflection, or a theatrical doubling. The notion of simulation and the term 'simulacrum' play a dominant role in Klossowski's work throughout the 1950s and 1960s.[19] According to one of Deleuze's most astute contemporary readers, James Williams, the simulacrum in *Difference and Repetition* 'brings together all the aspects of Deleuze's argument'. [20] The term simulacrum, of course, has a long history dating back to antiquity, to which Deleuze regularly refers, and to which he dedicates an appendix in *The Logic of Sense* (LS 253–79). Yet his interpretation of the modern simulacrum closely recalls Klossowski's use of the term. Towards the end of the chapter on repetition 'for itself' Deleuze describes the simulacrum in the following terms: 'simulacra are precisely demonic images, stripped of resemblance' (DR 167). Simulacra, here, are demonic not just because they are a bad resemblance or copy, but because they are phantasmatic images which are devoid of resemblance. This recalls very closely the terms of Klossowski's *Roberte ce soir* where fantastical images of giants and hunchbacks appear to sexually assault the eponymous heroine whilst declaiming perverted theological and scholastic discourse. Elsewhere Deleuze cites Klossowski's 1957 essay 'Nietzsche, Polytheism and Parody' in relation to the simulacrum and eternal return:

> Eternal return . . . has isolated the double or the simulacrum, it has liberated the comic in order to make this an element of the superhuman. That is why – again as Klossowski says – it is not a doctrine but the simulacrum of every doctrine (the highest irony). (DR 95)

This is, in fact, a rather curious citation or rather an apparent misquotation of Klossowski. In the 1957 essay on parody Klossowski's exact formulation is simply to affirm that the doctrine of return is a 'simulacrum of a doctrine' (SFD 226) (rather than 'the simulacrum of every doctrine'). He does indicate that Nietzsche, in his apprehension of eternity, sought to 'put the simulacrum in knowledge and knowledge in the simulacrum' (SFD 190). The words he uses, however, are rather different from Deleuze's attribution. For both Klossowski and Deleuze the simulacrum operates as a key term which articulates the Nietzschean thinking of eternal return, its figuration as a vicious or tortuous circle, and with this the loss of identity of a self construed as a fortuitous instance, mask or role. Deleuze's citation of Klossowski may be either playfully wayward or unconsciously imprecise. Either way it again represents the way in which Deleuze's repetition of Klossowski never occurs in a simple or straightforward manner, but always seems to, at some level, incorporate a divergence or difference from the original Klossowskian corpus or text.

INHERITANCE AS REPETITION

What appears to be most important about the relation of these two writers, however, is the way in which the very notion of origin, or of an identity belonging to a proper name, corpus or text, is overturned. If one were to say in any straightforward way that Deleuze, in the second half of the 1960s, 'inherits' key aspects of Nietzsche's thinking from the Klossowskian interpretation of eternal return, then the relation between the two would be assimilated to a logic of sameness. The two would 'share' a common ground of French post-war Nietzscheanism, and Deleuze's indebtedness to Klossowski would be clearly marked both in his explicit acknowledgements and in the way he implicitly yet persistently deploys Klossowskian language in order to think difference and repetition (as mask, circle, simulacrum, but also as reflection, disguise, travesty, doubling and soul). On one level the assimilation of the relation Deleuze–Klossowski into a logic which would imply commonality and sameness is both inevitable and necessary. It allows a specific trajectory of French Nietzscheanism to be historically traced and critically understood.

Yet on another level there is arguably a dimension of this relation which is inassimilable to such a logic of commonality or sameness. In both cases Klossowski and Deleuze are attempting an impossible reading of Nietzsche. Nietzsche's philosophy stands as an inaugural moment for a thinking which overturns any possibility of the inaugural, of the originary, or of the identity of a proper name (e.g. 'Nietzsche') which would authenticate the propriety and authority of an inaugural thinking. In their different ways the thinking and writing of both Klossowski and Deleuze aim to negotiate this paradox of thought. Both appeal to the simulacrum as a mode of repetition which internalises and affirms difference. The simulacrum, as thought, as figure, as sign, or as philosophical doctrine, does not so much repeat the identity of a body of text signed 'Nietzsche'. Rather it aims to repeat that which, within the Nietzschean text, is itself an impossible object of thought, a thinking of difference which is inassimilable to representation or to the work of a concept. In this sense both Klossowski and Deleuze aim to repeat that which is already repeated within the Nietzschean text as difference, as theatre, mask, or simulacrum.

It is in this sense also that Deleuze's repetition of Klossowski is itself a repetition of a repetition. This double repetition would not be entirely assimilable to a logic of inheritance governed by the repetition of sameness or identity. In the light of this, Deleuze's repetition of Klossowski in ways that diverge or differ from the original Klossowskian text emerges not just as a stylistic or playful flourish, but as a philosophical-rhetorical strategy. This strategy affirms that which is repeated as always (already) repetition, mask, or an internalised difference from itself: always, then, a simulacrum.

Downing College, Cambridge University

Notes

1. Interestingly at least two major thinkers for whom repetition plays a key role, Blanchot and Heidegger, are not mentioned in relation to this motif at all.
2. Apart from Nietzsche and Klossowski the only other reference to thinkers of eternal return in the bibliography is to Mugler's thinking of recurrence in ancient Greek thought.
3. Gilles Deleuze, 'Conclusion: Sur la volonté de puissance et l'éternel retour', in *Nietzsche*, edited by Martial Geroult (Les Cahiers de Royaumont Philosophie IV, 1967), pp. 275–86. See also *Difference and Repetition*, in particular, DR 312 n. 19, 66–7, 95.
4. Michel Foucault, 'La Prose d'Actéon', *La Nouvelle Revue Française*, March 1964.
5. 'Klossowski or Bodies-Language' (LS 280–301).
6. In particular Deleuze discusses *Roberte ce soir* (Paris: Minuit, 1954), *La Révocation de l'Édit de Nantes* (Paris: Minuit 1959), *Le Souffleur* (Paris: Pauvert, 1960) (collected as *Les lois de l'hospitalité* [Paris: Gallimard, 1965]), *Le Baphomet* (Paris: Mercure de France, 1965) and Klossowski's 1966 essay on Nietzsche, 'Oubli et anamnèse dans l'expérience vécue de l'éternel retour du même', in *Nietzsche et le cerle vicieux* (Paris: Mercure de France, 1969), pp. 93–103; *Nietzsche and the Vicious Circle*, trans. Dan Smith (New York: Athlone, 1997), pp. 56–66. All subsequent references to this essay will be to the English translation and will be preceded with the abbreviation VC.
7. Georges Bataille, *L'Expérience intérieure*, *Oeuvres completes*, vol. V (Paris: Gallimard, 1973), p. 49.
8. See, for instance, DR 1, 69, 127, 265, 277, 299.
9. Ferdinand de Saussure, *Course in General Linguistics*, trans. Roy Harris (London: Duckworth, 1983), p. 118.
10. Friedrich Nietzsche, *Thus Spoke Zarathustra*, trans. R. J. Hollingdale (Harmondsworth: Penguin, 1961).

11. Nietzsche, *Thus Spoke Zarathustra*, p. 161.
12. Interestingly, Klossowski's words in *Nietzsche and the Vicious Circle* are: 'Intensity is the soul of Eternal Return' (VC 217).
13. This point is made by Douglas Smith in his discussion of Klossowski and Deleuze, see Douglas Smith, *Transvaluations: Nietzsche in France 1872–1972* (Oxford: Clarendon Press, 1996), pp. 140–84.
14. Pierre Klossowski, 'Nietzsche, le polythéisme et la parodie', in *Un si funeste désir* (Paris: Gallimard, 1963), pp. 187–228. All references to this essay will be to the original French edition, preceded by the abbreviation SFD.
15. See SFD 226.
16. See in particular *Sade mon prochain* (Paris: Seuil, 1947; revised edition, 1967), *La vocation suspendue* (Paris: Gallimard, 1950), *Le Bain de Diane* (Paris: Pauvert, 1956). For an extended discussion of these and other fictional and theoretical works by Klossowski see Ian James, *Pierre Klossowski: The Persistence of a Name* (Oxford: Legenda, 2000). See also, Leslie Hill, *Writing at the Limit: Bataille, Blanchot, Klossowski* (Oxford: Oxford University Press, 2001).
17. Klossowski began his career as a secretary to a prominent Parisian psychoanalyst but was sacked after publishing his first article on the writing of de Sade. On Klossowski's biographical trajectory see Alain Arnaud, *Pierre Klossowski* (Paris: Seuil, 1990), pp. 181–91.
18. See *Nietzsche et la philosophie* (Paris: Presses Universitaires de France, 1962), p. 215.
19. Klossowski elaborates on his use of the term simulacrum on many occasions; e.g., at the end of his short monograph *Origines culturelles et mythoques d'un certain comportement des dames romaines* (Montpellier: Fata Morgana, 1968, 1986), in *Le Bain de Diane*, in his essay on Bataille, 'A propos du simulacra dans le communication de Georges Bataille', in *Critique* (Aug–Sept 1963), pp. 742–50. The term is also used in his fictional work; see for example, *Les lois de l'hospitalité*, p. 19.
20. James Williams, *Understanding Poststructuralism* (Cheshunt: Acumen, 2005), p. 72. Williams, however, does not mention the central role played by this term in Klossowski's writing nor Deleuze's close relationship to Klossowski.

19

Albert Lautman

Simon Duffy

Albert Lautman (1908–44) was a philosopher of mathematics working in the decades between the two world wars in the first half of the twentieth century. He postulated a conception of mathematics that is both formalist and structuralist in the Hilbertian sense. The reference to the axiomatic structuralism of Hilbert is foundational for Lautman, and it is because of this that his views on mathematical reality and on the philosophy of mathematics parted with the dominant tendencies of mathematical epistemology of his time. Lautman considered the role of philosophy, and of the philosopher, in relation to mathematics to be quite specific. He writes that: 'in the development of mathematics, a reality is affirmed that mathematical philosophy has as its function to recognize and to describe'.[1] He goes on to characterise this reality as an 'ideal reality' that 'governs' the development of mathematics. He maintains that 'what mathematics leaves for the philosopher to hope for, is a truth which would appear in the harmony of its edifices, and in this field as in all others, the search for the primitive concepts must yield place to a synthetic study of the whole'.[2]

One of the tasks, indeed the challenges, that Lautman set himself, but never carried through because of his early tragic demise – he was captured by the Nazis in 1944 and shot for being an active member of the resistance – was the task of deploying his mathematical philosophy in other domains. The commentator who, by taking up this challenge, shows the most assiduity in his engagement with Lautman is Gilles Deleuze. The mathematical work that is drawn upon and that plays a significant role in Deleuze's philosophical project is that of Lautman. Indeed, the speculative logic that Deleuze constructs as a part of his project of constructing a philosophy of difference is dialectical in the Lautmanian sense. The aim of this chapter is to give an account of this Lautmanian dialectic, of how it operates in Lautman's work, and to determine what, if anything, Deleuze does to this dialectic when it is incorporated into his project of constructing a philosophy of difference.

LAUTMAN'S AXIOMATIC STRUCTURALISM

What is quite clear in Lautman's work is that he was not concerned with specific foundational questions in mathematics, neither with those relating to its origins, its relationship to logic or to the problem of foundations. What he is interested in, rather, is shifting the ground of this very problematic by presenting an account of the nature of mathematical problematics in general.

Lautman had a wider and more precise schooling in both the French and German mathematics of the 1920s–30s than the majority of the mathematicians of his generation, who were often narrowly specialised.[3] Lautman, along with Cavaillès, was one of the introducers of the German axiomatic into a French context dominated at the time by the 'intuitionisms' of Poincaré, Borel, Baire and Lebesgue.[4] The two main ideas that are foregrounded in his primary theses in the philosophy of mathematics,[5] and which dominate the development of his subsequent work, are 'the concept of *mathematical structure* and the idea of the essential *unity* underlying the apparent multiplicity of diverse mathematical disciplines'.[6] It should be noted that, 'in 1935, the concept of structure' in mathematics 'had not yet been made completely explicit'.[7] Lautman's project is therefore novel. Lautman was inspired by the work of Hilbert on the axiomatic concept of mathematics to deploy the potential of an axiomatic structuralism in mathematics. The essential point that motivated this move was Lautman's conviction 'that a mathematical theory is predominantly occupied with the relations between the objects that it considers, more so than with the nature of those objects'.[8]

Lautman considers the idea that there is 'an independence of mathematical objects compared to the theories in which they are defined'[9] to be steeped in the analysis and geometry of the nineteenth century. He, by contrast, championed the modern algebra, and maintained that 'if classical mathematics was constructivist . . . modern algebra is on the contrary axiomatic'.[10] The introduction of the axiomatic method[11] into mathematics means that there is an 'essential dependence between the properties of a mathematical object and the axiomatic field to which it belongs'.[12] The isolation of 'elementary mathematical facts' that would function as building blocks is ruled out. Lautman can therefore claim that 'the problem of mathematical reality arises neither at the level of facts, nor at that of objects, but [rather] at that of theories'.[13] This of course is not to put mathematical facts *per se* into question. Lautman considered mathematics to be constituted like physics: 'the facts to be explained were throughout history the paradoxes that the progress of reflexion made understandable by a constant renewal of the meaning of the essential concepts'.[14] Rather than being isolatable elementary objects, mathematical facts, such as the 'irrational numbers, the infinitely small, continuous functions without derivatives, the transcendence of e and of ϖ, and the transfinite', 'were admitted by an incomprehensible necessity of fact before there was a deductive theory of them'.[15] He argues that mathematical and physical facts 'are organized thus under the unity of the concept which summarizes them'.[16]

Lautman's 'axiomatic structuralism' was the new mathematics that inspired the Bourbaki project which was influential in mathematics for several subsequent decades,[17] notably in the figure of Jean Dieudonné, who wrote the foreword to Lautman's collected works.[18] The structuralist point of view has been so influential on the development of mathematics since 1940 that it has become rather commonplace.[19] However, this was not yet the case when Lautman was writing.[20]

The first move that Lautman makes to develop his structural conception of mathematics is against the logical positivism of the Vienna Circle logicists. Lautman considered their effort 'to build mathematical concepts starting from a small number of concepts and from primitive logical propositions' to be in vain, because it 'loses sight of' what he refers to as 'the qualitative and integral character of the constituted theories'.[21] He argues that 'It is impossible to consider mathematical wholes as a result of the juxtaposition of elements defined independently of any overall consideration of the structure of the whole in which these elements are integrated'.[22] For Lautman, this impoverishment of logical positivism is the consequence of its conception of mathematics in propositional terms, as 'nothing more than a language indifferent to the content that it expresses'.[23]

Lautman also protests against the use made of Hilbert by the Vienna Circle logicists. Despite their claims to endorse the Hilbert programme,[24] Lautman is critical of the logicist interpretation of the term 'formalism', which he considers to be unrepresentative of Hilbert's thought.[25] While the logicists derive theorems in a formal system, such that the theorems are genetic or constitutive of the system, for Lautman, Hilbert is rather looking for theorems about formal systems, such as consistency or non-contradiction, completeness, decidability, etc.[26] Rather than confounding mathematical philosophy with the study of the different logical formalisms, Lautman considered it necessary to try to characterise mathematical reality 'from the point of view of its own structure'.[27] Lautman considered this to be a more accurate characterisation of Hilbert's meta-mathematical program, which, he argued, 'internalised the epistemological problem of foundations by transforming it into a purely mathematical problem'.[28]

Against the logicist interpretation of Hilbert's work Lautman argues that 'Hilbert substitutes for the method of genetic definitions that of axiomatic definitions, and far from wanting to rebuild the whole of mathematics starting from logic, introduced on the contrary, while passing from logic to arithmetic and from arithmetic to analysis, new variables and new axioms which each time broaden the domain of results.'[29] The (Hilbertian) axiomatic structural conception of mathematics that Lautman mobilises in his work is a nonconstructivist axiomatic, and he argues that 'Mathematics thus arises as successive syntheses where each stage is irreducible to the former.'[30] He continues by making the important point, again drawn from Hilbert, that 'a theory thus formalized is unable to bring with it the proof of its internal coherence; a meta-mathematics should be superimposed on it which takes the formalized mathematics as its object and studies it from the double point of view of non-contradiction and completeness'.[31] This double point of view distinguishes Lautman's concept of mathematics from the formalism of the logicists, which considered the study of mathematical reality to consist solely in the demonstration of the non-contradiction of the axioms which define it. The consequence of this 'duality of plans' that Hilbert establishes between 'formalized mathematics and the meta-mathematic study of this formalism' is that while the formalism is governed by 'the concepts of non-contradiction and completeness', these concepts are not themselves defined by this formalism. Hilbert expresses this governing role of meta-mathematical concepts over formalised mathematics when he writes that

> the demonstrable axioms and propositions, i.e. the formulas which are born from the play of these reciprocal actions (namely formal deduction and the addition of new axioms), are the images of thoughts that constitute the ordinary processes of mathematics developed up to now, but are not truths in the absolute sense. Truths in the absolute sense are rather the points of view . . . that my theory gives of the demonstration with regard to the resolvability and the non-contradiction of these systems of formulas.[32]

So, according to Lautman, the value of a mathematical theory is determined by 'the meta-mathematical properties that its structure incarnates'.[33]

While Lautman took a position against the version of logicism and formalism proposed by the Vienna Circle, he also distanced himself from the empirico-psychologising perspective of French mathematicians such as Léon Brunschvicg. Brunschvicg developed 'the idea that the objectivity of mathematics was the work of the intelligence in its effort to triumph over the resistance that the material on which it works opposes to it'.[34] Brunschvicg goes so far as to maintain that 'any effort of *a priori* deduction tends . . . to reverse the natural order of the mind in mathematical discovery'.[35] While Lautman follows Brunschvicg in distrusting all attempts 'to deduce the unity of mathematics starting from a small number of initial principles', including 'the reduction of mathematics to logic',[36] he doesn't endorse Brunschvicg's concept of mathematical philosophy 'as a pure psychology of creative invention'.[37] For Lautman, the task of characterising the mathematical real must be undertaken rather by 'mediating between' these two extreme positions. By extracting the minimal elements of each, the 'logical rigour' of the former and 'the movement of the intelligence' of the latter, Lautman proposes a third alternative characterisation of the mathematical real that is both axiomatic-structural and dynamic, where the fixity or temporal independence of the logical concepts and the dynamism of the temporal development of mathematical theories are combined.

THE METAPHYSICS OF LOGIC: A PHILOSOPHY OF MATHEMATICAL GENESIS

In order to do this, Lautman distinguishes two periods in mathematical logic, the first he characterises as 'the naive period', which goes from 'the first work of Russell until 1929', which is the 'date of the meta-mathematical work of Herbrand and Gödel'. The latter marks the beginning of what Lautman calls 'the critical period'. He characterises the first period as 'that where formalism and intuitionism are opposed in discussions which prolong those that had been raised by Cantor's set theory'.[38] These involved the criticism of classical analysis and the foundational disputes which were largely characterised by the dispute over the legitimacy of the actual infinite. While the formalists, as partisans of the actual infinite, claim the right to identify a mathematical object 'as a result of its implicit definition by a system of non-contradictory axioms', the intuitionists, on the contrary, maintain that 'to affirm the possibility of an unrealizable operation', for example, 'with regard to an object whose construction would require an infinite number of steps, or to a theorem that is impossible to check' because it relies on impredicative definitions,[39] 'is to affirm something which is either stripped of sense, or false, or at least undemonstratable'.[40]

Lautman's interpretation of the unity of mathematics distinguishes him from the constructivist perspective of his French intuitionist contemporaries (including Brouwer) because Lautman considered the actual infinite to be legitimate in its algebraic-axiomatic presentation. And, contrary to the intuitionists and constructivists, he grants to mathematical logic all the consideration which it deserves. That is, he accepts the logical principle of the excluded middle.[41] However, he maintains that 'logic is not *a priori* compared to mathematics, but that for logic one needs a mathematics to exist'.[42] He considered the simple idea that the logicists of the 'naive period' had made of 'an absolute and univocal anteriority of logic in relation to mathematics' to be 'out-of-date'.[43]

For Lautman, the philosophy of mathematics is not reducible to a secondary epistemological commentary on problematic logical foundations, nor to historical or *a fortiori* psycho-sociological research, nor to reflections on marginal movements such as intuitionism.[44] It is, however, precisely in the research of the critical period relating to the non-contradiction of arithmetic that Lautman considers a new theory of the mathematical real to have been affirmed. One that is 'as different from the logicism of the formalist as from the constructivism of the intuitionist'.[45] Lautman claims that between the naive and critical periods there is an 'internal evolution of logic', and he sets himself the task of disengaging from this new mathematical real 'a philosophy of mathematical genesis, whose range goes far beyond the field of logic'.[46]

While Hilbert's meta-mathematics proposes to examine mathematical theories from the point of view of the logical concepts of non-contradiction and completeness, Lautman notes that 'this is only an ideal towards which research is directed, and one knows at what point this ideal actually seems difficult to attain'.[47] This is an implicit reference to Gödel's second incompleteness theorem, which demonstrates that any non-contradictory formal system cannot demonstrate its completeness by way of its own axioms. Lautman concludes from this that 'Meta-mathematics can thus consider the idea of certain perfect structures, possibly realizable by effective mathematical theories, and this independently of the fact of knowing if there are theories enjoying the properties in question.'[48] What we have with the critical conception of the mathematical real is 'the statement of a logical problem without at all having the mathematical means of resolving it'.[49] What this means for Lautman is that the critical period marks the appearance of innovation in mathematics, not only at the level of results, but also at that of the problematic.[50] Lautman proposes to characterise the problematic 'distinction between the position of a logical problem and its mathematical solution'[51] by means of an 'exposé' of what he calls 'the metaphysics of logic'.[52] This takes the form of 'an introduction to a general theory of the connections which unite the structural considerations' of the critical axiomatic-structural conception with the 'affirmations of existence' of a particular dynamic conception.[53]

The particular dynamic conception of mathematics that Lautman deploys is further characterised when he qualifies his conception of the essential nature of mathematical truth as follows: 'Any logical attempt which would claim to dominate *a priori* the development of mathematics thus ignores the essential nature of mathematical truth, because this is related to the creative activity of the mind, and takes part in its temporal nature.'[54] Lautman is careful here to point out that mathematical truth is only partially related to the creative activity of the mind of the mathematician. In order to distinguish his account of dynamism from Brunschvicg's, Lautman considers it 'necessary to grasp, beyond the temporal circumstances of a discovery, the ideal reality which is solely capable of giving its sense and value to the mathematical experience'.[55] The lynchpin of this distinction is that Lautman conceives 'this ideal reality as independent of the activity of the mind'. For Lautman, the activity of the mind of the mathematician 'only intervenes . . . once it is a matter of creating effective mathematics', that is, effective mathematical theories.[56] This ideal reality is constituted by what he refers to as 'abstract Ideas'. Lautman proposes to call the relation between the independent activity of the mind of the mathematician and the ideas of this ideal reality 'dialectical', and he refers to these ideas as 'dialectical ideas'.[57] Lautman's principal thesis is that mathematics participates in a dialectic that governs (*domines*) it in an abstract way. He argues that the ideas 'which appear to govern the movement of certain mathematical theories', and which are conceivable as independent of mathematics, 'are not however susceptible of direct study'.[58] He goes on to claim that it is these dialectical ideas that 'confer on mathematics its eminent philosophical value'.[59] This is why Lautman considers mathematics, and especially 'modern mathematics' (and here Lautman is referring to the post-critical developments in algebra, group theory and topology), to tell, in addition to the constructions in which the mathematician is interested, 'another more hidden story [that is] made for the philosopher'.[60] The gist of the story is that there is a 'dialectical action [that] is constantly at play in the background and it is towards its clarification' that Lautman directs his research.[61] Lautman characterises this dialectical action as follows: 'Partial results, comparisons stopped midway, attempts which still resemble gropings, are organized under the unity of the same theme, and in their movement allow a connection to be seen which takes shape between certain abstract ideas, that we propose to call dialectical.'[62] Lautman argues that the nature of the mathematical real, and indeed the nature of physical reality, 'its structure and the conditions of its genesis are recognizable only by returning to the Ideas'.[63]

LAUTMAN'S SPECULATIVE LOGIC

This account of Ideas does commit Lautman to a version of Platonism. It is, however, a Platonism that is quite distinct from what is usually called 'Platonism' in mathematics, which consists rather in the practice of summarily indicating with the name 'Platonism' any mathematical philosophy for which the existence of a mathematical object is held as assured. Lautman considers this to be only one 'superficial understanding of Platonism'.[64] Nor does he 'understand by Ideas the models of which mathematical objects would only be copies'.[65] Lautman is here opposed to the Platonism traditionally founded on a certain realm of Ideas, which interprets mathematical theories as copies, reproductions, translations, or simple transpositions of eternal ideal models or Forms. Instead he wants to 'remove the idea of an irreducible distance between the "eidos" and its representation to affirm the productive power of ideas which are incarnated in the theories'.[66] What Lautman wants to do is restore to Ideas what he considers to be 'the true Platonic meaning of the term', that is, the understanding of these abstract dialectical ideas as 'the structural schemata according to which effective theories are organized'.[67]

Lautman characterises these structural schemata as establishing specific connections between contrary concepts such as: local–global; intrinsic–extrinsic; essence–existence; continuous–discontinuous; and finite–infinite. Lautman provides many examples of these contrary concepts, including the introduction of analysis into arithmetic, of topology into the theory of functions, and the effect of the penetration of the structural and finitist methods of algebra into the field of analysis and the debates about the continuum.[68]

The nature of mathematical reality for Lautman is therefore such that 'mathematical theories . . . give body to a dialectical *ideal*'.[69] This dialectic is constituted 'by couples of opposites' and the Ideas or structural schemata of this dialectic are presented in each case 'as the problem of establishing connections between opposing concepts'.[70] Lautman makes a firm distinction between concepts and dialectical Ideas: the Ideas 'consider possible relations between dialectical concepts',[71] or conceptual couples,[72] and 'these connections are only determined within the fields where the dialectic is incarnated'.[73] What Lautman is proposing is a speculative logic that considerably broadens the field and range of the meta-mathematics that he adopts from Hilbert. While meta-mathematics examines mathematical theories from the point of view of the concepts of non-contradiction and completeness, Lautman argues that there are 'other logical concepts, also likely to eventually be connected to one another within a mathematical theory'.[74] These other logical concepts are the conceptual couples of the structural schemata,[75] and Lautman argues that, 'contrary to the preceding cases (of non-contradiction and completeness)', each of which is bivalent, 'the mathematical solutions to the problems' which these conceptual couples pose can comprise 'an infinity of degrees'.[76]

So, for Lautman, Ideas constitute, along with mathematical facts, objects and theories, a fourth point of view of the mathematical real. 'Far from being opposed, these four conceptions are naturally integrated with one another: the facts consist in the discovery of new objects, these objects organize themselves in theories and the movement of these theories incarnates the schema of connections of certain Ideas.'[77] For this reason, the mathematical real depends not only on the factual base of mathematical facts but also on dialectical ideas that govern the mathematical theories in which they are actualised. Lautman thus reconsiders meta-mathematics in metaphysical terms, and postulates the metaphysical regulation of mathematics. However he is not suggesting the application of metaphysics to mathematics. Mathematical philosophy such as Lautman conceives it 'does not consist . . . in finding a logical problem of traditional metaphysics within a mathematical theory'.[78] Rather it is from the mathematical constitution of problems that it is necessary to turn to the metaphysical, that is to the dialectic, in order to give an account of the ideas which govern the mathematical theories. Lautman maintains that the philosophical meaning of mathematical thought appears in the incorporation of a metaphysics (or dialectic), of which mathematics is the necessary consequence. 'We would like to have shown', he argues, 'that this bringing together of metaphysics and mathematics is not contingent but necessary'.[79] Lautman doesn't consider this to be 'a diminution for mathematics, on the contrary it confers on it an exemplary role'.[80] Lautman's work can therefore be characterised as metaphysical, which, in the history of modern epistemology, characterises it as 'simultaneously original and solitary'.[81]

PROBLEMATIC IDEAS AND THE CONCEPT OF GENESIS

A key point for Lautman is that dialectical ideas 'only exist insofar as [they are] incarnated mathematically'.[82] Lautman insists on this point. He argues that 'the reality inherent in mathematical theories comes to it from the fact that it takes part in an ideal reality which is governing of the mathematics, *but which is only recognizable through it*'.[83] This is what distinguishes Lautman's conception from 'a naive subjective idealism'.[84]

The dialectical Ideas are therefore characterised by Lautman as constituting a problematic.[85] He argues that 'while the mathematical relations describe connections existing in fact between distinct mathematical objects, the Ideas of dialectical relations are not affirmative of an existing connection between any concepts whatsoever'.[86] They constitute rather a problematic, that is, they are 'posed problems . . . relative to the connections that are [only] likely to be supported by certain dialectical concepts'. As such, they are characterised by Lautman as 'transcendent (in the usual meaning of the term) in relation to mathematics'.[87] The effective mathematical theories are constituted in an effort to bring a response to the problem posed by these connections, and Lautman interprets 'the overall structure of these theories in terms of the immanence of the logical schemata to the sought after solution'.[88] That is, the conceptual couples of the logical schemata '*are not anterior to their realization within a theory*'. They lack what Lautman calls 'the extra-mathematical intuition of the urgency of a logical problem'. The fundamental consequence is that the constitution of new logical schemata and problematic Ideas '*depend on the progress of mathematics itself*'.[89] Mathematical philosophy such as Lautman conceives it consists in 'apprehending the structure of [a mathematical] theory globally in order to extract the logical problem which is both defined and resolved by the very existence of this theory'.[90] 'There is thus an intimate link', for Lautman, 'between the transcendence of the Ideas and the immanence of the logical structure of the solution of a dialectical problem within mathematics.' It is in direct relation to this link that Lautman characterises 'the concept of genesis'[91] that he considers to be operative in the relation between the dialectic and mathematics. However, 'the order implied by the concept of genesis is not the order of the logical reconstruction of mathematics' as undertaken by the logicists. For the latter, the genetic definitions 'of a theory give rise to all the propositions of the theory'; whereas for Lautman, although the dialectic is anterior to mathematics, it 'does not form part of mathematics, and its concepts are without relationship to the primitive concepts of a theory'.[92] Nor is the genesis conceived in the Platonic sense as 'the material creation of the concrete starting from the Idea', but rather as what Lautman describes as the genesis 'of concepts relative to the concrete at the centre of an analysis of the idea'.[93] Lautman defines the 'anteriority of the dialectic' as that of the 'question' in relation to the 'response': 'it is of the nature of the response to be an answer to a question already posed . . . even if the idea of the question comes to mind only after having seen the answer'.[94]

The dialectic therefore functions by extracting logical problems from mathematical theories. The apprehension of the conceptual couple, that is, the logical schema of the problematic Idea, only comes after having extracted the logical problem from the mathematical theory. This is the basis for Lautman's understaning of the genesis of concepts from the concrete that is operating in the dialectic. And, it is the logical problem itself, rather than the problematic Idea, that directly drives the development of mathematics. The problematic idea governs the extraction process that deploys the logical problem in the further development of new mathematical theories. So for Lautman, 'the philosopher has neither to extract the laws, nor to envisage a future evolution, his role only consists in becoming aware of the logical drama which is played out within the theories'.[95] This effort on the part of the philosopher to 'adequately comprehend dialectical Ideas' is itself 'creative of the system of more concrete concepts where the connections between the [concepts] are defined'.[96] The only '*a priori* element' that is able to be conceived 'is given in the experience of the urgency of the problems', which preceeds not only 'the discovery of their solutions',[97] but also the extraction of the logical problem from the mathematical theory under scrutiny.

THE VIRTUAL IN LAUTMAN

The method that Lautman uses in his mathematical philosophy is 'descriptive analysis'. The particular mathematical theories that he deploys throughout his work constitute for him 'a given' in which he endeavours 'to extract the ideal reality in which this material participates'.[98] That is, Lautman starts with mathematical theories that are already in circulation. For example, he incorporates all the new work in algebraic topology of the German mathematicians Alexandroff, Hopf and Weyl, and connects it to the work of Elie Cartan in complex analysis and to that of André Weil in what was then the emerging field of algebraic geometry.[99] He is also one of the first to anticipate the philosophical interest in algebraic topology, a branch of mathematics that was then under full development. In relation to these mathematical theories Lautman argues that while

> it is necessary that mathematics exists as an example where the ideal structures of the dialectic can be realised, it is not necessary that the examples which correspond to a particular dialectical structure are of a particular kind; what generally happens on the contrary is that the organizing power of the same structure is affirmed in different theories; they present affinities of mathematical structure which testify to the common dialectical structure in which they take part.[100]

One of the examples developed by Lautman is the operation of the local–global conceptual couple in the theory of the approximate representation of functions.[101] The same conceptual couple is illustrated in geometry.[102] Distinct mathematical theories can therefore be structured by the same conceptual couple.[103] Lautman sees in the local–global conceptual couple the source of a dialectical movement in mathematics that produces new theories. He argues that 'one can grasp closely the mechanism of this operation where the analysis of Ideas is produced in effective creation, where the virtual is transformed into reality'.[104] In the case of the example of the local–global conceptual couple, the new mathematical theory that was effectively created was Poincaré's qualitative theory of differential equations, or the theory of automorphic functions.[105]

According to Lautman, the problematic nature of the connections between conceptual couples 'can arise apart from any mathematics, but the effectuation of these connections is immediately mathematical theory'.[106] As a consequence, he maintains that 'Mathematics thus plays with respect to the other domains of incarnation, physical reality, social reality, human reality, the role of model where the way that things come into existence is observed.'[107] This is an important point for Deleuze, one which shapes his strategy of engagement with a range of discourses throughout his work. Lautman's final word on mathematical logic is that it 'does not enjoy in this respect any special privilege; it is only one theory among others and the problems which it raises or which it solves are found almost identically elsewhere'.[108] Lautman claims that 'for the mathematician, it is in the choice of original definitions and judicious axioms that true invention resides. It is by the introduction of new concepts, much more than by transformations of symbols or blind handling of algorithms, that mathematics has progressed and will progress.'[109]

DELEUZE AND THE CALCULUS OF PROBLEMS

At the time, opinion amongst mathematicians and philosophers was largely unfavourable to Lautman. Mathematicians were at odds with what was for them his incomprehensible 'philosophical speculation' and its 'subtleties'.[110] While the philosophers reproached him for what they considered to be a certain inaccuracy in his use of the term 'dialectical':[111] was it Socratic, Kantian or Hegelian?[112] It was another 30 years before an adequate account of the dialectic proposed by Lautman was able to be given. This was offered by Deleuze in his major work *Difference and Repetition*. Despite Deleuze's work, the confusion over the nature of the dialectic in Lautman remains pretty much intact, with quite recent commentators such as Jean Petitot – a French mathematician and philosopher of mathematics who, contraray to Lautman's peers, considers Lautman to be one of the most inspiring philosophers of the twentieth century[113] – suggesting that the dialectic proposed by Lautman is a Hegelian one.[114] It is only in recent work on Deleuze's engagement with mathematics that the significance of Lautman to the development of Deleuze's philosophy, and of Deleuze to the recent reception of Lautman's work, is being recognised.[115] Even Petitot proclaims that 'with Ferdinand Gonseth and very recently Jean Largeault, Gilles Deleuze is one of the (too) rare philosophers to have recognised the importance of Lautman'.[116] Jean-Michel Salanskis acknowledges that it was Deleuze's *Difference and Repetition* that led him to read Lautman's work and to appreciate its significance to the subsequent developments in mathematics, in particular to the Bourbaki project.[117] And both Petitot and Salanskis draw attention to the 'visionary and profound character of Deleuze's presentation of the notion of structural multiplicity'[118] in *Difference and Repetition* (DR 182–4).

It is in the chapter of *Difference and Repetition* entitled 'Ideas and the Synthesis of Difference' that Deleuze mobilises mathematics to develop a 'calculus of problems' (TP 570 n. 61)[119] based on Lautman's work.

> Following Lautman's general theses, a problem has three aspects: its difference in kind from solutions, its transcendence in relation to the solutions that it engenders on the basis of its own determinant conditions; and its immanence in the solutions which cover it, the problem being the better resolved the more it is determined. Thus the ideal connections constitutive of the problematic (dialectical) Idea are incarnated in the real solutions which are constituted by mathematical theories and carried over into problems in the form of solutions. (DR 178–9)

Deleuze explicates this process by referring to the operation of certain conceptual couples in the field of contemporary mathematics: most notably the continuous and the discontinuous, the infinite and the finite, and the global and the local. The two mathematical theories Deleuze draws upon for this purpose are the differential calculus and the theory of dynamical systems, and Galois' theory of polynomial equations. For the purposes of this chapter I will only treat the first of these,[120] which is based on the idea that the singularities of vector fields determine the local trajectories of solution curves, or their 'topological behaviour'.[121] These singularities can be described in terms of a given mathematical problematic – for example, how to solve two divergent series in the same field – and in terms of the solutions, as the trajectories of the solution curves to the problem. What actually counts as a solution to a problem is determined by the specific characteristics of the problem itself, typically by the singularites of this problem and the way in which they are distributed in a system.[122] Deleuze understands the differential calculus essentially as a 'calculus of problems', and the theory of dynamical systems as the qualitative and topological theory of problems, which, when connected together, are determinative of the complex logic of different/ciation. (DR 209).[123] Deleuze develops the concept of a problematic idea from the differential calculus, and following Lautman considers the concept of genesis in mathematics to 'play the role of model . . . with respect to all other domains of incarnation'.[124] While Lautman explicated the philosophical logic of the actualisation of ideas within the framework of mathematics, Deleuze (along with Guattari) follows Lautman's suggestion and explicates the operation of this logic within the framework of a multiplicity of domains, including, for example, philosophy, science and art in *What is Philosophy?*, and the variety of domains which characterise the plateaus in *A Thousand Plateaus*. While for Lautman a mathematical problem is resolved by the development of a new mathematical theory, for Deleuze, it is the construction of a concept that offers a solution to a philosophical problem; even if this newly constructed concept is characteristic of, or modelled on, the new mathematical theory.

One of the differences between Lautman and Deleuze is that while Lautman locates the ideas in a specifically Platonic and idealist perspective, the ideas that Deleuze refers to are rather more Kantian than Platonic[125], and Lautman's idealism is displaced in Deleuze's work by an understanding of the Lautmanian idea as 'purely' problematic. There is no ideal reality associated with ideas in Deleuze but rather ideas are constituted by the purely problematic relation between conceptual couples. Deleuze defines the 'Idea' as 'a structure. A structure or an Idea is . . . a system of multiple, non-localisable connections between differential elements which is incarnated in real relations and actual terms' (DR 183). For Deleuze, it is the problematic nature of the relations between conceptual couples that incarnate problematic ideas and which govern the kinds of solutions that can be offered to them.

What Deleuze specifically draws from Lautman is a relational logic that designates a process of production, or genesis, which has the value of introducing a general theory of relations that unites the structural considerations of the differential calculus to the concept of 'the generation of quantities' (DR 175). The process of the genesis of mathematical theories that are offered as solutions to mathematical problems corresponds to the Deleuzian account of the construction of concepts as solutions to philosophical problems.

The mathematical problematics that Deleuze extracts from the history of mathematics, following Lautman's lead, are directly redeployed by Deleuze as philosophical problematics in relation to the history of philosophy. This is achieved by mapping the alternative lineages in the history of mathematics onto corresponding alternative lineages in the history of philosophy, that is, by isolating those points of convergence between the mathematical and philosophical problematics extracted from their respective histories. The redeployment of mathematical problematics as philosophical problematics is one of the strategies Deleuze employs in his engagement with the history of philosophy. Deleuze actually extracts philosophical problematics from the history of philosophy and then redeploys them either in relation to one another, or in relation to mathematical problematics, or in relation to problematics extracted from other discourses, to create new concepts, which Deleuze and Guattari consider to be the task of philosophy (WP 5).

Deleuze is therefore very much interested in particular kinds of mathematical problematics that can be extracted from the history of mathematics, and in the relationship that these problematics have to the discourse of philosophy. He can therefore be understood to redeploy not only the actual mathematical problematics that are extracted from the history of mathematics in relation to the history of philosophy, he also redeploys the logic of the generation of mathematical problematics, that is, the calculus of problems, in relation to the history of philosophy, in order to generate the philosophical problematics which are then redeployed in his project of constructing a philosophy of difference. It is in relation to the history of philosophy that Deleuze then determines the logic of the generation of philosophical problematics as the speculative logic characteristic of a philosophy of difference.

THE SPECULATIVE LOGIC CHARACTERISTIC OF A PHILOSOPHY OF DIFFERENCE

This speculative logic, the logic of the calculus of problems, is determined in relation to the discipline of mathematics and the mathematical problematics extracted from it. It is not simply a logic characteristic of the relation between the history of mathematics and its related mathematical problematics, or between axiomatics and problematics,[126] or between what Deleuze and Guattari characterise as Royal science and nomad science. It is rather a logic of the generation of each mathematical problematic itself, or of nomad science itself. Deleuze writes that:

> It is sufficient to understand that the genesis takes place in time not between one actual term, however small, and another actual term, but between the virtual and its actualization – in other words, it goes from the structure to its incarnation, from the conditions of a problem to the cases of solution, from the differential elements and their ideal connections to actual terms and diverse real relations which constitute at each moment the actuality of time. This is a genesis without dynamism. (DR 183)

It is this logic that Deleuze redeploys in relation to the history of philosophy as a logic of different/ciation in order to generate the philosophical problematics that he then uses to construct a philosophy of difference.

Lautman refers to this whole process as 'the metaphysics of logic',[127] and, in *Difference and Repetition*, Deleuze formulates a 'metaphysics of logic' that corresponds to the local point of view of the differential calculus. He endorses Lautman's broader project when he argues that 'we should speak of a dialectics of the calculus rather than a metaphysics' (DR 178), since, he continues, 'each engendered domain, in which dialectical Ideas of this or that order are incarnated, possesses its own calculus. . . . It is not mathematics which is applied to other domains but the dialectic which establishes . . . the direct differential calculus corresponding or appropriate to the domain under consideration' (DR 181). It is not the particular method of the differential calculus which is applied to the dialectical logic to support its development, but rather the dialectical logic which determines the direct differential calculus which corresponds or is appropriate to its own development.

There is therefore a convergence between the logic of the local point of view of the differential calculus and the logic of the theory of relations that is characteristic of Deleuze's philosophy of difference. The manner by means of which an idea is implicated in the mathematical theory which determines it, converges with, or serves as a function or mathematical model of, the manner by means of which a philosophical concept is implicated in the philosophical problematic which determines it. There are 'correspondences without resemblance' (DR 184) between them, insofar as both are determined according to the same speculative logic, that is, according to the logic of different/ciation. The philosophical implications of this convergence are developed by Deleuze in *Expressionism in Philosophy* in relation to his reading of Spinoza's theory of relations in the *Ethics*,[128] and in *Cinema 1* and *Cinema 2* in relation to his understanding of Bergson's intention 'to give multiplicities the metaphysics which their scientific treatment demands' (B 112).

The problematic Ideas that 'it is possible to recover within mathematical theories', and that are 'incarnated in the same movement of these theories',[129] are characterised by the relations between the conceptual couples. These Ideas, which are recast by Deleuze as philosophical concepts, are used to develop the logical schema of a theory of relations characteristic of a philosophy of difference. It is in the development of this project that Deleuze specifically draws upon Lautman's work to deploy a speculative logic that, in *Difference and Repetition*, is determined in relation to the history of the differential calculus as the logic of different/ciation; in *Expressionism in*

Philosophy is determined in relation to Spinoza's theory of relations as the logic of expression; and in the *Cinema* books, is determined in relation to the work of Bergson as a logic of multiplicities.

Lautman outlined a 'critical' programme in mathematics that was intended to displace the previous foundational discussions that were occupied with the criticism of classical analysis. Against the logicist claim that the development of mathematics is dominated *a priori* by logic, Lautman proposes a 'metaphysics of logic', and calls for the development of a 'philosophy of mathematical genesis'. Deleuze responds to this call. His Lautmanian preoccupation with mathematics is primarily focused on locating what Lautman characterises as 'logical Ideas', which are recast by Deleuze as philosophical concepts to develop the logical schema of a theory of relations characteristic of a philosophy of difference. Lautman's work on mathematics provides the blueprint for adequately determining the nature not only of Deleuze's engagement with mathematics, but also of Deleuze's metaphysics, the metaphysics of his speculative logic.

University of Sydney

Notes

1. Albert Lautman, *Essai sur l'unité des mathématiques et divers écrits* (Paris: Union générale d'éditions, 1977), p. 23.
2. Lautman, *Essai sur l'unité*, p. 24.
3. See Jean Dieudonné in Lautman, *Essai sur l'unité*, p. 15.
4. Jean Petitot, 'La dialectique de la vérité objective et de la valeur historique dans le rationalisme mathématique d'Albert Lautman', in *Sciences et Philosophie en France et en Italie entre les deux guerres*, edited by J. Petitot and L. Scarantino (Napoli: Vivarium, 2001), p. 83.
5. Albert Lautman, *Essai sur les notions de structure et d'existence en mathématiques. I. Les Schémas de structure. II. Les Schémas de genèse.* (Paris: Hermann, 1938); Albert Lautman, *Essai sur l'unité des sciences mathématiques dans leur développement actuel* (Paris: Hermann, 1938).
6. Dieudonné in Lautman, *Essai sur l'unité*, p. 16.
7. Dieudonné in Lautman, *Essai sur l'unité*, p. 16.
8. Dieudonné in Lautman, *Essai sur l'unité*, p. 16.
9. Lautman, *Essai sur l'unité*, p. 145.
10. Maurice Loi, 'Foreword', in Lautman, *Essai sur l'unité*, p. 13.
11. The axiomatic method is a way of developing mathematical theories by postulating certain primitive assumptions, or axioms, as the basis of the

theory, while the remaining propositions of the theory are obtained as logical consequences of these axioms.

12. Lautman, *Essai sur l'unité*, p. 146.
13. Lautman, *Essai sur l'unité*, p. 147.
14. Lautman, *Essai sur l'unité*, p. 25.
15. Lautman, *Essai sur l'unité*, p. 25.
16. Lautman, *Essai sur l'unité*, p. 136.
17. The Bourbaki project explicitly espoused a set-theoretic version of mathematical structuralism.
18. Dieudonné in Lautman, *Essai sur l'unité*, pp. 15–20.
19. According to mathematical structuralism, mathematical objects are defined by their positions in mathematical structures, and the subject matter that mathematics concerns itself with are structural relationships in abstraction from the intrinsic nature of the related objects. See Geoffrey Hellman, 'Structuralism', in Stewart Shapiro (ed.), *The Oxford Handbook of Philosophy of Mathematics and Logic* (Oxford: Oxford University Press, 2005), p. 256.
20. Dieudonné in Lautman, *Essai sur l'unité*, p. 16.
21. Lautman, *Essai sur l'unité*, p. 24.
22. Lautman, *Essai sur l'unité*, p. 38.
23. Lautman, *Essai sur l'unité*, p. 23. The logicist thesis was that the basic concepts of mathematics are definable by means of logical notions, and the key axioms of mathematics are deducible from logical principles alone.
24. The main aim of Hilbert's programme, which was first clearly formulated in 1922, was to establish the logical acceptability of the principles and modes of inference of modern mathematics by formalising each mathematical theory into a finite, complete set of axioms, and to provide a proof that these axioms were consistent. The point of Hilbert's approach was to make mathematical theories fully precise, so that it is possible to obtain precise results about properties of the theory. In 1931 Gödel showed that the programme as it stood was not possible. Revised efforts have since emerged as continuations of the programme that concentrate on relative results in relation to specific mathematical theories, rather than all mathematics. See José Ferreirós, 'The Crisis in the Foundations of Mathematics', in *The Princeton Companion to Mathematics*, edited by Timothy Gowers, June Barrow-Green and Imre Leader (Princeton: Princeton University Press, 2008), Ch. 2.6.3.2.
25. Lautman, *Essai sur l'unité*, p. 282.
26. See Jean Largeault, *Logique mathématique. Textes* (Paris: Armand Colin, 1972), pp. 215, 264.
27. Lautman, *Essai sur l'unité*, p. 9.
28. Petitot, 'La dialectique de la vérité', p. 98. The term 'meta-mathematics' is introduced by Hilbert in 'Uber das Unendliche', *Mathematische Annalen* 95 (1926), pp. 161–90.

29. Lautman, *Essai sur l'unité*, p. 26.
30. Lautman, *Essai sur l'unité*, p. 26.
31. Lautman, *Essai sur l'unité*, p. 26.
32. David Hilbert, *Gesammelte Abhandlungen* (New York: Chelsea Pub. Co., 1965), p. 180. Cited in Lautman, *Essai sur l'unité*, p. 30.
33. Lautman, *Essai sur l'unité*, p. 27.
34. Lautman, *Essai sur l'unité*, p. 25.
35. Lautman, *Essai sur l'unité*, p. 25. See Léon Brunschvicg, *Les Étapes de la philosophie mathématique* (Paris: A. Blanchard, 1993).
36. Lautman, *Essai sur l'unité*, p. 25.
37. Lautman, *Essai sur l'unité*, p. 25.
38. Lautman, *Essai sur l'unité*, p. 87.
39. A mathematical definition is impredicative if it depends on a certain set, N, being defined and introduced by appeal to a totality of sets which includes N itself. That is, the definition is self-referencing.
40. Lautman, *Essai sur l'unité*, p. 88.
41. The law of the excluded middle states that every proposition is either true or false. In propositional logic, the law is written 'P V ¬P' ('P or not-P').
42. Lautman, *Essai sur l'unité*, p. 48.
43. Loi in Lautman, *Essai sur l'unité*, p. 13.
44. Petitot, 'La dialectique de la vérité', p. 81.
45. Lautman, *Essai sur l'unité*, p. 89.
46. Lautman, *Essai sur l'unité*, p. 89.
47. Lautman, *Essai sur l'unité*, p. 27.
48. Lautman, *Essai sur l'unité*, p. 28.
49. Lautman, *Essai sur l'unité*, p. 28.
50. Lautman, *Essai sur l'unité*, p. 211.
51. Lautman, *Essai sur l'unité*, p. 28.
52. Lautman, *Essai sur l'unité*, p. 87.
53. Lautman, *Essai sur l'unité*, p. 87.
54. Lautman, *Essai sur l'unité*, p. 140.
55. Albert Lautman, *Nouvelles recherches sur la structure dialectique des mathématiques* (Actualités scientifiques et industrielles. Paris: Hermann, 1939), p. 630.
56. Lautman, *Nouvelles recherches*, p. 630.
57. Lautman, *Essai sur l'unité*, p. 28.
58. Lautman, *Essai sur l'unité*, p. 29.
59. Lautman, *Essai sur l'unité*, p. 29.
60. Lautman, *Essai sur l'unité*, p. 28.
61. Lautman, *Essai sur l'unité*, p. 28.
62. Lautman, *Essai sur l'unité*, p. 28.
63. Lautman, *Essai sur l'unité*, p. 147.
64. Lautman, *Essai sur l'unité*, p. 143.

65. Lautman, *Essai sur l'unité*, p. 204.
66. See Catherine Chevalley, 'Albert Lautman et le souci logique', *Revue d'Histoire des Sciences* 40:1 (1987), p. 61.
67. Lautman, *Essai sur l'unité*, p. 204. See also pp. 143–4, 302–4; Emmanuel Barot, 'L'objectivité mathématique selon Albert Lautman: entre Idées dialectiques et réalité physique'. *Cahiers François Viète* 6 (2003), p. 7 n. 2.
68. See Chevalley, 'Albert Lautman et le souci logique', p. 60.
69. Lautman, *Essai sur l'unité*, p. 253.
70. Lautman, *Essai sur l'unité*, p. 253.
71. Lautman, *Essai sur l'unité*, p. 210.
72. Which are also referred to and operate as 'dualities'. See Charles Alluni, 'Continental Genealogies: Mathematical Confrontations in Albert Lautman and Gaston Bachelard', in *Virtual Mathematics: The Logic of Difference*, edited by S. Duffy (Manchester: Clinamen Press, 2006), p. 78.
73. Lautman, *Essai sur l'unité*, p. 253.
74. Lautman, *Essai sur l'unité*, p. 28.
75. Which he therefore also refers to as 'logical schemata'. See Lautman, *Essai sur l'unité*, p. 142.
76. Lautman, *Essai sur l'unité*, p. 28.
77. Lautman, *Essai sur l'unité*, p. 135.
78. Lautman, *Essai sur l'unité*, p. 142.
79. Lautman, *Essai sur l'unité*, p. 203.
80. Lautman, *Essai sur l'unité*, p. 10. From Lautman's correspondence with Fréchet dated 1 February 1939.
81. See Chevalley, 'Albert Lautman et le souci logique', p. 50.
82. Lautman, *Essai sur l'unité*, p. 203.
83. Lautman, *Essai sur l'unité*, p. 290.
84. Petitot, 'La dialectique de la vérité', p. 86.
85. Lautman, *Essai sur l'unité*, p. 211.
86. Lautman, *Essai sur l'unité*, p. 210.
87. Lautman, *Essai sur l'unité*, p. 212.
88. Lautman, *Essai sur l'unité*, p. 212.
89. Lautman, *Essai sur l'unité*, p. 142.
90. Lautman, *Essai sur l'unité*, p. 143.
91. Lautman, *Essai sur l'unité*, p. 212.
92. Lautman, *Essai sur l'unité*, p. 210.
93. Lautman, *Essai sur l'unité*, p. 205.
94. Lautman, *Essai sur l'unité*, p. 210.
95. Lautman, *Essai sur l'unité*, p. 142.
96. Lautman, *Essai sur l'unité*, p. 205.
97. Lautman, *Essai sur l'unité*, p. 142.
98. Lautman, *Essai sur l'unité*, p. 40.

99. Barot, 'L'objectivité mathématique selon Albert Lautman', p. 22.
100. Lautman, *Essai sur l'unité*, p. 213.
101. Lautman, *Essai sur l'unité*, pp. 32, 45–7. The 'global conception of the analytic function that one finds with Cauchy and Riemann' (p. 32) is posed as a conceptual couple in relation to Weierstrass' approximation theorem, which is a local method of determining an analytic function in the neighbourhood of a complex point by a power series expansion, which, by a series of local operations, converges around this point (pp. 45–7).
102. The same conceptual couple is illustrated in geometry by the connections between 'topological surface properties and their local differential properties', that is, between the curvature of the former and the determination of second derivatives of the latter, both in the 'metric formulation' of geoemtry in the work of Hopf (Lautman, *Essai sur l'unité*, pp. 40–3) and 'in its topological formulation' in Weyl and Cartan's theory of closed groups (pp. 43–4).
103. See Barot, 'L'objectivité mathématique selon Albert Lautman', p. 10; Chevalley, 'Albert Lautman et le souci logique', pp. 63–4.
104. Lautman, *Essai sur l'unité*, p. 209.
105. For an account of the role that this example of the local–global conceptual couple plays in Deleuze see Simon Duffy, 'The Mathematics of Deleuze's Differential Logic and Metaphysics', in Duffy (ed.), *Virtual Mathematics: The Logic of Difference*.
106. Lautman, *Essai sur l'unité*, p. 288.
107. Lautman, *Essai sur l'unité*, p. 209.
108. Lautman, *Essai sur l'unité*, p. 288.
109. Loi in Lautman, *Essai sur l'unité*, p. 12.
110. Petitot, 'La dialectique de la vérité', p. 99.
111. Lautman, *Essai sur l'unité*, p. 22.
112. Petitot, 'La dialectique de la vérité', p. 113.
113. Petitot, 'La dialectique de la vérité', p. 80.
114. Petitot, 'La dialectique de la vérité', p. 113. See also Barot, 'L'objectivité mathématique selon Albert Lautman', pp. 6, 16 n. 1. For a Deleuzian account of an alternative speculative logic to the Hegelian dialectical logic, one that implicates the work of Lautman, see Simon Duffy, *The Logic of Expression: Quality, Quantity and Intensity in Spinoza, Hegel and Deleuze* (Aldershot: Ashgate, 2006), pp. 74–91, 254–60.
115. Jean-Michel Salanskis, 'Idea and Destination', in *Deleuze: A Critical Reader*, edited by P. Patton (Cambridge: Blackwell, 1996); Salanskis, 'Pour une épistémologie de la lecture', *Alliage* 35–6 (1998) <http://www.tribunes.com/tribune/alliage/accueil.htm>; Daniel W. Smith, 'Mathematics and the Theory of Multiplicities: Deleuze and Badiou Revisited', *Southern Journal of Philosophy* 41:3 (2003), pp. 411–49;

Duffy, 'The Mathematics of Deleuze's Differential Logic and Metaphysics'.

116. Petitot, 'La dialectique de la vérité', p. 87 n. 14.

117. See Salanskis, 'Pour une épistémologie de la lecture' (in particular the section entitled 'Contre-temoinage').

118. Salanskis, 'Idea and Destination', p. 64.

119. When Deleuze and Guattari comment on 'the "intuitionist" school (Brouwer, Heyting, Griss, Bouligand, etc.),' they insist that it 'is of great importance in mathematics, not because it asserted the irreducible rights of intuition, or even because it elaborated a very novel constructivism, but because it developed a conception of problems, and of a calculus of problems that intrinsically rivals axiomatics and proceeds by other rules (notably with regard to the excluded middle)' (TP 570 n. 61). Deleuze extracts this concept of the calculus of problems itself as a mathematical problematic from the episode in the history of mathematics when intuitionism opposed axiomatics. It is the logic of this calculus of problems that he then redeploys in relation to a range of episodes in the history of mathematics that in no way binds him to the principles of intuitionism. See Duffy, 'Deleuze and Mathematics', in Duffy (ed.), *Virtual Mathematics: The Logic of Difference*, pp. 2–6.

120. For a brief account of Deleuze's enagement with Galois see Gilles Châtelet, 'Interlacing the Singularity, the Diagram and the Metaphor', trans. S. Duffy, in Duffy (ed.), *Virtual Mathematics: The Logic of Difference*, p. 41; Salanskis, 'Mathematics, Metaphysics, Philosophy', in *Virtual Mathematics* pp. 52–3; Salanskis, 'Pour une épistémologie de la lecture'; Daniel W. Smith, 'Axiomatics and Problematics as Two Modes of Formalisation: Deleuze's Epistemology of Mathematics', in Duffy (ed.), *Virtual Mathematics: The Logic of Difference*, pp. 159–63.

121. See Salanskis, 'Pour une épistémologie de la lecture'.

122. See Salanskis, 'Pour une épistémologie de la lecture'.

123. See Duffy, *The Logic of Expression*, where the complex concept of the logic of different/ciation is demonstrated to be characteristic of Deleuze's 'philosophy of difference'.

124. Lautman, *Essai sur l'unité*, p. 209.

125. For a critical account of Lautman's engagement with Kant see Petitot, 'La dialectique de la vérité'. See also Salanskis, 'Idea and Destination', for an account of the significance of Kant for Deleuze's engagement with Lautman. See Nathan Widder, 'The rights of Simulacra: Deleuze and the Univocity of Being', *Continental Philosophy Review* 34 (2001), pp. 437–53 for an account of Deleuze's reversal of Platonism and its implied idealism.

126. See Smith, 'Axiomatics and Problematics', for an account of the operation of the relation between Royal and nomad science and between axiomatics and problematics in Deleuze's work.
127. Lautman, *Essai sur l'unité*, p. 87.
128. See Duffy, 'Schizo-Math', *Angelaki* 9: 3, 2004, pp. 199–215 and 'The Mathematics of Deleuze's Differential Logic and Metaphysics'.
129. Lautman, *Essai sur l'unité des mathématiques,* p. 195.

20

Gilbert Simondon

Alberto Toscano

While the metaphysical troika of Spinoza, Nietzsche and Bergson[1] which oversaw Deleuze's tumultuous 'philosophical apprenticeship'[2] presents us with the potent, if controversial, image of a sort of philosophical counter-tradition – in which a Bergsonised Spinoza accompanies a Spinozistic Nietzsche and a Nietzschean Bergson – estimating Deleuze's relationship to the galaxy of often 'obscure' writers that populate his books (and lectures) is a difficult, and probably inconclusive, task. To begin with, Deleuze's practice of reference or citation poses some intriguing philological problems. At a remove from the ideological and procedural requirements of ordinary academic production, his references are not offered as tokens of authority, respectable citizens from the philosophical canon who could testify for the prosecution or the defence. There is a wilfully perverse, and not always persuasive, tendency in Deleuze sometimes to seek out authors with a pariah or occult status. But there is also, more importantly, an ethical imperative to rescue those 'minor' thinkers who have generated systematic speculative endeavours which the vagaries of 'molar' or 'royal' intellectual and academic consensus have sidelined. Raymond Ruyer and Gabriel Tarde come to mind. The latter's 'renaissance', for instance, has drawn much impetus from the long footnote in *Difference and Repetition* and the one-page homage to his work in *A Thousand Plateaus*.[3] Tarde's case is emblematic of the manner in which Deleuze is capable of beguilingly compressing ('implicating', he might say) whole interpretations of thinkers in a few lines.

It is also undeniable that Deleuze's own contemporary authority – marked by the proliferation of articles, collections, book series and most recently the founding of the journal *Deleuze Studies* – has been instrumental to the interest taken in authors whose work might have otherwise lain dormant. But what attitude is one to take vis-à-vis these thinkers who Deleuze so beguilingly, if often so fleetingly, cites? In my view, it would be a dire error to take any of these figures as the 'key' to Deleuze, or even as the basis for a critical reconstruction of his system. But what is the alternative, besides, as many have done, simply delving into the authors cited by Deleuze in their own right? After all, Deleuze himself seems to explicitly take an instrumental approach when it comes to the incorporation of the statements and theses of other thinkers and philosophers into the thrust of his own thinking. In the note accompanying the bibliographical chart in *Difference and Repetition* (whose diagrammatic arrangement is unfortunately lost in the English translation), Deleuze himself provocatively states that 'the accounts given remain completely inadequate from the point of view of the history of philosophy, since they are intended only to serve the needs of our researches' (DR 334).[4] This suggests that, as intellectually enriching as it may be for its own sake, the hunt for sources and influences will not endow Deleuze's texts with some kind of esoteric coherence, delivered by suitable philology and erudition (a trait which Deleuze, referencing Umberto Eco in the *Abécedaire*, was unguardedly contemptuous of). In my view, there are at least four approaches that might provide some way out of this hermeneutic impasse.

The first approach involves incorporating both Deleuze and his philosophical companions in the delineation of a problem that exceeds them both. This demands the more or less autonomous reconstruction of a problematic field, with its own tendencies, impasses, co-ordinates, and so on. Elsewhere, this is the approach I have taken vis-à-vis the genealogical vicissitudes of the problem of individuation, identifying in Simondon and Deleuze (alongside Peirce and others) suitable sources for the development of what I termed an 'ontology of anomalous individuation'.[5]

Second, it is possible to track the uses of a thinker in Deleuze as indices of Deleuze's own philosophical development, of the dislocation of certain concepts to new areas of concept-creation and the disappearance of others. Examples of this would be the radical demotion of Lacan from crucial thinker of the quasi-cause to principal culprit in the Oedipalisation of the subject; the delicate shift of Spinoza from ontological univocity to ethological immanence; or the cautious rehabilitation of Hegel at the start of *What is Philosophy?*

Third, Deleuze's own identification of the salient, determining or instrumentally useful aspects of a thinker can serve as the platform for an intervention into the conflicts of interpretation that inevitably accompany any philosophical reception. Of course, in order to rise above the vicarious imparting of the imprimatur of Deleuzian authority, this approach also requires an autonomous redefinition of the philosophical problem into which Deleuze's work can intervene.

The fourth involves a sharp eye for Deleuze's tactical use of certain borrowed and retooled concepts at key moments in the unfolding of his own thinking. It is interesting in this respect to recall Deleuze's own definition of the function of 'intercessors' in philosophy: 'Whether real or imaginary, animate or inanimate, you have to form your intercessors. It's a series. If you're not in some series, you're lost. I need my intercessors to express myself, and they'd never express themselves without me: you're always working in a group, even when you seem to be on your own.'[6] The intercessions of these virtual accomplices often take place at crucial junctures. As far as Simondon is concerned, his three most important intercessions are to be found in *Difference and Repetition* (where his theory of individuation provides the indispensable relay between virtual differentiation and actual differenciation [DR 244–54]), in *The Logic of Sense* (where Simondon is lauded for forging 'the first thought-out theory of impersonal and pre-individual singularities' [LS 344]), and *A Thousand Plateaus* (where Simondon provides Deleuze and Guattari with a seminal critique of hylemorphism and elements for the construction of a concept of matter qua machinic phylum [TP 408–10][7]).

In what follows, in an inevitably truncated and doubtless overly impressionistic manner, I'd like to move through these four approaches sequentially. First, I suggest that attention to Simondon's presence in Deleuze's thought permits us to move beyond the false alternatives presented by the recent debate on 'French Thought' and cybernetics. Second, in light of this discussion of Deleuze's complex (post-)cybernetic heritage, I show that the manner in which Simondon intercedes in *Difference and Repetition* and *A Thousand Plateaus* indicates an important shift in the desiderata of Deleuze's thought. Third, I combine the last two approaches by discussing how Deleuze's use of the notion of the disparate compares to political interpretations of Simondon's understanding of the powers of the pre-individual. Finally, I end by reconsidering Deleuze's statement that he 'part[s] company [with Simondon] only in drawing conclusions' in light of the two thinkers' estimations of the role of ethics in capitalist society.

CYBERNETICS AND ANTI-HUMANISM

In 2005, in the pages of the journal *multitudes*, François Cusset, author of the excellent intellectual history *French Theory*, launched an attack on the theses put forward by the Canadian sociologist Céline Lafontaine, about what she provocatively referred to as 'the American roots of French theory'.[8] Lafontaine had argued that despite the geographical, methodological and stylistic differences, the fortunes of 'French Theory' in American academia derive from the fact that it is essentially a message returning to its sender: a techno-scientific and anti-political intellectual paradigm forged in post-war America, laundered at the margins of French academia and contra-banded back into the US under the guise of a heterodox approach to the humanities. Structuralism and so-called post-structuralism are deemed to have integrated a whole host of cybernetic concepts (machine, entropy, information, plateau, structure, system, self-organisation, etc.) – concepts which serve as the bearers of a funda-mentally anti-humanist project that corrodes the very foundations of a concern with an autonomous and responsible human subject. They both partake of 'one and the same logic of desubjectivation'.[9] And poststructuralism, in the wake of cybernetics, results in a 'purely communicational representation of society'.[10]

Cusset has rightly cast doubt on Lafontaine's critique in terms of the simplistic model of intellectual causality it entails and, signifi-cantly, disputed the elision of the difference between first and second cybernetics in Lafontaine's account. Notwithstanding Cusset's useful juxtaposition of the problem of a *'non-dialectical* theory of differ-ence' shared by Deleuze, Derrida and others versus the tendency to holism of cybernetics as a science of control and communication, his contention that 'American' cybernetics and poststructuralist French thinkers have 'almost diametrically opposed' approaches, and that at best their 'local resemblances' and 'borrowings' are undermined by utterly incommensurable 'political programmes and ideological postures' remains unsatisfying. Not only does Cusset share with many critics of the cybernetic moment, including Lafontaine, a rather impoverished and nationally monolithic vision of it as a fundamen-tally technocratic *American* phenomenon, but he underestimates the seriousness of Deleuze's (and Guattari's) engagement with it.

Just as Lafontaine's model of intellectual influence is unsatisfactory, so Cusset's idea of different political uses of the same concepts seems insufficient. Inasmuch as he is right to point out that Lafontaine's juxtaposition of an emancipatory humanism of subjective autonomy and a technophilic anti-humanism is ultimately sterile, so should he recognise that Deleuze and Guattari are far too preoccupied with the *immanent* construction of alternatives to axiomatic capitalism to simply criticise it from an extrinsic ideological and political platform. Of course, their contempt for commodified communication and organicist utopias is ubiquitous, but it functions precisely by inoculating a political philosophy of difference with an arsenal of concepts – such as code, signal and field – endowed with a strong cybernetic pedigree. The turn to pragmatics in *A Thousand Plateaus*, for instance, can be conceived both as a use of a post-cybernetic approach against the signifying and subjectifying interiority of hermenutics, *and* as an immanent and constructive critique of the fetters that organicism imposes on cybernetics. Likewise, what Deleuze and Guattari regard as the identity of form(ation) and function(ing) and their critique of organicist brands of vitalism in *Anti-Oedipus*[11] can also be conceived as a development within and against cybernetics, rather than a merely external use of its concepts. In particular, it is the manner in which cybernetics opened up the possibility of a thinking of *operations*, introducing a language of 'controlling, commanding, communicating, moving, acting and reacting',[12] and scrambling the distinction between theory and practice which attracted Deleuze and Guattari, as they searched for conceptual vocabularies to think in and against capital.

But the complexity of Deleuze's (and Guattari's) relationship to cybernetics – in its various waves and derivations, for instance autopoiesis – is occluded, for both Lafontaine and Cusset, by insufficient attention to the French reception and critique of cybernetics in the 1950s. Deleuze's 'rescuing' of Raymond Ruyer, for instance, a unique neo-Leibnizian critic of the cybernetic paradigm, is difficult to fathom if we fail to grasp the idea that, to a certain extent, the kind of intellectual project issuing from the Macy conferences could be regarded as an important horizon (rather than a mere example or a determining influence) for the development of a 'new transcendental philosophy' in the post-war period. The case of Simondon is perhaps even more distinctive. Not only was Simondon, as Jean-Pierre Dupuy points out, a rare early French reader of the Macy conferences, but his intellectual project – linking a reflection on the technical object to an ontology (or ontogenesis) of individuation in the context of the attempt to axiomatise the human sciences – is entirely unintelligible without seeing it as working both within and against the cybernetic paradigm.[13] The very problems that Simondon delineates (and which Deleuze partly inherits) concerning the status of individuality, the question of finality and the possibility of breaking out of a humanist division of labour between ontology, psychology, sociology and the natural sciences are problems that cybernetics helps to introduce. Having said that, though Simondon is vitally influenced by the problematisation proper to cybernetics, he will distance himself from its fomalisations and solutions in the construction of an 'ontology of anomalous individuation'.[14] In particular, Simondon will fault cyberneticians such as Norbert Wiener for their excessive belief in the identity of living beings and self-regulating technical objects.[15]

One of the guiding ideas behind Simondon's highly original critical incorporation of cybernetics in his work of the late 1950s involves withdrawing the concept of information from its links to communication, noise and entropy, and recasting it as a crucial element in a thinking of ontogenesis, of the emergence or invention of new being out of a yet-unsynthesised field of pre-individual singularities – determinations not yet captured by the principles of identity, representation and the excluded middle.[16] This attention to information as a singular process of interaction also explains why Simondon, who was strongly influenced by the cybernetic ideal of an omni-comprehensive science or 'axiomatics' of information,[17] could not accept the reduction of information to a measurable quantity that would be merely contained (and already individuated) within a coded message. For, at its worst, the notion of a science of information synthesises the three main principles of individuation that come under Simondon's sustained attack: as unit-measure which atomistically composes organisation and quantifies degrees of order, it mimics *atomism*; as an expression of the unilateral relation between model and copy, it reinstates the Platonic *archetype*; finally, as a source of organisation which is separate from matter or 'substrate-independent', it is the latest heir to Aristotelian *hylemorphism*. Now, within his overall project of fashioning a general science of operations, or 'allagmatics',[18] bringing to the fore the 'dark zone' where individuation take place, Simondon is obliged to abandon any ontology that would ground the emergence of individuality in the pre-existence of individuated terms – whether these be matter and form, or sender and receiver. The process of in-formation is instead recast in terms of a model of innovative diffusion or contagion, which Simondon defines as 'transduction'. In this regard, we could say that Simondon retains from cybernetics the focus on operationality, but radicalises it by disputing the reliance of cybernetics on preconstituted individuals as the terms (or terminals) between which relations of command and communication obtain.

Persuaded that individuation, in whatever domain, can only take place by drawing on a pre-individual field, a 'metastable' domain composed of disparate virtualities (what he also calls a 'ground', *fond*), Simondon, drawing on scientific studies of crystallisation, rethinks the process of individuation as the result of the introduction of a 'form' in the guise of a structural 'germ' which catalyses the actualisation and reciprocal interaction of some of the virtualities that had hitherto remained at the pre-individual level. What the philosophical tradition identifies as form is thus not be thought of as a sudden imposition, but rather as the amplifying propagation of a structure, where a structured or individuated region of being serves as a principle of individuation, the model or form for other yet-unstructured and metastable regions (in this respect, the distinction between individuating and individuated is always relative). Transduction is thus a 'physical, biological, mental and social operation whereby an activity progressively propagates itself within a domain', and *'the notion of form must be replaced by that of information*, which presupposes the existence of a system in a metastable state of equilibrium which can individuate itself: information, unlike form, is never a single term, but the signification that emerges from a disparation'.[19] Simondon thus forwards the heterodox idea of chance as a source of meaning, inasmuch as information is 'impredictability in the variations of form'.[20]

METHODS OF DRAMATISATION

The concept of the disparate is particularly important for an understanding of Simondon's philosophy of interaction, and its changing role within the unfolding of Deleuze's own thought. Drawn from the physiological term for the integration of non-superimposable retinal images into unified visual perception, Simondon uses the idea of 'disparation' to reflect on how individuation implies the emergence or invention of a form of communication between hitherto incommensurable orders or potentials. As Deleuze noted in his 1966 review of Simondon, 'what essentially defines a metastable system is the existence of a "disparation", the existence of at least two different dimensions, two disparate levels of reality, between which there is not yet any interactive communication' (DI 87).[21] This conception of the disparate, which has pride of place in Chapter 5 of *Difference and Repetition*, is also crucial in providing Deleuze with another way of arguing for the *ontological* rather than epistemological character of *problems* as real-virtual complexes of unresolved difference which only the creation (or actualisation) of new beings can resolve.[22] Veritable interaction is thus thought of as an *event*, wherein individuation and communication are indissociable. It is worth noting how this concept of communication provides a manner of developing, in a heterodox direction, some of the founding tenets of cybernetics, while simultaneously providing the theoretical arsenal necessary to undermine the kind of communication 'which only works under the sway of opinions in order to create "consensus" and not concepts' (WP 6). Once again we can see how neither Lafontaine's Francophile model of Deleuze's anti-humanism as a kind of cybernetic fifth column for American technocratic imperialism, nor Cusset's subtler understanding of the political differend between poststructuralism and cybernetics, do justice to the sort of non-arborescent lineage at work in Deleuze's relationship to cybernetics.

The concept of disparation is also at the heart of Simondon's attempt to complicate the tendency of cyberneticians to engage in reflections on the analogies and isomorphies between men, machines, animals and societies as finalistic totalities characterised by various modalities of self-regulation.[23] The primacy of process over product, of genesis over individuality, dominates Simondon's account. It is around the possibility of a continued and creative interaction, under-stood as the renewed solution of the *problem* of disparation – of an intensive and dynamic difference – that Simondon distinguishes *individuation* from *individualisation*. Both living beings and technical beings are caught up in individualising processes to the extent that they never fully exhaust the metastable potentials of which they rep-resent a partial resolution. Indeed, as Simondon sets out in his book on the mode of existence of technical objects, the recurrent causality that qualifies individual autonomy depends on the coupling with an associated milieu (or an 'unconscious' psychic ground) from which the form of the individual draws its vitality.[24] Moreover, both living beings and technical objects, because of their inescapably 'problem-atic' nature and openness onto a 'milieu', are conceived of as involv-ing a necessarily 'collective' dimension – whether we are thinking of the formation of technical ensembles or the existence of transindivid-ual processes that compensate for the limits of psychic individuation. Individualisation thus takes place at the interface between pre-individual and supraindividual (or collective) dimensions of being. As Muriel Combes notes, 'the transindividual appears as what unifies not the individual and society, but a relation *internal to the individual* (what defines his psychism) and a relation *external to the individual* (what defines the collective): the transindividual unity of these two relations is thus a relation of relations'.[25] Simondon's philosophy can thus be defined as a relational ontology, resonating in many respects with contemporary tendencies towards 'interactionism'.[26] More specifically, Simondon's overall preoccupation with ontogenesis and 'allagmatics', and his work on technology and 'mechanology', are brought together in the ethical project of forging a 'technical culture' that would guide the interaction between men and technical ensembles, on the hand, and the 'metabolism' (to use Marx's expression) between man and nature on the other. I shall return to the issue of Simondon and Deleuze's ethico-political frameworks below, but first I want to inquire into how this complex of concepts and problems forged by Simondon can be seen to weave itself into the development of Deleuze's thought.

As the thinker who delves into the hidden abode of individuation and provides the conceptual tools to break with any vision of a determination of passive, undifferentiated matter by a determinate transcendent form (hylemorphism), Simondon can be said to play a crucial role in Deleuze's attempt in the late 1960s to construct what he called, in his creative reconstruction of structuralism, a 'new materialism' and a 'new transcendental philosophy' (DI 174).[27] Deleuze explicitly draws from Simondon (in conjunction with the Sartre of *The Transcendence of the Ego*) the idea of a transcendental *field* that would be populated by pre-individual singularities and would thereby constitute a non-subjective domain of multiplicities, a transcendental unmoored from the formal surveillance of a subject. As he writes in a note to *The Logic of Sense*: 'The five characteristics through which we have tried to define the transcendental field – *the potential energy of the field, the internal resonance of the series, the topological surface of membranes, the organization of sense, and the status of the problematic* – are all analyzed by Simondon' (LS 344).[28] And it is 'directly on his book' – i.e. on *L'individu et sa genese physico-biologique*, published in 1964 but originally intended as the first part of *L'individuation à la lumière des notions de forme et d'information* – that Deleuze relies to rethink the transcendental no longer in terms of categorial conditions of possibility, but rather via ontological conditions of realisation, conditions of 'the genesis of the living individual and the knowing subject' which are to be sought in operations at the level of pre-individual singularities.

More precisely, the role of Simondon and his theory of individuation is paramount in Deleuze's ontogenetic rethinking of structuralism and the transcendental in terms of thinking through the kind of operations that permit the passage from virtually differentiated Ideas to actually differen*c*iated beings. It is Simondon who allows Deleuze to reconsider structures as neither immaterial essences nor formal invariants, but instead as the pre-individual grounds of individuation. Ontogenesis is thus defined as the passage from one kind of multiplicity, the bearer of internal difference, to another, the denumerable and classifiable multiplicity of actual beings. Deleuze calls this genesis *static* because the structure itself, whilst providing the sufficient reason of actuality, has no causal role, precisely because it is not itself discretely individuated (or actualised). The concept of individuation drawn from Simondon thus comes to insert itself, as it were, in this disjunction between cause and genesis, in this crucial dissymmetry between structure and its incarnations, between the virtual and the actual.

In this new transcendental philosophy, structure cannot answer the 'What?' question, the question of essence, substance or universality. The transcendental cannot anticipate ontogenesis; it must follow, accompany, or repeat it. This is what Deleuze calls the 'method of dramatisation'.[29] Drawing on Simondon, individuation provides us with operational answers to the crucial question of the 'How?'. How do we pass from implicate differences to their explication? From ideas to beings? Ideas alone are not the source of genesis. Rather, a new materialism needs to confront those spatio-temporal dynamisms without which structuralism would merely remain a thought of the determination of passive matter by active form. Deleuze does not cease stressing the specificity of the virtual ideas implicated in each domain of production or 'indi-different/ciation', as well as the repercussions of the dynamisms on their differential composition. In other words, the theory of individuation drawn from Simondon allows us to think the very distinction between the virtual and the actual as a processual or differential, rather than a merely unilateral, one. Indeed, following Simondon's suggestion that the very distinction between the *a priori* and the *a posteriori* is a product of individuating processes rather than their condition, we could argue that virtual and actual constitute retrojections of the process of individuation.

However, while Simondon's contribution remains linked in Deleuze to this idea of individuation as dramatisation, it is also affected by Deleuze's increasing turn away from any allegiance to structuralism. This move can be read in the juxtaposition of a plane of immanence or plane of composition (linked to what Éric Alliez has usefully characterised as Deleuze's turn to an 'onto-ethology')[30] to a plane of organisation, with the latter functioning as a more or less explicit critique of the concept of structure. As Deleuze and Guattari write in *A Thousand Plateaus*, 'Here, there are no longer any forms or developments of forms, nor are there subjects or the formation of subjects. There is no structure, any more than there is genesis' (TP 266). Despite this break with the problem of genesis, Simondon's theorisation of pre-individual singularities remains formative, as it were, in the crucial concept with which Deleuze and Guattari displace structure: haecceity. In a sense, it could be argued that *A Thousand Plateaus* 'absolutises' the very dimension of spatio-temporal dynamisms and singularities which in *Difference and Repetition* seemed to mediate or schematise the dissymmetrical relationship between virtual and actual. Spatio-temporal dynamisms were defined as 'agitations of space, excavations of time, pure syntheses of speeds, directions and rhythms' (DI 96; translation modified). A haecceity, in turn, is *'defined only by a latitude and a longitude*: in other words the sum total of the material elements belonging to it under given relations of movement and rest, speed and slowness (longitude); the sum total of the intensive affects it is capable of at a given power or degree of potential (latitude)' (TP 260).

This shift in the role of Simondon is evident in the manner that he appears in *A Thousand Plateaus*, alongside Husserl, as a thinker not of virtual ideas as such, but of *'vague and material* essences' characterised by a 'corporeality' that distinguishes them from 'intelligible, formal essentiality or a sensible, formed and perceived, thinghood'. It is this thinking of a non-individuated material-ideality, dramatised by *'event-affects'* and no longer a 'kind of intermediary between the thing and the concept' which characterises, according to Deleuze, Simondon's anti-hylemorphic thought. Most significantly, the concept of a natural-artificial 'machinic phylum' as 'matter in movement, in flux, in variation, matter as a conveyor of singularities and traits of expression' appears to collapse what to some extent appeared as 'levels' of internal difference in *Difference and Repetition* (virtuality/ individuation by spatio-temporal dynamisms/actuality) onto a single plane. This only serves to intensify, of course, an image of thought which Deleuze also derives from Simondon's patient and meticulous description of processes of 'natural' and 'artificial' ontogenesis (e.g., the 'dramatisation' of brick-making in *L'individuation*). According to this view, 'matter-flow can only be *followed*' – not deduced or anticipated. The thinker in this regard is compared to the conceptual persona of the artisan, who engages in 'intuition in action', and his practice to that of metallurgy, where 'operations are always astride the thresholds, so that an energetic materiality overspills the prepared matter, and a qualitative deformation or transformation overspills the form' (TP 407–10). From the dramatisation of ideas to the modulation of matter, Simondon's thinking of individuation as dramatisation remains a powerful intercessor in Deleuze's philosophy of becoming, but the ways in which that intercession is modulated are important clues to the discontinuities in Deleuze's own thought.

THE UNEQUAL

What happens when we turn from Simondon's inflection of Deleuze's philosophical trajectory to Deleuze's own intercession into debates over Simondon's legacy? Much of the more interesting recent uptake of Simondon's work – by Paolo Virno, Muriel Combes, Bernard Aspe and Isabelle Stengers, among others[31] – has focused on the political resonances in his work, especially those deriving from *L'individuation psychique et collective* (the second part of *L'individuation à la lumière des notions de forme et d'information*) which was only published in 1989. Rather than merely mining Simondon for a set of concepts with which to format the political, the most interesting repercussions of his thought in this regard can be found in the way that it becomes both a testing ground and point of divergence for different approaches to the political. At the core of any discussion of Simondon and politics lies the question of the status accorded to his concept of pre-individual being. Here there are (at least) three possible readings.

The first interprets the pre-individual as an unresolved charge, carried by the individual as a *potential*, linking this concept to those of human nature and living labour. The pre-individual would thus name a non-reflexive, naturalisable capacity, namely the linguistic capacity to produce new statements. The circumstances of contemporary capitalism, and of the subjectivity that underlies it, would be such as to make this pre-individual potential surface, and politics could thus be considered as the insurrection of this capacity against the measures of domination imposed by capital and its mechanisms of control. A position of this sort can be encountered in Paolo Virno's very stimulating use of Simondon.[32]

A second reading sees the pre-individual as caught up in a twofold transindividual (or social) relation which concerns, on the one hand, an individual and what in it is more than itself, and, on the other, an individual and another by the means of their sub-representational emotional or affective comportment – in other words their unresolved pre-individual charge. Muriel Combes gives an apt name to this relation: the intimacy of the common. These two orientations in the political reading of Simondon, which one could respectively call *naturalist* and *relational*, share a certain view of the latency of the political (or of politics), which contrasts interestingly with Deleuze's reading of Simondon.

Deleuze turns to Simondon in one of the key moments of *Difference and Repetition*, at the beginning of Chapter 5. This text of pure metaphysics is nevertheless rich with indications for a political ontology. It begins by distinguishing between difference and diversity. The diverse is what is given, the phenomenon, but every 'phenomenon refers back to an inequality which conditions it', 'to a difference which is its sufficient reason'. This 'irreducible inequality', this transcendental injustice, is linked by Deleuze to the concept of a signal-sign system, in which the phenomenon is defined as a sign which 'fulgurates' between disparate and incommensurable series, giving rise to an *event of communication* that both synthesises and veils the heterogeneity from whence it emerges. Deleuze concludes as follows: 'The reason of the sensible, the condition of what appears, is not space and time, but the Unequal in itself, *disparation* such as it is comprehended and determined by difference in intensity, in intensity as difference' (DR 222–3). A politics of difference that was not merely to be understood as the conjunction of different particularities, which is to say as a politics of the diverse, would need to begin from here. By tracing the boundary-line between potential and virtual, Deleuze casts the pre-individual as a transcendental field populated by disparate singularities and series, rather than as reserve of creativity that could *express itself* in a given political occasion. This is one of the ways, of course, in which we could understand Deleuze's description of his own philosophy in terms of a vitalism of signs and events.

For Deleuze, the pre-individual is identified neither with human nature (in its neotenic or innate versions), nor with a 'common'. In both cases, that would involve a pre-emptive 'equalisation' of the Unequal, it would mean advocating a speculative optimism which would look at the pre-individual as the *pre-individual-of-humanity*, the latency of a collective life which is always already possible, and precisely not as something that leads us towards politics by its very 'inhuman', unconscious and properly unliveable aspect – what Deleuze refers to in *Essays Critical and Clinical* as that 'which overflows any liveable or lived matter . . . a passage of Life that traverses the liveable or the lived' (ECC 1). It is here that the concept of metastability, which we dealt with above, comes to the fore. As Deleuze says: 'what essentially defines a metastable system is the existence of a "disparation", the existence of at least of two orders of magnitude, two disparate levels of reality, between which there is not yet any interactive communication'. Could one ever qualify this disparate metastability, following the likes of Antonio Negri, as 'common'? Following the indications provided by Deleuze in *Difference and Repetition*, we could thus extrapolate from Simondon a conception of politics as the invention of a communication between initially incompossible series; the invention of a common that is not given in advance and which emerges on an ontological background of inequality.

ETHICS, TECHNICS, CAPITALISM

But this image of an inventive and aleatory politics of the unequal jars with what Deleuze calls Simondon's 'moral vision of the world', according to which 'the pre-individual, a "source of future metastable states", must remain associated with the individual'. For Deleuze, who will only really confront the moment of transindividuality with Guattari, some years after his review of 1966 and his use of Simondon in *Difference and Repetition* and *The Logic of Sense*, there is a sense in which this ethical moment risks a reintroduction of the 'form of the Self which [Simondon] had averted with his theory of disparity' (DI 89). Tellingly, and despite the formidable speculative efforts he expends in the dissolution of the Self, Deleuze does risk in *Difference and Repetition* a return to a *theoretical* ethics of the philosopher as 'pure individual' which is not so distant from Simondon's analogous concern with the exalted individuality of the inventor able to do justice, through his machines, to his pre-individual charge. It is in this vein that Deleuze writes of 'the universal concrete individuality of the thinker or the system of the dissolved self' (DR 259).[33] Arguably, it is only in the *Capitalism and Schizophrenia* volumes that Deleuze, with Guattari, manages to break with the fantasy of a purely philosophical ethics.

Though a sustained contrast between Simondon's desire for a 'technical culture' and Deleuze and Guattari's 'schizoanalysis' is certainly a worthwhile task, it is one that exceeds the limits of this intervention. By way of conclusion then, I simply wish to touch on the pertinence of Deleuze's doubts vis-à-vis Simondon's ethical preoccupation. This is a preoccupation that is most evident not so much in the texts on individuation but in the meticulous analyses of the various 'modes of existence' of technical objects, which is to say in the book where Simondon wrestles with the social and scientific legacy of cybernetic thought, *Du mode d'existence des objets techniques*. Here, Simondon displays what Combes has depicted as a normative thinking of becoming: the nihilistic misuse of technology is founded for him on a fetishism of utility which alienates the concrete individuality of technical objects, and thereby alienates men themselves. In the midst of the Cold War, Simondon's technical ethics of invention is designed as a way to bypass the conjunction of productivism and antagonism, as well as the critique of technology qua instrumental rationality. But how are we to move beyond (class) war and (meaningless) work? And can we find in the very genesis of technical objects the resources to generate a new ethics of interaction beyond the tripartite separation of man, nature and technics?

In *Du mode*, Simondon is very adamant that only a certain use of technics can properly configure the metabolic interaction between man and nature, inasmuch as the technical object is

> a stable mix of the human and the natural, it contains something human and something natural; it gives its human content a structure similar to that of natural objects, and allows the insertion in the world of causes and natural effects of this human reality. . . . A convertibility of the human into the natural and the natural into the human is instituted through the technical schematism.[34]

The technical schematism is explicitly aimed at replacing work in this metabolic function. Whereas the discussion of brick-making in *L'individuation* suggests the existence of a foreclosed knowledge in manual labour as 'in-formation', *Du mode* depicts work itself as the principal culprit of the crisis that a technical culture needs to remedy. It is only in the absence of technical objects that man needs to work and, as a 'bearer of tools', must himself accomplish a mediation between the species and nature. The prosthetic invention of a human-natural technical object frees man from the servile and dehumanising predicament of having to 'coincide with a reality that is not human'.[35]

This is why Simondon argues that there is a 'pre-capitalist alienation which is essential to work qua work'.[36] This alienation does not just take place at the individual level: the 'social community of work', as an 'interindividual relation', is itself alienating according to Simondon because it only takes place among beings who are individuated as 'somato-psychic men', that is, reduced to their labours. The true transindividual collectivity develops instead when 'human beings communicate through their inventions'.[37] The paradox here is that technical thinking is superior to work as a field of communication and a ground of collectivity because 'human nature' – 'what remains original and anterior even to constituted humanity within man himself'[38] – is carried and communicated better by technical objects than it is by the face-to-face social interactions of labouring men and women. But this transindividual form of collectivity, whereby men communicate with one another, with nature, and with what is in them more than themselves (pre-individual 'human nature') is instrumentalised under the conditions of modern productivism, which is dominated by what Simondon calls 'the morality of output'. An authentic, non-alienated form of social interaction would thus demand the integration of technical thought and social life, beyond work.

Simondon's is a deeply normative, even moral understanding of the interactions between men and technical objects (or machines), and a fortiori between men and men (with technical objects as intercessors and bearers of pre-individual 'human nature'). But is it possible to base the dream of an alternative 'technical culture' on a transindividual collectivity of inventors, interacting through technical objects just as technical objects and machines communicate with each other via men?[39] One of Simondon's gambits is that we can only terminate our alienation by terminating the servile alienation of machines themselves (a condition which is symptomatically signalled by our Asimovian nightmares of robot revolts) and surpassing the separation between work and invention (or between manual and intellectual labour). But this depends on thinking that – to the degree that 'work and capital lag behind the technical individual [which] does not belong to the same period as the work that activates it and the capital that frames it'[40] – it is by building collectivity and interaction from the fulcrum of invention that an instrumental, anti-technical culture can be surpassed and the antagonism between capital and labour circumvented.

It is here that Deleuze and Guattari's attempt to philosophise capitalism provides a potent antidote to the fantasy of an ethical escape out of a society characterised in terms of utilitarian productivism, and a rupture of the antagonistic circle of capital and labour. Maintaining the imperative of immanence and the refusal of holism – as well as maintaining what exceeds individuality as the proper concern of politics – means recognising that ethics alone cannot transcend, shape or contain capitalism considered in terms of something that arises out of 'the encounter of two sorts of flows: the decoded flows of production in the form of money-capital, and the decoded flows of labour in the form of the "free worker". Hence, unlike previous social machines, the capitalist machine is incapable of providing a code that will apply to the whole of the social field' (AO 33). A technical culture anchored in the figure of the 'technical individual' as the one who in a sense masters and possesses his own pre-individuality perhaps still belongs too much to the images of mastery and pacification that accompanied the emergence of cybernetics; its vision of ethics is one in which the passage of human nature through machinic prostheses will defuse the tendency towards molar (class) antagonisms. But is the juxtaposition of the inventor and the schizo, of Simondon's attempt to escape the twin ideologies of productivism (capitalism and socialism), on the one hand, and Deleuze and Guattari's penchant for intensifying capitalism's deterritorialising drives and 'reaching the furthest limits of the decomposition of the socius', on the other, a sign of an unbridgeable disparity? Leaving aside the clear differends in terms of ideological co-ordinates, I think it remains possible to argue, in line with Antonio Negri's methodological suggestion that a thinker's ethico-political outlook is best found in their metaphysics, that Deleuze and Guattari (like in other ways Virno, or Stengers) tapped into those ontological aspects of Simondon's thought – the disparate, the unequal, the modulation of matter – which push up against a tendency towards social holism and make possible a vision of the group or the transindividual as – to quote Michel Foucault's introduction to the *Anti-Oedipus* – 'a constant generator of de-individualisation' (AO xiv).

                    Goldsmiths College, University of London

Notes

1. We could plausibly add Hume to generate a quartet dominated by the concept of a transcendental or superior empiricism.
2. Michael Hardt, *Deleuze: A Philosophical Apprenticeship* (Minneapolis: Minnesota University Press, 1993).
3. David Toews, 'The New Tarde', *Theory, Culture & Society* 20:5 (2003), pp. 81–98.
4. In the case of Simondon, it is worth noting that Deleuze, though he mentions *Du mode d'existence des objets techniques* (Paris: Aubier, 1989), only cites *L'individuation et sa génèse physico-biologique*, the first part of Simondon's dissertation, published in 1964. The second part, *L'individuation psychique et collective*, was only published, at the insistence of François Laruelle, in 1989. They have recently been

brought back together into a single volume, *L'individuation à la lumière des notions de forme et d'information* (Grenoble: Millon, 2005).

5. Alberto Toscano, *The Theatre of Production: Philosophy and Individuation Between Kant and Deleuze* (Basingstoke: Palgrave, 2006).

6. 'Mediators', in N 121–34.

7. The discussion of Husserl and Simondon was first sketched out, with reference to metallurgy, in Deleuze's seminar of 27 February 1979, available at www.webdeleuze.com.

8. Francois Cusset, 'Cybernétique et 'théorie française': faux alliés, vrais ennemis', *multitudes* 22 (2005), pp. 223–31. Cusset was responding to Lafontaine's article 'Les racines américaines de la French Theory', *Esprit*, January 2005 (now translated as 'The Cybernetic Matrix of "French Theory"' *Theory, Culture & Society* 24: 5, 2007), as well as her book, *L'Empire cybernétique. Des machines à penser à la pensée machine* (Paris: Seuil, 2005).

9. Cusset, *L'Empire cybernétique*, p. 15.

10. Cusset, *L'Empire cybernétique*, p. 47.

11. AO 283–96; Toscano, *The Theatre of Production*, Chapter 6, Section 4.

12. Pascal Chabot, *La Philosophie de Simondon* (Paris: Vrin, 2003), p. 54.

13. Jean-Pierre Dupuy, *Aux origines des sciences cognitives* (Paris: La Découverte, 1999), p. 130. See also Chabot, *La Philosophie de Simondon*, p. 55. As Xavier Guchet has noted, Simondon had already drafted two unpublished articles on 'The Epistemology of Cybernetics' and 'Cybernetics and Philosophy' in the mid-50s which can justifiably be regarded as the matrix for the elaboration of his own thought. See Xavier Guchet, 'Simondon, la cybernétique et les sciences humaines. Genèse de l'ontologie simondonienne dans deux manuscrits sur la cybèrnetique', in M. Carbone, L. Lawlor and R. Barbaras (eds), *Chiasmi International 7: Life and Individuation* (Milan: Mimesis, 2005).

14. Toscano, *The Theatre of Production*, Introduction and Chapter 5.

15. Dupuy will actually argue that rather than being seen as a critic of cybernetic holism, Simondon should be lauded for realising that cybernetics is *not* holist, and that its models are artificial, that 'cybernetic totalities are always artificial', and therefore freed from the constraints of classical teleology. Dupuy, *Aux origines des sciences cognitives*, pp. 137–8.

16. See Toscano, *The Theatre of Production*, Chapter 5.

17. See Guchet, 'Simondon, la cybernétique et les sciences humaines'.

18. Simondon, *L'individuation*, pp. 559–66.

19. Simondon, *L'individuation*, pp. 32 and 35.

20. Dupuy, *Aux origines des sciences cognitives*, p. 130.

21. See also Alberto Toscano, 'La disparation. Politique et sujet chez Simondon', *multitudes* 18 (2004), pp. 73–82.

22. For Simondon's own account of the problem, as related to the distinction between the living and machines, as well as to the philosophy of Bergson, see *Du mode*, p. 144.
23. Simondon does nevertheless seek to retain the concept of analogy and to give it an ontological valence in terms of the operations of transduction. In this respect, he remains at odds with Deleuze's insistent condemnation of analogy and exaltation of univocity as the only admissible ontological stance.
24. The concept of 'milieu', which Deleuze uses in several of his books, could also be sourced to Simondon.
25. Muriel Combes, *Simondon. Individu et collectivité* (Paris: PUF, 1999), p. 47.
26. See Toscano, *The Theatre of Production*, Chapter 5.
27. DI 174.
28. LS 344.
29. Deleuze, 'The Method of Dramatisation' (DI 94–116).
30. Éric Alliez, *The Signature of the World, or, What is Deleuze and Guattari's Philosophy?*, trans. Eliot Ross Albert and Alberto Toscano (London: Continuum, 2004), pp. 53–84.
31. See the special section of *multitudes* 18 (2004), entitled 'Politiques de l'individuation: Penser avec Simondon'.
32. Virno has commented on Simondon in *multitudes* and in his introduction to the Italian translation of *L'individuation psychique et collective*. In English, see Virno's *A Grammar of the Multitude* (New York: Semiotext(e), 2002), pp. 78–80.
33. DR 259.
34. Simondon, *Du mode*, p. 245. Note the difference between this metabolic view of man and nature and the direct equation of Nature and Production in *Anti-Oedipus*.
35. Simondon, *Du mode*, p. 242.
36. Simondon, *Du mode*, p. 248.
37. Simondon, *Du mode*, p. 247.
38. Simondon, *Du mode*, p. 248.
39. Simondon, *Du mode*, p. 12.
40. Simondon, *Du mode*, p. 119.

Bibliography

Alexandrian, Sarane. *Histoire de la philosophie occulte*. Paris: Seghers, 1983.

Alliez, Éric. *The Signature of the World, or, What is Deleuze and Guattari's Philosophy?* Trans. Eliot Ross Albert and Alberto Toscano. London: Continuum, 2004.

Alliez, Éric, and Bonne, Jean-Claude. *La Pensée-Matisse. Portrait de l'artiste en hyperfauve*. Paris: Le Passage, 2005.

Althusser, Louis. *For Marx*. Trans. Ben Brewster. London: New Left Books, 1969.

——. 'Ideology and Ideological State Apparatuses (Notes Toward an Investigation)'. In *Lenin and Philosophy*. Trans. Ben Brewster. London: New Left Books, 1971.

Althusser, Louis, and Balibar, Etienne. *Reading Capital*. Trans. Ben Brewster. New York: Pantheon Books, 1970.

Alunni, Charles. 'Continental Genealogies. Mathematical Confrontations in Albert Lautman and Gaston Bachelard'. In *Virtual Mathematics: The Logic of Difference*. Ed. Simon Duffy. Manchester: Clinamen Press, 2006.

Antliff, Mark. *Inventing Bergson: Cultural Politics and the Parisian Avant-garde*. Princeton, NJ: Princeton University Press, 1993.

Aquinas. *Selected Philosophical Writings*. Trans. Timothy McDermott. Oxford: Oxford University Press, 1993.

——. *Summa Theologiae: A Concise Translation*. Ed. Timothy McDermott. Westminster, MD: Christian Classics, 1989.

Aristotle. 'Categoriae'. In *The Basic Works of Aristotle*. Trans. E. M. Edghill. Ed. R. McKeon. New York: Random House, 1941, 3–37.

——. *Metaphysics*, 2 vols. Trans. Hugh Tredennick. Cambridge, MA: Loeb Classics, 1933–35.

——. *Posterior Analytics*. Trans. Jonathan Barnes. Oxford: Clarendon Press, 1975.

Arnaud, Alain. *Pierre Klossowski*. Paris: Seuil, 1990.

Atlas, Samuel. *From Critical to Speculative Idealism: The Philosophy of Solomon Maimon*. The Hague: Nijhoff, 1964

Badiou, Alain. *Deleuze: The Clamour of Being*. Trans. Louise Burchill. Minneapolis: University of Minnesota Press, 2000.

Bains, Paul. *The Primacy of Semiosis: An Ontology of Relations*. Toronto: University of Toronto Press, 2006.
——. 'Subjectless Subjectivities'. In *A Shock to Thought: Expression after Deleuze and Guattari*. Ed. Brian Massumi. London and New York: Routledge, 2002, 101–16.
Balke, Friedrich. 'Eine frühe Soziologie der Differenz: Gabriel Tarde'. In *Eigentlich könnte alles auch anders sein*. Eds P. Zimmermann and N. Binczek. Cologne: Walther König, 1998.
Barot, Emmanuel. 'L'objectivité mathématique selon Albert Lautman: entre Idées dialectiques et réalité physique'. *Cahiers François Viète* 6, 2003, 3–27.
Bataille, Georges. *L'expérience intérieure*. In *Oeuvres completes*, vol. 5. Paris: Gallimard, 1973.
Baugh, Bruce. 'Death and Temporality in Deleuze and Derrida'. *Angelaki* 5:2, August 2000, 73–83.
Beach, Edward Allen. *The Potencies of God(s): Schelling's Philosophy of Mythology*. Albany: SUNY, 1994.
Beaulieu, Alain. 'Gilles Deleuze et les Stoïciens'. In *Gilles Deleuze. Héritage philosophique*, Ed. Alain Beaulieu. Paris: PUF, 2005, 45–72.
——. *Gilles Deleuze et la phenomenology*. Mons/Paris, Sils Maria/Vrin, 2004.
Beck, Lewis White. 'A Prussian Hume and a Scottish Kant'. In *Essays on Kant and Hume*. London: New Haven Press, 1978.
Beiser, Frederick. *The Fate of Reason: German Philosophy from Kant to Fichte*. Cambridge, MA: Harvard University Press, 1987.
——. *German Idealism: The Struggle against Subjectivism, 1781–1801*. Cambridge, MA: Harvard University Press, 1987.
——. 'Maimon and Fichte'. In *Salomon Maimon: Rational Dogmatist, Empirical Skeptic – Critical Assessments*. Ed. Gideon Freudenthal. Dordrecht: Kluwer Academic Publishers, 2003.
Benoist, Alain de. *Vu de droite: anthologie critique des idées contemporaines*. Paris: Copernic, 1977.
Bergen, Véronique. *L' ontologie de Gilles Deleuze*. Paris: L'Harmattan, 2001.
Bergler, Edmund. *The Basic Neurosis: Oral Regression and Psychic Masochism*. New York: Grune and Stratton, 1949.
Bergman, Samuel. *The Philosophy of Solomon Maimon*. Trans. Noah J. Jacobs. Jerusalem: Magnes Press, 1967.
Bergson, Henri. *Durée et simultanéité: a propos de la théorie d'Einstein. Duration and Simultaneity: With Reference to Einstein's Theory*. Trans. Leon Jacobson. Indianapolis: Bobbs-Merrill, 1965 [1922].
——. *Essai sur les données immédiates de la conscience. Time and Free Will: An Essay on the Immediate Data of Consciousness*. Trans. F. L. Pogson. London: George Allen and Unwin, 1910 [1889].

——. *La pensée et le mouvant: Essais et conférences.* In *The Creative Mind.* Trans. M. L. Andison. New York: Philosophical Library, 1946 [1934].

——. *L'énergie spirituelle: Essais et conférences. Mind-Energy: Lectures and Essays.* Trans. H. Wildon Carr. London: Macmillan, 1920 [1919].

——. *Les deux sources de la morale et de la religion. The Two Sources of Morality and Religion.* Trans. R. Ashley Audra and Cloudesley. Brereton, Westport: Greenwood Press, 1963 [1932].

——. Letter to W. R. Boyce Gibson. 9 February 1911. Gibson Papers, University of Melbourne Archives, Melbourne.

——. *L'évolution créatrice. Creative Evolution.* Trans. Arthur Mitchell. New York: Random House, 1944 [1907].

——. 'L'idée de lieu chez Aristote'. Trans. Robert Mosse Bastide. In *Mélanges.* Ed. André Robinet. Paris: Presses Universitaires de France, 1972, 1–56.

——. 'Life and consciousness'. In *Mind-Energy.* Trans. H. Wildon Carr. London: Macmillan, 1920 [1903].

——. *Matière et mémoire: essai sur la relation du corps à l'esprit. Matter and Memory.* Trans. W. S. Palmer and N. M. Paul. New York: Zone Books, 1991 [1896].

——. *Mélanges.* Ed. André Robinet. Paris: Presses Universitaires de France, 1972.

——. *Oeuvres.* Ed. André Robinet. Paris: Presses Universitaires de France, 1959.

Bernays, Paul. 'Review of: Essai sur L'Unite des Sciences Mathematiques dans Leur Developpement Actuel. Albert Lautman'. *Journal of Symbolic Logic* 5:1, 1940, 22.

Blay, Michel. *Reasoning with the Infinite: From the Closed World to the Mathematical Universe.* Chicago: University of Chicago, 1998.

Boehm, Rudolf. 'Les ambiguïtés du concept husserlien d'"immanence" et de "transcendence"'. *Revue philosophique de la France et de l'étranger* 84, 1959, 481–526.

Bogue, Ronald. *Deleuze on Music, Painting, and the Arts.* New York: Routledge, 2003.

Borch, Christian. 'Urban Imitations: Tarde's Sociology Revisited'. *Theory, Culture & Society* 22:3, 2005.

Boundas, Constantin V. 'Between Deleuze and Derrida'. *Symposium: Canadian Journal of Continental Philosophy* 9:1, 2005, 99–114

——. 'Foreclosure of the Other: From Sartre to Deleuze'. *The Journal of the British Society for Phenomenology* 24:1, 1993, 32–43.

——. 'The Ethics of Counteractualisation'. *Concepts*, hors série 2, 2003, 170–99.

Boyer, Carl B. *The History of the Calculus and its Conceptual Development.* New York: Dover, 1949.

Bransen, Jan. *The Antinomy of Thought: Maimonian Scepticism and the Relation between Thoughts and Objects.* Dordrecht: Kluwer Academic Publishers, 1991.

Brunschvicg, Léon. *Les étapes de la philosophie mathématique.* Paris: A. Blanchard, 1993 [1912].

Buzaglo, Meir. *Solomon Maimon: Monism, Skepticism, and Mathematics.* Pittsburgh: University of Pittsburgh Press, 2002.

Cavaillès, Jean, and Albert Lautman. 'La pensée mathématique'. *Bulletin de la Société Française de Philosophie* 40:1, 1947, 1–39.

Chabot, Pascal. *La philosophie de Simondon.* Paris: Vrin, 2003.

Chacornac, Paul. *Eliphas Lévi: rénovateur de l'occultisme en France.* Paris: Chacornac, 1926.

Châtelet, Gilles. 'Interlacing the Singularity, the Diagram and the Metaphor'. Trans. Simon Duffy. In *Virtual Mathematics: The Logic of Difference.* Ed. Simon Duffy. Manchester: Clinamen Press, 2006.

Chevalley, Catherine. 'Albert Lautman et le souci logique'. *Revue d'Histoire des Sciences* 40:1, 1987, 49–77.

Cloots, André, and Robinson, Keith (eds). *Deleuze, Whitehead and the Transformation of Metaphysics.* Brussels: Koninklijke Vlaamse Academie van Belgie voor Wetenschappen en Kunsten, 2005.

Cohen, Paul. *Set Theory and the Continuum Hypothesis.* New York: W. A. Benjamin, 1966.

Colwell, C. 'Deleuze and Foucault: Series, Event, Genealogy'. *Theory and Event* 1:2, 1997.

Combes, Muriel. *Simondon. Individu et collectivité.* Paris: PUF, 1999.

Conway, Daniel W. 'Tumbling Dice: Gilles Deleuze and the Economy of Répétition'. *Symploke* 6:1, 1998: 7–25.

Cooke, Alexander. 'Eternal Return and the Problem of the Constitution of Identity'. *Journal of Nietzsche Studies* June 2005, 16–34.

Couturat, Louis. 'On Leibniz's Metaphysics'. In *Leibniz: A Collection of Critical Essays.* Ed. Harry G. Frankfurt. Garden City, NY: Anchor Books, 1972.

Critchley, Simon. *Continental Philosophy: A Very Short Introduction.* Oxford: Oxford University Press, 2001.

Cusset, François. 'Cybernétique et 'théorie française': faux alliés, vrais ennemis'. *Multitudes* 22, 2005, 223–31.

Daniel, Stephen H. (ed.). *Current Continental Theory and Modern Philosophy.* Evanston, IL: Northwestern University Press, 2005.

D'Arcy, Philippe. *Wronski: philosophie de la creation. Présentation, choix de textes.* Paris: Seghers, 1970.

De Beistegui, Miguel. *Truth and Genesis: Philosophy as Differential Ontology.* Bloomington: Indiana University Press, 2004.

De Biran, Maine. *Exposition de la doctrine philosophique de Leibniz.* In *Oevres.* XI–1. Paris: Vrin, 1990.

De Saussure, Ferdinand. *Course in General Linguistics*. Trans. Roy Harris. London: Duckworth, 1983.

Dedron, Pierre, and Itard, Jean. *Mathematics and Mathematicians* (2 vols). Trans. J. V. Field. London: Transworld, 1974.

DeLanda, Manuel. *Intensive Science and Virtual Philosophy*. London: Continuum, 2002.

Deledalle, Gérard, and Huisman, Dennis (eds). *Les philosophes français d'aujourd'hui par eux-mêmes*. Paris: CDU, 1959.

Deleuze, Gilles. 'A quoi reconnait-on le structuralisme?' In *Histoire de la philosophie tome 8: Le XXe Siecle*. Ed. François Châtelet. Paris: Hachette, 1972. 'How Do we Recognise Structuralism?' Trans. Melissa McMahon and Charles Stivale. In Charles Stivale. *The Two-Fold Thought of Deleuze and Guattari: Intersections and Animations*. New York and London: Guilford Press, 1998.

——. 'Bergson 1859–1941'. In *Les philosophes célèbres*. Ed. Maurice Merleau-Ponty. Paris: Editions d'Art Lucien Mazenod, 1956, 292–9.

——. *Le Bergsonisme*. Paris: Presses Universitaires de France, 1966. *Bergsonism*. Trans. Hugh Tomlinson and Barbara Habberjam. New York: Zone Books, 1988.

——. 'Bergson's Conception of Difference'. Trans. Melissa McMahon. In *The New Bergson*. Ed. John Mullarkey. Manchester: Manchester University Press, 1999, 42–65.

——. *Cinema 1: The Movement Image*. Trans. Hugh Tomlinson and Barbara Habberjam. Minneapolis: University of Minnesota Press, 1989.

——. *Cinema 2: The Time Image*. Trans. Hugh Tomlinson and Robert Galeta. Minneapolis: University of Minnesota Press, 1989.

——. 'Coldness and Cruelty'. In *Masochism*. Trans. Charles Stivale. New York: Zone Books, 1989.

——. *Deux regimes de fou*. Paris: Editions de Minuit, 2003. *Two Regimes of Madness and Other Texts*. Trans. Michael Taormina. New York: Semiotext(e), 2006.

——. *Différence et répétition*. Paris: Presses Universitaires de France, 1968. *Difference and Repetition*. Trans. Paul Patton. New York: Columbia University Press, 1994.

——. *Empiricisme et subjectivité*. Paris: PUF, 1953. *Empiricism and Subjectivity*. Trans. Constantin Boundas. New York: Columbia University Press, 1991.

——. *Essays Critical and Clinical*. Trans. Daniel W. Smith and Michael A. Greco. Preface by Daniel W. Smith. Minneapolis: University of Minnesota Press, 1997.

——. *Foucault*. Paris: Minuit, 1986. *Foucault*. Trans. Sean Hand. Minneapolis: University of Minnesota Press, 1988.

——. *Francis Bacon: logique de la sensation* (2 vols). Paris: Éditions de la difference, 1981. *Francis Bacon: The Logic of Sensation*. Translation of the first volume by Daniel W. Smith. London: Continuum Press, 2003.

——. 'Hume'. In *Histoire de la philosophie 4 – les lumières: le XVIIIe siècle.* In Ed. François Châtelet Paris: Librairie Hachette, 1972.

——. *Kant's Critical Philosophy.* Trans. Hugh Tomlinson and Barbara Habberjam. London: Althone Press, 1983.

——. Lectures/Seminars. Available online at http://www.webdeleuze.com/php/sommaire.html

——. 'Lettre-préface de Gilles Deleuze'. In Jean-Clet Martin, *Variations: La Philosophie de Gilles Deleuze.* Paris: Payot, 1993.

——. 'Le "Je me souviens" de Gilles Deleuze'. *Nouvel Observateur* 1619, 1995, 50–1.

——. *Le pli: Leibniz et le baroque.* Paris: Editions de Minuit, 1988. *The Fold: Leibniz and the Baroque.* Trans. Tom Conley. Minneapolis: University of Minnesota Press, 1992.

——. 'L'idée de genèse dans l'esthétique de Kant'. *Revue d'Esthétique* 16:2, 1962–3, 113–36. 'The Idea of Genesis in Kant's Aesthetics'. Trans. Daniel W. Smith. In *Angelaki: Journal of the Theoretical Humanities* 5:3, December 2000, 57–70.

——. *L'ile déserte et autres textes.* Paris: Editions de Minuit, 2002. Ed. David Lapoujade. *Desert Islands and Other Texts.* Trans. Michael Taormina. New York: Semiotext(e), 2004.

——. 'L'immanence: une vie . . .', in *Philosophie* no. 47, September 1995, special issue on Deleuze, pp. 3–7. *Pure Immanence: Essays on a life.* Trans. Anne Boymen. Ed. John Rajchman. New York: Zone Books, 2001.

——. *Logique du sens.* Paris: Editions du Minuit, 1969. *The Logic of Sense.* Trans. Mark Lester and Charles Stivale. New York: Columbia University Press, 1990.

——. *Masochism.* Trans. Jean McNeil. New York: Zone Books, 1989.

——. 'Mathèse, science et la philosophie'. In Jean Malfatti de Montereggio, *La Mathèse, ou anarchie et hiérarchie de la science.* Paris: Griffon d'Or, 1946. 'Mathesis, Science and Philosophy'. Trans. Robin Mackay. In *Collapse* 3, 2007.

——. *Negotiations.* Trans. Martin Joughin. New York: Columbia University Press, 1995.

——. *Nietzsche et la philosophie.* Paris: Presses Universitaires de France, 1965. *Nietzsche and Philosophy.* Trans. Hugh Tomlinson. New York: Columbia University Press, 1983.

——. Online Seminars. Transcribed by Richard Pinhas. http://www.web deleuze.fr/sommaire

——. *Périclès et Verdi: la philosophie de François Châtelet.* Paris: Les Editions de Minuit, 1988.

——. '"A Philosophical Concept . . ."'. Trans. Julien Deleuze. In *Who Comes After the Subject?* Ed. Eduardo Cadava. New York: Routledge, 1991.

——. *Proust and Signs.* Trans. Richard Howard. Minneapolis: University of Minnesota Press, 2000.

——. 'Review of *Logique et existence* by Jean Hyppolite'. In *Revue philosophique de la France et de l'étranger* 94, 1954, 457–60.

——. *Spinoza et le problème de l'expression.* Paris: Minuit, 1968. *Expressionism in Philosophy: Spinoza.* Trans. Martin Joughin. New York: Zone Books, 1990.

——. *Spinoza: Practical Philosophy.* Trans. Robert Hurley. San Francisco: City Lights Books, 1988.

Deleuze, Gilles, and Guattari, Félix. *Kafka: Towards a Minor Literature.* Trans. Dana Polan. Minneapolis: University of Minnesota Press, 1986.

——. *L'Anti-Oedipe.* Paris: Les Editions de Minuit, 1972. *Anti-Oedipus: Capitalism and Schizophrenia.* Trans. Robert Hurley, Mark Seem and Helen Lane. New York: Viking Press, 1977.

——. 'Mai '68 n'a pas eu lieu'. *Les nouvelles*, 9 May 1984, 233–4.

——. *Mille plateaux.* Paris: Les Editions de Minuit, 1980. *A Thousand Plateaus: Capitalism and Schizophrenia.* Trans. Brian Massumi. Minneapolis: University of Minnesota Press, 1987.

——. *Qu'est-ce que la philosophie?* Paris: Editions de Minuit, 1991. *What is Philosophy?* Trans. Hugh Tomlinson and Graham Burchell. New York: Columbia University Press, 1994.

——. *Politique et psychanalyse* Paris: Alençon, 1977.

Deleuze, Gilles, and Parnet, Claire. *Dialogues.* Trans. Hugh Tomlinson and Barbara Habberjam. London: Althone Press, 1987 [1977].

Descombes, Vincent. *Modern French Philosophy.* Trans. J. Harding and L. Scott-Fox. Cambridge: Cambridge University Press, 1980.

Dickstein, S. *Katalog Dzieł Rękopisow Hoene-Wronskiego* [Catalogue des oeuvres imprimées et manuscrites de Hoëne Wronski]. Cracow: Nakładem Akademii Umiejetnośki, 1896.

Duffy, Simon. 'Deleuze and Mathematics'. In *Virtual Mathematics: The Logic of Difference.* Ed. Simon Duffy. Manchester: Clinamen Press, 2006.

——. *The Logic of Expression: Quality, Quantity and Intensity in Spinoza, Hegel and Deleuze.* Aldershot: Ashgate, 2006.

——. 'The Mathematics of Deleuze's Differential Logic and Metaphysics'. In *Virtual Mathematics: The Logic of Difference.* Ed. Simon Duffy. Manchester: Clinamen Press, 2006.

——. 'Schizo-Math: The Logic of Different/ciation and the Philosophy of difference'. *Angelaki* 9:3, 2004, 199–215.

Dumoncel, Jean-Claude. *La pendule du docteur Deleuze: une Introduction à l'anti-oedipe.* Paris: Cahiers de l'Unebévue, 1999.

Duns Scotus, J. *Philosophical Writings.* Trans. Allan Wolter. Indianapolis and Cambridge: Hackett Publishing Company, 1987.

——. 'Six Questions on Individuation from His *Ordinatio*, II. d. 3, part 1, qq. 1–6'. In *Five Texts on the Mediaeval Problem of Universals.* Ed.

and trans. V. Spade. Indianapolis: Hackett Publishers, 1994, 57–113.

Dupuy, Jean-Pierre. *Aux origins des sciences cognitives.* Paris: La Découverte, 1999.

Durkheim, Émile. *Les règles de la méthode sociologique.* Paris: PUF, 1973 [1895]. *The Rules of Sociological Method.* Trans. W. D. Halls. London: Macmillan, 1982.

Durutte, Camille. *Esthétique musicale. Technie ou lois générales du système Harmonique.* Paris: Mallet-Bachelier, 1855.

——. *Résumé élémentaire de la Technie harmonique, et complement de cette Technie, suivi de l'exposé de la loi de l'Enchainement dans la Mélodie, dans l'Harmonie et dans leurs concours.* Paris: Gauthier-Villars, 1876.

Echols, W. H. 'Wronski's Expansion'. *Bulletin of the New York Mathematical Society* vol. 2, 1893.

Erdmann, Johann Eduard. *A History of Philosophy*, 3 vols. Trans. W.S. Hough. London: George Allen & Unwin, 1890 [1878].

Ferreirós, José. 'The Crisis in the Foundations of Mathematics'. In *The Princeton Companion to Mathematics.* Ed. Timothy Gowers, June Barrow-Green and Imre Leader. Princeton: Princeton University Press, 2008.

Foucault, Michel. *Discipline and Punish.* Trans. Alan Sheridan. New York: Pantheon, 1978.

——. 'La Prose d'Actéon'. *La Nouvelle Revue Française.* March 1964.

——. 'Theatricum Philosophicum'. *Aesthetics, Method, and Epistemology.* Trans. Robert Hurley. New York: New Press, 1999.

——. *The Order of Things: An Archaeology of the Human Sciences.* New York: Vintage Books, 1994.

Freud, Sigmund. *The Standard Edition of the Complete Psychological Works of Sigmund Freud.* Ed. James Strachey. London: Hogarth, 1961.

Freudenthal, Gideon. *Salomon Maimon: Rational Dogmatist, Empirical Skeptic – Critical Assessments.* Dordrecht: Kluwer Academic Publishers, 2003.

Gernet, Louis. *The Anthropology of Ancient Greece.* Baltimore: Johns Hopkins University Press, 1981.

Gex, Maurice. 'La Psycho-biologie de Raymond Ruyer'. *L'age nouveau* 105, 1959, 102–9.

Ghyka, Matila. *Essai sur le rhythme*, Paris: Gallimard, 1938.

Ghyka, Matila. *The Geometry of Art and Life.* New York: Sheed & Ward, 1946.

——. *Le Nombre d'Or: rites et rhythmes pythagoriciens dans le développement de la civilisation occidentale*, Tome 1: Les rythmes; tome 2: Les rites. Paris: Gallimard, 2000 [1959].

Gilson, Etienne. *Being and Some Philosophers*, 2nd edn. Toronto: Pontifical Institute of Medieval Studies, 1952.

——. *History of Christian Philosophy in the Middle Ages*. London: Sheed and Ward, 1955.

Glendinning, Simon. *The Idea of Continental Philosophy*. Edinburgh: Edinburgh University Press, 2006.

Godwin, Joscelyn. *L'esotérisme musicale en France, 1950–1970*. Paris: Albin Michel, 1991. *Music and the Occult: French Musical Philosophies, 1750–1950*. Trans. the Author. New York: University of Rochester, 1985.

Godwin, Joscelyn (ed.). *Music, Mysticism and Magic: A Sourcebook*. London: Penguin Arkana, 1986.

Granger, Gilles-Gaston. 'Cavaillès et Lautman: deux pionniers'. *Revue philosophique de la France*, Philosopher en France 3, 1940–44, 293–301.

Grau, Albin. 'Hoëne Wronski'. In *Saturn Gnosis*. Graz: Geheimnes Wissen, 2006 [1929], 290–302.

Grogin, R. C. *The Bergsonian Controversy in France, 1900–1914*. Calgary: Calgary University Press, 1998.

Gualandi, Alberto, *Deleuze*, Paris: Les Belles Lettres, 1998.

Guchet, Xavier. 'Simondon, la cybernétique et les sciences humaines. Genèse de l'ontologie simondonienne dans deux manuscrits sur la cybèrnetique'. In *Chiasmi International 7: Life and Individuation*. Eds M. Carbone, L. Lawlor and R. Barbaras. Milan: Mimesis, 2005.

Hardt, Michael. *Gilles Deleuze: A Philosophical Apprenticeship*. Minneapolis: Minnesota University Press, 1993.

Harvey, David Allen. *Beyond Enlightenment: Occultism and Politics in Modern France*. Dekalb: Northern Illinois University Press, 2005.

Hegel, G. W. F. *Elements of the Philosophy of Right*. Ed. Allen W. Wood. Trans. H. B. Nisbet. Cambridge: Cambridge University Press, 1991.

——. *Hegel's Logic. Being Part One of the Encyclopedia of the Philosophical Sciences*. Trans. William Wallace. Oxford: Oxford University Press, 1975.

——. *Hegel's Science of Logic*. Trans. A. V. Miller. Atlantic Highlands, NJ: Humanities Press, 1989.

——. *The Phenomenology of Spirit*. Trans. A. V. Miller. Oxford: Oxford University Press, 1977.

Heidegger, Martin. *Being and Time*. Trans. Joan Stambaugh. New York: State University of New York Press, 1996.

——. *Beiträge zur Philosophie (Vom Ereignis). Gesamtausgabe*, vol. 65. Frankfurt: Vittorio Klostermann, 1989. *Contributions to Philosophy (From Enowning)*. Trans. P. Emad and K. Maly. Bloomington: Indiana, 1999.

——. *Nietzsche*, 4 vols. Trans. David Farrell Krell. San Francisco: Harper Collins, 1991.

——. *On the Way to Language*. Trans. Peter D. Herz. New York: Harper and Row, 1971.

——. 'Phenomenology and Theology'. In *The Play of Thinking*. Trans. James G. Hart and John C. Maraldo. Bloomington: Indiana University Press, 1976.

——. *What is Metaphysics?* Trans. R. F. C. Hull and Alan Crick. In *Existence and Being*. Chicago: Henry Regnery, 1970.

Hellman, Geoffrey. 'Structuralism'. In *The Oxford Handbook of Philosophy of Mathematics and Logic*. Ed. Stewart Shapiro. Oxford: Oxford University Press, 2005.

Hilbert, David. *Gesammelte Abhandlungen*, 3 vols. New York: Chelsea Pub. Co., 1965.

——. 'Uber das Unendliche'. *Mathematische Annalen* 95, 1926, 161–90.

Hill, Leslie. *Writing at the Limit: Bataille, Blanchot, Klossowski*. Oxford: Oxford University Press, 2001.

Holland, Eugene W. *Deleuze and Guattari's* Anti-Oedipus: *An Introduction to Schizoanalysis*. New York: Routledge, 1999.

——. 'Nonlinear Historical Materialism and Postmodern Marxism'. *Culture, Theory, Critique* 47:2, 2006, 181–96.

——. 'Spinoza and Marx'. *Cultural Logic* 2:1, 1998, http://clogic.eserver.org/2-1/holland.html

Hume, David. *A Treatise of Human Nature*. London: Penguin, 1985.

——. *An Enquiry Concerning Human Understanding*. London: Penguin, 1990.

——. *Dialogues Concerning Natural Religion*. Indianapolis: Hackett, 1980.

Husserl, Edmund. *Cartesian Meditations*. The Hague: Martinus Nijhoff, 1960.

——. *Husserliana. Gesammelte Werke*. Ed. S. Ijsseling. The Hague: Martinus Nijhoff Verlag, 1950.

——. *Ideas. General Introduction to Pure Phenomenology*. London/New York: George Allen/Macmillan, 1958.

——. *Logical Investigations*. London/New York: Routledge/Humanities Press, 1970.

Hyppolite, Jean. *Logic and Existence*. Trans. Leonard Lawlor and Amit Sen. Albany: State University of New York Press, 1997.

Igoin, Albert. 'De l'ellipse de la théorie politique de Spinoza chez le jeune Marx'. In *Cahiers Spinoza* 1, 1977, 213–28.

James, Ian. *Pierre Klossowski: The Persistence of a Name*. Oxford: Legenda, 2000.

Jones, Graham. *Difference and Determination: Prolegomena Concerning Deleuze's Early Metaphysic*. Unpublished PhD Dissertation: Monash University, 2002.

Joseph, Isaac. 'Gabriel Tarde: Le monde comme féerie'. In Tarde, Gabriel. *Les lois sociales*. Paris: Les Empêcheurs de penser en rond, 1999, 9–36.

——. 'Tarde avec Park. A quoi servent les foules?' *multitudes* 7, December 2001, 212–20.

Kant, Immanuel. *Critique of Judgement.* Trans. Werner S. Pluhar. Indianapolis: Hackett Publishing Company, 1987 [1790].

——. *Critique of Pure Reason.* Trans. P. Guyer and A. Wood. Cambridge: Cambridge University Press, 1997 [1781/1787].

——. *Critique of Pure Reason.* Trans. Norman Kamp Smith. London: Macmillan, 1990 [1781/1787].

——. Letter to Marcus Herz, 26 May 1789, in *Immanuel Kant: Philosophical Correspondence, 1759–99.* Ed. Arnulf Zweig. Chicago: University of Chicago Press, 1967.

——. *Prolegomena to any future metaphysics that will be able to come forward as science.* Trans. Gary Hatfield. Cambridge: Cambridge University Press, 1997.

Keller, Evelyn Fox. *The Century of the Gene.* Cambridge, MA: Harvard University Press, 2000.

Kerslake, Christian. 'The Somnambulist and the Hermaphrodite: Deleuze, Johann Malfatti de Montereggio and Occultism'. *Culture Machine,* 'Interzone' section. http://www.culturemachine.net/index.php/cm/article/view/243/225

Klossowski, Pierre. 'A propos du simulacra dans le communication de Georges Bataille'. *Critique* Aug–Sept 1963, 742–50.

——. *La vocation suspendue.* Paris: Gallimard, 1950.

——. *Le Bain de Diane.* Paris: Pauvert, 1956.

——. *Le Baphomet.* Paris: Mercure de France, 1965.

——. *Les lois de l'hospitalité* (*Roberte ce soir* [1954], *La révocation de l'Édit de Nantes* [1959] and *Le souffleur* [1960]). Paris: Gallimard, 1965.

——. 'Nietzsche, le polythéisme et la parodie'. In *Un si funeste désir.* Paris: Gallimard, 1963, 187–228.

——. *Origines culturelles et mythoques d'un certain comportement des dames* romaine's. Montpellier: Fata Morgana, 1986 [1968].

——. 'Oubli et anamnèse dans l'expérience vécue de l'éternel retour du meme'. In *Nietzsche et le cerle vicieux.* Paris: Mercure de France, 1969, 93–103. *Nietzsche and the Vicious Circle.* Trans. Daniel W. Smith. New York: Athlone, 1997, 56–66.

——. *Sade mon prochain.* Paris: Seuil, 1967 [1947].

Kuehn, Manfred. *Scottish Common Sense in Germany, 1768–1800.* Quebec: McGill-Queens University Press, 1987.

Lafontaine, Céline. *L'empire cybernétique. Des machines à penser à la pensée machine.* Paris: Seuil, 2005.

——. 'The Cybernetic Matrix of "French Theory"'. *Theory, Culture & Society* 24:5, 2007, 27–46.

Landgrebe, Ludwig. 'The Phenomenological Concept of Experience'. *Philosophy and Phenomenological Research* 34:1, 1973, 1–13.

Laplanche, Jean, and Jean-Baptiste Pontalis. *The Language of Psycho-Analysis.* Trans. Donald Nicholson-Smith. New York: Norton, 1973.

Lapoujade, David. 'From Transcendental Empiricism to Worker Nomadism: William James'. *Pli* 9, 2000, 190–9.

Largeault, Jean. *Logique mathématique. Textes*. Paris: Armand Colin, 1972.

Laruelle, François. *Nietzsche contre Heidegger*. Paris: Payot, 1977.

Latour, Bruno. 'Gabriel Tarde and the End of the Social'. In *The Social in Question. New Bearings in History and the Social Sciences*. Ed. P. Joyce. London: Routledge, 2002.

——. *Reassembling the Social: an Introduction to Actor-Network-Theory*. Oxford: Oxford University Press, 2005.

Laugwitz, D. *Bernhard Riemann: Turning Points in the Conception of Mathematics*. Trans. A. Shenitzer. Boston: Birkhäuser, 1999.

Lautman, Albert. *Essai sur les notions de structure et d'existence en mathématiques. I. Les schémas de structure. II. Les schémas de genèse*. Paris: Hermann, 1938.

——. *Essai sur l'unité des mathématiques et divers écrits*. Foreword by Jean Dieudonné, Olivier Costa de Beauregard and Maurice Loi. Paris: Union générale d'éditions, 1977. (Reprinted 2006. *Les mathématiques, les idées et le réel physique*. Paris: Vrin.)

——. *Essai sur l'unité des sciences mathématiques dans leur développement actuel*. Paris: Hermann, 1938.

——. *Nouvelles recherches sur la structure dialectique des mathématiques, Introduction de Jean Cavaillès et Raymond Aron. Actualités scientifiques et industrielles*. Paris: Hermann, 1939.

——. *Symétrie et dissymétrie en mathématiques et en physique. Le problème du temps. Introduction de Suzanne Lautman*. Paris: Hermann, 1946.

——. 'Symmetry and Dissymmetry in Mathematics and Physics'. In *Great Currents of Mathematical Thought*. Ed. F. Le Lionnais. Trans. R. A. Hall. New York: Dover Publications, 2004 [1971].

Lawlor, L. *The Challenge of Bergsonism*. London: Continuum, 2003.

——. 'Life: An Essay on the Overcoming of Metaphysics'. Available online at http://www.pucp.edu.pe/eventos/congresos/filosofia/programa_general/viernes/plenariamatutina/LawlorLeonard.pdf

Lazzarato, Maurizio. *Puissances de l'invention. La psychologie économique de Gabriel Tarde contre l'economie politique*. Paris: Les Empêcheurs de penser en rond/Le Seuil, 2001.

Leibniz, Gottfried Wilhelm. *New Essays on Human Understanding*, 2nd edn. Ed. Jonathan Bennett and Peter Remnant. Cambridge: Cambridge University Press, 1997.

——. *Philosophical Essays*. Trans. Roger Ariew and Daniel Garber. Indianapolis: Hachett Publishing Company, 1989.

——. *Philosophical Papers and Letters*, 2nd edn. Ed. Leroy E. Loemker. Dordrecht, Holland: D. Reidel, 1956.

Lévi, Eliphas. *History of Magic*. Trans. A. E. Waite, London: Rider, 1913 [1860].

Lévi, Eliphas [Alphonse Constant]. *Transcendental Magic*. London: Rider, 1896 [*Doctrine et ritual de la haute magie*, 1855].

Macherey, Pierre. *Hegel ou Spinoza*. Paris: Maspero, 1979.

McIntosh, Christopher. *Eliphas Lévi and the French Occult Revival*. London: Rider, 1972.

Maimon, Solomon. *An Autobiography*. Trans. J. Clark Murray. Urbana: University of Illinois Press, 2001.

———. *Versuch über die Transcendental-philosophie, mit einem Anhang über die symbolische Erkenntniß und Anmerkungen*. In *Gesammelte Werke* (II, VII). Ed. Valerio Verra. Hildesheim et al. 1965–1976, 2000.

Marx, Karl. *Capital* (3 vols). In *Marx/Engels Collected Works*. vol. 1. London: International Publishers, 1976.

———. *Grundrisse: Introduction to the Critique of Political Economy*. Trans. M. Nicolaus. New York: Vintage, 1973 [1939].

Marx, Karl, and Friedrich Engels. *The Communist Manifesto*. In *Marx/Engels Collected Works*, vol. 6. London: International Publishers, 1976.

Mates, Benson. *The Philosophy of Leibniz: Metaphysics and Language*. Oxford: Oxford University Press, 1986.

Matheron, Alexandre. 'Le *Traité Théologico-Politique* vu par le jeune Marx'. In *Cahiers Spinoza* 1, 1997, 159–212.

Merleau-Ponty, M. 'At the Sorbonne'. *The Bergsonian Heritage*. Ed. T. Hanna. New York: Columbia University Press, 1962, 133-49.

———. *Phenomenology of Perception*. Trans. Colin Smith. London: Routledge & Kegan Paul, 1962.

Meslet, Laurent. *Le psychisme et la vie. La philosophie de la nature de Raymond Ruyer*. Paris: L'Harmattan, 2005.

Milet, Jean. *Gabriel Tarde et la philosophie de l'Histoire*. Paris: Vrin, 1970.

Montferrier, A. S. de. *Encyclopédie Mathématique, ou exposition complète de toutes les branches des mathématiques d'après les principles de la philosophie des mathématiques de Hoëné Wronski* (4 vols). Paris: Amyot, 1834–40.

Moore, F. C. T. *Bergson: Thinking Backwards*. Cambridge: Cambridge University Press, 1996.

Morand, Max. 'Reflexions d'un physicien sur la Gnose de Princeton'. In *Cahiers Laïques* 174, 1980, 123–43.

Morot-Sir, E. 'What Bergson Means to Us Today'. In *The Bergsonian Heritage*. Ed. T. Hanna. New York: Columbia University Press, 1962, 35–53.

Moss, Lenny. *What Genes Can't Do*. Cambridge, MA: MIT Press, 2003.

Mourélos, G. *Bergson et les niveaux de réalité*. Paris: Presses Universitaires de France, 1964.

Mucchielli, Laurent. 'Tardomania? Réflexions sur les usages contemporains de Tarde'. *Revue d'Histoire des Sciences Humaines* 3, 2000, 161–84.

Mullarkey, John (ed.). *The New Bergson*. Manchester: Manchester University Press, 1999.
Nietzsche, Friedrich. *Beyond Good and Evil*. Trans. R. J. Hollingdale. London: Penguin Books, 2003.
———. *Sämtliche Werke. Kritische Studienausgabe*. Hrsg. G. Colli und M. Montinari. München: Deutscher Taschenbuch Verlag, 1967.
———. *Thus Spoke Zarathustra*. Trans. R. J. Hollingdale. Harmondsworth: Penguin, 1961.
———. *Untimely Meditations*. Trans. R. J. Hollingdale. Cambridge: Cambridge University Press, 1997.
Oyama, Susan. *The Ontogeny of Information*. Durham: Duke University Press, 2000.
Papus [Gérard Encausse]. *The Tarot of the Bohemians*. Trans. A. P. Morton. London: George Redway, 1896 [1889].
Papus. *La science des nombres*, Paris: Chacornac, 1934.
Parr, Adrian (ed.). *The Deleuze Dictionary*. Edinburgh: Edinburgh University Press, 2005.
Petitot, Jean. 'La dialectique de la vérité objective et de la valeur historique dans le rationalisme mathématique d'Albert Lautman'. In *Sciences et philosophie en France et en Italie entre les deux guerres*. Ed. J. Petitot and L. Scarantino. Napoli: Vivarium, 2001.
———. 'Refaire le Timée. Introduction à la philosophie mathématique d'Albert Lautman'. *Revue d'Histoire des Sciences* 40:1, 1987, 79–115.
Plato. *Collected Dialogues of Plato*. Ed. Edith Hamilton. Princeton, NJ: Princeton University Press, 1961.
———. *Republic*. Trans. G. M. A. Grube. Indianapolis: Hackett Publishing, Company, 1974.
Plotinus. *The Enneads*. London/New York: Penguin Books, 1991.
Plotnitsky, Arkady. *The Knowable and the Unknowable: Modern Science, Nonclassical Thought, and the 'Two Cultures'*. Ann Arbor: University of Michigan Press, 2002.
Pragacz, Piotr. 'Notes on the Life and Work of Józef Maria Hoëne-Wronski'. IMPAN website (Institute of Mathematics of the Polish Academy of Sciences), www.impan.gov.pl/-pragacz/download
Prentice, R. *The Basic Quidditative Metaphysics of Duns Scotus as Seen in His De Primo Principio*. Rome: Antonianum, 1970.
Read, Jason. 'Primitive Accumulation: The Aleatory Foundation of Capitalism'. In *Rethinking Marxism* 14:2, 2000, 24–49.
———. *The Micro-Politics of Capital: Marx and the Prehistory of the Present*. Albany: State University of New York Press, 2003.
———. 'Universal History of Contingency: Deleuze and Guattari on the History of Capitalism'. In *Borderlands E-journal* 2:3 (2003), http://www.borderlandsejournal.adelaide.edu.au/vol2no3_2003/read_contingency.htm

Reggio, David. 'Jean Malfatti de Montereggio: A Brief Introduction'. In *Working Papers on Cultural History and Contemporary Thought*, paper 1, November 2003. http://www.goldsmiths.ac.uk/ departments/history/ news-events/malfatti_intro.php

Reik, Theodor. *Masochism in Modern Man*. Trans. Margaret H. Beigel and Gertrud M. Kurth. New York: Grove Press, 1941.

Riemann, B. 'On the Hypotheses Which Lie at the Bases of Geometry'. Trans. W. K. Clifford. *Nature* 8, 1873, 14–17; 36–7.

Robert, Jason Scott. *Embryology, Epigenesis and Evolution: Taking Development Seriously*. Cambridge: Cambridge University Press, 2004.

Roudinesco, Elisabeth. *Jacques Lacan & Company: A History of Psychoanalysis in France, 1925–1985*. Trans. Jeffrey Mehlman. Chicago: University of Chicago Press, 1990.

Rubel, Maximilien. 'Marx à la rencontre de Spinoza'. In *Cahiers Spinoza* 1, 1997, 7–28.

Russell, B. *A History of Western Philosophy*. London: Counterpoint, 1984.

Ruyer, Raymond. *L'animal, l'homme, la fonction symbolique*. Paris: Gallimard, 1964.

——. *Eléments de psycho-biologie*. Paris: PUF, 1946.

——. *Esquisse d'une philosophie de la structure*. Paris: Alcan, 1930.

——. *La conscience et le corps*. Paris: Alcan, 1937.

——. *La cybernétique et l'origine de l'information*. Paris: Flammarion, 1954.

——. *La Gnose de Princeton: des savants à la recherché d'une religion américaine*. Paris: Fayard, 1977.

——. *Le monde des valeurs*. Paris: Aubier, 1948.

——. *L'humanité de l'avenir d'après Cournot*. Paris: Alcan, 1930.

——. *L'utopie et les utopies*. Paris: PUF, 1950.

——. *Néo-finalisme*. Paris: PUF, 1952.

——. *Paradoxes de la conscience et limites de l'automatisme*. Paris: Albin Michel, 1960.

——. *Philosophie de la valeur*. Paris: Armand Colin, 1952.

——. *La genèse des formes vivantes*. Paris: Flammarion, 1958.

Salanskis, Jean-Michel. 'Idea and Destination'. In *Deleuze: A Critical Reader*. Ed. P. Patton. Cambridge: Blackwell, 1996.

——. 'Mathematics, Metaphysics, Philosophy'. In *Virtual Mathematics: The Logic of Difference*. Ed. S. Duffy. Manchester: Clinamen Press, 2006.

——. 'Pour une épistémologie de la lecture'. *Alliage* 35–6, 1998. http://www. tribunes.com/tribune/alliage/accueil.htm

Santayana, G. *Winds of Doctrine and Platonism and the Spiritual Life*. Gloucester: Peter Smith, 1971.

Sauvagnargues, Anne. 'Actuel/Virtuel'. *Le vocabulaire de Gilles Deleuze*. Ed. R. Sasso and A. Villani. *Les Cahiers de Noesis* 3, 2003, 22–9.

——. *Deleuze et l'art*. Paris: Presses Universitaires de France, 2005.

Schelling, F. W. J. 'Stuttgart Lectures'. Trans. T. Pfau. In Schelling, *Idealism and the Endgame of Theory*. Albany: SUNY, 1994 [1810].

Schérer, René. 'L'impersonnel'. In É. Alliez et al., *Gilles Deleuze. Immanence et vie*. Paris: PUF, 1998, 70.

——. 'Préface. Fin de siècle–Une utopie esthétique'. In Gabriel Tarde. *Fragment d'histoire future*. Paris: Séguier, 1998, 7–37.

Schrag, Calvin O. 'Heidegger on Repetition and Historical Understanding'. *Philosophy East and West* 20:3, July 1970, 287–95.

Sheehan, Thomas. 'A Paradigm Shift in Heidegger Research'. *Continental Philosophy Review* 34, 2001, 183–202.

Simondon, Gilbert. *Du mode d'existence des objets techniques*. Paris: Aubier, 1989.

——. *L'individuation à la lumière des notions de forme et d'information*. Grenoble: Millon, 2005.

Smith, Daniel W. 'Axiomatics and Problematics as Two Modes of Formalisation: Deleuze's Epistemology of Mathematics'. In *Virtual Mathematics: The Logic of Difference*. Ed. Simon Duffy. Manchester: Clinamen Press, 2006.

——. 'Deleuze, Hegel, and the Post-Kantian Tradition'. *Philosophy Today, supplement* 44, 2001, 119–31.

——. 'Deleuze on Leibniz: Difference, Continuity, and the Calculus'. In *Current Continental Theory and Modern Philosophy*. Ed. Steve Daniel. Evanston, IL: Northwestern University Press, 2004.

——. 'Mathematics and the Theory of Multiplicities: Deleuze and Badiou Revisited'. *Southern Journal of Philosophy* 41:3, 2003, 411–49.

——. 'The Conditions of the New'. *Deleuze Studies* 1:1, 2007, 1–21.

——. 'The Doctrine of Univocity: Deleuze's Ontology of Univocity'. In *Deleuze and Religion*. Ed. Mary Bryden. London and New York: Routledge, 1999.

Stengers, Isabelle. *Penser avec Whitehead: une libre et sauvage création de concepts*. Paris: Seuil, 2002.

Sunden, Hjalmar. *La théorie bergsonienne de la religion*. Uppsala: Almqvist & Wiksell, 1940.

Tarde, Gabriel. *Ecrits de psychologie sociale*. Ed. Jean Millet and A.M. Rocheblave-Spenlé. Toulouse: Privat Editeur, 1973.

——. 'La croyance et le désir'. *Revue philosophique* 10, 1880, 150–80; 264–83.

——. *Les lois de l'imitation*, with a preface by Jean-Philippe Antoine. Paris: Les Empêcheurs de penser en rond/Le Seuil, 2001 [1890/1895].

——. *Les lois sociales*. With a preface by Isaac Joseph. Paris: Les Empêcheurs de penser en rond/Institut Synthélabo, 1999 [1898].

——. *L'opposition universelle*, with a preface by Jean-Clet Martin. Paris: Les Empêcheurs de penser en rond/ Institut Synthélabo, 1999 [1897].

——. *Maine de Biran et l'évolutionnisme en psychologie*, with a preface by Anne Devarieux. Paris: Les Empêcheurs de penser en rond/Institut d'édition Sanofi-Synthelabo, 2000 [1876].

——. *Monadologie et sociologie*. With a preface by Éric Alliez and a postface by Maurizio Lazzarato. Paris: Les Empêcheurs de penser en rond/Institut Synthélabo, 1999 [1893].

Thelke, Peter. 'Intuition and Diversity: Kant and Maimon on Space and Time'. In *Salomon Maimon: Rational Dogmatist, Empirical Skeptic – Critical Assessments*. Ed. Gideon Freudenthal. Dordrecht: Kluwer Academic Publishers, 2003.

Thoburn, Nicholas. *Deleuze, Marx and Politics*. New York: Routledge, 2003.

Toews, David. 'The New Tarde'. *Theory, Culture & Society* 20:5, 2003, 81–98.

Toscano, Alberto. 'La disparation. Politique et sujet chez Simondon'. *multitudes* 18, 2004, 73–82.

——. *The Theatre of Production: Philosophy and Individuation Between Kant and Deleuze*. Basingstoke: Palgrave, 2006.

Turkle, Sherry. *Psychoanalytic Politics: Jacques Lacan and Freud's French Revolution*. New York: Guilford, 1992.

Vax, Louis, and Wunenburger, Jean-Jacques (eds). *Raymond Ruyer, de la science á la théologie*. Paris: Kimé, 1995.

Vergez, André, and Huisman, Denis. *Histoire des philosophes illustrée par les textes*. Paris: Fernand Nathan, 1966.

Viatte, Auguste *Les sources occultes du Romantisme* (2 vols). Paris: Honoré Champion, 1928.

Villani, Arnauld. *La guêpe et l'orchidée*. Paris: Belin, 1999.

Virno, Paolo. *A Grammar of the Multitude*. New York: Semiotext(e), 2002.

Wacquant, Loïc. 'Durkheim et Bourdieu: le socle commun et ses fissures'. *Critique* 579/580, Aug–Sept 1995, 646–60.

Wahl, Jean. *Le malheur de la conscience dans la philosophie de Hegel*. Paris: Rieder, 1929.

——. 'Review of *Nietzsche et la philosophie* by Gilles Deleuze'. In *Revue de métaphysique et de morale* 68, 1963, 352–79.

——. *Vers le concret: étude d'histoire de la philosophie contemporaine, William James, Whitehead, Gabriel Marcel*. Paris: Vrin 2004 [1932].

Warrain, Francis. *Essai sur l'harmonices mundi ou musique du monde de Johannes Kepler*. Tome 1: *Fondements mathématiques de l'Harmonie*. Paris: Hermann, 1942.

——. *La synthèse concrète*. Paris: Chacornac, 1910 [1906].

——. *L'armature métaphysique de Hoëne Wronski*. Paris: Alcan, 1925.

——. *L'espace*. Paris: Fischbacher, 1907.

Warrain, Francis (ed.). *L'oeuvre philosophique de Hoëne Wronski* (3 vols). Paris: Vega, 1933.

Watson, Stephen H. 'Heidegger: The Hermeneutics of Suspicion and the Dispersion of Dasein'. Unpublished manuscript.

Weyl, H. *Space Time Matter*. Trans. Henry L. Brose. New York: Dover, 1952 [1918].

Whitehead, A. N. *Adventures of Ideas*. Harmondsworth: Penguin, 1948.

——. *Process and Reality*. New York: The Free Press, 1978.

——. *Science and the Modern World*. Cambridge: Cambridge University Press, 1927.

Widder, Nathan. *Genealogies of Difference*, Urbana and Chicago: University of Illinois Press, 2002.

——. 'The Rights of Simulacra: Deleuze and the Univocity of Being'. *Continental Philosophy Review* 34, 2001, 437–53.

Williams, James. 'Deleuze and Whitehead'. In *The Transversal Thought of Gilles Deleuze: Encounters and Influences*. Manchester: Clinamen, 2005.

——. *Gilles Deleuze's Logic of Sense: A Critical Introduction and Guide*. Edinburgh: Edinburgh University Press, 2008.

——. *Understanding Poststructuralism*. Chesthunt: Acumen, 2005.

Williams, Thomas A. *Eliphas Lévi: Master of Occultism*. Alabama: University of Alabama, 1975.

Wronski, Józef-Maria Hoëne. *A Course of Mathematics: Introduction Determining the General State of Mathematics*. London, 1821.

——. *Apodictique messianique*. Paris: Depot des ouvrages de l'auteur, 1876.

——. *Introduction à la philosophie des mathématiques et technie d'algorithmie*. Paris: Courcier, 1811.

——. *Mémoires sur l'aberration des astres mobiles et sur l'inégalité dans l'apparence de leur mouvement*. Marseille, 1801.

——. *Messianisme: union finale de la philosophie et de la religion, constituent la philosophie absolue*. Paris: Depot des ouvrages de l'auteur, 1831.

——. *Messianisme, ou réforme absolue du savoir humain*. Paris: Depot des ouvrages de l'auteur, 1847.

——. *Philosophie critique découverte par Kant, fondée sur le dernier principe du savoir humain*. Marseille, 1803.

——. *Philosophie de l'infini: contenant des contre-refléxions sur la métaphysique du calcul infinitésimal*. Paris: Depot des ouvrages de l'auteur, 1814.

——. *Programme du cours de philosophie transcendentale*. Paris: Firmin-Didot, 1811.

——. *Prospectus de la philosophie absolue et son développement*. Paris: Depot des ouvrages de l'auteur, 1878.

Žižek, Slavoj. 'Notes on a Debate "From Within the People"'. *Criticism* 46:4, Fall 2004, 661–6.

Notes on Contributors

Éric Alliez is Professor of Contemporary French Philosophy at Middlesex University. He is the author of *La Signature du monde, ou qu'est-ce que la philosophie de Deleuze et Guattari?* (1993), translated as *The Signature of the World* (2004), and (with Jean-Claude Bonne) *La Pensée-Matisse* (2005).

Paul Atkinson teaches in the Communications and Writing program at Monash University. His research focuses on the relationship between materiality and corporeality in Henri Bergson's writings on science, with particular emphasis on the relationship between immanent change and extended movement. His published articles explore a range of topics including Bergson's vitalism, cinema and foreseeability, time and recognition, the durational limits of affect and the implied movement in still images. He is currently working on a series of articles that explore the relationship between processual theories of time, aesthetics and narrative.

Bruce Baugh is Professor of Philosophy at Thompson Rivers University (Kamloops, Canada) and author of *French Hegel: From Surrealism to Postmodernism* (2003). His articles on Deleuze have appeared in journals such as *Man and World*, the *Journal of the British Society for Phenomenology*, *Social Semiotics*, *Angelaki* and *Symposium*.

Alain Beaulieu is Assistant Professor in the Department of Philosophy at Laurentian University, Canada. He is the author of *Gilles Deleuze et la phénoménologie* (2006) and co-editor (with D. Gabbard) of *Michel Foucault and Power Today: International Multidisciplinary Studies in the History of Our Present* (2006).

Ronald Bogue is a Distinguished Research Professor in the Comparative Literature Department of the University of Georgia. He is the author of *Deleuze and Guattari* (1989), *Deleuze on Cinema* (2003), *Deleuze* *on Literature* (2003), *Deleuze on Music, Painting, and the Arts* (2003) and *Deleuze's Wake: Tributes and Tributaries* (2004).

Constantin V. Boundas is Professor Emeritus of Philosophy at Trent University, and a member of the Trent Centre for the Study of Theory, Politics and Culture. His edited publications include *The Deleuze Reader* (1993) and, with Dorothea Olkowski, *The Theater of Philosophy: Critical Essays on Gilles Deleuze* (1994). His translations include (with Mark Lester and Charles Stivale) Gilles Deleuze's *The Logic of Sense* (1990), and Gilles Deleuze's *Empiricism and Subjectivity: An Essay in Human Nature* (1991). He is also the editor of *Deleuze and Philosophy* (2006) and General Editor of *The Edinburgh Companion to the 20th Century Philosophies* (forthcoming).

Simon Duffy is a Lecturer in the Department of Philosophy at the University of Sydney (Australia). His research interests include: early modern philosophy, European philosophy, and the history and philosophy of science and mathematics. He is the author of *The Logic of Expression: Quality, Quantity and Intensity in Spinoza, Hegel and Deleuze* (2006), and editor of *Virtual Mathematics: The Logic of Difference* (2006). He has also translated a number of Gilles Deleuze's seminars on Spinoza at www.webdeleuze.com.

Gregory Flaxman is an assistant professor in the English Department at the University of North Carolina, Chapel Hill. The editor of *The Brain is the Screen: Deleuze and the Philosophy of the Cinema* (2000), he has published articles on speech-act theory, psychoanalysis, postmodern fiction, the fate of critical theory, and philosophy. He is current finishing a book on fabulation and philosophy.

Eugene Holland teaches in the Department of French and Italian at Ohio State University. He specialises in social theory and modern French literature, history and culture. In addition to a number of articles on poststructuralist theory and particularly the work of Gilles Deleuze, he has published the books *Baudelaire and Schizoanalysis: The Sociopoetics of Modernism* (1993) and *Introduction to Schizoanalysis* (1999), and is currently working on books on citizenship and perversions.

Ian James completed his doctoral research on the fictional and theoretical writings of Pierre Klossowski at the University of Warwick in 1996. Since then he has been a Fellow and Lecturer in French at Downing College, University of Cambridge. He is the author of *Pierre Klossowski: The Persistence of a Name* (2000), *The Fragmentary Demand: An Introduction to the Philosophy of Jean-Luc Nancy* (2006) and *Paul Virilio* (2007).

Graham Jones is a lecturer at Monash University. He has taught at the University of Melbourne and Victoria University of Technology, and is a past president of the Australasian Society for Continental Philosophy, a member of the Melbourne School of Continental Philosophy and co-editor of *Sensorium: Aesthetics, Art, Life*. He is also the author of *Lyotard Reframed* (forthcoming).

Christian Kerslake is Research Fellow in Modern European Philosophy at Middlesex University, London. He is the author of *Deleuze and the Unconscious* (2006) and *The Problem of Immanence in Kant and Deleuze* (2008), and the editor of *The Origins and Ends of the Mind: Philosophical Essays on Psychoanalysis* (2007).

Melissa McMahon teaches in the Discipline of Philosophy at the University of Sydney, from which she recently received her doctorate on Deleuze and Kant's Critical Philosophy. She has produced numerous translations of Deleuze's writing and other French philosophers, including the seminars on Kant at www.webdeleuze.com. Her articles on Deleuze have appeared in Gary Genosko (ed.), *Deleuze and Guattari: Critical Assessments of Leading Philosophers*, vol. I (2001) and Charles Stivale (ed.), *Gilles Deleuze: Key Concepts* (2005).

Arkady Plotnitsky is a Professor of English and a Director of the Theory and Cultural Studies Program at Purdue University. He has published several books and many articles on British and European Romanticism, critical and cultural theory, continental philosophy, philosophy of physics, and the relationships among literature, philosophy and science. His most recent books are *The Knowable and the Unknowable: Modern Science, Nonclassical Thought, the 'Two Cultures'* (2002); *Reading Bohr: Physics and Philosophy* (2006), and a collection of essays, *Idealism Without Absolute: Philosophy and Romantic Culture*, co-edited with Tilottama Rajan (2004).

Jon Roffe is a member of the Melbourne School of Continental Philosophy (www.mscp.org.au), and editor of *Understanding Derrida*

(2004) and *Derrida's Heidegger* (forthcoming). He has published articles on Deleuze, Derrida and Merleau-Ponty, and is currently engaged in writing a comparative study of Deleuze and Badiou on ontology and politics.

Daniel W. Smith is an Associate Professor in the Department of Philosophy at Purdue University. He is the translator of Deleuze's *Essays Critical and Clinical* (1997) and *Francis Bacon: The Logic of Sensation* (2004), as well as Pierre Klossowski's *Nietzsche and the Vicious Circle* (1993).

Alberto Toscano is a Lecturer in Sociology and a member of the Centre for the Study of Invention and Social Process (CSISP) at Goldsmiths College, London. He is the author of *The Theatre of Production: Philosophy and Individuation Between Kant and Deleuze* (2006) and the co-editor of Alain Badiou's *Theoretical Writings* and *On Beckett*. He has written several articles on Simondon, Schelling, Badiou and contemporary social and political thought.

Nathan Widder is a Senior Lecturer in Political Theory at the University of Exeter. His *Genealogies of Difference* (2002) engages with ontological issues concerning identity, power, meaning, and difference by weaving together post-Hegelian philosophies of difference with strategic forays into ancient, early Christian, and medieval philosophy. He has written extensively on Deleuze's philosophy in book chapters and journal articles, which include publications in *Continental Philosophy Review* (2001), *Southern Journal of Philosophy* (2003), *Contemporary Political Theory* (2004), and *Philosophy Today* (forthcoming). His most recent book is *Reflections on Time and Politics*.

James Williams is Reader in Philosophy at the University of Dundee. His publications include *The Lyotard Reader and Guide*, with K. Crome (2006), *Lyotard and the Political* (2000), *The Transversal Thought of Gilles Deleuze: Encounters and Influences* (2005), *Gilles Deleuze's Difference and Repetition: A Critical Introduction and Guide* (2003) and *Gilles Deleuze's Logic of Sense: A Critical Introduction and Guide* (2008).

Index